To my dear [illegible], co-academic and patient editor.

[illegible]

HUMAN DIMENSIONS IN ORGANISED CRIME, MONEY LAUNDERING AND CORRUPTION

HUMAN DIMENSIONS IN ORGANISED CRIME, MONEY LAUNDERING AND CORRUPTION

Petrus C. van Duyne
Jackie Harvey
Georgios A. Antonopoulos
Klaus von Lampe
Almir Maljević
Jon Spencer
(eds.)

Human dimensions in organised crime, money laundering and corruption

Petrus C. van Duyne, Jackie Harvey, Georgios A. Antonopoulos, Klaus von Lampe, Almir Maljević, Jon Spencer (eds.) Wolf Legal Publishers (WLP), 2013

ISBN: 978-90-5850-983-3

This volume is based on the presentations of the authors at the eleventh Crossborder Crime Colloquium, hosted 21-22 May 2012 by Manchester University.
This project was supported by:
Tilburg University (the Netherlands)
Teesside University
Northumbria University
Heuni (Finland)

The Cross-Border Crime Colloquium is an annual event since 1999. It brings together experts on international organised (economic) crime to discuss the latest developments in empirical research, legislation and law enforcement, with a special geographical focus on Western, Central, and Eastern Europe. The Colloquia aim at building bridges in three respects: between East and West Europe, between scholars and practitioners, and between old and young. The Cross-border Crime Colloquium, so far, has been organised thirteen times:

2012 Manchester, UK
2011 Tilburg, the Netherlands
2009 Gent, Belgium
2008 Belgrade, Serbia
2007 Prague, Czech Republic
2006 Tallinn, Estonia
2005 Sarajevo, Bosnia and Herzegovina
2004 Berlin, Germany
2003 Ainring, Germany
2002 Ljubljana, Slovenia
2001 Bratislava, Slovakia
2000 Budapest, Hungary
1999 Prague, Czech Republic

Coverdesign: Maarten van Dijck

Copies can be ordered at:
Wolf Legal Publishers (WLP)
PO Box 313
5060 AH Oisterwijk
The Netherlands
E-Mail: info@wolfpublishers.nl
www.wolfpublishers.com

Human dimensions in organised crime, money laundering and corruption

List of authors

Meta Ahtik

University of Ljubljana, Faculty of law

Georgios A. Antonopoulos

Teesside University

Tihomir Bezlov

Centre for the Study of Democracy in Sofia.

Lieselot Bisschop

University College Ghent

Luis de la Corte Ibáñez

University of Madrid

Rowan Bosworth-Davies

Bosworth Fields Ltd

Alan Doig

University of Birmingham

Petrus C. van Duyne

Tilburg University

Michael Salinas-Edwards

University of Manchester

Martin Elliott

Northumbria University

Laura Requena Espada

University of Madrid

Philip Gounev
Centre for the Study of Democracy in Sofia

Andrea Gimenez-Salinas
University of Madrid

Jackie Harvey
Northumbria University

Colin King
University of Leeds

Klaus von Lampe
John Jay College of Criminal Justice

Ciril Keršmanc
Institute of Criminology at the Faculty of Law Ljubljana

Michael Levi
University of Cardiff

Anna Markovska
Anglia Ruskin University, Cambridge

Radu Nicolae
Centre for Legal Resource Foundation

Ugur Omurgonulsen
Hacettepe University

Georgios Papanicolaou
Teesside University

Brendan Quirke
Northumbria University

Atanas Rusev
Centre for the Study of Democracy in Sofia

Miroslav Scheinost
Institute of Criminology and Social Prevention, Prague

Alexey Serdyuk
Kharkiv National University of Internal Affairs

Melvin R.J. Soudijn
Dutch National Police

Back to human criminal size: an introduction

Petrus C. van Duyne

The human size and supersize

The old Greek sophist, Protagoras (490-420 BC) is attributed the aphorism: "*Man is the measure of all things: of things which are, that they are, and of things which are not, that they are not*". At first sight this looks over-obvious. Nevertheless there is an easily forgotten wisdom and consequence in it. The wisdom is a tautology: we are the ultimate yardstick. The consequence can be less comfortable as the 'human size' is often far from attractive: it implies banality, meanness or vulgarity, human traits that are far from admirable. Usually these traits are shunned because they conflict with the general desire to escape this banality and to present human beings and their deeds in greater dimensions than they are, whether in good or in evil deeds. This is not reprehensible even if it may imply a collective self-delusion. It is the foundation of expressive art and literature. Heroes and saints, Good versus Evil: usually represented in a bigger than human dimension. Such a great representation is a good cure against the generally drab existence of human beings.

This may be a proper observation, though of debatable general validity. For example, does this also apply to the *science* as a human undertaking? In principle, this should not be the case. Science is the domain of cool rationality, abstractions and accurate measurement: pale and bloodless. Researchers as 'servants' of science should be part of this paleness. However, this abstractness represents an ideal and not the real world of science: these humble scientists are stakeholders in an extra dimension: their contribution to the Truth.

The argumentation above implies an interesting duality: the humility of a servant on the one hand, and the elevation in serving the Truth on the other hand. Historically this is quite persistent: In the era of the scholastic philosophy the work of the scholars was always rising above themselves, being devoted to prove the existence of God and the infallibility of the Church's dogmata. Philosophers who tried otherwise, could find themselves condemned to revoke their heresy or end up on the stake. Reformation and Enlightenment secularised the status of science: the Truth became less divine but had to serve Mankind instead. Whether that is still bigger than human size, may be a matter of semantics, but a wise scholar knew he rather withheld his doubts. Only a lone wolf such as Friedrich Nietzsche dared to challenge the pomp in the 19th Century science and philosophy. His concept of a 'merry science' (fröhliche Wissenschaft) found no response. Science is a serious thing and deals with serious matters. This is not an abstract irony; it touches the daily work of every practitioner of science. Which researcher dares to be so audacious as to confess openly to do research just 'for the fun of it'? Universities as well as the Lords of the Research Grants and Subsidies have standards and the 'impact on society' ranks high on the evaluation scale of bigger aims. This may evoke an 'impact enlargement tendency' in many research grant bids. Modest, but realistic dimensions are not subsidisable.

Some research issues have a built-in 'supersize dimension' amplifier. Important examples are *safety* and *health*, often featuring in combination, which have a great amplification capacity if the right sensitive chord is touched. A highly sensitive chord is 'pandemic': once touched a whole health and related research machinery is set in motion. The 'Mexican swine flu' is a very recent and interesting example: with an insignificant casualty rate it succeeded to attract publicity and funds that dwarfed other global diseases that still cause millions of deaths per year. The pharmaceutical industry and scientists (some being stakeholders in that sector) thrived on this amplification of the problem size with the happy outcome of millions of unused vaccines.

In the past 25 years, *crime* has also enjoyed a very prominent place in this safety orbit as part of a highly successful combination: '*safety and crime*', lending amplification capacity to various crime themes. As far as the past 25-50 years are concerned organised crime and criminal finances are prominent successful examples of themes with such an amplification dimension capacity which was put into effect by a combination of policy makers, media and scientists (Van Duyne, 2004; 2012). Naturally, underneath all the up-sizing, there remains the humble human measure and proportion. This volume sheds light on this up-sizing and the human measure.

The underworld gaze

The statement that 'organised crime' has a built-in dimensions enlargement capacity meets immediately a refutation. Sutherland was one of the first pioneers in the field of organised crime though from the perspective of economic crime. Ten years after his first address in 1939 in which he drew attention to the issue of 'white collar criminals', he published his monograph under the same title. In the last part he qualified white collar crime as 'organised crime' (chapter 14). Though Sutherland has been influential and quoted time and again, the amplification capacity of his theory was modest and rather followed the political pendulum of conservative and liberal alternation in political power. His equation of white collar upperworld crime with organised crime produced regular citations in professional journals, but otherwise fell flat. What was lacking? The same that hampered the UN Congress in attempts to bring transnational (economic) organised crime to the fore in the 1980s (Van Duyne and Nelemans, 2012): a basic *underworld* dimension. To put it simply: historically organised crime without a sinister *underworld gaze* lacks dimension enlargement capacity: upperworld criminals are more akin to 'us' and when 'we' are the measure of all (criminal) things, then 'we' are not sinister.

In contrast, the 'organised crime' theme from the 'underworld gaze' fared most successfully: it was put solidly on the political agenda (as if Sutherland never existed): in the US in the 1950s and in Europe since the mid-1980s. Some countries were 'early birds', like Germany as elaborated by *Klaus von Lampe* in the first chapter, and Italy, for the obvious reason because of its various mafias. In 1992, the Sicilian Mafia triggered a real moral panic because of the killing of the two well-known judges Falcone and Borsellino. Moral panics inherently amplify threat dimensions (Woodiwiss and Hobbs, 2009) and the 'organised crime' fear which flared up in Europe was no exception: the threat as depicted by European policy makers was soon of an *Apocalypse-now* dimension (Van Duyne, 2004; 1995). In the course of the 1990s, as if this was not big enough, it was further amplified by adding the attribute of '*transnational*'. This aggravated threat is now enshrined in the UN Convention of Transnational Organised Crime of 2000, solemnly signed in Palermo and hosted by the most human (and allegedly criminal (Stille, 2007)) Silvio Berlusconi.

A parallel supporting amplifier was another global major threat: the *proceeds of crime* and the related money laundering. Initially targeting drugs and 'organised crime' the new policy now encompasses all (serious) crime-for-profit. The portfolio holder, the FATF, depicted an upsized financial threat with threatening dimensions: flows of crime-money undermining and infiltrating the financial markets and corrupting public administration alike (Tanzi, 1996; Quirk, 1997). Whether the supporting superlative figures of the volume of crime-money (one trillion dollar, then one trillion and a half) and laundering were credible or not, did not matter; downsizing calculations were simply ignored (Reuter and Greenfield, 2001; Reuter, 2007). The FATF, together with the IMF, OECD and the UNODC (2011) maintained a 'consensus range' of one

2-5% of the global GDP.[1] With the political objective achieved – the institutionalisation of a global anti-laundering regime (Stessens, 2000; Verhage, 2009; 2010) – few cared to reconsider the proposed dimensions of the crime-money threat or simply took the consensus as their point of departure.

Given these policy making successes, some chapters in this volume take a retrospective look at these topics. Have organised crime and money laundering been reduced after so many legislative and law enforcement efforts? Unfortunately, there is no clear answer to this question. Despite all rhetoric about the importance of both phenomena reliable data are still scarce, which is compounded by muddled definitions of the core concepts: money laundering and (transnational) organised crime. Funds for basic research are still scarce. As a matter of fact, the monster of Loch Ness has been more intensively researched than the whole organised crime and –money subject. Even at present, in the preface to the 2011 *Transnational Organised Crime Assessment* the executive director of the UNODC complains of the "*lack of information on transnational criminal markets and trends*", despite "*the gravity of the threat*" (UNODC, 2011). This is an interesting lamentation compared to other safety threats: at the first sight of a pandemic flu, a whole global apparatus of investigation, measurement and countermeasures is put into place at short notice. But after 25 years of OC threat we still have to resign to the sad complaint of the UNODOC executive director.

Looking back is an interesting mental history exercise that has been lucidly described in the chapter of *Klaus von Lampe* about *the debate on organised crime in Germany*. The author describes the onset and development of the 'organised crime' debate in Germany since the 1960s. He elaborates 30 years of threat projections as expressed by high-ranking police officers, prosecutors and occasional researchers from articles in two German professional journals covering a period till 1994. Subsequently he compares this with the available data, even if these do not always allow unambiguous interpretations. His elaboration makes clear that the organised crime debate started incorrectly, as with other countries, such as the Netherlands or the UK in the 1990s. It started with the common 'underworld gaze' mentioned before: the world of thugs and hoodlums *under* the decent society. This mental bias led easily to a 'crying wolf' about potential

---

1 The stand of these bodies is usually supported by economics, developing impressive models which are characterised by a fuzzy operationalisation of the essential concepts (see: Unger (eds. 2007), Walker and Unger (2009) and Walker (1995). Attempts of proper falsification are lacking; likewise none of these economist has been able to explain why in the two decades before the credit crises the alleged threat of crime-money and laundering failed to affect any of the main economies.

'mafia take-overs'. The author carefully collected and compared data, research findings and police situation reports. In the end he concludes that the empirical evidence does not reveal conspicuous developments: Yes there are criminal Italians residing in Germany and yes, some do have connections to Italian crime families, but as far as organised criminal groups are concerned, the share of German offenders remains dominant over the whole period. This also applies to multinational (*transnational*) organised crime groups: while the author does not deny their existence or the seriousness of the offences, there is no underlining of the official, by hindsight oversized threat dimensions with which the debate in Germany started. As far as Germany is concerned, the dimensions of the 'organised crime picture' is as 'flat' as (criminal) human beings usually are.

In the following chapter *Miroslav Scheinost* provides a retrospective view on the organised crime perception in the *Czech Republic*. Obviously, the criminal history of this country is very different from that of Germany: till its collapse in 1989, the socialist regime did not admit any crime problem, let alone something like 'organised crime'. After its fall, the awareness of crime changed: within four years the number of registered crimes rose fourfold while the existence of organised crime within the Czech Republic was admitted, but rather as something *alien*: first transiting the CR on its way to Germany or other countries and later targeting the Czech Republic itself. That was not a fantasy: in the first half of the 1990s, there were foreign organised crime groups taking advantage of the still transiting nature of the Czech society and law enforcement. The media and public were increasingly aware of it and later it had to be admitted that Czech offenders were also involved in organised crime groups (Scheinost, 2004).

According to the author, public and media attention was rather one-sided: these perceived forms of 'organised crime' concerned the 'usual suspects' from the underworld. The organisation of financial and economic crime, the upperworld, got less attention at the time, though the damage it inflicted was much bigger than 'traditional' organised crime. The recognition of 'upperworld' organised crime came much later in the 1990: yet it was still something different. not 'really' (underworld) organised crime and as such it lacked a 'dimension amplification capacity'. This changed during the following decade. In her reports the police began to warn against criminal penetration of the 'upperworld' through corruption and influencing policy making. Meanwhile the interest of the Czech public and media for the 'traditional' form of organised crime was waning. Instead the terms 'mafia' and 'godfather' were used figuratively to denote the sinister deeds of the political and entrepreneurial criminals with their numerous ties to the political decision makers. These were now viewed as another criminal species, more harmful than the 'usual suspects'. As far as the CR is concerned, and this may be true for other post-Soviet countries as well (von Lampe, 2005), the 'underworld gaze' appears to have been superseded by an upperworld organised crime awareness. Sutherland vindicated at last.

Elevating something of common human size to superlative dimensions can be a prolonged process; something an audience must get used to. This process is described by *Georgios A. Antonopoulos and Georgios Papanicolaou* in their chapter on migrants and the representation of 'organised crime' in the Greek press. They describe how in the last decade of the 20th Century two representations of public concern coincided but soon overlapped: 'organised crime' as a component of the public safety policy and the *migration issue*, which also became acute in the same decade. The eventual overlap was such that eventually ethnic migrant groups became identified as an organised crime threat (police Organised Crime Report, 2000), though *indigenous* crime groups failed to be recognised as such. In this process of upgrading the social nuisance of migrants to an organised crime threat, the media played an important role, which the authors investigated systematically. They elaborate how the press soon depicted the inflow of destitute migrants as a 'Trojan Horse' that delivered a multiple array of 'mafias', naturally all none-Greek and of a highly sinister, particularly Russian, nature. It appears that the media, by repeatedly presenting this image of migrant Organised Crime as a Big Threat infiltrating Greece, succeeded in hammering this into the awareness of the public.

What lesson can be drawn from these chapters? The chapters of von Lampe (Germany) and Scheinost (the Czech Republic) point at a waning fear of organised crime perceived with the 'underworld gaze' in respectively a small and big country of the EU, while in the CR attention is shifted to the criminal upperworld. Meanwhile, in Greece the representation of organised crime appears to be out of proportion, at least when foreigners are involved. Which yardstick is applied depends where one stands.

If the juxtaposition of these representations may be confusing, augmenting this confusion, we also have the Europol threat assessments as an official EU measurement: the Organised Crime Threat Assessments *Europol* issues since 2006. In these assessment measures are shifting: cross-comparing the documents shows that Europol arrives each year at new insights, some belatedly. In the 2011 OCTA organised crime would have become more flexible, poly-criminal and working in an increasingly collaborative atmosphere (what could mean they kill each other less frequently). Europol even detected that organised crime is at present using internet technology.[2]

Assessing threats is presented as an approach that intends to outline 'future oriented approaches'. This has a challenging sound: no backward burrowing in past events, but facing what is ahead of us. This is what Europol and the EU do since 2006 and every year the director of Europol writes to be "delighted" to present another OCTA. Should we share this annual delight of the director? There are many reasons not to do so. As Van Duyne (2006) and Van Duyne and Vander Beken (2008) pointed out, these Europol documents are supposed to be *evidence based*, however, with a *hidden* methodology which implies that nobody is in a position to judge their reliability and validity. Nobody knows what the data input of the 27 Member States looks like, nor how that multiple national input is converted into a (single?) database, what this looks like and how it is eventually processed into a threat analysis. This is a multiple 'hocus-pocus' methodology.

How this can result in a misleading EU threat assessment is convincingly explained in the chapter on the *Bulgarian Serious Organised Crime Threat Assessment* by *Atanas Rusev, Philip Gounev, Tihomir Bezlov*. According to the authors there is no valid Bulgarian database suitable as input for Europol's threat assessment. What remains of Europol's OCTAs if it is plausible to assume that Bulgaria is not the only EU-country with a flawed police data management and an unreliable input to Europol? Unfortunately the new methodology described in the EU Council draft methodology, issued 19 June 2012, does not address this flaw.[3]

As the authors are of the opinion that Europol's approach results in a distorted picture, the authors explore the *criminal market approach* that focuses on "*the number and types of actors that populate these illegal markets*". As examples they elaborate the heroin market and the illegal cigarette market. They demonstrate that by collecting data on the structure, actors (traders and customers), turnover and market value, one arrives at a more realistic assessment of illicit markets. The authors do not stand alone in this approach: we find the market approach spreading: in the Europol as well as the UN documents. For example, *Transnational Organised Threat Assessment* ('TOCTA', UNODC, 2011) puts the market

2 Europol has produced an annual Threat Assessments since 2006, mainly coloured by the 'underworld gaze'. Fraud was mentioned belatedly, 2008, without reference to earlier years: an old threat suddenly discovered.

3 Serious and Organised Crime Assessment – Methodology, 19 June 2012. Note of the Council of the European Union in which a new OCTA methodology is elaborated. While the paper contains theoretical improvements, in practical terms (completion by the police in the Member States) it may become a nightmare. The themes of reliability of input and validity of processing are lacking. See also footnote 4.

approach in the centre, though as mentioned before, the executive director regrets the lack of information. Nevertheless, it can be interpreted as an orientation to a more empirical and 'human size' tailored approach.

Such a tailor-made description is also provided by the following two chapters: a chapter on the organised crime situation in Spain and an elaborate description of the daily life of individual organising drug criminals. The OC situation in Spain is of interest because as the south-western 'criminal hub' (as mentioned in Europol's OCTA) it would fulfil a special function in transiting contraband from North Africa and Latin America to the rest of Europe. What kind of criminal organisations does that require? Based on extensive police material the authors *Andrea Gimenez-Salinas, Laura Requena Espada and Luis de la Corte Ibáñez* provide a sobering account of the identified criminal organisations. As far as the organisational structures in their sample are concerned, hierarchical and non-hierarchical organisations were equally present, but the hierarchical ones appear to be much smaller. The simple reason, according to the authors, is the trouble of management when hierarchical organisations expand. Horizontal and network 'organisations', if such loose structures still deserve that qualification, are more flexible and adaptable without the burden of management. Concerning the level of sophistication, the authors mention some identified technical high-level devices, but in general the technical level and knowledge were not conspicuous. The same applies to money laundering that consists mainly in physical moving around of cash. Altogether, the human "*profile seems different from the threatening profile shown in European reports.*"[4]

A closer look at the daily life of criminal (drug) entrepreneurs is provided in the chapter on *criminal risk mitigation* of *Mike Salinas-Edwards*, who closely followed 25 drug traders, mainly distributors, for a period of a couple of years. As all but one of his traders have never been arrested they form an exceptional sample, compared with the usual samples of known suspects from police sources. They traded in the UK as well as on a Mediterranean island on closed markets, partly distributing drugs in small quantities, partly importing bigger consignments from Asia. What was remarkable about these criminals as acting traders? As a matter of fact, very little. They were daily risk managers, whether shielding their information exchange (using common social media) or stashing and transporting their daily deliveries of contraband. Partly by learning from their peers'

---

4 A number of observations about Spain in the OCTA 2011 (also provided by the police) do not appear in the police data of this research project, making a critical look at the raw data input and processing of the Europol analysis (under whatever new methodology) all the more urgent. The whole chain of data input and processing must be accessible for methodological scrutiny: from village bobby till the output of Europol.

techniques, partly through self-education they learned to be disciplined in their methods and to keep a low social profile in an insecure market environment.

As remarked before, the criminal market approach is not new: it has been the focus in some of the first research projects (Van Duyne *et al.* 1990, 2003; von Lampe, 2003, 2005). In the past ten years this market perspective has come more to the fore again (UNODC, 2010). Does this reflect a silent departure from the one-sided Big Organised Crime Threat orientation, the 'underworld gaze' which dominated the onset of the organised crime debate and policy (Fijnaut *et al.*, 1998)? That is uncertain: once worded in official papers, a wrong start can have protracted consequences. Indeed, elements of it keep lingering on, for example at the Europol and UN level. However, the UNODC 2010 Transnational Organised Crime Threat Assessment is orderly built around criminal markets not all of them described from the usual 'underworld gaze': there are chapters devoted to environmental resources and counterfeiting of consumer goods and medicine. However, the concepts of economic or financial crime are missing, while the term money laundering occurs only five times in the main text. Relinquishing the 'underworld gaze' does not mean that one looks higher up, for example at the upperworld of criminal finances (or financial crimes).

Criminal finances: looking for the human size

Finding the 'realistic' human size is not easy, in particular in when it concerns criminal finances. If one wants to make realistic measurements one faces dimensions and yardsticks that rarely match. We have the *financial harm* and *volume* dimension: the alleged trillions of crime-money like strings of zeros behind the first positive digit(s) of official reports, a kind of threading beads from a well-filled basket and the more 'beads' in the number, the better. Next to that we have the *criminal law* dimension: investigation, prosecution and sentencing.

The financial Augean stables

When we look at the harm and volume dimension, we see the large dark outlines of big threats looming up. All transcending human reality? Here we encounter a refutation: the more than 50 billion Euro damage of Madoff, the hundreds of billions involved in the selling of 'triple A' junk bonds, the Libor scandal, Icesafe or Parmalat, they are all 'man-made'. 'Human size' does not need to be modest in its consequences. But above all these cases towers a bigger dimension: that of the mystical money-laundering volumes of the FATF, that first depicted dangerous financial Augean stables and subsequently imposed their special Herculean AML rescue regime to cleanse them (Levi, 2007; Stessen, 2000).

Against this background there are the dimensions of the criminal law handling of actual financial crimes, ranging from criminal market manipulation to fraud, deceit and embezzlement. In general these dimensions of case processing (prosecution and trial) do not look proportionate to the harmful financial consequences. Sometimes the criminal law apparatus does not come into action at all. *Ciril Keršmanc* and *Meta Ahtik* elaborate in their chapter on *deceptive practices in banking* three exemplar cases of systematic financial deception, ranging from local to international. Supervisors, but occasionally also states at least acquiesced to (if not profited from) the deceptive practices in these cases. The authors provide a readable explanation of the technical working of those financial deceptions. In essence it is an accountancy cheat: pretending to have a better balance sheet than actually exists – to be qualified as documentary fraud. This circular game can be illustrated for example, by letting a bad debtor repay his loan at the end of the year by giving a short term loan to another firm that loans it again to the bad debtor who quickly redeems his debt before 31 December. That is only temporary, however, because in January the situation is restored: the bad debtor had only disappeared from the books for a fortnight. This relatively simple scheme of a Slovenian bank was dwarfed by the Lehman Brother Holding Inc, in its sophistication as well as its consequences. The collapse of Lehman Brother reverberated worldwide. The same applies to the accountancy deception of the Greek state, with the help of Goldman Sachs acting as the accomplice for technical (dirty) work. It is interesting to speculate on the proportionality of the potential criminal law response compared with that of conmen such as Madoff and Stanford who *directly* harmed the interest of common investors. What really happened in these (global) deception cases described in this chapter? There were indictments in Slovenia, a criminal investigation in Greece (on-going) and in Iceland a real 'scapegoat conviction' of the ex-prime minister, though without punishment. But what happened to the other conspiracies to deceive, such as Goldman Sachs or the Libor manipulators?[5] The Herculean cleansing of the financial Augean stable merely swept just a few guilty mice of an insignificant dimension out of the barn and otherwise settled with the big players (Dorn and Levi, 2011).

5 It is not true that nothing happened from criminal law enforcement side. At the time of writing (December-February) the SFO arrested 3 persons connected to Libor manipulation. www.BBC-timeline, 19 December 2012

If the reader may think the 'classic' metaphor over-stretched, he should be reminded of the following cognitive tension. On the one hand people like the superhuman dimensions in many representations of reality, but on the other hand, they seek a neat 'classic Hellenic' harmonious balance in cause and effect. For example, in causal attribution 'big' consequences are preferably attributed to 'big' causes; and so are the small ones. Despite this psychological bias, such neat causal balances are not necessary, whether in normal life or in the financial field. Did the big Global Financial Crises unleash a big wave of fraud, or the other way round? Or was there not such a causal relationship? *Michael Levi* investigated in his chapter this potential relationship between financial and economic crimes and 'the' Global Financial Crisis. Of course, the author warns the reader of the methodological problems inherent in such a comparison. Financial/economic crime is very heterogeneous, the time series are far from reliable or comparable, while any (causal) nexus to the equally multi-facetted financial crisis has to take account of the time elapsed between the beginning of fraud schemes and their discovery. Various Ponzi-schemes, such as that of Madoff, predated the financial crisis for years and were only discovered because the financial crisis made continuation impossible. Whether the Global Financial Crisis is contributing to a substantial increase of fraud is equally difficult to determine. For many kinds of fraud schemes changing technology and opportunities seem to play a more important role than the crisis. For some other kinds of financial crime the relationship is more direct, if only because the crimes are committed out of misery and despair after dismissal or to maintain appearances of an affluent living standard. However, such financial-'existential' data are lacking, as are most data collections of fraud, that in most countries lack even a semblance of validity and reliability (a clear imbalance between seriousness and data management responsibility).

Levi's survey does not point at an 'harmonious' causal attribution; rather some kind of statistical fragmentation and chaos, which may be more characteristic for daily human (fraudulent) affairs than any kind of orderly statistical correlation. And within this chaos, and taking Levi's and Keršman's findings together, one finds nothing peculiar but old human tendencies: unbounded greed by a reckless financial elite scraping the loot; slack or even condoning supervisors of the same professional elite level (Dorn, 2010), and foot dragging or at least hesitating prosecution, also staffed by the more or less same social layer. This does not imply a deliberate non-action by a unified elite but rather a common uncertainty (Dorn and Levi, 2011; 43-46). In this state of disorder, at a certain point of time these 'human tributaries' flowed together and made the thin protective dikes break, followed by the superlative global credit flood.

An interesting aspect for further reflection is the Financial Action Task Force (FATF), guarding a global anti-laundering system (the 'Herculean' task) to further the integrity of the financial system. In the whole debate on the Global Financial Crisis this august body has remained deafening silent as if was guarding financial integrity on a different planet. Nevertheless, creating in concert non-collateral credits and selling these as 'safe' can be interpreted as a conspiracy to defraud, while the profits thereof represent 'proceeds'. However, the FATF is not focused on criminal money creation *inside* the banks, but on containing the global threat from 'outside' money that is at risk of flowing into the financial system.

What created the biggest Augean stable: 'inside' or 'outside' crime-money? By hindsight the criminal 'outside' money looks like a minor threat, but is nevertheless guarded by a monumental structure of supervision and regulations. In our metaphor: not the kind of humanly balanced Hellenic temple but rather a sort of ugly building of *Ceausescu* proportions of ever greater budgetary extensions (Harvey, 2011: 86). Despite the proportions of this AML-building, we should not forget that inside human beings are working: supervisors, compliance staff and the employees dealing with customers. This human aspect is the focus of the chapter by *Jackie Harvey, Rowan Bosworth-Davies* and *Martin Elliott.* They raise the question whether the regulatory system is a matter of ritual dancing according to a more or less mechanic choreography or something which is supported from some 'inner conviction' to improve the integrity of financial service providers. Against the background of Keršman's chapter and from what we know otherwise of the system of deliberate deception within the financial sector, the lofty aim of serving integrity "from the heart" sounds so naive that it is bound produce a burst of Homeric laughter.

As the authors do not share the cynical bias of the writer of this introduction, they carried out a proper research to assess the opinions of a sample respondents from the compliance sector of the financial service providers. While most of the interviewees agreed that some kind of regulatory system was required and positive to increase the reputation of the financial service sector, the 'inner conviction' was far from present. After all, anti-laundering compliance is a business cost, which could prevent losses (*e.g.* of fraud), but otherwise does not make money. In addition to that, the 'risked based system' which has replaced the 'rule based system', intended to relinquish a strict rule system, led to more (internal) rules, designed not to recognise but to *avoid* risks – not from launderers but from the supervisors. This could have been foreseen as the new risk-approach was imposed by one set of bureaucrats on a similar set of bureaucrats, while it is common knowledge that the last skill a bureaucrat is hired for is his capacity to face risks. So the outcome was as human as any psychologist would have predicted: a system of dancing rules to fend off risks from the potentially brow-beating or even punishing regulator. And the regulator and field inspectors, aren't they part of this tranquil choreography? According to the compliance officers most inspectors reflect the essence of this metaphor by mainly carrying out a routine procedure of tick-box inspection. Where is the real 'inner motivation'? The researchers cannot answer this question unambiguously.

Still, what drives the AML regime? 60% of the respondents believe that "*the international debate on money laundering is controlled by governments and the law enforcement lobby.*" The findings of Verhage (2009; 2011) and Gelemerova (2011) lend support to this statement: the AM-complex is maintained by all interested parties benefiting from it, governmental as well as private firms.

Some of these firms have an interest of their own to highlight certain potential forms of laundering which also happens to be their well-remunerated specialism as *Melvin Soudijn* observes in his chapter on *Trade Based Money Laundering*. In essence this way of laundering consists of using invoices to veil and justify the transfer of crime-money: increase or decrease of the value or the nature of the traded goods (if any goods are involved). This is an old trick for settling illegal accounts: *e.g.* dodging VAT and import duties as well as hiding large bribes. At present these predicate offences have an unavoidable laundering 'tail': once there are criminal profits, laundering must follow. Nevertheless, the worry about the laundering potential of 'licit' invoices was made public rather late: around 2005. There are various telling facets in the way this new danger was brought to the fore, which the author analyses accurately. In the first place there is an intertwining of interests between the FATF and an academic, Prof. Zdanowics, who started to bring this 'new' risk to the attention of the authorities. Zdanowics as well as the FATF had a shared interest in presenting this as a 'big threat'. For good reasons the latter will never present anything but as a big threat, otherwise it has no policy message. And Zdanowics established a company that maintains a website in which everybody can check whether commodity prices deviate suspiciously from a safe average. Of course, for a fee. As things go, Zdanowics was frequently fêted as a keynote speaker and the FATF could issue two reports (2006 and 2008) with (only) a couple of case studies. Both could now cross-refer to each other to underpin the gravity of the problem: intellectually I would qualify this as a sequence of suspicious transactions. Another facet is the way this trade based laundering is defined. As is so often the case in the field of laundering, the concept description looks analytically like a ragged table cloth, rarely able to delineate the phenomenon properly. The author observed casually that this does not seem to matter: "*Rather, the FATF does not engage in any critical debate. Lacking critical feedback [. . .] the definition remained somewhat ambiguous*", which is the way allegedly big problems retain their perceived size. However, the author's analysis of the shortcomings in using trade statistics and how one does not need in- or deflated invoices to present crime-money as licit income from trade, show otherwise: with every step of his analysis the problem appears to shrink. But not for the FATF or Zdanowics. Indeed, his casual remark cited above should have been put forward as a very fundamental aspect of the intellectual AML culture.

Guilty of crime-money, unless . . .

. . . Unless proven innocent. Sometimes big threats require a reversal of principles. This is the case with crime-money, one of the most conspicuous facets of the 'organised crime' threat. The display of criminal wealth reminds the law enforcement agents (and citizens) of a wrong state of affair that needs to be redressed. One may summarise this feeling as follows: "*Even if we cannot nail him in court, we should nail his money because he should not have it.*" Such a (resentful) wish is at odds with the legal principle in most constitutional states, namely that one cannot expropriate assets of suspected persons without conviction. That is what kings did during the *ancient regime*, an abuse abolished since the French Revolution. But now the question is raised whether that principle should not be set aside to address the threat of (transnational) organised crime threat and the assumed colossal criminal wealth?

In some countries, for example Ireland, this question was answered positively. *Colin King* relates in his chapter on *civil forfeiture of criminal assets* in Ireland how alleged criminal can be stripped of their assets without criminal conviction. This originated in the general heated atmosphere of fear of organised crime in the 1990s and after two shocking murders in 1996, a number of laws against organised crime were rushed through the legislator. Confiscation and forfeiture of 'illicit' assets without criminal convictions but in a civil procedure was one of the important innovations. This choice was made because a civil procedures does not require all the cumbersome criminal evidential rules and safeguards: the much lower standard of 'plausibility' is sufficient. The author gives a critical account of this Irish "experiment" (has already lasted 17 (!) years), the lack of transparency of the Asset Recovery Office, while he has to conclude his chapter with admitting that ". . . *less is known as to the extent and/or nature of organised criminal activity in Ireland. Reliable data concerning economic cost, market size, criminal income and wealth is notably absent*".

This sounds at the same time contradictory and familiar: a serious organised crime threat, a law that infringes on individual citizen's rights, a powerful but non-transparently functioning Criminal Asset Agency, and after 17 years ('experiment'!) still little is known about the targeted threat or the effects of the policy. Theis looks like an Irish variation of the international policy makers' ignorance or wilful avoidance of accountability.

The principle of unjustified or suspicious wealth and non-conviction based confiscation also plays a role in Romania. However, in this country the background is different: tackling *corruption* by confiscating the inexplicable wealth increase in a civil procedure, again because of the inefficiency of criminal law procedures. This policy, laid down in the Wealth Verification Law of 1996 was intended to discourage corruption and at the same time to solve the conflict about the constitutional principle that property is assumed to be acquired legally. The law also established an elaborate Verification procedure, which proved to be almost as cumbersome and unsuccessful as a criminal law procedure. The law was evaluated in 2004 and its outcomes appeared to be less than modest: the 16 commissions processed on average 2 cases per year. Three final decisions took between 5 and 9 years. It looked very much like a law in in-action: a display of foot dragging by an unwilling political elite and public administration, from the government downwards despite the many tough measures announced. In 2006/7, under pressure of the EU new laws were enacted and a National Integrity Agency was established, after much delay because of on-going petty wrangling and mud throwing between opponents. After that the Constitutional Court continued to create problems which in 2010 led to new amendments. Another couple of years were lost and in the end the mouse came out of the mountain: the 15 years of impotent policy against unjustified wealth yielded 7 final confiscation decisions. This meagre outcome should be interpreted against the background of a political and commercial elite bent on making impressive outward appearances while hiding their intention to guard their interest in the *status quo* even if it paid lip service to the debated principle: guilty of crime-money unless . . . .

Petrus C. van Duyne

Potemkin villages, silent resistance and realism

According to legend, Empress Catherina the Great of Russia visited the newly conquered Crimea and her lover and protégé, count Potemkin, wanted to impress her and her entourage by showing them thriving villages. There were none however, so he had fake villages built. Whether that is true or not, the concept of the 'Potemkin village' entered history and came to denote the presentation of an empty facade to keep up appearances, as is also the case in politics. In the previous section we encountered such a pretence in the Romanian anti-corruption policy. Of course, this is normal rationality, albeit deceptive. Entering such a Potemkin facade brings us right into the field of corruption, which is a form of 'rotten' decision making: pretending a legitimate decision making, while the outcome is determined by a hidden exchange of interests (Van Duyne, 2001).

The chapter by *Petrus C. van Duyne* concerns the *anti-corruption policy in Serbia* in a potential Potemkin village. Though the Serbian authorities have regularly proclaimed a new round in the fight against corruption (like in Romania), the meagre outcomes cast doubt on the real intentions: are these not just Potemkin villages? Therefore, the author raises the question: "Who really cares?" Reviewing the literature it appears that the answer to this question is: "few care and many take the initiative to bribery", either for some service or to stay out of trouble (with the police). Unsurprisingly the number of reported complaints of corruption and the subsequent criminal investigations and prosecution is low, as appears from the analysis of the database (2007-2009) of the Prosecution Service and the Courts. Of course, despite such meagre figures, there still could be a criminal policy behind them. However, apart from a special prosecution monitor system, which proved to be empty, no policy could be identified. The differences in case processing between court regions appeared to be both enormous and erratic, though unknown to the responsible ministries as well as to the prosecution offices and courts: nobody knew and nobody cared.

Doing research on corruption in Serbia is not popular: the research team found so many closed doors, that the system was characterised as a 'black box'. However, after the analysis of the erratic law enforcement data, the author concluded that the 'black box' could rather be qualified as a 'random box': almost nothing correlated with anything, whether one compared regions, years or criminal offence categories.

Nevertheless, under the pressure of the EU and GRECO, the Serbian government established institutions: the Anti-Corruption Council to advise the government and the Anti-Corruption Agency for a nation-wide overview.

However, the relationship between Council and government is such, that thus far the government has never replied to any letter or advice. The other institution, the Anti Corruption Agency, active since January 2010, proved to be completely impenetrable: it declined any cooperation or transparency. Though the ACA is tasked to monitor the anti-corruption policy, it performed that task on the basis of shady data while ignoring available statistical data, a transparent methodology or any help from outside academic experts. Nobody cared. The metaphor of the Potemkin village does not seem to be far-fetched, including a politically correct dancing in the village square.[6]

The next two chapters deal with the anti-corruption policy in Turkey. The title of the first chapter (with the question: *Is corruption a problem*?), written by *Ugur Omurgonulsen* already gives an indication that the basic attitude of the population may not differ essentially from that of Serbia ("who cares"). It seems that the problem awareness is in the first place again a matter of foreign attention: the EU, the IMF, World Bank and other bodies judge that there is a Turkish corruption problem. Under this outward pressure Turkish governments started to enact laws against corruption and established ethics and anti-corruption bodies. But: "*not only legal-institutional measures but also mentality changes as a fundamental element of integrity-based management are essential in combating corruption and unethical conduct*". These 'mentality changes' are the difficult targets to achieve: it involves the political elite (eager to retain their (corruptive) power, the bureaucracy (with a strong internal cohesion) and the business community competing with bribes for contracts. Doing something against corruption implies criticising the state. But the state is strong and unquestionable, while within the bureaucracy the ranks are closed. And the Turkish citizens? That depends on where you stand. For the real taxpayer, who has to bribe his way through a sluggish and cumbersome bureaucracy, corruption is an extra illegal taxation. For the lower working classes, the majority of the voters and earning (part of) their income from the grey economy, corruption appears to be less of a problem as it allows them to buy off control. So why should politicians strive for an effective anti-corruption policy if that would cost votes? "*It depends on where you stand*", which is also the title of the following chapter on corruption in Turkey by *Alan Doig and Brendan Quirke.*

The overview of the Turkish anti-corruption policy presented by the two authors reveals many similarities with that of Serbia (or the other countries in the region). There is no shortage of programmes, legislation, ratified international conventions, protocols and institutions behind which one does not find

6 Meanwhile, the first director was dismissed in November 2012 because her conduct damaged the reputation of the institution.

much content. Sometimes one finds a real building, but such as the *Prime Ministry Inspection Board*, which, however, appears to be too small. The civil society organisations are weak (also observed in Serbia by Trivunović *et al.*, 2007: 3), while the Turkish tradition of a strong central state allows NGOs only so much influence that it cannot not challenge the state. Add to this the bureaucratic tradition, and one has to conclude that there is no adequately prepared 'building lot' to set up a coherently designed and solid anti-corruption building. Actually, all the material for such a building must be imported, to which the cultural reality in Turkey (but also Serbia and other countries of the region, all erstwhile parts of the Ottoman empire) have to adapt. That evokes (silent) resistance camouflaged by the Potemkin villages of ratified conventions, laws and legal structures.

In discussions about corruption in countries such as Turkey and the neighbouring Balkan states references are often made to the 'complexity' of the situation as a kind of complementary explanation of the failing anti-corruption policy, particularly when it comes to implementation. In addition the abstract 'lack of political will' is added as a complementary explanation. However, these are abstract concepts veiling underlying banal human realities. 'Complexity' stands usually for the human capacity to create and maintain a state of disorder, while the 'political will' is actually little more than the personal preferences of cliques of persons within the perimeter of power. Corruption (or corrupted) policy is basically human relations management.

These 'complexities' compare badly with the policing and institution building in a really complex landscape. Such an example is provided by the maintenance of laws and regulations in the multiple faceted and institutional *environmental* policy. How this complicated law enforcement is maintained in *Belgium* has been accurately described by *Lieselot Bisschop* in her chapter on the *electronic waste export* from the port of Antwerp. The author describes how the transnational flow of electronic waste is supervised in Belgium. Given the multitude of agencies involved, perpetrators, the many competences of national and regional oversight bodies (six), the multi-layered private sector (production, transit and export) and the interests of the receivers of the e-waste (*Ghana*, in this study), given this composite landscape it is noteworthy that such a supervisory system works at all. Of course, it is work of man and far from flawless. It is also too complicated to be managed in a top-down way by the government. Instead, it is the task for a multi-actor governance, locally as well as internationally, which is no guarantee for success in stemming the e-waste (or other waste) to less regulated, developing countries such as Ghana. Within such a multi-actor governance there is a lot of pressure from various corners: governmental as well as from the private sector and civil society, but such that potential Potemkin villages will be soon exposed. It is interesting to observe that on the one hand, the actors in this field realise the size of the problem and that it is not easy to catch repeat offenders and 'big fishes', while on the other hand, they do not resort to 'organised crime' and 'mafia talk' to boost the importance of this portfolio. How easy would it not be to present the e-waste trade in terms of a 'waste mafia' accompanied with a boastful Waste Transnational Organised Threat Assessment, a 'WTOCTA'? Instead, in this chapter we find a down to earth realism eschewing supersized problem descriptions.

There is a weakness in the argumentation opposing sober human size realism to supersizing dimensions: they both involve a moulding the 'soft wax of a given raw material' to a desired outcome. And whether the outcome transcends or actually down-plays to human dimensions, it is all 'man-made'. Sometimes this 'man-made reality' can take hilarious-tragic proportions though. Dictator Ceausescu thought that his people would suffer less from the cold if he would order the weather forecast to state that the temperature was some degrees higher than actually measured. An example of man-made law enforcement reality, almost equally hilarious is described in the last chapter by *Anna Markovska* and *Alexey Serdyuk* on the dilemma of the Ukrainian policeman reporting crimes. Just as Ceausescu ordered frost to be thawed, so the Ukrainian Ministry of Interior sets targets of police successes. And success there will be! However, these must remain within safe limits and safe issues. For example, while opinion polls reveal that "*56% to 73% of all official contacts with the road traffic police is accompanied with bribery, not one single case of bribery was officially recorded*". For other crime categories, other aspects come to the fore in the kneading of the statistical criminal reality, which is not a matter of only putting thumbs roughly into the wax. The shaping must be smooth, also take care of the human interests of the work floor. Hence, police successes must be balanced over the years: too much success in one year implies one must work harder to be again successful in the next year. This has wider consequences than just keeping the up-going line of success smooth and comfortable to workload of the police force. It also affects profoundly the nature of case selection: more small cases add to desired statistics while more complicated organised crime and economic crime cases lower the success rate. Apart from higher-level political interests to de-prioritise such sensitive cases (or to launch corruption cases against opponents), the final result must please the Ministry of Interior and at the same time be credible. One can maintain that the whole official statistical criminal reality is the result of a well thought-out Potemkin building. Corrupt in its core, but rational in taking care of human realities.

Back to Protagoras

Under the banner of Protagoras' aphorism this chapter discussed the common bias to over-size human proportions. In this regard there is no self-exception to this bias for science: seriousness and pomp of language, together with external pressure to go along with what is expected politically these are all external amplifiers of proportions, to which may be added built-in amplifiers of the subjects themselves. Organised crime and crime-money are subjects that meet all these conditions for applying enlarged measures to the underlying reality. In recognition of this fallacy this volume looks back as well as comparing contemporary studies from the basic question: what is humanly real behind the pomp of the official debate that has by now turned into a stilled ritualised choreography? The findings of the studies highlight the validity of an old, but obvious adage: "Mobsters are human too" (Van Duyne, 2000). And with that was meant: do not attribute to them a heavier 'criminal burden' than their 'shoulders' can carry. Researching the organised crime phenomenon from this angle we arrive at the human measure of criminal things for what they 'really' are. And if in default of data (or access to them) researchers resort to describing again official structures and laws, it is time to remind them of saying of the historian Golo Mann (1992; 27): "*We speak (of) things but we mean men*" (Wir sagen Dinge und meinen Menschen").

Protagoras' statement allows no self-exception: policy makers are human too. They share the common bias and indulge in the enlargement of their threat dimensions and consequently their own enlargement. They can do so virtually unopposed; all the more as many of them belong or are related to the Lords of Grants and Subsidies. They are not likely to grant research from another angle than their own human measure – and researchers know that. This justifies a complementary research (Woodiwiss, 2003; Woodiwiss and Hobbs, 2008; Hobbs and Hobbs, 2012): Protagoras' thesis applied to policy makers too. With such a dual approach we may arrive at a proper Hellenic balance in researching this field: the human measure of organised crime and policy making.

Author's note: all numbers in this volume are in normal European annotation: the comma is for the decimals and the dot for the thousands

References

Dorn, N., Pozi finance and state capture: the crisis of the financial market regulation. In P.C. van Duyne *et al.* (eds.), *Cross-border crime inroads on integrity in Europe.* Nijmegen, Wolf Legal Publishers, 2010

Dorn, N. and M. Levi, Theorising the Security and Exchange Commission's 2010 settlement with Goldman Sachs. Legislative weakness, reintegrative shaming or 'temporary business interruption' for financial market power elites? In G. Antonopoulos *et al.* (eds.), *Unsual and unusual organising criminals in Europe and Beyond.* Apeldoorn, Maklu, 2011

Duyne, P.C. van, (Transnational) organised crime, laundering and the congregation of the gullible. Tilburg University 2011

Duyne, P.C. van, OCTA 2006: the unfulfilled promise. *Trends in Organized Crime*, 2007, *no. 3*, 120-128

Duyne, P.C. van, The creation of a threat image: Media, policy making and organised crime. In P. C. van Duyne, M. Jager, K. von Lampe and J.L. Newell (eds.), *Threats and phantoms of organised crime, corruption and terrorism.* Nijmegen, Wolf Legal Publishers, 2004

Duyne, P.C. van, Will 'Caligula go transparent?' Corruption in acts and attitude. *Forum on Crime and Society*, 2001, vol. 1, *nr. 2*, 73-98

Duyne, P.C. van, Mobsters are human too: behavioural science and organised crime investigation. *Crime, Law and Social Change*, 2000, *vol. 34*, 369-390

Duyne, P.C. van, *Het spook en de dreiging van de georganiseerde misdaad*, SDU, 's-Gravenhage, 1995

Duyne, P.C. van and T. Vander Beken, The incantations of the EU organised crime policy making. *Crime Law and Social Change*, 2009. vol. 51, 261–281

Duyne, P.C. van and M.D.H. Nelemans, Transnational organised crime: thinking in and out of Plato's cave. *Handbook of transnational crime*, Routledge, 2011

Europol, *OCTA 2011. EU organised crime threat assessment.* The Hague, 2011

Fijnaut, C., F. Bovenkerk, G. Bruinsma and H.G. van de Bunt, *Organised crime in the Netherlands.* Den Haag, Kluwer Law International, 1998

Gelemerova, L., *Money laundering in the context of globalisation.* Nijmegen, Wolf Legal Publishers, 2011

Harvey, J., Money laundering: phantoms, imagery and facts. In G. Antonopolis *et al.* (eds.), *Unsual and unusual organising criminals in Europe and Beyond.* Apeldoorn, Maklu, 2011

Hobbs, D. and S. Hobbs, A bog of conspiracy. The institutional evolution of organised crime in the UK. In F. Allum and S. Gilmour (eds.), *Routledge handbook of transnational organised crime.* London, Routledge, 2012

Lampe, K. von, Explaining the emergence of the cigarette black market in Germany. In P.C. van Duyne, K. von Lampe, M. van Dijck and J.L. Newell (eds.), *The organised crime economy. Managing crime markets in Europe.* Nijmegen, Wolf Legal Publishers, 2005

Lampe, K. von, Organising the nicotine racket. Patterns of criminal cooperation in the cigarette black market in Germany. In P.C. van Duyne, K. Von Lampe and J.L. Newell (eds.), *Criminal finances and organising crime in Europe.* Nijmegen, Wolf Legal Publishers, 2003

Lampe, K. von, Organized crime in Europe. In P. Reichel (ed.), *Handbook of transnational crime and justice*, Thousand Oaks, CA: Sage, 403-424

Levi, M., Pecunia non olet. The control of money laundering revisited. In F. Bovenkerk and M. Levi (eds.), *The organised crime community.* New York, Springer, 2007

Mann, G., *Deutsche Geschichte des 19. und 20. Jahrhunderts.* Frankfurt am Main, Fischer Taschenbuch Verlag, 1992

Reuter, P., Are Estimates of the Volume of Money Laundering either Feasible or Useful? Comments on the presentation by John Walker at the conference '*Tackling money laundering*' (fall, 2006), Utrecht, 2007

Reuter, P. and V. Greenfield, Measuring global drug markets: How good are the numbers and why should we care about them? *World Economics*, 2001, 4, 159–173

Scheinost, M., Organised crime politics in the Czech republic: A hard road from under-estimation to the European standard. In C. Fynaut and L.Paoli (eds.), *Organised crime in Europe.*Dordrecht, Springer, 2004

Stessens, G., *Money laundering, a new international law enforcement model.* Cambridge University Press, 2000

Stille, A., *The sack of Rome. Media + money + celebrity = power = Silvio Berlusconi.* London, Penguin Books, 2007

Sutherland, E.H., *White collar crime.* New Haven, Yale University Press, 1983. With introduction of G. Geis and C. Goff

Trivunović, M., V. Devine and H. Mathisen, *Corruption in Serbia 2007. Overview of problems and status of reforms.* Bergen, Chr. Michelsen Institute, 2007

Unger, B. (ed.), *The scale and impacts of money laundering.* Cheltenham, Edward Elgar, 2007

UNODC, *The globalisation of crime. A Transnational Organised Crime Threat Assessment.* Vienna, 2011

Verhage, A., *The anti money laundering complex and the compliance industry.* London, Routledge, 2011

Verhage, A., The holy grail of money-laundering statistics: Input and outcome of the Belgian AML-system. In: P.C. van Duyne *et al.* (eds.), *Cross-border crime inroads on integrity in Europe.* Nijmegen, Wolf Legal Publishers, 2010

Verhage, A., Between the hammer and the anvil. The anti-money laundering-complex and its interactions with the compliance industry. *Crime Law and Social Change*, 2009, vol. *no. 1*, 52, 9-32

Walker, J., Estimates of the extent of money laundering in and through Australia. John Walker Consultancy Services, September, 1995

Walker, J. and B. Unger, Measuring global money laundering: "The Walker gravity model". *Review of Law and Economics*, 2009 Vol. 5, no. 2, 822-853

Woodiwiss, M., Transnational organised crime: the strange career of an American concept. In: M.E. Bear (ed.), *Critical reflections on transnational organised crime, money laundering, and corruption.* Toronto, University of Toronto Press, 2003

Woodiwiss, M. and D. Hobbs, Moral panics and the rhetoric of organised crime policing in America and Britain. *British Journal of Criminology*, 2009, *49*, 106-128

Fears and forecasts
Notions about future trends in the early phases of the German debate on organised crime revisited

Klaus von Lampe[1]

Introduction

The debate on 'organised crime' in general, and in Germany in particular, has been repeatedly criticised for its lack of conceptual clarity and empirical underpinning, and for leading to policies that appear to rest on essentially a vague and ambiguous construct of social reality (Albrecht, 1998; Busch, 1991; Van Duyne, 2004; von Lampe, 2001). Or, put more bluntly, on stereotypes that "*owe more to Hollywood and police hype than to serious research*" (Naylor, 2003: 99). However, the lack of research does not automatically mean that the assumptions on which the mainstream discourse has rested, are false. The question is, to what extent the debate on 'organised crime' has relied simply on constructing a threat image, and to what extent it has been driven by realistic concerns. With the privilege of hindsight, a cautious answer to this question seems possible, especially when one focuses on one particular facet of the debate: predictions of the future development of 'organised crime'. Retrospectively it is difficult if not impossible to ascertain the accuracy of statements about the nature and extent of 'organised crime' for a given historical point in time. But to some extent it appears possible to judge past predictions of the development of 'organised crime', at least as far as these predictions pertain to broad trends which should have materialised in the meantime.

The purpose of this paper is to systematically examine such predictions within the context of the first 30 years of the German debate on 'organised crime', which can roughly be dated back to the time period from the mid-1960s to the mid-1990s, and to discuss these predictions with respect to two aspects.

First, what predictions have been made about the future of 'organised crime' in Germany, and to what extent, based on today's knowledge, have these predictions been accurate. Drawing on published law enforcement data, this chapter will argue that the generally pessimistic undertone of the 'organised crime'-debate is

1 Associate Professor, John Jay College of Criminal Justice (City University of New York).

contrasted with a development of the crime landscape that appears to be less dynamic and less dramatic than anticipated.

Second, the predictions are examined with a view to general ideas about the developmental dynamics of 'organised crime'. It will be argued that while these notions have been vague and ephemeral over the years, there is a persistent belief that Germany is under a manifest or latent threat of being taken over by foreign criminal organisations.

This point will be illustrated through a brief review of the reactions to three recent high-profile criminal cases: the serial murder of immigrant businessmen between 2000 and 2006 in various parts of Germany; the killing of seven Asians in a Chinese restaurant in a small town in North-West Germany in 2007; and the shooting dead of six Italians outside a pizzeria in the city of Duisburg in 2007.

Historical Background

The beginning of the German debate on 'organised crime' can be traced back to the 1960s when law enforcement officials began to notice a profound change in the crime landscape. The new crime landscape, it was alleged, was populated by offenders who were more intelligent and skilful than before, employing modern technologies and displaying strategic thinking (Hellmer, 1966; Niggemeyer, 1967). At the same time, crime appeared to be more and more an affair of internationally mobile offenders, or offenders that had relocated to Germany amidst the flow of labour migrants from Southern Europe (Bux, 1966; Ochs, 1964; Wehner, 1966; Westphal, 1969). It was in this climate that 'organised crime' first appeared as a theme in the West-German criminal policy debate.

Among the first voices that eventually would swell to a chorus was that of a police detective, Reinhard Steinke. He was the author of a paper about the Mafia in Italy and the U.S. which was published in a volume on international law enforcement in 1966 (Steinke, 1966). Steinke declared the Mafia the scourge of the future for Germany, arguing that the liberalised criminal procedure code, which had gone into effect in the previous year, would attract criminals from other countries and would make West-Germany their preferred domicile and area of operation. Steinke continued:

> "It doesn't require any prophetic talent to dare to predict that in 1966 and 1967 a crime boom will come upon us that can but evoke a terrible shudder. The Mafia will deliver its first great blow perhaps in the Cologne area. Presumably, at first only roadblocks will be erected and the motorists will be relieved of their cash. This should be followed by assaults on farm estates and the extortion of

business people, and certainly cases of kidnapping will be the next measures to intimidate the population." (Steinke, 1966: 149).

The media eagerly picked up on the issue. The *General-Anzeiger* in Bonn, seat of the government of West-Germany, asked in a headline "How big is the Mafia in Germany?" only to add: "First big blow expected in the Cologne area". The *Schwäbische Donau-Zeitung* in Ulm told its readers that the "Mafia prepares for an assault on Germany" and that the German police is helpless.[2]

Of course, the Mafia never set up any roadblocks anywhere in the country, nor have mafiosi become notorious for assaulting farm estates or engaging in kidnappings in Germany, although cases of the extortion of business people have been reported, typically in the case of restaurateurs of Italian origin (see Flormann and Krevert, 2001). So, while offhand, most of Steinke's predictions can be quickly discounted as rather bizarre horror scenarios, they did (and still do) strike a familiar note. His line of reasoning is, first of all, a variant of what American scholars have branded the 'alien conspiracy theory', the notion that 'organised crime' in the U.S., and by extension in Western Europe, is an imported phenomenon, rather than an outgrowth and integral part of the society where it exists (Potter, 1994; Smith, 1976).

But there is also a specific understanding of the developmental dynamics of 'organised crime' encapsulated in Steinke's thinking that has been resurfacing on occasion since then: the notion of a revolutionary rather than evolutionary process. It is a belief that a criminal group can establish itself in a new territory with a show of force in the form of blatant acts of violence.

The question that will be addressed in the following section is to what extent this notion of an 'alien take-over' is representative of the German discourse on 'organised crime', and how close to this and other scenarios the reality of crime in Germany has come over the past decades.

Methods and data

At the centre of the following discussion will be a systematic content analysis of the two leading German law enforcement journals *Die Polizei* and *Kriminalistik* covering the period from 1965 until 1994.

These two journals have been a major outlet for treatises by high ranking police officials and mid-level practitioners while also including scholarly contributions.

2 Cited in a book review in *Die Polizei*, 1966, p. 300.

The journals arguably provided the main forum for the discussion of 'organised crime' in Germany, at least during the time period in question. There seems to be a broad agreement among scholars that the German debate has been dominated by police officials and prosecutors (Albrecht, 1998; Busch, 1991; Kinzig, 2003). In fact, as I have shown elsewhere, the German media closely followed and took cues from the 'organised crime' debate within the law enforcement community (von Lampe, 2001).

In the absence of digitalised versions, print versions of *Die Polizei* and *Kriminalistik* were manually searched for content containing variations of the term 'organised crime' ('organisierte Kriminalität', 'organisiertes Verbrechen', 'organisiertes Verbrechertum'). This conceptual-history approach was chosen because it enables the scope of the material to be clearly and unambiguously defined for the purpose of the analysis. The importance of an article is determined strictly on a semantic level which leaves no room for interpretation. The downside is that articles that address, for example, mafia organisations or drug trafficking without using any synonyms of 'organised crime' are not included in the analysis; even though it could be argued that they are pertinent to the topic. However, such cases are fairly rare.

Overview of the organised crime debate in Germany 1965-1994

The initial analysis of the two law enforcement journals resulted in the identification of 452 articles and other items (book reviews, short reports, etc.) covering the period 1965 until 1994 that contained the term 'organised crime', 180 in *Die Polizei* and 272 in *Kriminalistik*. Figure 1 combines the data from both journals and shows the chronological distribution of the pertinent content (black columns). It also indicates for every year how often the discussion referred to the situation in Germany rather than only that in other countries (grey columns), and how often statements were made about the expected future development of 'organised crime' in Germany (striped columns), *i.e.* the kinds of statements which are the focal point of this chapter.

Figure 1

The 'organised crime' debate in *Die Polizei* and *Kriminalistik*, 1965-1994

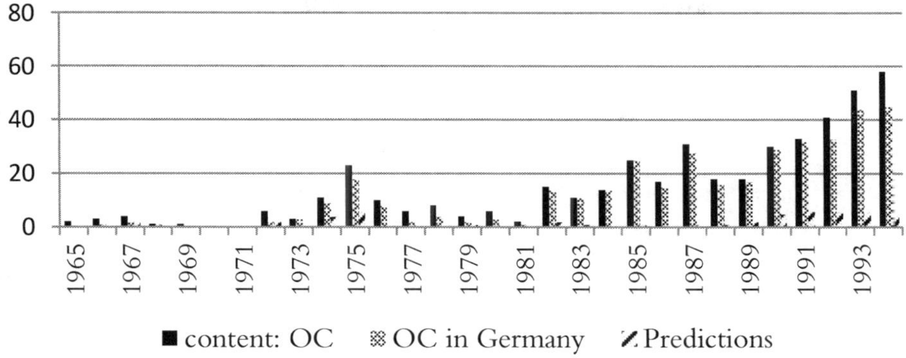

The data show that the prominence the concept of 'organised crime' had reached by the 1990s was not the endpoint of a linear process. Early peaks in the usage of the term 'organised crime' in 1967 and 1975 where followed, respectively, by phases where the term fell out of favour, only to emerge as a more or less consistently used term in the 1980s, and as an even more frequently used term in the first half of the 1990s.

As I have discussed elsewhere (von Lampe, 2001), these changes in the popularity of the term 'organised crime' are not so much linked to particular events in the real world of crime, but to events and developments in other spheres of society. For example, in the early 1970s a handful of police officials initiated a series of seminars at the national police academy and successfully lobbied for 'organised crime' to be the theme of the 1974 annual conference of the Bundeskriminalamt (BKA), Germany's federal police agency. A number of the articles in *Die Polizei* and *Kriminalistik* directly reflect these internal discussions within the German police. Likewise, after the attempt had failed in 1975, to establish an official definition of 'organised crime' against the backdrop of a struggle over competencies between the Bavarian police and the BKA, the term 'organised crime' all but vanished from the law enforcement literature. It was not until the early 1980s that the term 'organised crime' resurfaced; following a change in leadership in the BKA and a change of mind on the part of the Bavarian police (von Lampe, 2001).

It is also important to point out that the geographical point of reference for the debate changed over the years. Initially, in the 1960s, 'organised crime' was primarily seen as a phenomenon affecting other countries, namely the United States and Italy. Only a small share (36 percent) of the pertinent items identified from the time period 1965 - 1969 discuss the current or future existence of 'organised crime' in Germany. For the 1970s, the share of items addressing 'organised crime' in Germany increases to 68 percent, and to 92 percent and 86 percent, respectively, for the 1980s and 1990s. The slight relative decline in the focus on the situation in Germany during the 1990s can be explained by the emerging international debate on 'organised crime' and the changes in Eastern Europe which resulted in more articles in *Die Polizei* and *Kriminalistik* addressing phenomena in the former Soviet Bloc and at an international level.

Finally, the interesting pattern that is revealed by Figure 1 is that statements about the future development of 'organised crime' in Germany are fairly rare overall and for the most part are concentrated within two distinct phases of the debate. Of the 452 identified items in *Die Polizei* and *Kriminalistik* which address 'organised crime', only 51 contain some kind of prediction pertaining to Germany; most (38) of these statements either stem from the mid-1970s (1974 and 1975) or from the years 1990-1994. This suggests that during these periods, the crime situation was more commonly perceived as being dynamic compared to the period of the 1980s when 'organised crime' became recognised as an integral part of a rather static German crime landscape (see also von Lampe, 2001).

Predictions about the future development of 'organised crime' in Germany

Assumptions about the future development of 'organised crime' in Germany can be roughly grouped into three categories. According to one view, criminal organisations from countries such as Italy were expected to extend their areas of operation into Germany. Reinhard Steinke's 1966 paper (cited above), is one of the most elaborate examples in this category.

According to another view (see, *e.g.*, Niggemeyer, 1967: 168), the dominance of criminal organisations is envisioned for the future, but occurring as the result of endogenous processes rather than the infiltration of criminal groups from abroad. In this scenario, social and economic forces along with deficiencies in the legal and institutional frameworks in Germany were seen as the driving forces behind a process that supposedly would lead to conditions similar to those perceived to exist in the U.S. and Italy.

A third view (see, *e.g.*, Kollmar, 1974) saw forms of 'organised crime' specific to the German context developing with little influence from or similarities to the perceived situation in countries such as the United States and Italy.

Before going into more detail I need to stress that in most cases, predictions are contained only in brief statements that lack any elaboration of an underlying theory of the dynamics of 'organised crime'. Typically, future developments are simply extrapolated from a perceived status quo, or they are framed as approximations to an anticipated state of affairs, without a discussion of the processes that would bring about these changes.

Mafia infiltration

The concerns that established criminal organisations might expand their areas of operation into Germany had in part to do with the labour migration from Southern Italy and other parts of the Mediterranean since the 1950s and 1960s. Later, the influx of migrants more generally, namely the large numbers of asylum seekers in the 1980s and early 1990s, gave rise to fears that foreign criminals might gain a position of power in Germany. The concentration of migrants in urban areas, it was argued, could lead to marginalised subcultures which in turn would be fertile grounds for the development of 'organised crime', potentially centred on existing cells of traditional mafia organisations (Werner, 1982: 136). The endpoint of such a development was described as a situation where a criminal organisation, under the leadership of a 'capo' or 'godfather', gains control over a broad range of criminal activities (Sielaff, 1983: 419-420).

These developments were not necessarily seen as imminent or likely scenarios. The 'American example', for the most part, appeared as an admonition of what could happen if things went terribly wrong. That is, if the socio-economic conditions in Germany deteriorated and the legal and institutional framework for combating 'organised crime' had not been reformed as desired (Beuys, 1967: 67; Steinke, 1982: 98).

In later years, particularly in the 1990s, considerations of the socio-economic and legal-institutional development within Germany moved into the background, giving way to scenarios that emphasised the perceived globalisation of crime. These scenarios saw transnational criminal groups appearing and gaining influence in Germany as an outgrowth of an increasingly borderless world. At the centre of attention were, as before, mafia organisations from Italy, but also phenomena such as Chinese triads and Japanese Yakuza, and the so-called 'drug cartels' from Latin America. One of the main proponents of the debate, Alfred Stümper, a leading police official from the state of Baden-Württemberg, warned in 1990 in *Kriminalistik* that "*globally operating organised crime (has) reached a completely different dimension compared to earlier times*". The "*attempts by Colombian drug cartels*", he added, "are just one part of the overall threat" (Stümper, 1990: 4; see also Stümper, 1991: 696; 1992: 163). Likewise, in an article in *Kriminalistik* in 1993, a police detective, after noting a "*dramatic" increase in mafia related crimes in Germany, mainly as a result of "displacement effects*", predicted that "*the activities of the Mafia and other criminal organisations (will) further drastically increase*" (Koriath, 1993: 368).

Predictions of 'organised crime' beyond the 'alien conspiracy theory'

It is important to emphasise that scenarios of established foreign criminal groups gaining influence in Germany do not exhaustively characterise how future developments of 'organised crime' were envisaged during the mid-1960s through to the mid-1990s. In fact, numerically speaking, of the 51 articles in *Die Polizei* and *Kriminalistik* that include predictions, less than one-third (15) contain statements foreseeing the (increased) influx of foreign criminal groups in the near or distant future. A few other articles (8) contain predictions of an increasing "internationalization" of 'organised crime', but more in the sense of an increasing cross-border mobility and networking of criminals in different directions. By far the most common expectation, articulated in 46 of the 51 pertinent articles, is that 'organised crime' as a domestic problem will in some way or other get worse over time. Some of the reasons for this pessimistic outlook were assumptions that 'organised criminals' will become more sophisticated and will increasingly use modern technology and, as a result, will operate more profitably, will gain more importance relative to 'non-organised' criminals, and will gain more influence over the government, the economy and the media. The overarching concern in the law enforcement literature, however, has been that the police will not be able to effectively combat 'organised crime' (Schäfer, 1985: 582). Typical is the implicit or explicit juxtaposition of civil rights (of "*persons who obviously need to be considered a part of organised crime*") and "*the threat from an increasing spread and consolidation of criminal power*" (Sielaff, 1992: 754).

Interestingly, not a single article in *Die Polizei* or *Kriminalistik* could be identified where a future is envisioned with either less, or less serious 'organised crime'. In fact, one is hard pressed to find any voice in the German mainstream debate on organised crime with an optimistic undertone. In 1989 and 1990, the Bundeskriminalamt conducted a 'delphi study' on the threat of 'organised crime' with the participation of 26 experts from the fields of law enforcement, academia and the media (Dörmann, Koch, Risch and Vahlenkamp, 1990). When asked about the anticipated situation in the year 2000, all experts "*agreed that the share of OC of total crime will double*" (Dörmann *et al.*, 1990: 24). The authors add that it is "*remarkable that the representatives of the police assume lower shares for today as well as for the year 2000 compared to the other experts*" (Dörmann *et al.*, 1990: 24), and that according to only one expert the increase in 'organised crime' may slow to a halt by the mid-1990s and change into a downward trend as a result of the implementation of countermeasures (Dörmann *et al.*, 1990: 25).

Predictions of the future of 'organised crime' summarised

In a nutshell, then, the first 30 years of the German debate on 'organised crime' were marked by a pessimistic undertone whenever future developments were discussed. The expectations generally were that 'organised crime' will become more problematic and will gain more importance relative to 'non-organised' crime and *vis-a-vis* the legitimate spheres of society. Contrary to what one might expect, however, the notion of foreign criminal groups infiltrating Germany and eventually dominating the German underworld, while being a recurring theme, was not ubiquitous.

The development of 'organised crime' in Germany since the 1960s through the eyes of law enforcement

To evaluate past predictions one needs to contrast the envisioned scenarios with the actual developments that have taken place in the meantime. This is a tall order in the case of 'organised crime'. One would need to integrate and triangulate fragmented data spread across different kinds of sources, including law enforcement, the media, and empirical research. But even these sources combined would probably fall short of providing a clear and comprehensive picture. Within the scope of this chapter the focus will be on publically available law enforcement data to contrast past predictions in the law enforcement literature with how the reality of 'organised crime' has presented itself to law enforcement in the meantime.

Crime statistics

The conventional crime statistics, *Polizeiliche Kriminalstatistik* (PKS), just like the German Criminal Code, *Strafgesetzbuch* (StGB), do not contain a category or categories that would be indicative of the development of 'organised crime', irrespective of what specific conceptualisation of the term one chooses (von Lampe, 2005). 'Organised crime' is not a criminal offence under German law, and the "criminal association" offence contained in sec. 129 StGB is applicable only to a limited subset of criminal structures (Kinzig, 2004). Therefore, it appears impossible to pass a judgment on the relative importance of 'organised' and 'non-organised' crime. In fact, as far as can be seen from a cursory review of the more recent 'organised crime' debate, there is no perceived shift in terms of volume from 'non-organised' to 'organised' criminal activities over the past two decades.

The annual situation reports: quantitative changes

While the traditional crime statistics are inconclusive as regards the development of 'organised crime', what is available since 1991 are annual situation reports based on investigations that qualify as 'organised crime' cases according to Germany's official definition. This definition conceptualises 'organised crime' as a particular form of criminal conduct:

> "the planned commission of criminal offences determined by the pursuit of profit or power which, individually or as a whole, are of considerable importance if more than two persons, each with his/her own assigned tasks, collaborate for a prolonged or indefinite period of time, (a) by using commercial or business-like structures, (b) by using force or other suitable means of intimidation, or (c) by exerting influence on politics, the media, public administration, judicial authorities or the business sector".[3]

Figure 2
'Organised crime' investigations per year, 1991-2010

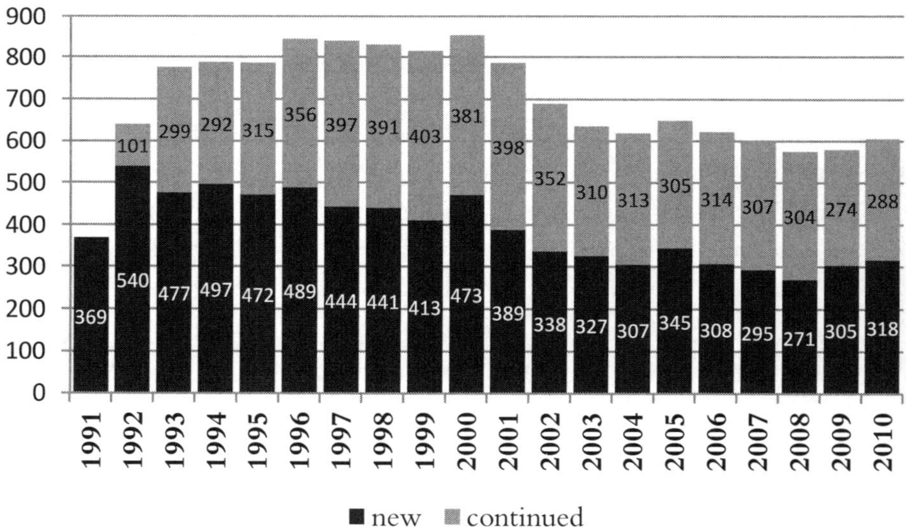

Source: Bundeskriminalamt

The annual situation reports indicate the number of 'organised crime' investigations conducted by German law enforcement agencies at the state and national levels, and they provide some details on the offenders and offences examined in the course

---

[3] Wording adopted from BKA (2011b: 9); however, one error in translation has been corrected.

of these investigations. Figure 2 shows that after an initial increase from 1991 until 1993, the number of reported 'organised crime' cases remained on a constant level until 2001. In the 2000s the number of 'organised crime' cases dropped back to levels seen during the early-1990s, even though the number of agencies contributing to the report had increased (von Lampe, 2005).

Of course, it is problematic to draw inferences from these figures about the actual extent of 'organised crime' and changes over time. As the drop in cases since 2001 suggests, the situation reports may simply reveal changes in the investigative resources invested in the area of 'organised crime' compared to other areas, namely the area of terrorism. Thus, it would be inappropriate to relate to the situation reports and to speak of a demise of 'organised crime' having taken place since 2001. At the same time, the situation reports, contrary to earlier expectations, cannot serve as evidence of an assumed quantitative increase in the importance of 'organised crime' in Germany either.

The annual situation reports: qualitative changes – influence-taking

Whereas quantitative trends are difficult to discern, the annual 'organised crime' reports may be better suited to capture certain qualitative changes, at least within the scope of what the German police is able to monitor. However, not all aspects that have been addressed in previous predictions of the future of 'organised crime' are incorporated in these situation reports. For example, it is not possible to deduce changes in the technological sophistication of criminal groups. But there are qualitative trends that may show up, namely with regard to the influence criminals exert on the legal spheres of society.

The situation reports contain information about the number of cases per year that involve influence-taking on decision-making processes in the realms of government, politics, courts, the media and business in accordance with alternative (c) of the official organised crime definition (see above). Yet, no clear trends become discernible. Between 1992 and 2002, the share of 'organised crime' cases reported to the BKA that involved influence-taking in some form, which also includes influence-taking outside of Germany, ranged from 15% to 23% (Bundeskriminalamt, 2003: 33). This share has risen to between 25% and 30% since 2003. But this increase seems to be the result of a clarification the Bundeskriminalamt made in 2002 with regard to the reporting criteria that have to be complied with when a case is submitted for inclusion in the situation report. The BKA pointed out that "*influence-taking*" is not only meant to include corruption offences defined in the German Criminal Code but also activities below that level, such as the creation of dependencies of office holders (Bundeskriminalamt, 2003: 8; Bundeskriminalamt, 2004: 5). Actual incidents of corruption in the legal sense are reported in only a handful of 'organised crime' cases each year. A similar picture emerges from the annual situation reports on corruption which the BKA has been issuing since 1994. Only a small fraction, at times less than 1% of the cases reported each year have been tied to 'organised crime' (Bundeskriminalamt, 2003: 32; 2005: 50).

Accordingly, the Bundeskriminalamt has rejected the notion that a close link between corruption and 'organised crime' exists in Germany. Rather, the data collected and analysed by the BKA suggest that corrupt practices are much more typical for 'legitimate' businesses than for criminal groups, and also that German corrupters are much more prevalent than foreign corrupters (Bundeskriminalamt, 2001: 3; 2003: 33; 2011a: 15-16). In addition, an in-depth analysis conducted by the BKA revealed that criminal groups dominated by non-Germans exert influence primarily in their home countries whereas German criminal groups typically draw on existing familial and friendship ties to influence decision-making processes (Bundeskriminalamt, 2003: 34).

Foreign criminal groups

Apart from the overall development of 'organised crime', the annual situation reports are designed to provide information about the make-up of the population of 'organised criminals' and in particular the role of foreign criminals. This provides an opportunity to see whether the prevalence of foreign criminals in the area of 'organised crime' has changed. However, upon closer inspection no clear trend in one direction or the other becomes apparent.

Figure 3
Share of selected nationalities among 'organised crime' suspects per year, 1991-2010

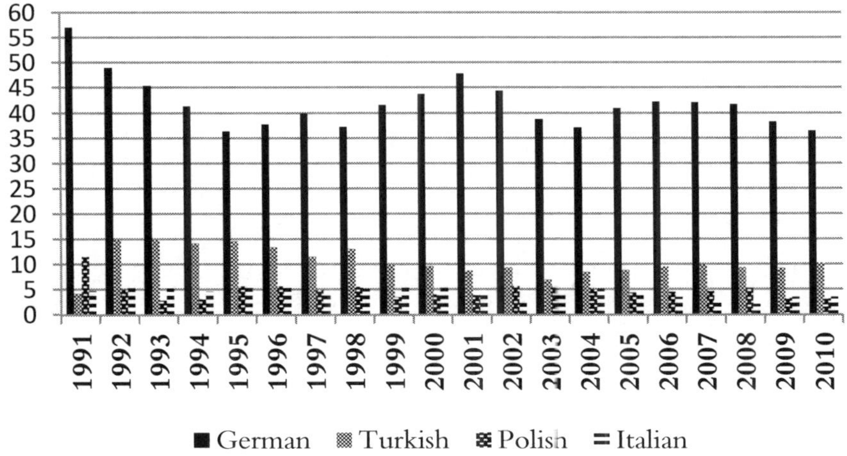

Source: Bundeskriminalamt

In 2010, German nationals were by far the largest group (3.515 or 36,5%) among a total of 9.632 'organised crime' suspects from 113 different countries. Suspects of Turkish nationality constituted the second largest group of suspected offenders with a share of 10,3% (996), followed by Italians with a share of 3,5 % (340) (Bundeskriminalamt, 2011b). This pattern is not substantially different from previous years, as Figure 3 indicates. While in the first year for which data were collected, 1991, a large proportion of 57,1% of suspects held German citizenship, the share of German nationals among 'organised crime' suspects has periodically decreased and then increased in the subsequent years. Following a decline until 1994, the share of suspects holding German citizenship rose from 36,4 % in 1995 to a peak of 47,9% in 2001 and another less prominent peak of 42,3 % in 2006, only to gradually decrease again to 1995-levels by 2010. The share of Turkish nationals, the largest group of foreign 'organised crime' suspects, has decreased from peaks at 14,8% and 14,6% in 1992 respectively 1995 to a low of 8,4% in 2003 and rebounded to a level of 10,3% in 2010. In comparison, the share of Italian suspects shows a downward trend overall, with levels above 5% in most of the years until 2000 and a share of around 3% in recent years. Other nationalities, such as Poland, former Yugoslavia, Romania, the Lebanon, Nigeria and Vietnam, have held similar single-digit shares for some or most of the time period between 1991 and 2010.

A slightly different picture emerges when one looks at criminal groups instead of individual offenders. Since 2003, the situation reports differentiate investigations by the nationality of the suspects who "*dominate*" a particular criminal group. This is different from the make-up of criminal groups because most of the 'organised crime' cases, 73,9 % in 2010, involve suspects from more than one country (Bundeskriminalamt, 2011b: 6).

According to these data, as well, Germans are the most prevalent actors in the German underworld, but to a lesser degree than the overall number of suspects suggests. On average, in 30,1% of 'organised crime' cases under investigation from 2003 until 2010, Germans were the main players, Turks were found to be in control in 12,1% of cases, compared to 4,2% Italian led groups and 5,1% Polish led groups.

Overall, the data from the annual 'organised crime' situation reports do not show a discernible trend towards an increasing importance of foreign criminals. Nor do the situation reports suggest that particular criminal groups from abroad, namely Italian mafia organisations, have established themselves as a dominant force. What the situation reports do suggest is that foreign criminals are part of an ethnically heterogeneous crime landscape with numerous links between criminals of different backgrounds.

Italian criminal groups in Germany

The picture that emerges from the situation reports of the role of foreign 'organised' criminals is in line with previous research sponsored by the Bundeskriminalamt. In the early 1970s, Hans Jürgen Kerner interviewed German investigators to determine the state of 'organised crime' in the country (Kerner, 1973). A similar study was again conducted in the mid-1980s, this time by Erich Rebscher and Werner Vahlenkamp (Rebscher and Vahlenkamp, 1988). Both studies described the German underworld essentially as a loose system of varying criminal alliances between criminals of different ethnic backgrounds without a permanent centralisation of power in the hands of any particular group. While the existence of ethnically homogeneous groups with hierarchical structures was acknowledged, these groups did not seem to play a central role. Given the recurring theme of an infiltration by foreign criminal groups, this aspect is particularly noteworthy and deserves closer inspection, especially with regard to Italian mafia organisations.

According to Kerner's analysis, Germany had been an area of operation for internationally mobile Italian offenders since at least the 1960s, while Italian migrant workers, in the eyes of the German police, did not constitute any particular crime problem (Kerner, 1973: 223). Italian professional criminals were prominently involved in crimes such as currency counterfeiting, the trafficking in stolen motor vehicles, serial burglary and robbery, often in cooperation with criminals from other countries, including Germany, France and Belgium. Italian professional criminals, thus, appeared to be part of a European crime network. In contrast, there was no indication of mafia organisations encroaching on Germany. In 1965, the Bundeskriminalamt had drawn up a list of 86 "Mafia-Bosses" who might attempt to infiltrate the German underworld. None of these individuals, however, appeared on the scene in the following years (Kerner, 1973: 223). "*The traditional Sicilian Mafia*," Kerner concluded, "*has so far not spread to other countries*" (Kerner, 1973: 235).

Rebscher and Vahlenkamp likewise found a significant presence of Italian criminals in Germany, particularly in the Southern and central parts of the country. They also noted that some investigators saw Italians as a special breed of criminals with regard to the cohesiveness of their networks, rivalled perhaps only by Yugoslavian offender groups and outlaw motorcycle gangs (Rebscher and Vahlenkamp, 1988: 26, 45). Italian criminals allegedly had a strong sense of belonging to a particular criminal group or 'family', with group leaders enjoying a degree of authority largely unknown among German criminals (Rebscher and Vahlenkamp, 1988: 26). Yet this higher degree of cohesion apparently did not translate into a greater influence or position of power within the underworld and in the broader societal context. "*It is not appropriate to speak of an importation of foreign OC-conditions into the Federal Republic of Germany*," Rebscher and Vahlenkamp concluded, even though "*foreign offender groups have had their part in shaping OC in the Federal Republic*" (Rebscher and Vahlenkamp, 1988: 140).

In connection with the drafting of the first organised crime situation report, analysts of the Bundeskriminalamt revisited the question of a mafia infiltration into Germany based on a review of pertinent investigations from the years 1989 until 1991. During this time span, 62 cases involving members of the Sicilian Mafia, Camorra, 'Ndrangheta and Sacra Corona Unita, the four main Italian mafia organisations, had been under investigation by German law enforcement agencies. The cases pertained primarily to drug dealing, the trafficking in stolen motor vehicles, violations of Germany's gun laws, and extortion. The analysis confirmed the presence of Italian mafiosi, particularly from the lower ranks, in Germany. However, it remained unclear to what extent Italian mafia organisations had established bases of operation on German soil (Gehm and Link, 1992: 494).

A decade later, another analysis of the state of 'organised crime' in Germany based on police intelligence suggested that such bases did indeed exist (Flormann and Krevert, 2001). Five examples for the presence of Italian mafia organisations were presented to underscore this claim.

The most detailed case involved a 'Ndrangheta cell with branches in several mostly southern German towns. Members had to obtain permission to commit crimes such as extortion, theft, robbery, fencing and drugs, and they had to share their crime proceeds with the group hierarchy. Interestingly the group was dismantled by the police with the help of several informants, and the investigation had been triggered by an Italian restaurateur who had turned to the police for help against three Italians who had demanded protection payments (Flormann and Krevert, 2001: 66).

By the late 2000s, following the 'Duisburg massacre' of 2007, which I will discuss further below, the 'Ndrangheta moved to the centre of attention. In the previous years, among the Italian mafia organisations the Camorra had been perceived to constitute the main threat to Germany (Förster, 2007).

In an internal report from 2008 that has been leaked to the press, the Bundeskriminalamt listed the names of more than 750 individuals with assumed 'Ndrangheta links residing in Germany. The report also notes that leading members of certain 'Ndrangheta clans have relocated to Germany in the past (Ohnewald, 2010). Yet from the content that has been disclosed in the press it is not clear what should constitute the "*qualitative leap*" in the 'Ndrangheta presence that the report claims has occurred in recent years (Ohnewald, 2010).

What appears to be established knowledge is that 'Ndrangheta members have been involved in criminal and legal economic activities in Germany for decades. Legal investments pertain particularly to restaurants, construction and the real estate sector with which, it is alleged, large sums of illegal proceeds are being laundered (Reski, 2009). It also seems that the cells existing in Germany are in a structural sense integral parts of 'Ndrangheta clans in Calabria (Forgione, 2011). Yet there is no clear evidence that the influence of the 'Ndrangheta in the German underworld and upperworld has grown in absolute terms, or relative to the influence of other criminal groups. In particular, there is no indication that 'Ndrangheta cells in Germany have been able, or even have tried to establish the kind of territorial control and the selling of protection which constitutes the core business of mafia organisations in Italy (see Campana, 2011; Varese, 2011) and which has been envisioned in the German 'organised crime' debate since the 1960s as a possible development. Even those who blame the German public and the German police for ignoring the threat posed by the 'Ndrangheta implicitly support this assessment. Francesco Forgione, for example, in his book *Mafia Export*, argues that the true reason why the 'Ndrangheta has established bases of operation in Germany is the cocaine trade and the need to have a logistical infrastructure for receiving and transporting drug shipments arriving at north-western European ports such as Antwerp and Rotterdam (Forgione, 2011: 131-132). And the economic and political influence of the 'Ndrangheta in Germany is still measured primarily in terms of the number of restaurants owned and operated by 'ndranghetisti and by the ties they establish to politicians who frequent these restaurants (Forgione, 2011: 143; Ohnewald, 2010).

The current picture of 'organised crime' in Germany

It is important to re-emphasise at this point that this chapter does not intend to present an exhaustive assessment of the situation of 'organised crime' in Germany. Further the possibility cannot be excluded that under the surface other and much graver developments have taken place. My purpose, though, is not to speculate but to contrast past predictions with what is known about the state of 'organised crime' today through the lens of the law enforcement community.

I would argue that there is no sufficient basis for claims that truly fundamental changes have taken place since the 1970s, either quantitatively or qualitatively, that would correspond to the pessimistic outlook from 20 to 50 years ago on the future development of 'organised crime' in Germany. There have been forms of crime decades ago, some might even claim centuries ago (Weschke, 1986: 317), that involve fairly sophisticated offenders who cooperate on a more or less continuous basis and who pose a challenge for the police and the criminal justice system. When speaking of an absence of fundamental changes, therefore, I assume that the situation has remained at a rather high level of severity over the past few decades.

Rebscher and Vahlenkamp, in their analysis of the situation in the mid-1980s spoke of local offender networks without a distinguishable overall organisation which constituted the typical form of criminal structures in the urban areas in Germany. These local 'scenes' or 'milieus' were populated by individuals who knew each other and cooperated as the need and opportunity arose according to the logic of a particular criminal activity on a short or more long term basis (Rebscher and Vahlenkamp, 1988: 24, 31-35). Connections between the local 'milieus' existed through influential individuals who occupied the higher rungs in an informal status hierarchy (Rebscher and Vahlenkamp, 1988: 38).

Some foreign criminals, Rebscher and Vahlenkamp (1988: 66) report, kept a distance to local crime 'milieus' for various reasons, such as a lack of acceptance and language difficulties. Others had gone through a process of adjustment or even absorption into the criminal 'milieus' in Germany (Rebscher and Vahlenkamp, 1988: 139). Overall, peaceful coexistence rather than violent competition characterised the relationship between 'organised' criminals, irrespective of their ethnic background. Cases of violent conflict were rare and were typically linked to the intrusion by foreign criminals into an area or market without the consent of the existing, ethnically mixed local crime network (Rebscher and Vahlenkamp, 1988: 103-104).

Attempts to gain influence over public officials were made through sponsoring activities and by targeting the individual weaknesses of office holders, however, without the use or threat of violence, even when recruitment efforts failed (Rebscher and Vahlenkamp, 1988: 131-132).

When one looks at the annual 'organised crime' reports and other assessments by German law enforcement agencies, but also at the scarce academic research in this area (Kinzig, 2004; Sieber and Bögel, 1993; van Duyne, 1996; von Lampe, 2003; 2007), it seems that this description has remained valid and that from the perspective of the law enforcement community this is the way 'organised crime' in Germany continues to present itself today.

Three high profile murder cases

In contrast to the picture of a rather static or only gradually changing crime landscape, there appears to be a latent notion persisting in the public conscience and in the minds of at least some law enforcement officials that the crime situation can change drastically within a fairly short time span. This notion is linked, it seems, to stereotypical imagery of foreign mafia organisations ruthlessly using violence in pursuit of their interests in gross defiance of state authority and civil society: the very imagery one can find at the beginning of the German 'organised crime' debate half a century ago with speculations about impending mafia roadblocks.

To illustrate this point, it is interesting to consider three notorious crime cases that have captivated the imagination of law enforcement authorities and the media. The three cases that are briefly discussed here are arguably among the most publicised cases of multiple murders in recent German history. They all have in common not only an unusually high number of victims: between six and nine. They are also similar in that they have evoked images of sinister mafia organisations behind the killings: in one case Turkish or Kurdish criminal groups, in one case Chinese triads, and in one case the 'Ndrangheta. Only in the latter case, it turned out, was there an element of truth to these speculations.

The so-called Ceska killings

Between 2000 and 2006, eight men of Turkish origin and one man of Greek origin between the ages of 21 and 50 were shot dead in different German cities: two in Munich, one in Hamburg, one in Rostock, one in Dortmund, one in Kassel, and three in Nuremberg. All victims were killed inside or nearby businesses of the kind that are typically run by migrants. The only concrete link between the crimes was the use of the same gun, a Ceska 83, cal. 7,65 (Przybilla, 2010).

The German police invested vast resources in an effort to identify and apprehend the perpetrator or perpetrators. Up to 160 officers were assigned to the case in the state of Bavaria alone where five of the nine murders had been committed. The main thrust of the investigation was directed at an assumed 'organised crime' background, even though leads in this direction, if at all, existed only with regard to three of the nine victims. The very "*criminal inconspicuousness of the victims*," one investigator surmised, could indicate that they had links to an "*OC group*" (Leyendecker, Goetz and Richter, 2012).

It was not until 2011 that the truth came to light. The killings had been committed by neo-Nazis with an apparent xenophobic motivation (Heise, Röbel and Stark, 2012).

The massacre in Sittensen

The second case involved a Chinese restaurant in the small town of Sittensen, located between Hamburg and Bremen. Seven Asians between the ages of 28 and 57 were shot and killed inside this restaurant one night in February 2007. The victims included the couple who owned the restaurant and five employees.

The media were quick to speculate that the killings were the act of a Chinese triad which had attempted to collect protection payments (von Lucius, 2007). The police, unlike in the case of the Ceska murders, avoided a fixation on an 'organised crime' angle in initial statements and were fortunate that a coincidence helped to solve the case within hours. At a road block two Vietnamese were apprehended without the necessary papers and a subsequent search of their vehicle produced a hand-drawn map of the restaurant in Sittensen. Eventually two pairs of brothers and a former employee at the Chinese restaurant, all of Vietnamese origin, were convicted for what turned out to be a robbery that had got out of hand (*stern.de*, 2009).

The Duisburg massacre

The third case I want to briefly discuss is the now infamous Duisburg massacre. On 15 August 2007, at about 2 a.m., six Calabrians between the ages of 16 and 38 were shot dead outside an Italian restaurant in Duisburg, a town in the Ruhr region. Once again, the media, without hesitation, took the killings as a sign that "*The Mafia is on its way to Germany*", as one newspaper headline announced (*Berliner Morgenpost*, 17 August 2007).

There was little time for speculation, however. With the help of the Italian authorities it quickly became known that the six men in Duisburg had fallen victim to a family feud that had pitted two 'Ndrangheta clans from the Calabrian town of San Luca against each other since 1991. Some members of the two clans had relocated to Germany over the years and, as it seems, had formed 'Ndrangheta cells in fairly close proximity to each other here (Piller, 2008; Reski, 2009).

The Duisburg killings have been interpreted in different ways by the German law enforcement community. Some feared that mafia wars could spread to Germany (Förster, 2007). For the most part, however, the Duisburg massacre has been viewed as evidence of what had already been known before, an established, and perhaps growing 'Ndrangheta presence in the country, while the murder itself, the blatant use of violence, is considered atypical for that presence (*Zeit Online*, 2007).

Conclusions

A lot more could be said about the three cases, and a lot still remains in the dark. At the time of writing, the exact motives behind the Duisburg killings are still somewhat in doubt, and the Ceska killings are the subject of parliamentary inquiries to determine why the German authorities failed to recognise the right-wing extremist background of these crimes. Yet for the purpose of this chapter the short descriptions of these events and the imagery they have evoked should suffice to establish a point: In the German debate on 'organised crime' there is a fundamental uncertainty about the developmental dynamics of illegal markets, criminal networks and illegal power structures. I would argue that this uncertainty has opened the door to stereotypical imagery taking hold of the perceptions of law enforcement and the public.

In the case of the Ceska killings, the problem has become most obvious. It seems that a few hints, such as the nationality of the victims and the mode of killing, because they fit a particular stereotypical imagery, led investigators to focus on an 'organised crime' angle and to discount the possibility of right-wing extremist offenders. At the same time, comparing the evidence against a more coherent model of 'organised' criminal behaviour might have exposed sufficient inconsistencies in the 'organised crime' hypothesis so that it would have been given less weight in the investigation.

To avoid any misunderstanding, the point being made here is not, with the benefit of hindsight, to show the blindness of investigators. I am also not arguing that an 'organised crime' angle should have been dismissed outright. The point is that while mafiosi of some sort might have been behind the Ceska killings as well as the Sittensen killings, it would have been an unlikely scenario because the modus operandi in these cases, as in the case of the Duisburg massacre, did not represent a recipe for success for 'organised' criminals in the social context in which they occurred. Rather, in all three cases the crimes suggested a high degree of irrationality on the part of the perpetrators (see *e.g. BZ*, 2007).

The ease with which mafia imagery surfaces may also be explained in part by a certain uneasiness and even disbelief that one can sense in the debate on 'organised crime' regarding the tools that are being employed to assess the crime picture in Germany, namely the annual situation reports and ad hoc analyses prepared by the BKA. As argued in the first part of this chapter, there are no real fundamental differences discernible between the situation of 'organised crime' described by the police officers interviewed by Kerner (1973) and by Rebscher and Vahlenkamp (1988), and the situation of 'organised crime' reflected in the annual situation reports and internal analyses prepared by the BKA since the early 1990s, at least to the extent the content of these analyses has been publicised. This means that, as I have also pointed out, the pessimistic predictions made between the mid-1960s and mid-1990s, namely those of a mafia take-over, have not materialised in a measurable way. The available assessments are either inconclusive, for example with regard to the relative shares of 'organised' and 'non-organised' crime, or they show no clear trend in one direction or the other, for example with regard to the share of foreign nationals amongst 'organised crime' suspects.

Of course, one may wonder how it is possible that no fundamental changes in the crime picture have taken place over the past few decades despite fundamental changes in the geopolitical landscape. And an argument can indeed be made that the analytical instruments currently employed by the German police are not suitable for measuring important changes. The situation reports, for one, are supposed to contain only reliable information generated in the course of a criminal investigation. This means that soft data are not included. For example, if a businessman of Italian origin invests more money than can be explained by his legal business activities, but only a suspicion exists that this person is laundering illicit funds for an Italian mafia organisation (see Reski, 2009), this will not show up in the annual BKA situation reports. Yet, the existence of this kind of 'soft information' does not answer the question of how conclusive it really is. After all, if 'soft information' points at a drastically worsening situation, why does it not lead to the 'hard information' of criminal investigations?

Therefore, from the perspective of an empirical researcher, suspicions of mafia infiltration remain just that: suspicions, until solid data have been put on the table. For the time being, the discrepancies between past predictions and the current situation of 'organised crime' remain and provide support for the sceptic stance empirical researchers have taken *vis-a-vis* official and journalistic claims relating to 'organised crime'.

References

Albrecht, H.-J., Organisierte Kriminalität – Theoretische Erklärungen und empirische Befunde, in: Deutsche Sektion der Internationalen Juristen Kommission (ed.), *Organisierte Kriminalität und Verfassungsstaat*. Heidelberg: Müller, 1998, 1-40

Berliner Morgenpost, Die Blutfehde der kalabrischen Mafia, 17 August 2007, http://www.morgenpost.de/content/2007/08/17/politik/916232.html

Beuys, W., Gefahren durch organisiertes Verbrechertum?, *Die Polizei – Kriminalpolizeiliche Tagespraxis*, 1967, 65-68

Bundeskriminalamt, *Lagebild Korruption Bundesrepublik Deutschland 2000*. Wiesbaden: BKA, 2000

Bundeskriminalamt, *Lagebild Organisierte Kriminalität 2002 Bundesrepublik Deutschland*. Wiesbaden: BKA, 2003

Bundeskriminalamt, *Ausfüllanleitung zum 'Raster für die Erhebung von OK-Verfahren zur Erstellung eines Lagebildes OK'*. unpublished manuscript, 2004

Bundeskriminalamt, *Bundeslagebild Korruption 2004*. Wiesbaden: BKA, 2005

Bundeskriminalamt, *Korruption Bundeslagebild 2010*. Wiesbaden: BKA, 2011a

Bundeskriminalamt, *Organised Crime National Situation Report 2010*, Wiesbaden: BKA, 2011b

Busch, H., Die Debatte um Organisierte Kriminalität in der BRD, *Bürgerrechte and Polizei (CILIP)*, 1991, *no.2*, 6-16

Bux, n.a., Intensivere Bekämpfung der Hehlerei, *Die Polizei*, 1966, *no.* 7, 215-218

BZ, Wie mächtig ist die Mafia in Deutschland?, 17 August 2007

Campana, P., Eavesdropping on the Mob, *European Journal of Criminology*, 2011, *no. 3*, 213-228

Dörmann, U., Koch, K.-F., Risch, He. and Vahlenkamp, W., *Organisierte Kriminalität – wie groß ist die Gefahr?* Wiesbaden: BKA, 1990

Duyne, P.C. van, The phantom and threat of organised crime, *Crime, Law and Social Change*, 1996, *no.* 4, 341-377

Duyne, P.C. van, The creation of a threat image: Media policy making and organised crime, in: P.C. van Duyne, M. Jager, K. von Lampe and J.L. Newell (eds.), *Threats and Phantoms of Organised Crime, Corruption and Terrorism.* Nijmegen: Wolf Legal Publishers, 2004, 21-50

Flormann, W. and Krevert, P., *In den Fängen der Mafia-Kraken*, Hamburg: E.S. Mittler and Sohn, 2001

Förster, A., So leise läuft's Business, *Berliner Zeitung*, 17 August 2007 http://www.berliner-zeitung.de/archiv/kriminalitaet---nach-den-morden-in-duisburg-fahndet-die-polizei-im--ndrangheta-milieu--bisher-hat-sich-die-mafia-in-deutschland-eher-unauffaellig-betaetigt--die-ermittlungen-koennten-ihre-geschaefte-jetzt-stoeren--so-leise-laeuft-s-business,10810590,10498082.html

Forgione, F., *Mafia Export*, Munich: Goldmann, 2011

Gehm, V. and M. Link, Organisierte Kriminalität: Das aktuelle Lagebild, *Kriminalistik*, 1992, *no. 8-9*, 491-496

Heise, T., S. Röbel and H. Stark, 'Sieg oder Tod', *spiegel.de*, 2012 http://www. spiegel. de/spiegel/a-809419.html

Hellmer, J., Kriminalpolitische Besinnung - Grundsätzliche Gedanken zur Bekämpfung der Kriminalität, *Kriminalistik*, 1966, *no. 6*, 287-290

Kerner, H.-J., *Professionelles und organisiertes Verbrechen.* Wiesbaden: BKA, 1973

Kinzig, J., Organisierte Kriminalität in Deutschland: Begriff – Rechtliche Maßnahmen – Empirische Erkenntnisse, *Angewandte Sozialforschung*, 2003, *no. 1-2*, 27-40

Kinzig, J., *Die rechtliche Bewältigung von Erscheinungsformen organisierter Kriminalität.* Berlin: Duncker and Humblot, 2004

Kollmar, H., 'Organisierte Kriminalität' - Begriff oder Bezeichnung eines Phänomens, *Kriminalistik*, 1974, *no. 1*, 1-7

Koriath, G., Verdeckte Ermittler, *Kriminalistik*, 1996, *no. 8-9*, 535-542

Leyendecker, H., Goetz, J. and Richer, N., 'Die NSU-Morde sind unser 11. September', *Süddeutsche.de*, 26 April 2012 http://www.sueddeutsche.de/ politik/untersuchungsausschuss-zum-nsu-die-nsu-morde-sind-unser-september-1.1343041

Naylor, R.T., Towards a General Theory of Profit-Driven Crimes, *British Journal of Criminology*, 2003, *no. 1*, 81-101

Niggemeyer, B., Technik des Verbrechers und Technik der Kriminalpolizei, *Die Polizei*, 1967, *no. 6*, 166-172

Ochs, S., Die betrügerische Kfz-Anmietung als internationales Delikt und ihre repressive und präventive Bekämpfung, *Die Polizei*, 1964, *no. 10*, 289-294

Ohnewald, M., Im Schlaraffenland, *FAZ Online*, 6 October 2010 http://www.faz.net/aktuell/politik/inland/mafia-in-deutschland-im-schlaraffenland-1604753.html

Piller, T., 'ndrangheta auch in Deutschland stabil, *FAZ Online*, 14 August 2008 http://m.faz.net/aktuell/gesellschaft/kriminalitaet/kalabresische-mafia-ndrangheta-auch-in-deutschland-stabil-15491.html

Potter, G., *Criminal Organisations*, Prospect Heights, IL: Waveland, 1994

Przybilla, O., Es geschah am helllichten Tag, *Süddeutsche.de*, 6 August 2010 http://www.sueddeutsche.de/bayern/2.220/mysterioese-mordserie-es-geschah-am-hellichten-tag-1.984861

Rebscher, E. and W. Vahlenkamp, *Organisierte Kriminalität in der Bundesrepublik Deutschland*, Wiesbaden: BKA, 1988

Reski, P., Die Mafiosi von nebenan, *Die Zeit*, 13 August 2009, 11-13

Schäfer, H., Das Ende der Selbsttäuschung, *Kriminalistik*, 1985, *no. 12*, 582-583

Sieber, U. and M. Bögel, *Logistik Organisierter Kriminalität*, Wiesbaden: BKA, 1993

Sielaff, W., Bis zur Bestechung leitender Polizeibeamter?, *Kriminalistik*, 1983, *no. 8-9*, 417-422

Sielaff, W., Rauschgiftkriminalität, *Kriminalistik*, 1992, *no. 12*, 749-756

Smith, D.C., Mafia: The Prototypical Alien Conspiracy, *The Annals of the American Academy of Political and Social Science*, 1976, 75-88

Steinke, W., Das organisierte Verbrechen, *Kriminalistik*, 1982, *no. 2*, 78-100

stern.de, Lebenslange Haft für Mörder von Sittensen, 13 May 2009 http://www.stern.de/panorama/massaker-im-china-restaurant-lebenslange-haft-fuermoerder-von-sittensen-700694.html

Steinke, R., Die Mafia – Geißel der Vergangenheit oder Schrecken der Zukunft?, in: H.J. Hoeveler (ed.), *Internationale Bekämpfung des Verbrechens*. Hamburg: Verlag Deutsche Polizei, 1966, 128-150

Stümper, A., Sicherheit in Europa, *Kriminalistik*, 1990, *no. 1*, 2-8

Stümper, A., Farbe bekennen, *Kriminalistik*, 1991, *no. 11*, 695-697

Stümper, A., Internationale Kriminalität im Aufbruch, *Die Polizei*, 1992, *no. 7*, 161-166

Varese, F., *Mafias on the move*. Princeton, NJ: Princeton University Press, 2011

von Lampe, K., Not a process of enlightenment: The conceptual history of organisedc crime in Germany and the United States of America, *Forum on Crime and Society*, 2001, *no. 2*, 99-116

von Lampe, K., Organising the nicotine racket, in: P.C. van Duyne, K. von Lampe and J.L. Newell (eds.), *Criminal Finances and Organising Crime in Europe*. Nijmegen: Wolf Legal Publishers, 2003, 41-65 von Lampe, K., Making the second step before the first: Assessing Organised Crime, *Crime, Law and Social Change*, 2005, *no. 4-5*, 227-259

von Lampe, K., Criminals are not alone, in: P.C. van Duyne, A. Maljevic, M. van Dijck, K. von Lampe and J. Harvey (eds.), *Crime Business and Crime Money in Europe*. Nijmegen: Wolf Legal Publishers, 2007, 131-155

von Lucius, R., Ein Fall von Schutzgelderpressung, *FAZ Online*, 6 February 2007 http://www.faz.net/aktuell/gesellschaft/kriminalitaet/mord-von-sittensen-ein-fall-von-schutzgelderpressung-1411103.html

Wehner, B., Analyse der Kriminalitätsentwicklung, *Die Polizei*, 1966, no. 11, 337-344

Werner, A., Organisierte Kriminalität: Fiktion oder Realität?, *Kriminalistik*, 1982, *no. 3*, 131-136

Weschke, E., Netzstruktur Kriminalität, *Kriminalistik*, 1986, *no. 6*, 297-317

Westphal, K.-H., Der Zuhälterparagraph und die Polizei, *Kriminalistik*, 1969, *no. 9*, 476

Zeit Online, Mafia ante portas, 31 August 2007 http://www.zeit.de/online /2007/34 /Mafia-Duisburg

Organised crime in a country of transition after twenty years

Miroslav Scheinost[1]

Introduction

Criminological analyses of organised crime usually focus on the phenomenon itself, on its development, forms, the structures of its functioning and on its fields of interest. Criminologists are also occasionally asked about threats of organised crime and about the possibilities of responses. But the impact of criminological knowledge on the 'public mind' or the public representation of organised crime is only limited.

While criminologists present their knowledge in professional articles and publications, the picture of organised crime in 'public eyes' rather depends on its presentation in the media. Criminological knowledge on organised crime is only one – and not the prevalent – source of information for media along information coming from police reports and from their own sources of investigative journalism. The collected information is moreover usually recast into the form supposed to be attractive for readers thereby creating a popular imagery of what organised crime is supposed to be.

Public opinion naturally reflects this media picture as do the politicians and policy makers who in addition project into this popular imagery their own interests and concepts. The related policy against organised crime therefore is not based upon (more or less) valid research based analyses and information but from the general, rather popular discourse on organised crime in which all these pieces of knowledge, information, views, opinions and interests are blended. To be fair it is necessary to admit that criminologist and criminological research also contribute to one part of this discourse. They may (certainly only partly) influence it but they are also influenced by the general stream of thinking when they offer the research topics that seem to be promising in order to obtain grants and subsidies. The presentation of the picture of organised crime and the role of fear of organised

1 The author is director of the Institute of Criminology and Social Prevention, Prague

crime in public opinion and in policy-making is nicely shown in the study of Van Duyne (2011).

When we deal with the development of organised crime we, therefore, can focus either on this phenomenon itself and try to find and verify its substantial forms and changes, or we may take into account the shape and shift in the general discourse on organised crime. It is true that as criminologists we must first and foremost accurately collect the information on the phenomenon itself. However, if we also look at the historical context, it is interesting to analyse and evaluate the way in which organised crime has been presented and discussed, not only among experts but also in the public domain, primarily within the media (see von Lampe, 2012).

That is why it is important to elaborate the perception and understanding of organised crime in the public discourse. This is illustrated through looking at the period of transformation in the Czech Republic (CR). The shift in understanding organised crime in this period and in this country may shed light not only on the state of recognition of this phenomenon but on the state and development of the society as a whole.

The beginning and the history

It is worthwhile to remember that the term 'organised crime' entered general awareness in the CR only after 1989. Before the collapse of the previous socialist regime it was simply not possible – with regard to the dominant ideology – to admit to the very existence of anything such as 'organised crime' in this (or indeed in any) socialist society. In the minds of the public this category of crime did not occur and if it did so, it was only as something transmitted through books and in films; something connected with a specific tradition, capitalist countries and regions abroad. This state of affairs was also reflected within the existing law. The Czechoslovak penal code existing at that time did not contain the term 'organised crime' and did not take into account the possibility of such forms of crime. The only term near approaching the concept was the notion of an 'organised *group*'. But this was used to designate the cases of several offenders associated together in order to commit some separate concrete crime. Actually, this was more about temporary cooperation around a specific offence.

Not having a word to denote a phenomenon does not mean that it does not exist. As a matter of fact, a lot of criminal organisation takes place, certainly at a higher level. This was the case for organised prostitution (Trávníčková, 1995) or for the illegal exchange of foreign currency (Scheinost, 2001). However, these criminal activities were not understood as comprising organised crime either in the wording of the law or in terms of common language, in spite of the fact that they bore all the features of organised crime. The only difference being that there was no cross-border overlap because the borders were hermetically sealed and all contact with external countries carefully supervised (Scheinost, 2001: 34; Nožina, 2004: 441-442). Thus, organised crime until 1989, represented something alien and distant. Its existence in the Czech society began to be acknlowedged only after the emergence of the profound political, social and economic changes that occurred during the period of transition.

The beginning of this period can be characterised as a time of great expectations over the future. The majority of people enjoyed the open space of liberty and definitely awaited a positive improvement in social and economic development. They also believed that the way was now open for their own ambitions for social advancement and success.

There was, however a degree of childish naivety in these expectations. An opinion poll in 1992 showed that 45% of people interviewed anticipated an improvement in their situation in the near future; 40% a slight improvem;ent and only 14% epected a deterioration of their situation (Svítková, 1992). A Different study in the same year found that 59% of respondents anticipated an improvement in their personal circumstances that woul take place immediately whilst 36% expected improvements within next three years (Rezková, 1992). In 1994, a follow-up study discovered that improvement in living standards within one year was anticipated by 33% of people; and by 64% within five years (Mladá fronta Dnes, 1994).

Table 1
Expectations of people – percentage of respondents

1992 [1)]	45 - improvement of the situation in near future 40 - slight improvement 14 - aggravation of situation
1992 [2)]	59 - chance to enhance personal ability is great 36 - this chance will be even greater in three years
1994 [3)]	33 - awaited better level of life within one year 64 - awaited better level of life within five years

Source: 1) Svítková, 2) Rezková, 3) Mladá Fronta Dnes

There was no place for doubts or fears. If there were some fears for the future they were psychologically hidden in some corner and affected only a small part of the population (the 14% found in the year 1992). This scepticism was expressed mostly by people with only a basic level of education; people with higher levels of education were predominantly optimistic in their expectations. Warnings about the possible risks arising from the speed of transformation and criticism of some of the transformation processes were not taken as seriously as perhaps they should have been. The risks were not taken into account, at least during the first phase of transformation until the second half of the 1990s.

The transformation of the economy and of society included enormous shifts in ownership, extensive privatisation of the state property as well as basic transformation of the state administration including that of law enforcement . The speed of this process was declared as being more important than ensuring its strict regulation. This situation challenged existing norms and standards of behaviour, the 'internalised values' of people. Former Socialist values had to be replaced by liberal and capitalist (free-market) ones. These changes also encouraged the opening of 'windows of opportunity': with some people soon recognising such windows also opened at the edge of the law and indeed, in some cases, beyond it. The implications of these opportunities were far-reaching. The risk of serious forms of crime became a reality, if remaining unrecognised at the time.

Nevertheless the Czech society kept its confidence and optimism longer than in some other transforming states such as Slovakia. It was referred to as a 'patient society'. Even in comparison with such closely tied countries as Czech Republic and Slovakia the studies referred to in Table 1 found a noticeable difference in expectations. The 36% of respondents in the CR who anticipated an improvement in their own circumstances within the next three years was higher than in Slovakia which was only 30%; similarly for the 10% of respondents in the CR who anticipated a negative outturn was matched by 29% in Slovakia! (Rezková, 1992). However, in the face of widening social differentiation and a failure to meet expectations, this optimism was graduallt replaced by scepticism at least for a substantial part of population. Indeed, reality fell far short of (too high) expectations. For example: in a comparison of the results of repeated public opinion surveys about the economic situation and material life conditions that were carried out by the agency of Sociological Institute of the Czech Academy of Science in 1997, we find that in 1997 the Czech respondents evaluated the level and state of the Czech economy as being better than in the Polish, Hungarian, Slovenian economy. But by 2001, Czech citizens rated their economy and economic situation worse in comparison with that of these countries. Similarly comparing these studies carried out in the Czech Republic, Poland and Hungary in 2001, shows the Czechs as most pessimistic with regard to further development (CVVM, 2008).

Figure 1
Development of crime rate in the CR

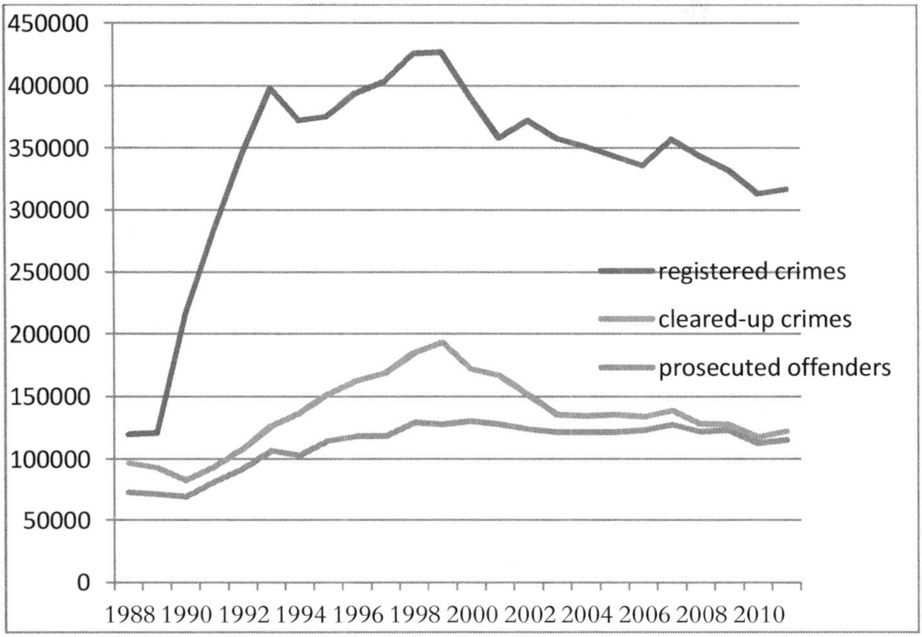

Source: Statistics of the Czech Police

There was evidence of a rapid growth in criminal activity, in part facilitated by the transformation. For the period from 1989/1990 until 1993, the number of registered crimes tripled. The rapid increase in the level of registered crime, especially that of property crime, caused a corresponding increase of the fear of such crime. Crime began to be gradually perceived as an important social problem and the issue of the existence of serious forms of crime such as organised and economic started to be recognised and discussed.

Understanding the phenomenon of organised crime

Against this background, the activities of organised criminal groups gradually began to be noticed by the police, media and judiciary. A characteristic of this initial period was the fact that organised crime was not understood as the product of the criminogenic potential of domestic conditions but was seen as the consequence of the adverse changes in Czech social conditions by organised groups *penetrating from abroad*.

Such a penetration of course existed indeed. There were many factors that could be viewed as being favourable for criminal activities coming from abroad and developing on the Czech territory. These included the advantageous geographical location of the CR, the anticipated entry into the EU, weakened social and formal controls, instability of legal systems, weak law enforcement authorities. The CR became a transit route for transnational illegal trafficking in a diverse range of commodities (especially drugs) and of illegal migration. These routes were quickly established through the Czech territory serving as it did as a transit country for both the east-west and south-north contraband movements. But gradually the CR grew from a transit route into a target country.

These foreign groups were at first involved in drug trafficking, illegal migration, prostitution, racketeering etc. (Macháček and Rumpl, 1997). They were not connected with activities run in the legitimate economy. Though some information did appear about the investment of criminal organisations in legitimate business activities (textile and leather goods, restaurants, bistros) and in real estate (housing) especially by Italian, Chinese and Russian groups (Macháček and Rumpl, 1997). These 'upperworld' activities were at the time not seen as comprising substantially unlawful or indeed criminal operations.

This implies that at the first half of the 1990s, the penetration by foreign criminal organisations did take place. For this reason organised crime was presented as the result of these alien organisations. The concept of organised crime became conterminous with foreign organised groups and their activities. With regard to the domestic criminal scene it was interpreted as some kind of incentive that gradually recruited domestic co-offenders, suppliers and customers.

The risk of exploitation of the changing social and economic conditions from 'inside' by Czech organised criminal offenders remained to a large extent unnoticed. In this manner organised crime remained represented in the media and thus understood in the public mind in a very biased manner.

This way of presenting organised crime was confirmed by the initial content analysis of the Czech press reports carried out as part of a research project on organised crime carried by the *Institute of Criminology and Social Prevention* in 1993-1995. It covered the first eight months of 1993. State-wide newspapers (eleven in total excluding tabloids) and three magazines were monitored. Even during this relatively short period, there were some 100 reports, or articles on organised crime, which evidences the relative interest in this topic (Scheinost, 2011:208). "*Organised crime sells*", as show by Van Duyne (2004) in his analysis of the media seduction by organised crime and of the interaction between the media, law enforcement agencies and the public (we may add to this triangle the policy-makers) that is documented using examples from the U.S., Russia and Netherlands.

Daily newspapers at the time, concentrated mainly on information about penetration by organised groups from abroad, or on those comprising foreign nationals residing in the Czech Republic. In terms of the country of origin of foreign groups, the press drew attention to groups coming from countries comprising the former Yugoslavia, Italy, Bulgaria, Albania and those of the former Soviet Union. Only very seldom was mention made of groups arising from outside Europe.

Though causality is always difficult to determine, there is a relationship between the frequency of media reports about organised crime and on its activities and threats and the fear-of-crime by citizens. Subsequent to 1993, organised crime began to be seen as an urgent problem as shown by public opinion polls (Scheinost, 2011: 210). These polls were regularly conducted using a sample size of about 1000 respondents. The following table shows the opinions of people about social and political problems felt as being 'urgent'.

Table 1
The time trend for assessing problems as 'very urgent'
Five most frequently mentioned issues

	92/10 %	**93/10** %	**94/10** %	**95/4** %	**96/10** %	**97/10** %	**98/10** %	**99/5** %
Corrupt., econ. crime	-	70	77	73	70	79	82	76
Unemployment	44	40	42	37	26	38	58	74
organised crime	-	68	73	66	68	65	71	64
economic reform	69	53	42	41	33	53	57	64
general crime	73	83	79	76	72	65	72	62

Source: Research Institute of Public Opinion, Prague

Wording of question: In your opinion, how urgently must the following problems in our society be resolved? (The number expresses the percentage of those who listed the problem as urgent. Numbers in the heading of the table indicate year and month when the inquiry was carried out.)

It can be said that the fear of organised crime was not only a matter of concern for Czech citizens. Fear of organised crime had been dominant in Europe for over two decades at the end of the twentieth century until it was overshadowed by the fear of terrorism (see van Duyne, 2006:178).

First response

Subsequent to the first half of the 1990s, the legal provisions against organised crime were gradually adopted – concepts, laws, special units in the police and in the public prosecutor office. The first governmental strategy in the fight against organised crime was adopted in 1996 (with a number of updates in subsequent years, with the most recent in 2011). This first response included a broad list of legislative and administrative measures (Scheinost, 2004: 880). The intention of this strategy and of the measures that it introduced was to enhance the measures against organised crime, making them sharper and more effective but also to hamper the 'penetration' of organised criminals from abroad which had been perceived as the major threat.

With hindsight it would appear that the public attention, media and public administration were concentrated on one 'branch' of organised crime – let us say the 'classic' or 'traditional' variety. This was represented by extended criminal organisations and groups operating on a transnational basis to carry out business in goods and services.

Such organisations were no myths and they really came from abroad, they developed their activities and, depending on their nature, they also developed contacts with Czech collaborators. Attention was concentrated on these groups. Subsequent to this, the existence of mixed groups or those composed only of Czech offenders but linked to these international groups , began to be recognised. These foreign, mixed and domestic groups gradually delimited their areas of interest, sometimes via conflicts and violence.

Different activities went through periods of boom and decline (*e.g.* boom of illegal migration in the period of Balkan conflicts, or trafficking in stolen art items during the 1990s), others, such as drug trafficking, were seen to be constantly profitable.

This 'branch' of organised crime, comprising the 'ususal suspects' can be regarded as 'traditional' or 'classic organised crime' (see Abadinsky, 1994); it may also be designated, in spite of higher profitability as a 'lower' form of organised crime connected with lower social strata, at least at the executive level.

Organised or 'organising' crime in the economic area

Aside from this form or 'branch' of organised crime there was of course also another form of serious crime which was not seen to be visibly connected with the existence of organised criminal groups and thus for a relatively long time did not attract any special attention. This concerns illegal or semi-legal activities that were committed within the economic and financial sector, predominatly by its own professionals.

In contrast with the above mentioned underworld 'branch', these forms of financial and economic crime were facilitated through the transformation of the Czech economic environment. They arose from the 'inside' and were committed mostly by Czech offenders, though in many cases there was international overlap especially with regard to financial criminal transactions.

The period of transformation provided an ideal environment for the growth of similar activities, in particular with regard to the privatisation of state property, the development of private enterprises and extensive capital transfers. In this "*misty and inarticulate*" situation when economic regulations were only just being created and in consequence, the semi-legal and illegal economic activities were for a long time outside the circle of interest of law enforcement agencies, thus their danger was underestimated (Baloun *et al.*, 2005).

Offenders from abroad also became involved in these activities, *e.g.* by investment of illegal profits but the core and substantial part of this kind of crime should be attributed to the Czech offenders. However, these activities were for a long time, not presented as organised crime even in those cases where the 'traditional' traits of organised crime were evident including the use of violence, *e.g.* as in the so-called 'light fuel oils' cases.

The cases of 'light fuel oils' appeared as a typical 'white-collar crime'. They consisted of large scale tax evasion, or tax fraud. The offenders exploited different taxation rates of chemically identical and, in terms of appearance, indistinguishable products – light fuel oil (lower tax rate) and motor gasoline (higher tax rate). The criminal activities were committed by mostly Czech offenders who were able to exploit this double taxation rate and the gaps in the laws and regulations which facilitated its perpetration. But aside from its classification as white-collar crime, these cases also showed the typical features that were usually attributed to organised crime. These features include the existence of a group of offenders; organised and well-planned activity; continuity; division of tasks, the functioning of networks of suppliers, agents and customers; international connection;, corrupt behaviour; conflicts and their resolution through violence. Nevertheless, these cases were presented only as economic crime and not as organised crime.

Other well-known were the cases of so-called '*tunelling*' of which the following example.

> One of the prominent cases of tunnelling in the history of the Czech transformation was the case of *CS Funds*. This investment company had, since 1995, been run by the controversial financial grouping Motoinvest and in February 1997 was sold to the unknown firm Austel Enterprises. However, before the sale, the stock in the accounts of CS funds was exchanged for cash. This happened twice more over a period of several weeks after the holder of

> CS Funds had been changed. Subsequently in March 1997, 1,24 billion Czech crowns disappeared from CS Funds and reappeared in the accounts of several foreign companies. Money on accounting records was replaced by some worthless stock, for example, the stock of a non-existent poultry farm that moreover never reached the accounts of CS Funds (Baloun *et al.*, 2002).

The commission of these forms of economic crime as described in the two examples of light fuel oils and tunelling was quite sophisticated and the activity was well organised. Committing these crimes required a certain level of expertise in economic, financial and tax matters as well as knowledge of bank operations. To this should be added the social skills and experience, required to keep open the channels of communication for practical information or direct collaboration with the staff of banks, privatisation committees *etc.* But in contrast to the activities belonging to the 'first branch' these organised forms of upperworld economic and financial crime may occur without establishing specific criminal organisations. More often they take advantage of the existing entrepreneurial environment and of official structures and institutions, which is totally rational as a means of blending into the surroundings.

It is often the *modus operandi* to establish shell companies for these fraudulent operations as a legitimate commercial vehicle, which functionally operate as a smokescreen, usually to siphon off the money. This type of crime was typical during the first phases of economic transformation. The question is whether it may be classified as comprising organised crime and if so, how it can be differentiated from other manifestations of organised crime.

In contrast to the 'classic' organised crime the offenders of economic crime usually do not offer any goods or services to customers or clients. They directly damage their targets without giving anything in the way of counter value. The typical *modus operandi* is fraud, embezzlement or gathering of ill-gotten benefits gained by corruption or by other means skimming off their victims. There are exceptions to this pattern, however: with fraud schemes concerning labour or high-taxed commodities actual services and goods are delivered – against a reduced price. However, comparing the amount of profit for the perpetrators, the social and economic harm of this kind of crime and the sophisticated organisation of activities, it is at the same level as the traditional organised crime and, according to Van Duyne and Soudijn, (2010) can be even higher.

As a result of such sharp practices the perpetrators accumulated huge wealth during the period of transformation and above all, gained indispensable influence over those in the public life, state administration and policy makers. The side-effect was a decline of public trust in the legitimacy of the newly created entrepreneurial strata. Of course, this is not only the case of the Czech Republic.

Plywaczewski writes about the two ways in which different strains of criminal operation gathered strength in Poland in the early 1990s. The first originated in the upper levels of power and responsibility (the so-called 'top-down' variety of organised crime), as corrupt public officials and politicians who exercised control over strategic sectors of the economy abused their positions. The second type involved criminal activities at low-lying levels of society which then crept upwards: in this 'bottom-up' organised crime the traditional criminal underworld – reorganised and newly stimulated – formed the source of the crime networks (Plywaczewski, 2004: 467). Póczik also wrote in a similar vein about the developments in Hungary (Póczik, 2011).

Present situation

At present the danger arising from these forms of crime is known and declared both in the media and in official documents but unfortunately it occurred only after the expansion of the power of many of the players in this branch. In spite of this declared danger and maybe due to the previous underestimation of these unlawful or semi-lawful economic activities there are still gaps in the relevant Czech legislation. The initial governmental strategy against organised crime stressed the importance of the tools of penal and police law. After their adoption, the Czech legislation became quite comparable with that existing in most of the European countries. But what is still missing is the tools that could limit the space for the operations and influence of the perpetrators of economic and financial crime. During the twenty years of transformation of the country *e.g.*, the Law on State Administration has still not been adopted (it has been 'under preparation and discussion' for this period); the same is the case with mandatory property declaration and the regulation of lobbying. The drafted abolishment of the so-called anonymous stock has been repeatedly rejected.

The report on the security situation in the CR, a document that is drawn up each year by the Czech police and submitted to the government and to Parliament notes both the stabilisation of the 'traditional' organised crime (underworld) in the CR and also the considerable risks stemming from the impact of hidden economic and financial interests on the policy or policymakers (Zpráva o bezpečnostní situaci, 2011). Corruption is noted especially in connection with contacts between entrepreneurs and officials in particular with regard to the management of public property and public budgets.

This report also draws attention to the slow decline in violent crime (murders, extortion, injury) and the shift towards non-violent crime, mostly of an economic nature (tax fraud and evasion, credit fraud, internet crime). Dubious business practices have been found in relation to tenders for both government and public contracts.

The report points to the enormous profits acquired from these types of economic crimes and generated in an organised and professional way that allows the perpetrators to operate on the edge of the law and aviod attention from law enforcement authorities. At the same time the report stresses that the most serious manifestations of organised crime can be seen through applying hidden pressure on the decision making process within the public administration, law enforcement authorities and judiciary and indeed even on the legislative process itself.

It is possible to say that the initial misunderstanding and underestimation of the threat of the upperworld form of organised crime, (the 'second branch') has been addressed. With hidsight the underestimation and hence late reaction have been paid for dearly: through a ssubstantial growth in the wealth and influence of people connected with this organised – rather organising – economic and financial crime. These risks and threats are now at least understood as expressed in the police report on security as well as in the media. How is that reflected in the written media?

In 2011, the Institute of Criminology and Social Prevention carried out a new press analysis concerning reporting of organised crime. This analysis encompassed the three most popular Czech daily papers for the period May to July 2011 (Luptáková, 2012).

Among other things, a significant shift in terminology was found. During the monitored period the use of the term organised crime was rare and somewhat exceptional. There was no use in connection with domestic events and it occurred only a few times with regard to the news from abroad. Sometimes the term 'mafia' was used, but in the figurative sense *i.e.* referring to the case of conflict between the former supreme state prosecutor that used the term 'judicial mafia' for designation of some members of the judiciary. Likewise the term 'mafia' was also used in connection with the activity of some lobbies – pharmaceutical, coal *etc.* – and their effort to influence the public administration.

In contrast, a great deal of attention was directed by journalists to sinister practices that happen on the borderland between business and policy. This attention corresponds to the warning contained in the police report on the security situation about the influence of financial and economic crime on the public life. In this connection the term 'godfather' was much more frequently used than the phrase 'organised crime'.

The term 'godfather' is basically a journalistic one used similarly to the word 'tunnelling'. It has also been used by politicians (in particular if they want to undermine their political opponents designating them to be supported by 'godfathers'); in general it very quickly became within last two or three years, a part of common language.

In the current context this term is not used in the sense of an identification of the supreme boss of a criminal organisation as it was in the literature or movies on 'classical' organised crime, but as a designation of powerful and rich entrepreneur or financier who acts as sponsor of political parties, who manipulates politicians at least at the regional level. This 'godfather' is often characterised as a 'controversial' entrepreneur –used in media as a euphemism for entrepreneurs acting at the edge of the law and probably beyond it. This term is connected with an impression that the links of 'godfathers' to the criminal sphere are not proved but are very plausible. We may interpret the meaning of this term as not directly belonging to the criminal underworld but rather as generating the image of a suspicious background, of shady practices, sinister pressure within the public sphere, misuse of power and evasion of the democratic procedures of the administration. Simply said the 'godfather' is the powerful man behind the political scene pulling many strings.

We can conclude that the subject of the 'first branch' of organised crime is no longer seen by the media as as being as attractive and important as it appeared to be in the 1990s in spite of the fact that it has not been dismissed from the scene and is still considered as highly profitable. The organised crime picture is so far no longer linked to the penetration of organised groups from abroad.

The press analysis documents that more attention is now drawn to the risk of vulnerability of the state by the influence of controversial entrepreneurs – *i.e.* by the second, 'upperworld branch' of organised crime that was, for a long time, ignored. Its protagonists are not presented as a part of lower social strata. The shift of the interest of media and subsequently of public opinion and interest from the 'first branch of organised crime to the 'higher' sphere of shady economic activities and hidden influence on policy, is apparent.

The survey of public opinion on the issue of organised crime, carried out by the *Institute of Criminology and Social Prevention* in August 2010, assessed opinions on organised crime in a representative sample of the population in the scope of 999 respondents aged 15 years or older.

This research affirmed the above mentioned shift. The problem of organised crime does not attract primarily interest by the general population. Only 10% of respondents stated that they were interested in the problem of organised crime.

Table 2
The problem of organised crime is . . .:

Answer	Percentage of respondents
Very interesting	10
Interesting but only marginally	34
I have little interest	31
I have no interest	24

Source: ICSP - Survey on public opinion – August 2010

Concurrently the respondents interviewed in this survey do not deny the existence of organised crime in the CR. A full 70% of respondents say that organised crime occurs in the CR and another 25% state that it probably does. It seems that people know about organised crime but no longer take it for as interesting a matter as was the case in the past. Also the view about the perpetrators of organised crime seems to be more realistic: 28% of respondents answered that it was mainly foreigners who were involved in organised crime; 4% of respondents said mainly Czechs were involved; but 63% of respondents shared the opinion that both foreigners and Czechs are involved in committing organised crime.

Asked for their opinion about the best way to act against organised crime, respondents mentioned that the most effective policy would be to make punishments more severe. But immediately following on in second place, the respondents expressed the wish for a more effective confiscation of the proceeds from crime, anti-corruption measures and greater supervision over allocation of public tenders (Scheinost, 2011:212). This could be interpreted as arising from a better understanding of the threat of organised crime for the society that includes the impact of the 'second branch' – organising economic crime in the upperworld of public life, policy and public administration.

The 'shadows of the godfathers' can probably be observed behind the attitude of citizens towards the behaviour of politicians expressed in the findings. Asked what type of behaviour by politicians people would not be willing to overlook, 73% of respondents answered the contacts with 'mafias' and 37% referred to corruption.

In the frame of expert inquiry, made by the *Institute of Criminology and Social Prevention* in 2010, the experts – mostly police officers serving in police units specialised in organised crime – were asked about the predicted changes in the nature and activities of organised crime in the relatively short term up to 2015 (Cejp, Scheinost, 2012). Most of them predicted, in general, a continuing expansion of organised crime into the sphere of the economy and business.

In the opinion of experts crime in the economic sphere, which produces high profits, is set to rise. The experts mentioned especially that extensive fraudulent banking transactions and the 'tunnelling' of subsidies from the national budget and EU funds can be anticipated. The experts assumed that organised crime will respond to the adoption by the Czech Republic of the Euro, with an increase in cases of currency counterfeiting. Sophisticated fraud in the field of taxes will proliferate (with a view to fictitious exports and price increases with the addition of VAT refunds). Increases in the fraudulent evasion of excise duty on fuel, alcohol and cigarettes are predicted; real estate fraud will become ever more common. Organised crime will invest more in the legal economy. Organised criminal groups will use information technology more than they do at present. Further growth will occur in credit card abuse and document forgery.

In sum, qualified economic and financial crime is expected to rise. This means that its significance will increase and attempts by its protagonists (let us say the "godfathers") to affect the public life and public policy will be aided by the accumulated assets.

Conclusions

The present development, as registered by the police, by experts as well as by researchers, formulates the premise that economic crime will inosculate with organised crime in an increasing way, in other words, economic crime will increasingly move into the realm of organised crime and *vice versa*. The border between organised and economic – 'organising' – crime will, therefore, be less and less transparent. Maybe this distinction should now be considered obsolete.

Organised crime and economic crime function in a certain symbiosis; they are intertwined. This interaction compounds their power and influence, their seriousness and the threat they pose. The interlinking of organised and economic crime and their increased influence on politics, the economy, government, media, public life, *etc.*, is the biggest threat and risk for the future. These risks have now been reflected in media.

There are concerns that organised crime will strengthen its links with central, regional and local government, and that it will influence the legislature and the executive branch, all through the corruption of staff at the relevant decision making levels, in particular concerning the allocation of large public contracts. There are attempts to influence and sponsor political parties, along with efforts to influence the work of the courts, public prosecutors, and the police, and to engage in corruption.

There we come again to the phenomenon of 'godfathers' that substantially contributes to the decline of trust in the state, policy and politicians. This decline is connected with the current disappointment with the low level of social and political development that has taken place within the last decade. It also stems from the failure to meet the high expectations shared by people entering the transformation and is exacerbated by the difficult situation arising from the economic and financial crisis, that affects a great number of citizens. These trends result in the general decline of trust in the future capacity of state and politicians to act as good administrators for the public good.

In this respect the impact of the second branch of organised crime – or organising crime – should be considered as substantially more dangerous than the first, the classical one. The classical organised crime is a source of fear and sometimes generates criticism against the police, judiciary or concrete politics, but it is this "second upperworld branch" that undermines the trust of people in the democratic system itself that leads to the resignation, feelings of powerlessness and willingness to accept the radical and non-democratic solutions made by the "strong hand".

References

Abadinsky, H., *Organized crime.* Nelson Hall, Chicago, 1994

Baloun, V., M. Scheinost, Economy and crime in the society in transition - the Czech Republic case. In: P.C. van Duyne, K. von Lampe and N. Passas (eds.), *Upperworld and Underworld in Cross-Border Crime.* Wolf Legal Publishers, Nijmegen, 2002, pp. 43-60

Baloun, V., Kadeřábková,D., Scheinost,M., 2005 Adventure capitalism and economic crime in the countries of transition: the case of the Czech Republic. In: P.C.van Duyne, K.von Lampe, M.van Dijck, J.L.Newell (eds.), The Organised Crime Economy. Managing Crime Markets in Europe. Wolf Legal Publishers, Nijmegen 2005. pp. 143-162

Cejp, M. and M. Scheinost, Organised and economic crime: A common problem. In: A. Šelih and A. Završnik (eds.), *Crime and transition in Central and Eastern Europe.* Springer 2012, pp. 157-178

CVVM, Sociologický ústav Akademie věd ČR, Hospodářská situace a materiální životní podmínky v ČR, Polsku a Maďarsku z pohledu veřejného mínění [CVVM, Sociological institute of Czech academy of science, Economic situation and material life condition by public opinion] 2004, www.cvvm.cas.cz/upl/zpravy/100321s_ev40213.pdf

Duyne, P.C. van, The creation of a threat image: Media, policy making and organised crime. In: O.C. van Duyne, M. Jager, K. von Lampe and J.L. Newell (eds.), *Threats and phantoms of organised crime, corruption and terrorism*. Wolf Legal Publishers, Nijmegen 2004

Duyne, P.C. van, The organisation of business crime. In: P.C. van Duyne, A. Maljevic, M. van Dijck, K. von Lampe L.J. and Newell (eds.), *The organisation of crime for profit*. Wolf Legal Publishers, Nijmegen 2006

Duyne, P.C. van, *Transnational) organised crime, laundering and the congregation of the gullible*. Tilburg University, 2011

Duyne, P.C. van and M.R.J. Soudijn, Crime-money in the financial system: what we fear and what we know. In: M. Herzog-Evans (ed.), *Transnational Criminology Manual, Volume 2*, Nijmegen, Wolf Legal Publishers, 2010

Kosík,S., J. Souček and J. Zátorský, Organizovaný zločin v České republice [Organised crime in the CR]. Kriminalistika 1/1996Luptáková,M., Názory české veřejnosti na problematiku organizovaného zločinu a vliv denního tisku na utváření těchto názorů [Views of the Czech public on organised crime matters and impact of newspapers on the their formation]. Trestněprávní revue 2/2012, pp. 37-42

Macháček, Z. and T. Rumpl, Zahraniční skupiny organizovaného zločinu a jejich aktivity na českém území [Foreign organised groups and their activities on the Czech territory]. In: Nožina, M., Mezinárodní organizovaný zločin v ČR [International organised crime in the CR], ÚVM, Praha 1997

Nožina, M., The Czech Republic: A cross-roads for organised crime. In: C. Fijnaut and L. Paoli (eds.), *Organised crime in Europe: Concepts, patterns and control policies in the European Union and beyond*. Springer 2004, pp. 435-466

Mladá Fronta Dnes [newspaper], 23.2.1994

Plywaczewski, E.W., Organized crime in Poland: Its development from "Real Socialism" to the present time. In: C. Fijnaut and L. Paoli, (eds.), *Organised crime in Europe: Concepts, patterns and control policies in the European Union and beyond*. Springer 2004, pp. 467-498

Póczik, S., Paper presented at the conference Creating a Security Sphere in the Wider Central Europe, Prague 2011

Rezková, M., Možnosti uplatnění schopností před listopadem 1989, dnes a zítra [Chance to enforce personal abilities before November 1989, today and tomorrow]. Sociologické aktuality 9/1992

Scheinost, M., Transnational organised crime and cross-border trafficking in human beings in the Czech Republic. In: Van Duyne,P.C., Ruggiero,V., Scheinost,M., Valkenburg,W. (eds.), Cross-border Crime in a Changing Europe. Nova Science Publishers, New York 2001, pp. 33-48

Scheinost, M., Organised crime policies in the Czech Republic: A hard road from under-estimation to the European standard. In: Fijnaut,C., L. Paoli (eds.), *Organised crime in Europe. Concepts, patterns and control policies in the European Union and beyond*. Springer 2004, pp.879-898

Scheinost,M., Organised crime, the media and the sentiments of the public. In: Antonopoulos G. *et al.* (eds.), Usual and unusual organising criminals in Europe and beyond. Profitable crimes, from underworld to upper world. Maklu, Apeldoorn, 2011, pp. 207-214

Svítková, T:, Vzpomínky na budoucnost [Remember to future], Sociologické aktuality 5/1992

Trávníčková, I., Prostituce jako jedna z možných aktivit organizovaného zločinu [Prostitution as one of possible activities of organized crime]. IKSP, Praha 1995

von Lampe, K., Fears and forecasts: Notions about future trends in the early phases of the German debate on organised crime revisited. Paper presented at the 13th Cross-border crime colloquium, Manchester 2012

Zpráva o situaci v oblasti vnitřní bezpečnosti a veřejného pořádku na území České republiky v roce 2011 [Report on situation in the sphere of internal security and public order on the territory of Czech Republic]. Ministry of Interior of the CR 2012

Migrants and 'Organised Crime' in the Greek Press (1991-2011)

The Politics of Representing the 'Organised Criminal Other'

Georgios A. Antonopoulos and Georgios Papanicolaou[1]

Introduction: the world as a constructed representation

In this chapter we are taking a more concentrated look at the representation of the link between migration and organised crime in the major Greek national daily newspapers since 1991. As we have pointed out in our work previously (Antonopoulos 2009; Papanicolaou 2011; Papanicolaou and Antonopoulos 2010), during this period established concepts and public perceptions of security and public safety in Greece have been re-codified around the idea of organised crime as a threat linked directly to the question of ethnicity. It is true that this development coincides with genuine major changes in that country's social fabric and life. For the first time in her modern history Greece emerged in 1990-91 as a destination country for eastern European and wider migratory movements. Even though it is still difficult to provide accurate figures due to a large number of undocumented migrants, the last Greek Census in 2001 recorded 797.091 foreigners, in their majority Albanian but also other eastern European and Asian nationals, in a total population of 10.964.020 (ESYE, 2001). These trends have continued unabated during the first decade of the 21st Century. Migratory inflows are now widely understood to have ignited wholesale transformations of the country's economic, political and cultural life, particularly in urban areas, whose formal and underground economies have hosted large numbers of foreigners.

No matter how dramatic, such change cannot be taken to account directly for the degree to which ethnicity almost monopolises today's perceptions of organised crime. 'Ethnic crime groups' have been frequently and explicitly identified as organised crime threats in official reports and accounts of criminality. Consider for

1 Georgios A. Antonopoulos is Reader in criminology at Teesside University, UK. Georgios Papanicolaou is Senior Lecturer in criminology at Teesside University, UK.

example the Hellenic Police's Annual Organised Crime Reports (AOCR), which have made repeated and prominent reference to the 'threat' posed by the non-indigenous 'organised crime groups': the 1999 AOCR suggests that "*the ethnic crime groups that constituted a specific threat . . . in 1999 were the Albanians, Russians, Bulgarians, Romanians, Turkish, Iraqi, and in some cases Pakistani and groups of Bangladeshi nationals . . .*" (MPO, 2000: 2). Similar formulations can be found in the AOCR editions published in subsequent years. What is remarkable about this tendency is that indigenous crime groups involved in racketeering and corruption particularly in association with urban nightlife (the godfathers of the night) have never failed to capture the attention of both authorities and public historically and certainly well before the 1990s. More interestingly, their activities have rarely underpinned notions of organised crime: in fact, in the period preceding the late 1990s Greek authorities and society, more generally speaking, did not possess a concept of organised crime as a kind of activity linked to ethnic crime groups, either as ethnic groups or 'organised' groups. Rather, beginning originally from the 1970s and continuing even well into the 1990s, 'organised crime' as a term had been used to refer to terrorism (Xenakis, 2004). But today, against the background of the extreme political right in Greece having conducted their May 2012 electoral campaign on the single issue of 'sweeping the country clean' from the migrant criminals, the association of organised crime with migrant ethnic groups is virtually unchallenged in Greek public perceptions and even policy debates.

How was this development possible? What kind of real or imaginary social, political and cultural problems has such a particular concept of organised crime hinged upon in Greece at the dawn of 21st Century, and how has it addressed them? The introduction of particular constructions of organised crime and of specific manifestations of it in technical terms (*e.g.* the trafficking and smuggling in human beings or drugs) has been seen as the product of pressures, including the exercise of international influence, at the top of policy making (Papanicolaou, 2011; Xenakis, 2004). The ensuing regularisation, diffusion and acceptance by the wider society of a notion of organised crime as an *ethnic* threat points to a wider process of social construction of reality. This in its turn lent support to a criminal law legitimisation involving a wider set of apparatuses. Prominent within this institutional nexus are the media, to whose discourse we direct our attention in the following pages: given that "*virtually all human experience is inseparable from mediatised experience*" (Barak, 2010: 1), the media have the potency to shape perceptions of 'lived' realities, both collective and individual. It has become common place to accept this capacity when it comes to media representations of crime (Ericson *et al.*, 1991). Their performance of the same instrumental role has been recognised in the construction of the question of '(transnational) organised crime' (see, *e.g.*, Van Duyne, 2004; 2011).

We examine here the construction of the link between migrants and organised crime in the Greek print media, using a large sample of reports from nine major national dailies (see the next section) between 1991 and 2011. While this strategy arguably excludes the most powerful agents of contemporary mediamatic experience of crime, radio and, of course, television, there are important reasons to justify this choice. Firstly, electronic media have been a recent development in Greece, as the operation of non-state run radio and TV stations was only allowed in the late 1980s. Secondly, not only the Greek public has consistently relied primarily (albeit at falling rates in the past decade) on print media for information and 'sober' news analysis, but also electronic media organisations have emerged as ancillary operations to print journalism: most Greek TV stations are integrally tied to print media corporations, and the most influential TV news commentators also maintain regular columns in major dailies. So while it is true that electronic media offer 'superior' dramatisations of social reality and of crime, they are by no means superior to print media as regards content and commentary, despite the fact that the latter's influence has been shrinking due to the general decline of reading in general and newspapers in particular (European Journalism Centre, 2010). We are thus confident that newspaper reports are a highly suitable place to begin deciphering the contribution of media in general in the representation and social construction of the link between migrants and organised crime in Greece.

Methods and data

Qualitative content analysis was the method of researching how migrants and 'organised crime' have been presented within the Greek Press. Qualitative content analysis is used to refer to any qualitative data reduction and sense-making effort that makes a volume of qualitative material, and attempts to identify core consistencies and meanings (Quinn Patton, 2002). *Qualitative* implies an emphasis on processes and meanings that are examined "*but not measured in terms of quantity, amount or frequency*" (Labuschagne, 2003: 100). Qualitative content analysis has an important advantage in that it allows the researcher to have valuable historical insights over time. Our analysis was performed by means of a very specific process and has involved several methodological decisions. There were, namely, four steps in our content analysis:

1. Identification of the data set.

The titles and content of 647 newspaper articles found on the internet[2] were systematically described and classified with a view to identifying specific textual characteristics (Krippendorff, 1980: 23). 'Organised crime' covers a wide range of phenomena (see von Lampe, 2008), which may be described in a variety of ways in press reports. There may be mention of specific activities, structures, and the general context in which 'organised crime' takes place. To identify these in every newspaper's electronic archive, we used combinations of a number of alternative and relative search terms: 'organised crime', 'criminal organisation', 'network', 'cluster', 'illegal markets', 'black market', 'black economy', 'immigrants', 'aliens', 'smuggling', 'trafficking', 'counterfeiting', 'piracy', 'fraud', 'drugs', 'money laundering'. Articles from nine major daily newspapers were selected, namely '*To Vima*', '*Eleftherotypia*', '*Eleftheros Typos*', '*Ta Nea*', '*Adesmeftos Typos*', '*Ethnos*', '*Kathimerini*', '*Apovegmatini*, and '*Proto Thema*' over the period from 1991 to 2011. In addition, a large number of newspaper articles from the researchers' personal archives were used for the same period.

There are numerous local, regional and national dailies in Greece today (including special financial/business and sports newspapers). However the above were selected firstly because they have been the most widely read national newspapers in the period under consideration. For example, the total sales of the above group would represents on average 75% of all newspapers sold in the week 20-26 June 2011 (To Vima 2011). Secondly, the selection of these titles was intended to ensure a degree of continuity in the sample, since in the period under study the vast majority of these dailies have circulated uninterruptedly; the only exception is '*Proto Thema*', a Sunday publication which is relatively new, but captured quickly a significant portion of the Sunday newspapers market. In terms of content and style of reporting, it should be noted that the division between 'broadsheets' and 'tabloids' is of little relevance in Greece (technically speaking most of the titles in our sample are actually published in tabloid format). Rather, the most important division in the Greek press is that between political dailies and sports dailies, while non-political dailies (*e.g.* the daily '*Espresso*' which focuses on celebrity and gossip) and financial press occupy rather marginal positions in the newspaper market in terms of sales. Most political dailies in Greece have a mixed readership in terms of class and educational backgrounds, the dividing line between them typically being drawn in terms of political affiliation (see European Journalism Centre, 2010).

---

2 Specifically on www.mme.gr, the Greek mass media website where almost all of the Greek newspapers, magazines, television channels and radio stations are listed.

Thus, the titles in our sample are all regarded as practicing professional journalism and are, therefore, more likely to voice more informed, 'objective', non-emotive and balanced views about migrants and 'organised crime' (see Sparks, 2000; Conboy, 2006). While their political affiliations and proclamations range between the centre-right and the centre-left, interestingly, they all appear to have taken a 'common line' regarding the representation of migrants and (organised) crime and the insecurity they 'cause' (see Panousis, 2011a; 2011b), and a common interpretative repertoire, which transcends party politics.

2. Choice of unit of analysis.

It was decided that the unit of analysis of our study at this stage would be themes such as 'offenders'. Thus, no attention was paid to the number of times an item or an 'element', as Harmon and Boeringer (2004: 404) call it, appears in a story and/or in the data set as a whole. Moreover, no particular effort was made to quantify each item/element/story devoted to each theme, although occasionally we are referring to the volume of articles on a particular issue.

3. Coding of articles.

Initially, we coded the collected articles based on the taxonomy (categories into which the articles were coded) developed by Konstantinidou (1999) in her remarkable study of the representation of Albanian criminality in the Athenian Press in the late 1990s. Specifically two of her categories were adopted: a) The representation of migrants, and b) the representation of migrant criminality and fear of crime. These initial categories are distinct and mutually exclusive as there is no overlap among them (see Tesch, 1990). They are also are exhaustive as all articles fit in one of the categories. By 'reducing' the collected articles to the aforementioned categories, and by examining the articles of each category several patterns relating to our study were apparent *e.g.* 'the migrants as organised criminals' and 'the migrants as victims of organised crime'.

4. Analysis of data.

After the coding of articles three files were formed for one for each of the aforementioned categories or themes:

a. The migrants as 'organised criminals';
b. the migrants as victims of 'organised crime'; and
c. The representation of migrant 'organised criminality'.

We started analysing the data by focusing at each file (theme) at a time. At this point it should be mentioned that, as Ryan and Bernard (2000) suggest, "*no matter how the researcher actually does the coding, by the time he or she has identified the themes and refined them to the point where they can be applied to an entire corpus of texts, a lot of . . . analysis has already been done*" (Ryan and Bernard, 2000: 781). The process of analysis involved reading through the articles in each file at least twice, attempting to draw possible generalisations and conclusions, and manually writing down concept occurrences. Again, however, there was some reference to aspects of reporting that had nothing to do with themes but with features of the article such as photographs and maps. A number of newspaper titles *as primary data* are cited indicatively within the text and at the footnotes.

As with any study the present study has certain limitations, which should be acknowledged at this stage. The first one has to do with the representativeness of the sample. For some newspapers that could not be found on the internet (archive) at the time of the data collection e.g *Eleftheros Typos* and *Apogevmatini*, and relatively newer newspapers such as *Proto Thema* it is extremely difficult to determine the 'representativeness' of the sample or to refer to earlier representations of the phenomenon of 'organised crime'. The second limitation is subjectivity. It is not obvious what exactly the journalist had in mind when writing the article, and how the authors of this chapter perceived it. Thirdly, there is no analysis of the way the readers receive the information and representations provided by the Greek Press, how they 'decode' the 'meanings', and whether there is "*a conjecture on the part of the reader*" (Eco, 1992: 64) that highlight the texts' intention and purposes (see also Chiricos *et al.*, 1997). Finally, there are language limitations: the meaning (and sometimes the zeal and passion) of headlines in Greek can often be distorted when the titles are translated into English.

'Bad news is good news' - the representation of migrant 'organised criminality'

Crime rates began to rise in Greece in the early 1980s and at faster rates in the early 1990s, particularly as regards serious crime, including homicide, robbery, assault, and drug-related crimes (Kourakis, 1998). Given the absence of robust data and analyses, which is a continuing problem in Greece, it is a mute point whether the trends witnessed in the 1990s have been a continuation of those of the 1980s. Far less uncertain is the fact that in public perceptions and policy debates the faster rise of crime rates in the early 1990s was quickly associated with the issue of migration and the rising fear of crime (see, *e.g.* Karydis, 1996). At the same time, it is equally certain that the large influx of migrants, which has continued unabated since the beginning of the 1990s, began to be perceived as a source of social disorganisation and disruption of everyday life. This has been a more wide-ranging development, which did not merely involve established patterns in the labour market, but also affected the housing market, the quality of social services, and ultimately the very quality of everyday life particularly in the larger urban centres of Greece (for an overview of research, see Stratoudaki, 2008). 'Organised crime' through its link with migration thus appears to be the device around which the Greek press has attempted to represent the accelerated pace of social change within a more cohesive narrative that maximizes their prospects for commercial competitiveness and success (Vryzas, 1997) in an era of intensified news commodification.

Building on the objective experience of the social change brought about by the influx of migrants, the newspapers have *regularly* focused on migrants and 'organised crime' through the accumulative function of everyday 'organised crime' news reports (see Liska and Baccaglini, 1990; Schlesinger *et al.,* 1991), and they have secured a sense of 'news-ness' through the recycling of the same or similar stories on 'organised crime' and migrants. In this way they have successfully constructed a link between rising serious crime with migration either directly or indirectly and thereby have largely contributed to the creation of perceptions of 'organised crime waves'.[3]

The Greek Press describes 'organised crime' as an *imported* feature that is partly a side-effect of the increased immigration in the country, partly of the increased migration from East to West and from South to North a process in which Greece is presented[4] as simply a '*crossroads*'[5], and partly as the effect of expansion of foreign 'mafias'. Inadvertently what is suggested is that the pathogenies of the Greek social environment have nothing to do with 'organised crime'.[6] 'Organised crime', as reported in one of the articles examined, is "*a catastrophic threat, a Trojan horse whose corrosive penetration threatens the societal structures*" (Chatzidis, 2000: N14)[7], and which

3 For example: "The exportation of crime from Russia".

4 In what follows we present the results of our analysis and therefore we only quote characteristic headlines and extracts from the news reports we have examined for illustrative purposes. These extracts appear *italicized* in the main text, whereas further quotations serving, where necessary, to convey more robustly to readers a 'feel' of how migrants are represented in the press, are included in footnotes. The translations from Greek are ours.

5 "Crossroads for Mafiosi", "Greece is the Crossroads of the Cigarette Mafia", "Chinese Invasion in the Contraband Cigarettes Too".

6 It should be noted that, in the newspaper articles we examined, we came across only *one* case in which, although foreigners and specifically nationals from the formers Soviet Union were identified as the main actors in the cigarette smuggling scene of Greece, an emphasis on the legal context was placed. This was an article in the financial section of the daily *Kathimerini* titled "The Lost Battle of Competition" in which the author highlighted the Greek state as the party mostly responsible for the smuggling of tobacco products due to the inevitable retail price wedges high taxation creates (Konstantinidis, 2005).

7 "*Deportation of Foreign Criminals*", "*Crime became more organised than our state: The Mafiosi got in our lives before the governmental bodies took any precautions*", "*The Police are Absent*", "*The*

has corruptive effects on otherwise law-abiding Greek citizens (see Mandrou, 2009).

The country is also represented as the "*paradise for illegal markets*" (Kalliagopoulos and Tsioutsias, 2003: 22; Tsarouchas, 2002a) and the Greek economy as a whole is also portrayed as being at risk due to the foreign illegal marketers. In an article appearing in the Greek daily *Ethnos*, for instance, it is estimated that the illegal trade of several commodities by 50.000 *migrants* results in €2 billion in taxes being evaded on an annual basis and whole commercial sectors becoming extinct (Kolonas, 2008). In the same article the Chair of the Commerce Association of Piraeus is quoted to state that

> ". . . *the illegals have been operating uninterruptedly for many years now, without paying taxes, making a profit at the expense of consumers, healthy commerce, the local community, Greek economy and employment. They put small and medium businesses in serious danger, [and] weaken the legal, healthy commerce* . . ." (in Kolonas, 2008: 34).

In a similar vein, the Chair of the Commercial and Industrial Chamber of Athens, noted that these illegal trade activities involve ". . . *imported smuggled goods*" and what he suggested towards the '*eradication*' of the illegal trade was – among others – tighter control of the borders (in Kolonas, 2008: 35). In another article appearing in the newspaper *To Vima*, physical piracy committed *by foreigners* is identified as one of the reasons for the 'Death of Discography' in Greece (Skintzas, 2008).

In this representational context specific ethnic groups have a greater journalistic appeal such as the Italians[8] – with all the connotations this group may have with regards to 'organised crime' – the Albanians (often referred to as the 'apprentices' of the Italian Mafia), nationals of African countries, Yugoslavians, Bulgarians, Romanians and Russians. In one article we came across, titled '*Imported Underworld War*', Greece was reported to be the meeting place for 60 Russian 'arch-godfathers' from the former Soviet Union, the United States, Israel and W. Europe who supposedly discussed the settling of feuds between so called 'families' (Lambropoulos, 2010). In another article dating back to 1999 the concern was the ease with which Russian 'mafiosi' could pay US$ 65.000 each to obtain a Greek passport and extend their activities uninterrupted in Greece and beyond (Alisanoglou and Nesfyge, 1999). The obsession with ethnic groups such as the Russians, in particular, is hardly a phenomenon that can be traced in Greece alone since the end of 1980s. Rawlinson (1998: 346) notes that "*[t]he 'Russian Mafia' offers a perfect synthesis of mafia 'octopus' with 'Red Terror'* . . .". The identification of *migration* and 'organised crime' also

Police in Breakdown", "*Kaminis [Mayor of Athens]: We Cannot Face Organised Crime*", "*25 Greek Companies are the Window of the Bulgarian Mafia*".

8 "*The Italian Mafia Spread its Tentacles to Greece*".

serves the objectives of crossing a *threshold* of news. According to Jewkes (2011) crime-related events need to meet a level of drama, if they are to be considered newsworthy. If an event (or a series of events) works within an 'international medium', they pass the threshold. 'Organised crime' including migrants exactly because of the international/transnational aspect it has or it is perceived to have, and because it is perceived to be of greater magnitude than conventional crime, easily meets the international threshold of newsworthiness.

'Organised crime' in general or individual manifestations of 'organised crime' are represented as the business of hierarchical, 'mafia-type', rigid 'organisations' and groupings with 'Mr. Bigs' on their top, irrespectively of whether such structures really exist in Greece. This image is maintained despite the scepticism of the international (see Reuter, 1984; van Duyne, 1996; Levi, 2002) and part of the Greek academic community (Antonopoulos, 2009; Papanicolaou and Antonopoulos, 2010) on the existence of this type of structures which connote durability and "*an existence and behaviour independent of the behaviour of [their] members*" (von Lampe, 2004: 230). Newspaper titles referring to the 'sexy' notions of 'Mafias', 'Cartels', 'Lobbies', 'Syndicates', 'Czars' and 'Godfathers' such as are commonplace and *consistent* in the last twenty years that we have examined and represents the period in which the country was transformed in a host country for migrants. Examples are:

> "The Mafia has camped in four Greek cities", "The Mafia of Cigarettes", "Following the Cigarette Mafia Trace", "The Cartel of the West Coast", "Mafia a la Greca", "Greece is the Refuge of the Russian Mafia", "The Russian Mafia had a Rendezvous in Greece", "The Mafia of Luxury Passenger Cars", "The Mafias of the Stolen Passenger Cars", "The Gun Warehouse in Thessaloniki Leads to the Hit men Syndicate", "The Czars of Crime with the Greek Names" or "The Godfathers of the Night".

It would be interesting to note that even when other terms such as 'networks' or 'clusters' (*speires*) are used on the title or the body of the newspaper article, the description of the entities involved in the organised criminal activities point to hierarchy and rigidity rather than fluid and dynamic social systems that consist of patterns of relationships among people/actors (see Wasserman and Faust, 1994). For example, in 2005 an article in the newspaper *Ta Nea* referred to a dismantled *network* exploiting deaf people; however, in this network the emphasis was on a Ukrainian 'leader' called the 'Clown' and his 'sub-leader' called the 'Doll' (Nesfyge, 2005).

It is also significant that when the terms 'Mafias', 'Cartels', 'Syndicates' etc. are used to refer to migrant 'organised criminality' a 'reliable' source is very rarely used on the specific issue. Although crime journalists increasingly rely on the police or other law enforcement agencies for technical or other information (see Chibnall, 1975; Fishman, 1981), in most of the articles the journalists make the *assumption about the structure of the 'organised crime' entity involving migrants.* When it comes to the immigration-crime nexus in general, Panousis (2011b) notes that the issue is presented by non-specialist journalists who obtain information from the internet as well as other colleagues. Evidently, there is great room for discretion on the part of the journalists in the context of crime reporting and a tendency to impute meaning on the basis of a range of taken for granted commonsensical understandings and expectations about 'organised criminality', which is one way or another identified with rigid structures and with non-Greeks. However, even when a presumably 'reliable' source is used, the information is twisted to fit pre-conceived ideas about 'organised crime'. For example, in 2007, one of us was interviewed by the Greek, centre-left, daily newspaper *Eleftherotypia* on his research on cigarette smuggling and the organisation of the particular trade. Antonopoulos clearly expressed his concerns about the obsession of the media, law enforcement and the political sphere with hierarchical structures and offered information that might help establish an alternative view. Namely, that the market could be based primarily on networks involving individuals often acting on improvisation and for their own financial benefit. He even offered a number of case studies of *individual* entrepreneurs such as *Greek* students studying in foreign country universities who simply capitalised on differential prices of tobacco and otherwise were *socially isolated* marketers. Yet, the article was published titled '*The Pyramid of Contraband Cigarettes*' and the major focus was on the foreigners involved in the business.

Apart from the nature of migrant 'organised criminality' put forward, the Greek newspapers use technical ways of constructing and enhancing meaning. Priyadarsini (1984 cited by Williams and Dickinson, 1993: 36; see also Konstantinidou, 1999) noted that many crime reports are more passionate when they are 'highly graphic', when they involve 'sensational portrayals' and 'embellished descriptions'. In this sense the Greek Press either uses very artistic, metaphoric titles[9] or systematically uses photographs, which constitute a continuous message and "*totally exhaust its mode of existence*" (Barthes, 1977: 18; Sontag, 1970). The presentation of photographs/mug-shots of apprehended foreign offenders, especially those coming from countries of the former Soviet bloc and being involved in violent crimes as part of their 'organised criminal activities', regularly appear in newspaper articles (*e.g.* the mugshots of Russian 'organised criminals' Selivestrov, Tatarenkov and Solonik in Nesgyge, 1998). The characteristic visual aesthetic of the mugshot impresses on the general public the signs of difference in the criminal. In this way it

9 "On the Routes of Heroin Albanian is Spoken", "Greece is Under Albanian Occupation", "Crime in Greece speaks Albanian".

feeds an ideological process, reinforcing a particular view on the nature and background of 'organised criminality' committed by the 'Other' (Hall, 1981: 226; Jermyn, 2003: 190).

Moreover, the newspapers systematically use crime statistics and reports offered by law enforcement authorities (*e.g.* the Annual Reports on Organised Crime). In addition: maps embellished with legends containing dramatic and sensational accounts[10], verbal impression, moralistic vocabulary (which, in our case, is the result of ethnic clichés becoming conventional wisdom) (see Cameron, 1996). All this goes under 'scandalous' titles in order to give the everyday crime news process a touch of a police drama. It also focuses on some empirical manifestations of 'organised crime' such as: fraud, contract killings, loan sharking, migrant smuggling, trafficking of women for sexual exploitation, the gun trade, the human organs trade, the exploitation of children, CD/DVD piracy, money laundering as well as green 'organised crime', which are not included in what the newspapers would call as 'traditional' criminality even though many of these activities did exist before the early 1990s.[11] The re-'discovery' of these supposedly 'new' organised criminal activities becomes "*sufficient to give [them] prominence*" (Jewkes, 2011: 46).

In those articles dealing with *entrepreneurial* manifestations of 'organised crime' identified with migrants, newspaper articles use what van Duyne (2004: 29) calls the 'golden key' of making an 'organised crime' story plausible: the *big* money obtained by 'organised criminals' and specifically money that is evaded by the authorities and often diverted out of the country. Given that journalists, just as the majority of people, have little, inadequate, or no knowledge of the finances of 'organised crime', itself an issue considered newsworthy, they reproduce such 'money' figures. These are made available by national or international organisations or business federations on the issue supposedly giving a touch of certainty and authority into what is a highly uncertain business (see, for instance, Kanellopoulos, 2000; Tsarouchas, 2002b).

In addition, and apart from making direct and indirect references to 'organised crime' and using 'organised crime' signifiers, newspapers choose to introduce an 'organised crime' element to cases in which such elements do not exist. This is the case with a number of high profile incidents in the late 1990s, which led to a further consolidation of the '*organised* criminal other'. These incidents were viewed

---

10 E.g. "The Ionian Sea is Surrendered to the Italian Mafia".

11 "*Terror Over the City*", "*HELP! Save Us from the Albanians*", "*Greece, a country-hostage of the Albanian criminals*", "*The maps and statistics of criminality*", "*Crime in Greece Speaks Albanian*", "*The business of organised crime*", "*The routes of mafia: the geography of organised crime in Eastern Europe and the Balkans*", "*Illegal Sex is the Heavy Industry of Greece now – 45 million drachmas is the Profit for Every Alien Prostitute*", "*733.000 Pirated CDs*", "*Albanians Stole 30 Tonnes of Wood from the Forrest*".

through the prism of 'organised crime', even though evidence of a link between the individuals 'starring' in the incidents and 'organised crime' was absent. For example, the case of Flamur Pisli, a young Albanian, who being armed with an AK-47 and two hand grenades, held the passengers and the driver of a bus as hostages in May 1999. One of Pisli's requests, namely to be given passage to Albania, was granted. The Greek media were talking about "*a reception that the Albanian mafia was organising for Pisli*" and about "*some members of the Albanian mafia cheering for the hostage-taker's success*" (see Hatsios and Kantouris, 1999). However, Pisli was a socially isolated offender and no 'Albanian mafia' link was ever established.

In some other cases, the newspapers play up as 'organised crime' or as 'networks' activities that are committed by *two* individuals. As Levi (2008) suggests, associating a criminal activity or 'conventional' criminals with 'organised crime' is a very functional way of enhancing the seriousness of crime, whereas Scheinost (2011) notes that such an association inevitably leads to an increased scope of 'organised' activities.

Finally, the victims of 'organised crime' committed by migrants are used as a medium of representation for migrant 'organised criminality'. Specifically, the newspapers focus on some aspects of 'organised criminality', which arguably influence the perception the readers have of the migrant offenders. Since, as Heath (1984: 275) argues, "*the readers do not appreciate criminals who choose their victims randomly*", the Greek Press highlights some conditions in which the organised criminal activity (carried out by the "Other") took place (see Bowling and Phillips, 2002) as well as some personal characteristics of the 'actors'. According to Chermak (1995) and Jewkes (2011), crime victims supply an emotional –often sensational – element to the crime story. In particular certain characteristics they possess such as age, sex, and vulnerability (on which the newspapers and the media in general focus), not only automatically 'grab' the readers' attention, but also constitute the basis of the evaluation of the foreign 'organised criminal'. From a Durkheimian point of view this evaluation may help the 'evaluators' sustain in-group standards and norms as well as energise and reinforce their (and, of course, their readers') moral codes and identity. By mentioning the '*dramatis personae*', as Barthes (1962 cited by D'Elia, 1999: 160) would suggest, "*an emotional essence is being created, which intends to reinforce the stereotype*" of migrant 'organised criminality'. Thus, in the newspapers, the organised criminal 'Others' not only exploit people but these people are handicapped, for example deaf, as was the case of the Ukrainian leader called the 'Clown' and his sub-leader, the 'Doll' (Nesfyge, 2005). Not only do they produce pornographic material, but in this they are accused of exposing children as well.[12]

---

12 "*Thessaloniki becomes the centre of crime: dangers from the mafia, the drug trade, and child pornography on the internet*".

Not only do they force minors to regularly engage in begging but they also force children to drink shampoo so that they look sick and receive the pity and sympathy of the passer-by as was the case with Hamit, a 14-year-old Albanian Roma exploited by his 'patron' (Karatziou, 2002). The presence of children, in particular, in an 'organised crime' story also ensures that the media contribute as active partners to what Jenkins (1992) calls 'morality campaigns'.

Generally, the Greek Press focuses on what Innes (2004), following Eco's (1976) work on semiotics, calls 'signal crimes'. As Innes (2004: 15) argues, "*[t]he manufacture of a signal crime via mass mediated communication involves a crime incident being constructed by journalists through their use of particular representational and rhetorical techniques and interpreted by audiences as an index of the state of society and social order*". As is shown in other research studies (see Saint-Jacques *et al.*, 2011), the emphasis on a vulnerable victim and the publication of stories on these 'signal crimes' contribute significantly to adoption of relevant laws and a 'demand' for more efficient control mechanisms.

'The usual suspects': the migrants as 'organised criminals'

Generally, as elsewhere, in order for the Greek Press to consolidate news as credible, it has to be built upon commonsense understandings within society (Konstantinidou, 1999). As Bignell (1997: 92) argues, given that the press pursues, 'easy', 'quick' and most importantly 'continuous' communication with its readership, it uses the most approachable 'self-evident' logical consequences through an entirety of meanings and myths, and a series of arguments, with stereotypes playing an important role in these narratives (see also Vryzas, 1986). The method of *simplification*, as Jewkes (2011) defines this provision of reduced themes and 'easy' or 'simple' messages, serves two functions. Initially, the attention of the reader is not strained, and secondly, because of the restriction to the range of possible meanings, the readers' critical reading capacity is suspended or bended, and a 'consensus' about the news is more easily reached (Jewkes, 2011). In this process of 'making news' regarding criminal acts the stories are based on some features or stereotypes, not necessarily germane to the story *per se* which, simultaneously, fail to communicate the complexity of the 'organised crime' phenomenon in the country or even single manifestations of the phenomenon or related incidents.[13]

The 'race' or ethnic origin of a person may be irrelevant to the reporting of a criminal act committed, according to a journalistic convention (Howitt, 1998). Mentioning this constitutes a breach of the code of ethics of journalists with the Greek National Council of Radio-Television which specifies that any mention to the ethnicity of offenders and suspects should be avoided (see Panoussis, 2011b). Nevertheless, the newspapers in Greece systematically represent the migrants negatively through the use of the nationality of 'organised criminals'. Thus, what is present in many articles is not only a tautological or redundant form where the nationality of the migrant offender(s) or suspect(s) is highlighted[14], but also a strategy of substitution where the nationality may be veiled or omitted from the title or the body of the article. In the latter case, it can be presented in the form of an adjective or a noun, which refers to the stereotypical characteristics and perceived cultural qualities of the particular (migrant) group (Guillaumin, 1972 cited by Konstantinidou, 1999: 113). This process makes the point about the organised criminal 'Other' even when the nationality at stake in a particular representation has nothing to do with the term.[15] The result is the same in both representations since the nationality or its substitute is used as 'keywords' that include and mean everything else.

By using these semantic schemes two clearly different and *juxtaposed* groups exist (see Konstantinidou, 1999; Markovska, 2004 for Estonia; Lundgren *et al.*, 2009 for Norway): on the one hand there are the migrants, 'Them', the Albanians, the Russians, the Romanians, the 'thugs', the 'Mafiosi', the 'merciless', the 'armed', and 'dangerous', and on the other hand, there are the Greeks, the 'quiet', the 'law-abiding', the 'insecure', and – very importantly – the 'victims'. It appears that differentiating between groups of people, and in particular between 'Us' and 'Them' is a common characteristic of human societies (Tajfel, 1969), and as Fiske (1989) suggests, these forms of social differentiation function to define an individual's identity and confirm their sense of belonging or exclusion.

The 'Others' are depicted as the root of evil, the (external) 'enemies within' and as 'organised crime' itself in Greek newspapers. The terms appearing in the newspaper article title or body not only make groups, and in our case migrants, 'com-

---

13 In relation to drug trafficking, the veteran Colombian journalist, Sierra (2010: 38), argues that the public learns only "the tip of the iceberg of a phenomenon whose complexity barely becomes mere brushstrokes in the vast mural of information".

14 "*The Albanians Come First in Criminality*", "*Manhunt for the Romanian Thugs*", "*The Murder of the 29 year old was a vendetta among the Albanians*".

15 "*The Mafia of the Greek Riviera*", "*Fierce Crime Committed by the Cosa Nostra*", "*The Mafiosi Killed the Farmer*".

prehensible', but they also do it, according to Fowler (1991), creatively. Influenced by a philosophy and mentality of a Lombrosian flavour, when it comes to the representation of 'organised crime', and in particular this of the 'Other', the journalistic ideology, which has to choose between competing theories of criminal behaviour, attributes violence that comes to 'organised crime' (itself an element fulfilling the objective of a drama), and crime in general, primarily to *individual pathology* (Chibnall, 1977). Individual pathology and propensity to criminal behaviour are being presented by the Greek Press as essential characteristics of the 'Other', and as characteristics generally absent from the esoteric Greek 'virtue-system'. Thus, even when 'organised crime' *appears to be a Greek case*, as with the rivalry among groups of extortionists (also involved in other 'organised crime' activities) euphemistically called the 'Godfathers of the Night', *Russian* hitmen were called to do the 'job' (Ta Nea, 2007).

Simultaneously, however, the public is never informed of the realities behind the stories (see Howard, 2001). In contrast to crime stories in which the offenders' actions are presented as the product of individual pathology as well in case in which individual pathology is not part of the picture, *migrant* 'organised criminals' are never interviewed in order for more and detailed information about the 'motives' and offence technicalities to be provided. This *individualisation* (Jewkes, 2011) and human interest in 'organised crime' has another side effect: it becomes the vehicle for legal *organisations* that commit what could be described as 'organised criminal activities', such as multi-national corporations, banks, law enforcement agencies and governments, to escape negative attention or the labelling of their activities as 'organised crime' (see, for example, the 'light heating oils' case in the Czech Republic; Scheinost, 2011).

The Press is part of the social order of a particular context, and exists in a situation in which it perpetuates the cultural 'traditions' and/or cultural assumptions of this context (Hall *et al.*, 1978). In fact it is this function of perpetuating the cultural traditions that helps the Press to exist. In essence, the relationship between the cultural tradition and the Press is a vicious cycle involving a kind of mutual amplification. As the British 'cultural legacy', according to Hartman and Husband (1973), contains deprecating elements for a foreigner, the Greek tradition also contains elements derogatory to foreigners and in particular migrants who do not belong to the so called 'respectable' foreigners.

'The unusual victims' - the migrants as victims of 'organised crime'

The representation of migrants as *victims* of 'organised crime' in the Greek Press is a further important and interesting dimension to the general theme of migrants and 'organised crime' exactly because – as it will be shown – it reinforces stereotypes of the migrant as offender in 'organised crime' via its *unpredictability* (see Jewkes, 2011; Konstantinidou, 2003). What can be seen particularly after 2000 is that the same newspapers with a different 'linguistic register and tone of voice' (Bignell, 1997: 91) this time attempt to make a distinction between 'law-abiding' and 'non law-abiding' migrants. This distinction, however, transcends the index of inclusion/exclusion of migrants on the basis of the national identity that exists in the Greek context (see Pavlou, 2001) and which occasionally results in a positive or negative treatment of specific ethnic groups. A second dichotomy is being created with the same actors but this time with different 'roles' and attached qualities. It is the Greeks who are being presented as the 'Mafiosi' who in cooperation with other – *foreign*, according to the Press – 'criminal networks' make a living out of the misery and destitution of migrants.[16] A similar case has been the representation of the cockle-picker disaster in 2004 in which eighteen cockle pickers have died after becoming trapped by rising tides in Lancashire's Morecambe Bay in North West of England, thought to be forced to pick cockles by 'organised criminal groups'. According to Levi (2005), this was one of the cases that assisted in the 'good' migrants being included in the representational picture of migrants.

When the migrant victims of 'organised crime' are removed from the background (or even obscurity) to the forefront of the representation of 'organised crime', their victimisation and suffering is the very *raison d'être* of the story (Reiner *et al.*, 2001). Human trafficking of women (and children) for the sexual exploitation offers a set of good examples for this account (see also Spencer, 2008 for UK). Women primarily from the former Eastern bloc are always represented – by journalists, 'embedded' academics (van Duyne, 2011), state agencies and

16 "*Exploited Women*", "*Prostitution: Totally Black Pink*", "*Lucrative Trade in Migrants*", "*Gold-bringing Huts*", "[The Authorities] *See Illegal Network of Legalisation of Migrants*", "*Four hundred and forty four Kurdish were hanged like grapes from the wooden bulwark of the slave-ship*", "*Dead at the snow the illegal immigrants from Pakistan and Georgia, who attempted to cross borders at mount Beles*", "*Six Migrants Die Off the Island of Lesvos*", "*Human Sacrifice at the Mine-fields*", "*The fight for the hospitalization of the foreigners: The tricks of the illegal networks*", "*The Female Migrants Have a Double Pain*", "*'Cruises' for Undocumented Migrants in the Aegean Sea*", "*Human Trafficking Network is Dismantled*", "*How Far is Calabria?*", "*Sensitisation for the Victims of Trafficking*", "*Shock from a Case of Slavery in Ilia*".

representatives of the 'rescue industry'— as 'innocent', 'scared' *victims* who are "*caught in the net of traffickers*", brought into Greece under false pretences, and are always *manipulated* and *forced* into prostitution by them (see Nikolakopoulos, 1996). In his article appearing in *Eleftherotypia,* Lazos (2003: 41), a university professor, recognises trafficked women as the third type of women in 'constant maltreatment', and describes them as "*women who are not even disposable, they are useless. They are the women that only in the hand of the trafficker obtain the value that he gives them*".

Two plausible explanations can be offered in relation to the trend of focusing on the migrant victims of 'organised crime'. First it may constitute an exercise in what Tuchman (1972) calls the 'strategic rituals' of balance and objectivity by reporting both sides of the story (migrants as 'offenders' and 'victims' in 'organised crime'). A similar case is presented on a different phenomenon and a unique context which involves the conflict between two ethnic groups, and the reporting of Palestinian casualties in the Israeli press (Korn, 2004). A second explanation for this tendency can perhaps be traced not to any significant change on the quality of perception of migrants (and their identification with 'organised crime'), but to the newsworthiness of the 'new victim' of 'organised crime'. After almost a decade of being represented as offenders, as 'organised criminals', now the migrants appear to have the capacity to attract more public attention as 'unusual'. 'Unusualness' is typically understood as a traditional value in journalism and a key criterion for the selection of news: the more unusual a crime, criminal or victim, the more newsworthy it is. But arguably, this selection mechanism also happens to be rather biased against ethnic or racial minorities (McBride, 2005: 31; see also Lambropoulou, 1999).

However, although the Greek Press presents this inverted stereotype, the outcome is not any different. By mentioning, again, the nationality of the exploited or victimised – by 'organised crime'– migrants, these contrast with the 'assumed' general migrant characteristics and 'virtues' that appear to be already consolidated in the Greek social consciousness. In essence the Press continue inadvertently to postulate that *e.g.* the migrants are generally prone to 'organised criminality', and the Greeks or the Greek society/economy as whole are generally the victims. As Konstantinidou (1999) puts it, from the moment the nationality of the foreigners appears at the title or in the body of the article, the 'meaning' is trapped into the contrast Greek-'Other' with all the complications this may have. In Howitt's (1998: 150) words, "*an asymmetry exists, which stems from routine features of the news*". As, for example, the majority of the journalists in the United States, who are white, immediately counterbalance any tendency to see white criminals as *typical* of white people, in the same way Greek journalists counterbalance any tendency to see 'organised criminality' as the typical feature of the majority of the Greeks; or labour, honesty, conformity to the law, and victimhood as typical migrant features. No matter the focus of the negative stereotype, the newspapers in Greece provide, as Quinney (1970) would suggest, a distinctive social reality about 'organised crime' (see also Sherizen, 1978), in which the migrants are identified mainly as 'organised crime'-*doers*.

Conclusion – uncovering the coverage of migrants and 'organised crime'

The press in Greece, as in any other country, plays a major role in the construction of social reality. Contrary to Giulianotti's (1997) claim that it is extremely difficult to have homogeneity in the messages, meanings and representations conveyed, given the plethora and wide diversity of media sources, our analysis indicates that the features of the reporting 'organised crime' involving migrants for the period 1991-2011 has remained consistent both temporally and in terms of the different newspapers concerned, regardless of political affiliation, readership background and other factors. We stress again here that all the newspapers we have sampled represent the higher end of the Greek press in terms of content and commentary quality. Such remarkable homogeneity and consistency can be explained only with reference to the integrationist role of the media as an ideological apparatus, an idea which can easily be found to underpin extant criminological discussions of media and crime (*e.g.* Cohen, 1972; Cohen and Young, 1981; Hall *et al.*, 1978). This role is inevitably connected with the drawing of boundaries between those who are entitled and do participate in the established social order and 'the Others' who embody change and the threat that is associated with change. In Greece during the 1990s the influx of migrants engendered a particularly fluid social environment, a wholesale perception of disorganisation and an acute sense of threat to which the authorities and the established institutions were unable to mount a robust response (see, *e.g.* Papanicolaou and Antonopoulos, 2010; Karydis, 1996).

It is not by coincidence that the Greek newspapers have adopted the philosophy and 'themes' of what we can call the orthodox school, when it comes to the definition of 'organised crime' and the 'organised criminal'. In the absence of adequate mechanisms for the investigation, analysis and management of a newly emerging social reality, we must recognise that notions of 'organised crime' as robust criminal structures can readily offer a cohesive *vision* of a social reality that lacks cohesion, a vision that articulates explicitly on the most prominent feature of 'otherness': the migrant populations. 'Organised criminality' was thus represented on one hand, as a foreign *structure*, an alien body, as it were, within Greek society, and on the other hand, as an attribute of certain ethnic groups or foreigners in general, and as an exotic, imported reality, which stripped of any contextuality and reference to structural processes, is profoundly inimical to the presumably ethically sound features of the Greek economy and society (see a similar account on Serbian 'organised crime by Nikolić-Ristanović, 2004). Needless to say, this representational framework leaves no space for competing accounts which are more appreciative of the complexity and even the beneficial economic and social aspects of migration; unsurprisingly, such competing accounts are duly neutralised or outright neglected (see, for example, Antonopoulos, 2009; Papanicolaou and Antonopoulos, 2010).

The framework we lay out above accounts well for both the temporal and thematic consistency of the newspaper articles we have discussed. Clearly, newspapers in Greece have constructed and reinforced a double dichotomy between 'organised crime' and established society (what Van Duyne, 2004, calls 'underworld' and 'upperworld') on one hand and Greek/migrants, 'Us'/'Others' on the other hand. Within this framework the migrants are taken to possess certain characteristics and 'virtues' totally different from those of the Greeks and thus, by virtue of their 'organisation' represent a total threat – recall Shelley's (1999) notion of 'organised' as the new 'authoritarianism'. If generally offenders are deviants, then migrant 'organised criminals' are triply deviant. Being foreigner and being 'organised criminals' adds to more layers of deviancy. However, when there is an inversion of the characteristics and virtues of the two groups (migrants and Greeks), the result is the same as the majority of the articles have presented the migrants negatively. In this way the reference to the 'organised criminals' foreign nationality invites, in our view, the readers to make the connection of this nationality with 'organised criminality'. The instances when the Greek Press attempts to make a distinction between 'law-abiding' and 'non law-abiding' migrants has not had any different outcome but to reinforce the stereotype the migrants generally possess, that of the 'organised criminal'.

Because, as Lichtenstein *et al.* (1978 cited by Williams and Dickinson, 1993: 34) note, 'fear sells', and because the readers have an enormous 'thirst' for news with representations of 'organised crime' (and crime in general) which is not analogous to this for other social issues (see Roberts and Stalans, 1998), the newspapers focus on the sensational aspects of 'organised criminality' and, very importantly, attribute elements of the nature of organised crime to activities that are clearly not 'organised' and involving socially isolated offenders. In this way they create a 'moral panic' of 'organised crime' which is added to the social anxiety of conventional migrant criminality. However, it should be mentioned that the issue of a supposed link between media coverage and 'moral panic' and fear of crime is quite complicated and not always direct (see Chadee and Ditton, 2005). Through the use of quantitative and qualitative elements of reporting crime the Greek Press creates a climate of insecurity heavily linked with the presence of the 'Other' in the country.

The Greek press, the 'twin factor' of social segregation (Young, 1971: 4), identified migrants with 'organised crime' and illegality in general, described the migrant 'organised criminal' stereotype and 'analysed' it. At the same time it was unable to consolidate the representation of migrant as 'organised crime' victim. While doing it created a 'moral panic', and consequently amplified and consolidated the aforementioned stereotype that is difficult to erode. People, who do not know the exact amount of crime committed in their locality (see Sever, 2003; Lane and Meeker, 2003) or have a pragmatic perception of 'organised crime', are fed with this information, and these meanings and stereotypes that are provided by the Greek Press. Thus, it is plausible to argue that the media will have at least some impact on the public's understanding of the particular issue. Identifying this impact should be the next step in research endeavours of Greek criminologists.

References

Alisanoglou, P. and L. Nesfyge, 'Me US$ 65.000 oi Rossoi Mafiosi Ginontai Ellines', *Ta Nea,* 1999, August 27

Antonopoulos, G.A., Public reporting of criminal activities to the police in Greece: Is there a difference when the offender is migrant? *European Journal of Crime, Criminal Law and Criminal Justice,* 2006, 14(2), 135-160

Antonopoulos, G.A., Are the 'Others' coming?': Evidence on 'alien conspiracy' from three illegal markets in Greece. *Crime, Law and Social Change,* 2009, 52(5), 475-493

Antonopoulos, G.A., J. Tierney and C. Webster, Police perception of migration and migrants in Greece. *European Journal of Crime, Criminal Law and Criminal Justice,* 2008, 16(4), 353-378

Barak, G., Mass media and the social construction of crime. Presentation at the annual meeting of the ASC, San Francisco, United States, November, 2010

Barthes, R., The photographic message. In S. Heath (ed.) *Image, text, music-Roland Barthes.* (pp.15-31) London, Fontana, 1977

Bignell, J., *Media semiotics.* Manchester, Manchester University Press, 1977

Bowling, B. and C. Phillips, *Racism, crime and justice.* Harlow, Longman, 2002

Cameron, D., Style policy and style politics: A neglected aspect of the language of news. *Media, Culture and Society*, 1996, 18, 315-333

Chadee, D. and J. Ditton, Fear of crime and the media: Assessing the lack of relationship. *Crime, Media Culture,* 2005, 1(3), 322-332

Chatzidis, K., Ta Plokamia tis kai stin Ellada Aplose i Italiki Mafia', *Ta Nea,* 2000, July 20, p.N14

Chermak, S.M., *Victims in the news: Crime and the American news media.* Oxford, Westview Press, 1995

Chibnall, S., The crime reporter: A study. *Sociology*, 1975, 9(1), 49-66

Chibnall, S., *Law and order news: An analysis of crime reporting in the British press.* London, Tavistock, 1977

Chiricos, T., S. Eschholz and M. Gertz, Crime, news and fear of crime: Towards an identification of audience effect. *Social Problems*, 1997, 44, 342-357

Cohen, S., *Folk devils and moral panics.* London, MacGibbon and Kee, 1972

Conboy, M., *Tabloid Britain: Constructing a community through language.* Abingdon, Routledge, 2006

D'Elia, A., I Parekklisi tou Ksenou Metanasti sta Mesa Enimerosis: Apotalesmata Erevnas sto Salento'. In A. Koukoutsaki (ed.), *Eikones Eglimatos.* (pp.143-181) Athens, Plethron, 1999

Duyne P.C. van, The phantom and threat of organised crime. *Crime, Law and Social Change,* 1996, 24(4), 341–377

Duyne, P.C. van, The creation of a threat image: media, policy making and organised crime. In P.C. van Duyne, M. Jager, K. von Lampe and J.L. Newell (eds.), *Threats and phantoms of organised crime, corruption and terrorism: critical European perspectives.* (pp.21-50) Nijmegen, Wolf Legal Publishers, 2004

Duyne, P.C. van, *(Transnational) organised crime, laundering and the congregation of the gullible.* Tilburg, Tilburg University, 2011

Eco, U., *A theory of semiotics.* Bloomington, In., Indianapolis University Press, 1976

Eco, U., Overinterpreting texts. In S. Collini (ed.), *Interpretation and overinterpretation.* (pp.45-66) Cambridge, Cambridge University Press, 1992

Ericson, R.V., P.M. Baranek and J.B.L. Chan, *Representing order: Crime, law, and justice in the news media.* Milton Keynes, Open University Press, 1991

ESYE, *Census 2001.* 2001. Available online: http://www.statistics.gr

European Journalism Centre, Medial landscape: Greece', *European Journalism Centre.* 2010 Available online at http://www.ejc.net/ media_ landscape/arti cle /greece/

Fishman, M., Police news: Constructing an image of crime', *Urban Life*, 1981, 9, 371-394

Fiske, J., *Understanding popular culture.* London, Routledge, 1989

Fowler, R., *Language in the news.* London, Routledge, 1991

Garofalo, J., Crime and the mass media: A selective review. *Journal of Research in Crime and Delinquency*, 1981, 18(2), 319-350

Giddens, A., *Modernity and self-identity.* Cambridge, Polity Press, 1991

Giulianotti, R., Drugs and the media in the era of post-modernity: An archaeological analysis. *Media, Culture and Society*, 1997, 19(3), 413-439

Hall, S., The determination of news photographs. In S. Cohen and J. Young (eds.), *The manufacture of news.* (pp.226-243) London, Constable and Robinson, 1981

Hall, S., C. Critcher, T. Jefferson, J., Clarke and B. Roberts, *Policing the crisis.* London, Macmillan, 1978

Harmon, D. and S.B. Boeringer, A content analysis of internet-accessible written pornographic depictions. In S. Nagy Hesse-Biber and P. Leavy (eds.), *Approaches to qualitative research: A reader on theory and practice.* (pp.402-407) New York, Oxford University Press, 2004

Hartman, P. and Husband, C., The mass media and racial conflict. In S. Cohen. and J. Young (eds.), *The manufacture of news: Deviance, social problems and the mass media.* (pp.270-283), London, Constable, 1973

Hatsios, G. and K. Kantouris, Perase stin Alvania o Kakopios me tous Omirous', *Ta Nea,* 1999, May 29, p.28

Heath, L., Impact of newspaper crime reports on fear of crime: Multi-methodological investigation. *Journal of Personality and Social Psychology*, 1984, 47(2), 263-276

Howard, K., Is it a crime to seek refuge? *Criminal Justice Studies*, 2001, 43(1), 18-20

Howitt, D., *Crime, the media, and the law.* London, Wiley, 1998

Innes, M., Crime as a signal, crime as memory. *Journal of Crime, Conflict and the Media*, 2004, 1(2), 15-22

Jenkins, P., *Intimate enemies: moral panics in contemporary Great Britain.* Hawthorne, NY, Aldine de Gruyter, 1992

Jermyn, D., Photo-stories and family albums: Imaging criminals and victims on Crimewatch UK'. In P. Mason (ed.) *Criminal visions* (pp.175-191). Cullompton, Willan, 2003

Jewkes, Y., *Media and crime.* 2nd edition. London, Sage, 2011

Kalliagopoulos, F. and N. Tsioutsias, Paradeisos gia to Paraemporio i Ellada. *Oikonomiki Kathimerini,* 2003, September 11, p.22

Kanellopoulos, L., Paidia tou Dromou', *Ta Nea,* 2000, December 11, p.N21

Karatziou, N., Oi Oliver Twist tis Alvanias', *Eleftherotypia,* 2002, December 15

Karydis, V., *I Eglimatikotita ton Metanaston stin Ellada: Zitimata Theorias kai Anteglimatikis Politikis.* Athens, Papazisis, 1996

Konstantinidis, S., I Hameni Machi tou Antagonismou. *Kathimerini,* 2005, October 23

Konstantinidou, C., I Eglimatikotita ton Alvanon Metanaston ston Athinaiko Typo. In A. Koukoutsaki (ed.), *Eikones Eglimatos.* (pp.103-141) Athens, Plethron, 1999

Konstantinidou, C., Ta Mesa Mazikis Epikoinonias kai i Paragogi Noimatos. Part B', *Epitheorisi Koinonikon Erevnon,* 2003, 111/112, 53-125

Kolonas, C., O Mavros Tziros ton € 5 Dis ton Chrono Apeilei tin Oikonomia. *Ethnos,* 2008, August 25, pp.34-35

Korn, A., Reporting Palestinian casualties in the Israeli press: The case of Haaretz and the Intifada. *Journalism Studies,* 2004, 5(*2*), 247-262

Kourakis, N., Report on the development of criminality in contemporary Greece. *Poiniki Dikaiosyni*, 1998, 1(*3*), 239–248.

Krippendorff, K., *Content analysis.* Newburn Park, Ca., Sage, 1980

Labuschagne, L., Qualitative research: Airy fairy or fFundamental?' *The Qualitatıve Reporter,* 2003, 8(*1*), 100-103

Lambropoulos, V., Eisagomenos Polemos tou Ypokosmou. *To Vima,* 2010, June 24

Lambropoulou, E., *I Kataskevi tis Koinonikis Pragmatikotitas kai ta Mesa Mazikis Epikoinonias.* Athens, Ellinika Grammata, 1999

von Lampe, K., Not a process of enlightenment: the conceptual history of organised crime in Germany and the United States of America. *Forum on Crime and Society*, 2001, 1(2), 99-116

von Lampe, K., Making the second step before the first: assessing organised crime – the case of Germany. *Crime, Law and Social Change,* 2004, 42, 227-259

von Lampe, K., Organised crime research in Europe: development and stagnation. In: P.C. van Duyne, J. Harvey, A. Maljevic, M. Scheinost and K. von Lampe (eds.) *European crime-markets at cross-roads: Extended and extending criminal Europe.* (pp.17-41) Nijmegen, Wolf Legal Publishers, 2008

Lane, J. and J.W. Meeker. Ethnicity, information sources and fear of crime. *Deviant Behaviour,* 2003, 24(1), 1-26

Lazos, G., Gynaikes se Monimi Kakopoiisi. *Kyriakatiki Eleftherotypia,* 2003, August 31, p.41

Levi, M., The organisation of serious crimes. In M. Maguire, R. Reiner and R. Morgan (eds.), *The Oxford Handbook of Criminology.* 3rd edition (pp.878-913) Oxford, OUP, 2003

Levi, M., Organised business crime in the news. *Criminal Justice Matters,* 2005, 59(1), 20-21

Levi, M., The media construction of financial white-collar crimes. *British Journal of Criminology,* 2006, 46, 1037-1057

Levi, M., White-collar and organised crime in the media. Presented at the *Crime Narratives in Context Network* seminar series 2008/09. Cardiff, November, 2008

Liska, A.E. and W. Baccaglini, Feeling safe by comparison: crime in the newspapers. *Social Problems,* 1990, 37, 360-374

Lundgren Sørli, V. and K. Ingvaldsen. Organised crime in Norway: An imported phenomenon? In K. Ingvaldsen and V. Lundgren Sørli (eds.), *Organised crime: norms, markets, regulation and research. (pp.83-118) Oslo, Unipub,* 2009

Mandrou, I., I EYP ston Polemo kata tou Eglimatos. *Kathimerini,* 2009, July 19

Markovska, A., Representations of organised crime in Estonian printed media. In Nevala, S. and Aromaa, K. (eds) *Organised Crime, Trafficking, Drugs.* (pp.157-173) Helsinki, HEUNI, 2004

McBride, J., Covering crime. *Wisconsin Interest,* 2005, Winter, 31-37

MPO, *Etisia Ekthesi gia to Organomeno Eglima stin Ellada, Etous 1999.* Athens, MPO, 2000

Nesfyge, L., Oi Tsaroi tou Eglimatos me ta Ellinika Onomata. *Ta Nea,* 1998, July 4, 22-23

Nesfyge, L., Kykloma Kofon Ekmetallevotan Kofous. *Ta Nea,* 2005, August 3

Nikolakopoulos, D., Allodapes sta Dihtya ton Kyklomaton tis Somatemporias. *To Vima,* 1996, September 1

Nikolić-Ristanović, V., Organised crime in Serbia – media construction and social reaction'. In G. Meško, M. Pagon and B. Dobovšek (eds.), *Policing in Central and Eastern Europe.* (pp.1-10) Ljubljana, University of Maribor, 2004

Panousis, G., MME kai Eglimatikotita ton Metanaston - Ena Proto Panorama. *Ati,* 2011a, 2(9), 18-20

Panousis, G., Media, crime and criminal justice. In L. Cheliotis and S. Xenakis (eds.), *Crime and punishment in contemporary Greece.* (pp.65-75) Oxford, Peter Lang, 2011b

Papanicolaou, G., *Transnational policing and sex trafficking in southeast Europe: policing the imperialist chain.* Basingstoke, Palgrave Macmillan, 2011.

Papanicolaou, G. and G.A. Antonopoulos, Organised crime and migrants in the labour market: the economic significance of human smuggling and trafficking in Greece. In: P.C. van Duyne, G.A. Antonopoulos, T. Vander Beken, J. Harvey, A. Maljevic and K. von Lampe (eds.), *Cross-border crime inroads on integrity in Europe* (pp.277-308). Nijmegen, Wolf Legal Publishers, 2010

Pavlou, M., Oi Lathremporoi tou Fovou: Ratsistikos Logos kai Metanastes ston Typo Mias Ypopsifias Mitropolis. In A. Marvakis, D. Parsanoglou and M.

Pavlou (eds.), *Metanastes stin Ellada.* (pp.127-162) Athens, Ellinika Grammata, 2001

Quinney, R., *The social reality of crime.* Boston, Ma., Little Brown and Co., 1970

Rawlinson, P., Mafia, media and myth: representations of Russian organised crime. *Howard Journal of Criminal Justice,* 1998, 37(4), 346-358

Reiner, R., Media made criminality: The representation of crime in the mass media. In: M. Maguire, R., Morgan and R. Reiner (eds.) *The Oxford Handbook of Criminology.* 3rd edition (pp.376-416) New York, Oxford University Press, 2002

Reiner, R., Commentary. In: L. Cheliotis and S. Xenakis (eds.), *Crime and punishment in contemporary Greece.* (pp.77-85) Oxford, Peter Lang, 2011

Reiner, R., S. Livingstone and J. Allen, Casino-culture: Media and crime in a winner-loser society. In K. Stenson and R. Sullivan (eds.), *Crime, risk and justice: the politics of crime control in liberal democracies.* (pp.174-194) Cullompton, Willan, 2001

Reuter, P., *Disorganised crime.* Cambridge, Ma., MIT Press, 1983

Roberts, J. and L.J. Stalans, Crime, criminal justice, and public opinion. In: M. Tonry (ed.), *The handbook of crime and punishment.* (pp.31-57) New York, Oxford University Press, 1998

Ryan, G. and H.R. Bernard, Data management and analysis methods. In N.K. Denzin and Y.S. Lincoln (eds.), *Handbook of qualitative research.* 2nd edition (pp.769-802) Thousand Oaks, Ca., Sage Publications, 2000

Saint-Jacques, M-C., P. Villeneuve, D. Turcotte, S. Drapeu and H. Ivers, The role of media in reporting child abuse. *Journal of Social Service Research,* 2011, 1-13

Sever, B., The minority population/police strength relationship: exploring past research. *Criminal Justice Studies,* 2003, 16(2), 153-171

Scheinost, M., Organised crime, the media, and the sentiments of the public. In G.A. Antonopoulos, M.S. Groenhuijsen, J. Harvey, T. Kooijmans, A. Maljevic and K. von Lampe (eds.), *Usual and unusual organising criminals in Europe and beyond – Liber Amicorum Petrus van Duyne.* (pp.207-214) Apeldoorn/Antwerpen/Portland, Maklu, 2011

Shelley, L., Transnational organised crime: the new authoritarianism. in H.R. Freeman and P. Andreas (eds.), *The illicit global economy and state power.* Lanham, Maryland, Rowman and Littlefield Publishers, 1999

Sherizen, S., Social reaction of crime news: All the news fitted to print. In C. Winick (ed.), *Deviance and the mass media* (pp.203-224). Beverly Hills, CA., Sage, 1978

Sierra, A., Is there an independent journalistic narrative on drugs? In Open Society Foundations (eds.), *Coverage of drug trafficking and organised crime in Latin America and the Caribbean.* (pp.31-52), 2010. Accessed at: http://www.soros.org/initiatives/media/articles_publications/publications/austin-forum-20110515/austin-forum-20110515-en.pdf

Skintzas, G., O Thanatos tis Diskografias. *To Vima,* B2, 2008, January 20, 12-13

Sparks, C., The panic over taboid news. In C. Sparks and J. Tulloch (eds.), *Tabloid tales.* (pp.1-40) Lanham MD, Rowman and Littlefield, 2000

Spencer, J., Media constructing organised crime concepts in an extended criminal Europe. In P.C. van Duyne, J. Harvey, A. Maljevic, K. von Lampe and M. Scheinost (eds.), *European crime-markets at crossroads* (pp.43-61), Nijmegen, WLP, 2008

Stratoudaki, C., *Research on migrants in Greece: research fixations and pending issues.* Athens, National Centre for Social Research, 2008

Tajfel, H., Cognitive aspects of prejudice. *Journal of Social Issues*, 1969, 25(4), 79-97

Ta Nea, Rossoi Ektelestes ston Polemo ton Nonon', *Ta Nea,* 2007, October 23

Tesch, R., *Qualitative research.* New York, Falmer, 1990

To Vima, Circulation of newspapers from 20.6.2011 to 26.6.2011 nationally', To Vima, 2011, July 2. Accessed at http://www.tovima.gr/media/article/?aid=409179

Tsarouchas, K., I Ellada 'Paradeisos' ton Lathremporon. *To Vima,* 2002a, July 28, p.A31

Tsarouchas, K., '600.000.000 Euro o Tziros tis Porneias', *To Vima,* 2002b, March 10, p.A44

Tuchman, G., 'Objectivity as Strategic Ritual', *American Journal of Sociology,* 1972, 77(4), 660-679

Vryzas, K., O Entyposiasmos sta Mesa Mazikis Enimerosis. *Epitheorisi Koinonikon Erevnon,* 1986, 61, 107

Vryzas, K., *Pagosmia Epikoinonia kai Politistikes Tautotites.* Athens, Gutenberg, 1997

Wasserman, S. and K. Faust, *Social network analysis.* Cambridge, Cambridge University Press, 1994

Williams, P. and J. Dickinson, Fear of crime: read all about it? The relationship between newspaper crime reporting and fear of crime. *British Journal of Criminology*, 1993, 33(1), 33-56

Young, J., Deviancy amplification in industrial societies. In S. Cohen (ed.), *Images of deviance.* (pp.3-4) London, Pelican, 1971

Xenakis, S., International norm diffusion and organised crime policy: the case of Greece. *Global Crime*, 2004, 6, 345-373

Zarafonitou, C., *O Fovos tou Eglimatos.* Athens, Sakkoulas, 2002

European lessons from the Bulgarian Serious Organised Crime Threat Assessment

Atanas Rusev, Philip Gounev and Tihomir Bezlov[1]

Introduction

When organised crime threat assessment reports were introduced over a decade ago, they aspired to be an improved version of the traditional organised crime situation reports with the key difference of being 'forward oriented' rather than merely descriptive (Zoutendijk, 2010). Drawing on the premise that policing was or should be 'intelligence led', they borrowed the intelligence approach to analysing threats, and applied it to crime analysis.

The approach took on a special popularity in the European Union, where a number of countries (the UK, Belgium and the Netherlands) adopted such analysis as the basis for their counter-organised crime policies. In 2006 EUROPOL produced the first European Organised Crime Threat Assessments (now transformed into *Serious and Organised Crime Threat Assessment – SOCTA)* (EUROPOL, 2006), thus mechanically imposing the organised crime threat assessment (OCTA) analytical model to all 25 EU countries. The United Nations Office on Drugs and Crime (UNODC) took the OCTA inspiration even further, producing in 2009 the first Global Organised Crime Threat Assessment(UNODC, 2010).[2]

This chapter argues that the current methodologies and the basic premise of OCTA reports, in particular the ones put forward by international bodies (Europol / UNODC), result in a distorted picture of the threat from organised crime (OC). In most countries the OCTA approach is subverted by the lack of intelligence led-policing, by the poor quality and manipulated information which OCTA analysts use, and by the unwillingness of governments to prioritise organised crime policies based on objective analysis rather than political considerations. In countries where

1 The authors are researchers at the *Centre for the Study of Democracy* in Sofia.

2 The United States has also produces some threat assessments, such as the Gang Threat Assessment. In 2010 the Obama administration produced an Organised Crime Threat Assessment, which although not public, an FBI official described as 'standard threat assessment' (Interview by Philip Gounev with an official responsible for US OCTA, Washington, Nov. 16, 2011).

political will is missing, OCTA reports are likely to provide only a semblance of an intended threat assessment. For all other countries, though, this chapter suggests some overall methodological approaches that aim to bridge the intelligence gaps and assess the intelligence needs.

The Europol approach has been criticised on many levels, including the adopted operational definitions of 'threat', and the overall methodology that has been applied. Specific criticisms were addressed to the main data collection tool – *i.e.* the survey questionnaire employed by EUROPOL (Van Duyne, 2007), which resulted in subsequent efforts by the agency to adjust and improve the data collection methodology. This approach has a number of vulnerabilities such as contributions of differing quality, political filtering, and aggregating data from divergent national reporting systems.

This paper does not aim to assess and criticize the methodology of Europol, UNODC or any other national police service. It rather aims to show, from a Member State perspective, why such reports tell little about the size of the threat and which threats should be prioritised. For the purposes of the proposed methodology it is not necessary we do not need to engage in the debate about defining the term 'threat' and its appropriateness.

The proposed methodology that is provided below goes further than previous efforts to assess organised crime threats. Instead of simply providing data on the size of the illicit markets, we attempt to provide an *estimate of the number and types of actors that populate these illicit markets*. The main usefulness of this approach is that it (1) shows the size of the existing intelligence gaps and (2) provides baseline information from which to develop priorities.

This paper draws on a two year project, funded by the European Commission and led by the Center for the Study of Democracy (CSD) which aimed to develop a methodology and produce the first national OCTA report for Bulgaria[3]. During the two year project, about 200 in-depth interviews were conducted with a variety of officers from various law enforcement agencies (General Directorate for Combating Organised Crime, Criminal Police, Economic Police, Ministry of Interior, National Customs Agency, National Revenue Agency, State Agency for National Security), private sector representatives (tobacco producers, oil, alcohol companies, banks, insurance companies); and offenders (street drug dealers, prostitutes and pimps). Most insightful was the secondment of one of the authors, who spent several months alongside the analytical unit at GDCOC in developing the report.

---

3 The project was implemented with the Bulgarian Ministry of Interior and was supported by UK's Serious and Organised Crime Agency and Europol. More information about the project and its outputs are available at www.csd.bg/bocta.

The current chapter starts with an analysis of the reasons why the OCTA approach is difficult to implement in many countries. We then suggest a different methodological approach and two examples of how it could be implemented. The two examples we provide focus on the illicit tobacco and the illicit drugs markets. The suggested approach, which uses the 'market actor' as an analytical unit can be applied and used to overcome the deficiencies and thus produces far more realistic and meaningful results for the purposes of resource and policy prioritisation.

The politics of counter-organised crime policies

The concept of OCTA was first introduced in Bulgaria in the light of the accession to the European Union in 2007 as the country had to contribute to Europol's OCTA reports. Up until this point, the Bulgarian law-enforcement agencies did not produce any type of threat assessment. What existed instead were annual reports that the Ministry of Interior, the Customs Administration, the State Agency for National Security, and the National Revenue Administrations produced independently from each other. These were mostly focused on reporting on the investigative activities conducted during the preceding year, but also contained elements of situational reports. These separate situational reports are produced on an ad-hoc basis coveing specific criminal activities.

The task of collecting and putting together Europol's OCTA data was assigned to the General Directorate Countering Organised Crime (GDCOC), a specialised police force, which covers most, but not all areas covered by the Europol report. For instance, motor vehicle crimes, organised begging, pick-pocketing, immigration related crimes, prostitution, some types of customs frauds (*e.g.* smuggling of oil products), lay outside its remit. Furthermore, GDCOC has overlapping responsibilities with the Criminal Police, which investigates almost all OC and economic crime cases covered by GDCOC (with the exception of cultural goods crimes, trafficking in human beings, and extortion racketeering). The Border Police leads the investigations on migrant smuggling networks, while the National Customs Agency has its own small investigation unit focusing on customs frauds (including smuggling of excisable goods). The National Revenue Agency gathers information on tax frauds. Moreover, the national counter-intelligence agency, the *State Agency for National Security* is also tasked with collecting intelligence, amongst other things, on some forms of organised and economic crime, including corruption.

Therefore, in theory, the GDCOC should mainly be responsible for collating information from all other law-enforcement agencies, and supplementing this information with its own data. In practice, that has never taken place, as none of the other agencies have supplied GDCOC with any information to feed into Europol's SOCTA, or to enable the production a national SOCTA report. The reasons for this are certainly complex. The key to understanding is that an organised crime threat assessment is neither needed nor necessary at the strategic level. On the one hand, because there is no particular counter-organised crime policy model within which to fit in, and on the other hand, because decisions at the strategic level are primarily politically motivated. How did this develop?

After the dissolution of State Security apparatus[4] and its joint intelligence database *ISKRA* ('sparkle') in the early 1990s tens of thousands of investigators and intelligence officers were dismissed. What followed was a period of chaos in law-enforcement and the criminal justice system. The main characteristic of this chaos was the concentration of meaningful analytical information within a small circle of political appointees within the Ministry of Interior and Law Enforcement. The lack of any systematic approach to gathering, storing, evaluating the quality, and sharing of intelligence data (in Bulgaria usually referred to as 'operational information') pushed investigators towards considering information above all as their own personal asset. This asset allowed them to extort money from criminals or politicians, to ensure the stability of their posts, in short – to trade against influence. This more or less continues to be the case at present. Therefore, the absence of an intelligence system even within the police services under the Ministry of Interior, let alone within other intelligence or law-enforcement agencies, has sustained the utility of this 'privatised' intelligence data.

The reason why OCTA reports have no basis in Bulgaria is because Europol's (or other EU Member States') policy model '*analysis* → *counter-organised crime strategy / operational planning* → *identifying intelligence needs and tasks*' does not exist in Bulgaria. Policies are not based on analysis on data which are private assets. It would not be an exaggeration to claim that there are no policies regarding organised crime. Rather, law enforcement operations are haphazard, opportunistic, and largely politically motivated. As such they are rarely coordinated with other administrative measures (*e.g.* tax or customs authorities measures). Instead, counter-organised crime priorities (both investigation and intelligence gathering) are subject to a number of other principles:

- Political influence and priorities
  - international investigations (especially joint investigation team), which end up with a foreign official (head of Europol or the FBI) publicly praising Bulgarian police and political leadership for cooperation.

4 State Security is the KGB equivalent in Bulgaria as it combined political police with counter-intelligence functions.

  - o criminal structures related to political opponents (or without any political backing)
- 'Low-hanging fruit' – police units / prosecutors may go after criminal structures that are politically unproblematic
- Avoiding complex cases – police units try avoiding complex cases, either because they may turn up to be politically sensitive, or because they do not result in a quick solution of the case (which reduces their professional evaluation)
- Media / public pressure – both politicians and police units find it difficult to avoid investigating cases which become the focus of public attention.

As a result of the above priorities, attempts to draft situational reports or even OCTA reports based on 'operational information', *i.e.* collected in the course of ongoing investigations, will result in a highly distorted picture. Consequently this national contribution to Europol's SOCTA would be equally unreliable.

Political influence remains the most significant structural impediment to developing an OCTA or to delivering a meaningful contribution to Europol's SOCTA. In Bulgaria, the political influence over law enforcement services is much greater than in Western Europe. The level of police independence and politically independent investigations is minimal. In a country in which during the past 20 years the grey and illicit economies reached a proportion of 30-40% of the GDP, the police and the security services were acting as a shadow regulator of the economy. In this informal capacity the Ministry of Interior has become the embodiment of hidden power. For the ruling political elite the MoI and the police have become the key instrument ensuring that the economic elites act as their political supporters and financiers.

The heavy political influence brought to bear on the law enforcement agencies inevitably has an effect on the intelligence information flows within the system, as it imposes specific priorities at the operational level, which have little to do with objective analyses.

The above model of political meddling in police affairs explains the other major constraints for developing OCTA. One is the lack of a national intelligence model and an intelligence data base that connects police departments and the various police agencies (let alone interagency intelligence sharing). There are only rudimentary intelligence systems that some (but not all) police forces share. Another issue is the lack of analytical capacity. The analytical units lead a 'shadowy life' and are considered little more than 'statistical and information offices'. Almost all analysts have only police academy and police operations background with very little advanced analytical skills. The majority have no internet or email access in their daily work environment.

Alternatives to existing SOCTA methodologies

The case of Bulgaria is hardly unique, as most countries around the world have no reliable intelligence gathering systems. Even in countries where significant resources are spent on gathering, evaluating, and analysing intelligence, there are intelligence gaps. Estimating the size and nature of these intelligence gaps is a challenging task, and may be more art than science. The proposed method in this chapter aims at contributing towards the develop of a set of reliable methods to measure at least the 'known unknowns'. These proposed methods rely on intelligence data themselves, but employ macro data analysis to find out:

- The total number of players, or 'illicit entrepreneurs', in a market for illicit goods or services and
- Estimate the number of illicit entrepreneurs that populate the various wholesale levels or other players working on retail levels of a market.

While this may have limited use at the operational level, it is quite important on a strategic and management level, as it allows for a better allocation of resources for the monitoring of performance and to set goals.

The described situation indicates that an alternative approach to information gathering should be considered, if more realistic OC threat assessments are to be constructed. Existing data like the number of offences, number and quantity of seized illicit goods (*e.g.* drugs, tobacco) have limited added value, as these rather depict the law enforcement activities and efforts at countering these organised crime activities. On the other hand, a criminal markets approach could be used as a viable and cost-effective alternative. For example changes in the size of the drug market can provide information about the net effects and impact of the supply reduction policies and the day-to-day law enforcement activities (Kilmer & Pacula, 2009). The market size data combined with some additional data on market structure could also serve as a starting point in estimating the number of participants within a given criminal market. Therefore, it allows comparisons to be made with other criminal markets regarding their crime threat potential.

The value of this approach has already been recognised by UNODC, which produces estimates of the size of the global drug markets in their annual world drug reports, as well as recently by EMCDDA (EMCDDA, 2010). Yet law enforcement authorities rarely rely on such analysis for strategic planning, prioritising and allocation of resources, though it could be a more cost-effective way to shed a light on and overcome the gaps in the intelligence data gathered.

The first national serious and organised crime threat assessment in Bulgaria also relied extensively on this approach, proving its viability despite some minor weaknesses and drawbacks. Two examples are provided below of the application of the approach to the heroin market and the illicit tobacco market.

The heroin market in Bulgaria

Cross-border trafficking and trading in illicit drugs are among the essential income sources for organised crime in Bulgaria. Bulgaria is a transit country for drug trafficking and the role of Bulgarian organised crime groups is shaped by the geographic location of the country on the Balkan route for smuggling heroin from Afghanistan to Western Europe, as well as for smuggling synthetic drugs and their precursors from Europe towards the Middle East. The Bulgarian market for illicit drugs is relatively small compared to most drug markets in Western Europe. Nevertheless, it comprises many actors with substantial financial potential and influence. During the last 20 years there has been a well-established retail market for heroin, and growing markets for synthetic drugs, cannabis and cocaine.

The hierarchical structures and the strict territorial zoning have been characteristic of the drug markets in Bulgaria for the period 1998 – 2008. The heroin market was the first drug market that the big organised criminal structures, known in Bulgaria as 'groupirovki', captured in the mid-nineties. This process transformed the entire drug market in the country from a place populated by numerous small importers and retailers into a well-structured market which is divided amongst a few big players (CSD, 2007). The political pressure on law-enforcement to increase its effectiveness in dismantling these groups in the run-up and following Bulgaria's accession to the EU in 2007 fractured the drugs market again into a population of numerous small actors. In 2009 and 2010, especially, many of the middle and high level market players were arrested.

There are other factors which contributed to a change in the market structure as well. First, the steady fall of the heroin use in the past 10 years, which was additionally furthered by a major supply shortage in the streets during 2010 and 2011. Many users turned to available substitutes such as methadone. The heroin supply shortage also led to a reduction in purity and rise in the retail prices. The key difference from the 1990s market is that the prevalent consumption in 2011 changed from heroin to that of amphetamines and cannabis.

The proposed assessment methodology focuses on the estimation of two key indicators of the level threat from organised crime:

- estimating the number of market players at the different levels;
- estimating the overall criminal potential and harms caused by 'organised crime'.

We consider the first one in more detail, and outline a possible way in which the second one may be estimated.

Sources of information and overall approach

The proposed method of estimation uses indicators, most of which come sources other than law enforcement: prevalence of drug use, purity-adjusted price of drugs, or typical quantities consumed by drug-users. Other necessary data, such as knowledge about market structure and operation (*e.g.* average number of clients of a street drug dealer per day, average number of street dealers buying from a wholesaler, number of whole-sale levels) could also be collected either via interviews with drug users / drug dealers / social workers, or in the course of investigations / intelligence gathering. Some of the above data is systematically collected on an annual basis and regularly published by the EMCDDA and UNODC. For the purpose of the present analysis, we conducted 25 in-depth interviews with heroin users, heroin dealers and police officers in 2011 in Sofia. Data from some investigations was also used.

Estimating the number of market players

The basic formula used to estimate the number of market players relies on a bottom-up approach, where the starting point is the total number of *drug-users*. It then uses data on the number of customers that each drug dealer sells to, and the average number of dealers that buy from each consecutive wholesale level of the market. A similar approach was applied for estimating the number of amphetamine type stimulants (ATS) dealers in Canada (Bouchard, et al., 2012), though existing research for Canada and USA report lower user-to dealer ratios (MacCoun & Reuter, 2004; Tremblay, et al., 2009).

Number of heroin users

There is only one official estimate of the number of heroin users in Bulgaria, which was produced by the REITOX National Focal Point in 2005 using the Treatment Multiplier method (NFP, 2005). The estimation then was for 20.000-30.000 heroin users. In 2011 the National Focal Point published their estimate of the *problem* drug users, based on a Capture-Recapture (NFP, 2011) method that arrived at 31.316 users[5]. The REITOX National Focal Point indicates that 84,8% of all clients entering treatment in 2010 are heroin users(NFP, 2011). Taking into

5 This estimate is based on a statistical analysis. When a confidence interval of 95% is applied the broader range of the evaluation is between 23.050 and 42.920 users.

account the share of heroin users among all users entering treatment would provide for around 26.000 heroin users out of total average number of problem drug users. The two estimates produced by the National REITOX Focal Point are quite identical and imply that the prevalence of the heroin use in Bulgaria has not changed between 2005 and 2011.

At least three major factors have contributed to the overall decrease in the heroin use in the last ten years in Bulgaria. First of all the access to opiate substitution treatment has grown substantially, as the implementation of the *National Programme for Development of a System of Methadone Maintenance Programmes in Bulgaria 2006-2008* led to six-fold increase in the access to methadone treatment. In 2005 there were only five methadone programmes with a capacity for treatment of 770 patients while at the end of 2010 there are 30 programmes with a capacity for treatment of 5.230 patients.[6] At the same time, the treatment demand data suggests at in the past ten years there was a twofold decrease in the number of clients seeking first-time treatment in all other types of drug-treatment programmes. The share of users entering treatment for first time dropped from 43% in 2001 of all users to 20% in 2010 and the mean age of all users entering treatment increased from 22,2 years in 2000 to 29 years in 2010, which indicates a steadily aging population of problematic drug users. In addition to this, the proportion of clients with more than 5 years of drug use history entering treatment in 2010 is about 60%, which is triple the share in 2001 (National Focal Point on Drugs and Drug Addictions 2011:54). The fall in the number of users entering drug treatment programmes for a first time suggests that the 25.000 estimate from 2005, should be lowered to the range of 10.000-12.000 people.

Market organisation and number of participants

Knowledge about the structure and the *modus operandi* of the heroin distribution network provides additional details needed to estimate the number of participants within the heroin market. This information should be collected either with interviews with heroin users and dealers or retrieved from investigation and intelligence data. This kind of data provides a fairly good basis for making assumptions, especially when trying to estimate the number of participants in a local or regional heroin market. The number of distribution levels or the density of the retail distribution networks vary across cities, so estimations based on micro level would be expected to be more accurate as well as diverse.

The organisation of the heroin distribution network in Sofia resembles to a great extent the structure described by Preble and Casey in New York (Preble and

6 Official data provided by the Bulgarian Ministry of Health

Casey, 1969). It has been described in detail by Bezlov in 2007 (CSD, 2007) on the basis of qualitative data collected through in-depth interviews with heroin users, heroin dealers and police officers. There are five levels in the distribution network, starting from the consumers (heroin users) at the first level, street dealers at the second level, weight dealers ('gram dealers') at the third level, connection (base, lieutenant) at the forth and kilo connection (captain) at the fifth level. Up to 2008 the distribution networks used to be vertically integrated from top to bottom, which allowed for maximisation of profit and monopolisation of the distribution network in Sofia. The dismantling of these big vertically integrated criminal networks in 2009-2010 led to the emergence of 2-3 four-level distributors and many more three level groups, which took over the retail market. The wholesale level ('connections' and 'importers') ceased exerting control over retail distribution in order to minimise the risks of arrest.

Existing estimations of the National REITOX Focal Point show that the population of heroin users in Sofia is half of total the heroin user's population within Bulgaria (NFP, 2006), which would make 5.000-6.000 heroin users in Sofia, if we use 10.000-12.000 users as a baseline. Interviews with street dealers in 2011 in Sofia show that a street dealer sells heroin to between 20 and 100 users per day (5 - 35 grams street purity), depending in which part of the city he operates and how he sells: on the phone, or at a street corner (the so called 'posta'). Usually dealers in the central parts of the city working at a 'posta' have more clients. The street dealers never pay in cash for the heroin – it is provided by the weight dealer and they are supposed make payments depending on their daily revenues. Usually a weight dealer works with 2-4 street dealers. The weight dealers supply the heroin from the 'connection'. Within the three-level distribution networks 'gram' dealers operate independently and supply heroin from different 'connections', while within the four level criminal networks the criminal leader supplies the heroin for his 'gram' and they are only allowed to supply from him.

Table 1

Assessment of the number of participants of the heroin market

Task	How	Result
Estimate number of heroin users Estimate number of drug users served by one street dealer	Use of surveys (*e.g.* capture-recapture method) Interviews / intelligence data	6000 High: 100 Low: 20
Find out number of street dealers	Divide total number of users (6000) by the average number served by one dealer (20 or 100)	High: 300 Low: 60 Average: 100
Estimate number of street dealers buying from one wholesaler ('weight' dealer)	1. Interviews with street dealer / intelligence data 2. Average quantities sold by 1st level wholesalers	High: 4 Low: 2
Find out number of 'gram dealers' (low-level wholesalers)	Divide number of street dealers (300) by the average number of street dealers served by one wholesaler (10)	High: 100 Low: 20 Average: 33
Estimate number of wholesale levels and number of players in each level	Intelligence data / interviews	Not available

Estimates of the number of players in the upper levels may become difficult, as in 2010-2011 many of the heroin 'gram' dealers in Sofia started to operate independently. 'Gram' dealers supply heroin from a 'connection'. Within the *three-level* distribution networks 'gram' dealers operate independently and supply heroin from several different 'connections', while within the *four level* criminal networks the criminal leader supplies the heroin for his 'gram' and they are allowed only to supply from him. Only three out of eight districts in Sofia were supplied exclusively by four level distribution networks in 2010-2011, according to the information from the field interviews.

Taking this methodology a step further to estimate the total number of players in the drugs market is also challenging. Although surveys of drug-users may be used to estimate the total number of users of other drugs (cannabis, cocaine, or amphetamines), these are likely to underestimate the total number of users. Moreover within cannabis, amphetamines and cocaine markets there are regular users, which form a small consumer core next to a wide periphery of non-regular users, who buy drugs occasionally. In addition, many drug dealers or criminal networks may deal in more than one type of drug. Intelligence sources may provide information about the number of criminal networks or dealers that deal with more than one type of drug. This in turn, could be used to extrapolate about the total number of players. For instance, if one knows that 40% of all dealers and groups deal in heroin as well as in all other types of drugs, the data about number of heroin drug dealers could be used to estimate the total number of drug market players. There are certainly complexities about this approach, but triangulating such data with information about the numbers of drug users from surveys could provide insight into the entire drugs market.

Estimating the overall criminal potential

The overall potential size of the criminal market can be assessed based on the overall size of the market and the revenues earned at each level. The estimation of the size of the **national** heroin market, in terms of revenues, builds upon the methodology suggested by Kilmer and Paccula (2009) and is adapted according to the available data sources in Bulgaria. The estimation of the revenues at the different levels of the heroin distribution requires market information for each level, as well as some intelligence or field information on how these criminal networks function.

The first step in the assessment of the criminal potential of the heroin market follows the general formula: '*Size of market = Number of users * Pure grams consumed per 1 year * Purity adjusted price per gram*'. The sources and data available of the number of heroin users in Bulgaria have already been discussed in the previous section. The purity adjusted prices are not collected and systematically analysed in Bulgaria. Data on heroin prices is collected in the course of police investigations and reported regularly to EMCDDA and UNODC. Regional Drug Councils provide price data based on reports from workers in prevention and health programmes. Purity data is based on analysis of samples of drugs seized by the police and by the custom's authorities. Despite some deficiencies in data collection about price and purity certain 'best guess' estimates can be produced using purity adjusted prices, which allows for an idea of the minimum and maximum extend of the heroin market. The selected approach follows the one suggested by Kilmer and Pacula (2009) with slight modifications. Three different purity adjusted prices and respectively expenditure estimates are produced employing three different levels for heroin purity. The provided mean for heroin purity by EMCDDA (2009) is used as a midpoint and minimum and maximum values for purity are set within the range (-20%; +20%). For the purpose of the above estimates we use the minimum and maximum heroin prices provided by the police and the midpoint is calculated as a geometric mean[7] of the two values.

Data on daily or annual dosage of heroin consumed by users in Bulgaria has not been systematically collected. The UNODC in its estimations on the Southeast Europe heroin market assumes that the average quantity consumed is 30.6 grams pure heroin per user (UNODC, 2009), and Kilmer and Paculla (Kilmer & Pacula, 2009) – 30 grams pure heroin. Therefore, below we use the same estimate - 30 pure grams.

Following the suggested formula one can easily produce the size of the heroin market in Bulgaria (Table 2).

Table 2

Estimation of heroin market expenditures on retail level (2009 data).

		Min.	Mean	Max.
A	**Annual value of market in million of Euros** (A=B*11.500 users*30 grams pure heroin consumption per annum)	**20,01**	**23,1**	**45,4**
B	Purity adjusted price per gram (B= C/D)	€ 58	€ 67	€ 132
C	Retail price per raw gram	€ 30	€ 21	€ 15
D	Purity	51%	31%	11%

Source: Own estimates based on retail price per raw gram and purity taken from EMCDDA Statistical bulletin 2009.

In order to estimate the criminal potential at each level of the distribution chain one should not only account for the price of heroin at each level, but also for its level of purity. At each level of the heroin distribution chain the heroin is adulterated, as a means of maximising profit but also as a way to respond to irregular supply. In most cases distributors at each level cut the heroin with adulterants in a ratio of 1:1, although this is not a fixed rule. Taking into account the adulteration and the user-street dealer and the street-dealer to 'gram'-dealer ratio (Table 3), as well as the prices of heroin at each level, one can calculate revenues at the levels shown below *only for the city of Sofia* (Table 3).

7 To account for the highly skewed nature of drug price data Kilmer and Pacula (2009: 11) suggest the use of geometric mean instead of arithmetic mean when generating drugs price information from ranges. The *geometric mean* is different from the arithmetic mean, but the price difference in this example is small, as the arithmetic mean would have given a price of 22,5.

Table 1
Structure of heroin distribution network in Sofia

Distributor	Heroin Purity	Adulteration	Price per gram in euro	Grams sold per month (low)	Grams sold per month (high)	Revenues per month in euro
'Gram' dealer	15%-20%	1:1	30	150	2100	4.500-63.000
Street dealer	7%-10%	1:1	40	150	1050	6.000-42.000

The proposed methodology has the potential to yield far more accurate results, although in countries like Bulgaria it is constrained by the quality of the data collection system. For example, the established data collection system does not allow for precise estimates of the purity adjusted prices on street level, as price data sets does not have a direct relation to the purity data sets. Moreover the price data sets produced by the Ministry of Interior are not consistent with the datasets produced by the Regional Drug Councils. Available data sets very often do not provide basic statistics (mean, mode, median) or provide just the mean value, while minimum and maximum values vary (for example EMCDDA data for 2009 shows that heroin purity varies between 1,2 and 67%). This wide range suggests that statistics collected do not distinguish between purity at retail level and purity of heroin on wholesale level. Along with this there are no data available on a regional or city level, nor are there any data collected on a monthly basis. Establishing a better data collection system could provide a way to overcome these deficiencies. Possible solutions could be improvement of the collection of price and purity data based on seizures of drugs by the law enforcement agencies or undercover purchases made by police agents (Kilmer and Hoorens, 2009).[8]

The illicit tobacco market

In 2009 and 2010, the sale of contraband tobacco products (both legally produced and counterfeit) became one of the fastest growing organised criminal activities in Bulgaria. The majority of illegal cigarettes sold in Bulgaria are the so called 'illicit whites' – not counterfeit cigarettes. 'Illicit whites' are low quality, low-price, legally produced, little known brands of cigarettes typically smuggled from outside

8 Kilmer and Hoorens (2009) - Understanding illicit drug markets, supply-reduction efforts, and drug-related crime in the the European Union. RAND. p.38

the EU. In Bulgaria there are both: domestically produced and smuggled illicit whites. In either case, they are illegally distributed, avoiding VAT and excise taxes. After a steep increase of tobacco excise taxes in 2008, following Bulgaria's accession to the EU, the size of the illegal market tripled. In 2009 – 2010, the customer basis for illicit tobacco products grew and the number of retail dealers multiplied. Cross-border smuggling and domestic supply routes and distribution infrastructure became well established. The new excise taxes were structured in such a way that the prices of the lowest class cigarettes increased the most, fuelling demand for illicit cigarettes.

In 2009 Bulgaria had the second highest smoking prevalence in the EU – 39% of the population were active smokers (The Gallup Organisation, 2009). Moreover the excise levels in the EU have been introduced in relation to the average income in the 'old' Member States, which are about three times higher than the average income in Bulgaria, which in turn meant that the affordability of a packet of cigarettes in Bulgaria is about three times lower than in West European countries. Growth of the illegal cigarettes market was further facilitated by the economic crisis and unemployment growth. The growth of the illicit market for cigarettes is also based on the well-known premise from economics that the demand for cigarettes is highly elastic. The increases in prices do not immediately force consumers to stop purchasing the product. Rather, consumers adjust their behaviour gradually and may seek substitute products, which in the case of Bulgaria are the illicit cigarettes. Therefore the comparative analysis of the dynamics of the licit and illicit segments of the market is key to understanding the overall market dynamics.

Data sources and approach

Unlike the drugs market, there is abundance of quantitative data about the tobacco market, generated by both tobacco and marketing companies, as well as by the tax and health authorities. This makes it easier to produce much more accurate estimates of the size and structure of the illicit market. For the purpose of these estimates there are different indicators for tracking market trends and developments (consumer surveys, 'retail audit' surveys by marketing companies, surveys based on collecting empty cigarette packs from streets, official data on paid excise and VAT taxes). Unless triangulated, though, no single data sources would yield reliable results. In addition, interviews with cigarette dealers, including of illicit cigarettes and data from investigations provides additional information on the market structure and operations.

For the purpose of the present research close to 530 interviewees were carried out in 9 different locations and border crossings in Bulgaria with police (150) and customs investigators (50), border guards (30), illegal cigarettes dealers at various levels (100), tobacco companies and distributors (50), and consumers/small dealers of illegal cigarettes (150). Some of these multiple interviews were carried out over the course of the two years of the project.

While the methodology for the heroin market is based on a bottom-up approach that takes as a starting point the estimate for the 'number of heroin users', for the illicit tobacco market 'number of users' is not an appropriate analytical category. Even though, tobacco users, generally consume (on average) a constant amount of cigarettes on a daily basis, the number of illicit cigarettes consumed fluctuates. There is a significant proportion of consumers who buy illicit cigarettes on irregular basis. Therefore, the approach presented here is based on estimating the number of illicit 'cigarette sticks' sold. Using this category as a starting point the methodology uses interview and intelligence data to find the average sales and the number of retailers and wholesalers. The rest of this chapter goes over the process of presenting detailed estimates for the illicit tobacco market in Bulgaria.

Table 4.
Estimating the threat of illicit tobacco

Task	How
Find out the number of licit cigarettes sold for a baseline year when the illicit market is at its lowest	Use of retail audits and data on excise duty paid
Estimate the drop in licit sales	Use of retail audits and data on excise duty paid
Find out the growth in illicit sales and the number of illicit cigarette sticks sold	1. Find out the number of people who quite smoking (from consumer surveys) 2. Compare the drop of licit sales with the drop in the number of smokers. The difference between the two = illicit market 3. Use empty pack / consumer surveys to triangulate the growth in illicit sales
Estimate number of street dealers	1. Interviews with street dealer / intelligence data 2. Average quantities sold by 1st level wholesalers
Find out number of 1st level wholesaler	Divide the number of street dealer by average number of street dealers served by one wholesaler
Estimate number of wholesale levels and importers	Intelligence data / interviews

Estimating the illicit market size

The most precise data are the national statistics on the excise tax paid for import, production and sales of tobacco products, which are produced by the National Customs Agency. The excise tax paid provides the volume of tobacco sticks sold at the domestic market on a monthly and annual basis, though the figures should be adjusted for goods for transit to third countries, tax fraud, seasonal and tax increase effects. The analysis of the annual data on paid excise for the period 2001-2011 was picked as a *first step of the assessment of the illicit tobacco market*, as it illustrates well the history of harmonisation of the excise levels in Bulgaria with the average levels in the EU. The review of the existing annual data on paid excise tax shows that since 2001 there has been a constant decrease in the size of the legal market, which is driven by the harmonisation of the Bulgarian excise tax level with that of the EU. The years 2007 and 2008, immediately after Bulgaria's EU accession are considered to have had the lowest share of illicit tobacco for a number of reasons. The economy was still booming, the state monopoly over the tobacco market had been just removed and all multinational companies were aggressively extending their distribution networks with low-priced cigarettes. Also, all land-border crossing duty-free operators, which were a major source of contraband cigarettes (CSD, 2007), were shut down.

The above facts make 2008 the most suitable baseline for comparison, as the illicit market was at its lowest point, before the steep rise in the excise tax in the beginning of 2010. The data shows that for the period 2009 and 2010 there is a 44,5% decrease in the size of the licit market for cigarettes from 19,1 billion sticks in 2008 to 10,6 billion sticks in 2010.

Additional sources of data for the share of the illegal market are the *ad hoc* household surveys, which provide data for the tobacco smoking prevalence in the population. The juxtaposition of smoking prevalence data with paid excise per stick is *the second step in the illicit tobacco market assessment*. It allows not only for a validation the actual consumption of tobacco products, but also enables an adjustment for the decrease in consumption due to the increases of retail prices. For the period 2009-2011 the data collected by CSD within household surveys shows about an 18% drop in consumption rates. In 2012 the smoking prevalence was at 36% and the number of cigarettes smoked per day to be 15,1 (TNS Opinion & Social, 2012).

The consumer's data could then be used to estimate of the overall consumption of cigarettes in the country applying:

*Annual consumption = Number of users * Number of cigarettes per day * 365 days*

The difference between the annual consumption (according to consumer surveys) and the annual legal sales (supply of cigarettes) produces the size of the black market. Yet, smoking prevalence data should be used with caution as various household surveys produce different smoking prevalence numbers. Applying the multiplier to the rate of 39% prevalence of smoking among the Bulgarian population produces 21-22 billion sticks consumption annually for 2008. The comparison of existing prevalence data shows that there was at least 25% decrease in consumption in the period 2008-2011.

This brings about the need to introduce additional data about the illegal market in order to adjust the real illicit volumes through triangulation of data, which is the *third step in the illicit tobacco market assessment.* Most of the tobacco companies regularly conduct the so called 'empty pack surveys', which produce a relatively sound indicator for the level of illicit tobacco consumption. The method is based on collection and analysis of used empty cigarette packs in randomly selected areas in big cities.[9] Empty pack survey data about Bulgaria for the period 2007-2008 obtained from tobacco companies show that 10-14% of all cigarettes consumed were illicit. This was the lowest share during the past ten years and equals 1,33 - 2,68 billion sticks for 2008. By 2010 it reached 34%.

The fourth and last step of the illicit tobacco market assessment uses market retail-audit data. This type of data is considered to be the most reliable measurement of what is actually sold legally. The market retail audit is a method which collects retail data based on the monitoring of invoices of a sample of retail outlets across the country. Monthly retail audit data is more precise than paid-excise duty data, and it is a better tool with which to monitor monthly market variations.[10] It can be used to validate the official government statistics, as well as to adjust for certain seasonal effects or hoarding effects when an increase in excise is expected for the coming year. Along with this Customs' data cannot be used for assessing monthly changes in retail sales, as payments of excise tax are made in advance and does not reflect the real purchases made in retail stores and therefore does not allow for the real dynamics of the tobacco product sales.

The comparison of retail data and paid excise data clearly demonstrates the reliability of the market retail audit surveys, as on annual basis the difference in results for 2008 and 2009 showed merely 0,02% a deviation and for 2010 only

---

9 The 'empty pack' method is used in the largest study of the illegal cigarette market within the EU which is conducted with the support of major cigarette producing companies (KPMG LLP, 2012)(KPMG LLP, 2012). The introduction of these surveys in Bulgaria is in 2007 and since then they have been conducted on annual base in 14 major cities and since 2010 bi-annually in 21 major cities and a number of small settlements.

10 Companies sometimes pay the duty in advance and it is difficult to estimate the exact monthly sales.

3,3%. This allows us to draw the assumption that the monthly retail data will also be as accurate and, therefore, can be used as an early warning indicator for increase in the illicit cigarettes sales provided that there is no sharp reduction in smoking prevalence. The market retail audit data is so sensitive that it provides indications for increases in illicit sales within weeks of them having taken place. Moreover they are far more precise on a monthly basis compared to custom's data as the purchasing of excise stamps is made in advance and is susceptible to seasonal and other short-term effects.

The pooling of the different data sources provides the overall picture of (licit and illicit) tobacco consumption, presented in Figure 2 below. Taking 2008 as a benchmark for its lowest share of illegal sales (1,6 billion sticks with paid excise sold monthly = 19,2 billion) and comparing it with 2010 (900-910 million sticks with paid excise duty sold monthly) shows a gap of 691 million sticks on a monthly basis. Part of this gap is explained by a 25% decrease in consumption, indicated by surveys of smoking prevalence. In 2008, the empty packs survey data shows that only 10-14% of all cigarettes consumed were illicit, which amounted to 1,33 - 2,68 billion illicit sticks annually. In 2010, the size of the illegal market was between 30% and 40% of all cigarettes sold. For the same year, the total revenues from the sale of illegal tobacco products reached € 250 million, or 16 – 18% of total consumption.

Figure 2
Consumption of legal and illegal cigarettes (2008-2011).

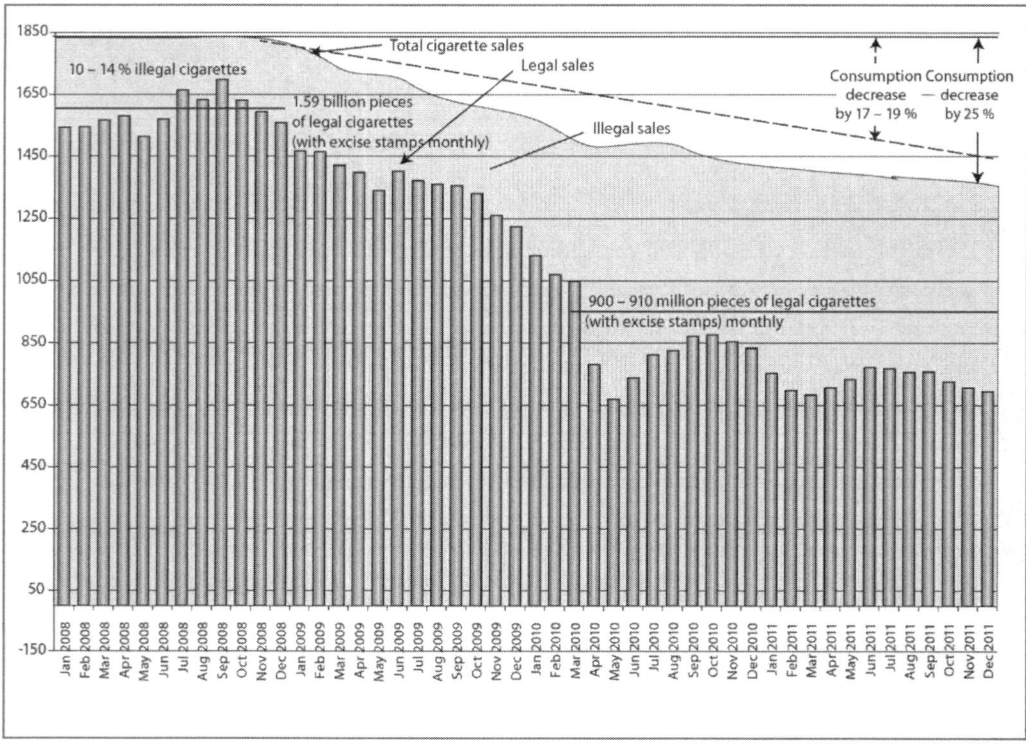

Source: *Estimates based on data from Nielsen retail audit (Monthly Retail Audit 2008 – 2011); empty pack surveys; National Crime Survey (2008 – 2011).*

Assessing the structure and players in the market

Data on the structure and organisation of the networks involved in the illicit tobacco distribution can be obtained through information gathered within criminal investigations and interviews with market participants. The knowledge about the structure and organisation coupled with data on sales is the basis for an estimation of the number of participants involved. The analysis shows that hundreds of stable criminal structures have emerged in Bulgaria within a period two years. The typical criminal network functions at one or two levels and does not cover the entire range of activities related to importing and distribution of illegal cigarettes. They usually focus on a particular phase of the process. For instance, large-scale importers and the manufacturers do not control the wholesale and retail trade; mid-level networks do not engage in import and manufacturing.

At the highest level of this structure are Bulgarian and Greek entrepreneurs with significant financial resources, including 2 – 3 legitimate manufacturers and

5 – 7 importers. The manufacturers provide part of their production to criminal entrepreneurs who avoid paying excise duties and/or VAT on the quantities they sell. These entrepreneurs use two main schemes. The most commonly used one includes fictitious export and relocation of the products to warehouses for illegal distribution. In the second scheme, cigarettes are exported and, following a complex string of transfers of ownership, they are eventually smuggled back into the country.

Large-scale importers work mainly with the so-called 'Greek hub': a concentration of criminal networks in large Greek ports which controls the contraband of cigarettes via Greece. The criminal entrepreneurs smuggle illicit whites, manufactured in the Middle East (mainly in Dubai), Greece, the former Soviet republics or even Southeast Asia. The illicit whites are sold by producers legally to importers. After being resold and reshipped several times, including through duty free zones (*e.g.* Mersin in Turkey), they are smuggled into illegal warehouses in Greece, and are then further exported to other EU countries, including Bulgaria. The contraband imports are negotiated between large importers/manufacturers and Bulgarian mid-level criminal entrepreneurs.

Another source of illegal cigarettes in Greece is the local illicit production facilities which usually produce counterfeits of leading brands. Several factories were uncovered in the past few years.

Monthly sales of nearly 300 million cigarette sticks suggest hundreds of thousands of consumers and thousands of participants in the illegal distribution. The daily illegal sales are estimated at 500.000 cigarette packs, which indicates that the retail distributors involved are between 5.000 and 10.000 selling between 5 and 10 cartons (1 carton contains 10 cigarette packs) of cigarettes per day. If distributors at the mid and high level, shuttle traders, security providers, couriers, those working in warehouses and retail storage were to be added, the total number of regular participants in the illegal cigarette trade would amount to as many as 15.000 (Table 7). The number of participants up the distribution chain (various wholesale levels) is estimated based on intelligence and interviews data.

Table 7
Illicit tobacco distribution network (2010-2011)

Distributor	Role	Price paid per pack[11]	Volume of sales (monthly)	Monthly profits (euros)
Large importer	Between 5-10 importers, who organize the large scale smuggling of illicit cigarettes (2-7 containers monthly each of them).	€ 0,35 per pack (€ 175.000-200.000 per container)	62,5-75 mln packs (25-30 containers or 12.500-15.000 master cases)	175.000 – 600.000
Wholesale importers	According to expert estimations – 20-50 high level distributors. Each importer is expected to work with 4-5 wholesalers. They organize the mid- and low level of the retail distribution.	€ 0,60 – 0,85 per pack	100.000 – 125.000 packs (200-250 master cases)	27.000-125.000
Middle level distributor	80-250 mid level distributor, who is supplied by importers	Average € 1,00	10.000-15.000 packs (20-30 master cases)	1.500-2.200
'Master case' dealer	350 – 950 low level wholesalers– some of them sell illegal cigarettes under the counter in small shops, while majority supplies networks of street dealers.	Average € 1,10	1.000-1.400 packs (2 -7 master cases)	150-2.000
Street dealer	Between 5,000 and 10,000 street level distributors. When adding guards and other logistics people – the number involved reaches 15,000.	Average € 1,25	1.500-3.000 (50-100 packs daily)	200-400

11 The prices vary widely as there is no perfect market information. The average prices for the lower levels are the prices that we heard about in the course of interviews most often, but are not systematically averaged. Therefore in statistical terms it more correctly to speak of 'mode' value.

The knowledge of the structure of the illicit tobacco distribution networks, coupled with the regional sales data from tobacco companies allows for an estimation of the number of participants and turnovers on a regional level. Such estimates were made for Bulgaria's 28 administrative regions (CSD 2012:44). As a baseline we used the regional sales data provided to us by several big tobacco companies. Similarly to the national estimates, we used the drop in licit sales between 2008 and 2010, to estimate growth in illicit sales on a regional level. Regional estimates are more challenging as empty pack surveys do not cover all administrative regions through a representative sample. Also, consumer surveys rarely use large enough samples to provide regional data. Therefore, regional data on the number of consumers who quit smoking is not available, and national averages need to be used instead.

The proposed regional analysis was tested in Bulgaria. The results of the analysis were discussed with investigators within the regional GDCOC or Criminal Police departments in nine different regions. The feedback was mixed and showed both advantages and deficiencies of the approach. Prior to meeting with each district we had their annual activity report so we knew exactly how many illicit tobacco cases they have handled in the same period. In a few police districts investigators claimed that the numbers were grossly exaggerated. The long debate in these districts usually left us with the impression that officers were not investigating cigarettes cases, either because it was considered politically sensitive or because in some way they profited from this. In the majority of districts, we observed that investigators generally agreed with the estimates, and they had knowledge about most of the market actors. This information, howeve, was was not displayed anywhere; neither in their activity reports nor in the GDCOC intelligence database.

Conclusion

The collection of macro-data, such as the types of market data suggested in the analysis of the market for illicit cigarettes is not cheap, and the use of tobacco companies proprietary sales data may be sensitive, but the approach is not untenable, as tobacco companies are generally cooperating in the EU and US with law-enforcement in the combat against illicit tobacco products. The commissioning of consumer, victimisation, or retail audit surveys to supplement intelligence data is also expensive, but most likely cheaper than making significant investments in gathering additional intelligence.

The main advantage of the proposed method is that in countries where OCTA-type reports are not possible due to the absence of a 'national intelligence model', the proposed methodologies could be a good substitute to help shift political priorities or to seek accountability about government policies. In Bulgaria, the first *Serious and Organised Crime Threat Assessment* (CSD, 2012) caused havoc in the political leadership, mostly because the European Commission saw it as the only objective and measurable assessment of the state of organised crime in the country.

The proposed approach will also strengthen political control over the police, as it calls for the use of sources that are alternative to those obtained from police intelligence. The police can no longer be the sole 'guardian' of the crime threat related data. The approach which we suggest could be further improved by extracting more relevant market information from police investigation files (about revenues, sales, or the structure of illicit enterprises), or even interviews with persons in custody.

The application of the proposed methodology can certainly be expanded beyond the 'markets' for illicit goods and services. Crime victim surveys and police statistics could also be used to gain insight into the total number of actors involved in a certain criminal activity. Matching crime victim survey data about the total number of crimes with intelligence and/or self-reported data about the average crime activity (*e.g.* burglaries or car-thefts per month or per year), could indicate the number of criminal groups or entrepreneurs involved.

References

Bouchard, M. et al., 2012. Estimating the Size of the Canadian Illicit Meth and MDMA Markets: A Multi-Method Approach., s.l.: Department of Public Safety Canada.

CSD, 2007. Effective Policies Targeting the Corruption - Organised Crime Nexus in Bulgaria: Closing Down Duty-Free outlets. [Online] Available at: http://www.csd.bg/artShow.php?id=9182 [Accessed 18 September 2012].

CSD, 2007. Organized Crime in Bulgaria: Markets and Trends., Sofia: Center for the Study of Democracy.

CSD, 2012. Serious and Organised Crime Threat Assessment, Sofia: s.n.

Duyne, P.C., OCTA 2006: the unfulfilled promise. *Trends in Organised Crime*, 2007, p. 120–128.

Duyne, P. C. van, Organised crime (threat) as a policy challenge: a tautology. *Journal of Criminal Justice and Security*, 2010, pp. 355-366.

Duyne, P. C. van and T. Vander Beken, The incantations of the EU organised crime policy. *Crime, Law and Social Change*, 2008, pp. 261-281.

EMCDDA, 2009. Statistical bulletin 2009 (archive). [Online] Available at: http://www.emcdda.europa.eu/stats09/ppp [Accessed 18 September 2012].

EMCDDA, 2010. First European conference on drug supply indicators.A joint initiative to develop sustainable options for monitoring drug markets, crime and supply reduction activities.. Brussels, EMCDDA.

EUROPOL, 2006. EU Organised Crime threat Assessment, The Hague: European Police Office.

Kilmer, B. and S. Hoorens, Understanding illicit drug markets, supply-reduction efforts, and drug-related crime in the European Union. s.l.: RAND Corporation, 2009

Kilmer, B. and R.L. Pacula, Estimating the size of the global drug market. A demand-side approach., s.l.: RAND Corporation, 2009

Kilmer, B. and R.L. Pacula, Estimating the size of the global drug market. A demand-side approach., s.l.: RAND Corporation, 2009

KPMG LLP, 2012. Project Star 2011 Results. [Online] Available at: http://www.pmi.com/eng/tobacco_regulation/illicit_trade/documents/project%20star%202011%20results.pdf [Accessed 18 September 2012]

MacCoun, R. J. and P. Reuter, *Drug war heresies. Learning from other vices, times, and places.* Cambridge: Cambridge University Press, 2004

NFP, 2005. 2005 National Report (2004 data) to the EMCDDA, Sofia: National Focal Point on Drugs and Drug Addictions.

NFP, 2006. 2006 National Report (2005 data) to thr EMCDDA, Sofia: National Focal Point on Drugs and Drug Addictions.

NFP, 2011. 2011 National Report (2010 data) to the EMCDDA, Sofia: National Focal Point on Drugs and Drug Addictions.

Preble, E. and J. Casey, Taking care of business - The heroin user's life on the street.. *International Journal of The Addictions*, 1969

Sheptycki, J., H. Ben Jaffel and D. Bigo, *International organised crime in the European Union*. 2011 [Online] Available at: http://www.europarl.europa.eu/studies [Accessed 18 September 2012].

The Gallup Organisation, 2009. Survey on Tobacco, s.l.: EUROBAROMETER.

TNS Opinion and Social, 2012. Attitudes of Europeans towards Tobacco, s.l.: Eurobarometer.

Tremblay, P., M. Bouchard and S. Petit, S., The size and influence of a criminal organization: a criminal achievement perspective. *Global Crime*, 2009, p. 24–40

UNODC, Addiction, crime and insurgency. The transnational threat of Afghan opium., Vienna: United Nations Office on Drugs and Crime, 2009

UNODC, The Globalization of Crime. A Transnational Crime Threat Assessement., Vienna: United Nations Office on Crimes and Drugs, 2010

Zoutendijk, A., Organised crime threat assessments: a critical review. *Crime Law and Social Change*, 2010, p. 63–86

The profile of a sample of criminal organisations acting in Spain during the last decade

Andrea Gimenez-Salinas, Laura Requena and Luis de la Corte[1]

Introduction: knowledge about Spanish organised crime

As a number of recently published reports have shown (OCTA, CICO, SOCA, etc.), Spain is a country that has a very high profile in global organised crime (De la Corte and Giménez-Salinas, 2010). In particular, its geographical position has made it a neuralgic centre for many illicit trade routes reaching and crossing the European continent. The list of routes includes: trafficking of several types of drugs consumed in Europe, such as cocaine produced in the Latin American countries, or hashish from Morocco; trafficking of immigrants arriving illegally from the North of Africa and South America, and human trafficking for the purposes of sexual and or labour exploitation from Eastern Europe, South America and North Africa; and trafficking in illegally exported vehicles from western Europe to northern Africa, through the Maghreb countries, to Eastern European countries such as Romania or Bulgaria.

Spain plays a relatively important role in global organised crime despite the lack of publicly accessible information and statistical data. Reports issued by CICO (Centre for Intelligence against Organised Crime), the principal Spanish national body dedicated to investigating organised crime, are not available to the public or to academic researchers. At present, moreover, official statistics do not allow dimensions to be gauged or the characteristics of organised criminality in Spain to be analysed in any adequate and independent manner.[2] To overcome such

1 The authors are professors and researchers at the Institute of Forensic Sciences and Security of Autonomous University of Madrid.

2 The regulatory dispersion of legal definitions of offenses related to organised crime makes almost impossible the measure of its dimensions in an easy, transparent manner and comparable to other countries (Giménez-Salinas *et al.*, 2009).

obstacles, our research team tried to reach the Guardia Civil (Spanish Civil Guard[3]), one of the two principal Spanish police agencies, who provided authorisation to collect and analyse data on a sample of operations carried out by one of their specialised units in the fight against organised crime, namely the UCO (*Central Operational Unit*).

Following the methodology applied previously in other studies (Van Duyne, 1996; Kleemans *et al.* 1998, 2002; UNODC, 2002), our research team was able to collect and analyse an abundance of information regarding multiple dimensions of a wide sample of organisations that form part of the organised crime category (Gimenez-Salinas, 2009; Gimenez-Salinas et al, 2011). The aim of the study was to provide a profile of Spanish criminal organisations of the sample as well as to gain a deeper understanding of its structural and internal characteristics. Nevertheless, the results presented in this chapter only refer to information about the following four aspects:

a. the organisations' internal structure and their internal division of functions;
b. the means of protection and defence most commonly used by the criminal organisations studied;
c. the relations established between legal companies and criminal organisations, referring specially to their use as cover for illicit activities; and
d. the type and intensity of the relationships and synergies generated among criminal groups.

A preliminary profile can be described with these features that will allow an assessment of the complexity and dangerousness of an organisations' profile. In this sense, some questions should be answered by this research: Is Spanish organised crime a significant threat to our economic and social order? Is Spanish organised crime more dangerous than European organised crime? With that purpose, we will explain the methodology used in the following section.

Data sources and methodology

As mentioned earlier, the aim of this study was to create a profile of the criminal organisations operating in Spain, as well as a profile of the members that make up those organisations. This organisational profile was defined on the basis of three distinct dimensions:

---

3 We have been able to conduct this research thanks to the help of specialized units of the Guardia Civil. Nevertheless, opinions and statements shown in this paper are authors' responsibility.

- the internal characteristics of the organisations themselves,
- the illicit markets they participate in and
- the instrumental activities they simultaneously, engage in such as money laundering, corruption and violence.

Knowledge of the latter activities not only illustrates how criminal organisations operate, but also helps to distinguish among them depending on their criminal potential and their dangerousness. To describe individual profiles for the members of the criminal organisations information was collected with regard to their socio-demographic features, their criminal records and the function and position they occupy within the organisation.

The data sources used were police reports on operations carried out in Spain by the UCO, Guardia Civil, against criminal organisations between 1999 and 2010. This sample was selected taking into account the illegal market developed and will be described in the following sections. It should be noted that the sample is not representative due to its small size and the fact that selection was on the basis of accessibility to the researchers. The police selected the operations in order to have a variety of illegal activities but the selection was biased by the accessibility of operations.

Spanish police reports include abundant data regarding each investigation and the characteristics of each organisation and of its members. In particular, each police report contains the investigative techniques employed in the criminal investigation performed by the police agents: entry and search, intercepting telecommunications, seizure of assets, photographic reconnaissance, interrogation, shadowing, *etc.* It must be stressed that throughout the full process of collecting and analysing data, investigators have at all times kept the identity of each investigated subject anonymous, thus safeguarding their privacy rights.

At the beginning of the investigation, two templates were set up in which the information available from police reports could be put and organised systematically, to facilitate the subsequent generation of a database allowing for comparisons between all the police investigations included in the sample. By means of the first template[4] data were gathered on the organisations, looking at three major areas for analysis:

---

4 To design this template, several pre-existing models were used as reference: principally the annual reports of EUROPOL (OCTA), the United Nations report "Results of pilot survey of forty selected organised criminal groups in sixteen countries" (2002) and the document edited by Savona, Lewis and Vettori (2003) "EUSTOC: Developing an EU statistical apparatus for measuring Organised Crime, assessing its risk and evaluating Organised Crime policies". Before applying the template, the first draft of the questionnaire was reviewed by experts from both Spanish national police corps: Guardia Civil and National Police Corps. After the corrections and modifications proposed by this

a. the organisations;
b. main and secondary illicit markets developed by the organisations;
c. instrumental activities carried out by organisations: violence, corruption and money laundering.

Table 1 summarised the most significant variables collected in the spreadsheet for the mentioned areas:

Table 1
Most significant variables collected by areas of research

Research areas	Variables (i.e.)
Features of organisation	Number of people under arrest Organisation task in Spain Structure Location of main head Division of labour Collaboration with other groups Technical and complex means deployed Use of experts Security means employed Infiltration of police bodies Use of legal enterprises
Illegal markets	Dedication to more than one market Main illegal market Second market exploited *Modus operandi* Revenues Geographical location International activities
Instrumental activities	Corruption in Spain an abroad Obstruction of justice in Spain and abroad Money laundering activities Violence inside and outside organisations Homicides committed Other instrumental activities

The second data collection template was designed in order to gather specific information on members belonging to the organisations under investigation with reference to socio-demographic variables: age, sex, nationality, level of education, marital status, legal work, legal status in Spain and country of residence. In addition we gather information about their main task and hierarchical position within the criminal organisation structure and their criminal records.

subject matter experts had been incorporated, researchers drew up a final data collection template, with a total of 77 questions and sub-questions on the variables considered of interest to the study.

Due to space constraints, we cannot give information on all variables and areas in this chapter. The results of the research presented in this paper only concern the analysis of four particular variables: a) organisations structure and division of labour, b) protective measures developed, c) legal facilitators for organised crime groups and d) collaboration between groups.

Sample description

The study sample comprises a total of 74 criminal organisations, defined as those criminal groups featuring in the investigation and, after analysing each case, identified as being independent.[5] The criterion chosen for selecting the operations to include in the sample, was the main illegal market carried out by each criminal organisation. It must be pointed out that some of these organisations may have more than one illegal market, which is why the percentages can be more than 100%.[6]

Table 2 below shows the distribution of the sample as a function of the main activity carried out.

Table 2
Sample distribution of organisations by main illegal markets[7] (N=74)

Main Illegal Market	Frequency	Percentage
Robberies	31	42%
Drug trafficking	27	11%
Money laundering	8	11%
Trafficking vehicles	5	7%
Concealment of stolen goods (receiving)	11	15%
Forgery	7	9%
Trafficking in human beings	4	5%
Smuggling arms and others	3	4%
Fraud	5	7%
Smuggling immigrants	2	3%
Violence, extortion and kidnapping	5	7%
Total	108*	120%

* Organisations can be engaged on more than one market.

5 In a single police operation, several groups could be researched; in this case, we considered them to be independent and gave them different identifiers. In other words, the measuring unit was established as the organisation, not the police operation.

6 Sample selection was conditioned by availability and access to the operations carried out in each department. Although the UCO centralises many of its nation-wide organised crime operations, not all were fully available for review.

7 The main illegal market of each organisation was defined as: the most significant activity providing the economic revenue to the organisation. As we can see, some organisations share more than one main illegal market. That is the reason why percentages sum up more than 100% (108 organisations).

The sample distribution shown in Table 2 includes an overrepresentation of robberies due to the fact that the department co-operating with us was specialised in these kinds of operations. Nevertheless, taking into account the official data provided by the Ministry of Interior during the last decade (see Figure no. 1), the distribution by illegal market of organised crime groups arrested in Spain is rather similar, except in case of drug trafficking and robberies. Those illegal markets are underestimated and overestimated in our sample respectively in comparison with official data.

Figure 1
Mean percentage of organised crime groups arrested between 1997and 2007 by illegal market[8]

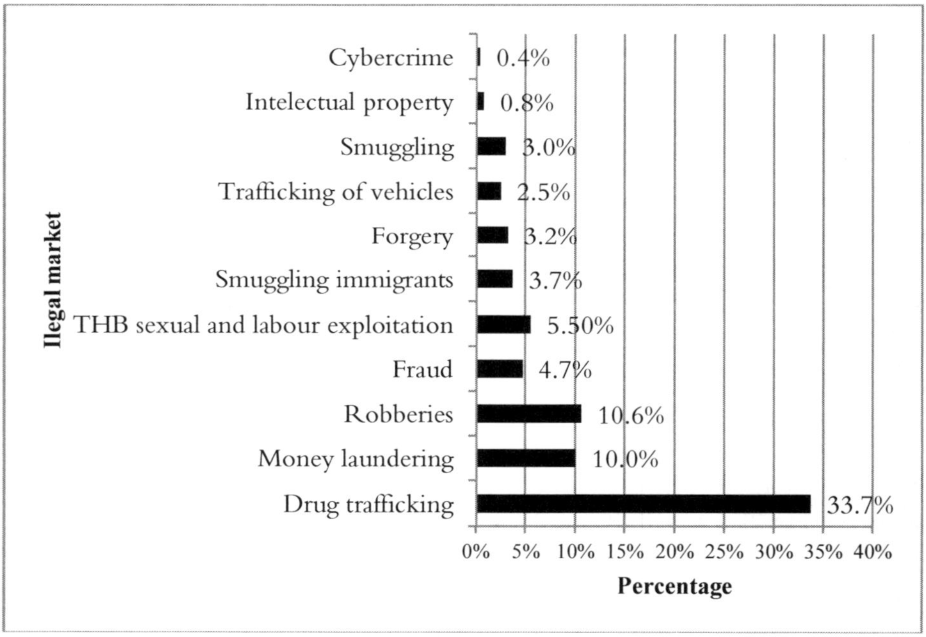

Source: Official data provided by the Ministry of Interior (1997-2007)

According to official data, drug trafficking (cocaine and hashish) is the most significant illegal market developed in Spain, followed by organised robberies and trafficking in human beings for sexual and labour purposes. In a secondary position, the following activities are shown: smuggling immigrants, forgery, other types of smuggling (art, jewellery and arms) and trafficking vehicles. Money laundering scores high as an accompanying offence.

---

8 The reliability of those data is limited due to the existing missing data provided by the national reports when a yearly comparison is done.

Size and composition of the criminal groups

The sample includes organisations of between three and 100 members[9], although the majority of groups studied are small or medium sized. In fact, the distribution over member intervals was as represented in Figure 2:

Figure 2
Distribution of the sample by members of each organisation

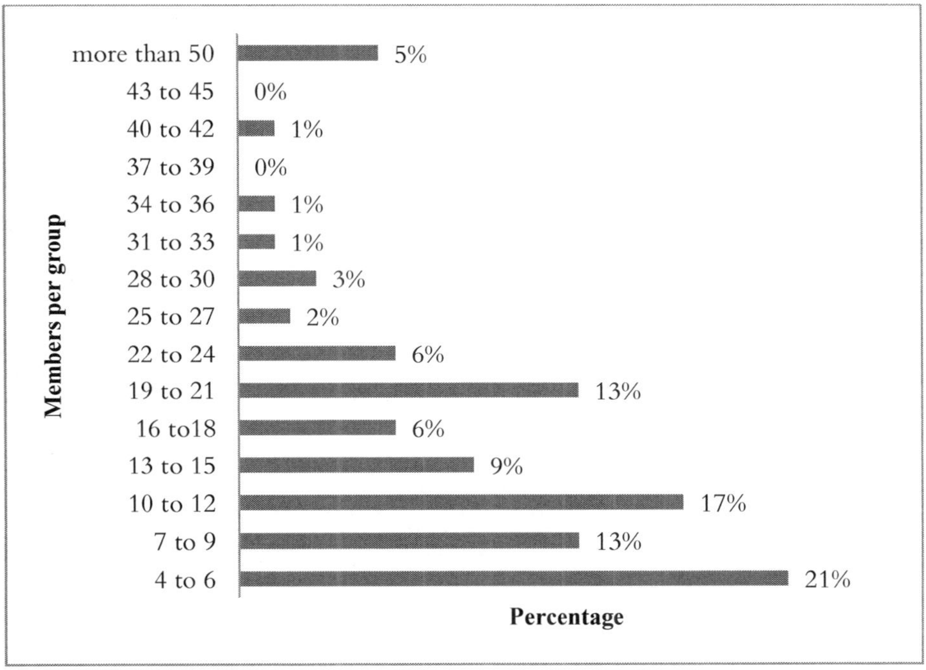

Source: authors' investigation

With regard to nationality, the vast majority are Spanish nationals, 2% consist of groups of European nationals (Bulgarians, Romanians, Portuguese, French or Italian), 3% are nationals of African countries (Morocco and Algeria), 1,5% are from North America (United States of America and Mexico) and 7% come from South American countries such as Colombia or Ecuador.

9 The size of the organisation does not reflect the real size, as we found it in the files, it reflects the number of members arrested by the police of each organisation. Nevertheless, it can be an indicator of the organisation significance in volume terms.

Main findings

The following section describes the main findings of the profile of Spanish criminal organisations regarding three specific topics:

a. the organisations' internal structure and their internal division of functions;
b. the means of protection and defence most commonly used by the criminal organisations studied;
c. the relations established between legal companies and criminal organisations, referring specially to their use as cover for illicit activities; and
d. the type and intensity of the relationships and synergies generated among criminal groups.

The characteristics do not allow for designing a deep profile of the organisations but provide a preliminary assessment of the complexity and sophistication of the criminal organisations actin in Spain. It will allow us to know more about the most prevalent organisation structures, the most appreciated criteria for task assignment inside the organisations, the protection strategies used by the organisations, the level of penetration of legal facilitators in the Spanish main illegal markets; and the methods most commonly used for money laundering. Finally, we will know if the relational patterns maintained amongst the organised crime groups are collaborative or competitive.

Organisation structure and division of tasks

Analysing the structure of organised crime groups is a complex task and results are always conditioned by the data source used. Our study, based on secondary data, allows as sole reference the interpretation made by the police of the internal structure discovered in the course of the investigation. In this sense, we know from several studies (Reuter, 1984; Adler, 1985; Pearson and Hobbs, 2001; Desroches, 2007; Morselli, 2009; Natarajan, 2000; Gimenez-Salinas *et al.*, forthcoming) that this information tends to over-represent the hierarchies within these organisations on account of the investigators own inclinations. Aware of these limitations, we also gathered information on the functions and roles played by the members of each organisation, in order to contrast this against the structure defined by the police investigators.

The reference framework used to distinguish and classify the structures within the organisations studied was taken from a United Nations report published in

2002.[10] This report established five types of such structures, of which three (standard hierarchy, regional hierarchy, clustered hierarchy) can be considered hierarchical structures and two (core group and criminal network) are network structures.

Following the UN report, the five typologies identified can be defined shortly as follows:

- *Standard hierarchy*: Single hierarchical group with strong internal systems of discipline.
- *Regional hierarchy*: Hierarchically structured groups, with strong internal lines of control and discipline, but with relative autonomy for regional components.
- *Clustered hierarchy*: A set of criminal groups which have established a system of coordination/control, ranging from weak to strong, over all their various activities. - *Core group*: A relatively tightly organised but unstructured group, surrounded in some cases by a network of individuals engaged in criminal activities.
- *Criminal network*: A loose and fluid network of individuals, often drawing on individuals with particular skills, who constitute themselves around an ongoing series of criminal projects.

The Figure 3 provides a graphic description of the five categories of organised crime structures.

Figure 3
UN typology of organised crime structures

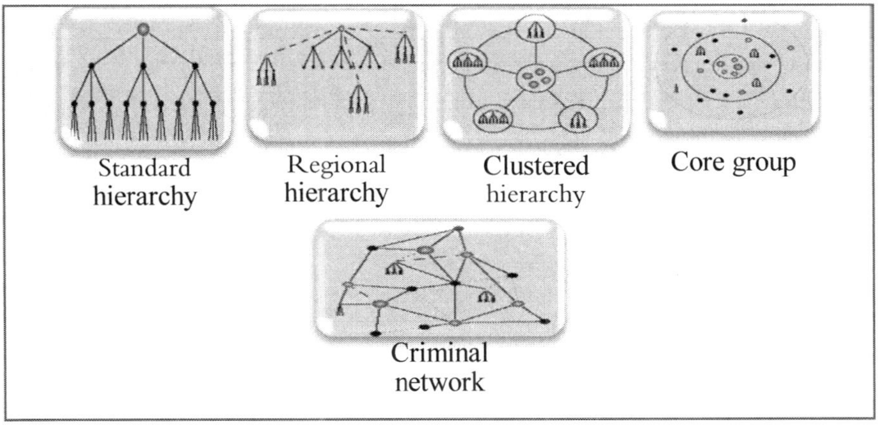

Source: UNODC, 2002.

[10] UNODC. (2002). *Results of pilot survey of forty selected organised criminal groups in sixteen countries*. Available at: http://www.unodc.org/

Furthermore, our research incorporated a sixth structure type, which we labelled *horizontal*. These sixth structure type identified (horizontal) was added at a later stage after analysis of the data, because it represents a relationship pattern that had not been classified by United Nations. This structure type includes associations in which members occupy practically the same hierarchical position and do not have clear-cut leaders commanding the whole group. A typical example of this is the organisation identified in 2007 whose activity was systemised theft. Initially, it appeared that groups whose main activity is theft should not be included in the category of organised crime, but in this case the group comprised 122 members, of which 47 ended up as being indicted by the Spanish courts. That same organisation had members from at least 25 different countries, where they had been operating for the last four years. According to the police sources consulted, revenue from thefts carried out in Spain reached the sum of € 2.100.000. The organisation was active from Monday to Friday all over Spain. Every week, a group of representatives held a meeting to decide which cell of members would carry out actions during the following week. Each cell was independent, was renewed on a weekly basis and a different coordinator was assigned as manager (each cell was named after the person designated as coordinator ("So-and-so's" group). Tasks were assigned according to criteria of availability of personal means, (vehicle, *etc.*), and members' functions were fully interchangeable.

Figure 4 describes the structural distribution of the six types, and the distribution taking into account two global groups: hierarchical and network structures. By categories, as shown in Figure 4, *regional hierarchy* type structures are prevalent in this sample, representing almost 30% of the sample according to type. Nevertheless, *network* type structures have a similar percentage, being in a secondary position (27%). After that, standard hierarchy (17%) and horizontal structure (18%) are the next significant categories.

From a global viewpoint (Figure 4 right side), hierarchical and network structures have similar distribution, even if hierarchical structures are more prevalent in the sample.

Figure 4
Organisations distribution by their structure (N=74)

Structure distribution by UN categories	Structure distribution by two main categories: Hierarchical and network

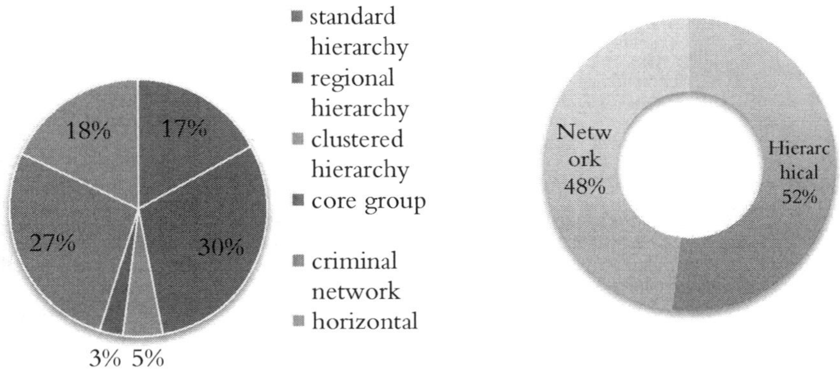

Among hierarchical structures, the regional hierarchy is the most common. Taking an example of this type of organisation we can illustrate its structure.

This case concerns a criminal organisation that deals in human trafficking from Morocco to Spain, profiting from a fee of € 6.000 that is charged to each immigrant. As soon as the "customer" accepts the deal, a member of the organisation in Morocco provided an air ticket from Casablanca to Sao Paulo (Brazil), with a stopover in Madrid-Barajas. The reason for choosing Madrid for the transfer was the agreement between Morocco and Brazil that eliminated the requirement for a visa for citizens of these two countries. Once the "customer" was on Spanish soil, a member of the organisation showed him how to leave the airport unnoticed. From the airport, the individual had then to take a taxi to an address where he would receive false identity documents on which he could circulate legally. The organisation offering this service was made up of a total of 23 members, in Morocco and Spain. The members in each country maintained relations of a hierarchical nature, but still operated with relative independence, while the nucleus was in fact situated in Morocco.[11]

[11] These results must be taken cautiously as our sample contains more small and medium sized groups than large ones, and for this reason the conclusions reached regarding organisations must be seen as preliminary and requiring further empirical evidence.

Organisation structure and size

Contrary to what one would expect, the larger organisations (with a smaller representation in our sample) generally present a reticular or horizontal structure, characterised by equivalent hierarchical positions and the absence of leaders in command of the organisation. The clustered hierarchy structure appears as the most typical among medium size organisations. In addition, it is interesting that hierarchical structures are more prevalent in organisations with fewer members than in large organisations[12], although among the majority of small organisations the prevailing structure is the horizontal type (see Figure 5).

Figure 5
Structure distribution by organisations size

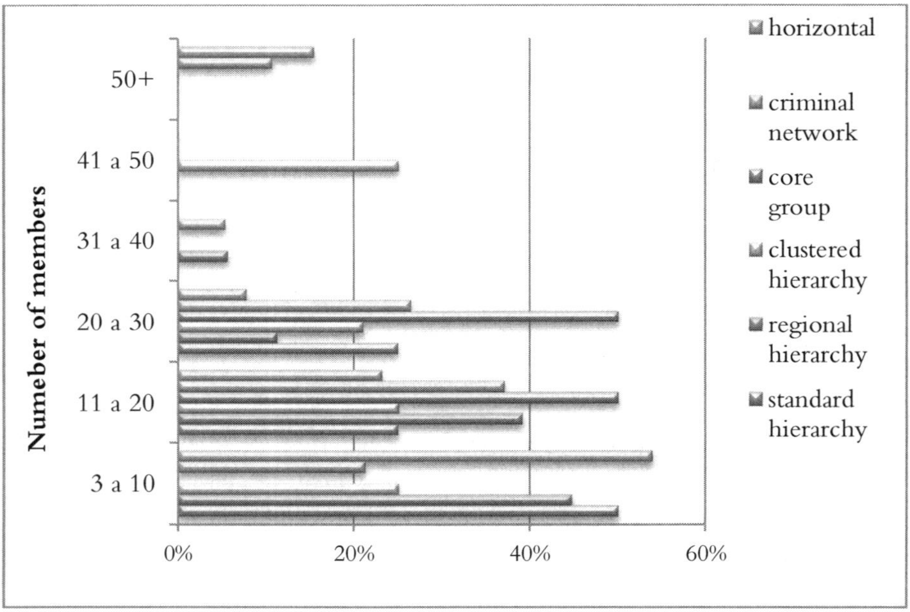

The widespread presence of grid type organisations is congruent to the results of other comparable research in which the organisational structure has been studied with regard to different illegal activities. Some ethnographic studies relating to the sale of drugs to lower echelons (retailers and distributors: Adler, 1985; Natarajan, 2000, 2006; Benson and Decker, 2010) and higher levels (wholesalers: Reuter and Haaga, 1989; Natarajan and Belanger, 1998) show that such groups make up reticular, rather than hierarchical, structures. Similarly, studies that have related different illegal activities (Bruinsma and Bernasco, 2004; Williams, 1998, 2001),

12 One must bear in mind in these results that over- representation of small and medium sized groups in our sample is influencing the outcome.

have revealed that groups participating in activities such as drug trafficking or other illegal activities such as human trafficking and illegal immigration are not criminal organisations as we know them from a traditional point of view, but are highly compartmentalised while their hierarchical loyalties are not so prominent.

Internal division of functions

Our study also yielded information on the extent of the division of tasks within each organisation, and the criteria underlying such division. As shown in Figure 6), out of the 74 organisations that were analysed, 89% presented a clear task division, although not always following the same criterion. Of all the organisations with clear task division, 68% reflected this division in their structure and organisational flowchart (see Figure no. 6).

The prevalent criterion regarding internal division of functions is the accumulated experience depending on the time spent in carrying out those functions (55%). This is the case of individuals that are experienced and have special driving skills or those who are expert in manipulating drugs, such as cocaine.

The second most prominent criterion is related to *access to contacts* (50%) or individuals skilled in expanding or developing the illicit business, or providing a front for it. Examples to illustrate these functions are members with trading contacts who deal in the sale of articles, and can facilitate the sale of stolen goods on legal markets. Similarly, this group comprises individuals who know the managers of nightclubs or cabarets where the group can negotiate the sale of women trafficked in from East European countries for exploitation by prostitution.

The third criterion for assigning functions is the *possession of a privileged access route to certain resources* that are needed for the activity (43%), as the case of individuals who have direct access to sales terminals where they can obtain fraudulent duplicates of credit cards, or the means of transport to camouflage illegal goods.

Finally, the speciality or *expert knowledge* of a given function is relevant only in 24% of cases. This is the case of members of a criminal organisation who have the technical training to handle and repair geographical positioning systems that allow objectives to be targeted, or for forging identity documents with the use of specific software. The low percentage of this type of expertise may be a consequence of the type of activities included in our sample, as the majority of these lack the complexity that would demand subject matter experts for most of the assigned functions. Nevertheless, it may also imply that most forms of organised crime active in Spain are rather simple since our sample represent the most significant illegal markets developed in our country.

Figure 6
Frequency of tasks assignment over all organisations (N=74)

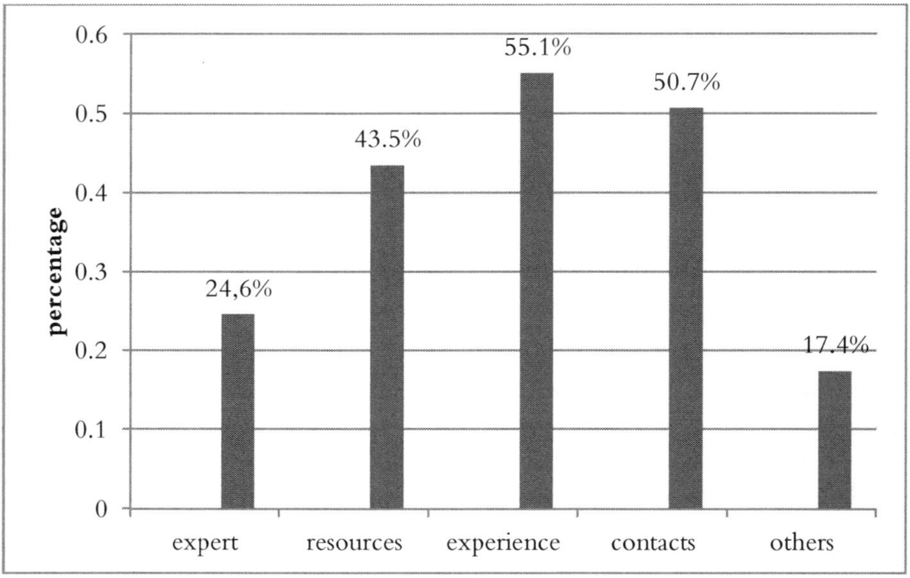

Figure 7 shows the task assignment broken down by illegal market. As can be seen, the experience is a significant task assignment criteria in illegal markets such as receiving, robberies or drug trafficking. Having relevant contacts is an appreciated criterion for money laundering and trafficking of vehicles. Possession of resources is valued in activities such as falsification of money, documents or credit cards and smuggling of immigrants. Finally, expertise is a significant criteria in falsifications or frauds. Nevertheless, what is relevant from Figure 7 is that all criteria are useful in almost every illegal market but differing by degree of significance.

Figure 7
Frequency of Task assignment criteria by illegal market

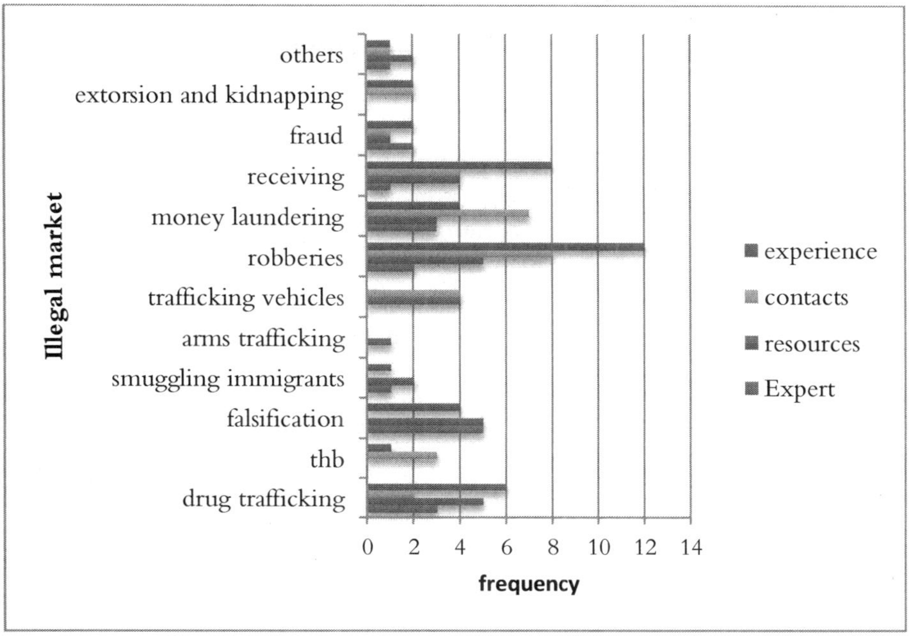

Protective Measures used by organisations to avoid detection

Assessment of the threat or the magnitude of a phenomenon such as organised crime is a complex task that requires a multi-dimensional approach. One such crucial dimension is the protective or defensive measures taken by these criminal organisations to avoid being detected. Large or mafia-type organisations usually use complex measures of protection that involve corruption practices, violence on a large scale and sophisticated defensive methods that can only be identified through intensive intelligence work (Paoli, 2002; Van Dijk, 2007).

This research programme did not set out to detect the existence of such methods, but rather to find out, from the data gathered during previous investigations, what types of protective means are used by organisations up to 50 members organisations with limited resources to implement complex defensive methods.

With reference to the type of protective measures used, the following information was collected covering three categories:

a. *generic* measures: these include all types of activities intended to avoid detection and act as a front to cover the group's illegal activity;

b. *defensive* measures: all actions intended as a response to an attack or intrusion by the police;
c. *counter-measures:* measures used by groups that suspect they have been detected by the police.

Naturally, criminal organisations use some kind of generic protective measure to avoid detection. One of the most widely used measures found in this first category is the use of multiplex telephone terminals with prepaid cards. This method makes it difficult to identify the user and affords greater protection. However, a new regulation has recently been implemented in Spain prohibiting telephone companies from selling this type of card without initially registering the user's data. This will reduce the number of telephone numbers individuals can contract to their name. Another widely used protective measure among criminal organisations consists of frequent changes of address, increasing geographic mobility of group members.

Secondly, we found that 42% of groups used defensive measures. Among these, we have identified examples of attempts to run policemen over when attempting to stop a vehicle belonging to the criminal organisation at highways checkpoints, and the use of brutal violence against property or people to avoid being seen by witnesses or detected by the police.

In 60% of the organisations we have identified countermeasures such as anticipating police actions. We have seen many examples of the measures employed by organisations to transport goods or persons in which drivers display great skill in eluding the police involving changes in driving techniques, the use of detectors or radars, *etc.* Likewise, in an operation involving house thefts, organisation members blocked the exits from the village with tree trunks to prevent the police from entering and arresting them.

It is also interesting to analyse the distribution of the protective measures by illegal markets to see which activities are "more protected" or show a higher degree of protection. As can be seen in the Figure 8, the organisations using more countermeasures are involved in: extortion and kidnapping, drug trafficking and receiving. Defensive measures are used mainly in organisations involved in extortion and kidnapping, fraud, receiving and robberies. Nevertheless, attending to the protection capacity or the accumulated measures of protection, we can see that the most protected organisations are preferably implicated in extortion and kidnapping and receiving.

Figure 8
Existence of countermeasures and defensive measures in the organisations by illegal markets[13]

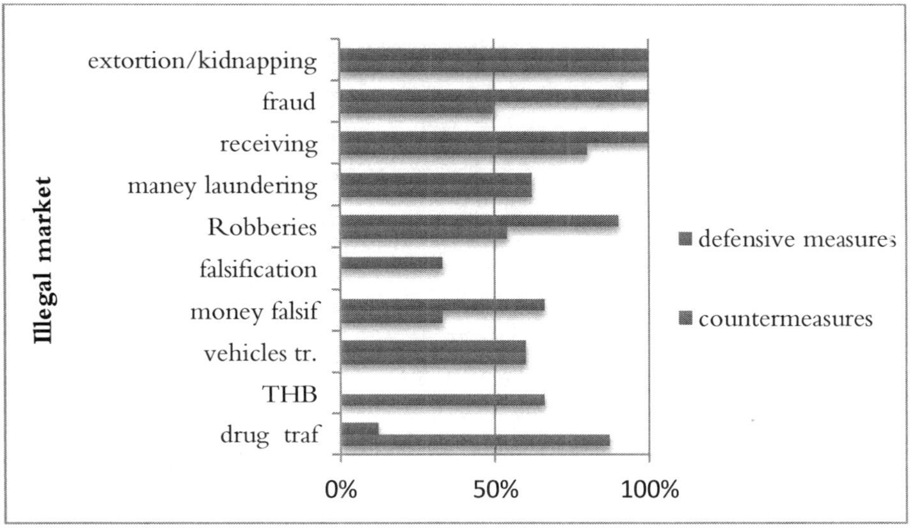

In addition to the function performed by the security measures adopted, we also set out to evaluate the sophistication of these protective measures. On the data collection template, we identified different internal forms of protection according to their degree of complexity: the first type of information concerns the possible use of secure communications as a simple protective mechanism available to any type of organisation. The second measure, by 'second degree' of sophistication, on which we collected data, concerned the presence in the organisation of an internal security service; *e.g.* members were given the specific task of controlling security within the organisation. Thirdly, we want to consider the possibility that some organisations comprised an intelligence cell or group with a mission to gather information on police movements. Finally, the last stage in protective measures we took into account was the possible routine of habitual use of corruption methods (bribes or payments to officials in exchange for immunity).

As can be seen in Figure 9, the most common protective measures applied by criminal organisations in our sample are distributed in a gradual manner. The most frequent are the two simplest: the use of secure communications (85%) and an internal security service (78%), while the presence of an internal intelligence service (16%) and corruption methods (10%) were the least common options.

---

13 The percentages represent the percentage of organisations using defensive and countermeasures among the organisations implementing the specific market.

Figure 9
Type or protective measures undertaken by organisations

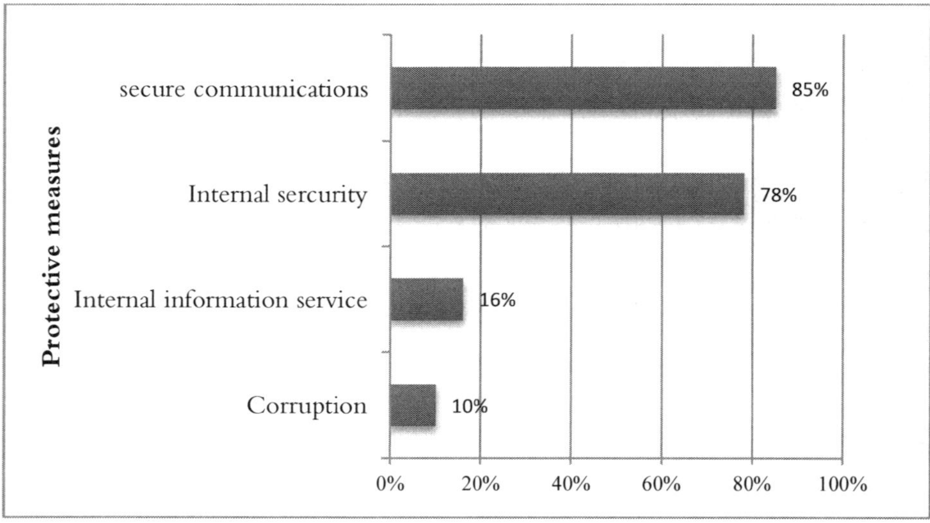

Considering those measures by the principal illegal market developed by the organisations, we found (see figure no. 10) that most frequent activities developed by organisations having an internal security service (78%) are: trafficking in human services, forgery, falsification of credit cards or document fraud and receiving. Less common in the global sample is to have an internal information service (16%), and these services have been found in organisations related to fraud activities, robberies, falsification of documents and credit cards, vehicles trafficking and trafficking of human beings. Finally, corruption activities to protect illegal markets have been detected namely in extortion and kidnapping activities, frauds, drug trafficking and receiving. From a global point of view, the activities that were apparently being more protected are frauds, forgery and trafficking of human beings.[14]

[14] This information should be interpreted carefully because the information collected could be biased by the description available in the police files.

Figure 10
Protective measures by illegal market

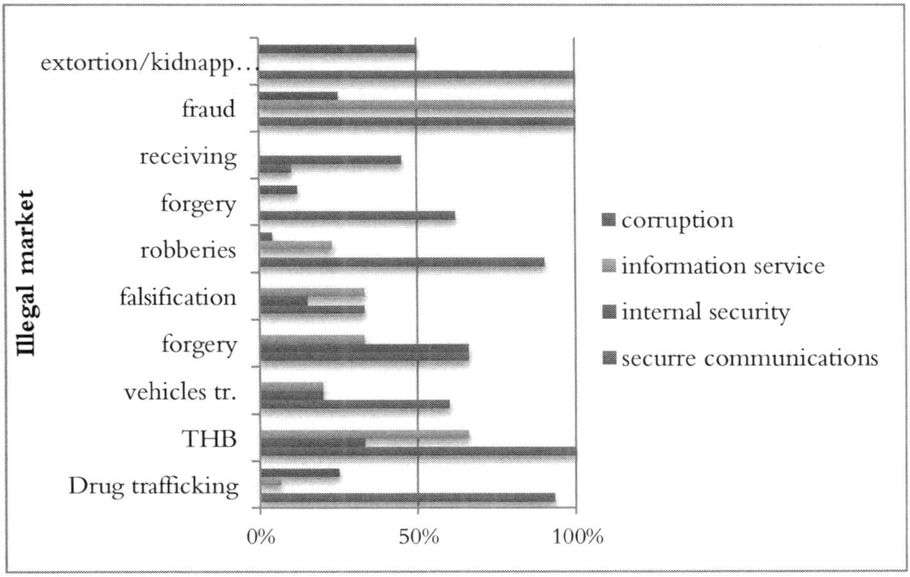

Another aspect related to the variety and nature of protective measures employed by criminal organisations involves the use of technical or technological means, generally becoming more sophisticated the greater the organisation survival or capacity (Gambetta, 1993; Skaperdas, 2001). To gauge the technical sophistication of the defensive and protective measures deployed by the organisations investigated in this study, our data collection template was designed to include three categories:

a. use of *technological*, or the use of resources needing technical skills or knowledge to manage them;
b. use of *computational* means, or the use of computer technologies to develop their activities;
c. use of *technologically complex* means, or the use of sophisticated equipment requiring high technician skills.

The data thus collected show that the majority of the organisations studied (54%) used complex technological means. Within this category we found means ranging from satellite telephones (hard to detect by the Spanish Security Forces) or frequency inhibitors, usually used by groups involved in burglary. 32% of the organisations regularly used technological means such as decoders to inhibit security systems on vehicle starter engines and control panels, GPS-GSM technology, radio-frequency scanners, Point-of-Sale Terminal systems for the purpose of making counterfeit bank cards, *etc.* Only 14% used computational technology as means of protection. This type of tool involves chiefly tailor-made software for forging ID documents or bankcards[15], or for geographical positioning and searching. The percentage for the use of these is low, as their use depends fundamentally on the organisation's access to such means and the presence of experts among their ranks.

From a global point of view, the organisations of our sample use technological means to develop their activities even thought they cannot be described as extremely complex. In addition, though they need personnel with special skills to manage those resources, this cannot be considered a high sophisticated expertise.

Legal allies in the practice of illegal activity

The association between criminal enterprise and the legal world is common practice, which serves at least three ends. On the one hand, it is a form of protection against scrutiny when criminal organisations create front companies or use middlemen to mask their illegal activity and remain undetected. On the other hand, it is a means of hiding the proceeds of crime through investment or business activities, which launder the revenues from various sources. Finally, it can also be part of the *modus operandi*, *e.g.* in smuggling operations when legal association is needed to sell the illegal commodity. In turn, the professionals or entrepreneurs who collaborate with criminal organisations in these ways derive extra revenues from the illegal activities.

The protection that legitimate businesses can provide for criminal organisations is often complemented by services facilitating the criminal activity. As an example of this dual role we can cite cases involving vehicle traffic whose perpetrators work closely with garages that enable them to counterfeit or forge license plates and modify the chassis in order to prevent identification of a stolen vehicle. Multinational operations related to drug trafficking groups commonly use transportation or exporting companies in order to smuggle narcotics into Spain (*e.g.*, companies manufacturing rubber or stage flooring whose products can be used to conceal cocaine).

Relationships between criminal organisations and legitimate business partners may occur at two levels. At one level we might find a deal involving a fee between an independent legal company and a criminal group. Our analysis in this regard suggests that 68,9% of organisations surveyed established partnerships with legal Spanish businesses (61,5%) or foreign firms (7,4%), in terms of collaboration or concealment. Among this group the most frequently used commercial sector is the

15 In case of forgery or document falsifications software is part of the modus operandi and cannot be counted as additional technical means but we have considered its addition to assess technical complexity and sophistication of organisations.

service industry (45,9%) mainly involving catering businesses such as bars or restaurants. Secondly, 17,6% of the organisations use a variety of small businesses to meet their objectives, including: scrap yards, bakeries, antique dealers or jewellers, strip clubs to exploit trafficking of women, etc. Thirdly, construction and real estate companies have been used in 12,2% of cases to conceal criminal activity. The large quantities of materials stored on building sites and the large spaces available allow goods to be easily hidden and for exchanges to be carried out conveniently. Finally, 1,4% used the agricultural sector for the same purpose. One of the clearest examples of the latter is provided by trafficking of human beings for labour exploitation, the agricultural sector being the most used for this purpose. The remoteness of cultivation areas makes it difficult to control activities, thus favouring illegal business activities.

A second level of collusion with the legal economy has been identified in 9,8% of the criminal organisations which are involved in the management and ownership of legal businesses, created as covers for illegal activities (by bogus shareholders). Similarly, 6,8% of these organisations set up companies with active participation in the (bogus) boardrooms for the same purpose. Both forms of concealment by front companies are frequently found in organisations dedicated to drug trafficking, especially cocaine. Finally, this second level of activity tends also to be linked to money laundering, as well as for cover purposes. Below we shall review the data on methods used by criminal organisations for money laundering through companies, information not always accessible to police investigations.

As mentioned above, collaboration or use of legal firms may also be aimed at money laundering. In these cases legitimate businesses are created to give the appearance of legality of funds obtained from illicit activities. There have been cases of businesses, such as restaurants or bars, set up to disguise profits from illegal activities. In general, real estate and construction are the most vulnerable sectors for investments destined for money laundering. However, the number of criminal organisations examined in our research that laundered money through the construction and real estate sectors is relatively low (21,5%). More specifically, 9,5% of organisations surveyed had such companies located in Spain while 9% had equivalent companies located outside the country. Only 3% of organisations had invested in real estate or construction firms that were not their own property. In that sense, our results are similar to those found by other researchers (Van Duyne, *et al.*, 2010). They analysed the role of the money-crime in the legal financial system and found that the threat was overestimated according to the reality, and the real state is less affected than is generally assumed.

The relatively low proportion of cases of legitimate businesses being used for money laundering purposes deserves further explanation. First, the majority of police investigations analysed did not include information about the procedures used for the laundering of illegally obtained monies. This information is particularly sensitive and requires more arduous and lengthy investigations whose outcome may not have been available at the time of reviewing the police files. Secondly, it was found that over half of the sample used informal methods to transfer funds so as to avoid local detection and to be able to launder the money in the countries of origin of the contraband or trafficked persons. The most frequently used method was to send funds physically (by land, sea or air) or by various methods of transferring funds. In these latter cases funds were transferred by banks in several smaller amounts, or through companies that specialise in wiring money abroad that were used extensively before the financial crisis. Since the early 2000s there has been a significant increase in the immigrant population which led to a considerable increase in remittances to their countries of origin. This increase in remittances generated a significant niche market for many companies sending legal and illegal savings at a time when Spanish law was more lax in identifying the sender of small quantities.

Collaboration between criminal groups

The final purpose of this chapter is to discuss the relationships and synergies between criminal organisations. The traditional view we have of the relationship between organised crime groups relates more to competition and avoidance than to strong collaborative relationships. One of our working questions was to know the existence relations between organisations with the premise that relations of hostility and confrontation could be more likely to exist in environments characterised by weak state or police control rather than in well-controlled environments. In other words, direct confrontation and violence in an illegal environment within the European framework is too risky and could attract police detection, thanks to a long tradition of measures to combat organised crime and the existence of specialized enforcement agencies. Empirical evidence seems to confirm our premise in the sense that cooperation prevails over rivalry or competition between groups and support a cooperation trend revealed by others (Williams, 2002). Nevertheless, to provide consistency to our hypothesis we need more research on that using other research methods.

Data and evidence from criminal investigations concerning the relationships between groups show that partnership is more likely than competition. 60,8% of organisations were found to have relationships with other criminal groups, especially those engaged in organised crime related activities. The most frequent relationship occurs between criminal organisations performing a similar illegal market-based activity (97,8%), and in only one instance did the criminal organisation maintain relations with a terrorist group. Groups can share *resources* (*i.e.* when they share arms or falsified documents with other groups), *personnel* (*i.e.* when they use a financial or technical expert from others), *contacts* (*i.e.* shearing organisations for falsification of documents or for helping to recover some debts, etc) or experience (*i.e.* how to have access to protected infrastructures or to have credit card data). They can also have transactions in order to develop their activities (*i.e.* money, drugs, arms, *etc.*).

The relationship was classified as a) *permanent* or constant, b) *occasional* when mutual relationship between organisation is provided from time to time or c) *sporadic* when the relationship has occurred on one occasion. In 24% of the cases there was permanent collaboration or a continuous exchange of services and resources between them. Collaboration has been occasional in 27% of cases. Less common is sporadic collaboration that occurs in only 8% of cases. Amongst collaborating organisations, those composed of Spanish citizens were most frequent (35%), followed by European organisations (17%) and South American (10%).

As it is shown in Table 3, the illegal market where collaboration takes place more frequently is in drug trafficking (synthetic, cocaine and hashish), fraud, extortion, trafficking vehicles and money laundering. Low collaborating patterns are shown in robberies and falsifications.

Table 3
Frequency of collaboration by illegal market

Crime category	N	Frequency	%
Hashish	9	7	77,7
Cocaine	16	14	87,5
Synthetic	1	1	100
Traf. vehicles	5	4	80
Falsification	2	1	50
Forgery	3	2	66,6
Robberies	31	14	45,1
Money laundering	8	6	75
Fraud	1	1	100
Extortion	4	3	75
Total	80	53	

Collaboration between criminal organisations may have different motives and purposes depending on the common interests. Several reasons for collaboration were identified (Table 4). The most common reason is the need for a resource to which the other organisation has access. Half of the organisations which cooperate, come together to obtain materials or human resources necessary to both parties (60,8%). This need for resources leads to the direct transaction of goods or services in 25,7% of cases of collaboration. The second motive of collaboration stems from the need of one party to gain access to contacts or facilitators owned by the other party for the exercise of an illegal business activity. 19% of partner organisations have shared contacts: suppliers, dealers, forgers, *etc.* The third main reason for collaboration is to share another organisation's staff or resources, a kind of "outsourcing" (14% of cases). Finally, in a smaller proportion of cases (5.4%), collaboration takes the form of a transfer of funds.[16]

Table 4
Motives of collaboration between organisations (N=72)

Type of collaboration	Percentage
Experience sharing	15
Use of resources	25,7
Use of staff	7
Use of contacts	19
Transaction of goods	25,7
Resource sharing	7
Transaction of funds	5,4

Conclusions

The results shown so far allow us to draw some tentative conclusions about the nature of a sample of criminal organisations that have operated in Spain during the decade since 2000. In the sample we found, firstly, that hierarchical and networked organisations are distributed equally.

Hierarchical structures were commonest amongst small and medium sized groups, whilst network structures are common in small as well as large groups. Our study suggests that larger organisations can survive even if they lack a traditional, complex structure. It also seems that networked structures, representing half of the sample, could be gaining in numbers amongst criminal organisations operating on Spanish soil, frequently with horizontal structures. This could also been explained

16 These results may be influenced by the difficulty of obtaining information from the police investigation. The data presented may be under represented by not including information from police files.

by the fact that large groups are more difficult to manage by hierarchical structures than smaller ones.

On another level, the revised data confirms that the availability of specialist expertise, contacts and privileged access to key resources required for illegal business activity are the criteria determining the division of labour and allocation of responsibilities and tasks within organisations in our Spanish sample. This also demonstrates that the anticipated knowledge about this kind of information (access to contacts or resources and expertise) of key members could be extremely useful from the police investigation point of view. In addition, it seems that expertise is the less common criteria for task assignment. This means, that forms of organised crime in Spain showing in our sample are rather simple.

Regarding the protective measures used, a large percentage of organisations use countermeasures to avoid detection by police and extensive use of applied technology for protective purposes. In terms of the illegal activity implemented drug trafficking, extortion and kidnapping, and receiving are the prevalent activities using countermeasures. Nevertheless, taking into account all protection means, organisations executing extortion and receiving are the most protected.

The extensive involvement of legal entities in Spanish criminal organisations is consistent with results found elsewhere (Passas, 2002). Nevertheless, collaboration is the most common relationship between legal and illegal partners and front companies are found in 10% of the cases. As demonstrated by other researchers, economic penetration in real estate and legal business is exceptional and less common than generally assumed (Van Duyne *et al.*, 2010). With reference to money laundering, the Spanish sample of medium sized organisations shows extensive use of physical movement of money as a way to evade a highly involved financial system. This information should prompt increased controls on these types of activity.

Finally, we found that cooperation between criminal organisations is the commonest form of relationship. These trends represent a major challenge for Spanish law enforcement agencies since the scope of criminal organisations operating in Spain may be multiplied by the support received from each other. These synergies should be taken into account when designing strategies for combating and preventing an increasingly cohesive, networked phenomenon (Von Lampe, 2008).

The outcome of this research highlights empirical evidence about characteristics of Spanish organised crime that can be useful to assess the threat posed for economic and social society. According to international organised crime threat assessments, Spanish organised crime poses a serious threat for European societies and should be controlled to decrease European organised crime. Evidence coming from our sample shows that the common profile of criminal organisations is mainly reticular, and hierarchical organisations tend to be small in size. In addition, their protective measures and sophistication in technology and expertise are modest. Laundering of funds and economic penetration is rather low, being the transfer of funds the most common method to launder the money. Definitely, this preliminary profile seems different from the threatening profile shown in European reports. Moreover, those findings correspond with a low profile stated by other authors about organised crime in other European countries (Van Duyne, 1996; Paoli, 2002; Von Lampe, 2008). This does not mean that organised crime activities are not a big issue in our country and that we do not have big organisations developing their activities. Those conclusions are only suitable for the most prevalent profile of criminal organisations.

References

Adler, P. A., *Wheeling and dealing: An ethnography of an upper-level dealing and smuggling community*. New York, Columbia University Press, 1985

Benson, J. S. and S.H. Decker, The organisational structure of international drug smuggling. *Journal of Criminal Justice*, 2010, 38: 130-138.

Bruinsma, G. and W. Bernasco, Criminal groups and transnational illegal markets: A more detailed examination on the basis of social network theory. *Crime, Law and Social Change,* 2004, 41: 79–94

De la Corte, L. and A. Giménez-Salinas (2010). *Crimen.org. Evolución y claves de la delincuencia organizada*. Barcelona: Ariel, 2010

Desroches, F., Research on upper level drug trafficking: A review. *Journal of Drug Issues*, 2007, 37: 827

Dijk, J.J.M. van, Mafia markers: assessing organized crime and its impact upon society. *Trends in Organized Crime*, 2007, 10: 39-59.

Duyne, P. C. van, The phantom and threat of organised crime. *Crime, Law and Social Change*, 1996, 24, 341-377.

Duyne, P.C. van, M.R.J. Soudijn and T. Kint, Bricks don't talk: Searching for crime-money in real estate. In: P.C. van Duyne, S. Donati, J. Harvey, A. Maljevic and K. von Lampe (eds.), *Crime, money and criminal mobility in Europe*. Nijmegen, Wolf Legal Publishers, 2009

Fickenauer, J.O. and E.J. Waring, *Russian mafia in America: immigration, culture and crime*. Boston, Northeastern University Press, 1998

Gambetta, D., *The Sicilian mafia: The business of private protection.* Cambridge: Harvard University Press, 1993

Gimenez-Salinas Framis, A., L. De La Corte, L. Requena and M. De Juan, La medición y evaluación de la criminalidad organizada en España: ¿Misión imposible? *Revista Española de Investigación criminológica*, 2009, 7

Gimenez-Salinas, A., L. Requena, L. y De la Corte, ¿Existe un perfil de delincuente organizado? Exploración a partir de una muestra española. *Revista electrónica de Ciencia Penal y Criminología*, 2011, 13, 3.

Giménez-Salinas, A., H. Román, L. Nieto, A. Martínez and S. Fernández, Estructuras y liderazgo en cuatro redes españolas dedicadas al tráfico de drogas. *Revista Española de Investigación Criminológica*, 2012, 10

Haller, M.H., Illegal enterprise: A theoretical and historical interpretation. *Criminology*, 1990, 28, 207-235

Hobbs, D., The Firm: organisational logic and criminal culture on a shifting terrain. *British Journal of Criminology*, 2001, 41, 549-560

Kleemans, E. R., E.A.I.M. van den Berg, and H.G. van de Bunt, Georganiseerde criminaliteit in Nederland: Rapportage op basis van de WODC-monitor [organised crime in the Netherlands: Report based upon the WODC-monitor]. The Hague: WODC, 1998

Kleemans, E. R., M.E.I. Brienen and H.G. van de Bunt, Georganiseerde criminaliteit in Nederland: Tweede rapportage op basis van de WODC-monitor [organised crime in the Netherlands: Second report based upon the WODC- monitor]. The Hague: WODC, 2002

Morselli, C., *Contacts, opportunities and criminal enterprise.* Toronto, Ontario, Canada: University of Toronto Press, 2005

Morselli, C., *Inside Criminal Networks.* New York, Springer, 2009

Natarajan, M., Understanding the structure of a drug trafficking organisation: A conversational analysis. *Crime Prevention Studies*, 2000, 11: 273-298

Natarajan, M., Understanding the structure of a large heroin distribution network: A quantitative analysis of qualitative data. *Journal of Quantitative Criminology*, 2006, 22: 171-192

Natarajan, M. and Belanger, M. (1998). Varieties of upper-level drug dealing organisations: a typology of cases prosecuted in New York City. *Journal of Drug Issues*, 28, 4: 1005–1026

Paoli, L., Paradoxes of Organized Crime. *Crime, Law and Social Change*, 2002, 39(1), 51-97

Passas, N., Cross-border crime and the interface between legal and illegal actors. In P.C. van Duyne, K. von Lampe and N. Passas (eds.), *Upperworld and underworld in cross-border crime.* Nijmegen, Wolf Legal Publishers, 2002

Pearson, G. and D. Hobbs, *Middle market drug distribution*. London: Home Office Research, Development and Statistics Directorate, 2001

Reuter, P., *Disorganised crime: Illegal markets and the mafia*. Cambridge, MT, The MIT Press, 1984

Reuter, P.H. and J. Haaga, *The organisation of high-level drug markets: An exploratory study*. Santa Monica, CA: Rand, 1989

Savona, E., J. Lewis and B. Vettori, *EUSTOC: Developing an EU statistical apparatus for measuring organised crime, assessing its risk and evaluating organised crime policies, Final Report*. Trento, Italy, Transcrime, 2003

Skaperdas, S., The political economy of organized crime: providing protection when the state does not. *Economics of Governance*, 2001, 2, 3: 173-202

UNODC. 2002. *Results of pilot survey of forty selected organised criminal groups in sixteen countries*. Available at: http://www.unodc.org/

von Lampe, K., Organized crime in Europe: conceptions and realities. *Policing*, 2008, 2, 1, 7-17.

Williams, P., The nature of drug trafficking networks. *Current History*, 1989, 97: 154-159

Williams, P., Transnational criminal networks. In: J. Arquilla and D. Ronfeldt (eds.), *Networks and netwars: the future of terror, crime and militancy*. RAND, Santa Monica, CA, 2001

Williams, P., Cooperation among criminal organizations. In M. Berdan and M. Serrano (eds.), *Transnational Organized Crime and InternationalSecurity. Business as usual?* Boulder: Lynne Reinner Publishers, Inc, 2002

"It's not like Sainsbury's! We don't keep stock of anything."
How drug dealers mitigate risk

Mike Salinas-Edwards[1]

Introduction: risk reduction within drug markets

Little empirical research has addressed the operations of closed-market drug dealers. To date, most research relating to illicit-drug markets focuses on retail-level dealers functioning within 'open-markets': such markets are often geographically situated within marginalised urban communities and are operated by individuals of matching marginal status (undereducated and underemployed males). Studies relating to 'middle-class' closed-market dealers are rare, while studies addressing the wholesale or importation trade (*i.e.* 'upper-level' dealing) are particularly scant (Desroches, 2007). Thus, the operational procedures of drug distribution that are most widely documented relate to lower-socioeconomic open drug-markets. Based on ethnographic fieldwork this paper offers an in-depth insight into how a network of predominantly 'middle class' British drug dealers mitigated risks at various levels of the trade.

Studies demonstrate how various kinds of offenders attempt to limit the risk of capture and punishment. Whether these offenders are car thieves (Cherbonneau and Copes, 2005), sexual predators (Beauregard and Bouchard, 2010), individuals trying to elicit sex from prostitutes (Holt *et al.*, 2009) or drug dealers, the evidence suggests that once potential hazards have been identified (*i.e.* points of exposure), risk-mitigation strategies are developed and employed. Understanding what these self-protective strategies are and how offenders develop their appreciation of risk is an ever-constant concern for criminologists, policy makers and law enforcement officers, alike – particularly with regards to the illicit drugs trade. However, scholarly research that may inform policy or policing is somewhat limited within contemporary drug markets.

The majority of studies documenting drugs markets centre mainly on the *retail* of goods (*i.e.* 'street-level' dealing). Indeed, Geoffrey Pearson (2007) stated:

---

1 The author is an ESRC funded doctoral student at The University of Manchester

"*research evidence and funding is disproportionately directed towards 'demand side' issues [. . .] as a consequence, the massive public expenditure on enforcement and intelligence measures against illicit drugs [at all levels] is underpinned by a pitifully thin evidence base*" (2007: 76). Indeed, even fewer studies provide us with *any* data regarding 'upper-level' trading operations (the most prominent being: Adler, 1985; Van Duyne, 1996; Dorn *et al.*, 1998; Pearson and Hobbs, 2001; Zaitch, 2002; Desroches, 2005; Decker and Chapman, 2008, Benson and Decker, 2010).

Many of the key studies addressing the risks of retail drug distribution derive from the *open-market* context, and include: Jacobs (1996a, 1996b), Jacobs and Miller (1998), Aitken *et al.* (2001), Hutton (2005), Johnson and Natarajan (1995), VanNostrad and Tewksbury (1999) and May *et al.* (2004), with ethnographic studies providing additional resources of information (*e.g.* Bourgois, 1996; Anderson, 1999; Venkatesh, 2000). Yet their application to the modern day U.K. context is questionable. Open markets have tended to operate in inner-cities or urban settings (Harocopos and Hough, 2005). Such public markets were readily accessible to customers with few restrictions in terms of who could procure drugs from the dealers (May and Hough, 2004). Individuals who operated in open markets were often geographically bound to particular public settings (*e.g.* a certain street corner, outside a grocery shop, etc.), and were frequently linked to street gangs (*e.g.* Fagan, 1989; Klein *et al.*, 1991; Esbensen and Huizinga, 1993). Although open markets have been documented in the U.K (e.g Kings Cross in London during the mid-1990s, see May *et al.*, 2001), their presence has most readily been identified within large U.S. and European inner cities such as Philadelphia (Anderson, 1999), Chicago (Venkatesh, 2000), Oslo (Sandberg, 2008), Rotterdam (Van DeMheen *et al.*, 2004), Frankfurk and Milan (Paoli *et al.*, 2000). Findings and conclusions drawn from such a context cannot be readily transferred to the 'closed', friendship networks that predominate in the U.K. This applies in particular to the ways and methods of risk mitigation. After all, also operating in a closed market of friends implies working in a dangerous and hostile environment. This chapter will describe how drug entrepreneurs coped with risks.

Problems with past research regarding drug market risks

Closed markets offer participants far greater protection from law-enforcement than the open markets. They are less visible (*i.e.* detectable) and are thus less susceptible to 'control' from law-enforcement agencies (Mark, Kleinman and Smith, 1990: 85). Customers have to be acquainted with a dealer in order to be supplied (often achieved via a referral). Consequently, closed market dealers do not openly tout their product or elicit stranger sales. However, studies detailing closed market drug dealing are far more rare (*e.g.* Waldorf *et al.*, 1995; Dunlap, Johnson and Manwar, 1994; Ward, 2010; Mohamed and Fritsvold, 2010), with markets facilitated by "the silent majority" (Mohamed and Fritsvold, 2010: 2) particularly under-researched. This silent majority refers to the "*off-the-radar collection of middle-class and upper-class drug [dealers] whose deviant behaviours are largely unknown beyond the limits of their social networks*" (2010: 2). Indeed, research has tended to focus on dealers operating within the low-socioeconomic groups (exceptions to this trend are Adler's 1985 ethnography on upper-level markets; Waldorf et al., 1995; and Mohamed *et al.*'s 2010 study on university campus dealers).

One major factor may have lessened the usefulness of many earlier studies: the growth in digital communication. The mobile phone has potentially revolutionised drug markets and its instrumental use is only now being studied. Natarajan and Clarke (1995) identified the use of telecommunications in arranging deals within open markets of the 1990s (specifically via payphones). Yet more recently McEwen (2011) described the use of pre-credited phones among dealers. Despite studies (such as Moore, 2006) suggesting a significant number of drug users use of mobile phones to procure their drugs, research documenting how these forms of digital communication are facilitating criminal trades is inadequate. To-date, no research has addressed the use of contemporary digital mediums (*e.g.* social network media) to which many mobile phone users (including drug dealers) have access.

Thus it can be argued that there is a lack of knowledge relating to contemporary dealing. It may also be argued that criminological knowledge regarding distribution is predominantly skewed towards the study of lower-end distribution, committed largely by marginalised communities, in a society that functioned prior to the sharp rise in mobile phone ownership. Since the advent of this device the need for open markets has decreased (May *et al.*, 2004) and shifts from *open* to *closed* markets have been observed in the U.S., aided by this device (Aitken *et al.* 2002). New research is needed in order to resituate previously identified risk-mitigation techniques and to identify the new methods being employed. An understanding of these measures' success is also needed if law-enforcements are to better appreciate or develop their own efforts at combating the trades.

Methods

This research is based on six years of ethnographic fieldwork with 25 individuals from May 2006 to September 2011. Access to this social network was secured several years ago when I conducted participant observations of the group for my undergraduate dissertation. This research assessed the group's 'cafeteria style' offending, particularly their affinity for violent confrontations as well as minor forms of 'hustling'. I maintained contact with the participants following fieldwork, further developing rapport. Access to others in their ever-developing network snowballed from these original participants and relationships of trust with many of these other individuals progressively developed. All of the 'core' group were aware of my research, yet it was participants who decided whether or not affiliate members (*i.e.* other peers of theirs) knew my researcher stance.

Key participants kept me up-to-date with the group's on-goings during my postgraduate research studies. I intermittently met with group members during the 48 months prior to the one-year's intensive fieldwork. I made notes and talked informally about developments regarding their lives and their expansion into the illicit markets.

During the intensive fieldwork year I spent every-second week in the field detailing individual and group activities. Upwards of 8 hours each day were dedicated to the overt observations of various participants, particularly those who did not work regular '9 to 5' jobs. In the evening I would frequent one of the businesses owned or managed by group members, at one of their houses or in one of the group's rendezvous/chilling areas (*e.g.* a particular park or car parks). I would accompany certain participants for entire days, if I felt my presence was welcomed and safe. Observational data, documented conversations and in-depth recorded semi-structured interviews were maintained during this period. During the course of conversation issues were often mentioned that would elicit an immediate questioning. Any informal interviews were quickly written up in an anonymised form either as a note on my mobile phone, or on the computer as soon as I returned to my residence (or the morning after particularly late nights); placing an audio-recorder in front of a participant whilst with their peers could often cause individuals to either 'clam-up' or boast, thus less formal conversations and observations provided the greatest body of data. In addition I also collected social network data on the group, and was granted access to financial records of four key participants.

Almost all of the protective strategies documented were observed throughout the network, however this paper draws predominantly on case studies from a selection of participants. During the intensive fieldwork-year these individuals were formally interviewed on their perceptions of risk and risk mitigation techniques they employed.

The research primarily focused on the group's involvement in their local drugs market, a medium-sized town (referred to in this chapter as '*Tanners Town*') based in the North of England. However, aspects of the research also addressed the distribution markets and networks that were based elsewhere in the U.K and abroad. Aspects of the fieldwork took place on a Mediterranean island while key participants were importing drugs and distributing these products to the seasonal British workers.

The level of access afforded to the network has generated a detail of data rarely achieved in the study of underground markets, in particular closed drugs markets. Adler (1985) used a similar approach in her 'groundbreaking' contribution to upper-level drug market literature. More recently this approach has exposed an 'elite' group of middle-class, American university closed-market drug dealers operating with apparent impunity, who the authors term 'anti-targets' (see Mohamed and Fritsvold, 2010). Unlike studies that rely on samples of offenders taken from institutional settings through prisons, court programmes or probation etc. (*e.g.* Reuter and Haaga, 1989; Pearson and Hobbs, 2001; Decker and Chapman, 2008), this study's participants were active offenders who could mostly be described as 'successful' in their crimes and who could not have been accessed via the methods cited above. Only one of the dealers was ever incarcerated for his offences, while another was arrested and convicted for a lesser drugs-related offence. Of the other 17 individuals who had involvement in the markets described, none were ever arrested or prosecuted. Due to the unobtrusive nature of closed market trading and the participants' 'success' at avoiding punishment, such a group may fall short of much criminological scrutiny. The ethnographic approach offered privileged access to a group whose illicit trade would have otherwise remained unknown and offers an understanding of how successful drug dealers avoid the state's legal enforcement.

Results

a. Characteristics of the dealer group

Research participants were embedded within a loose social-network, which facilitated a highly profitable illicit drugs market. Of the 25 participants, 19 had some involvement in drugs during the research period. Those six individuals not involved in the trade were still 'core members' of the network yet their roles and relations remained strictly social. Despite facilitating a lucrative drugs trade, the group's identity remained rooted in hedonistic and social enjoyment. The observed market included only one female dealer. This ethnically diverse group consisted of young White and British-Pakistani males in their early to late twenties. Despite more than half of the participants having been raised in lower income households the majority of the group were living 'middle class' lives, living comfortably as a consequence of their legal and illegal successes (note: by the end of fieldwork legitimate wages ranged on average between £20.000-£40.000).

The group functioned, intermittently, over a six-year period.. Of the 19 individuals who *had* engaged in drug sales a small number (n=4) continued to operate on a daily basis, while the remainder (n=15) had, over the final 12 months, began to lessen their involvement in the drugs trade and focus their efforts primarily on legitimate endeavours (full-time employment, pursuit of qualifications, establishing and running legitimate businesses).

Participants primarily managed drug delivery services at the retail level (n = 18) on a nightly basis. Though dealers' commodities of stock changed over time, the drugs most commonly sold were cocaine (n = 12), cannabis (n = 7) and ketamine- a horse sedative that can be used 'recreationally' (n = 4). *Cocaine* was retailed in either single 'gram' units or in multiples of 3 (where a discount would be applied). 'Grams' of cocaine were sold at £40. Those who ran *cannabis* delivery services at the retail level sold their product in single units weighing approximately 2 grams and charged £20. *Ketamine* sales were primarily facilitated by some of the cocaine dealers, though one former cocaine dealer limited his product to ketamine after moving away from *Tanners Town*. Ketamine retailed at £25 a gram: however, orders placed in multiples of 7 grams ("quarter ounces") were heavily discounted.

In addition to retail level sales, six individuals also had involvement in the wholesale of the following drugs over the observation period:

- Two individuals sold cocaine in half-ounce multiples (with maximum amounts rarely exceeding 71g per transaction);
- Two individuals (one of whom wholesaled cocaine) dealt ketamine in half-ounce multiples (with maximum amounts rarely exceeding 255g per transaction);
- Two individuals were involved in the cultivation of cannabis and its wholesale in one-ounce multiples (with maximum amounts rarely exceeding 255g per transaction);
- One individual sold cannabis in one-ounce multiples and in kilogram-multiples.

The group had links with Ireland (Eire), a Mediterranean island (referred to in this paper as *The Island*) and South-Central Asia. Five of the group had imported quantities of drugs onto *The Island* over several years. This included several kilograms of ketamine that were sold at retail and wholesale levels, as well as several ounces of high-level purity cocaine that was then adulterated and sold at retail level. Each shipment of ketamine weighed exactly 1 kilogram. Each transport of high-quality cocaine weighed 1 ounce and was couriered *internally* (*i.e.* a 'mule') before being diluted with benzocaine at a 1:6 ratio on The Island. Kilograms of ketamine were also transported from South-Central Asia to the U.K. before being brokered to customers in Ireland.

Network members had the ability to engage or disengage in the sale of illicit drugs, as and when desired or needed. This flexibility was made possible because of their established investments within legitimate society. Nearly all the participants had job skills and were highly employable. 'Job skills' ranged from academic qualifications such as, a Bachelor or Masters degree, qualifications and skills acquired in the armed forces, vocational qualifications such as skilled technician training, or a solid work history. Many worked in reputable occupations (*i.e.* high-level engineering, building surveying, the banking sector), others were in full-time study and a small number had established their own businesses. Only two of the participants remained unemployed for a period greater than 12 months.

Finally, the markets that these participants engaged in were 'closed'. Referrals and intermediaries were required before participants would "talk business".

> *Sol, Cocaine Wholesaler*: "If 'Johnny' off the street came up to me and was like, 'Any chance you'd be able to sort us a half [ounce] of Charlie [cocaine]?' I'd tell them, 'I dunno what you're talking about pal".

An informal 'vouch' on behalf of an intermediary served as a character reference. Trading could commence once this introduction had been made. Transactions were discreetly arranged over the phone (either verbally or via coded text messages) and conducted privately (generally in the customer's home).

b. Risks for all Involved in drug distribution

Many of the fundamental risks associated with drug distribution were present for *all* the individuals involved in the illegal drugs trade, regardless of *drug type* or the *level* at which they operated. Many of the dealers identified similar probable points-of-exposure regarding their illegal operations. Likewise, the group's perceptions of the evidential requirements needed for a successful prosecution were much the same; such risks related to the physical evidence intrinsic to their trade; communication records, financial records (*e.g.* lists of debtors), and of course, the drugs themselves. Consequently, many methods employed to mitigate these perceived risks were the same for all participants.

The risks of drug transit

As noted above, the observed markets were 'closed'. Passing trade was not elicited and transactions were generally conducted in the privacy of customers' homes. One of the perceived main risks was a chance encounter with the police whilst drugs were being transported. As the drugs were stored in 'stashes' during times of inactive trading (see 'Storage and the Dead Letterbox stash'), it was predominantly during its transportation that these individuals were in direct proximity with their illegal commodity for a prolonged amount of time. Being pulled over by the police was an infrequent but ever-present risk as retail deliveries were made on an almost nightly basis. Units were separately bagged, ready for orders placed previously. The sheer quantities of drugs being transported, on behalf of cocaine wholesalers, risked far tougher penalties if caught, but a single weekly journey (necessary for the weekly resupply of retailers) limited the likelihood of a chance encounter.

Vehicle stashes

As with the transportation of most other contraband such as cigarettes or alcohol resourceful means of hiding the drugs during transit were developed (von Lampe, 2011), These were often unobtrusive design shortcomings (*ibid*) that permitted access to a small area of the car by removing panels or forcing a gap between two panels. These stash compartments were not restricted for the use of larger consignments (*e.g.* the 'pucks' of cocaine weighing 4,5 ounce) but were also employed as storage for single units *en route* to end-users. Indeed, these dealers rarely drove their vehicles without having stashed their own personal supply of cannabis so as to mitigate even minor repercussions from the police. Though limited in space, such compartments suited the needs of all retailers who required temporary storage while *en route* to customers.

Communication interception and retrieval

Telecommunications were an essential part of the operation. As McEwen (2011: 140) states, "*mobile phones facilitate [drug dealers] interactions by making the social organisation of the transaction more efficient and less predictable*". Mobile phones ensured a direct link to suppliers or customers whenever communications were needed to coordinate logistics, payments or threaten debt enforcement.

Participants believed information communicated via mobile phones could be retrieved following the seizure of the handset or alternatively, via its interception (if the authorities had been made aware of a phone number facilitating criminal trading). If the police confiscated a suspect's phone, a device's SIM card (a removable chip which contains an internationally unique number) had the potential of granting access to the user's calls and call history, as well as text messages ('SMS messages' *i.e.* 'short message service'), although discussions during the calls would remain unknown, the messages could be read in their original form. However, if a phone number was linked to criminal activity then the police could intercept any subsequent calls and text messages. In addition, by triangulating the signal of an active phone, police could determine the location of the phone's user allowing them to track the movements of suspected criminals (Mellers, 2004).

Though participants viewed the likelihood of the police employing interception surveillance methods as fairly small, they were well aware that messages could be easily retrieved (the one participant who was successfully prosecuted, had his conviction for distribution secured on the basis of text messages the police had been able to retrieve from his handset).

One technique guarded against both the risk of telecommunication interception and data retrieval: the frequent changing of mobile phone numbers, specifically of the 'SIM card'. The replacement of the SIM was seen by many of the dealers as a basic "principle" of protection against prosecution. SIMs were incredibly cheap (as little as 99 pence) and could be purchased at various informal outlets (*e.g.* newsagents and markets) and simply inserted into any phone for immediate use. This made the use of such a method both effortless and affordable. Other studies (May *et al.*, 2001, 2004) similarly showed dealers regularly changing their handset as a means of altering their phone number. Indeed, the use of "burners" (cheap phones with a pre-paid call-time allowance) allowed dealers to dispose of the handset once credit was exhausted (McEwan, 2011). Though the exchanging of phones is a seemingly common phenomenon, the use of replacement SIMs has not as yet been documented. Such a straightforward method undermined law enforcement's ability to identify and track numbers by continually altering the identifying feature (*i.e.* the unique phone number).

Telephone network providers began incentivising the registration of SIMs. Once registered, crediting the number with (for instance) £15, gave the user a set amount of free call time or monthly bundles of text messages.

> *Sol, cocaine wholesaler.* "The thing is, it adds up. Having to phone around all day, sending texts all days, chasing people up, sorting things, arranging things, what else . . . just everything. You're always having to get in touch with people. You're spending a tenner [£10] a day just on that; might as well put 15-20 quid's worth of credit on as soon as you get it and [the provider] gives you a load of free calls and texts. That way, you're only spending a fraction of what you would otherwise".

Individuals who regularly changed their number and wanted 'free' call times and messages would ask a friend, often a female, to call the registration-line and give false details. Once activated, the SIM would be used in a dealer's mobile phone, with all phone calls relating to business being made via this bogus person's telephone number. This observation confirms that false personal information *is* being provided to mobile phone operators as a means of protection (a question posed by McEwan, 2011).

Very often their new numbers would by-pass individuals where no recent 'business' transactions had occurred, selectively updating those who were actively sourcing their product from them. These individuals would send out a generic message to all those they believed would require contact regarding their trade. Active dealers and customers would regularly receive a message from their supplier reading: "New number, Miller", or "Its Blaine, got some pucker ['*good*'] stuff". Individuals in the network were *au fait* with the meaning of such a text: *this is the number to use if you require the specific drug*. These selective updates removed either former or stray 'players' from the communication network, helping to maintain a level of insulation. All of the participants perceived telecommunication as a potential evidential source for the police yet the rigour with which SIMs were changed, varied. The wholesalers appeared most fearful of their telecommunications being intercepted by the police and of the amount of data stored on the device. Generally, retailers who had been operating within one of the markets for any prolonged period (more than a few months) were more alert to this perceived risk than those who had just started trading. At times, some 'novice' dealers would use a *registered* SIM as their point of contact for customer before a fellow dealer raised this 'error' of practice.

Modern forms of communication

Studies have long shown the instrumental importance of telecommunications in drugs markets. Natarajan *et al.* (1995) observed how public payphones once helped to connect customers with dealers. In the latter years of the twentieth century, pagers and mobile phones emerged as another 'tool' of the dealers' trade (for an early example of its prevalence see Hobbs, 1995: 24), with research even suggesting a move from open to a form of closed market dealing, facilitated by this apparatus (Aitken *et al.*, 2002). Yet, it should be stressed that in the 'digital age' dealers, as with much of the population, are progressively embracing newer forms of digital technology that are allowing ever more connections between individuals.

Dealers in the observed network progressively utilised 'digital age' technologies in the logistical planning of their deals as such technologies became more commonplace; this included social media websites and smartphone messaging applications. The emergence of 'smartphones' (phones that provide users with access to the Internet using either 3G signal or 'Wi-Fi' signals) allowed for even greater access to these modes of messaging. The most popular smartphones used by participants provided 'smartphone-to-smartphone' data and messaging transfer, allowing for the instant exchange of written script, audio recordings and digital photographs (*e.g.* 'iMessage' and 'Blackberry Messenger'). I was aware of numerous participants using these new software applications as well as social-networking sites to arrange for the transport of ketamine from abroad.

These technologies have provided resourceful criminal entrepreneurs with an array of instruments to 'exploit' (Kampschor, 2009). With the use of these 'tools' having been documented among the socially oppressed in the recent Middle Eastern uprisings (the 'Arab Spring') its application by young Western adults engaging in an illicit trade is unsurprising and to have been expected.

As "*law enforcement agencies around the world are trying to take this technology out of the hands of suspected criminals*" (McEwen, 2011: 135), the number of formats digital communications are taking are continuing to increase. To-date, no research has acknowledged the potentials for such media to facilitate drug dealing (or any other form of criminal market) despite the U.K. government's plans to extended powers of surveillance to the public's email and social medias in a bid to undermine serious crimes such as terrorism (Guardian newspaper, 02-04-12).

Coded language

As has been observed elsewhere the use of codes in telecommunications was a means of "*insulating their activities [. . .] from law enforcement*" (McEwan, 2011:141). Basic methods of encryption or coding were used during most telecommunications between individuals in the group, particularly in text messages. In addition, more-seasoned dealers maintained a physical record of debts (known as a 'tick list') using a simplistic code. The use of code words in place of blatant criminal lingo or names of fellow-participants was another attempt at limiting an indisputable evidential link between the wholesalers, the retailers and the end-users.

There was an unwritten rule (but one vehemently enforced through threats): *refrain from using drug names or specific volumes/sums from digital messaging*. Mobile phone calls were the preferred means of communication because they, unlike text messages, were not retrievable on an *ad hoc* basis: all that existed once the call ended was a log of the two phone numbers, the time of the call and its duration. The perceived likelihood of a falsely registered SIM, less than a month old, being intercepted by police was viewed as slim; thus most of the participants appeared reassured and 'safe' when conversing on their mobile. Yet there were daily instances when communication over the phone was not possible: either because the dealer was at work (a legitimate job) and unable to talk simply because of commitments and/or because it was not suitable to discuss a potentially suspicious transaction in the company of someone unaware of their trade (*e.g.* a colleague or parent). Thus, text messages were vital in delivering pieces of information when verbal communication was not appropriate for either party or when an individual could not be reached via a phone call. In these instances code-talk was essential as any message had the potential of being retrieved.

Because Sol's wholesaling operation ran on continual flows of credit (termed "black credit" by one participant) and because of the large number of individuals indebted to him each week, it was essential he maintained up-to-date records of which retailers owed him, together with the amount. The other wholesalers in this study (except Miller- a cocaine and ketamine wholesaler) relied on memory because the number of debtors was far less. Sol's concern with maintaining wholesale tick-lists was the dubiousness of having a list of names (all of whom were drug dealers, possibly known to the authorities) adjacent to a list of figures. Lists needed to be physically accessible and readily decipherable to Sol and his 'grafter' (Sol's assistant), whilst simultaneously appearing both innocuous (to avoid arousing anyone's suspicion) and justifiable (if needed, to a jury).

> *Sol*: "[It is a physical list,] it's a shopping list. For example [...] 'Persil Washing Powder £1,50'- would be a lad called Percy owes £150. There's loads of things it could be, mate. Coz people have got daft names [nicknames], haven't they? [. . .] There's lots of variations. And then just put it in a good place. For [a time] that was stuck to the fridge with a fridge magnet, plain sight".

Sol and the grafter created a simplistic means of storing important financial information by using terms commonly seen around people's kitchens, but which also carried word-associations with debtors' nick-names. These names proved useful for establishing private word-associated encryption. Others, whose custom-base was far smaller in size, relied on memory rather than records: this carried the obvious risk of being forgotten or becoming inaccurate. Financial losses through any inaccurate recollection could be factored in by retailers and some simply did not mind losing out on small sums from debtors because "*they give you that much money . . . I'm happy whatever*". Debts to wholesalers were much greater but were often spread to just a handful of retailers. I was aware of two cocaine retailers who had devised a means of coding on their mobile phones, using a contact's second phone number to store the sum (in between two 'marker' numbers). Several of the retailers physically recorded financial debts without coding, but were careful to store such lists in obscure locations in or around their residence. Any retailer who feared potential police activity and who did not want any such physical list relied on memory. It is worth noting one wholesaler had been storing debt-lists on his phone as a 'note': one evening, having been made aware of his unguarded technique the wholesaler's peers openly criticised him and commented on the necessity of such protective practises.

The intention of those employing codes was to make it problematic for police and prosecutors to demonstrate an unquestionable link to criminality through their communiqués or their financial records. However, it was not evident whether dealers even considered such codes to be potentially identifiable or usable by the police or prosecutors as evidence of their trade.

c. Risks with retail distribution

Two main aspects of retail dealing carried the greatest risks. As one participant concisely surmised:

> *Cliff*: One: is your stash [primary stock] being found; two: is being caught with it on you. Basically it's them [physically] linking the drugs to you. There's not much chance of them finding your stash or getting you with anything on you if you do basic things [. . .]. As I never have it in me house, that's me number one rule, and never carry it on me, other than hidden in that car, I can't see how they'll actually link me to me coke" (5 years into his dealing career).

The biggest risks faced by the retailers came from their requirement to store a week's worth of stock. Retailers had to ensure that the product with which they had daily contact with was out of sight at all times, away from their residence and securely hidden while in transit (see 'Vehicle stashes'). At the onset of their dealing careers drugs were often stored at home. As their enterprises expanded, drugs gradually began to be stored at friends' houses (for a small fee). Three cannabis dealers continued to store their stock in the homes of friends, offering either a small cash sum or an amount of the drug as payment. During the research a more convenient means of storing cocaine stock (the most in-demand drug) became apparent.

Storage and the 'Dead Letterbox' stash

A sufficient supply of stock was required to fulfil orders throughout the week. Having a ready supply not only maximized profits but helped retain customers. If a retailer ran out of stock they risked losing not only immediate sales, but future ones too as customers were forced to find an alternative source for the drug. Thus the availability of drugs was essential for retailers, so too was its storage, but where should one keep an abundance of an illegal substance? For individuals involved in the sale of cannabis, its sheer bulk and pungent aroma limited storage to either their own residence or (for the larger 'operations' s) a trusted peer's house/garage. Yet for cocaine and ketamine retailers whose stock was small the answer was simple: a 'stash'.

In espionage practices used throughout the globe a 'Dead Letterbox' was a technique employed, in which two parties were able to pass items between each other discreetly and without having to meet, thereby facilitating the concealment of their operation. The 'primary-stash' was a similar concept: a discreet location known to the relevant parties (*i.e.* a dealer or dealing partnership) in which a container storing the week's stock was hidden. A stash maintained a distance between the cocaine stock and a dealer's residence, stored in a location unlikely to be found. The Dead Letterbox permitted access to the drugs as and when needed, and meant individuals within a partnership could pass drugs to one another without the need of a hand-to-hand transaction. This proved useful if delivery duties changed during the course of an evening.

The choice of location for a Dead Letterbox stash was unique to each dealer/dealing partnership. Sites were mainly located off country lanes, in lay-bys away from residential or agricultural buildings, ideally "*a back lane where you wouldn't even think there was a road*" (Cliff). The location of the stash needed to tick multiple boxes in order to be seen as providing a discreet and accessible site:

- Proximity to residence
- Quiet (few houses (if any), minimal traffic)
- Provide cover (when accessing or hiding the drugs)
- Situated on a lengthy straight road (to give an early indication if traffic is coming)

Dead Letterbox locations changed frequently. For a time Bear and Cliff's cocaine was stored in a sealed, plastic 'butty box' buried in a 'shallow' patch of soil, just off a quiet lane. This required a few seconds frantic digging, a task which neither enjoyed:

> *Bear*: "Going to the stash point in *Tanners Town*, diggin' it up, that was always a sketchy fuckin' thing. Used to hate it, going down some little dark lanes . . . fuckin' hell!"
> *Cliff*: [It] scares me when I think back [. . .] Just took too long and looked too dodgy."

As a solo retailer, Cliff decided that the time spent in the vicinity of his primary-stash could be greatly reduced by keeping the stock above ground. By packaging the single units (grams) into 'new' and tiny plastic bags Cliff was able to fit 20 'grams' (almost half of his entire week's stock) into a container the size of a small egg. These unobtrusive containers were then hidden in a bramble bush or patch of nettles next to a 'marker'. Because of the container's modest size and durability it no longer needed burying. By placing his stash directly on the side of the country lane, Cliff could park-up, leave the vehicle with the engine still running, retrieve the necessary number of units from the stash (approximately a metre from the car), replace the container in the stash point and be back in the car within a ninety second time period. The container was small enough to store in the car's 'stash' when in transit.

Time spent in the vicinity of the stash was clearly the tensest aspect of their 'job' (note: separate units would have been weighed out following the weekly resupply, usually in a trusted customer's home, before being taken to the Dead Letterbox location). Individuals were at their most exposed during these times and dealers risked being linked to their entire consignments. But these stash sites were vital as they, above all other precautions, offered individuals a necessary 'peace of mind' at home:

> *Cliff*: "Early mornings are primetime for getting raided. That's when they like to do it. If you've got stuff on you or at the house you get paranoid and get worrying what happens if they do decide to kick the door in [. . .] Going to bed you can get sketchy [anxious]. But if [it's] stashed, you've got nothing to worry about. Even if they do come knocking [. . .] Say they come and you've got stuff hidden in the house then you'll be shitting yourself and, you know, you'd probably make it obvious that you've got something to hide, but if you know they've got no chance of finding anything you can relax."

d. Risks with wholesale distribution

This section focuses on one of the cocaine wholesalers, Sol. His market was the most profitable in the network and at its peak weekly sales generated him profits above £3.000. Yet two key characteristics of this market presented Sol with a unique set of risks.

Firstly, the weekly consignment of cocaine being transported from the source city (known here as *Top City*), processed (adulterated and/or weighed) and delivered to retailers could equate to half a kilogram. Such amounts were enough to ensure a custodial sentence. Being caught with such quantities of drugs would prompt penalties far tougher than those faced by the retailers and the drugs could not be so easily justified (*e.g.* claiming it for one's personal consumption). From the outset of his wholesale endeavours Sol worried about the logistical necessities of his trade, rightly fearing the police would soon be aware of his illicit business and attempt to seize him together with his drugs.

Secondly, *all* retail-level dealers acquired their weekly drug consignments on 'tick' (*i.e.* on loan).. With no legal forms of redressing unsettled contracts (a "*transactional risk*", Cross, 2000) Sol relied on violence as a means of "*resolving disputes*" (Reuter, 1985:25). Sol's debts were "*chased up*" and enforced via the threat or use of violence. He viewed such behaviour as the sole means of ensuring "*contract compliance*" (Pearson and Hobbs, 2001:41). Violent rebukes not only ensured Sol's ability to repay his debt in a given week, but also dissuaded other retailers from defaulting on their debts in the future. Violence was indispensable: it helped maintain a steady, weekly equilibrium of credit and cash flow that was essential to this market but risked drawing attention to him and his trade from the authorities.

Clearing stock

The amount of cocaine couriered from '*Top City*' only ever equalled the sum of the orders placed that week. No surplus of stock was ever brought back to the town because all weekly orders from retailers would be fulfilled in one night. Overnight storage was rare; usually the 'grafter' (Sol's assistant) collected the bulk consignment and had it 'bashed' (*i.e.* adulterated), weighed and passed to the retailers within a four-hour time period. Though cocaine residue would, of course, be detectable on the associated paraphernalia (scales, work-surfaces where the drugs were weighed and bagged, knives for cutting, *etc.*), the cocaine itself was almost never stored, making it difficult for a potential prosecution to judge the exact quantities that were being distributed. When required, the cocaine could be stored overnight at a predetermined 'stash' point (see 'Storage and the 'Dead Letterbox'). Sol was more concerned with cocaine being in his or his grafter's possession, than giving it on loan to retailers.

> *Sol*: "I'd rather get it all out, rather it be on people's heads than in [my grafter's] possession [. . .] As soon as I've got anything I just want it all out the same day- everything's out! It's not like Sainsbury's! We don't keep stock of anything".

Sol's reference to the British retail supermarket, Sainsbury's, indicates how distinct his operation was from those retailing the cocaine who needed to maintain sufficient stock to supply customers over a seven-day period. The size of the weekly orders remained at the retailer's discretion. Sol hoped that the necessary evidence needed to prosecute either him or his grafter was weakened without actually seizing this substantial consignment of cocaine stock.

Sourcing out the labour

Despite not coming into contact with the police, Sol felt it prudent to distance himself from the two main aspects of his trade: the physical logistics and the enforcement of debts. Sol employed individuals to conduct business on his behalf; these have previously been termed 'runners' (Pearson and Hobbs, 2001) but were referred to by this group as 'grafters'. Indeed, when the police came in numbers to search his properties Sol had little that directly linked him to his trade. Such a technique was justifiable only when turnover and profits were substantial, thus only one other participant (a cannabis broker) used grafters to undertake such tasks.

1. Sourcing out the labour: 'the grafter'

By employing the services of 'grafters' Sol immediately lessened both his direct and indirect involvement in the trade. Sol took managerial accountability and was responsible for compiling weekly orders from the retailers and forwarding an appropriate wholesale order to the *Top City* contact (via his mobile phone). Yet it was the grafter who undertook all logistical duties. It was Sol's 'name' attached to the product, it was his reputation which backed the black credit agreements and for over two years it was he who would "*break [your] fuckin' legs*" (former grafter, figuratively speaking) if you failed to repay the debt. Yet his physical involvement was so detached that the police raids on his properties proved fruitless.

Knowing who held the grafting role was essential (no grafter, no drugs!). Yet the 'grafting' role changed several times each year, sometimes switching hands as often as once a month. Thus another layer of insulation between Sol and the cocaine was created (Dorn *et al.*, 1998) with a continued avoidance of any physical proximity to the drug, the bags, the weighing equipment, the hydraulic press (which compacts the cocaine and diluting substance into one 'puck') or the customers.

> *Sol*: "The last year and a half, two years, I never seen it. I would purposefully avoid where it was. It wouldn't be in the house. I wouldn't even like a gram near me really—unless I was having a sniff" (Sept, 2010).
>
> *Sol*: "I don't even let the grafter or any of my mates bring it [cocaine] in the house . . . Years ago we'd have the odd party where we'd have it out and we'd all be on it, but that's coz we were daft . . . Wiser now, no fucker's allowed it near me" (Aug, 2011).
>
> (Note the change in attitude between the two dates, "wiser" and more cautious).

Prosecuting Sol by attempting to link him to any physical evidence would have been almost impossible. Because so few people were aware of who held the role (their name was not associated with the product being sold) seizing the grafter together with the drugs would have been, in the face of it, equally as difficult.

2. Sourcing out the labour: 'the muscle'

Sol's ultimate debt collection methods were self-admittedly "*ruthless*" to those who failed to adhere to rescheduled payment dates. Various overt tactics had been used to intimidate heavily indebted retailers and force their repayment: threats being made outside debtors' homes, the threatening of family members or spouses, their front doors being "*kicked in*", physical assaults and even kidnapping in the most extreme cases.

> *Sol*: "We're very forceful in the way that we do it [. . .] I've had people's mum and dad have to pay me, you know what I mean! [. . .] I had to meet [a debtor's mother] in a car park. She was crying and begging me not to give him anything again, etcetera, etcetera".

Debt collection proved just as intrinsic and vital as the logistical side and Sol was certainly successful at forcing repayments, or recouping the debt by alternative methods (*e.g.* "working-off" their remaining balance by engaging in manual labour for him). Yet towards the latter half of fieldwork observations, as overt police scrutiny befell him and his businesses, Sol had no other option but to out-source this essential role.

Sol turned to a peer who had served a prison sentence for past violent conduct. He was paid a weekly wage (a relatively meagre £100) to ensure the continuation of Sol's insurance policy; "*If you haven't got the money, you fuckin' get your head bashed in*"' (Former Grafter). His reputation superseded that of Sol's in terms of his aggression and fighting ability, a point that even Sol alluded to. His elevated reputation made the 'chasing-up' of debts easier. With two "big guys" now demanding repayments, all but a minority ensured the money was paid upon demand. However, even with the added physical kudos, there were still 'tough' individuals who needed to be coerced into repaying the debt:

> *Sol*: "I got two lads who are on the thing [debtors' list] at the moment. One's called [Mr. X], [local football hooligan], couple of rum brothers, thinks he's something- he owes me money. He was testing his luck last week but I got hold of him and he's made a good payment. It could of come to a big fuckin' ruck there [violent confrontation], but he ended up paying me. Another Lad [Mr Y], [local football hooligan], still does a bit [of cocaine retailing] and thinks he's hard [. . .] He's been a fuckin' pain in the arse, but I heard off him yesterday [. . .] I am gonna be seeing that money this weekend"

"It's not like Sainsbury's! We don't keep stock of anything."

The addition of 'The Muscle' meant that any such 'rucks' between wholesaler and retailer were avoided, thereby reducing the number of overt, violent acts needed for operations to continue. When physical intimidation was still required, Sol resigned himself to "staying at home", sending this man in his place.

e. Risks with cross-border trading

The tentacles of trade

While the majority of drugs distributed by this group remained within the U.K (cocaine, anabolic steroids, cannabis) the participants' network had begun to extend its tentacles of trade beyond the U.K. boundary. Utilising friendship ties, five of the participants were able to establish additional avenues across borders where drugs could be sourced or sold. These markets offered greater financial returns. The five individuals intermittently capitalised on these trade links over a 5-years period. At the peak of this trade, kilogram packages of ketamine were being transported from South-Central Asia to the U.K. and to a Mediterranean island. A large proportion of this product was also being forwarded on from the U.K to Ireland via ferry. This international, yet intimate trade ended as quickly as it had developed (primarily a consequence of soured relations between players) and those who had used it to their advantage were able to walk away having earned some modest returns.

'The Island'

Having spent consecutive summers working as seasonal summer-staff (working as bar "reps" which included dealing drugs) Bear and Cliff both understood 'The Island's' demand for illicit drugs as well as the market's high-profitability. The bar was popular with tourists and operated as a discreet (yet open) party drug outlet. Bear and Cliff had entered into a seasonal 'workers' culture; populated by like-minded hedonistic young men and women who were employed by the bars and clubs of the Mediterranean Island. This culture was categorised by nightly partying and almost daily recreational drug use.

Cutting out the middlemen: transporting drugs abroad

Aware of the high worker demand for drugs on the Mediterranean Island, Bear, Cliff and another friend, Miller, returned the following year, this time as semi-partnered, autonomous traders (*i.e.* not working for a bar or club). Rather than sourcing their drugs on the island (where wholesale prices were comparably high) they couriered their own bulk stock. This increased their profits and cut out the island's middlemen. Miller's personal penchant for cocaine steered him in his decision to courier packages of 'pure' cocaine, to 'process' it on the island and to retail it to workers and tourists. Bear and Cliff believed their best avenue for high turnover in drugs sales came from helping feed the ketamine habits of the seasonal worker population. Ketamine had proved to be one of the most prevalent drugs among this sub-cultural cohort and was a logical choice in terms of product.

In order to avoid more stringent airport controls and checks they felt it prudent to travel by vehicle across mainland Europe. This allowed them to take all the luxuries they wanted for a 5-months extended vacation (air-conditioning unit, games consoles, *etc.*) and allowed them to surreptitiously transport the drugs. Transporting kilograms of ketamine across several national borders required a different approach to their usual method. The consignment had to be "hidden in plain sight", in areas or in containers which would not necessarily look suspicious under x-ray or from a physical search. Their transportation method involved dissolving the ketamine in water, transferring the solution into empty bottles of 'spring water' and driving across borders (and on ferries) with it packed among countless other items. Once they had moved into their apartment on the Mediterranean Island, the solution was cooked until the water had evaporated and what remained was the ketamine. Miller flew out to the island to join his two friends. Acting as his own 'drugs mule' Miller ended up making multiple flights to and from the U.K. with his 'pure' supply sealed and stored within his person (this technique has been documented in various other markets (see Zaitch, 2002; Pearson and Hobbs, 2001). Once the cocaine had been diluted with benzocaine, the ketamine 'cooked' and both drugs weighed, the three dealers took all but a small amount of their stock to a discreet location: a secluded part of one of the island's rural areas, hidden by trees and bushes. For the duration of the season this became their primary 'stash'.

An alternative mode of cross-border transportation

While living in South-Central Asia one of the group was able to secure a bulk load of ketamine direct from its manufacturing plant. Aware of participants' demand for ketamine he had been sending packages to three of the group members. The consignments were packed within a range of consumables (spices, protein supplements *etc.*) and the ketamine itself was vacuum-sealed within one of these packages, which were then posted to the U.K. to a bogus name. The addresses belonged to paid associates of the group. If 'caught' these individuals agreed to "*play dumb*" (though whether they would indeed remain close-mouthed or pass information regarding the *intended* recipient was unknown). Numerous packages were sent in this manner, unabated by law enforcement. These loads were split into ounces and sold to retailers across the U.K. (many to the friends they had met on the Mediterranean island). Bear and Miller both utilised a shared contact in Ireland (a friend from the Mediterranean Island) to forward thousands of pounds worth of their product, until one month the contact defaulted on his debt and severed contact with the two.

Another observed method included simply storing a kilo of stock within a toiletry container and packing this amongst the suitcase luggage.

The possible success of risk-mitigation techniques

There was no way of accurately identifying whether many of the group's risk-mitigation strategies had any effect on their ability to evade capture and punishment. The only way of assessing a strategy's success was during any confrontations with law enforcement.

Cases existed where individuals would have otherwise been caught 'red handed' or successfully prosecuted had it not been for these strategies. For instance, there were several occasions where multiple police units had conducted exhaustive searches of Sol's (the cocaine wholesaler's) home and his business with the aid of 'sniffer' dog units. Also Sol's phone was confiscated by the authorities on two of these occasions, allowing the police to read any undeleted text messages (potentially access sent and received messages) and whatever call logs remained on the phone. As a consequence of his insulating strategies (there was no cocaine to be found, no messages with explicit references to drugs or money, and no paraphernalia that would indicate his role as a trader) "*they had nothing*" (Sol). In another example of successful risk-mitigation measures, Cliff was able to walk away 'clean' after having been pulled over and thoroughly searched by the police. At the time Cliff was in possession of nearly 20 units of cocaine, all ready for Friday night distribution (usually the peak trading day). Yet having stashed these in his vehicle's hidden compartment he was able to "*play it cool*", he even managed to "*act disbelievingly*" towards their allegations/suspicions of selling a 'Class A' substance; as an honest man would (managing his image via a 'front stage' performance similar to that documented by Jacobs and Miller, 1998). Following a thorough search and some roadside questioning, the officers explained the vehicle's registration had been suspected as being associated with the delivery of drugs in a local housing estate.

There are also examples that show how the failure to adhere to a "basic" strategy led to prosecutions. One retailer was caught with only two grams of cocaine on his person; the police secured their confession due to the explicit text messages on his phone. In another example an affiliated broker failed to stash a kilo of cocaine. A chance encounter with the police led to the vehicle being searched and the drugs being found.

A comment from a police source (responsible for the county in which the group operated) indicated his awareness of the main protective measures used by participants (specifically, distancing themselves from the drug). His statement also alludes to the difficulties of *proving* that such individuals deal and suggest that the measures taken by the participants may indeed have some success.

> *Police source*: "[. . .] how many people are known to be selling drugs *actually* out of their house? I think, personally, it's a low number [. . .] you can rest assured that if everybody in [the area] knows so and so's dealing drugs, then it's not a surprise to the police [. . .] What I would say to people is; "*You might say 'Steve' down the road's selling cocaine*"- right, well, fantastic! We *know* Steve down the road's selling cocaine, but the problem is proving that Steve down the road is selling cocaine. That's the issue. Unless he actually has it in his house, which he'd have to be an absolute numpty [idiot], unless he has it sitting in his living room sitting in little separate bags with people's names on, next to a wad of cash – you know, proving it, that's the problem [. . .] I think it's only the small-time people who are gonna keep anything in their house [. . .] You don't need solid evidence to get a warrant, but you've *got* to find something when you're there, it's got to be justified hasn't it [. . .] A lot of intelligence is saying; "That person is selling drugs and they keep it somewhere in a field, in [a nearby village]" [. . .] it's just difficult [to prove] isn't it"

This front-line officer was resigned to the fact many dealers could easily mitigate their primary means of enforcement. His constabulary had priorities and resources that differed significantly from larger cities and their efforts targeted overt crimes or acts of deviancy with obvious victims (*e.g.* anti-social behaviour and burglaries). Drug dealing was a criminal activity with "*no victim*". Thus, it appears that the standardised protective strategies employed by the vast number of dealers *would* limit the risk of being successfully prosecuted.

Conclusion

"*The ability to sense and avoid harmful environmental conditions is necessary for the survival of all living organisms*" (Slovic, 1987:236).

The findings in this chapter suggest that these drug dealers progressively developed and employed a variety of strategies they believed insulated them from the evidence of their criminal trades. This discreet nature of their businesses guarded them from the police, whose priorities tended to be victim-orientated (*i.e.* robberies, thefts and anti-social behaviour). Because the observed markets were closed, operations were far less exposed than in open markets. Dealers functioned without intruding upon the local environment; they were not geographically bound to a public territory, nor were they required to elicit sales from customers. Of course such markets were not infallible and a chance encounter with police risked exposing the dealer and his trade. In addition, larger-scale dealers who operated for several years could often develop a reputation, either for being 'flash' or for being 'tough' (a consequence of having to enforce debt recovery). Maintaining 'low profiles' was difficult when reputations continued to develop. Thus, the majority of the risk-mitigation strategies identified in this paper focused on limiting the amounts of evidence that *could* be used in a prosecution.

'Knowing' what the police *could* and *had* used to secure successful prosecutions was essential in the development and implementation of risk-mitigation techniques. The group's 'forensic awareness' (Beauregard and Bouchard, 2010) progressed during the course of their involvement within these markets. Their own experiences and those of their affiliates formed the foundation of their 'knowledge' regarding police techniques. High-profile media news stories, representations of law enforcement in police documentaries, and non-academic 'criminal' literatures also helped to develop their awareness. Intermittent police activity (*e.g.* raids, surveillance on some, arrests, and being pulled over under suspicion of drug related offences) all served to keep participants on the alert. Such police activity was indeed rare, but clearly a present risk. "Close calls" also served as an impetus for stringent strategies ensuring their fates did not rest solely on the (in)competencies of an officer (*e.g.* failing to make a thorough search of a drawer or failing to identify "key" evidence such as a hydraulic 'press' machine used to compact cocaine pucks). Observations indicate that the majority of the participants employed the 'standard methods' of protection (changing phone numbers, stashing the drugs, *etc.*). Without individually calculating the potential risks (or even considering if such strategies were necessary) many of the participants simply imitated their peers' protective behaviours. The rigour of their strategies varied significantly from the wholesalers to retailers and also between individual retailers. The wholesale traders were far more stringent in the application of their protective techniques, acutely aware of the tougher penalties they faced if caught.

Yet, by engaging in closed-markets and by employing the strategies discussed in this paper, these participants limited the profitability and scope of their illicit-enterprises. Firstly, the implementation of these techniques made their trade less efficient and more time consuming (particularly the need to stash one's primary stock). Secondly, dealers were unable to elicit passing trade, nor sell to individuals without an intermediary vouch. They were unable to promote or 'market' their product to a wider market, regardless of its product. Their customer bases were dependent solely upon the social networks which they had each developed over their lifetime and the snowballing of 'trusted' custom. They relied on the clandestine nature of the market to protect them from the law yet at the same time this secrecy limited turnover and profit.

Lastly, the use of contemporary digital media to facilitate aspects of the trade demonstrates that criminals, as with the broader population (in particular teens and young adults), are adapting to modern forms of communication. Such an observation supports Eck and Gersh's (2000: 245) observation of "*common, everyday, off-the shelf technology that is easy to learn and not particularly expensive*" being employed by dealers. Though the progression towards the adoption of these new medias by participants was not intended to undermine enforcement efforts, the utilisation of alternative communicative links potentially limited the use of more common police efforts (*e.g.* SMS text retrieval). With such an increase in digital formats, the interception of criminal communiqués may prove ever more problematic. If we are to fully appreciate how criminal markets develop and evolve further research is needed on the use of modern social medias that help to facilitate the ever-increasing "Glocal" economy (Hobbs, 1998).

References

Adler, P., *Wheeling and dealing: An ethnography of an upper-level drug dealing and smuggling community*. New York, Columbia University Press, 1985

Aitken, C., D. Moore, P. Higgs, J. Kelsall, and M. Kerger, The impact of a police crackdown on a street drug scene: evidence from the street, *The International Journal of Drug Policy*, 2002, vol. 13, 193-202

Anderson, E., *Code of the Street: Decency, violence and the moral life of the inner city*, London, W.W. Norton and Company, 1999

Beauregard, E., and M. Bouchard, Cleaning up your act: Forensic awareness as a detection avoidance strategy. *Journal of Criminal Justice*, 2010, vol. 38, 1160-1166

Benson, J., S. Decker, The organizational structure of international drug smuggling. *Journal of Criminal Justice*, 2010, vol. 38, 130-138

Bourgois, P., *In Search of respect: Selling crack in El Barrio*. Cambridge, Cambridge University Press, 1996

Cherbonneau, M., and H. Copes, 'Drive it like you stole it': Auto theft and the illusion of normalcy. *British Journal of Criminology*, 2005, vol. 46, 193-211

Cross, J., Passing the buck: Risk avoidance and risk management in the illegal/informal drug trade. *International Journal of Sociology and Social Policy*, 2000, vol. 20, *no. 9/10*, 68-94

Decker, S., and M.T. Chapman, *Drug smugglers on drug smuggling*. Philadelphia, Temple University Press, 2008

Desroches, F., *The crime that pays: Drug trafficking and organised crime in Canada*. Toronto, Canadian Scholar's Press, 2005

Dorn, N., L. Oette, and S. White, drugs importation and the bifurcation of risk. *British Journal of Criminology*, 1998, vol. 38, *no.4*, 537-560

Dunlap, E., B. Johnson, and A. Manwar, A successful female crack dealer: Case study of a deviant career. *Deviant Behaviour*, 1994, vol. 15, 1-25

Duyne, P.C. van, The phantom and threat of organized crime. *Crime, Law and Social Change*, 1996, vol. 24, *no.4*, 341-377

Eck, J.E. and J.S. Gersh, Drug trafficking as a cottage industry. *Crime Prevention Studies*, 2000, Vol.11, 241-271

Esbensen, F., and D. Huizinga, Gangs, drugs, and delinquency in a survey of urban youth. *Criminology*, 1993, vol. 31, *no. 4*, 565-589

Fagan, J., The social organization of drug use and drug dealing among urban gangs. *Criminology*, 1989, vol. 27, 633-669

Harocopos, A., and M. Hough, Drug dealing in open-air markets. *Problem-Oriented Guides for Police Series,* 2005, Washington D.C., U.S. Department of Justice, Guide No.31,

Hobbs, D., *Bad business*. Oxford, Oxford University Press, 1995

Hobbs, D., Going down on the glocal: The local context of organised crime. *The Howard Journal of Criminal Justice*, 1998, vol. 37, *no.4*, 407-422

Holt, T.J., K.R. Blevins, and J.B. Kuhns, Examining diffusion and arrest avoidance practices among Johns. *Crime and Delinquency*, 2009, doi:10.1177/0011128709347087, 1-24

Hutton, F., Risky business: Gender, drug dealing and risk. *Addiction Research and Theory*, 2005, vol. 13, *no. 6*, 545-554

Jacobs, B.A., 'Crack dealers' apprehension avoidance techniques: A case of restrictive deterrence. *Justice Quarterly*, 1996a, vol. 13, *no. 3*, 359-381

Jacobs, B.A., Crack dealers and restrictive deterrence: Identifying narcs. *Criminology*, 1996b, vol.34, 409-431

Jacobs,. B.A, and J. Miller, Crack dealing, gender, and arrest avoidance. *Social Problems*, 1998, vol. 45, *no. 4*, 550-569

Johnson, B.D., and M. Natarajan, Strategies to avoid arrest: crack sellers' response to intensified policing. *American Journal of Policing*, 1995, vol. XVI, *no. 3/4*, p 49-69

Kampschor, B., Cell phones ideal for crime. In: *Organized Crime and Corruption Reporting Project*, August 11th, 2009. Available at; http://www. Reportingproject.net/ (consulted April, 2012).

Klein, M., C. Maxson, and L. Cunningham, "Crack" street gangs and violence. *Criminology*, 1991, vol. 29, *no. 4*, 623-650

May, T., A. Harocopos, P.J. Turnbull, and M. Hough, Serving up: The impact of low level police enforcement on drug markets, *Crime Prevention and Detection Series Paper 133*. Policing and Reducing Crime Unit, Home Office, London, 2001

May, T., and M. Hough, Drugs markets and distribution systems. *Addiction Research and Theory*, 2004, vol. 12, *no. 6*, 549-563

Mark, A., R. Kleinman, and K.D. Smith, State and local drug enforcement. In Search of a Strategy, 1990. *Crime and Justice*, vol. 13, 69-108

McEwan, R. N., Tools of the trade: Drugs, law and mobile phones in Canada. *New Media Society*, 2011, vol. 13, 134-149

Mellers, B., Forensic examination of mobile phones. *Digital Communication*, 2004, vol.1, 266-72

Mohamed, A.R., and E.D. Fritsvold, *Dorm room dealers: Drugs and the privileges of race and class*. London, Lynne Rienner Publishers, 2010

Moore, K., Sort drugs make mates: The use and meaning of mobiles in dance music club culture, In: K. O'Hara *et al.* (eds,) *Consuming music together: social and collaborative aspects of music consumption technologies*. New York, Springer, 2006

Natarajan, M., R. Clarke, and B. Johnson, Telephones as facilitators of drug dealing. *European Journal on Criminal Policy and Research*, 1995, vol.3, *no. 3*, 137-153

Natarajan, M., and M. Belanger, Varieties of drug trafficking organizations: A typology of cases prosecuted in New York City. *Journal of Drug Issues*, 1998, vol. 28, 1005-1025

Pearson, G., and D. Hobbs, Middle market drug distribution. *Home Office Research, Development and Statistics Directorate*, 2001, Home Office Research Study 227

Pearson, G., Drugs markets and dealing: From 'street dealer' to 'Mr Big. In: M. Simpson et al., *Drugs in Britain: supply, consumption and control*. Hampshire, Palgrave MacMillan, 2007

Paoli, L., and M. Planck, *Pilot project to describe and analyse local drugs markets - First phase final report: Illegal Drug markets in Frankfurt and Milan*. Lisbon, EMCDAA, 2000

Reuter, P. *The organization of illegal Markets: An economic analysis*, Honolulu, University Press of the Pacific, 1985

Reuter, P., and J. Haaga, *The organization of high-level drug markets: An exploratory study*. Santa Monica: RAND, 1989

Sandberg, S., Black drug dealers in a white welfare state: Cannabis dealing and street capital in Norway. *British Journal of Criminology*, 2008, vol. 48, *no.5*, 604-619

Slovic, P., Perception of risk. *Science*, 1987, vol. 236, *no. 4799*, 280-285

Van DeMheen, D. and P. Gruter, Interventions on the supply side of the local hard drug market: Towards a regulated hard drug trade? The case of the city of Rotterdam. *Journal of Drug Issues*, 2004, vol.34, *no. 1*, 145-161

VanNostrand, L. and R. Tewksbury, The motives and mechanics of operating an illegal drug enterprise. *Deviant Behavior: An Interdisciplinary*, 1999, vol. 20, 57-83

Venkatesh, S. A. *American project: The rise and fall of a modern ghetto*. Cambridge MA, Harvard University Press, 2000

von Lampe, K., Re-conceptualizing transnational organized crime: Offenders as problem solvers, 2011, *International Journal of Security and Terrorism*, vol.2, *no.1*, 1-23

Waldorf, D., and S. Murphy, Perceived risks and criminal justice pressures on middle class cocaine sellers, *Journal of Drug Issues*, 1995, vol.25, 11-32

Ward, J., *Flashback: drugs and dealing in the Golden Age of the London rave scene*, Devon, Willian Publishing, 2010

Zaitch, D., *Trafficking cocaine: Colombian drug entrepreneurs in the Netherlands*. The Hague, Kluwer Law International, 2002

Learning the ABCs of deceptive practices in banking

Ciril Keršmanc and Meta Ahtik[1]

The debate and method in the criminological context

Critical criminologists tend to expound the idea that substantive and procedural criminal law has (so far) evolved primarily as an instrument to control the poor and those without any political influence (the 99%) and is as such (currently) inappropriate for sanctioning those with power (the 1%) (*e.g.* Kanduč, 1997). While not a critical criminologist himself, Edwin H. Sutherland opened the hunting season on the 1% by focusing on what he defined as white collar crime.[2]

Sutherland's White Collar Crime (1983) is an appropriate common denominator to bring the following discussion into a criminological context. Chapter 10 in the second part of White collar crime entitled "Financial manipulations" is of particular importance for our discussion. In it Sutherland focuses on "*practices of corporations or of their executives which involve fraud or violation of trust. These practices include embezzlement, extortionate salaries and bonuses, and other misapplications of corporate funds in the interest of executives or of the holders of certain securities; they include public misrepresentation in the form of stock market manipulations, fraud in sale of securities, enormous inflation of capital, inadequate and misleading financial reports and other manipulations*" (Sutherland, 1983: 153).

The author himself notes that his statistical analysis is not complete. Levenstein's famous observation that statistics are like bikinis, in the sense that what they reveal is suggestive, but what they conceal is vital, holds especially true for complex

---

1 Ciril Keršmanc, LL.M., Junior researcher at the Institute of Criminology at the Faculty of Law Ljubljana and a criminal law Ph.D. student at the University of Ljubljana, Faculty of Law. [ciril.kersmanc@pf.uni-lj.si] Meta Ahtik, Ph.D., Assistant Professor at University of Ljubljana, Faculty of law (Member of the Chair of Legal and Economic Sciences).

2 As is generally known, Sutherland's term was criticized early on due to its inherent ambiguity and vagueness. One of its harshest critics was Tappan, who denounced it as creating a criminological no-man's land between civil law and criminal law by pointing out that ". . . the term has spread into vacuity" (Tappan, 1947: 98,99). Wheeler and Kahan provide a succint overview of the white collar crime idea and its spin-offs and ascribe its endurance to the fact that it »reflects deeply felt concerns that make psychological and social sense, even if they present logical ambiguities." (Wheeler and Kahan, 2002).

economic crime. Deisinger commented in 1983 that we are dealing with a relatively uncharted territory which is of vital importance (Deisinger, 1983: 190). Namely, such types of crimes usually stay hidden in the (undetected) dark figure of (economic) crime. That is to say, despite valiant efforts in a few countries[3], even today "*fraud data elsewhere in the world are too poor and/or intermittent to provide an adequate basis for knowing whether fraud is rising or if more of the 'dark figure' of undetected fraud has been discovered*" (Levi and Smith, 2011:1). Furthermore "*even in the best countries fraud data are quite poor and this is an area that requires some redress if empirical criminology is not to continue to neglect white collar crimes*" (Levi, 2012: 270).

It should therefore come as no surprise that Sutherland in his time relied heavily on individual court cases and newspaper articles for his analysis. In the chapter on financial manipulations he paints the picture case by case thus presenting us with generic subtypes of individual contentious practices (Sutherland, 1983: 153-173). Using this method Sutherland subtly avoids what Mills critically described as abstracted empiricism that fetishes the Method and the Technique on the one hand, as well as the cloudy obscurity of overly abstract concepts (Mills, 2000: 50-75; 223-226) on the other hand.

This chapter tries to emulate Sutherland's method with a view on presenting the evolution of deceptive practices in banking. It could be said that it falls into the group of papers contributing to the discussion on financial manipulations in White Collar Crimes' Chapter 10.[4] Content wise, one final word of wisdom by Sutherland seems appropriate, namely that "*[m]any of white collar crimes can be appreciated only by persons who are experts in the occupations in which they occur. A corporation often violates a law for a decade or longer before the administrative agencies or the public becomes aware of the violation*" (Sutherland, 1983: 59). This means that for a relevant analysis of the contentious practices one must provide some prior technical clarifications and context. In addition to that, a scientific approach that makes social science matter also requires that we identify a specific social problem and critically evaluate the solution to the problem which is being proposed by those in power (Flyvbjerg, 2001).

The problem we will be addressing are the exorbitant bonuses in the banking sector and the regulatory problems and failures connected to it. Following the presentation of the UK prime minister's road towards a 'moral capitalism' in the

---

3 Levi and Burrows offer an in depth analysis of problems with measuring the impact of fraud in the UK and paint a rather dim picture of the state of data collecting, especially in connection to complex (business) frauds (Levi; Burrows, 2008) that are the focus of this paper and at the centre of the white collar crime concept. See also Levi *et al.*, 2007.

4 Coincidence would have it that the practices covered in this particular chapter usually precede bankruptcy proceedings which are referred to as "Chapter 11" proceedings in the US.

next section we proceed to show through individual case studies how it would most likely lead us to a dead end or rather back to where we started off in the first place, even if it was meant as anything more than mere political puffery. The type of case selection we are using in this paper is information-oriented selection. As Flyvbjerg noted:

> "When the objective is to achieve the greatest possible amount of information on a given problem or phenomenon, a representative case or a random sample may not be the most appropriate strategy. This is because the typical or average case is often not the richest in information. A-typical or extreme cases often reveal more information because they activate more actors and more basic mechanisms in the situation studied. In addition it is often more important to clarify the deeper causes behind a given problem and its consequences than to describe the symptoms of the problem and how frequently they occur. Random samples emphasising representativeness will seldom be able to produce this kind of insight; it is more appropriate to select some few cases chosen for their validity (Flyvbjerg, 2006:229)."

Given that one of the aims of the paper is to present the evolution of deceptive practices in banking we are analysing what we consider to be paradigmatic cases (Flyvbjerg, 2006: 230)[5] for each of the three identified evolutionary stages in deceptive banking practices – the local, the international and the public-private partnership or collusion phase.

---

5 Flyvbjerg summarizes various strategies for the selection of samples and cases in two big groups: A. Random selection (with either a random sample or a stratified sample) and B. Information-oriented selection (with either 1. Extreme/deviant cases, 2. Maximum variation cases, 3. Critical cases and 4. Paradigmatic cases). ". . . a case can be simultaneously extreme, critical and paradigmatic. He defines paradigmatic cases as those that one uses to "develop a metaphor . . . those that characterise more general characteristics of societies in question" (Flyvbjerg, 2006: 230, 232). He goes on to ask himself "How does one identify a paradigmatic case? How does one determine whether a given case has metaphorical and prototypical value" and provides the following answer: "...the paradigmatic case transcends any sort of rule-based criteria. No standard exists for the paradigmatic case because it sets the standard . . . Like other good craftspeople, all that researchers can do is use their experience and intuition to asses whether they believe a given case is interesting in a paradigmatic context and whether they can provide collectively acceptable reasons for the choice of case." In the end it is up to the reader to asses if our case selection for deceptive practices in banking meet the standard.

The road to "moral capitalism" – a dead end?

David Cameron, who in a speech on 19-1-2012 put forward his vision of a "moral capitalism":

> "Markets can fail . . . where they work properly, open markets and free enterprise can actually promote morality. Why? Because they create a direct link between contribution and reward; between effort and outcome . . . First, we need to be clear about the very specific mistakes of the last decade. Second, we need to put the right rules and institutions in place to correct them . . . The bonus culture, particularly in the city has gone out of control . . . the link between risk, hard work, success and reward has been broken . . . As the governor of the Bank of England reminded us (this week) excessive undeserved bonuses reduce lending that is available to small businesses. Large rewards for failure, when companies are suffering, means that even less is left over for customers and for shareholders" (Cameron, 2012a; Cameron, 2012b).

These are the words of the British prime minister. The governor of the Bank of England, Mervyn King, went even further with the articulation of the central problem "*. . . a market economy rests not just on incentives, but on the acceptance that the distribution of rewards is fair*" (West, 2012).

Time has shown that the initial political and legislative response to the global financial and economic crisis (now turning into a social one as well) was a miss in many countries. As Dorn put it "*The belated regulatory activism and policy responses of 2008-2009, including rescuing private sector actors who had taken unsustainable market positions, remain controversial . . . The crisis and the rescues will have consequences that will be felt for decades.*" (Dorn, 2010: 235). The segment of the 'financial crisis management' policy which is of particular interest for our debate is how the governments tackled the broken link between contribution and reward in the banking sector.

In the UK they proposed a maximum limit on bank bonuses for those banks that received state aid (Winning and Guevarra, 2012). The UK is of course not the only state where excessive bonuses are being paid out either directly in the form of cash or indirectly in the form of option contracts and the possibility of their subsequent capitalisation. "Obscene" bonuses in the banking sector were high on the agenda for the president of the US for a while, that is before he proposed the so called "Financial Crisis Responsibility Fee" in 2010 ("Massive profits and obscene bonuses motivated bank tax", 2010).[6] The EU tackled the problem with its

---

6 Interestingly enough the proposed measure has not been adopted (yet). Initially the measure provided for an additional tax of "0,15% on the liabilities of large financial

Directive 2010/76/EU with which it amended Directive 2006/48/EC and 2006/49/EC as regards capital requirements for the trading book and for re-securitisations, and the supervisory review of remuneration policies. Slovenia for example implemented the said Directive into its legal system via an amendment to the Banking Act in July 2011. According to the change, the system of rewards in the banking sector is supposed to be based on a longer track record (several years) of positive results (see Simoneti, 2010: 55-65). The local outrage regarding a 1 million Euro bonus paid out to the former CEO of the biggest Slovenian bank, NLB, prompted the adoption of the Act on additional taxation of a part of managers' incomes in the period of financial and economical crisis (2009).[7] This Act preceded the abovementioned legislative enactments in the UK, US and the EU. As one of the sponsors of the bill commented: "*the extra taxation will neutralise payments of undeserved bonuses and rewards to management boards in the time of financial and economic crisis*" ("Poslanci složni glede dodatnega davka", 2009).

While the identification of excessive bonuses as a problem seems to be correct, we should ask ourselves whether the described legislative approaches address the underlying cause of the problem. An undifferentiated approach to bank bonuses can turn out to be problematic. Instead of resolving the causes systemically, current legislative measures are addressing the symptom, while the real cause remains undiagnosed and untreated. We should also ask ourselves whether or not the assumption that we are dealing with a short term acute problem limited to the time of the financial and economic crisis is correct.

Even though the problem is much more visible in the time of the crisis, it is rooted in the period of economic growth. It is then when the lax borrowing standards and the battle for profits result in loans which are unlikely to be repaid later on (Levi, 2012: 285). Times of economic growth also give rise to numerous 'innovative' contracts in the banking sector and in general, whose function is not financial intermediation between those with assets and those without. Instead, their main aim becomes "merely transferring assets from one drawer to another" and their "by-products" of various transactional fees and commissions covering all the participants to the transactions. Such transactions incrementally increase the balance sheets of the agents in the financial sector, while they lead to financial deepening of

---

institutions. It would apply only to those companies with assets of more than $50 billion – a group estimated at about 50." The provision can at the moment still be found in a proposed bill called "Rebuild America Act", currently before the US House of Representatives H.R.5727.IH (http://thomas.loc.gov/cgi-bin/bdquery /z?d112:h.r. 05727:) and the US Senate S.2252.IS (http://thomas.loc.gov/cgi-bin/bdquery/z?d1 12:s.02252:) under subtitle D "Making Wall Street Take Responsibility". Mere political puffery? We shall see when the US presidential elections pass, if not before.

7 The Act is popularly known in Slovenia as the »Kramar Act« - i.e. it was named after the CEO who received what was deemed an unacceptable bonus.

an economy and can result in bloated GDPs.[8] What is of particular relevance is the fact that such bloated balance sheets are among the factors that form the basis for paying out bank bonuses and rewards. On top of the incentive system itself, there are other various forms of accounting manipulations that have the same effect.[9]

The ABCs of deceptive practices in banking

Finances can be complicated and deceptive finances even more so. For this reason we will elaborate our thesis by means of a number of actual cases incrementing the complexity of deception as well as the system. Each of the following case studies adds another layer of complexity to the story and brings to light additional deficiencies of our regulatory framework and the "Cameron" hypothesis. The selected cases are in our opinion paradigmatic examples of the evolution of deceptive practices in banking.

We start by examining specific issues raised by our local paradigmatic case study "Com-pact" (Section **a**). Then we take a look at how the process of globalisation provided additional venues and opportunities for deceptive practices by circumventing or at least hindering the work of "local" regulatory agencies in our second paradigmatic case - The Lehman Brothers Inc. "Repo 105" (Section **b**). While the previous case studies are limited to the private sector, we take a look at how in the next phase of the evolution private (inter)national agents start to provide their deceptive services to individual states to circumvent their international obligations. We point out how in the end states themselves succumb to (systemic) temptation and internalise or at the very least acquiesce to deceptive practices which they are supposed to be curtailing (Section **c**).

a. Examining the local phase – The 'Com-pact' paradigm case

It does not happen very often that the Bank of Slovenia (BoS) conveys a notice to the prosecutor's office that a crime has allegedly been committed. In the case

---

8 One could argue that the mere scale of financial transactions on a global level brought us to the point where a substantial part of economic growth is dependent on various financial products (leading to an increase in the proportion of financial services in relation to the real sector) and as such in a way fictitious.

9 An important factor in the increase of the scale of accounting manipulations were (in many instances justifiable) 'fair market value' valuations of assets in the balance sheets of the companies. Notable among abuses of this sort are for example Parmalat and Enron (*see* Belak, 2008: 9; Koletnik and Kolar, 2008: 85).

which we call "Com-pact"[10] it did just that back in 1997. Based on the notice filed by Slovenian main banking supervisory and regulatory authority, several indictments were brought to the prosecutor's office against four top management members of a privately owned bank. The investigation phase of the proceedings focused on several different offences, however the one of particular interest to us is the charge of abuse of position or rights under article 244 of the Slovenian Penal Code (Official Gazette of the Republic of Slovenia, 63/1994).[11]

The management team was charged to have circumvented the regulatory framework set by BoS, which required banks to maintain special reservations in their balance sheets as a protection against potential losses due to bad loans. What they essentially did was a temporary loan swap for the duration of the reporting period. As a result of the swap the bank's balance sheet showed a profit, while it should have shown a loss. The fictitious or falsely demonstrated profit was distributed among the accused together with other shareholders and management members.

Because understanding the technique is the key to spotting similar deceptive practices elsewhere, we need to delve a bit further into the technicalities of the transaction. The regulatory framework set out by BoS had rules regarding how the banks have to classify their loans. An individual loan could be classified as an A, B, C, D or an E loan, A being the highest rating. There were objective and subjective criteria for rating an individual loan. The rating was done by banks themselves and was (at least in theory) supervised by BoS. The objective criteria were based on how regular loan repayments from a certain borrower were – its track record so to speak. The subjective part of the criteria was more of a grey area and was left up to

---

10 The docket number of the case at the first instance court in Ljubljana was I K 6226/2010. Since 1997, when the proceedings started, two of the suspects died (the circumstances of their deaths were not suspicious), the other two were acquitted by the first instance court in December 2011. The prosecutor filed an appeal, however given the statute of limitations it is unlikely that the case will end any differently even if the prosecutor is successful with his appeal.

11 At the time of the act itself, Article 244 read as follows: "(1) Whoever, in the performance of an economic activity, abuses his position or acts beyond the limits of the rights inherent in his position or fails to perform any of his duties with a view to procuring an unlawful property benefit for himself or for a third person or to causing damage to the property of another, whereby such conduct does not constitute any other criminal offence, shall be sentenced to imprisonment for not more than five years.
(2) If a large loss of property has been caused or a large property benefit acquired through the committing of the offence under the above paragraph and if the perpetrator intended to cause such loss of property or to gain such property benefit, he shall be sentenced to imprisonment for not more than eight years." This article has since been amended and renumbered – the same crime can now be found under Article 240 of the Slovenian Criminal Code (Official Gazette of the Republic of Slovenia 55/2008 with subsequent changes).

the banks themselves from the start. In any case, depending on the quality of their loans/borrowers the banks were required to form special reservations in their balance sheets as a protection against potential losses due to bad loans. The lower the rating of the borrower the larger the percentage of the required special reservations in terms of the given loan. What is essential to understand is that the special reservations reduced the banks' profit/bottom line. In case a certain bank had a particularly bad loan structure, the reservations would increase, potentially to the point at which the bank showed no profit at all, but a loss. This was actually what would have happened in our "Com-pact" case, were it not for the following "trick" the accused came up with.

Not long before the date of drawing up the bank's balance sheets, they reached a deal with their borrowers to temporarily swap their loans until after the reporting period. The bank on its books no longer showed exposure to borrower E (lowest rating), but instead to borrower A (highest rating). As a result fewer special reservations had to be made. Once the reporting period was over they returned to the initial position. The following diagram shows exactly how the transaction itself was completed.

Figure 1
Diagram of a temporary loan swap of bank's borrowers with different ratings

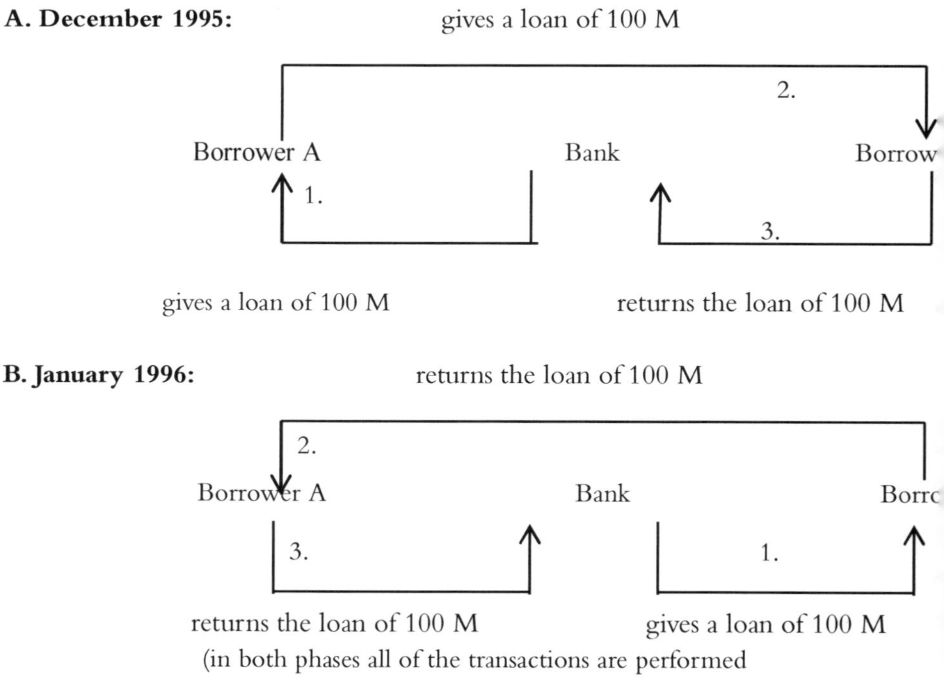

(in both phases all of the transactions are performed on the same day/at the same time)

The diagram shown above represents not a case of an individual transaction, but the method which was used by this particular bank in several combinations of its commercial borrowers with ratings A and E – hence the name of this paradigmatic case "Com-pact". The technique itself had several variations as well. Essentially the same transactions could be carried out via regular loan/credit contracts and the creation of an actual cash flow (real deposits and withdrawals). Alternatively the second phase of the transaction could be achieved by netting. We can even start off with an assignation: the original borrower E (assignor) gets a loan from borrower A (obligor) and gives an order to pay the amount of the credit to the bank (assignee) so his debt is temporarily paid off. Beforehand the bank gives A a short term loan which covers the amount of the loan given to E by A.

The 'Com-pact' technique seems to have no other purpose than cleaning the bank's balance sheets in order to paint a better financial picture which ultimately makes it possible to pay out dividends to shareholders and bonuses to the management teams. What should also be emphasised is that the 'fictitious/false' profits result not only in real dividends and bonuses, but can also lead to an extra income for the state through taxation. Thus even the state itself indirectly (though unknowingly) participates in the spoils, which raises the issue of its incentive to actively pursue such machinations. At least as long things go well, the scheme continues. But the blame game starts when things begin going badly in an (inevitable) economic downturn for the bank or for the economy. The system which was there to prevent bad loans and provide a safety net was effectively dismantled in the "Com-pact" case, the bank in question went down.

Event though BoS was the one who ultimately brought the contentious practice to the prosecutor's notice, there seems to have been a tacit tolerance/acquiescence for it up to that point. At the final hearing the judge read, among others, a statement of one of the witnesses who testified that what they were doing was being done in other banks as well and that they understood the position of BoS to be that "it was not desirable, but also not punishable".[12]

Summe (2011) points at a similarly complacent stance by the US Securities and Exchange Commission (SEC) regarding the notorious Lehman Brothers Holding Inc. case.:

> ". . . Lehman Brothers consistently ignored its own risk thresholds through its commercial real estate investments . . . the SEC ignored the bank's disregard of those risk limits. In addition, the bank's stress test omitted the inclusion of its riskiest assets, its commercial real estate portfolio." As Mr Valukas testified: "The SEC was aware of these excesses and simply acquiesced". . . "The

12 It should be noted however, that the witness in question was at the time an employee of the bank which conducted the transactions.

liquidity of the investment bank was alarmingly low . . . [T]he bank's liquidity pool included assets used as deposits with its clearing banks which was a clear breach of regulatory guidelines. The SEC knew of this breach, but it again acquiesced . . . [T]he bank relied on a quarter-end approach to lover its leverage ratio by moving certain assets off its balance sheet on a temporary basis. The SEC never appears to have inquired about this practice, despite the fact that most other banks had ceased using this approach" (Summe, 2011).

It is the last of the irregularities which Summe indicates that will be the focus of our next (sub)section.

b. Examining the global phase – The "Lehman Brothers Holding Inc." paradigm case

15. September 2008 is the date when the "Chapter 11" bankruptcy proceedings were started for one of the largest investment banks in the world - Lehman Brothers Holding Inc. (LBHI). According to some, this date was also the break-out point of the ongoing global financial and economic crisis.[13] On 11 March 2010, a 2208 page long report with a 38 page long table of contents was published as part of the bankruptcy proceedings *In re* Lehman Brothers Holdings, Inc. (Report of Anton R. Valukas [Report], 2010). The entire third volume of the Report is dedicated to the analysis of the accounting gimmick called 'Repo 105' (Report, 2010: 732-1053).[14] What follows are some of the highlights of the technique from the Report, which in our opinion demonstrate the global paradigm of deceptive practices in banking.

The business strategy of LBHI was based on aggressive growth and consequently also on a high financial leverage[15] (they borrowed a lot). This strategy was nothing unusual in the period of a protracted and continuous economic growth worldwide. LBHI stood out only in terms of scale. At the first signs of an economic downturn, the management team of LBHI consciously decided to increase its leverage ratio (borrowing even more) counting that things are going to turn around sooner rather than later, when they will ultimately capitalise on their investments. However, in the meantime it was of vital interest to them to keep

13 For the causes of the crisis, its start in the USA and its spread worldwide, see for example Štiblar, 2009: 102-119.

14 Repo 105 has since found its place in wikipedia: http://en.wikipedia.org/wiki/Repo_105

15 Leverage (ratio) is a measure of a company's financial health so to speak: it is basically defined in financial terms as a fraction between company's borrowings and stockholders' funds.

their financial rating in line with that of its competitors to secure further loans.

Net leverage[16] was one of the key financial indicators for the rating agencies and also for LBHI's lenders. As a result this financial metric was an important factor for LBHI's stock price and the amount of bonuses paid out either in the form of shares or stock options to its management. There was therefore a strong incentive for everyone involved to improve this financial indicator. This is where the accounting gimmick 'Repo 105' came into place.

Repurchase agreements (repos) are temporary sales of financial assets with an obligatory repurchase. The sale of financial instruments is followed by repurchase on a set date in the future of the same amount and kind of financial instruments at a pre-agreed price (Mishkin, 2006: 29; Čok, Košak and Berk Skok, 2012:10; Rozman, 2010: 1107).[17] With an ordinary repo, the transaction was recorded as a loan/credit and the temporarily 'collateralised' financial instruments or other assets were still recorded in LBHI books. With 'Repo 105', on the other hand, the transaction was recorded as a 'true' sale and the financial instruments went off the LBHI books. LBHI used the money it received to bring down its other loans. The overall effect of the transaction was an artificially lowered/deceptive net leverage ratio (Report, 2010: 752-763).[18]

So how did one (re)qualify a repo transaction from a loan to a sale for accounting purposes? LBHI legal team found a lacuna in the now obsolete[19] Statement of Financial Accounting Standards – SFAS 140 issued by the US Financial Accounting Standards Board (FASB). The distinguishing factor was whether or not we can establish that there was a "surrender of control" regarding the financial instruments that were being transferred. The SFAS 140 set out how to

---

16 Lehman's net leverage ratio was calculated as net assets divided by tangible equity capital. Net assets were calculated from total assets by excluding cash and securities segregated and on deposit for regulatory and other purposes, collateralized lending agreements and identifiable intangible assets and goodwill. Tangible equity capital was composed of stockholders' equity and junior subordinated notes and excluded identifiable intangible assets and goodwill.

17 Repurchase agreements are used by numerous central banks (including the ECB) as an instrument to achieve their monetary policies. Commercial banks and other economic subjects conduct repo transactions for any of the following reasons: 1. Need for liquidity, 2. Need for a specific type of securities, 3. Collateralized loans, 4. Insurance against interest rate risks, 5. Adjustment of the investment structure, 6. Increasing exposure as a strategy to capitalise on market expectations (Čok, Košak and Bert Skok, 2012: 12-13; Snoj, 2001:48).

18 To use an automobilistic analogy to demonstrate the overall effect of the trick; imagine you are buying a car and have narrowed down your choice to either car A or car B which are identical in every way except with respect to how much gasoline they consume. A uses 17 l/km and B uses 15 l/km – for a rational consumer the decision is obvious. Compare with data in Table 2.

19 The upgraded version of the same standard can now be found under "Codification Topic 860 Transfers and Servicing" of the US Accounting Standards Codification.

determine, if the criteria of surrendering control have been met.[20]

Because LBHI could not obtain a legal opinion in the US which would confirm that their repo transactions do indeed meet the criteria of a 'true sale', they sought legal council from their more innovative legal cousins in the UK. The UK based law firm Linklaters issued an opinion based on the UK legal system and exclusively for the UK subsidiary of LBHI – LBHIUK. In it, they find that, we can indeed consider repo transactions to be a true sale, if the underlying financial assets are liquid enough, *i.e.* there is a market for them and they can be readily bought and sold on this market.[21] Based on this opinion 'Repo 105' transactions were conducted through LBHIUK for all of the members of LBHI. In this way they were excluded from consolidated balance sheets of LBHI in the US.[22] As the FASB held that "*when the collateralization was between 98% and 102%, a repo borrower maintained effective control over transferred assets and consequently the assets could not be moved off the borrower's balance sheet*" (Report, 2010: 778, footnote 2999). The show of a true sale required an above standard premium in the percentage of the collateralised assets (Report, 2010: 777). LBHI considered that the above standard premium starts with at least 5% – hence the name 'Repo 105'. LBHI therefore paid an above standard premium for its 'repo trick'. One can get an idea of the cumulative (direct) cost and scale of "Repo 105" transactions for LBHI when we factor in that the transactions began as early as 2001 (The people of the State of New York v. Ernst & Young LLP, 2010: para. 20).[23]

---

20 According to SFAS 140 The following criteria had to be met:
"1. The transferred assets have been isolated from the transferor-put presumptively beyond the reach of the transferor and its creditors, even in bankruptcy or other receivership.
2. Each transferee (or, if the transferee is a qualifying special-purpose entity (SPE), each holder of its beneficial interests) has the right to pledge or exchange the assets (or beneficial interests) it received, and no condition both constrains the transferee (or holder) from taking advantage of its right to pledge or exchange and provides more than a trivial benefit to the transferor.
3. The transferor does not maintain effective control over the transferred assets through either (1) an agreement that both entitles and obligates the transferor to repurchase or redeem them before their maturity or (2) the ability to unilaterally cause the holder to return specific assets, other than through a cleanup call."

21 A continental lawyer needs but to remember what he was thought in school regarding *genus* and *species* to understand the gist of the opinion. Namely if there is little or no liquid market for the financial instrument, the object is more of a *species*. This means that it cannot be substituted at given that it must be returned later on – there was therefore no surrender of control. Alternatively if the financial instrument is liquid/marketable, then it is a generic thing, meaning it can be substituted by a generic thing of the same kind and quality. In such a case, surrender of control is plausible as Linklaters opined.

22 The variations in the technique itself is detailed in the Report, 2010: 788-792.

23 Based partly on the Report from the bankruptcy proceedings, the Attorney general of the State of New York filed a so called Martin Act suit against LBHI's auditors Ernst & Young LLP who gave their stamp of approval on LBHI's deceptive balance sheets between 2001 and 2008. Ernst & Young is supposed to have received $ 150 ml for its services from LBHI

Table 1
The growth of 'Repo 105' transactions and the effect of the transactions on LBHI reported net leverage

Reporting period per quarter:	'Repo 105' use in billion $	Reported net leverage	Leverage without 'Repo 105'	Difference	Difference (in %)
Q4 2007	38,6	16,1	17,8	-1,7	-10,5
Q1 2008	49,1	15,5	17,3	1,8	-11,6
Q2 2008	50,4	12,1	13,9	-1,8	-14,8

This case is a prime example of how the globalisation of financial markets, without accompanying global standards and regulations can be (ab)used.[24] The direct effect on LBHI's financial metrics can be discerned from Table 1 above.[25] Among the indirect effects were also bonuses and rewards for LBHI's management team either in the form of stocks or stock options. The famous Thomas theorem states that "when people define situations as real, then they are real in their consequences". Creative interpretation of accounting standards made it possible for the LBHI's management team and a select few of informed shareholders who "capitalised" their shares before the crash to create real personal wealth by painting a false picture of the financial state of their company. Despite the fact that in the LBHI case we are dealing with a systematic, planned, technically sophisticated and brilliantly executed deception with (arguably) systemic harms, the authors of this paper are currently unaware of any confirmed convictions of the perpetrators who executed it. But given the planned and systematic nature of these integrity breaches, two criminal elements are clearly identifiable: intent and cooperation, sufficient for conspiracy.

How can we achieve Cameron's vision of a "moral capitalism" in a globalised

(The people of the State of New York v. Ernst & Young LLP, 2010: para. 10). In comparison with the scale of the "Repo 105" transactions, the amount of damages requested does not appear to be significant. From the initial "soft" limit 20-30 billion USD in 2002, the (ab)use of "Repo 105" transactions more than doubled in LBHI's last four financial quarters from $ 24 billion in Q4 of 2006 to $ 50,38 billion in Q2 2008 (The people of the State of New York v. Ernst & Young LLP, 2010: para. 26). As a reference point with regards to scale: the estimated value of the Slovenian GDP in 2008 according to the IMF stands at $ 54,6 billion.

24 See Dorn, 2010:246 and Prentice, 2005 for more in connection to 'jurisdictional shopping' also known as 'regulatory arbitrage'.

25 Table 1 is a slightly adapted table which can be found in the Report, 2010: 748.

world with no globally accepted and enforced standards? As we shall see in the next (sub)section deceptive practices in banking transcend the private sector and have begun to corrupt states themselves, that is if one builds on the assumption that they were not corrupt before.

c. Public-private partnership or collusion phase – "The Great Vampire Squid(s)" paradigm case

In the previous two case studies we have analysed deceptive practices perpetrated by private (international) companies or rather their agents acting alone for individual private gain. For the final phase of the evolutionary development of deceptive practices in banking we will take a closer look at how a state – a public entity – directly engaged deceptive services of a private international investment bank in order to join an exclusive 'gentlemen's club'.

In what has become an iconic reference Taibbi (2009) described yet another of the world's largest investment banks, Goldman Sachs, as "*a great vampire squid wrapped around the face of humanity, relentlessly jamming its blood funnel into anything that smells like money*". He went on to point out that there is "*an extremely unfortunate loophole in the system of Western democratic capitalism, which never foresaw that in a society governed passively by free markets and free elections, organised greed always defeats disorganised democracy*" (Taibbi, 2009). Which brings us to our next case study on how Goldman Sachs "*helped*" Greece.[26]

In order to introduce the Euro a country has to fulfil the so called 'Maastricht criteria', among them being the prescribed maximum share of public debt in the gross domestic product (GDP) and a maximum budget deficit in GDP. The former should not exceed 60 % and the latter should not exceed 3 % of a country's GDP. Greece failed to fulfil the criteria in 1999, when the Euro was introduced by twelve EU members, but deceptively managed to comply with the criteria before 2001. In this period various investment banks offered complex financial products with which governments could postpone part of their liabilities into the future. Not only Greece, all Mediterranean countries allegedly used such products intensively (Balzli, 2010).

The complex financial products, used in the Greek case were different types of swaps.[27] As mentioned by a Goldman Sachs' spokeswoman, this was only one of

---

26 There is a growing consensus that Goldman Sachs has been involved in several other disputable activities (more in: Fisher, Cregan, Di Giulio and Schutze, 2011).

27 Exchange of one type of asset, cash flow, investment, liability, or payment for another; most common are currency swaps, interest rate swaps etc.

"*several techniques that many European governments used to meet the terms of the treaty*" (Dunbar and Martinuzzi, 2012).

Greece's debt managers reached a deal with US investment bank Goldman Sachs. The deal involved cross-currency swaps in which government debt issued in dollars and yens was swapped for euro debt for a certain period in order to be exchanged back into the original currencies at a later date. This type of transactions represents a normal method of government refinancing.[28] However, in the Greek case, Goldman Sachs developed a particular type of a swap (Balzli, 2010). Not actual, but fictional (historical) exchange rates were used, which made about 2% of the Greek debt disappear from its national accounts (Dunbar and Martinuzzi, 2012).

Since Eurostat's reporting rules were not adapted for recording (very complex) financial derivatives in a State's financial records, this debt did not appear in Greek debt statistics. Therefore the official budget deficit reached only 1,2% of GDP in 2002, but was revised up to 3,7% in 2004 and later on to 5,2% (Dunbar and Martinuzzi, 2012). Apparently Eurostat itself allowed the use of the so-called off-market rates in swaps until 2008.[29] However, they had to be included in statistics afterwards, which Greece failed to do (Hope, 2011). In contrast with swaps traded on exchanges whose exchange-rate is public, exchange rates of over-the-counter swaps remained secret (Dunbar and Martinuzzi, 2012).

Of course the deal proposed by Goldman Sachs was not a humanitarian act, just the opposite: it was extremely lucrative for the investment bank. According to Spyros Papanicolaou, chief of the country's debt-management agency between 2005 and 2010, the price of the 2,8 billion Euros borrowed went up from 600 million Euros to 5,1 billion Euros. Former (heading the agency from 1999-2004) and current chiefs of the debt-management agency agree that the country did not understand what kind of product it was buying[30] and was not capable of properly assessing the risks of this act (Dunbar and Martinuzzi, 2012).[31]

After a three year grace-period the repayment should have been taken place in the following fifteen years. However, the complexity of the instrument caused the initial payments as foreseen by Greek authorities to drastically increase after the events of September 11th. Several changes of the formula used for calculations were made during following years, but each proved to have even worse consequences

28 For example: country has its debt issued in US dollars but for meeting its current obligations it needs Euros – the swap is performed to assure the country the right currency.

29 As was mentioned above, 2008 marks the beginning of a widespread world financial crisis.

30 The statement was given by the functionaries who had a leading role in conducting business with Goldman Sachs.

31 Use of financial derivatives for improvement of financial records using Goldman Sachs' services had proved to be very costly also for Harvard University, Jefferson County (Alabama) and Pforzheim in Germany (Dunbar and Martinuzzi, 2012).

for Greece. When trying to search for price comparison in international markets the authorities were told that the deal would have been cancelled, if the details of the deal would be revealed to the public (Dunbar and Martinuzzi, 2012).

Greece continued to hide its actual deficit and debt figures even after 2008. True numbers were revealed when a new and independent statistical office was established. As a result the budget deficit for 2009 jumped from 12,4% to 15,4% (Donadio, 2012). Of particular interest is what followed. The Greek authorities started a criminal investigation against the chief of the Statistical Office (Elstat) Andreas Georgiou (a former IMF employee) appointed by the IMF and the European Commission in 2010 with a mission of cleaning up Greek statistics after years of manipulations. Elstat finally revealed the real state of Greek debt and budget deficit which triggered a strong reaction among Elstat employees – several of the Elstat board members resigned and a criminal investigation was launched against Georgiou. He is now being investigated for "*betraying the country's interests*" and could face lifetime imprisonment (Hope, 2011). As stated by a member of the Elstat's board, the deficit was allegedly exaggerated by Elstat "*so it would become larger than that of Ireland [and Greece] would be forced to adopt painful austerity measures*". This act is considered problematic because it forced Greece into a painful savings program that is further reducing its GDP and worsening the economic standard of its inhabitants.

The end of the road – The Saga of Iceland's Geir Haarde

For the home stretch of our analysis we have to turn back to the concept of 'moral capitalism' and the issue of its systemic unsustainability – its entropic potential, if you will - for a moment. Dorn argues that

> "Market innovations in the 1990s included the construction of complex and opaque financial instruments (in US parlance, 'securities) involving high levels of leverage and even greater levels of trading... These globally-disseminated and legal market innovations share the key feature of illegal Ponzi frauds - they can continue until a significant proportion of market participants seek to make withdrawals... Minsky suggests, that periods of stability lull market players (and regulators) into thinking that the stability is an inherent and defining aspect of the financial system. In such a situation, more risky financial tactics are adopted, as investors believe they can have high profits without risk (risk having been banished in this sphere of stability). More speculative patterns emerge and, as

> this way of thinking spreads form the professional investment world to the whole population, Ponzi styles of investment become generalised. Minsky says that 'the greater the weight of speculative and Ponzi finance, the greater the likelihood that the economy is a deviation-amplifying system (Minsky, 2008: 203)'. The suggestion is that far from being a departure from market norms, Ponzi schemes become the emerging norm at a certain (turning) point in the cycle. This perspective has until recently been of little interest to orthodox economists, however, it appears to be an idea whose time has come." (Dorn, 2010: 237, 242)

We concur with Dorn and Minsky and point to the downfall of the Icelandic banking sector in which one can recognise a paradigm case for a 'deviation-amplifying system' that Minsky speaks of.

However, in what is a stark contrast to the Greek example, Iceland is actively pursuing those who were not active enough in preventing the modern Icelandic financial saga.[32] Besides starting an investigation against bank managers, Iceland actually prosecuted one of the highest politicians in the period before and during its financial crisis – its ex-prime minister. Geir Haarde was the first politician in the world who faced a criminal trial in connection with the Global Financial Crisis.[33] He was tried in front of a special court (Landsdómur) established in 1905 to hear cases against elected officials. This was the first use of this court in Iceland's history, indicating that the crisis that hit Iceland was an event unprecedented in hundred years (Stothard, 2012a). Haarde was tried following the issuance of a parliamentary report in 2010 that accused certain political leaders (including Haarde) of "gross negligence" for the lax oversight of the banks in the run-up to the crisis. Later on the parliament voted to indict Haarde. Nonetheless, some critics say that the indictment was politically motivated – Haarde was the only one accused, while others mentioned in the parliamentary report, ministers in Haarde's government and members of the currently leading party, were left out (Stothard, 2012a).

---

32 In 2008 when the financial crisis started spreading around the world, Icelandic banks' balance sheets reached about 800 % of Icelandic GDP. Since they mostly financed on interbank lending markets and deposits came from outside Iceland, towards the end of 2008 they were no longer able to refinance their loans (no one was willing to lend them) (Waibel, 2010). A large part of banks' assets and liabilities was denominated in foreign currencies which further hindered Icelandic central bank's ability to act as a lender of last resort (Buiter and Sibert, 2008: 1-2). Icelandic financial sector was simply too large for such a small country.

33 This trial is otherwise a part of an investigation of criminal wrongdoings in the banking sector that already resulted in formal indictments – former chief executive and chairman of the failed Kaupthing Bank was charged with fraud and market manipulations (Stothard, 2012a).

Dorn's position regarding the possibility of criminalising specific aspects of conduct that led to the financial crisis is clear-cut

> ". . . such discussion is irredeemably idealist, meaning that 'it ain't gonna happen': one would have to attack not isolated individuals but whole social swathes. In reality, the opposite has happened, with the responsible institutions and social class being re-capitalised at public expense. Neither are we likely to see regulators or policy-makers prosecuted criminally for their roles in the financial crisis: even civil actions against regulators seems largely absent (as of late 2009). Yet there is public anger, but trying to stoke it higher is likely to result in bringing down just a few vulnerable individuals, whilst further distracting attention from the historical dynamics that have brought us to this juncture." (Dorn, 2010: 255).

Is Iceland's ex-prime minister Geir Haarde the exception that proves the Dorn rule? Haarde faced criminal trial in front of a special constitutional court and was found guilty only of failing to properly inform other ministers of the potential troubles developing in Iceland, but he will face no punishment and his legal costs will be paid by the government. Haarde was acquitted of other, more serious charges against him. Interestingly, among them was also the accusation that he failed to move Landsbanki's UK Icesave accounts into a subsidiary (Stothard, 2012b), which would (formally)[34] worsen the position of foreign depositors.

There is a term of Greek origin called *catharsis* meaning "*a purification or purgation that brings about spiritual renewal or release from tension*". Could it be said that the saga of Iceland's ex-prime minister Geir Haarde is cathartic? In light of the sanctions, or rather the lack of them, we are in the end brought back to reflect on the opening quote, namely that substantive and procedural criminal law is currently inapt for sanctioning the 1% in power.

Concluding remarks

How does one draw a line between something that is clearly a deceptive business practice and something that has already crossed into the domain of illegality? Ultimately the decision regarding illegality, especially the qualification 'criminal', is in the hands of the courts. However, without being judgmental, academic discourse can lend a helping hand in adjusting the judges' focus by providing

34 *De facto* depositors of the failing Icelandic branches were repaid by their home deposit guarantee schemes (i.e. UK and Dutch), but this repayment is considered as a loan to Icelandic authorities. Case is being tried by the EFTA Court.

"context clues" regarding a practice that has become an issue, potentially a criminal one.

As time goes by "*the initially deviant or 'sinful' nature of certain business practices seems to purify and is erased (ex post facto)*" (Kanduč, 2004; 141–154). We believe that criminology can progress also by identifying and analysing such business practices. That is why the paper focused on a number of what we believe to be paradigmatic cases showing the evolution of deceptive practices in banking.

It is important to point out that it was not the Global Financial Crisis which caused the practices, but it was the other way around. At least in the 'Repo 105' construction the contentious practice was brought to the public eye thanks to the financial crisis which effectively prevented its 'normalization'.

As the 'Com-pact' case study – ordinary loan/credit contracts – showed, when looking at a certain legal construction in isolation, it is often, if not always, difficult to find anything wrong with it in the narrow, legally-dogmatic sense. The question of illegality appears before our eyes when we start to ask ourselves "how, why and in what way" did the management team manage to conjure up profit where there was in fact a loss. We need to take a look at the deceptive constructions in a broader context, especially when we are dealing with sophisticated abuses and deceptive practices that fall in the domain of white collar crime. As the Report in LBHI concluded, financial statements can be misleading and can cause colourable responsibility even if they do not break the accounting rules in a technical sense (Report, 2010: 963). The same applies for the construction in the 'Com-pact' case. Every time a judge or another official finds himself facing such a case, a certain amount of insight and determination is needed to break through the deceptive legal form. Unfortunately there is no abstract formula for the judges as to when it is acceptable to go past the form – the individual judge himself and the transparent balancing of interests is the only guarantee that in a concrete case the judge's decision is justified. Because of the judge's role, other state regulatory, supervisory and prosecutorial agents can be less courteous when assessing the potential illegality of a deceptive practice – without their initial (re)action there will be no case law to (re)formulate enforceable standards and the show will go on.

Our selected cases showed that there is an apparent lack of (re)action from existing supervisory and regulatory agencies. It was not the SEC which brought the deceptive practices of LBHI to light, but the financial crisis and its subsequent bankruptcy, arguably the worst one in the last 80 years. It is also safe to assume that it was the impending bankruptcy which caused the prosecution of the Slovenian 'Com-pact' case. What is relatively worrying, but seems to be endemic, is that BoS tolerated the contentious practices and that it acted upon them relatively late in the game.[35]

On top of the understaffing of the regulatory agencies, we also have to consider their lack of motivation to proceed with investigations and bring them to a close, once they identify them. As was demonstrated in the 'Com-pact' case, the state takes its share of the spoils via taxes. That is why regulatory independence is vital. However, even if such independence is achieved, there is a tendency to overlook minor infractions in view of safeguarding the appearance of the overall stability of the system which is also one of the indicators of their effectiveness.[36] The banks profit from such complacency, their investors are in the dark as to what is going on and their sources of financing are cheaper. All this leads to higher profits and bigger bonuses. An error in judgment as to what constitutes a "cosmetic issue" on the one hand, and what constitutes a criminal breach that can have devastating consequences can be costly for the entire society on the other hand. It is especially problematic because the consequences only begin to show up in the long run, once it is already too late.[37] The (deceptive) business practice has already been 'normalised' and spread through the system.

Deceptive practices in banking are evolving together with the complexity of the global financial system. As we have seen with the Greek case, even states can succumb to similar tactics with a helping hand from skilled practitioners of the craft. The techniques which were covered in this paper can reappear in an evolved form at anytime, anywhere. The so called "stress tests" that were and will be performed by the European Banking Authority (EBA) are probably a good place to look for the newest tricks. The banks being tested are highly motivated to pass the tests and they are also the ones which send the EBA their data.

Considering all of the above, we can safely conclude, that the concept of "moral capitalism" which was proposed by the British PM, David Cameron, is an illusion. The presented cases suggest that the system of incentives in the capitalist market economies is not conducive to a moral behaviour. Our legislators are fighting the symptoms and not adequately addressing the problem of systemic

---

35 During the trial it was also hinted by the defence that BoS was not even-handed in its measures and that its enforcement and supervision was more comprehensive when it came to (smaller), privately owned, banks. See more on internal structural conflicts of the state in prosecuting "too big to fail" cases in Jager, 2011.

36 Dorn outlines another aspect of regulatory capture/rapture, not in terms of "capture by the market of particular staff or sections witihin market regulators, but rather a wider process of intellectual capture of the framework of thinking, and mood, of regulators, central banks and state treasury departments (Dorn, 2010: 252, in depth on state capture 243-251)."

37 See more on the quality of the regulatory environment in Slovenia in Vehovar and Jager, 2007.

incentives and the failure of our immune system which has itself become infected. There is no cure for financial AIDS yet.

References

Ahtik, M. and B. Gramc, Denarni trg Evropske monetarne unije. *Bančni vestnik*, 2006, *55*/7-8, p. 33-37

Bajt, A. and F. Štiblar, *Ekonomija. Ekonomska analiza in politika.* Ljubljana: GV založba, 2004

Balzli, B. (2.8.2010). How Goldman Sachs helped Greece to mask its true debt. *Spiegel Online.* Availabe at: http://www.spiegel.de/international/europe/0,1518,676634,00.html

Belak, V., Kreativno računovodstvo in njegov vpliv na računovodske izkaze. *Računovodstvo, davki, pravo*, 2008, 1/7-8, 8-19.

Brussels, J. C. and K.H. Athens, EU demands details on Greek swaps. *Financial Times* (15-2-2010). Available at: http://www.ft.com/cms/s/0/cc82f954-1a3f-11df-b4ee-00144feab49a.html#axzz1oC1VefoU

Cameron, D., New Statesman - Full transcript | David Cameron | Speech on "moral capitalism" | New Zealand House, London | 19 January 2012. Available at: http://www.newstatesman.com/uk-politics/2012/01/economy-capitalism-market

Cameron, D., Cameron: bank bonuses out of control | Video | Reuters.com. (19-1-2012b) Available at: http://www.reuters.com/video/2012/01/19/cameron-bank-bonuses-out-of-control?videoId=228816786

Cochrane, J.H. and L, Zingales, Lehman and the Financial Crisis. *Wall Street Journal* (15-9-2009). Available at: http://online.wsj.com/article/SB10001424052970203440104574403144004792338.html

Čok, M.,M. Košak and A.Berk Skok. *Institucionalni razvoj finančnega okolja v Sloveniji: repo-trg in efektivna obdavčitev dohodkov pravnih oseb.* Ljubljana: Ekonomska fakulteta, 2012

Deisinger, M., Gospodarski kriminal v SR Sloveniji. *Revija za kriminalistiko in kriminologijo*, 1983, *34*(3), 189-198

Dimitrova-Grajžl, V., P. Grajžl and J. Šušteršič, in K. Zajc, (2012). Court output, judicial staffing and the demand for court services: Evidence from Slovenian courts of first instance. *International Review of Law and Economics*, 2012, 32(1), 19-29

Direktiva 2010/76/EU o spremembi direktiv 2006/48/ES in 2006/49/ES v zvezi s kapitalskimi zahtevami za trgovalno knjigo in za relistinjenja ter v zvezi z nadzorniškim pregledom politik prejemkov, *Uradni list L 329.*

Donadio, R., Greek statistician under scrutiny for budget estimates before Euro Crisis, *The New York Times*, 6-4-2012

Dorn, N., Ponzi finance and state capture: The crisis of financial market regulation. In: P.C. van Duyne, *et al.* (eds.), *Cross-border Crime Inroads on Integrity*, Oisterwijk: Wolf Legal Publishers, 2010, 235-255

Dunbar, N.; and E. Martinuzzi, Goldman secret Greece loan shows two sinners as client unravels. Bloomberg, 6-3-2012. Available at: http://www.bloomberg.com/news/2012-03-06/goldman-secret-greece-loan-shows-two-sinners-as-client-unravels.html

European Central Bank (2011). *Financial Stability Review.* Available at: http://www.ecb.int/pub/fsr/html/index.en.html

Fisher, J., C. Cregan, J. Di Giulio and J. Schutze, Economic crime and the global financial crisis, *Law and Financial Markets Review*, 2011, 276-289

Flyvbjerg, B., *Making social science matter: Why social inquiry fails and how it can succeed again.* Cambridge, New York, Melbourne, Madrid: Cambridge University Press, 2001, 2007

Flyvbjerg, B., Five misunderstandings about case-study research. *Qualitative Inquiry*, 2011, *12(2)*, 219-245

Gorton, G., Questions and answers about the financial crisis. 2010. Available at: http://online.wsj.com/public/resources/documents/crisisqa0210.pdf

Hope, K., Greece's statistics chief faces criminal probe. *Financial Times*, 27-11-2011

Huisman, W., Corporate crime and crisis: Causation scenarios. *Sociology of Crime, Law and Deviance*, 2011, *16*, 107-125

Jackson, R., The Big Chill, *Financial Times*, 15-11-2008

Jager, M., The politics of the Zemono Building Cartel on the sunny side of the Alps. In: *Usual and unusual organising criminals in Europe and beyond: Profitable crimes, from underworld to upper world – Liber Amicorum: Petrus C. van Duyne,* Antwerpen: Maklu, 2011, 105-119

Kanduč, Z., Gospodarski kriminal in ekonomsko nasilje: kriminološke in kazenskopravne perspektive. *Revija za kriminalistiko in kriminologijo*, 1997, *48*(1), 11–26

Kanduč, Z., Kriminaliteta, delo in podjetništvo. *Revija za kriminalistiko in kriminologijo*, 2004, *55*(4), p. 370–388

Kanduč, Z., Družbena kriza, nacionalna država in »varnostno vprašanje« v kriminološki perspektivi. *Revija za kriminalistiko in kriminologijo*, 2011, *62*, 2, 141–154

Kazenski zakonik (KZ). *Uradni list RS*, (63/1994).

Koletnik, F. and I. Kolar, Forenzično računovodstvo. Ljubljana: Zveza računovodij, finančnikov in revizorjev Slovenije, 2008

Levi M. and J. Burrows, Measuring the impact of fraud: a conceptual and empirical journey. *British Journal of Criminology* 2008, 48 (*3*), 293–318

Levi, M., Fraud vulnerabilities, the financial crisis, and the business cycle. In: *Contemporary issues in criminological theory and research. The role of social institutions* (269-293). Belmont: Wadsworth Cengage Learning, 2012

Levi, M. and R.G. Smith, Fraud vulnerabilities and the global financial crisis. In: *Trends and issues in crime and criminal justice*, 2011, (*1-6*). Australian institute of Criminology

Levi, M., J. Burrows, M. Fleming and M. Hopkins (with the assistance of Matthews K.) The nature, extent and economic impact of fraud in the UK. London: Association of Chief Police Officers., 2007, Available at: http://www.cardiff.ac.uk/socsi/resources/ACPO%20final%20nature%20extent%20and%20economic%20impact%20of%20fraud.pdf "Massive profits and obscene bonuses" motivate bank tax. (14-1-2010). Available at: http://www.usatoday.com/money/economy/2010-01-14-obama-bank-tax_N.htm

Mills, C.W., *The sociological imagination.* New York: Oxford University Press, 1959, 2000

Minsky, H., The financial instability hypothesis. In: *Economics as a social science: readings in political economy.* North Melbourne: Pluto Press, 2003, 201-203

Mishkin, F.S., *The economics of money, banking and financial markets.* (8th ed.) Boston: Addison Wesley, 2006

Muhič, D., *Požari v naravi.* Ljubljana: Gasilska zveza Slovenije, 2004

Peeraer, M., *Spremljanje poslovnih dogodkov v bankah v skladu z MSRP.* Ljubljana: ZBS, 2009

Poslanci složni glede dodatnega davka. (23-9-2009). Available at: http://www.delo.si/clanek/88749

Prentice, R., Regulatory competition in securities law: a dream (that should be) deferred. *Ohio State Law Journal*, 2005 66 (6), p.1156-1230

Report *In re* Lehman Bros. Holdings Inc., No. 08-13555. (2010). Available at: http://jenner.com/lehman/

Rozman, R., Repo posli in dogovori o izravnavi v slovenskem pravu. *Podjetje in delo*, 2010, *26*/6-7, p. 1106-1113

Simoneti, M., Bankers' pay and the financial crisis: policy debate and new regulation. *Bančni vestnik*, 2010, *59*/11, p. 55-65

Sklep Banke Slovenije o razvrstitvi aktivnih bilančnih in zunajbilančnih postavk bank in hranilnic. *Uradni list RS*, (55/93)

Sklep o ocenjevanju izgub iz kreditnega tveganja bank in hranilnic. *Uradni list RS*, (28/2007 z nadaljnjimi spremembami)

Sklep o višini in načinu oblikovanja rezervacij za zavarovanje pred potencialnimi izgubami bank in hranilnic. *Uradni list RS*, (66/93)

Snoj, A., Repo posli. *Prikazi in analize*, 2001, *9*/5, 47-63

Stothard, M., Iceland's former PM denies negligence, *Financial Times*, 5-3-2012a

Stothard, M., Former Icelandic PM guilty of negligence, *Financial Times*, 23-4-2012b

Summe, K., Misconceptions about Lehman Brothers' bankruptcy and the role derivatives played. *Stanford Law Review Online*, 2011, *64*, 16

Sutherland, E.H., *White collar crime – the uncut version with an introduction by Gilbert Geis and Colin Goff.* New Haven in London:Yale University, 1983

Štiblar, F., *The impact of the global crisis on Montenegro and the Western Balkans.* Podgorica: Centralna banka Crne Gore, 2009

Taibbi, M., The great American bubble machine. Rolling Stone, 9-7-2009. Available at: http://www.rollingstone.com/politics/news/the-great-american-bubble-machine-20100405

Tappan, P.W., Who is the Criminal? *American Sociological Review*, 1947, *12*, 96-102

The people of the State of new York *v.* Ernst & Young LLP. (21.12.2010). Office of the Attorney General of the State of New York:
http://www.ag.ny.gov/media_center/2010/dec/dec21a_10.html

Vehovar, U. and M. Jager, Corruption, quality of governance, and economic growth: The Slovenian dilemma between true reform from within and mere façade. *Monatsschrift für Kriminologie und Strafrechtsreform*, 2007, *90* (2/3), 126-139

Vlahek, A. and M. Ahtik, Kartelni dogovor o višini Euriborja? *Pravna praksa*, 2012, 31/10

Waibel, M., Iceland's financial crisis – Quo Vadis, *International Law*, 2010, (5)

Wheeler, S. and D.M. Kahan, White collar crime: History of an idea. In: *Encyclopedia of Crime and Justice*, Macmillan Reference USA, 2002

Weiner, J., Biggest mistake of the financial crisis: Lehman Bros. bankruptcy. *Politics Daily*, 15-9-20012. Available at:
http://politicsdaily.com/2009/09/15/biggest-mistake-of-the-financial-crisis-lehman-bros-bankruptcy/

West, M., Bank of England Governor slams bank bonuses. *CNBC.com*. 25-1-2012.

Available at: http://www.cnbc.com/id/46127919/

Winning, N. and V. Guevarra, U.K. Caps Part-State Bank Bonuses. *Wall Street Journal*, 19-1-2012. Available at: http://online.wsj.com/article/SB1000142405297020461650457717068402320

Financial crimes and the global financial crisis

Michael Levi[1]

Introduction

The aim of this chapter is to examine the links between the financial crisis and fraud. This is an issue that has been the subject of much discussion in the media, and some in academic circles (*e.g.* Deflem, 2011; Wang and Holtfreter, 2012; Piquero, 2012). It has become increasingly clear that a prime generator of the financial crisis was the wholesale mis-selling of sub-prime mortgages and their wrapping into derivatives that took no real account of their underlying probability of being repaid (McLean and Nocera, 2011; Sorkin, 2010). The labelling of such misconduct as 'fraud' is legally perilous, since a curious aspect of the economic crisis is that almost none of its key precipitators – corporate or individual – have been prosecuted. This makes it difficult to speak of trends in elite fraud with any certainty (and safety from defamation) so that the denotation 'deception' may be pointing more at dishonest behaviour by the middle classes and below, and by criminal 'outsiders'. As this is not a chapter on semantics it suffices to indicate that demarcations in the field of financial crimes remain difficult. Here, I turn to examine the overlap between fraud and financial crimes.

Fraud in the context of financial crimes

Fraud is a deceptively simple word covering a very broad territory. It is a way of making money illegally via deception, whether that deception is directly person-to-person in real space or occurs in virtual space, usually without physical contact between offender and victim. Fraud is committed by spreading false stories or via the use of deceptive physical or e-documents or via Personal Identification Numbers. It may be committed using everyday transactions and stories, sometimes using genuine or phoney businesses as tools for the deed.

---

1 The author is Professor of Criminology at Cardiff University

Fraud is a partially overlapping sub-set of 'financial crime'. The latter is a heterogeneous term whose denotation has been expanding substantially over time, and now includes:

1. frauds of different types (*modus operandi*) with different victims (from wealthy corporations and High Net Worth Individuals to the very poor and from very rich to very poor governments);
2. 'market abuse' such as insider dealing/trading (which covers a range from corrupt relationships between investors and insiders to giving talks about company prospects to some important analysts before releasing results to the general market, giving the former an unlawful competitive advantage);
3. money laundering (of all crimes, increasingly including tax fraud[2]);
4. financing of terrorism (mostly since 2001) and (since 2008) of Weapons of Mass Destruction proliferation, sometimes using deceptive documents; and
5. (transnational) bribery (usually by corporates paying public officials in developing countries, but also paying officials in their own – wealthy or poor – countries), covering up the act and money transfers by deceptive documents.

Some of these offences – like fraud – have existed in some form for centuries though even there, legislative changes have been needed to qualify them as criminal, for example to cope with the evolution of technology or moral awareness. This is the case with offences which are new since the 1980s (such as insider dealing/trading and money laundering). Others still typically are only a few years old or are in a process of major adaptation (like the financing of terrorism and of the proliferation of weapons of mass destruction, and transnational bribery). In addition, offences involving Intellectual Property, environmental crimes, *etc.* can be treated as part of 'financial crime', if only via their role (with all other offences) as part of the ever-extending list of 'predicate crimes' for money laundering offences. Indeed, to the extent that most crimes for gain lead to concealment or transformation of *some* proceeds, it is arguable that all such crimes *ipso facto* become 'financial crimes'. Consequently those who facilitate them and the movement of moneys from them are liable to increased risks of 'criminalisation', at least in principle. This implies a huge extension of what 'financial crime' and its

2 Though countries vary substantially in how they define 'tax fraud'. Switzerland for example restricts it to active deception (e.g. falsification of data in tax submissions made to it), excluding omissions and non-reporting of tax obligations elsewhere. So if someone with a Swiss account does not need to file tax documents in Switzerland, they cannot commit tax fraud there and cannot normally be extradited for this. On the other hand, since 2008, there has been a great deal of international action on mutual cooperation in tax matters and in withholding tax arrangements, though these too are subject to sophisticated avoidance mechanisms. See de Willebois *et al.* (2012), Sharman (2011), Shaxson (2011) for good contemporary analyses.

subdivisions constitute, which evokes criticism from the more 'purist' analysts like Van Duyne (2011), because of conceptual dilution and decrease of clarity.

It may be useful to regard 'financial crime' – and its sub-sets 'money laundering' and 'corruption' –as a floating signifier, a moral category of illicit capitalism which contains whatever pressure group politics succeeds in criminalising and placing therein. An almost universal core component of its control is the passage of criminal laws and regulatory processes, meeting ever evolving Financial Action Task Force (FATF) criteria.[3] For example, anti-money laundering legislation (AML) must henceforth cover both tax evasion and the financing of WMD proliferation (FATF, 2012). Within this bureaucratic category of 'financial crime', the amount of fraud that gets investigated from victim reports or via Suspicious Activity Reports or from other intelligence-led (*e.g.* criminal informant) sources can easily be widely extended or can be reduced in favour of profit-generating asset forfeiture investigations. For example, Gannon and Doig (2010) have shown how within British police forces, fraud investigation resources have been reallocated to financial investigations of 'organised crime' to generate more recovered assets in which the police share. What initially would be counted as 'organised crime' might then be transformed into 'financial crime' on the list of police efforts and priorities.[4] Deconstructing the origins and relevance of data on fraud and other financial crimes is necessary in order to assess the reliability of trend data.

The fraud-crisis nexus

The relationships between financial crimes and 'the' Global Financial Crisis (or rolling crises) can take several forms. First, what was the impact of financial crimes (compared with other socio-economic phenomena) as a *cause* of economic crisis? Second, what have people *argued* or *asserted* about the impact of the financial crisis on financial crimes? And third, what does the *evidence* tell us about the impact of the financial crisis on financial crimes – volume and organisation – and, separately, on their control.

---

3 There are echoes here of the classic Sutherland/Tappan arguments of the 1940s over whether white-collar crime really is 'crime' (Braithwaite, 1985; Geis and Goff, 1983) and the extension of this into the title "*It's Legal but It Ain't Right: Harmful Social Consequences of Legal Industries*" (Passas and Goodwin, 2005).

4 The way of police reporting reflects the development in criminalisation and prioritising. For example, drug trafficking arrests were first recorded as drug cases only, then as organised crime plus drug offences; while in the past decade almost all multi-offender crimes-for-profit are also mentioned as 'money laundering': an unavoidable accompanying second or third offence.

Crime and crime control are loosely coupled because the 'crime triangle' argues that crimes result from the combination of the dimensions of motivated offenders, situational opportunities and capable guardianship. (Though opportunities and guardianship are harder to separate than the framers of situational crime prevention theory appreciate.) Particularly in economic crimes, their constituent parts are typically more complex than in the household and street crimes to which the model has usually been applied (though see Bullock *et al.*, 2010). In the financial field we need to focus on changes in all three dimensions for each sub-type of crime in order to try to account sensibly for changes in financial crimes. Whatever conclusion one comes to, it is worthwhile trying to disentangle the data and the connections, not just to reveal more about the 'known knowns' and the 'known unknowns', but also to focus on what form the relationships take.

There are two key components of the control of financial crimes: public and private sector efforts. Both of these involve regulating in the sense of managing the problem, but with different criteria. For the private sector, theory suggests that (at least on short-run models) firms should stop spending money on control when the costs of control exceed the costs of fraud. However, the author's interviews with industry managers suggest that in reality, this expenditure stops earlier, because management expect a high Return on Investment (ROI) on 'security' or fraud management as well as on their normal business. Such investment decisions are made on estimated benefits, which estimations are difficult to make scientifically: but fraud risk managers are accountable for their judgments, even if demonstrating savings is often a matter of guesswork.[5]

For the public sector, such a logic may apply to spending on reducing benefit and tax frauds, but that is unlikely because broader social criteria may properly apply to reduce the extent to which 'social security scroungers' and, to a far lesser extent, 'tax evaders' can be publicly allowed to flaunt their amorality in public. So though the private sector also engages in regulating fraud and other 'business crimes', the overall regulation of financial crimes is primarily a governmental task that requires careful management in case there is an uncontrollable surge in the repression of 'entrepreneurial' and 'wealth creating' activities of elites themselves (Levi, 2009). Nevertheless, as public anger has mounted about the job losses and (in parts of the USA, housing desolation) caused by a combination of the financial crisis and mortgage origination frauds (Nguyen and Pontell, 2011), this has generated pressures for tougher criminal justice and regulatory responses to the City of London and Wall Street. (Similar pressures exist in Greece and some other parts

5 Whims and personal preferences may play a part in investment decisions generally, quite apart from any biosocial pressures of which financial services and other businesspeople may be quite unconscious (Coates, 2012).

of the Eurozone to show that action is being taken against tax avoidance and evasion by elites, as social welfare is slashed.) Yet in contrast to the large numbers prosecuted in the earlier Savings and Loan crisis of the 1970s, no senior bankers or mortgage grantors had been prosecuted by late 2012 in the UK or USA for their role in the Global Financial Crisis. The impacts elsewhere in Europe are variable, since they have become entangled in the crisis of the Eurozone.

In Iceland and the Irish Republic, bankers (and governments/regulators) have been heavily blamed for the economic collapse, while there have been a very small number of elite prosecutions there. Marxist authors might consider that the recent rise in prosecutions of insider dealing, cartels and corporate bribery represents a 'bread and circuses' diversionary tactic to show that action is being taken against more elite offenders (Barak, 2012). Such a hegemonic structuralist account lacks direct evidence, but this does represent something that prosecutors and regulators can do to show they are taking some serious action against some firms and individuals, however relatively unimportant insider dealing may be to the overall economy and even to the financial services sector. In a concerted crack down (12 October 2011), the US authorities charged 530 people, 'including 172 executives' (though presumably not elites, who would not have been in this sort of business) for allegedly trying to defraud homeowners in arrears on their homes and facing foreclosure.[6] These offences as well as these reactions occurred after the Global Financial Crisis, and therefore are irrelevant the explanation of the Global Financial Crisis, but they are relevant to the impact of the global financial crisis on the opportunity to fraudsters offered by many people who still have assets they are desperate not to lose.

The heterogeneity of fraud

Fraud has highly diffuse consequences, affecting consumers, donors (*e.g.* of EU subsidies, social security and tax allowances and refunds), investors rich and poor (including all of our pension funds), lenders, *etc.* The media and government tend to look unhelpfully at 'fraud' as if it were one homogeneous problem, and (as in money laundering) tend to swallow or even to produce ever-larger figures presented under the banner of 'awareness raising'. Despite very large error margins in estimation, what we do know is that fraud is a very large sum, and it is larger than other forms of property crime. *Some* fraudulent trading, mortgage frauds, *etc.*, were stimulated as well as revealed by the Global Financial Crisis: as Levi (2008a)

6 http://www.fbi.gov/news/pressrel/press-releases/financial-fraud-enforcement-task-force-members-reveal-results-of-distressed-homeowner-initiative

noted, slippery slope and intermediate frauds often occur when existing business owners lie (or launder for others) in the hope of continuing to trade until business improves, or intentionally turn to fraud to preserve their lifestyles. However, losses from fraud were almost certainly less than those from bad lending decisions by bankers against commercial and domestic property, etc., even discounting 'bad loans' to non arms-length borrowers/elite political cronies made by such as the Kabul Bank.

There is a tendency to make categories of fraud incoherent. Thus, the Kroll Global Fraud Report 2011-12, conducted in collaboration with the prestigious Economist Intelligence Unit uses the following figure[7]:

Figure 1

Chart VI: Proportion describing themselves as highly vulnerable to the following frauds

	Survey Average	Over 10% of revenu[e] lost to fraud
Corruption and bribery	24%	51%
Theft of physical assets	13%	24%
Management conflict of interest	13%	24%
Vendor, supplier or procurement fraud	13%	19%
IP theft	13%	17%
Information theft	13%	17%
Regulatory or compliance breach	11%	30%
Financial mismanagement	10%	27%
Market collusion	9%	24%
Internal financial fraud	9%	15%
Money laundering	8%	30%

It is difficult to see what many of these – including money laundering – have to do with fraud, nor how such a large proportion of companies can be said properly to be vulnerable to losing more than 10% of their revenue to laundering (which - excluding frauds against them – costs them nothing), to regulatory breaches (likewise), *etc.* The report stated that despite heightened levels of concern, the

7 http://www.krolladvisory.com/media/pdfs/KRL_FraudReport2011-12_chartVI.jpg. As usual in surveys of this kind, the sampling remains obscure, but we are told that 1265 executives (half of them chief officers) were polled from a broad range of business sectors and parts of the world.

overall prevalence of (composite) fraud decreased to 75% of the 1.265 companies, from 88 % in 2010. Management conflict of interest (21%), vendor, supplier or procurement fraud (20%) and internal financial fraud (19%) all saw large increases. The incidence of corruption and bribery nearly doubled from 10 to 19%.[8] On average fraud cost companies 2,1% of earnings in 2010-11, which is equivalent to a week of revenues over the course of a year. Eighteen percent lost more than 4% of revenues to fraud in the year, while 53 companies, or one quarter of that sub-group, lost more than 10% of revenues to fraud. Despite these impressive sounding figures, given the flexible 'definition' of fraud, it is difficult to know what these data mean. I am including them because corporate fraud surveys are an important data source, but equally, the fact that their methodology is seldom transparent raises significant problems for judgments about their validity, especially when one understands that the sponsors and authors usually have a self-serving motivation for threat inflation. Indeed data credibility is an important issue for those who seek to plan policing and prevention 'rationally', *i.e.* taking into account sound evidence rather than the discourse of fear-mongering.

Some selected figures

The best and most effortfully compiled national data on fraud are to be found in the UK. Following up the costs of fraud review of Levi *et al.* (2007), the National Fraud Authority (NFA, 2010) estimated UK fraud losses at about £30 billion in 2009: around £621 a year for every man, woman and child in the UK (though given the uneven distribution of losses, such average figures are statistically valueless, if rhetorically valuable in justifying the importance of anti-fraud measures to otherwise uninterested criminal justice, government and media audiences). By 2010, this figure had risen to £38,4 billion, then almost doubling to £73 billion in 2011, though some of these rises resulted from an expansion of the areas of fraud researched (NFA, 2011, 2012). These cover a variety of sorts of victim. One survey cited in the NFA estimate found that 54% of small businesses have been a victim of fraud or online crime in the last twelve months (Federation of Small Businesses, 2009); and 30% considered some form of fraud to be the type of crime that had the biggest impact on small business (Federation of Small Businesses, 2010: 7). In 2008, four per cent of all insurance claims by value (excluding life insurance) were deemed fraudulent, against three per cent in 2007 (Association of British Insurers, 2009); and – though no trend data or sources are given, an average of 100 new

8 The report does not mention the possibility that these rises may have been an artefact of better control and detection measures, perhaps prompted by fresh anti-bribery legislation and the raised prosecution rate of such offences.

victims of share sale frauds contact the police each week. These victims report losses ranging from £3.000 per person up to more than £1 million.[9] Well over half the total detected losses from fraud arises in the public sector, at least in the UK (NFA, 2011, 2012): it is hard to tell whether that proportion has been rising or falling since the Global Financial Crisis.

Currently, reasonably long time series cost data are available in the UK only for payment card frauds (Financial Fraud Action UK), some aspects of identity frauds (CIFAS) and – until 2009 when they were stopped - for external frauds against government departments (UK Treasury). There are also data over time for social security fraud and error (Department of Work and Pensions) and fraud against local authorities and some national non-departmental bodies (the Audit Commission, awaiting abolition in 2013 as part of the UK government's 'localism' agenda), but not for tax fraud. These are all now subsumed into the NFA annual fraud indicator. Fraud cost and incidence surveys carried out by accounting/consulting firms in many parts of the world since the mid-1980s are intermittent and cover mainly large corporations (Levi, 1987; Levi *et al.*, 2007; Levi and Burrows, 2008; Levi and Williams, 2012). They are not panel studies, which follow up the same firms over time. We cannot be very confident that data show us whether fraud or almost any sub-component of it (other than plastic fraud or identity fraud, which are well reported) has changed.

Many estimates of fraud are based on very limited evidence, derive from institutional profile-raising, and take on a life of their own as 'facts by repetition', seldom critiqued either by media, always hungry for sensational headlines (Levi, 2006), or by pressure groups. On the other hand, if we rely on cases brought to conviction, the data may be absurdly low in both harm caused and case complexity. The most subtle cases of fraud are hardest to prove beyond a reasonable doubt in the minds of juries or judges. Therefore, they may be dropped under the 'reasonable prospect of conviction' criterion in the Code for Crown Prosecutors in England and Wales, and equivalents in most other jurisdictions.

Any given year's data of disclosed frauds will be a mix of crimes which, because of delays in identification and reporting, as well as the spread of time over which *some* frauds have been committed, have occurred over several preceding years. This time variable is a particular problem for evaluating the impact of economic trends. The elapsed time from fraud to discovery and then from discovery to criminal justice action (if any) means that many of the larger frauds coming to light in 2008-2012 will have been committed some years before. There has been no opportunity in this chapter for the individual case analysis that would be a desirable alternative

[9] http:www.attorneygeneral.gov.uk/nfa/WhatWeDo/FraudFacts/Pages/TheCostofFraud tousall.aspx

to aggregate data, but the following examples illustrate this time lapse clearly. The Madoff case is the exemplar of a long maturing Ponzi scam in which credibility of the principal persisted for longer than a decade, though the underlying business was almost entirely fake (Van de Bunt, 2010; Markopoulos, 2010). An example of lengthy elapsed time from fraudulent to business-detected awareness is 'rogue trading' in the form of illicit (and – more importantly – unsuccessful) betting on market trends, for example by Nick Leeson at Barings in 1995 (http://www.nickleeson.com) and by Jérôme Kerviel at Société Générale in 2007–8 (whose appeal against conviction and imprisonment was in 2012 rejected by the French courts). In both cases the accused alleged that more senior managers turned a blind eye to the risk taking, because they were incompetent (Barings) or because they stood to gain if the risks paid off (both Barings and Société Générale). More recently, trader Kweku Adoboli was accused of losing UBS $2,25 billion between 2008 and 2011 by deceiving his management about trades, risking losses of $12 billion: his trial commenced in September 2012. The beginning of these losses post-dated the Global Financial Crisis, but had no obvious connection with it, either in motivation or opportunity. In essence, they were all cases in which traders found ways of breaching their dealing limits without detection and, having lost significant sums in early trading, carried on trading in the hope/expectation that they would be able to recoup those losses. Whether others behaved similarly but were more fortunate in their later dealing (or gambling) and remained forever undetected is unknown.

Fraud and 'Organised Crime'

There is much discussion of the role of organised crime, both generally and in relation to (always growing) involvement in fraud and other forms of financial crime. This has been extensively commented on elsewhere (Gelemerova, 2011), and I will not review it further here. In 2009, former UNODC head Antonio Da Costa asserted that in the course of the financial crisis, banks anxiously sought capital, including criminal capital, to keep them afloat, citing (with one eye on libel laws) as an example Wachovia Bank's alleged laundering of $480 million in Mexican drug money (*The Observer*, 13 December 2009): however this, and other similar allegations, seem implausible on a large scale.[10]

Fraudsters are more diverse in terms of socio-economic status and age than are other 'organised offenders', though they sometimes operate in national or ethnic

10 http://online.wsj.com/article/SB10001424052748704532204575397543634034112.html

networks transnationally (Levi, 2008a, 2008b). Very serious frauds can be committed by solo actors. According to reviews of its forensic cases by KPMG (2007), typical internal fraudsters act alone, are middle aged and have usually been employed by the company for six or more years. By 2011, though this may merely reflect changing composition of reports to KPMG rather than real changes in the organisation of fraud, this had changed to the typical fraudster acting in collusion and being employed for more than 10 years (KPMG, 2011). Over half commit twenty or more frauds, usually over some years (though these are all people whose frauds are serious enough and whose victims are wealthy enough to engage KPMG).

Software advances have shown that what would previously have been seen as isolated frauds, if fraud at all, are actually part of an 'organised' network. For example between accident management companies, car hire firms, valuers, and a pool of people willing to make false claims for whiplash and other injuries. Thus it is tempting to see these trends as an effect of the Global Financial Crisis and (at least partly independently) of the inexorable movement of 'organised crime' into fraud (Levi, 2008a; Association of British Insurers, 2012), but many 'organised frauds' preceded the Global Financial Crisis undetected, and in any event, this looks more like the dissemination of techniques by imitation.

Fraud entails many different sorts of harm which were likely to be driven by different factors, including what we do to prevent them and prosecute them. A rise in crime rates can be an indication that the quality of life has got worse, but in this case, the substantially greater cost of fraud figure is far more likely to reflect improved knowledge than a real rise. We should appreciate that any given sector of fraud risk consists of the interaction between motivation, criminal ingenuity and the opportunities that we give criminals by the way potential victims and 'third party guardians' watch over our assets and intervene (or otherwise). All three of these can change over time. Box (1997) examined the links between recession, crime (including corporate crimes) and punishment in earlier eras, but very little data were available on white-collar crimes. Those expecting a rise in fraud due to the recession/Global Financial Crisis are not only loosely tempted by fears of 'Apocalypse Soon', but also by the alleged invasion of 'organised crime', the corruptibility of the professionals, 'teckies' (technology obsessives) and of the middle and working classes fearful of their jobs and wanting to make a quick profit before they lose their access to rich crime opportunities.

Volume fraud trends

Unlike some high value frauds, 'volume crimes' such as credit and debit card fraud usually come to light promptly (though seldom as promptly as burglaries and vehicle thefts). Since 2006, payment card fraud data in the UK have displayed a broad downwards trend in fraud on lost or stolen cards, due to the introduction of Chip and PIN. A more recent (2009-10) drop is observed in counterfeit frauds on skimmed and cloned cards, which previously had risen substantially, mainly being used overseas to side-step Chip and PIN controls. There was a slower, modest rise in cards obtained by identity theft; and a less obviously explained very recent drop in card-not-present frauds over the phone and internet. The only type of card fraud having shown an increase in the number of fraudulent transactions between 2009 and 2010 was account take-over (up from 66.000 to 84.000) (Financial Fraud Action UK, 2011). Online banking fraud losses rose substantially in 2009 and 2010 – perhaps due to improved awareness and reporting, but also reflecting increased phishing for passwords and sophisticated bank site-cloning – before falling, as banks worked harder on prevention.

Card fraud losses in 2010 totalled £365,4 million, 60 per cent of the losses in 2008 (and a record low in the past decade as a ratio to turnover). Total fraud losses on UK cards fell by 7% between 2010 and 2011 to £341 million. This is the lowest annual total since 2000 and follows on from a fall of 17% in 2009-10. Card fraud losses as a proportion of total turnover – at 0,06% – continue to decrease and fell by 33% in 2009-11 (Financial Fraud Action UK, 2012). In 2011 online banking fraud losses totalled £35,4 million – a decrease of 24% from the previous year and a very large fall from £59,7 million in 2009. Following annual decreases since 2007, 2011 saw a 17% increase in cheque fraud losses. The main reason given for this rise (and supported by the data on sub-types) is an increase in fraudsters stealing genuine cheques and altering the payee name, or using details from genuine cheques to create counterfeits. So from those data, it seems clear that the financial crisis had no negative effect on card fraud in the UK, and the recent rise in cheque fraud is attributable to other factors.

Payment card fraud in Europe generally increased after 2006, peaking in 2008. However, 2011 levels are €121 million more than in 2006. A notable exception is the UK, which accounted for 45% of the total in 2006 and now accounts for 29%, a reduction of €177 million. It has been asserted that criminals have shifted their focus to new opportunities within the European continent, as anti-fraud measures in the UK become stricter.[11]

---

11 (FICO, 2012, www.fico.com/fraudeurope)

In the UK, data collected by fraud prevention service CIFAS – a not for profit organisation which acts as a rule-based clearing house and store for a variety of frauds on member organisations (many of which are also frauds on individuals) – indicate a rise in identity takeover frauds, as 'new credit' becomes harder to get, generating displacement to impersonating existing account-holders. Such frauds emerge quite quickly.

Figure 2

Trends in credit frauds on UK CIFAS database 2007-2011

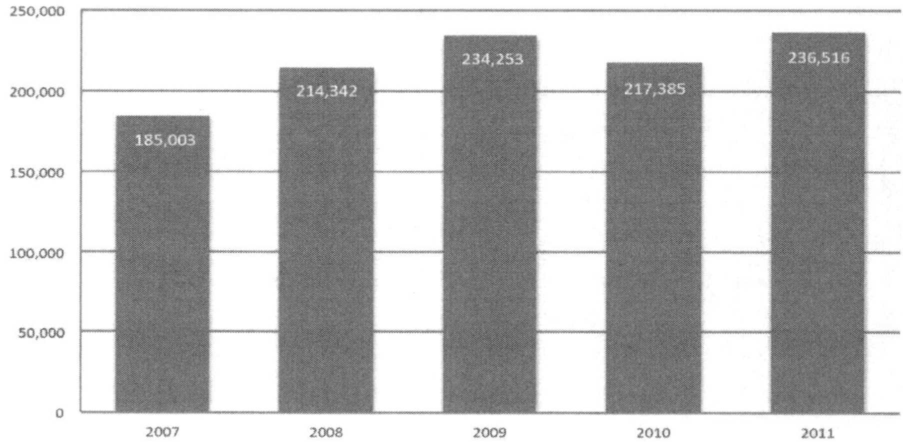

According to CIFAS (2012), Identity Fraud and Facility Takeover Fraud[12] account for 58% of all frauds, and rose by 10% and 18% respectively 2010-11. Misuse of Facility Fraud increased to nearly 54.000 frauds in 2011 and is the second largest fraud type. As fraud is not merely committed by anonymous third party criminals, 'first party frauds' (by the person who applied for credit) are also important. The migration to new products identified first in 2009 has continued, with 2011 witnessing the emergence as a fraud target of the 'payday lender'.[13] By analogy with

12 *Identity Fraud* is cases of false identity and identity theft. *Application Fraud/False Insurance Claim* relates to applications or claims with material falsehood (lies) or false supporting documentation where the name has not been identified as false. *Facility Takeover Fraud* occurs where a person (the 'facility hijacker') unlawfully obtains access to details of the 'victim of takeover', namely an existing account holder or policy holder (or of an account or policy of a genuine customer or policy holder) and fraudulently operates the account or policy for his own (or someone else's) benefit.

13 Licensed firms such as Wonga that controversially but lawfully lend money for a very short time at very high interest rates until workers get paid and then can repay them unless they lose their jobs or are persuaded to roll the debt over. Their own loan practices have been

the Cressey model of embezzlement, some people experiencing financial stresses will see submitting fraudulent applications for goods and services as a way of easing that pressure (albeit temporarily). Counterbalancing this increase in those who are willing to lie to gain credit and services, there is still a risk averse culture in many organisations which translates into high credit score thresholds. This means that many fraudulent applications are failing to pass that scoring threshold and are being declined. Therefore, never reaching those organisations' fraud teams and not being recorded as 'fraud' even though they are fraudulent attempts.

This decline in opportunities for credit frauds plausibly (but not demonstrably) resulted in the transferring of criminal attention to products that are not subject to the same level of credit assessment. This might account for the explosion in frauds recorded against the likes of mail order from 2008 to 2010. The rewards per single act that the fraudster obtains for a successful fraud against a mail order company will be smaller than those which they would obtain if they could fraudulently acquire a credit card, but their chances of success are likely to be higher. As controls tightened around mail order, and lending conditions became more stable, fraudsters moved away slightly from attacking mail order at application stage. The personal data that had been harvested fraudulently, however, allowed them to try to take over existing mail order accounts (evidenced by an increase of over 40% in the number of Facility Takeover Frauds against mail order products).

The steady increase in the number of cases of Identity Fraud against communications products (almost exclusively mobile phones) gathered pace in 2011, due to the emergence of the smart phone as both valuable for resale and aspirational to possess. Such smart phones are more difficult to obtain than a standard mobile phone contract due to more stringent verification and vetting procedures because the firm stands to risk losing more from unpaid internet access. Some identity fraudsters feel that there is a greater chance of getting the phone that they want if they use someone else's identity, even that of a family member. Other fraudsters attempt to obtain large quantities of these devices to resell, as there is a ready market.

In short, identity fraud trends reveal the variations over time, reflecting the intersections between motivated offenders, situational fraud opportunities and organisational interventions. *Prima facie*, this has more to do with trends in technology and the relative safety of different products than it does the Global or any other Financial Crisis.

---

much criticised for encouraging people to take on debts they have great difficulties in repaying.

Figure 3

Identity fraud in different commercial arenas, CIFAS database 2007-11

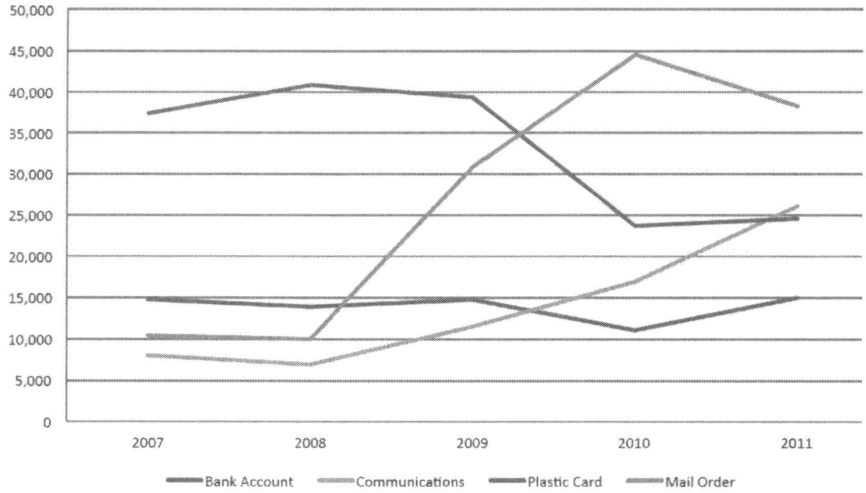

Langton (2011) reviewed identity theft data from US national surveys, 2005-10, though this was not explicitly linked to the Global Financial Crisis. In 2010, 7% of households in the United States - about 8,6 million households - had at least one member age 12 or older who experienced one or more types of identity theft victimization. This represented an increase from the 5,5% of households, or 6,4 million households, that were victims of one or more types of identity theft in 2005. The increase in identity theft from 2005 to 2010 was largely attributable to an increase in the misuse or attempted misuse of existing credit card accounts. The percentage of households in which an existing credit card account was illegally used increased by about 50%, from 2,5% to 3,8%. The percentage of households that experienced the misuse of personal information to open a new account or for another fraudulent purpose declined by about 30%, from 0,9% in 2005 to 0,6% in 2010. This may reflect the greater difficulty of getting new credit. So the trends and data are broadly consistent in the UK and US.

Insurance frauds

No comparable data are available for other countries, but a UK study by the Association of British Insurers (2009) estimated that in 2006, £2,1 billion of fraud was committed and the insurance industry detected £0,5 billion (23%) of this (so £1,6 billion was undetected). In 2008, they estimated that £2,7 billion of fraud was committed and the insurance industry detected £0,7 billion (27%). So making the heroic assumption that these data are valid, between 2006 and 2008, while total fraud increased, the proportion of total fraud that the UK insurance industry detected increased by 16%.[14] The Association of British Insurers (2009, p. 7) argues:

> "To date (July 2009), our research finds that there are clear indications that the recession, which began in the third quarter of 2008, is leading to an increase in general insurance fraud. While these indications are clear, they are not conclusive. They include:
>
> - An increase in 'walk-aways' where the claimant drops the claim in response to enquiries from the insurer.[15]
> - Significant increases in the proportion of 'suspect' claims and in applications for insurance where underwriting fraud to reduce the level of premiums is suspected.
> - An increase in the proportion of claims referred for investigation that are proven to be fraudulent. This is in part due to improved processes for 'flagging' suspect claims. It is also thought this reflects an increase in the level of fraud. Estimates of the increase in fraud – in particular opportunistic fraud – are not available from all the insurers we interviewed but have been put in the range of a 15-25% increase in Q1 2009 compared to Q1 2008.
> - An increase in very amateur attempts at claims fraud indicating that otherwise honest customers are attempting to make fraudulent claims for the first time.
> - Interviews with loss adjustors indicating that detected fraud, while on an upward trend anyway, dramatically increased in 2008 suggesting an increase in the underlying level of total fraud. One loss adjustor had detected 41% more fraud in 2008 compared to 2007, another estimates a fraud increase of between 15% and 21%, varying by line of business. However, these estimates are likely to be also the pickup on improved flagging of suspect claims for passing to loss adjustors by insurers which would increase the success-rate of loss-adjustors.
> - Research by Royal Sun Alliance showing that the number of people in Britain who think insurance fraud is acceptable increased dramatically (from 3,6 to 4,6 million people) between March 2008 and January 2009.
> - An increase in calls to the Insurance Fraud Bureau's 'Cheatline' . . . . Over the course of 2008 alone, the volume of calls more than doubled. This in-

14 The improved detection performance is plausible in the light of changes in the forensic analysis of insurance claims by voice stress and data linkage software.

15 Though some or all of this rise may represent more risk-aware insurers behaving sceptically. Alternatively, claimants may drop their claims as they expect the 'small print' conditions will defeat anyhow the attempt at compensation.

> crease is in part due to higher public awareness of the Cheatline and the new facility allowing online reporting. It also appears that the public attitude towards fraudsters has hardened: many callers cite the fact that they are motivated to call as they have to pay increased premiums as a result of the activity of fraudsters. Subject to these caveats, the large increase in calls to Cheatline may be indicative of an increase in opportunistic claims fraud."

Insurers also reported that claims on lost LCD TVs, high-end watches and laptops had increased by as much as 35% between 2007 and 2008, though it is possible that much of this was the result of a rise in genuine crime rates for those items, which are attractive because of the resale opportunities and values. Savings ratios have been declining as people shift to a credit mindset, but credit has tightened due to the LIBOR market and the liquidity capital ratios imposed under Basel II. People are more willing in recent years to walk away from their homes in negative equity, and mortgage holders are readier to push for forced sales of properties in a poor market. Consequently, the time lag may diminish. However, the most recent UK recorded crime and victimisation survey statistics (ONS, 2012) show a general fall over time in (mostly non-fraud) acquisitive crime 1995-2011, though this drop is viewed with scepticism by the general public. Earlier Home Office statistical model predictions of general crime rises in the United Kingdom as a consequence of unemployment and reduced incomes have not hitherto been realised.

The Association of British Insurers study also (2009: 15) also generated its Figure 7 below, though changes in fraud recording procedures that might have affected this graph and might have driven recent recorded data upwards artificially are not discussed. This suggests a slight inverse but lagged relationship between changes in the unemployment rate and recorded fraud and forgery statistics. However, this evidence is not strong for the impact of unemployment on lower volume insider frauds, since payment card and social security frauds constitute a large proportion of recorded fraud and forgery cases and would mask any trends in insider fraud.

Figure 7 - Unemployment rate vs fraud and forgery offences (1971 - 2007)

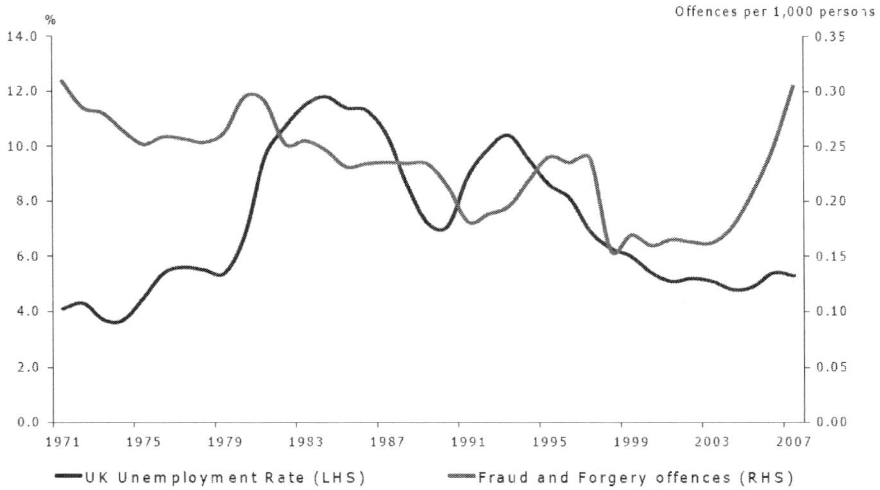

Note: Fraud and Forgery offences are for England and Wales only. Various definition changes occur throughout.
Source: Office For National Statistics (2009), Home Office (2009) and World Bank (2009).

In 2011, £983m of fraud was detected (Association of British Insurers, 2012). This was 7% higher than the value of fraud detected in 2010 and comprises 138.814 fraudulent insurance claims. Home insurance was the area where insurers detected the largest proportion of frauds, with 71.000 bogus or exaggerated claims. Dishonest personal motor insurance frauds were the second largest area of insurance fraud with 37.000 frauds uncovered. They were also the most costly, totalling £441m. 7% of all motor claims in 2011 were fraudulent compared to 5% in 2010. This allegedly reflects the rise in fraudulent whiplash claims, often encouraged by a small minority of corrupt professionals.

In short, there is evidence that the public are relatively tolerant of low level insurance frauds, and increased pressures to make money from relatively harmless offences plus a rise in organised insurance fraud (and in its detection) can be seen. But the connection of organised fraud with the Global Financial Crisis is doubtful.

Mortgage frauds

The Key Findings in a report by the FBI (2009) state that:

> "A decrease in loan originations and an increase in defaults and foreclosures continued to dominate the downward trend in the housing market in 2008. While the amount of mortgage fraud cannot be precisely determined, industry experts agree that there is a direct correlation between fraud and distressed real estate markets . . . The downward trend in the housing market during 2008 provided a favourable climate for mortgage fraud schemes to proliferate. Several of these schemes have the potential to spread if the current economic downward trend, as expected, continues into 2009 and beyond. Increases in foreclosures, declining housing prices, and decreased demand place pressure on lenders, builders, and home sellers. These and other market participants are perpetuating and modifying old schemes, including property flipping, builder-bailouts, short sales, and foreclosure rescues. Additionally, they are facilitating new schemes, including reverse mortgage fraud, credit enhancements, condo conversion, loan modifications, and pump and pay in response to tighter lending practices."

However, this has failed to take sufficient account of the lagged effect of the fraud identification process, and that the frauds began typically *before* the financial crisis, though the general report usefully outlines the precipitating factors behind the mortgage fraud crisis and suggests that the rate of deception accelerated as brokers sought to retain their commission bonuses in a falling market. (See the mortgage fraud updates in FBI, 2011, 2012.) Many of the situational opportunities to defraud are fairly widespread over time, so variation is likely to be accounted for in terms of the spread of techniques among the wider population, expectations of the corruptibility of others, and changes in motivation, including the fear of downward economic mobility. McLean and Nocera (2011) argue that the US mortgage market experienced a rush to poor quality lending, as even those firms that began with a disciplined model of loans to sub-prime borrowers became caught up in a rush to business as other firms came in and lent recklessly, using credit derivatives as a bottomless pit to recycle future bad debts as badly priced triple-A rated Collateralised Debt Obligations (CDOs), investment-grade 'securities' backed by a pool of bonds, loans and other assets. The analogy here might be to Gresham's Law, in which bad money drives out good. Such frauds were added to by firms – whether complete scams or merely genuine but predatory lenders – who gouged advance fees from householders desperate to retain their homes: a kind of secondary victimisation.

Discussion

Two decades ago, Weatherburn (1992, p. 8) concluded that:

> "[T]here would appear to be no reason to expect the criminogenic effects of sustained economic deprivation to be any quicker to dissipate than they were to arrive . . . In the final analysis, the effect of passing economic crises, even severe ones such as the current recession, would seem less important to the future course of crime trends, than the overall pattern of economic development. Uncontrolled and rapid economic development, chronically high levels of unemployment in certain sectors of the economy, and the existence of a marginalised under-class of individuals and families living in poverty are all conditions which can just as easily be found in booming as in contracting economies . . . . Nothing could be more inimical to law and order than an economy which generates rapidly rising living standards for some and an abundance of criminal opportunities for the remainder."

The present circumstances are as good an opportunity as any to test this model. Thus far, general crime rates have not followed the upwards path expected, but how likely is this to be true of financial crimes? The reactions of people to often dramatic changes in their financial circumstances and their social prestige (and in their *expectations* of upwards socio-economic mobility) are central. In the particular case of white-collar crimes (see Simpson and Weisburd, 2009), the anxieties among well-paid (and often highly competitive and wealth-oriented) professionals about the personal and corporate impact of the Global Financial Crisis gives plausible grounds for concern about what extra crime risks will be generated. These might take the form of greater willingness to trade off the risk of prosecution (for fraud and/or for laundering the proceeds of fraud and other crimes) against extra income from doing extra business that may be needed to maintain existing lifestyles or even survive (Levi, 2008a; Piquero, 2012). Pushed by trade union and nationalist concerns in the West, lower paid white-collar workers – for example in overseas (and domestic) call centres and banks – may be tempted to engage in fraud and money-laundering on behalf of organised crime groups. These phenomena are not recent but workers may be more motivated to take-up such opportunities (Van Duyne and De Miranda, 1999), especially if outside criminals are more emboldened to make corrupt offers or extortion demands.

Chief executives have been able to allocate to the company expenditures that, in fact, were largely or wholly personal. Though on a vastly different scale, they are not alone in this. Also kleptocratic dictators in developing countries filled their enlarging coffers because of the increased desperation of sales divisions of international corporations. At present this may be counteracted by the increased activism of prosecutors noted recently in the United Kingdom as well as the United States, under pressure from domestic audiences such as NGOs and international ones such as anti-bribery and anti-money laundering bodies.

Accountants, bankers and lawyers cannot readily manipulate clients' accounts or set up trust and other corporate secrecy vehicles if they no longer work for firms, though they (and anyone else) can make up *imaginary* firms and may have a pretext for corporate instructions to firms ("Starting a new phase in my life – wonderful opportunities for new investments in country or product x"). If others have confidence in them, such entrepreneurs can develop new businesses that may generate new manipulative possibilities, but this would usually take longer at times of recession.

At a lower level, staff in call centres cannot so easily copy and extract personal data of account-holders if they have been fired. If still employed, they may be more tempted to defraud if they consider that they may shortly become unemployed and/or that the company will show no loyalty towards them. (Though their *ability to offend* may be reduced by physical opportunity controls such as the absence of USB and CD drives on computers and rapid integrity checks.) Under such circumstances, *voluntary* compliance via procedural legitimacy (Tyler, 2009) becomes much harder to achieve. (Financial and social pressures to offend may also be affected positively or negatively by fear of redundancy and peer group pressures, though threats from organised crime groups may not be Global Financial Crisis-related.)

Knowledge of criminal techniques should be differentiated from *opportunity and motivation to offend,* though offending may be inhibited if people do not believe that they have enough technical knowledge to commit any particular sort of fraud that they contemplate. *It is the expectation or fear that one may become unemployed that presents the extra risk here.* In addition, social engineering opportunities make firms and government departments vulnerable to outsiders who can be ex-employees or in collusion with employees, but also just may have sufficient expertise to 'pass' as staff. Impacts of the Global Financial Crisis on professionals elsewhere may impact any country (even those like Australia that have suffered less) because, given international finance and trade – both for business and individuals – we may be the victims of frauds originating elsewhere, and expatriate professionals who lose their jobs may return home and exercise their skills illicitly. On the other hand, there are significant segments of technologically sophisticated people in Eastern Europe who have never had sufficient economic opportunities to meet their wants, so, except in reducing their future expectations, the downwards shift in economic status implied by the term Global Financial Crisis has not happened for them. Nevertheless, the greater time available to the unemployed can give greater room for experimentation, and criminal attempts are seldom punished or even logged by targets or financial intermediaries.

The crime triangle of motivation, opportunity, and capable guardians can be applied to fraud, and it is here in human and technological changes to these parameters that one may search for an explanatory framework. *A priori*, it would appear that different skill sets, commercial/personal background and formal qualifications will be needed for different fraud offences, and the barriers to entry depend on the starting point of any given individual or network *in relation to the practical opportunity and criminal justice obstacles that confront them.*

In most countries of the world, a distinction is made between laissez-faire opportunities to set up and work in commerce and some restrictions (normally simple criminal record and indebtedness checks) applied to people who want to work in the financial services sector, largely on the grounds that the latter can directly steal funds from the public. It is important to understand such restrictions in a global context rather than the traditional nation-state perspective of regulation and criminal justice.

Sometimes what is needed for the accomplishment of fraud is compliant colleagues – both inferiors and superiors – who do not ask critical questions. This was the case with Nick Leeson and Barings Bank, where as a leading trader, Leeson was surrounded with Singaporean subordinates and colleagues who were passive, and with British superiors who understood little about trading and were content to take the results he fed them that inflated their own large bonuses (Leeson, 1999).

Many of the larger cases in which corporate vehicles are used as a vehicle for fraud begin in good economic times, when there is an atmosphere of optimism among lenders, and large bonuses for corporate takeover activity (though recent bonuses have been much larger than in earlier eras). These bonuses sometimes have a criminal function in the *modus operandi*. Some corporate fraudsters paid staff on much higher than normal market salaries to ensure their loyalty or wilful blindness when facing alternative employment on much lower salaries. Alternatively, as in the Madoff and Stanford scandals, they may employ small firms of accountants who are dependent on them, whether or not they were active participants in the frauds. Such alleged scams are facilitated by trust combined with pressure on investors to get higher than average returns (and by greed). By contrast with credit card skimmers who may need to be helped by an army of people to use the card numbers they have skimmed before the breach of identity is realised and reported, there may be no need for conscious co-conspirators in other frauds, depending on the chain of authority within large corporate or governmental settings and their competence. What some offenders are able to do is simply to deploy the range of global corporate mechanisms available in a free enterprise society where there are insufficient capable guardians to stop them misusing the disguises offered by the corporate form or the authority and power of a corporate role. Enron offered a dazzling array of Special Purpose Vehicles to hide transactions. This was long before the Global Financial Crisis, and it is moot whether the impact on fraud of the crisis was affected by the Sarbanes-Oxley Act 2002[16] and other supervision measures introduced in the aftermath (see Tillman, 2009, for some insights). So for volume frauds, there does appear to have been an increase in some areas, but for larger corporate frauds, there is not yet any firm evidence. As Warren Buffet (2001) noted some years before the Global Financial Crisis: "*You only find out who is swimming naked when the tide goes out.*"

This brings us back to the issue of what we choose to call fraud and what we choose to call 'organised crime'. In the credit boom, as competition between lenders pushed banks' profit margins to very low levels, they needed a new revenue stream. In the UK, Payment Protection Insurance (PPI) quickly became a huge profit generator and an easy way to keep headline interest rates on loans artificially low, as it was combined together with personal loans and mortgages but was not included in the apparent overall cost. Borrowers thought they had a good rate of interest, while the "hidden" charges meant that lenders could still generate huge profits. As Goff and Moore put it[17]: "These tactics enabled banks to shift about 20m PPI policies by 2006. Between 2001 and 2010, when certain PPI sales were banned, regulators estimate that the industry sold £34bn of the insurance." It has led to compensation payments exceeding £10 billion, and some substantial fines also. There is no doubt that this was a highly organised form of misconduct, but it has never been characterised officially as fraud. If it has been, some interesting questions of personal and corporate criminal liability would have been raised, but perhaps it would have been even harder for victims to get compensation for products on which the small print excluded so many of them from actually claiming.

To summarise: In essence we know very little about the causal relationship of the Global Crisis and financial crimes. There are insufficient data for trend analysis, the data are fragmented because of the particularities of fraud schemes and their perpetrators. The population of perpetrators is heterogeneous, which makes

---

16 As a result of this legislation, top management must now individually certify the accuracy of financial information; penalties for fraudulent financial activity are more severe; outside auditors who review the accuracy of corporate financial statements were given greater independence; the oversight role of boards of directors was enhanced.

17 October 28, 2012, http://www.ft.com/cms/s/0/67e137ac-1e94-11e2-be82-00144feabdc0.html#ixzz2AwpohNoh.

generalisation tentative if not yet mistaken. Elite financial crimes look to be independent of economic cycles, perhaps with the exception of loan and mortgage fraud, which recedes as banks apply stricter risk thresholds and inter-professional conspiracies are highlighted by past misconduct coming to the surface. Bankruptcy fraud will increase, usually in the form of embezzlement from the bankrupt's corporate or individual assets. These are usually 'crimes of desperation'. As for 'organised crime', we have to confront the verities taken for granted by many. How likely is it that 'they' will put their money in tottering banks? There is not much evidence beyond mere assertion. As 'the' organised crime is little more than a crude political and law enforcement construction, there is some plausibility in the statement that organising business criminals are more likely to pull money *out of* the banks than entrusting it to them. Unless, that is, they are afraid that the 'sentinels of the banking industry' (Favarel-Garrigues et al., 2008) and/or of financial intelligence units are watching them, might identify them as malefactors *and* will do something about it. As the chief of police in an updated version of *Casablanca* might have said, "Make suspicious activity reports on the usual suspects".

References

Association of British Insurers, *General insurance claims fraud*. London, Association of British Insurers, 2009 http,//www.abi.org.uk/Media/Releases/2009/07/40569.pdf

Association of British Insurers, *No hiding place: Insurance fraud exposed*. London, Association of British Insurers, 2012

Barak, G., *Theft of a nation: Wall Street looting and federal regulatory colluding*. Lanham, Rowman and Littlefield Publishers, 2012

Box, S, *Recession, crime and punishment*, 1987

Braithwaite J, White collar crime. *Annual Review of Sociology*, vol. 11, 1-25, 1985

Buffet, W, *Berkshire Hathaway 2001 Chairman's Letter,* 2001 http://www.berkshirehathaway.com/2001ar/2001letter.html

Bullock, K., R Clarke, and N Tilley (eds.), *The situational prevention of organised crime*. Cullompton, Willan, 2010

Bunt, H.G. van de, Walls of secrecy and silence: The Madoff case and cartels in the construction industry. *Criminology and Public Policy*. 9 (3): 435-453, 2010

CIFAS, *Fraudscape: Depicting the UK's fraud landscape (2012 Edition)*, London, CIFAS, 2012

Coates J, *The hour between dog and wolf: Risk-taking, gut feelings and the biology of boom and bust*. London, Fourth Estate, 2012

Deflem M, Introduction: criminological perspectives of the crisis. In: Deflem M. (ed.) *Economic crisis and crime*. Bingley, Emerald Group Publishing Limited, 2011

Duyne, P.C. van and M.D.H. Nelemans, Transnational organised crime: thinking in and out of Plato's cave. *Handbook of transnational crime*, Routledge, 2011

Duyne, P.C. van and H. De Miranda, The emperor's cloths of disclosure: hot money and suspect disclosures. *Crime, Law and Social Change, 3:* 1999, 245-271

FATF, *International standards on combating money laundering and the financing of terrorism and proliferation - the FATF Recommendations*, Paris, OECD, 2012

FBI (2011) 2010 Mortgage fraud report: Year in review. http://www.fbi.gov/stats-services/publications/mortgage-fraud-2010/mortgage-fraud-report-2010

FBI (2012) Financial crimes report to the public: Fiscal Years 2010-2011. http://www.fbi.gov/stats-services/publications/financial-crimes-report-2010-2011

FTC (2012) Consumer sentinel network data book January – December 2011, Washington DC, Federal Trade Commission

FICO (2012) Evolution of card fraud in Europe. www.fico.com/fraudeurope

Favarel-Garrigues, G., T. Godefroy and P. Lascoumes, Sentinels in the banking industry: Private actors and the fight against money laundering in France, *British Journal of Criminology* 48(1), 1-19, 2008.

Federation of Small Businesses, *Inhibiting enterprise: Fraud and online crime against small businesses*, 2009

Federation of Small Businesses, *Localism and tackling crimes against business*. 2010

Financial Fraud Action UK, *Fraud – the facts 2011*. London, Financial Fraud Action UK, 2011

Financial Fraud Action UK, *Fraud – the Facts 2012*. London, Financial Fraud Action UK, 2012

Gannon, R. and A. Doig, Ducking the answer: Fraud strategies and police resources. *Policing and Society*, 2010, 20, 1.

Geis, G and C. Goff, "Introduction" in E.H. Sutherland, *White-collar Crime: The Uncut Version*, New Haven: Yale University Press, 1983

KPMG, *Profile of a fraudster survey 2007*, London, KPMG, 2007

KPMG , *Who is the typical fraudster?* London, KPMG, 2011

Langton, L., Identity theft reported by households: 2005-2010. Washington DC, Government Printing House, 2011 http://bjs.ojp.usdoj.gov/content/pub/pdf/itrh0510.pdf

Leeson, N., *Rogue trader*. London, Sphere, 1999

Levi, M., The Media construction of financial white-collar crimes. *British Journal of Criminology*, 2006, 46: 1037-1057

Levi, M., *The phantom capitalists: the organisation and control of long-firm Fraud.* 2nd edition. Andover, Ashgate, 2008a

Levi, M., 'Organised Fraud': Unpacking research on networks and organisation. *Criminology and Criminal Justice*, 2008b, 8(4), 389-420

Levi M., Suite revenge? The shaping of folk devils and moral panics about white-collar crimes. *British Journal of Criminology*, 2009, 49 (1): 48-67

Levi, M., J. Burrows, M. Fleming and M. Hopkins (with the assistance of K. Matthews) T*he nature, extent and economic impact of fraud in the UK*. London, Association of Chief Police Officers, 2007 http://www.cardiff.ac.uk/socsi/resources/ACPO%20final%20nature%20extent%20and%20economic%20impact%20of%20fraud.pdf

Levi, M. and J. Burrows, Measuring the impact of fraud, a conceptual and empirical journey. *British Journal of Criminology*, 2008, 48(3), 293-318

Levi, M. and R Smith, Fraud vulnerabilities and the global financial crisis. *Trends and issues in crime and criminal justice* no.422. Canberra, Australian Institute of Criminology, 2011

Levi, M. and M. Williams, *eCrime reduction partnership mapping study*, 2012 http://www.cardiff.ac.uk/socsi/resources/Levi%20Williams%20eCrime%20Reduction%20Partnership%20Mapping%20Study.pdf

McLean, B. and J. Nocera, *All The Devils Are Here: Unmasking the Men Who Bankrupted the World*, London, Viking, 2011

Markopoulos, H., *No one would listen: A true financial thriller.* Hoboken, John Wiley, 2010

Muriel, A. and L. Sibieta, *Living standards during previous recessions.* IFS Briefing Notes No. 85, 2009 (http://www.ifs.org.uk/publications/4525)

NFA, *Annual fraud indicator 2010.* London, National Fraud Authority, 2011

NFA, *Annual fraud indicator 2011.* London, National Fraud Authority, 2012

Nguyen, T.H. and H.N. Pontell, Mortgage origination fraud and the global economic crisis: A criminological analysis. *Criminology and Public Policy*, 2010 9(3), 591–612

Passas, N. and N. Goodwin, *It's legal but it ain't right: Harmful social consequences of legal industries.* Ann Arbor: University of Michigan Press, 2005

Piquero, N.L., The only thing we have to fear is fear itself: Investigating the relationship between fear of falling and white-collar crime. *Crime and Delinquency*, 2012, 58 (3): 362-379

Sharman, J., *The money laundry.* New Haven, Princeton University Press, 2011

Shaxson, N., *Treasure islands.* London, Bodley Head, 2011.

Simpson, S. and D. Weisburd (eds.), *The criminology of white-collar crime*. New York, Springer, 2009

Sorkin, A., *Too big to fail: Inside the battle to save Wall Street*, London: Penguin, 2010

Tillman, R., Reputations and corporate malfeasance, collusive networks in financial statement fraud. *Crime, Law and Social Change*, 2009, 51, 365–382

Tyler, T., Self-regulatory approaches to white-collar crime: The importance of legitimacy and procedural justice. In: S. Simpson and D. Weisburd (eds.), *The criminology of white-collar crime*. New York, Springer, 2009

Wang, X. and K. Holtfreter, The effects of corporation- and industry-level strain and opportunity on corporate crime. *Journal of Research in Crime and Delinquency*, 2012, 49(2): 151-185

Weatherburn D., Economic adversity and crime. *Trends and Issues in Criminal Justice* No. 40. Canberra, Australian Institute of Criminology, 1992

de Willebois, E., J. Sharman, R. Harrison, J.W. Park, and E. Halter, *The puppet masters: How the corrupt use legal structures to hide stolen assets and what to do about It*. Washington DC, World Bank, 2011

AML Compliance: Rituals of Engagement or Improvements in Integrity?

Jackie Harvey, Rowan Bosworth-Davies and Martin Elliott[1]

The UK Anti-Money Laundering Framework

Rules and legislation are like the choreographic indications of dance steps: they specify and set out expected conduct on a stage. In such circumstances, it is hoped that the dancers integrate these indications and convert them into an inner value to be translated into the beauty of the dance. However, the indications can also be followed without inner conviction, technically correct, but without heart or soul, like an outward ritual of compliance. It is possible that legal frameworks and regimes may function in a similar manner. This is more likely in those cases where they cover a broad social and economic space, with many participants who are obliged to conform, either out of conviction or to avoid being brow-beaten by stage's technical director. There are many examples of this, but the money laundering stage may be a typical representative of 'choreographic' legislation lacking 'inner' acceptance but characterised by outward ritualistic dancing. What is to be observed?

The choreography within the UK legal framework for money laundering has been developing since the early 1990s and is contained within a range of primary legislation although primarily located within the Proceeds of Crime Act 2002 (POCA), as amended by the Serious Organised Crime and Police Act 2005 (SOPCA).

The regulatory side of this legislation was, in the first instance, focused upon the financial services sector, however, the scope has been gradually extended to encompass a range of 'at risk' sectors, including activities undertaken by professional advisers, the legal and accounting profession, who are traditionally viewed as the 'gatekeepers' to the financial system. Despite the observation by Levi (2003: 111) that the UK authorities are identified as "*the greatest devotee of anti-money*

1 The authors are respectively Professor at Newcastle Business School, Northumbria University, Director Bosworth Fields Ltd and researcher at Newcastle Business School, Northumbria University. Corresponding author: jackie.harvey@northumbria.ac.uk

laundering provisions within the European Union" being seen as exceptionally diligent; the development and application of AML is rather like "*driving a car by only looking in the rear view mirror*" (Doig, Harvey, Artinghall and Howell, 2011: 51). Given the dynamic nature of criminal activity, it is inevitable that policies are always implemented or adjusted in response to, rather than in prevention of, money laundering. This is simply because criminals, as rational agents, continually respond to such new rules and regulations by adjusting their behaviour. Thus despite ensuring adherence to compliance requirements, it cannot be assumed that conventional approaches or best practice solutions are perfect.

Under the requirements of the money laundering regulations, regulated institutions are required to have in place systems and procedures that enable them to do two things. Firstly they need to be able to verify the identity of their customer (this is reported as know your customer or KYC) and, secondly, they are required to effectively implement the Suspicious Activity Reporting regime (SARs). More recently international standards (as set out in the 2007 money laundering regulations[2]) have moved towards a wider appraisal of the risks associated with a particular customer referred to as 'Customer Due Diligence' (CDD) with assessment taking place at the commencement of the business relationship and at other times during that relationship according to an internal estimate of 'risk'. The purpose behind this risk-based approach was to enable reporting entities and banks in particular, to tailor their scrutiny and AML efforts in a more cost effective manner with the argument being that it would enable greater concentration to be directed towards those clients deemed to be 'more risky' and help, therefore, reduce the costs of compliance.

The problem to arise from implementing this approach is that the institutions, who still have to demonstrate that the measures in place are appropriate for the risk, felt that they needed rather more clarity and direction from the regulators. The latter for their part, were trying to divest some of the decision making surrounding the former 'rule-based' approach as they sought to transfer interpretational responsibility into the market place. It is, therefore, something of a paradox that an apparent attempt to reduce regulation by shifting from a rule based to a risk based approach has actually resulted in greater internal regulation. This is simply reflective of a dismantling of rules increasing uncertainty. Firms eschew uncertainties so they counteracted its presence with a plethora of own rules, systems and procedures, with which they sought to 'demonstrate' their compliance (Geiger and Wuensch, 2007; Harvey, 2008; Levi and Reuter, 2006; and Gill and Taylor, 2003). Ross and Hannan (2007: 106) comment on the transference of interpretational responsibility

---

2 Statutory Instrument Number 2157, 15th December, 2007

between the regulated and the regulators, by observing "*. . . the requirements on agencies imposed by the risk-based approach involve a significant element of uncertainty.*"

Of course, the notion of due diligence did not arrive with AML, having been legally enshrined in UK financial markets through the 1986 Financial Services Act and prior to this formal legal incorporation, it was seen to operate informally through the colloquial concept of the 'sniff test'. The 'sniff test' can be seen to describe an informal internal code of morals and ethics that operates within an institution. This test was more of a professional feeling or 'instinct' employed to ensure that market participants or their employing institutions did not get involved with anything remotely likely to bring them into contact with activities that might cause embarrassment. This was also fraught with risks and uncertainties, but was out of the sight of the prying eyes of regulators. The AML system of compliance and oversight changed this by adding a new external control and sanction dimension but has this furthered an internal change to genuine integrity or has it simply evoked ritualistic dancing as evidenced through simple rule-compliance? What is to be observed are they dancing from the heart or merely executing the steps?

This chapter seeks to understand the additional compliance dimension that has come about as a result of the development of the AML framework and questions whether the additional measures introduced as part of the AML framework make an appreciable difference to the intrinsic integrity of either the regulated sectors and by extension, to the individual institutions or whether they merely add to the existing elaborate rituals of engagement that form the basis of the relationship between the regulators and the regulated sector, described by Moran (2000: 11) as:

> "a constant battle of wits between the surveyors and the surveyed – a battle where rituals of verification abound, and where enormous energy goes into those rituals and into their subversion."

Integrity and the role of compliance

The approach on the part of the regulators has been to assume that internal integrity, rather than being a construct intrinsic to and part of the fabric of an institution can, instead, be forced into existence through regulation. As eloquently stated by Moran (2000: 10) "*we audit, and we regulate, when we cease to trust*". Without doubt, integrity is of critical importance to the financial sector and is integrally linked with the concept of reputation. Indeed Harvey and Lau (2009: 59) commented that "*Far from being an objective construct, reputation is, like beauty, in the eye of the beholder and thus not easily defined*". Clearly trust is linked to confidence, because "*Scandals and unethical behaviour in financial institutions erode confidence in such firms*" (Venard and Hanafi, 2008: 481). Such sentiments can similarly be applied to the wider regulated sector particularly where it embraces the professions whose very office rests on client trust and confidentiality. Historically, bankers in particular would have been more comfortable with a code of ethics that demanded discretion rather than disclosure in the dealings of their clients. This position was illustrated by a comment made by the Money Laundering Reporting Officer (MLRO) from a financial institution interviewed by the principal author in June 2009 as part of this study, who stated: "*Traditionally you were taught only to give very limited information, the idea of any cooperation between banks and law enforcement was an anathema*". AML introduced an external dimension to the compliance construct and the associated scrutiny of business relationships and transactions for potentially illegal activities thus challenging the presumed confidentiality of that relationship.

Of course, from the perception of the regulator, the key component in ensuring that regulated entities adhered to any regulatory framework rests with its enforcement and integral to this is the role of compliance, more specifically that of internal compliance. However, if such rituals exist, one might expect to find that attempts to regulate as a means to engender integrity merely result in evidence of compliance for compliance sake. In other words: simply executing the steps. Hence the responsiveness to the regulations by those subject to them is critical for their effectiveness: "*The institutions and locations where regulation takes place affect both the outcome of the regulatory process and the legitimacy of the rules and practices produced*" (Cooper and Robson, 2006: 415). Indeed to the extent that those tasked with implementation might doubt their effectiveness, the legitimacy would be seriously undermined.

Given the important role and perceived complexity of the financial sector, there has been a certain acceptance of a more closed system of regulatory scrutiny operating between the regulator and the regulated sector itself played out with very clear rules of engagement. But how far does that acceptance go? Clearly the compliance officer faces considerable conflict in executing his role. Assumption of the mantle of internal policeman suggested that the 'sniff test' had failed and that firms required a firmer prod towards ensuring effective internal governance. This inevitably creates a conflict for the individual compliance officer as they are employees of the same institutions they are required to 'police'. Mindful of their contribution to cost rather than profit, they might well be drawn towards ensuring that they could demonstrate the execution of their function. That they can do by showing that they prevented the exposure of their employers to anything that might result in regulatory intervention and thus possible financial loss through disciplinary action or damaging public scrutiny.

The principal regulatory body, the Financial Services Authority (FSA) have interpreted the money laundering laws and associated regulations and defined them in a series of requirements and compliance actions that they have placed upon the regulated sector. Just as the individual compliance officer protects the integrity of his company, so the regulator needs to be able to demonstrate probity of his sector through inspection of the ensuing systems and procedures adopted by the institutions. If indeed, we are witnessing an engagement with *rituals* it might be anticipated that compliance mechanisms will comprise a meticulous display demonstrating the outward appearance of compliance: highly organised and well-composed, systems will be well documented; and apparent controls will be in place. The overwhelming impression will be one of compliance and orderly conduct, regardless of whether any meaningful results are being achieved. Hence investment in systems and procedures is viewed as providing concrete evidence of an institution's commitment to fulfilling obligations. In fact, what will be demonstrated, as articulated by Harvey and Lau (2009), is sanction-avoiding compliance. In this regard it is interesting to consider the comments made in an interview with the MLRO from the gaming sector that was conducted by the principal author in June 2009, again as part of this study:

> "Risk to [name of company] of non-compliance is what drives the company to be compliant – otherwise we will lose our license to operate. The driver is not to identify proceeds of crime but to be showing to be seen as compliant and diligent."

Likewise the comments of an interviewee from the accounting sector carried out at the same time in June 2009:

> "There is a problem with resources for a firm this size – we ignore stuff and keep our fingers crossed. Small companies will have a manual and it will all be kept up to date. If you are larger you can afford some overhead staff . . . . A lot of analysis is done because we have to do it but it is totally meaningless . . ."

The view from the front line

The quotations given above come from three interviews undertaken at the same time as an electronic survey of MLROs that was facilitated by the Institute of Money Laundering Prevention Officers (IMLPO) and which took place in the summer of 2009. The questionnaire aimed to understand the rationale, conviction and effectiveness of AML compliance as well as to establish where MLRO's perceived the real risks of money laundering to be, and what impact these risks have on their industry sector. In other words, it was hoped to gain clarity of understanding about whether the approach to AML compliance executed by the dancers was truly from the heart. The survey was launched on May 15th 2009 and held open for a period of four weeks until June 12th. During that time a total number of 36 members of IMLPO responded to the survey. To set this in context, there are just over 200 members, of which around 100 could be described as active.[3] Against this, the response rate of 18%, although low, it is still at an acceptable enough level to be able to undertake some analysis.

Respondents' demographics

As shown in Table 1 respondents came from a wide range of regulated sectors.

Table 1
Respondents' primary business area

Institution's primary business activity	number
Accounting	6
Asset management	1
Broking	1
Financial services	8
Gaming	4
Insurance	6
Legal	1
Private banking	1
Retail banking and building societies	7
Other	1
Total	36

Similarly, respondents worked for a range of size of institutions both in terms of turnover (range from less than £0,5m to £500m plus, modal value £500m plus) and number of employees (range from 10-100 to over 50.000, modal value 1001-10.000). It should be noted, however, that the majority of respondents came from the very large commercial backgrounds which has to be borne in mind when looking at the results: 61% (17) had a turnover greater than £100m of which 43% (12) had turnovers in excess of £500 million; 28% employed more than 10.000 people while 61% had more than 1.000 employees.

3 Information obtained in a telephone conversation with the IMLPO.

Figure 1
Size of organisations responding: number of employees and turnover

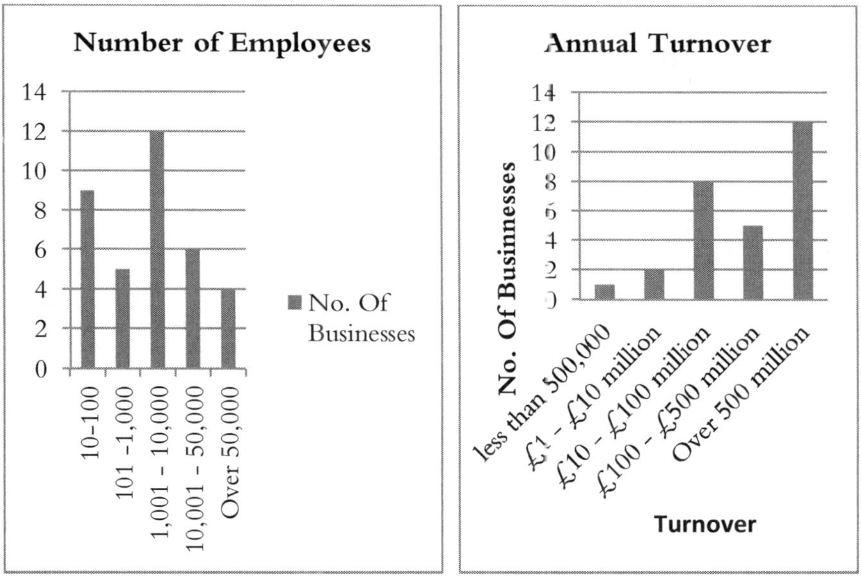

Likewise respondents were from a range of geographic areas within the UK, although as might be expected the largest number were from London (42%). For the majority of respondents (14) the AML compliance and investigation function was conducted by a group of 2-5 people, although six respondents had a department of more than 20 people. A number of the respondents either had oversight as MLRO over a wide geographic or functional area or indeed had additional duties alongside that of MLRO. Finally the greater majority of respondents have significant years of service and experience inside their institution, with over a quarter of them having more than 20 years service. Five respondents came into compliance having had a former role in the police and eight answering the question had a prior position within compliance or audit elsewhere suggesting compliance is increasingly viewed as a profession.

Figure 2
Location of respondents and Size of compliance function

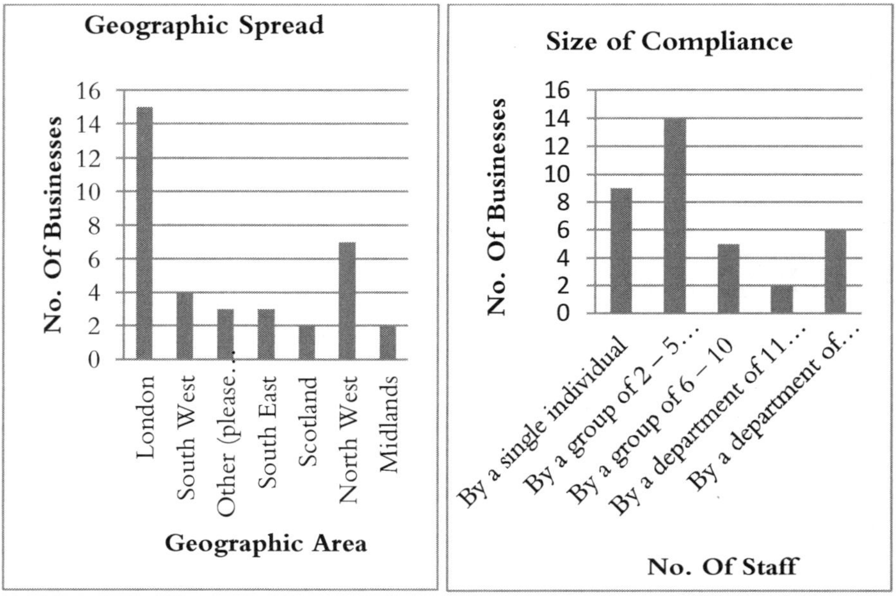

It is worth commenting that 7 out of 12 of the businesses with a £500million plus turnover have 10 or less compliance staff, two have only a single person undertaking this function. Interestingly, it is the two out of three companies in the Gaming industry, with £550million plus turnovers that have only a single person carrying out compliance, with the third company having only between 2 and 5 people. The 25% of firms that have 20 plus people in a department dealing with compliance are, as might be expected, from the banking and financial services area.

Results from the survey

The answers to the questions were scored using a five point Likert scale although for ease of interpretation they are presented grouped into agree/disagree and neither agree nor disagree. The question results, provided in Appendix 1, are grouped according to four broad areas: those around the regulations themselves; those in relation to the regulators/SOCA; those covering the organisation responding and finally those focusing on implementation, cost and effectiveness. The discussion that follows takes on a further level of granularity focusing on sub-sections within these broad areas.

Rationale for compliance - reputation and disclosure

62% of respondents noted no disclosure in annual reports and accounts or in Corporate Social Responsibility (CSR) reports, a finding that is consistent with Harvey (2008). Further, there is no clear pattern of disclosure with respect to businesses required to publish annual reports with between half and two thirds of financial services, retail banks and insurance sectors making public statements around AML compliance (Figure 3). It would appear from this and prior interviews conducted by the first author (Harvey, 2008) that many institutions refuse to make any public statement or announcement of their AML compliance activities. As previously concluded by Harvey and Lau (2009), compliance procedures are not perceived to be a business-enhancing feature. Indeed there was no real consideration of the relative nature of AML controls. A third thought that their competitors were less rigorous than themselves (**Q 33**) in terms of AML procedures although the majority (44%) had no view on this. Neither was there any indication that the public demonstration of AML compliance could be used to provide competitive advantage (**Q 35**): 26% agreeing or strongly agreeing, 37% disagreeing or strongly disagreeing and 32% being indifferent. Contrast this, however, with the answers for two questions, both of which identify damage to reputation as a major risk from money laundering: Compliance is viewed as protecting reputation with 78% agreed with the statement that protection of reputation is the most important function of compliance (**Q 17**) (although it would perhaps be strange to see an alternative response); likewise 80% agreed or strongly agreed that the main risk of money laundering was to reputation (**Q 43**).

Figure 4
Public disclosure rates

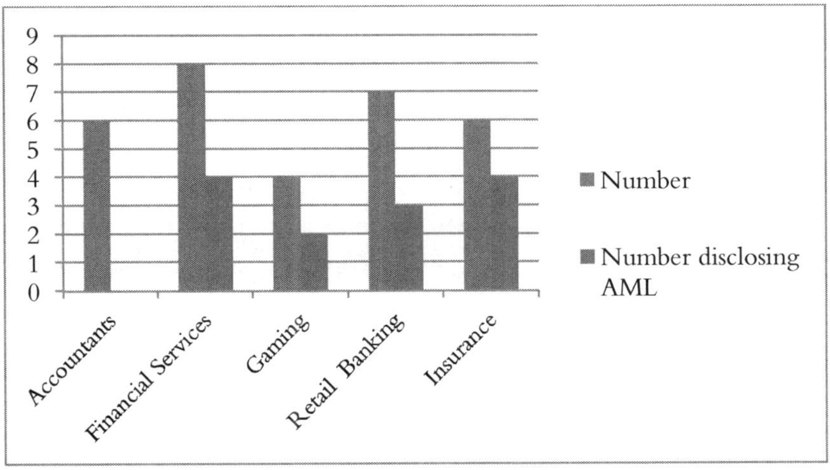

92% either agree or strongly agree that it is important to have a strong regulatory framework given how significant the financial sector is to the UK economy **(Q 21).** Yet despite such strong support for the regulatory framework and the clear identification that money laundering would cause reputational damage, nearly 25% (8/36) of firms believed that their organisation does not benefit from the current money laundering regulation with a further six firms neither agreeing nor disagreeing. Five of the accountants and four of the financial services companies were among the group believing they got no benefit or that they had no opinion on the statement. It is also interesting to note that a final question (**Q 53**) indicated that only 40% of companies feel that AML procedures assure customers and enhance their reputation, 37% neither agree nor disagree and approximately 20% disagree or strongly disagree.

Cost of compliance - budgets

The survey of compliance officers, noted that AML budgets ranged from tens of thousands up to millions, with the majority of respondents indicating an annual spend of between £100.000 and £200.000. There is a traditional reluctance by institutions to divulge annual expenditure on AML, being viewed as a business overhead (Harvey, 2008). Hence one third of respondents indicated that they could not answer the question or, were unable to as the data were not recorded (**Q 14**). One respondent noted, however, a rather worrying zero spent on AML because compliance was "*done as additional tasks outside company time*" with no costs incurred by the company. Overall half (18) of the firms believed that bigger companies bear the brunt of the compliance costs (**Q 49**); as might be expected, of those that agreed, most were 'bigger' organisations: four retail banks; four financial services groups and a building society.

A different question that asked about the importance of value for money arising from the AML compliance function (**Q 42**) indicated that 25 respondents (69%) either agreed or strongly agreed that this was essential that anti-money laundering compliance had to demonstrate value for money. A different question, phrased in terms of the importance of maintaining integrity of the financial sector enquired about the perceived reasonableness of the compliance costs to which 20 agreed (61%) with the remainder holding either no opinion (21%) or disagreeing (21%) that these costs were reasonable (**Q 29**). Interestingly in direct contrast to this 55% agreed or strongly agreed that money laundering compliance was a significant cost to their business, 18% disagreed or strongly disagreed and 18% were indifferent (**Q37**). It is hardly surprising that despite the apparent importance of regulation and of its compliance in terms of integrity, there is no real desire to dwell upon the costs that are imposed.

Demonstration of compliance - activity

Given a defensive mindset, it would be rational for those within the compliance field to overstate importance and significance of their role in dealing with AML (Harvey, 2008 and Aldridge, 2008). Thus 86% respondents gave the answer that AML is key to fighting international organised crime (**Q 18**) and a further 81% (29 out of 36) also believe compliance with money laundering regulation helps prevent other economic crime **(Q 19).** It is interesting that such arguments continue to be presented despite increasing evidence that they do not hold in practice (Alldridge, 2003; Van Duyne *et al.*, 2005; Reuter and Truman, 2006; and Harvey and Lau, 2009).

The dichotomy apparent in the minds of practitioners is illustrated by the 92% agreeing that a strong regulatory framework is required, while only 61% (22 respondents) said they benefitted from AML (**Q 22**). It can be observed that 30 (83%) thought that the system of checks and balances (**Q 23**) would make laundering within their firm difficult, (although three admitted that they thought laundering could occur). Interestingly, in direct contrast to this, a third of respondents believe their organisation is likely to be targeted by criminals trying to launder illicitly acquired funds (**Q 26**). Of this group, four were financial service groups, four were retail banks, one was a private bank and one other a law company. But contrast this with the 18 (50%) who said there was little money laundering through their types of organisation (**Q 38**), (five of the six accountancy companies believed there was little laundering throughout their industry, along with three of the insurance companies), although 8 (22%) thought they would be a target for terrorists for financing purposes (**Q 31**). Of these, three were financial services firms, two retail banks, two insurance companies and the other a gaming company. While the majority saw a clear role for AML in disrupting organised crime, there was considerably less certainty with respect to international terrorism as only just over half thought that money laundering controls are a key component of winning the war against international terrorism (**Q 36**). Curiously in response to a statement concerning the amount of money laundering through their geographic region (**Q 39**), 63% disagree or strongly disagree that there is very little money laundering through their part of the country, only 13% agreed and 21% neither agreed nor disagreed. It would be expected that the majority of those disagreeing with the statement could be found in London (12), they were not confined to this geographic area: two were in the South East; one in Scotland; two in the South West; four in the North East with the others not specifying.

Of the 14 (39%) firms who do not believe there is a need to continually tighten money laundering regulations (half of respondents thought that they should be) only one of these was a retail bank (arguably the most likely place where illicit funds would enter the financial system **(Q 45)**). The rest of this group of respondents who stated that regulations were tight enough, not surprisingly, came from the legal, accounting and gaming sector, although they also included a private bank and three of the financial services groups.

19 respondents (53%) thought that AML is too focused on customer identification (**Q 20**) (hitherto the main area of focus for the FSA has been on KYC checking), although 29 (83%) thought that their customers were aware of the reasons for identity checks (**Q 24**) and there did not appear to be much concern over the potential for lost business as a result of compliance procedures (**Q 25**) although 12 or 34% did see this as a problem for them. It is interesting to note that a further question concerning the time consuming nature of due diligence (**Q 30**) indicated 11 in agreement (33%) although 15 (44%) disagreed that this was the case. Nearly 60% agreed or strongly agreed with the statement "*International money laundering regulations do not sufficiently take into account commercial realities faced by the business sector*" (**Q 47**), 32% were indifferent and the remainder disagreed.

It is difficult in the light of this to comment on the extensiveness of checking of client identities when engaging in KYC checks. However, even with transaction monitoring systems in place (**Q 9**), the majority of respondents believed that detecting suspicious activities as opposed to unusual transactions was difficult: 44% of respondents said that they could do that, although the majority were unable to so or were unsure (**Q 48**). It is fascinating, considering how many proprietary Transaction Monitoring systems that now exist on the market, that 42% of respondents admitted that they did not use any. The 58% of the companies that utilised Electronic Transaction Monitoring Systems comprise all of the retail banks, the one building society, private banking company and life and pensions provider. Four out of six and five out of seven of the Insurance and Financial Services Groups respectively also use these services. The majority of accountants and all of the Gaming industry respondents did not use these systems, possibly due to the fact that accountants are dealing with money already in the financial system. The majority (but not exclusively) of non-users fell into the non-financial services sector but some of these companies had fairly large turnovers.

Interestingly on a question over status (**Q 40**) 53% agree or strongly agree that compliance staff are highly regarded in their company, 16% said the opposite and 24% were indifferent – given the desire for self-legitimisation it might have been expected that the response here would have been 100%. Although nearly 85% agreed or strongly agreed that suspicions of trained staff were regarded seriously and acted upon, worryingly two organisations disagreed and a further two failed to have an opinion (**Q 41**). One potential risk area identified from the survey arises from the number of respondents that report having additional responsibilities over and above their functions as MLRO 'diluting' their work. An open question on performance measures elicited a range of interesting responses many of which demonstrated application of complex internal methods on monitoring and of probable self-legitimation:

> "We undertake assurance activity including the understanding of local procedures and how AML requirements are incorporated. In addition to this key staff within the business are interviewed to test their knowledge of the procedures and obligations under the ML regulations."
>
> "Number of SARs submitted, training and awareness (checking of staff knowledge) other forms still being worked on."
>
> "First time right AML compliance rate account operating AML compliance rate. Ongoing KYC Compliance rate. PEP Rates. SAR Rate Disclosures Rates."
>
> "Regular meetings with business areas re-assessment of SARs, standards of CDD, compliance with Sanctions and PEP regime; Regular annual audit of AML, regular 'self assessment' reporting from all areas of the Group; AML sign off required for all product and service development issues."

As would be expected, a number monitored volume of SARs submitted although one respondent noted

> "None, how can you measure this? No. of reports made, both internally and to SOCA? How can such number be related to the totality of what actually exists? How can you measure 'unknown unknowns?'"

Regulatory inspection and the political dimension

The majority of respondents appear to rely on internal rather than external scrutiny of their AML procedures with 23 using this method although a further 11 had used both internal and external, in the prior 12 month period (**Q 11)**. One respondent noted no risk assessment had been conducted. Internal reviews, whilst of some value, do not necessarily provide the degree of independent analysis as accorded through an external review. Although it is very likely that cost will have had an influence on this decision as the regulations state an internal risk assessment is sufficient (and although not stated, much cheaper).

Two questions about the FSA indicated that the majority of respondents did not have a view as to whether the focus of inspection visits was on breaches of procedure rather than with possible money laundering (**Q 15**), although 14 (39%) agreed this to be the case. It is interesting to note that the answer to a further question that probed about the focus of the FSA on documentation of systems and procedures (**Q 32**) indicated less than one third or 27% agreeing this to be the case, while the majority (20 or 56%) did not hold an opinion. As to their thoroughness on a visit (**Q 16**) only 10 (27%) agreed or strongly agreed this to be the case, with the majority of the rest failing to have an opinion on how thorough such visits were with seven disagreeing with the statement. The answers in this section suggest that most respondents did not really engage with the purpose and outcome of an FSA visit seeing little value to themselves.

Whilst 60% of respondents believe the international debate on money laundering is controlled by governments and the law enforcement lobby, 14% disagree and 26% have no views on the subject (**Q 27**). 80% said they would like to see greater consultation with industry in regards to future AML (**Q 28**). Of concern for the regulator is the fact that there is no clear indication that feedback from SOCA is helpful in shaping AML policy (**Q 46),** the majority (42%) had no view. They should also be aware of the fact that only 7 out of 34 respondents knew who at SOCA deals with their reports (**Q 51**). Similarly 70% believe they are not kept informed of prosecutions from the information they supplied, 10% believe they are and 15% don't know (**Q 50**). The same proportion (70%) are surprised there are not a greater number of money laundering prosecutions in the UK **(Q 52).**

A question about voluntary compliance by non US financial institutions with US laws this did not elicit any strong response. There was quite a mixed response to the statement "*Non US financial institutions will voluntarily comply with US laws, which do not apply to them in their own countries, to demonstrate good corporate citizenship to US authorities*", (**Q 34**) 34% agreed or strongly agreed, whilst 29% disagreed and 29% neither agreed nor disagreed. It may be that there is little attention paid to the issue.

Discussion

This chapter has sought to consider whether the additional requirements of AML compliance have enhanced integrity or merely provided another avenue for engagement with ritual. To return to the original analogy, are the compliance 'dancers' merely going through their routines, doing sufficient to avoid the attention of the stage director or are they truely interpreting and living each move of the dance? From the discussion of the results of the small survey of compliance professionals it is clear that the traditional rhetoric and mantras around the rationale for AML in protecting integrity and reputation are widely upheld. However, there remains a clear dilemma for these practitioners (as identified by Harvey and Lau, 2009 and Verhage, 2008) between the importance of their function and the cost overhead that they introduce. Whilst most thought that their institution benefitted from the existence of the legislative framework and appeared to accept the arguments surrounding its deterrent effect on organised crime, the results showed no clear indication as to whether there was as a result any profound increase in integrity within the sectors covered.

The previously identified move to deregulation through the adoption of a risk-based framework paradoxically appears to have complicated systems and procedures and to have produced a corresponding rise in internal measures of self-efficacy, with complex internal performance measures being introduced. What is further demonstrated, when looked at overall, is the degree to which anti-money laundering practice within industry sectors appears to beginning to polarise into sector methodologies as each company does sufficient to ensure they mirror the activity of their competitors but without incurring the cost of going beyond this. This is not surprising, as each industry has a different view of their exposure to the money laundering phenomenon. With reliance mainly on internal review and with the suggestion that the FSA visits veer toward a 'tick-box' exercise seeking to ensure compliance with procedural process, it is unlikely that additional methods or approaches will be adopted.

It is likely that money laundering prevention does not rank highly in the ambitions of financial services providers and those other firms who are subject to the Money Laundering Regulations, principally because there is little material benefit to be gained. As noted by Harvey and Lau (2009: 98) "*It is argued that the banks, in particular, will be compliant with legislation and be willing to perform the consequent outreach services for law enforcement due to concern over reputation, certainly, but more probably due to their desire to avoid regulatory censure.*" If this is the case it might be expected that AML does little to enhance integrity but is merely seen as a ritual of engagement – something that has to be done but with little conviction.

Probably compliance staff can justify their role and it is perhaps appropriate to conclude with the following comment from an MLRO of a financial institution interviewed in June 2009

> "*not because most people think this* [AML] *is a moral crusade or anything like that, but there is . . . an end that you can see . . . something which is a good thing, it is just a question of whether what you are doing contributes to that end whatsoever or whether actually you have misunderstood the end in the first place. Part of that is also . . . that it is hard to decry what you do on a daily basis and just to say I think this is a complete waste of time, even though sometimes you might do.*"

This rather suggests that compliance officers themselves are uncertain as to whether their actions objectively contribute to genuineness of integrity. From their perspective this has to be the preferred outcome otherwise they are dancing without conviction and only engaging in the rituals.

References

Alldridge, P., *Money Laundering Law: Forfeiture, confiscation, civil recovery, criminal laundering and taxation of the proceeds of crime*. Hart Publishing, Oxford, 2003

Bonvin, J. and P. Dembinski, Ethical issues in financial activities. *Journal of Business Ethics*, 2002, *v*ol. 37, 187–192

Cooper, D. and K. Robson, Accounting, professions and regulation: locating the sites of professionalization. *Accounting Organizations and Society*, 2006, vol. 31, 415–444

Duyne, P.C. van, M.S. Groenhuijsen and A.A.P. Schudelaro, Balancing financial threats and legal interests in money-laundering policy. *Crime, Law and Social Change*, 2005, vol. 43, 117 – 147

Gill, M. and G. Taylor, The risk-based approach to tackling money laundering: Matching risk to products. *Company Lawyer,* 2003, vol. 24 , *no* 7, pp 210 – 213

Geiger, H. and O. Wuensch, The fight against money laundering: An economic analysis of a cost-benefit paradoxon. *Journal of Money Laundering Control*, 2007, vol. 10, *no. 1*, pp 91 – 105

Harvey, J., Just how effective is money laundering legislation? *Security Journal*, 2008, vol. 21, *no 3*, 189 – 211

Harvey, J., and S. Lau, Crime-money, reputation and reporting. *Crime Law and Social Change*, 2009, vol. 52, 57-72

Hoffmann, V., T. Trautmann and J. Hamprecht, Regulatory uncertainty: a reason to postpone investments? Not necessarily.s*Journal of Management Studies*, 2009, vol. 46, *no* 7, 1227-1253

Levi, M., Following the criminal and terrorist money trails. In P.C. van Duyne, K. von Lampe and J.N. Newell (eds.), *Criminal Finances and Organising Crime in Europe*. Nijmegen, Wolf Legal Publishers, The Netherlands, 2003

Levi. M. and P. Reuter, Money Laundering. *Crime and Justice*, 2006, vol. 34. 289 – 376

Moran, M., The Frank Stacey Memorial Lecture: From command state to regulatory state. *Public Policy and Administration*, 2000, vol. 15, *no 4*, winter

Reuter, P. and E. Truman, E., Anti-Money Laundering Overkill? It's time to ask how well the system in working. *The International Economy*, 2005, winter, 56 – 60

Ross, S. and M. Hannan, M., Money laundering regulation and risk-based decision-making. *Journal of Money Laundering Control*, 2007, vol. 10, *no 1*, 106-115

Venard, B. and M. Hanafi, Organizational isomorphism and corruption in financial institutions: empirical research in emerging countries. *Journal of Business Ethics*, 2008, vol. 81, 481–498

Verhage, A., Compliance and AML in Belgium: a booming sector with growing pains. *Journal of Money Laundering Control*, 2009, vol. 12, *issue 2*, 113 – 133

Appendix 1 : Survey Questionnaire Responses

Number	Question	Agre e	Neither	Disagree
Questions about the regulations				
21	Given the significance of the finance sector to the UK it is vital to have a strong regulatory framework	97%	3%	0%
45	There is a need to continually tighten money laundering controls	50%	11%	39%
18	AML controls are a key component in fighting organised crime	86%	8%	6%
52	It is surprising that there are not greater numbers of prosecutions for money laundering within the UK	75%	19%	6%
19	AML helps deter other types of economic crime	81%	6%	14%
27	The international debate on money laundering tends to be closely controlled by governments and the law enforcement lobby	60%	26%	14%
28	I would like to see greater consultation with business over the future direction of AML	80%	20%	0%
47	International money laundering regulations do not sufficiently take into account commercial realities faced by the business sector	52%	29%	20%
34	Non US FIs will voluntarily comply with US laws to demonstrate good corporate citizenship to the US authorities	38%	31%	34%
44	It is likely that non-US banks voluntarily comply with OFAC in order to avoid enforcement by US authorities	63%	34%	3%
Questions about the regulators/SOCA				
15	Inspection visits by the FSA are more concerned with breaches of regulation	39%	47%	14%
16	The FSA examination of compliance	27%	53%	20%

	has been thorough			
32	On inspection visits the FSA have tended to focus more on documentation of systems and procedures than on overall approach	27%	56%	17%
46	The response/feedback from SOCA is extremely helpful in determining our AML policy development	23%	42%	36%
51	I know the person at SOCA who deals with reports from my institution	21%	15%	64%
50	We are kept informed of any prosecution resulting from information supplied by my institution	11%	17%	72%
Questions about the organisation				
17	My organisation believes that protection of reputation is the most important function of its compliance policies	78%	8%	14%
43	The major risk to my organisation is risk to reputation	84%	6%	11%
22	My organisation benefits from the existence of AML	61%	17%	22%
53	We feel our AML compliance procedures reassure our customers and enhance our reputation	42%	39%	20%
33	Our competitors have less rigorous AML compliance procedures than ourselves	36%	44%	20%
23	The system of checks and balances within my organisation makes money laundering difficult	83%	8%	8%
26	My organisation is very likely to be targeted by organised criminals for laundering	34%	23%	43%
38	There is very little money laundering through my type of organisation	50%	19%	31%
39	There is very little money laundering through my region of the country	50%	19%	31%
31	My organisation is very likely to be targeted by terrorists for financing	22%	19%	58%

	purposes			
Questions about the implementation, cost and effectiveness of AML				
20	AML compliance activity is too focused on customer identification	53%	11%	36%
24	Customers are aware of the reasons for identify checks	83%	9%	9%
30	KYC procedures are too time consuming for business with a time sensitive value	33%	24%	44%
25	It is possible that we lose genuine new business because of compliance procedures	34%	33%	34%
29	Given the overriding importance of maintaining integrity of the financial system the AML costs to my institution are reasonable	59%	21%	21%
37	ML compliance is a significant cost to our business	60%	20%	20%
42	As a business overhead it is essential that AML compliance demonstrates value for money	69%	19%	11%
35	Demonstration of our AML compliance gives us a competitive advantage	28%	33%	39%
40	The status of compliance staff is regarded as high in my organisation	58%	26%	17%
41	Suspicions of trained staff are regarded seriously and acted upon	89%	6%	6%
48	It is very difficult to identify suspicious rather than just unusual activity	44%	17%	39%
49	Bigger institutions bear the brunt of compliance costs	50%	19%	31%

A critical approach to Trade-Based Money Laundering

Melvin R.J. Soudijn[1]

Introduction

The Financial Action Task Force (FATF), an influential international organisation for combating money laundering and terrorist financing, is continually calling for more codification, regulation and standardisation of all types of financial and business transactions. Not because new laundering dangers arise, but because the organisation seems to have the mindset of a lawyer wishing to plug the smallest possible hole. If it was up to the FATF, each financial or business transaction would have to adhere to special regulations. A well-known example with respect to the financial community (and its researchers) is the FATF's "40 recommendations and 9 special recommendations to combat money laundering and financing of terrorism" (FATF, 2001, 2003, 2009). As of 2012, these 49 recommendations have been reshuffled and re-integrated in a new report (FATF 2012).

Of course, trying to combat money laundering and terrorism financing is a respectable cause. However, the problem with trying to regulate all aspects of business and finances for the sole purpose of detecting and countering money laundering, is that it places a heavy burden on the persons or organisations involved and can even stifle competition (Razavy and Haggerty 2009). A good example of the over-zealous promotion of 'due diligence' and 'know your customer' principles is the scare created around the international flows of goods. In this connection, the FATF uses the phrase Trade Based Money Laundering (TBML) to refer to money laundering that makes use of the channels of the trade system. In the view of the FATF, these flows provide excellent opportunities for criminals to move their money around undetected (FATF 2006, 2008). The reasoning of the FATF is as follows.

Firstly, anti-money laundering regulations are strongly focused on flows of cash and on the financial system; in consequence there is a danger that ordinary trade

1 The author works for the Dutch National Police. This article is written in a personal capacity.

flows may be overlooked. But international trade is susceptible to abuse, arising from the enormous volume involved and the complexity of its financing.

Secondly, the FATF assumes that if the risks and costs of one method of money laundering increase, it is only logical that other methods will become more attractive. The success of the measures taken thus far "*may have the unintended effect of increasing the attractiveness of the international trade system for money laundering and terrorist financing activities*" (FATF 2006: 1). Besides this, the international exchange of information between customs agencies is patchy, and resources for identifying illegitimate transactions in trade flows are scant.

However, the FATF cannot indicate the exact extent of crime displacement of this kind, and no data is available on the phenomenon. In consequence there are only a couple of case studies available that highlight the methods used for TBML: manipulation of the price of goods; the stated quantities; or the product description (FATF 2006; 2008). Nevertheless, the FATF urges customs agencies and financial institutions to be aware of these sorts of methods and to make use of red flag indicators as an early warning system for TBML (FATF 2006). Goods whose prices lie considerably above or below their true value, for example, should be flagged as a possible case of over- or under-invoicing and therefore for potential laundering.

Others have argued along similar lines on the importance of TBML. Probably the most well-known person in this area is Professor John Zdanowicz (see *e.g.*: Zdanowicz, 2004; 2004a; 2009). Besides numerous presentations given as a keynote speaker on TBML, he set up the consultancy firm International Trade Alert, Inc., which "*provides international trade consulting and international trade analysis to private sector firms, U.S. and foreign governments, and international agencies*".[2] The analysis is carried out by statistically filtering out abnormal price patterns from international trade transaction data as reported by the United States Department of Commerce. For a fee, clients can check on Zdanowicz's website as to whether the price of a certain trade product lies within the margins of legitimate international trade or whether it should set off alarm bells. According to his website, clients range from attorneys, trade boards and banks to the Central Intelligence Agency and US Treasury department. Naturally, Zdanowicz' company thrives in line with the increase in the severity of the problem for which he sells solutions.

The two reports by the FATF and the work of Zdanowicz have been very influential in shaping the image of TBML in the research literature (see *e.g.* Delston and Walls, 2009; Liao and Acharya, 2011; Sulivan and Smith, 2011) and law enforcement (see *e.g.* FinCen 2010; USDOS, 2009; Freis 2010). In such articles, TBML has almost become synonymous with the method of over- and under-invoicing. It is a given that this method occurs, but there is otherwise not an

2 http://www.internationaltradealert.com/index.html

absence of development in this particular field of research. Existing insights are often rehashed without adding any new cases. Sometimes international trade figures are compared revealing a large number of potential cases of TBML (Ferwerda *et al.* 2011; Zdanowicz 2009). However, these numbers are never taken to the next step by testing their implied assumptions, implicitly taking as proven what still has to be proved. It appears that over- or under-invoicing in international trade flows is automatically seen as money laundering. For all it is worth, there could be perfectly legitimate reasons for any statistical deviations. Furthermore, there is little or no further critical reflection about the meaning of the terms employed or the manner in which data are collected.

With a view to breathing new life into the discussion about TBML, this chapter addresses three problems that have beset the research thus far: a fuzzy definition of the issue, tunnel vision, and statistical distortion. In each case, the question is raised as to what extent these problems can be resolved.

The structure of this chapter is as follows. The first section looks in more detail at exactly what the FATF means by TBML. The FATF's definition serves as the 'industry standard', but is not without its drawbacks. The section on tunnel vision makes clear that TBML need not necessarily be a matter of dubious dealings with prices or goods, but can also take place using the genuine market value. Information for this section was obtained by interviewing persons from Dutch law enforcement. This involved interviews with three people from the tax authorities and five people from the National Police on five police investigations involving TBML. The section on statistical distortion examines the various limitations inherent to import and export figures. This was prompted by the realisation that too little attention has been paid to the various exceptional circumstances in international trade that can provide equally valid reasons for deviating from market prices. In each case, a possible solution to the problem is put forward. This chapter ends with a general discussion on TBML and on its prevention.

The FATF definition of TBML

A clear definition is crucial for research. For after all, how can you research something unless you know what you are researching? How can you verify or reject a hypothesis if data can be used arbitrarily? Moreover, in areas of focus such as organised crime, terrorism or money laundering, definitions are not merely a matter of academic quibbling, but also have legal consequences. A criminal accused of being a member of a criminal organisation can expect a more severe sentence. A suspect who falls under the category of 'terrorism' is subject to more invasive investigative powers than a 'normal' criminal. If companies or premises are financed with criminal money, 'money laundering' is deemed to be involved and such assets may be confiscated. So in these cases the terminology used has an impact on the legal reality (Beare, 2003; Mitsilegas, 2003; van Duyne, 2003). It is therefore important to take a closer look at the definition of TBML.

It is impossible to tell from the research literature when exactly the term TBML emerged and who was the first person to coin it. Zdanowicz refers to early studies from the 1960s and 1980s, in which "*abnormal international trade pricing patterns*" prompted suspicions that money was being transferred across borders illegally (Zdanowicz 2009: 856).

Although these and other early studies mentioned already the abuse of the regular trade flows, it was only from 2006 that the term TBML began to gain currency. This was the year in which the FATF published its first report on TBML. The aim of the report was to make the authorities aware of the dangers of TBML. In the introduction, the report posits that there are three main methods of moving criminal money (FATF 2006: 1). The first method makes use of the financial system itself, using wire transfers, for instance. The second method involves the physical moving of cash, by such means as hiding it in hand luggage. The third method involves the moving of value "*using methods such as the false documentation and declaration of traded goods and services*" (FATF 2006:1). This third method is what the FATF has designated as TBML, which it then went on to define as:

> "the process of disguising the proceeds of crime and moving value through the use of trade transactions in an attempt to legitimise their illicit origins" (FATF 2006: 3).[3]

In 2008, the FATF published a second report on TBML (FATF 2008). The term had now been expanded to TBML/FT, with FT standing for financing of terrorism. The definition was also expanded slightly:

> "the process of disguising the proceeds of crime and moving value through the use of trade transactions in an attempt to legitimise their illegal origins *or finance their activities* [author's own emphasis]" (FATF 2008: 1).

The FATF is an authoritative intergovernmental institution responsible for developing policies for combating money laundering (and terrorist financing), so the terminology and examples from the two reports have been adopted by many government bodies and researchers (see for example Liao and Acharya 2011; Zdanowicz 2009; Brayshaw 2009; Delston and Walls 2009).

3 The FATF considers cases of over- or under-invoicing primarily designed to gain a tax advantage as a case of customs fraud rather than trade-based money laundering (FATF, 2006 p. 5).

However, precisely because the FATF is accorded such high status and is involved in inspecting the implementation of anti-money-laundering policies in its member countries, one would expect the reports to be exempt from criticism, which proves to be wrong. Rather, the FATF does not engage in any critical debate. Lacking critical feedback, it is not strange, then, that the definition has remained somewhat ambiguous, and contains inconsistencies and undeveloped terms. This argument can be developed as follows.

Firstly, the 2006 report states, for instance, that the primary focus lies on the international goods trade. A footnote to this report hints that the connection between TBML and the international trade in services warrants further research (FATF 2006: 1). In the second report (FATF 2008), this reservation has been set aside, and the description of the various techniques of TBML speaks throughout of goods *and services*. But this distinction cannot be inferred from the definition itself, which consistently mentions only the goods trade.

Secondly, the FATF's introduction to TBML also states that TBML concerns cases with an international dimension, and the various examples cited to illustrate TBML all relate to international trade. However, the definition makes no allusion to an international component, speaking only of 'moving value through the use of trade transactions'. By this definition, TBML could equally take place at the local or national level.

Thirdly, there is the lack of clarity about what precisely is meant by the 'trade transactions' themselves. This is never explained. Where physical goods are concerned, a trade transaction generally concerns the sale and purchase of these goods by two parties, the seller and the buyer. But this brings the danger that a whole range of transactions can be grouped under the heading of TBML. By way of illustration:

> Let's say X has acquired some money through criminal dealings and uses this to buy an expensive car. He knows a dodgy car dealer who will accept large amounts of cash without reporting the transaction as suspicious to the Financial Intelligence Unit (although such reports are compulsory in many countries). X then sells the car to an unsuspecting third party, now by wire transfer.

Following the FATF's definition, X has now attempted to "legitimise the illegal origins" of the "proceeds of crime" by purchasing and reselling a car (in this way "moving value through the use of trade transactions").

If, in accordance with the FATF's 2008 report, a trade transaction can also refer to services, the ball game really is wide open. Services could include supplying non-physical goods to another party. Building on the previous illustration:

> Let us imagine, for instance, that X asks a front man to put the car in his name for payment. For a small fee, the front man registers the car in his name. At the same time, X continues to have the car at his disposal. However, the value of the car has been transferred from X to the front, so it has been 'moved'.

Again, following the FATF's definition, X and the front man have entered into a trade transaction for certain services, aimed at shielding the criminal assets (the car) that X wants to enjoy. Following this line of argument, virtually every money laundering transaction could fall under the heading of TBML. Needless to say, this was never the original intention of the FATF.

Fourthly, there is also a lack of clarity with the addition of "or finance their activities" to the original definition. This creates a dual objective for TBML: to legitimise the illegal origins of the proceeds of crime or to finance "their activities". Quite apart from the question of who "their" refers to and what their "activities" are, this clause implies that the objective of legitimising criminal assets is no longer necessary, thus undermining the definition still further. By way of example:

> Suppose that a group of criminals smuggle cocaine into Europe. This shipment is not intercepted and they are able to sell the cocaine realising a large profit. However, the criminals have no plans to retire but want to make an even bigger return. They therefore invest the original cocaine profits in the purchase of a new consignment of cocaine in South America. Once again, the cocaine is smuggled to and sold into Europe.

Effectively this amounts to a trade transaction whereby the original proceeds of crime (from the first cocaine transport) are concealed in new assets (the second consignment of cocaine). After all, if the second consignment were to be intercepted, it would probably be impossible to trace the fact that it was financed from the proceeds of the initial transport. So this situation again fulfils the definition of the TBML, because though admittedly we are now dealing with criminal assets, the aim is no longer to legitimise the proceeds of crime, but to finance the activity of 'transporting cocaine'. So that means that every drug trafficker is automatically guilty of TBML, since it is common knowledge that they acquire new supplies by using the proceeds of their previous drug transactions.

The FATF's definition is, therefore, far from coherent. If ever a third FATF report on TBML is to be published, the terms used warrant stricter definition in order to make clear that the focus lies on the international trade in (bulk) goods that is financed from the proceeds of crime.

Tunnel vision

The FATF definition of TBML does not necessarily need be a problem if it is understood simply as what sociologists refer to as a 'sensitising concept'. In this case, a concept can remain entirely open, but still indicate a direction in which to look. Further theories can then be developed in this direction. The situation is somewhat similar to the discussion around organised crime. There is a great deal of ambiguity about what the precise definition of 'organised crime' should be, but that does not stop researchers from studying it.[4] Within a general framework, they can study and elaborate in depth the specific issues they find important: such as the role of corruption; violence; or illegal market transactions (Albanese 2000, Anderson 1995, Jacques and Wright 2011, Reuter 1983).

As stated in the previous section, the TBML definition has also some severe shortcomings as a delineation of the problem, since, by this purported definition, virtually any criminal act involving money can be labelled TBML. However, the reports do clearly indicate that attention should be focused on fraudulent trading of *legal* goods on the legitimate international markets. There is no mention of the shipping of illegal goods or the provision of illegal services, as can be deduced from the TBML techniques described (FATF 2006, 2008). What the FATF has in mind can be summarised as follows:

- *Over-invoicing.* The seller acquires surplus value for the goods at point of sale by overstating the price of the goods in the invoice or other documentation.
- *Under-invoicing.* The buyer acquires surplus value for the goods at point of sale by understating the price of the goods in the invoice or other documentation.
- *Multiple invoicing.* The seller can account for several payments by sending several invoices for one and the same trade transaction (either for goods or services).
- *Under-shipment.* The seller sends fewer goods, or goods of inferior quality, than stated on the invoice. The true value of the goods sent is thus lower, so that this method is in fact very similar to over-invoicing.
- *Over-shipment.* The seller sends more goods, or goods of superior quality, than stated on the invoice. The true value of the goods sent is thus higher, meaning that this method is in fact very similar to under-invoicing.
- *Phantom shipment.* No goods or services are supplied, and all documentation is false.

Furthermore, the FATF reports (2006, 2008) mention the existence of the Black Market Peso Exchange (BMPE). This phenomenon is viewed specifically in

4 For a survey of over 160 definitions of organised crime, see the website set up by Klaus van Lampe: http://www.organized-crime.de/organizedcrimedefinitions.htm

relation to South America.[5] The BMPE is described as a complex form of (trade based) money laundering, whose motivation lies in unfavourable exchange rates for legal trade. The BMPE system works as follows:

> Colombian criminals approach a peso broker to exchange their proceeds from the American drug market from dollars into Colombian pesos. The broker then finds legal traders who need dollars to import goods (refrigerators, for instance) from the U.S., but are put off by the unfavourable local exchange rate. The broker then makes his 'cocaine' dollars available to the legal trader, who uses them to import the goods from abroad, sells them for pesos on the local market, and hands the proceeds over to the broker at the pre-arranged exchange rate.

In the BMPE construction, the drug trafficker is only tangentially involved in the legal flow of goods. He takes his dollars to the broker and receives pesos in exchange. What the broker does with the dollars is not relevant for the drug trafficking organisation, which need not even be aware of what goods are imported. Although, the BMPE variant does not necessarily involve misrepresentation of the price of the goods or the quantities purchased, the goods associated with such transactions are often said to be smuggled into the country to avoid duties and taxes (FATF 2006: 8). But that is a different phenomenon. The reader of the FATF reports therefore could still be left with the idea that TBML in a non-American context never takes place on the basis of the 'true value' of the goods: deviation from 'true value' is therefore, not a necessary element.

We can infer from the above overview of TBML techniques that the focus of the FATF lies squarely where there is "*misrepresentation of price, quantity or quality of imports or exports*" (FATF 2006: 3). But that brings us to the second shortcoming of the FATF reports: tunnel vision.

It seems that TBML can only occur if prices are manipulated (with the exception of BMPE). The consequence of this focus is that the countermeasures the FATF proposes are also specifically geared towards these types of crimes. The FATF recommends the training of staff within organisations that come into contact with TBML in order to help them recognise anomalies. Customs agencies, tax authorities, financial intelligence units, law enforcement agencies, and the banking sector are thus urged to develop a system of red flag indicators to identify any deviation on the true value, quantity and quality of the goods shipped.[6]

---

5 The BMPE seems to be first and foremost a South and North American affair. Not a single article or report on the BMPE refers to the same mechanism being used in a European or Asian context, for instance. And nowhere is the theoretical question raised of whether Euros could be exchanged for pesos in the same way.

6 For an overview of all the proposed measures, see the 'Red Flag Indicators' section in the first FATF report on TBML (FATF 2006).

However, it still has to be proven that such countermeasures are productive. As the Wolfsberg Group[7] succinctly commented on the red flag-method, the role of financial institutions is limited simply because some 80% of all international trade payments are made by open accounts (Wolfsberg Group, 2009). This means that buyer and seller agree the terms of the contract whereupon the goods are delivered to the buyer who then arranges a clean or netting payment through the banking system. In these circumstances, the bank has no access to the terms of the trade transaction, *nor is it willing to*. It can simply not be demanded from the financial sector to physically inspect every transaction of goods or to check the genuineness of invoices.

Furthermore, it would be a misconception to think that TBML cannot occur in the case of the shipment of goods at their true value. In the Netherlands, the National Crime Squad and regional police forces have encountered several cases of TBML in recent years which have had nothing to do with misrepresentation of the stated price, quality or quantity of goods. Quite the contrary, in these cases legal goods were traded and transported on the international market at normal prices. The following case study is illustrative of this form of TBML:

Case 1

In the course of an investigation of cocaine smuggling from Africa to the Netherlands, a telephone conversation involving the main suspect was intercepted. He lived in the Netherlands and told his girlfriend to bring a certain sum of cash money to the Dutch company D. This company traded in potatoes and fruit. Enquiries with company D revealed that the suspect's girlfriend was funding the export of cargoes of potatoes and fruit to companies in Africa. These goods were shipped at their true value. The girlfriend (and others) paid for these goods on behalf of companies E and F. But these companies were also in the hands of the drug trafficker, and the money given to company D turned out to be the proceeds of cocaine trafficking. Using the legitimate company D, the original proceeds in Euros had already been shipped to Africa where they could easily be converted to local African currencies without arousing suspicion.

Searches of the suspect's premises turned up receipts showing that several hundred thousands of Euros had been paid to company D in cash. When the manager of company D was asked why he agreed to receive such large cash payments, he

7 The Wolfsberg Group is an association of 11 global banks, which aims to develop financial services industry standards, and related products, for Know Your Customer, Anti-Money Laundering and Counter Terrorist Financing policies. Members are Banco Santander, Bank of Tokyo–Mitsubishi UFJ, Barclays, Citigroup, Credit Suisse, Deutsche Bank, Goldman Sachs, HSBC, JPMorgan Chase, Société Générale and UBS.

replied that he had not been suspicious because Africa lacked a good banking system and "*trade is trade*". He seemed to forget, however, that his other long-standing, legitimate African clients always managed their payments through bank transfer. Apparently the lure of profit outweighed due diligence.
A slightly different case involving trade with Africa runs as follows.

Case 2

A man from Sierra Leone came into contact with a Dutch trader in agricultural machinery. The man from Sierra Leone subsequently bought several machines, each worth between 10.000 and 15.000 euro. These prices were paid in cash because the man indicated that wire transfers involving Africa would be complicated.

After a couple of transactions, the man asked the Dutch trader if he could make use of the Dutch company's account in order to pay for a shipment of rice from Vietnam. This shipment, worth 200.000 euro, was to be delivered to Sierra Leone. The manager of the company agreed and the African brought him 200.000 in cash. The company deposited the cash and made a transfer to the Swiss bank account of the rice merchant. Shortly afterwards, the man from Sierra Leon was arrested for the smuggling of cocaine.

In case 2, we cannot be absolutely sure that the rice was actually delivered at regular market price because the shipment did not cross any European borders and could not be checked by the Dutch investigators. However, the cocaine trafficker had made a habit of using legitimate companies to pay for cocaine shipments. This never aroused suspicion because he always paid fair prices without employing illegal methods of under- or over-invoicing.

In both cases, the Dutch traders involved were not aware of the link with cocaine smuggling. They may have been more careful accepting large cash payments, but were not seen as money laundering suspects.
In the next example, the companies were more involved.

Case 3

A man from Curaçao is the organiser of a large-scale cocaine smuggling operation into the Netherlands. The cocaine is sold on the Dutch market for which he receives Euros. This poses a problem as he lives in Curaçao and, therefore, needs to bring his profits out of the Netherlands and exchange them into local currency. Two Dutchmen, brothers, offer their services. One lives in Curaçao where he has trading company K that receives wholesale products from other companies in the Netherlands. The other brother lives in the Netherlands. For a fee of five percent, they arrange for the drug dealer to bring his cash to the brother living in the Netherlands. With this money, he buys

> wholesale products at appropriate market prices. At least one other company was knowingly involved in the arrangements and accepted these large cash payments. One occasion involved the acceptance of a stack containing 3.750 twenty-euro notes The goods were subsequently shipped to the company K in Curaçao and thereafter sold. The proceeds were deposited in the bank account of the company K. These sums were then withdrawn by the brother in Curaçao and handed over to the drug dealer. The Dutch investigators believe that the company K moved some 2,5 million Euros in a period of about three years.

Of course, one could argue about whether this was an efficient way to launder money. After all, once the drugs proceeds had been converted into the bank account of company K., they had already entered into the financial system without arising suspicion. To take the money out again seems unnecessary, unless it was done to interrupt the money trail to confuse those trying to follow it.

The motives of the suspects involved, whatever these were, are not relevant for the purpose of this section. What these three cases show is that detecting TBML is difficult, if not impossible, when working on the basis of the examples put forward by the FATF reports. After all, if the goods are shipped in accordance with their true value, quantity and quality, they will identical to normal trade flows, and thus no anomalies will be detected.

Moreover, one could come up with various hypothetical examples of TBML in which goods are shipped at their true value and therefore difficult to spot. For example, a trader could stipulate in a payment agreement that the counterparty will receive a 20% reduction if he pays within 30 days, or that he must pay an extra fee of 20% if he fails to pay within the agreed period. This is effectively a legal form of over- or under-invoicing. Or one party in a deal purportedly complains on receipt of goods that the quality is unacceptable. He demands redress, and the other party returns part of the cost price. Matters such as this can legitimately be agreed between parties in trade and the disguise cannot in any way be traced through the customs systems.

Statistical distortions

Although the preceding section argued that TBML does occur with goods that are shipped in accordance with their true value, quantity and quality, this does not mean that methods such as over- and under-invoicing do not exist. They do exist, as cases in the reports of the FATF (2006, 2008) illustrate. To detect this kind of abuse, the comparison of international trade data is seen as providing an effective solution (FATF 2006, 2008; Zdanowicz, 2009). The mean price for the trade in a given commodity is calculated, and outliers are viewed as an indication of possible money laundering. The definition of an outlier can be set, for example, at over 50% above or under average country price, for instance (Zdanowicz, 2009).

This brings us to the third and final problematic area: the use of statistics to detect TBML. The process of identifying outliers is often depicted in very rosy terms, but in fact it is far from certain that the figures are as cut and dried as is often suggested. One of the few researchers that published such concerns is Nitsch (2010). Building on his remarks, I would like to point out the following pitfalls.

It is not known, for instance, to what extent distortions may arise as a result of the authorities' data-entry processes. These could be subject to human error: if the employee entering the data puts a decimal in the wrong place, the figures can be multiplied (or reduced) by a factor ten or a hundred.

Nitsch (2010) points out that U.S. trade data categorising goods according to commodity codes (the method used by Zdanowicz) is less pure than it might initially appear. Nitsch holds that prices within a given product code can vary quite significantly according to their quality. In addition, the product categories appear to be extremely detailed (the system distinguishes 28.985 product categories), but on closer inspection they may turn out to be very broad. This too can lead to broad variations within one and the same category.

Another inherent weakness of the system is that the price data recorded is strongly influenced by the number of transactions within a given category. In the case of a product code in which little trade takes place, just one new transaction with a deviating price can substantially alter the mean. A transaction that was formerly not suspicious can suddenly become an 'outlier', or indeed *vice versa*.

Nitsch (2010) has also written about the statistical limitations of bilateral data comparisons. For instance, one country may calculate the value of its exports at the initial point of departure, or free on board (f.o.b.), whereas another country calculates imports at the value at the point of final destination. In that latter case, cost, insurance and freight (c.i.f.) are most likely to be included in the calculation.

It is also important to point to the plethora of legal guidelines and directives which countries impose for the regulation of trade flows, but which may in turn lead to further distortions. Take export subsidies, for instance, which may also prove an incentive for traders to overstate the value of their goods. This higher value may indeed be picked up by statistical analysis, but in this case it is related to subsidy fraud rather than money laundering.

Import duties can also lead to distortions. The author was told of an old example from the 1980s which involved the importation of raisins from Turkey. The EU had stipulated that those who imported Turkish raisins under a certain invoice value would be required to pay a compensatory duty. Since Turkish raisins were cheap, but importers wanted to avoid paying duties of this kind, many of them submitted false invoice amounts. Importers stated a higher value, but in fact paid their Turkish suppliers the regular, much lower, cost price. If the trade prices for Turkish raisins were to be analysed at the international level, it would emerge that they were two or three times as expensive when exported to Europe, than to other parts of the world. This situation of distorting market prices by levying import duties could still occur today with other products. Again, this has nothing to do with money laundering in the FATF meaning of the term.

Another example that would distort statistical analysis is the preferential treatment former colonies receive in the EU. For example, goods imported from Suriname, a former colony of the Netherlands, are allowed to be imported cheaper because of preferential tax treatment. This could lead international producers to move their product to Suriname in order to re-export it at an immediately cheaper price to the Netherlands.

In short, trade data can be distorted because of all kinds of exceptional tax circumstances. But even when over- and under-invoicing are indeed detected, it is not necessarily related to TBML. Deliberately misleading the Customs or tax authorities by submitting false invoices is certainly a criminal offence that can be qualified as fraud, but fraud is not necessarily tantamount to money laundering, though that depends on the extension of the laundering definition.

Discussion

This chapter focused on three aspects of Trade Based Money Laundering (TBML), that to date have not been jubject to a thorough debate. First of all, the definition was put under the microscope and dissected. Although the FATF, the primary body on financial anti-money laundering recommendations by which countries are judged, has a definition in place, this is really too broad to be useful. Virtually every criminal transaction could be categorised as TBML. It would therefore be better not to speak of the FATF definition anymore, but of the FATF description.

Secondly, on the basis of the cases described by the FATF, the focus is on one particular type: TBML involving the misrepresentation of the value, quantity or quality of the traded goods. As a result, the emphasis in detecting and combating TBML has come to lie very much on one type of approach: the analysis of 'price anomalies' as a signal of over- or under-invoicing. However, what can be learned from real investigations is that goods can also be shipped at their true value within the context of TBML. Checks based on the price or weight of the goods in question would not have singled out these shipments

Thirdly, the question of whether detecting TBML on the basis of statistical trade data is effective should be questioned. The data may be distorted for several reasons which are not related to money laundering. Moreover, any discrepancy that is indeed recognised could just as much point to fraud (or capital flight) instead of money laundering. Proponents of a statistical approach will counter that the real work only starts once the outliers have been identified: after all, an outlier is merely an indicator that something untoward is going on. Further investigation will then be required to establish whether this is a case of TBML or something else. As yet, however, using outliers to identify and act on cases has scarcely been used.

One can also try to develop money-laundering indicators that can pick up TBML even when genuine flows of goods against normal market value are involved. At first sight, this may prove to be difficult, if not impossible, working on the basis of the examples put forward by the FATF reports. After all, if the goods are shipped in accordance with their true value, quantity and quality, they will not differ from normal trade flows, and no anomalies can be detected.

But the cases discussed in the section 'tunnel vision' also show that opportunities for detection exist. These arise from the manner in which payment is made for the goods. One constant that emerged from the Dutch cases was that, without exception, the goods were paid for *in cash.* Cash payments of this kind open up excellent opportunities for the business and banking sector to detect TBML. Even better, there is no need for more obligations in monitoring trade transactions by financial service providers. Strict compliance with the existing obligation to report unusual transactions is sufficient. Three sorts of signals can be distinguished.

The first signal lies in the nature of the payment itself. The criminals often pay for the goods using small denominations of banknotes. This means that the companies, in their turn, will have to pass on or deposit these notes. For instance, in case three, goods were paid for with a stack containing 3.750 twenty-euro notes. An employee of the company had to physically carry out several transactions, as the bank's cash deposit machine would only accept 300 notes at a time. Cash transactions of this kind are extremely unusual for most companies. This could have prompted the bank in question to report a suspicious transaction.

The second signal could be that a company that formerly carried out all its payment transactions by wire transfer, suddenly deviates from its customary payment patterns and starts depositing large sums of cash as is in case 1. The company director accepted large payments in cash because of his desire to accommodate new African clients. Changes of this kind should also not go unnoticed/unreported.

The final signal lies in a flow of goods that is uncharacteristic of the business sector or enterprise in question. The Dutch investigations uncovered TBML when an agricultural machinery company suddenly imported a large consignment of rice from a different continent from where it normally did business, which it then paid for in cash. Or a garage that suddenly imports a cargo of toys from China. In order to pick up such signals, it is obviously essential to be well acquainted with the company and its regular trading activities, and this will not always be the case. However, if a cash payment has already set off alarm bells with a bank's compliance department, anomalous trade transactions may perhaps be the decisive prompt to report the matter to the Financial Intelligence Unit.

References

Albanese J.S., The case of organized crime. *Journal of Contemporary Criminal Justice*, 2000, *16*(4), 409-423

Anderson A., Organized crime, mafias and governments. In: G. Fiorentini and S. Peltzman (eds.), *The Economics of organized crime*. Cambridge: Cambridge University Press, 1995

Beare, M.E., Purposeful misconceptions: Organized crime and the state. In E.C. Viano, J. Magallanes and L. Bridel (eds.), *Transnational organized crime; Myth, power, and profit*. (pp. 157-168). Durham: Carolina Academic Press, 2003

Brayshaw, E., Combating trade-based money laundering calls for a united front. *Anti-Money Laundering,* 2009, *19*, 14-17

Delston, R.S. and S.C. Walls, Reaching beyond banks: How to target trade-based money laundering and Terrorist Financing outside the financial sector. *Case Western Reserve Journal of International Law*, 2009, 41(1), 85-118

Duyne, P.C. van, Medieval thinking and organized crime economy. In E. C. Viano, J. Magallanes and L. Bridel (eds.), *Transnational organized crime; Myth, power, and profit* (pp. 23-44). Durham: Carolina Academic Press, 2003

FATF, *FATF IX Recommendation*. Financial Action Task Force (FATF), 2001

FATF, *40 recommendations*. Financial Action Task Force (FATF), 2003

FATF, *Trade Based Money Laundering*. Financial Action Task Force (FATF), 2006

FATF, *Best practices paper on Trade Based money laundering*. Financial Action Task Force (FATF), 2008

FATF, *Methodology for Assessing Compliance with the FATF 40 Recommendations and the FATF 9 Special Recommendations.* Financial Action Task Force (FATF, ed.), 2009

FATF, *International Standards on Combating Money Laundering and the Financing of Terrorism and Proliferation - the FATF Recommendations.* Financial Action. Paris: Task Force (FATF), 2012

Ferwerda, J., M.A.C. Kattenberg, H-H. Chang, B. Unger, L.F.M. Groot and J.A. Bikker, *Gravity models of trade-based money laundering.* Tjalling C. Koopmans Research Instituten, Utrecht, 2011, 11(16)

FinCen, *Advisory to financial institutions on filing suspicious activity reports regarding trade-based money laundering.* Department of the Treasury Financial Crimes Enforcement Network, Washington, 2010

Freis, J.H., jr., Prepared remarks of James H. Freis, jr. Director, Financial Crimes Enforcement Network. *Florida International Bankers Association 2010 AML Conference.* Miami, Florida, 2010

Jacques, S. and R. Wright, Informal control and illicit drug trade. *Criminology*, 2011, *49* (3), 729-765.

Liao, J. and A. Acharya, Transshipment and trade-based money laundering. *Journal of Money Laundering Control*, 2011, *14* (1), 79-92.

Mitsilegas, V., Countering the chameleon threat of dirty money: 'hard' and 'soft' law in the emergence of a global regime against money laundering and terrorist finance. In A. Edwards and P. Gill (eds.), *Transnational organised crime: Perspectives on global security* (pp. 195-211). London: Routledge, 2003

Nitsch, V., *The dynamics of illicit flows from developing countries*, Paper presented at the World Bank conference September 14-15, 2009

Razavy, M. and K.D. Haggerty, Hawala under scrutiny: Documentation, surveillance and trust. *International Politcal Sociology,* 2009, (3), 139-155

Reuter, P., *Disorganized crime: The economics of the visible hand.* Cambridge, Massachusetts: MIT Press, 1983

Sullivan, C. and E. Smith, *Trade-based money laundering: Risks and regulatory responses.* Canberra: Australian Institute of Criminology, 2011

USDOS (2009). *International narcotics control strategy report: Volume II Money laundering and financial crimes.* United States Department of State Bureau for International Narcotics and Law Enforcement Affairs

Wolfsberg Group (2009). *The Wolfsberg trade finance principles.* The Wolfsberg Group.

Zdanowicz, J.S., Detecting money laundering and terrorist financing via data mining. *Communications of the ACM*, 2004, 47 (*5*), 53-55

Zdanowicz, J.S., Who's watching our backdoor? *Business Accents*, 2004a, *1* (1), 26-29

Zdanowicz, J.S., Trade-based money laundering and terrorist financing. *Review of Law and Economics*, 2009, *5* (*2*), 856-878

Following the money trail: 'Civil' forfeiture of 'criminal' assets in Ireland

Colin King[1]

Introduction: the context

During the 1990s, there was significant concern as to the level of crime in Ireland, particularly those activities relating to organised crime (O'Donnell and O'Sullivan, 2003; Campbell, 2008). Matters came to a head in the Summer of 1996 following the murder of a member of An Garda Síochána (Irish police), Detective Garda Jerry McCabe, and that of the investigative journalist Veronica Guerin.[2] In the wake of these murders, a number of enactments were hastened through the Oireachtas (Irish legislature). These included the Disclosure of Certain Information for Taxation and Other Purposes Act, 1996; the Proceeds of Crime Act, 1996; the Criminal Assets Bureau Act, 1996; the Criminal Justice (Drug Trafficking) Act, 1996; and the Criminal Justice (Miscellaneous Provisions) Act, 1997. In addition, the government announced its intention to hold a referendum on the issue of bail, which culminated in the Bail Act, 1997. Such measures were designed to hit back at the "*professional thugs*" (Seanad Éireann, Criminal Assets Bureau Bill, 1996, Second Stage, October 09, 1996, vol.148, col.1547, per Senator Mulcahy), "*drug barons*" (Dáil Éireann, Private Members' Business – Organised Crime (Restraint and Disposal of Illicit Assets) Bill, 1996, Second Stage, July 02, 1996 vol.467, col.2486, per Deputy Gregory), "*home grown Mafia*" (Dáil Éireann, Private Members' Business – Organised Crime (Restraint and Disposal of Illicit Assets) Bill, 1996, Second Stage, July 02, 1996 vol.467, col.2442, per Deputy Shatter), and "*godfathers of crime*" (Dáil Éireann, Private Members' Business – Measures Against Crime: Motion, July 02, 1996 vol.467, col.2396, per Deputy Harney), who were seen as a scourge on Irish society. Against a backdrop of growing concern surrounding organised crime, it was perhaps inevitable that there would be

1 The author is Lecturer in Criminal Law and Evidence at the University of Leeds.

2 Detective Garda Jerry McCabe was murdered by members of a terrorist organisation during an armed robbery on June 6, 1996, while Veronica Guerin was murdered by a criminal gang on June 26, 1996.

significant substantive and institutional reform of the criminal justice system (see, for example, Meade, 2000). The conventional approach of police investigation, prosecution, conviction and punishment was perceived not to be working – particularly in relation to organised crime - so a new approach was called for. In the words of Deputy O'Donnell,

> "We need to reconsider this matter. If traditional methods fail we must devise new ones. If we cannot punish, deter or reform these people we must set a new aim, to stop them from operating their evil trade. This Bill, which forms the basis of that new approach, is long overdue. We have given the courts power to seize the assets of those convicted of certain crimes and to restrain the assets of those facing certain criminal charges, but given the difficulties experienced in getting convictions, or even gathering evidence, a new power is needed to restain [sic] the use of assets outside the context of criminal proceedings. To date we have dealt only with assets which are the fruits of past crimes. What we need to do now is prevent assets being used as the seeds of future crimes. To put it another way, if we cannot arrest the criminals, why not confiscate their assets?" (Dáil Éireann, Private Members' Business – Organised Crime (Restraint and Disposal of Illicit Assets) Bill, 1996, Second Stage, July 2, 1996 vol.467, col.2435)

In a similar vein, it was said that "*The conventional criminal justice system is simply not equipped to bring the so-called crime bosses to justice since they can rarely be directly linked with the execution of a crime. They can, however, be linked with the enormous profits generated by their crimes.*" (Dáil Éireann, Private Members' Business – Organised Crime (Restraint and Disposal of Illicit Assets) Bill, 1996, Second Stage, July 02, 1996 vol.467, col.2463, per Deputy E.Byrne) The seizure of illicit assets, then, in the absence of a criminal conviction, was pushed to the fore of the fight against organised criminal activity. As those at the upper echelons of organised criminal activity were seen as often being outside the reach of the criminal law, recourse to the civil process was thought to be the only viable way to target their ill-gotten gains, given difficulties associated with post-conviction forfeiture (cf. Lusty, 2002: 351; Simser, 2009: 20). This "new"[3] approach was to be implemented by an innovative multi-agency body – the Criminal Assets Bureau (CAB). Together, civil forfeiture provisions and the Criminal Assets Bureau constitute what is widely regarded on the international stage as a successful model in tackling organised crime, in particular in targeting illicitly obtained assets. The focus of this chapter, then, is

3 Civil forfeiture had previously been used against subversive activities, under the Offences Against the State (Amendment) Act, 1985 – the constitutionality of which was upheld in *Clancy v Ireland* [1988] IR 326

to demonstrate that, notwithstanding the many plaudits, there exists a number of concerns with both civil forfeiture and the Bureau. Specifically, this chapter engages with the rights of the individual and how the individual is negatively affected by this alternative approach to crime control.

What can we learn from the Irish experience?

While civil forfeiture does represent "*a significant extension in the powers available to the State to deal with the proceeds of crime*" (Performance and Innovation Unit, 2000: para.5.3), it must also be recognised that it has been subjected to scathing criticism often on the grounds that it allows the State to circumvent due process values even though it is pursuing criminal law objectives under the guise of a civil process (see, for example, Lea, 2004; Piety, 1991). For example, one constant criticism has been that it is unfair for a person to be deprived of assets where the State has not established beyond reasonable doubt that that person has committed a criminal offence. Moreover, even though allegations of criminal wrongdoing might be made in the civil forum, the presumption of innocence does not apply. This is particularly problematic where, following an acquittal in criminal proceedings, a person is faced with civil proceedings seeking forfeiture of assets based on the same allegations and evidence as used in the criminal process.

The Irish legislation provides a useful model for understanding civil forfeiture. In adopting such a radical measure, in the Summer of 1996, the Irish State was at the forefront of the move to seize illicit assets, absent criminal conviction, and the Irish model has influenced a number of other jurisdictions in developing similar legislation[4] (Simser, 2009; Kennedy, 2006). The use of the civil process in this manner has been validated by the Irish Supreme Court, which has explicitly held that enhanced protections inherent in criminal procedure do not apply in proceedings seeking civil forfeiture (*Murphy v GM, PB, PC Ltd, GH; Gilligan v CAB* [2001] 4 IR 113). Jurisprudence from the Irish courts has also proved influential in other jurisdictions, and it is significant that civil forfeiture is now reaching the highest courts in other common law jurisdictions (see, for example, *Chatterjee v Ontario (Attorney General)*, 2009 SCC 19 in Canada and *Gale v Serious Organised Crime Agency* [2011] UKSC 49 in the UK). There are also increasing moves towards the adoption of an EU civil forfeiture regime (European

4 Civil forfeiture legislation can also be found in, *inter alia*, Australia (e.g. Criminal Property Confiscation Act, 2000), Canada (e.g. Civil Forfeiture Act, 2005), New Zealand (Criminal Proceeds (Recovery) Act, 2009), UK (Proceeds of Crime Act, 2002), and the United States (e.g. Civil Asset Forfeiture Reform Act, 2000).

Commission, 2008), and the Irish experience is playing a crucial role in this regard. One example of this is that the Criminal Assets Bureau (the designated Irish Asset Recovery Office for the purposes of Council Decision 2007/845/JHA) is playing a key role in attempting to allay concerns as to the validity of civil forfeiture (especially important in the context of securing recognition of orders in jurisdictions where civil forfeiture does not exist) through, for example, delivering presentations demonstrating how the Irish model has withstood constitutional scrutiny at the domestic level and how this fits in with rights under the European Convention on Human Rights. The Bureau also provides support at the European level in seeking to achieve recognition of non-conviction based orders in appropriate cases. The Bureau is explicit in its desire "*to reach a point where Member States, who do not wish to adopt non-conviction based forfeiture regimes themselves, at least acknowledge the legitimacy, within the Human Rights context of such orders and therefore recognise such orders or requests in the context of investigations conducted under that regime.*" (CAB, 2011: para.7.3).

Notwithstanding such 'encouraging' developments, the Irish approach to civil forfeiture merits further examination. While there have been many plaudits, this has not been matched by concern for the rights of the individual and for the rule of law. This chapter addresses that deficiency. The chapter first outlines the relevant provisions governing civil forfeiture in Ireland and the multi-agency body established to target illicit assets. The chapter then engages with the due process concerns that stem from civil forfeiture as a method of crime control. By resorting to the civil process in order to pursue criminal law objectives enhanced procedural protections inherent in criminal procedure are pushed to one side in the interests of efficiency and expediency. This is aptly demonstrated by discussion of the presumption of innocence (which does not apply in civil forfeiture proceedings) and the applicable standard of proof (that is, the lower civil standard of the balance of probabilities). Alongside concern as to the rights-based ramifications of civil forfeiture, there are a number of concerns surrounding the multi-agency Criminal Assets Bureau. The Bureau is widely lauded as an innovative, and successful, aspect of the Irish approach to seizing illicit assets, yet, here too, there exists significant concerns in relation to the sharing of police powers (in the absence of appropriate training and disciplinary regulations), the sharing of information across State agencies, and the absence of transparency and accountability.

The outlines of the Proceeds of Crime Act

The Proceeds of Crime Acts, 1996 - 2005 (herein POCA) are concerned with property that constitutes, directly or indirectly, "proceeds of crime", which is defined as "*any property obtained or received at any time (whether before or after the passing of this Act) by or as a result of or in connection with criminal conduct*" (POCA, s.1(1)). As mentioned before, the procedure set down in the Act operates outside the conventional criminal justice system. There is no requirement that a person be convicted of a criminal offence before action may be taken under the Act. Indeed, it is not even necessary that criminal proceedings be instituted against a person. The Proceeds of Crime Act operates in the civil sphere. Yet, it would not be appropriate to describe proceedings under the Act as private litigation. It is, in fact, the use of public law powers, by the State, in the civil courts (Ashe and Reid, 2007: 306). The long title of the Proceeds of Crime Act provides that it is

> "An Act to enable the High Court, as respects the Proceeds of Crime, to make orders for the preservation and, where appropriate, the disposal of the property concerned and to provide for related matters."

This Act allows the court, prior to the trial of an action, to restrain a person from dealing with assets where the court is satisfied that those assets represent proceeds of crime and are of a certain value. As Finnegan J. noted in *McKenna v EH*, the Act of 1996 "*creates a statutory right to an injunction to preserve the assets said to be the proceeds of crime.*" ([2002] 1 IR 72, 81). Ultimately, a person might be deprived of any rights in the property concerned. What follows is a brief overview of the Irish civil forfeiture schema, to demonstrate the intricacies of the Irish approach and also to flag up pertinent issues that will be discussed later in relation to due process concerns.

Interim Order

An application for an order under section 2 of the Proceeds of Crime Act, 1996 (an interim order) can be brought by a member of An Garda Síochána not below the rank of Chief Superintendent or by an authorised officer of the Revenue Commissioners (ie tax official). Where the court is satisfied as to certain prerequisites (set out below), it may grant an order under section 2 restraining a person from disposing of, or otherwise dealing with, specified property. The rationale underlying this is to ensure the preservation of assets suspected of being, or deriving from, proceeds of crime until the full hearing. It will usually (but not always) be essential for such an order to be granted *ex parte* – that is, without notice to the party against whose assets an order is sought. The rationale behind bringing an *ex parte* application, in the first instance, is to ensure that the assets concerned cannot be dissipated, or removed from the jurisdiction, pending the full *inter partes* hearing, thus ensuring that a judgment in favour of the applicant can properly be executed (see, for example, *FMcK v D.C., S.T. and B.H. Ltd* [2006] IEHC 185).

An interim order under section 2 operates in a similar manner to equitable remedies, such as the Mareva injunction. An interim order prohibits a person from disposing of, dealing with, or diminishing the value of the property concerned during a 21 day period from the date the order was granted. This is to ensure that assets will be preserved pending the full hearing. An interim order can only be granted where the court is satisfied that the property concerned is, or was acquired with, the proceeds of criminal activity and is of a certain value. Before the court can grant the order, there must be sufficient objective evidence, on the civil standard of proof (POCA, s.8(2)),[5] that the relevant property represents proceeds of crime. A significant feature of the Act is that it permits opinion evidence of a member of An Garda Síochána, not below the rank of Chief Superintendent, or an authorised officer of the Revenue Commissioners to be admitted as evidence (POCA, s.8(1)). Where the court is satisfied that the property concerned represents proceeds of crime, it must then go on to consider whether it is appropriate to grant an interim order – it is left to the discretion of the court whether such an order would be appropriate in the circumstances. Subject to being discharged, an interim order expires 21 days from the date of its making, unless an application for an order under section 3 (an interlocutory order) has been brought in respect of any of the property in question (POCA, s.2(5)).

Interlocutory Order

Although usually preceded by an interim order, there is no requirement that an interim order be in place before an application for an order under section 3 (an interlocutory order) can be brought. An interlocutory order is similar to an interim order. Where it appears to the court that a person is in possession or control of specified property that represents proceeds of crime, and the value of that property is not less than €13,000 then the court shall grant an interlocutory order (POCA, s.3(1)). An interlocutory order prohibits a specific person(s), or any other person having notice of the order, from disposing of, dealing with, or diminishing the value of the property concerned (POCA, s.3(1)). Note, though, that there is a significant difference between interlocutory orders (as conventionally understood)

5 The relevant standard is the balance of probabilities. Cf. *Banco Ambrosiano SPA v Ansbacher and Co Ltd* [1987] ILRM 669; *Masterfoods Ltd v HB Ice Cream Ltd* [1993] ILRM 145

and the statutory interlocutory order as contained in s.3 of the Act of 1996. Conventional interlocutory orders are not final orders, they are merely ancillary relief. The procedure under s.3, however, is of a different mould. It is, in fact, to be regarded as the trial of the action (*Murphy v GM, PB, PC Ltd, GH; Gilligan v CAB* [2001] 4 IR 113; *FJMcK v AF and JF* [2002] 1 IR 242).

Opinion evidence is again admissible at this stage, even though the effect of an interlocutory order is much more far-reaching than an interim order (Ashe and Reid, 2007: 330). Significantly, there is no discretionary element here. Where the court is satisfied as to the above prerequisites then it must grant an interlocutory order, unless the respondent, or any other person, produces evidence to satisfy the court that the property in question does not represent proceeds of crime (POCA, s.3(1). See, for example, *McKenna v MON* [2006] IEHC 428). Unlike an application for an interim order, the court need not be "satisfied" as to the evidence of the applicant. The court will not, however, grant an interlocutory order where it is established that the value of the property is less than €13,000 (POCA, s.3(1)). Moreover, the court will not grant such an order where it is satisfied that there would be a serious risk of injustice (POCA, s.3(1)). This latter safeguard has been described by two practitioners as

> "an important safeguard, not only having regard to the admissibility of evidence of belief on behalf of the applicant, but also having regard to the fact that the respondent may have had no connection with the commission of the crime to which the proceeds related. There is, as yet, no judicial guidance on this provision. However, it would appear to enable the court to protect people who have, in good faith, acquired property, who have no knowledge of the true nature of the business conducted by the individuals with whom they had been dealing and where it would be unfair to grant the order". (Ashe and Reid, 2001: 259)

On the other hand, however, another practitioner has described it as "*a vague and intangible yardstick and it is not immediately clear how it would operate in practice.*" (O'Higgins, 1996: 12) A further safeguard is that, at any time during which an interlocutory order is in force, the respondent, or any other person claiming ownership of the property concerned, can apply to the court to have the order discharged or varied (POCA, s.3(3)). In practice, this also opens up the possibility of victims of crime applying to the court to have their rights recognised (see, for example, the case of CAB v Matthew Schachter, discussed in CAB, 2008: para.5.4).

Subject to being discharged, where an interlocutory order is granted, it will normally continue in force until the determination of an application for a disposal order in relation to the property concerned, the expiration of the ordinary time for bringing an appeal from that determination or, if an appeal is brought, the determination or abandonment of that appeal or any further appeal or expiration of the ordinary time for bringing any further appeal, whichever is the latest (POCA, s.3(5)). With both interim and interlocutory orders, where the property in question is subject to a forfeiture order or a confiscation order under the Criminal Justice Act, 1994, or a forfeiture order under the Misuse of Drugs Act, 1977, then the order under either section 2 or 3 shall be varied or discharged as appropriate (POCA, s.3(7)).

Disposal Order

The interim and interlocutory orders have been described as *"essential stages en route to a final destination, namely the permanent confiscation of the property in question."* (Murphy and Galvin, 1999: 29) Where an interlocutory order has been in force for not less than seven years in relation to specified property, the court, on application to it, may grant an order under section 4 (a disposal order), directing that the property, or part thereof, be transferred, subject to any terms and conditions specified by the court, to the Minister for Finance or to such other person as determined by the court. Post-2005, there is now provision for a disposal order to be granted before the seven year period has elapsed where all the parties to the action so consent (POCA, s.4A). Although it would appear that the court has a discretion whether or not to grant a disposal order, the court must in fact make a disposal order in relation to any of the property concerned unless it is shown to its satisfaction that that particular property does not represent proceeds of crime (POCA, s.4(2)). Before deciding whether to grant an application under section 4, the court must allow any person claiming ownership of any of the property concerned the opportunity to be heard by the court and to show cause why an order should not be made (POCA, s.4(6)). Moreover, a disposal order shall not be made where the court is satisfied that there would be a serious risk of injustice (POCA, s.4(8)).

The effect of a disposal order is to deprive the respondent of his rights (if any) in the property concerned; consequent to the making of an order the property will be transferred to the Minister for Finance or to any other person to whom the order relates (POCA, s.4(4)). The Minister may sell or otherwise dispose of any such property and any money thus realised shall be for the benefit of the Exchequer (POCA, s.4(5)).

The Criminal Assets Bureau

Even before the Summer of 1996 there had, for some time, been many calls to ensure that the resources of the State were better co-ordinated to combat criminal activity. Alongside substantive measures, a new "*special unit to target criminal assets*" was to be established (Dáil Éireann, Criminal Assets Bureau Bill, 1996, Second Stage, July 25, 1996, vol.4668, col.1024, per Minister Quinn). Indeed, the establishment of such a unit has been described as "*a necessary adjunct*" to the adoption of civil forfeiture (Dáil Éireann, Criminal Assets Bureau Bill, 1996, Second Stage, July 25, 1996, vol.4668, col.1031, per Deputy McCreevy). Known as the Criminal Assets Bureau, the unit is headed by a Chief Superintendent from An Garda Síochána, and is composed of officials from different state agencies working together for crime control purposes. The Bureau was officially brought into existence on October 15, 1996 (SI 310/1996 Criminal Assets Bureau Act, 1996 (Establishment Day) Order, 1996) although it had been operating on an *ad hoc* basis prior to this.

The Criminal Assets Bureau Act, 1996 (herein, CAB Act) was, according to its long title, introduced in order to establish the Criminal Assets Bureau and to define its functions.[6] The Bureau brings together State officials from An Garda Síochána, the Revenue Commissioners and the Department of Social Protection under the umbrella of one multi-agency body. The Bureau represents a concerted effort to bring three separate agencies together without traditional barriers to cooperation hindering their work. The Bureau is, however, much more than a multi-agency body. It is, essentially, a policing unit that is able to harness the powers and resources of separate agencies to pursue policing objectives. In introducing the Bill, establishing the Bureau, before the Dáil, Minister Quinn stated:

> "The criminal activities of major criminals are multi-faceted and our response to these require new ways of directing the resources of the State and new structures through which the dedicated and determined efforts of the Garda, Revenue and Department of Social Welfare can be channelled most effectively."

6 The objectives of the Bureau are: to identify assets that derive, or are suspected to derive, directly or indirectly, from criminal conduct; to take appropriate action to deprive persons of such assets or to deny them the benefit of such assets; and to carry out investigations, or other preparatory work, in relation to the above objectives. (Criminal Assets Bureau Act, 1996, s.4, as amended). The remit of the Bureau involves: the confiscation, restraint of use, freezing, preservation or seizure of assets identified as deriving or suspected of deriving from criminal conduct; ensuring that the proceeds of criminal conduct, or suspected criminal conduct, are subjected to tax; and the investigation and determination of claims for benefit under social welfare legislation. (Criminal Assets Bureau Act, 1996, s.5, as amended).

(Dáil Éireann, Criminal Assets Bureau Bill, 1996, Second Stage, July 25, 1996, vol.4668, col.1025)

The benefits of this are axiomatic, for example there is the pooling of professional expertise, improved management of resources, and it allows the surpassing of individual capacities by improving efficiency and reducing costs of managing investigations (Lemieux, 2010: 266). And, as is proclaimed by the Garda Commissioner in the most recent annual report:

> "The Bureau is in its 15th year and among the most notable aspects which have contributed to the successes achieved to date has been the multi-agency and multi-disciplinary approach chosen at its inception. The approach has proven to be one of the most enduring features in terms of the effectiveness of the Bureau" (CAB, 2011: 'Letter to Minister from Commissioner').

As Murphy and Galvin (1999: 30) note:

> "A dominant and novel characteristic of the Government's response in 1996 to the upsurge in drug-trafficking and organised crime was the adoption of a multi-agency approach. For the first time in the history of the State, the resources of the Garda Síochána, the Revenue authorities and the Social Welfare authorities were combined to produce a more effective weapon to combat organised crime. The vehicle through which these resources would be pooled was a new statutory agency, namely the Criminal Assets Bureau (CAB)".

As the Hederman Committee (2002: para.10.52) pointed out:

> "The traditional police approach of securing convictions against the offenders has been complemented by a strategy that focuses on the wealth that is believed to derive, directly or indirectly, from organised crime. By combining the knowledge and skills of the Revenue Commissioners and the social welfare officers with those of the Garda Síochána, it will be easier to identify suspects who appear to be enjoying a lifestyle which grossly exceeds their publicly declared income and capital."

The Bureau is widely lauded for its successes. Annual reports regularly proclaim, somewhat self-congratulatory, that the Bureau "*has had another successful year in the context of pursuing its statutory remit.*" (CAB, 2011: 'Letter to Minister from Commissioner'). The 2010 report goes on to say "*It is self-evident that organised crime continues to pose a serious threat to society and in this regard, the Bureau continues to demonstrate its effectiveness as an integral part of the law enforcement response to criminal conduct of this nature.*" (CAB, 2011: 'Letter to Minister from Commissioner').

According to the Minister for Justice, Equality and Law Reform, Dermot Ahern:

> "The Criminal Assets Bureau has been at the forefront of the fight against organised crime, including drug trafficking, in this jurisdiction since its inception in 1996. The significant successes that the Bureau continues to achieve by its operations demonstrates the effectiveness of its approach in pursuing illegally gotten gains." (Dáil Éireann, Written Answers – Criminal Assets Bureau, vol.661, September 24, 2008)

Such self-congratulatory assessment rests on the value of assets realised by the Bureau. In 2010, for example, €2.810.902,52 was realised under section 4 of the Proceeds of Crime Act (CAB, 2011: para.4.12), while in 2009 €1.263.388,69 was realised under sections 4 and 4A of the Act (CAB, 2010: para.4.12). On their own, however, such figures tell us very little as to the effectiveness of the Bureau in the fight against organised crime. In the absence of reliable data on organised crime groups (eg economic cost, market size, criminal income, *etc.*) these figures in the annual reports fail to provide a proper performance measurement (cf. Naylor, 1999).

Now that the Irish model governing civil forfeiture, and the agency tasked with implementing that legislation, have been outlined, there are a number of concerns that must be addressed.

Due Process Concerns

The 'civil' forfeiture of 'criminal' assets, under the Proceeds of Crime Act, raises serious concerns about circumventing traditional due process protections that are inherent in the criminal process. By resorting to the civil process, the State, conveniently sidestepping the rights of a suspect/ accused, seeks to exact criminal punishment for wrongdoing under the cloak of civility. In resorting to civil procedure, "the legislature", according to Fellmeth (2005: 5),

> "can achieve – and currently does achieve – precisely the same policy goals as it could using criminal law, in nearly the same manner, and without the inconvenience of affording to the suspect or defendant the enhanced protections and procedures nominally guaranteed by the Constitution in criminal cases."

He goes on to say,

> "The result is to ensure the efficient control of private behaviour without the need to honor such pesky rights as the guarantees against double jeopardy and excessive fines, and most importantly, the requirement that the state prove its

cause beyond a reasonable doubt before inflicting punishment on a defendant." (Fellmeth, 2005: 6)

While this radical approach, in which crime control objectives are pursued in the civil process, has been justified on grounds of inadequacies of the conventional criminal justice approach and in the interests of efficiency and expediency (Farley, 1994), Fellmeth (2006: 728) argues that this "*fails to address why some unknown amount of economic savings should relieve the state of the duty to afford EPP* [that is, enhanced procedural protections] *to defendants before forcing them into a position of serving as a negative example or of suffering punishment to deter one's own speculative future misbehaviour without an offer of proof beyond a reasonable doubt and other EPP.*" Moreover, in relation to the claim that the conventional criminal justice system is inadequate to tackle organised crime (See, for example, Seanad Éireann, Proceeds of Crime Bill, 1996, Second Stage, July 26, 1996, vol.148, col.1377, per Senator Neville ("drug super criminals . . . cannot be touched by the State forces of law and order")), it is clear that police and prosecution authorities have a vast arsenal available to them with which to tackle criminal behaviour. In recent decades, this array of powers has been further enhanced and there is a demonstrative shift towards the crime control model at the expense of due process norms (see, for example, Campbell, 2008b). Indeed, it is apparent that the Criminal Assets Bureau, the primary body responsible for proceedings under the Proceeds of Crime Act, utilises its civil/ administrative persona to target those that are suspected, accused and/ or convicted of involvement in criminal activity, particularly that activity associated with organised crime (See, for example, "*Killer made £720,000 in drugs deal*", *Irish Times*, July 30, 1999; "*After comfortable start, 'Dutchy' devotes rest of his life to crime*", *Irish Times*, June 20, 2009; "*Couple oppose Cab order to seize house, ring and cash*", *Irish Times*, March 19, 2010). And, of course, given that it purports to operate outside the conventional criminal process, procedural safeguards that are insisted upon in the criminal process do not apply. In essence, enhanced procedural protections that are mandated in criminal proceedings are rendered nugatory. The difficulty that arises, then, is that a person can be subjected to what is essentially a criminal punishment, but is stripped of important due process protections.

This can be illustrated by discussion of the presumption of innocence and the applicable standard of proof. Given that civil forfeiture operates in the civil realm, the presumption of innocence does not attach.[7] As Ashworth (2006: 270) points out, "*What could be simpler, then, than for a government to circumvent the presumption by*

7 The European Court of Human Rights has, however, recognised that the presumption might, in appropriate situations, be engaged in civil proceedings. See, for example, *Bochan v Ukraine* App. No.7577/02 May 3, 2007, para.78; *Lutz v Germany* [1988] 10 EHRR 182, para.60

promoting legislation that provides for the imposition of civil orders on citizens?" Yet, given that proceedings seeking 'civil' forfeiture (of 'criminal' assets) will usually include allegations of wrongdoing on the part of the respondent is there not an argument that it would be appropriate for the presumption to apply? This argument is strengthened when we consider that a successful application for forfeiture will expose that person to stigma and/or community condemnation (Hart, 1958: 406). The contention that the presumption of innocence ought to apply is further strengthened in situations where an individual has been acquitted in a criminal trial but then confronted with civil forfeiture proceedings based upon the same allegations and evidence as had been used in the criminal proceedings. For example, how can the civil trial make a finding adverse to the respondent without, in some way, casting doubt on the validity of the previous acquittal in criminal proceedings? (Mahmutaj, 2009) If the civil trial does, *de facto*, impute criminal liability, surely the presumption ought to be afforded a continuing influence. To say that civil forfeiture is not concerned with a criminal charge, and therefore there is no role for the presumption of innocence, ignores the reality of the situation, namely that such proceedings (if successful), post-acquittal, essentially serve to undermine the criminal acquittal. As Naylor (1999: 41) points out,

> "in those cases where a criminal process is implemented, and the person charged found innocent, the U.S. government can re-litigate the same facts against that person's property using civil criteria with the onus reversed. Not only does punishment in the form of property forfeiture then occur, but the owner has been to all intents and purposes found guilty, in the eyes of not just the state but of all of his/her fellow citizens, of the very offense for which he/she was previously acquitted."

Related to arguments concerning the presumption of innocence is a concern surrounding the applicable standard of proof in civil forfeiture proceedings, namely the balance of probabilities. Given that proceedings under the Proceeds of Crime Act are, arguably, concerned with criminal punishment, there is a strong argument that a heightened standard of proof ought to apply. Indeed, it might even be appropriate for the criminal standard of proof beyond reasonable doubt to be insisted upon. In *Gough v Chief Constable of the Derbyshire Constabulary*, concerning football banning orders, it was said the civil standard of proof "*is flexible and must reflect the consequences that will follow if the case for a banning order is made out. This should lead the justices to apply an exacting standard of proof that will, in practice, be hard to distinguish from the criminal standard*" ([2002] QB 1213, 1242-1243). In *McCann*, a case concerning anti-social behaviour orders, Lord Hope of Craighead, in holding that the appropriate standard in proceedings for an ASBO was the criminal standard, stated:

> "But it is not an invariable rule that the lower standard of proof must be applied in civil proceedings. I think that there are good reasons, in the interests of fairness, for applying the higher standard when allegations are made of criminal or quasi-criminal conduct which, if proved, would have serious consequences for the person against whom they are made". (R (McCann) v Crown Court at Manchester; Clingham v Chelsea Royal London Borough Council [2003] 1 AC 787, 826)

While the Irish courts have not been willing to go down such a route, the Supreme Court, albeit in a different context, has recognised that "*the more serious the allegation made in civil proceedings, then the more astute must the judge be to find that the allegation in question has been proved.*" (*O'Keeffe v Ferris* [1997] 2 ILRM 161, 168) In another case Hamilton CJ stated:

> "The standard of proving a case beyond reasonable doubt is confined to criminal trials and has no application in proceedings of a civil nature. It is true that the complaints against the plaintiff involved charges of great seriousness and with serious implications for the plaintiff's reputation. This does not, however, require that the facts upon which the allegations are based should be established beyond all reasonable doubt. They can be dealt with on "the balance of probabilities" bearing in mind that the degree of probability required should always be proportionate to the nature and gravity of the issue to be investigated . . . . I am satisfied that in inquiries, such as conducted in this case, the standard of proof to be applied is not standard of proof required in a criminal case but is that applicable to all proceedings of a civil nature, namely "the balance of probabilities" a standard which takes into account the nature and gravity of the issue to be investigated and decided." (Georgopoulus v Beaumont Hospital Board [1998] 3 IR 132, 149-150)

It might well be argued, though, that civil proceedings, seeking forfeiture of property on the basis that that property constitutes proceeds of crime, should be regarded as more severe than conventional civil proceedings and, as such, ought to attract a higher standard of proof than the civil standard of proof.[8] For example, the loss of property and potential social stigmatisation might be seen as, at the very least, akin to a fine imposed in criminal proceedings (Jensen and Gerber, 1996: 427; Stahl, 1992-93: 301). Downward pressure on the standard of proof has been described as "*indicative of increased support for a risk management standard, premised on efficiency rather than certainty, as opposed to a more traditional criminal standard that placed a premium on*

---

8 Admittedly, though, this would go some way to undermining one of the primary rationales underpinning the adoption of civil forfeiture.

accuracy and was designed to afford individuals every possible benefit of law." (Kilcommins and Vaughan, 2006: 109. Kilcommins and Vaughan refer to the Proceeds of Crime Act, sex offender orders, and post-conviction confiscation of assets as evidence of this downward pressure.) If, however, the Irish courts were to adopt a similar approach to that in *McCann*, and insist upon the criminal standard of proof in proceedings concerning forfeiture of assets under the Proceeds of Crime Act, this would go a long way towards respecting the rights of the individual. Were there a requirement that property could only be forfeited where it is shown, beyond reasonable doubt, that that property constitutes proceeds of crime then the 'civil' forfeiture of 'criminal' assets would be much less objectionable.

Concerns surrounding information access and powers

By virtue of its presence in the administrative realm the Criminal Assets Bureau has enhanced capabilities and access to information when compared to the conventional police force. Indeed, the Bureau is also in a position to circumvent many of the checks and balances that apply to the police due to this administrative persona. This raises concerns, as, where a body seeks to inflict criminal punishment; there is an expectation that such potential for punishment will be accompanied by appropriate safeguards. That does not appear to be the case with the Criminal Assets Bureau, though. In fact, it is apparent that the Bureau is primarily concerned with using its extensive armoury of powers to target particular forms of criminality, particularly that which is associated with organised crime. It is plain to see that the Bureau is, in essence, a cog in the criminal justice apparatus – exercising police powers, in conjunction with enhanced powers and resources due to its multiagency nature, in the pursuit of criminal law objectives. This shall be examined further here in the context of police powers and the sharing of information across different State agencies.

The powers and duties vested in a bureau officer are those that that officer has already by virtue of being a Garda, a member of the Revenue Commissioners, or an officer of the Minister for Social Protection. For example, a bureau officer who is a member of the Revenue Commissioners retains all his powers and duties under the Revenue Acts. A bureau officer shall continue to have all the powers and duties vested in him by virtue of his position as either a Garda, an officer of the Revenue Commissioners or an officer of the Minister for Social Protection, whether that be for purposes related to the Criminal Assets Bureau Act, 1996 or otherwise (CAB Act, s.8(8)). The significance of this is that bureau officers can exercise their own individual powers in carrying out the work of the Bureau, and for other purposes.

Bureau officers are not, however, conferred with any extra powers solely by virtue of appointment to the Bureau.[9] As was pointed out in the Dáil:

> "The essence of the bureau is that each of the three agencies will bring their own powers and expertise to the bureau and, by means of section 8 of the Bill, will exercise these powers in a mutually supportive and concerned manner." (Dáil Éireann, Criminal Assets Bureau Bill, 1996, Second Stage, 25 July, 1996, vol.468, cols.1025-1026, per Minister Quinn)

Significantly, a bureau officer may be accompanied or assisted in the exercise of his powers or duties by such other persons as he considers necessary (CAB Act, s.8(6)(a)).[10] This is stated very broadly and would appear to include assistance by non-bureau officers. Presumably, this provision was deemed necessary to allow technical experts to assist in the work of the Bureau, but the broad manner in which this is provided for does not confine assistance to such persons. Further, there is no limitation as to the background or qualifications of a person who may provide assistance, nor is there any limit as to the number of such people that may be involved in the Bureau's work. This could potentially open the door to the temporary engagement of large numbers of Gardai, Revenue officials, Social Welfare officials, or indeed any other person. The most significant aspect here is that there is no express requirement that a person providing assistance meet any standard of training or be subject to disciplinary regulations. Any person could apparently be asked to assist a bureau officer where that officer deems it "necessary". Bureau officers are drawn from a pool of qualified and suitably trained people. No such qualification or prescribed standard of training, however, is required of persons accompanying or assisting bureau officers under this provision.

As significant is that a bureau officer who assists another bureau officer in this regard shall be conferred with the powers and duties of that other bureau officer for the purposes of assisting him (CAB Act, s.8(6)(c)). This is far-reaching in that it allows non-police officials to be bestowed with policing powers where they are assisting a Garda bureau officer. Thus, for example, where an officer of the Revenue Commissioners, acting as a bureau officer, assists a member of the Garda Síochána, acting as a bureau officer, then that officer of the Revenue Commissioners will be bestowed with the powers and duties of a Garda, for the purposes of assisting that other bureau officer. Again, this raises concerns as to the

---

9 S.58 of the Criminal Justice Act, 2007, amending s.8 of the Criminal Assets Bureau Act, 1996, does, however, make provision for Revenue bureau officers and Social Welfare bureau officers to attend and participate in the questioning of a detained person in certain circumstances.

10 Any information, documents or other material obtained by bureau officers under subsection (6) shall be admitted in any subsequent proceedings. CAB Act, s.8(6)(d)

standard of training provided. Bureau officers will have their own expertise, and training, from their role as a member of the Garda Síochána, a Revenue official, or a Social Welfare official as the case may be. Moreover, they will be subject to a particular disciplinary regime. Bestowing upon bureau officers, when acting as such, the powers of other bureau officers raises its own concerns. One obvious example is where a non-Garda bureau officer assists in an entry, search and seizure. Where such a power is exercised by a person who does not possess adequate training and experience, it is more likely that breaches of substantive protections (for example, under Article 8 of the ECHR) will occur (Joint Committee on Human Rights, 2005: para.1.54-1.55). As Harfield (2006: 751) has noted in relation to civilian employees of the Serious Organised Crime Agency being afforded police, customs and/or immigration powers, as required,

> "In adopting the position that police powers are no longer exclusively for police officers to execute, the Government has altered radically the relationship of the citizen to the use of police powers and the accountability inherent there".

So, where two or more bureau officers assist each other then those officers will be conferred with the powers of the others. While this might be regarded as enhancing flexibility and expediency, there remains a concern that this represents a radical step in extending police powers to non-police officials.

The Bureau's role in 'information gathering' also merits consideration here. A bureau officer may exercise or perform his powers or duties based upon any information received from another bureau officer or based upon any action taken by that other bureau officer in the exercise or performance of that other bureau officer's powers or duties for the purposes of the Criminal Assets Bureau Act, 1996. Any information, documents or other material thereby obtained by bureau officers shall be admitted in evidence in any subsequent proceedings (CAB Act, s.8(5)). This is not restricted to proceedings initiated by the Bureau itself. Such information, documents or other material may be used in proceedings taken by Gardai, the Revenue Commissioners, or the Department of Social Protection. This is a hugely significant power particularly in the realm of crime control. It could even be suggested that bureau officers are tasked with compiling information from a wide variety of sources, made possible by the multi-agency nature of the Bureau, and then reporting back to their parent authorities with this information. According to the Minister for Finance,

> "Provision is made to ensure that information, documents or material obtained by officers or officers assisting each other may be admitted in evidence. The bureau officers will be able to share information with each other and to disclose this information or material to their "parent" authorities. It is important for the

effectiveness of the bureau to maintain these links especially in the case of the Garda, as such information on the activities of criminals or suspected criminals will be of material use to the Garda authorities generally in discharging their responsibilities for combating crime." (Dáil Éireann, Criminal Assets Bureau Bill, 1996, Second Stage, 25 July, 1996, vol.468, cols.1028-1029)

By drawing on the expertise of Gardai, Revenue officials and Social Welfare officials the Bureau is able to provide much more detailed information to the Garda Síochána, the Revenue Commissioners and the Department of Social Protection than would otherwise have been possible. Traditionally, information could only be used for the purpose for which it had been collected. Essentially, information in the hands of, for example, the Revenue Commissioners was treated as confidential and could not be disclosed to other authorities.[11] The multi-agency character of the Criminal Assets Bureau, however, facilitates access to information that may have been gathered for an entirely different purpose. Indeed, one former bureau legal officer has described this as "*the bedrock of* [the Bureau's] *success*" (Barrett, 2007: 230. In *CAB v Craft* [2001] 1 IR 121, 133 O'Sullivan J stated "*The members of the Criminal Assets Bureau are entitled to exchange information amongst themselves and clearly they would be in dereliction of duty if they failed to do this in an appropriate case.*"). Given the scope and sensitivity of material held by the relevant agencies, there are potentially huge consequences in allowing the Bureau access to such material. This is even more troubling when we consider that a person under investigation by the Bureau may be required to produce material for inspection (for example, under s.9 and s.14A of POCA), with the result that such material could then be made available to other State authorities for wholly unconnected purposes. Given that 'administrative' information could potentially be used for criminal law purposes, this is particularly worrying.

The significance of this power is reinforced by the provisions of section 8(7) of the Act. For the purposes of the Criminal Assets Bureau Act, 1996, a bureau officer may only disclose information to another bureau officer, or a member of the staff of the Bureau; any member of the Garda Síochána for the purposes of Garda functions; any officer of the Revenue Commissioners for purposes relating to revenue; any officer of the Minister for Social and Family Affairs for the purposes of the Social Welfare Acts; or with the consent of the Chief Bureau Officer, any

11 In a submission to the Law Reform Commission, the Revenue Commissioners emphasised that "it is a fundamental principle of the tax code that taxpayers are entitled to expect that any information provided by them is treated in confidence for tax purposes only and that such information and their tax affairs will not be disclosed to third parties." (Law Reform Commission, 1991: 64). The LRC (1991: 65), however, was of the view that there is "room for co-ordination of the activities of the Revenue and the criminal law without affecting the integrity of the tax collection code."

other officer of a government department or of a local authority for purposes relating to that officer's powers or duties. Again, this would appear to provide authority for an information-sharing procedure whereby policing, tax and social welfare investigations can call upon sources and information that they previously had no access to. This is particularly so in the absence of any meaningful limitations on the disclosure of information, which appears to fly in the face of data protection legislation. Admittedly, internal guidelines might well impose restrictions on the sharing of information, but as has been pointed out elsewhere

> "reliance on management controls to guarantee the appropriateness and proportionality of using and disclosing personal information does not satisfy the requirement that interferences with the right to respect for private life must be in accordance with the law, if there are insufficient legally binding safeguards in the legislation itself." (Joint Committee on Human Rights, 2005b: para.2.15. Cf. *Leander v Sweden* [1987] 9 EHRR 433, para.51)

Moreover, where internal guidelines are not published they cannot be regarded as an adequate safeguard against unwarranted interference with privacy rights. It would appear, then, that there are inadequate safeguards governing the disclosure of information by Bureau officials.

Significantly, the legislation provides that information obtained in this manner is admissible as evidence in subsequent proceedings. Section 8(7) states that "*information, documents or other material obtained by a bureau officer or any other person under the provisions of this subsection shall be admitted in evidence in any subsequent proceedings.*"

It would therefore appear that information gleaned by the Criminal Assets Bureau may subsequently be used by other authorities – including, but not limited to, the Garda Síochána, the Revenue Commissioners or the Department of Social Protection - in subsequent proceedings.[12] Going one step further, it is not clear whether a trial judge would have any discretion to exclude such material – section 8(7) provides that such material *shall be admitted in evidence* (But, see the decision in *CAB v* Hunt [2003] 2 IR 168. Cf. *Blanchfield v Judge Harnett* [2001] 1 ILRM 193). A further concern here is that information gathered by the Bureau, whether for administrative purposes or for the purposes of a potential civil forfeiture action, might be passed to An Garda Síochána and form the basis of a criminal prosecution. An exception to this is provided for under section 9(2) of the Proceeds of Crime Act in that where the court orders a respondent to file an affidavit specifying the

12 For an analogous situation, see *Re Barnroe Ltd, Director of Corporate Enforcement v Rogers* [2005] IEHC 443 where it was argued that evidence obtained during a criminal investigation ought not to be subsequently used in a civil application for disqualification of a company director.

property which he is in possession or control of, or his income, and sources of income, for a specified period, then such an affidavit is not admissible in subsequent criminal proceedings against that person or his spouse (except for proceedings for perjury arising from statements in that affidavit).

Accountability Issues

While the Bureau is afforded significant powers, this has not been matched with concern as to transparency and accountability. The only formal accountability requirement is that the Minister for Justice and Equality is to be presented with a report, by the Garda Commissioner, which details the activities of the Bureau during the previous year (CAB Act, s.21). As we shall see, such "accountability" is severely lacking. The structure of such reports generally follows the same format from year to year. Chapter one provides a brief and somewhat superfluous introduction, before chapter two provides an overview of the number of personnel and any changes concerning personnel numbers during the year in question. Chapter three essentially just states the amount of money expended during the year (€6.531 million in 2010). Chapter four is the only chapter of any real substance (purportedly at least) in relation to transparency and accountability. This chapter is entitled "Actions taken by the Bureau", and gives an overview of the number of search warrants (126 in 2010[13]) and production orders (233) obtained; the number of receivership orders (15) obtained; the number of orders obtained, and number of respondents, under each of the different provisions of the Proceeds of Crime Act; the number of revenue actions initiated (and those under appeal) and the global figures for tax/ interest assessed, demanded, and collected; and the number of social welfare actions as well as the monetary amount of social welfare overpayments that were identified and assessed, and the recovery of monies related to such overpayments. This chapter further provides a brief summary of "other investigations", which discloses that a number of people have been arrested and/ or charged with revenue offences, fraudulent claims for social welfare benefit, money laundering offences, corruption, and offences concerning intimidating and threatening bureau officers under section 13 of the CAB Act. While the information contained in this chapter is very basic, it does reinforce concerns that the Bureau, although purportedly an administrative multi-agency body, is concerned with pursuing criminal law objectives. Chapter five of the annual report provides an overview of litigation and caselaw concerning the Bureau, while

13 Figures here refer to the 2010 report unless otherwise indicated.

chapter six gives information as to the Bureau's cooperation and/or engagement with other jurisdictions, the EU, and the Camden Assets Recovery Inter-Agency Network.[14] Finally, chapter seven serves as a concluding chapter, which, at times, simply regurgitates earlier comments but also flags up how the Bureau intends to address specific issues that are identified (eg the impact of the economic downturn).

The annual report is to be presented by the Garda Commissioner to the Minister for Justice and Equality. In practice, the Chief Bureau Officer sends this report to the Commissioner who, in turn, forwards it to the Minister. The Minister can also request, again through the Commissioner, information as to the general operations of the Bureau (CAB Act, s.21(3)). Outside of this, there does not appear to be any mechanism for holding the Bureau to account. Moreover, the efficacy of such accountability is open to question. Although annual reports are prepared these, understandably, are sketchy on details. As we have seen, these reports simply provide a general overview of the work of the Bureau, for example the number of actions taken pursuant to the Proceeds of Crime Acts, Revenue legislation or Social Welfare legislation. As was emphasised in the 2005 annual report, "*For operational effectiveness and statutory confidentiality reasons the Bureau is required to keep specific details of many of its actions confidential.*" (CAB, 2006: 7) This, however, raises significant concerns as to the absence of any real democratic accountability – as the legislature simply plays a passive role in receiving the annual reports (den Boer, 2002: 283).

It is difficult, then, to get a detailed insight into the workings of the Bureau. And as Bowling and Murphy (2007: 33) note in relation to the Serious Organised Crime Agency in the UK, "*In the absence of proper public accountability, scrutiny – whether this is through research, parliamentary committee or through openness to public debate – becomes even more important.*" Regrettably, though, the Criminal Assets Bureau does not appear to be open to such scrutiny. While the Bureau does have available an extensive array of powers, this has not been matched with equally extensive accountability measures (den Boer, 2002: 279). The Criminal Assets Bureau is a multi-agency body, dominated by the police, pursuing policing objectives. This represents a significant new development in policing. While the Bureau undoubtedly has the potential to enhance the efficacy of law enforcement, it also has the potential to move important aspects of policing beyond traditional democratic checks and balances (Similar concerns have been expressed in the

14 The Camden Asset Recovery Inter-Agency Network (CARIN) is an informal network dedicated to improving cooperation in all aspects of tackling the proceeds of crime. The CARIN permanent secretariat is based in Europol headquarters. Cf. http://www.assetrecovery.org/kc/node/baf520a5-fe6d-11dd-a6ca-1120cbf9dd3.0;jsessionid=A7306C9765B694E5F9A47E36A18BAD59(accessed September 19, 2012)

context of police agencies involved in civil forfeiture in the United States. See, for example, Blumenson and Nilsen, 1998: 93). By bringing together the extensive powers of police, revenue and social welfare officials, the Bureau creates one of the most powerful agencies in the State yet, at the same time, concern as to democratic accountability and transparency is, regrettably, eschewed.

Conclusion

'Following-the-money' is an increasingly common tool in the armoury of the State, especially in the fight against organised crime (for a critique, see Naylor, 1999). Until relatively recent years, follow-the-money techniques have centred upon anti-money laundering and post-conviction forfeiture. The attractions of the civil approach, though, which is not dependent upon successful criminal prosecution, are now widely promulgated and adopted across the globe, (Kennedy, 2006) often with little or no consideration as to the due process implications.

By imposing 'punishment' in the civil arena, the State is able to avoid certain 'obstacles' that, supposedly, affect efficiency and expediency in the criminal process. Thus, the presumption of innocence is neatly sidestepped as civil forfeiture proceedings are not, *de jure*, regarded as being concerned with criminal matters. There are, however, difficulties with this in that civil forfeiture proceedings will often involve allegations of wrongdoing against a respondent that expose that person to community condemnation and/or stigma. And, of course, a respondent faces the prospect of being deprived of property on the basis that that property represents proceeds of crime, even though the respondent himself might not have been convicted of any criminal offence. That has serious implications for the presumption of innocence. So too does the State benefit from the 'civil' nature of such proceedings in that the lower standard of proof – the balance of probabilities – applies. This makes it easier for the State to bring 'criminals' to account for their wrongdoing, which severely undermines the rights of the individual. Concern surrounding civil forfeiture is reinforced by the wide array of powers bestowed upon the Criminal Assets Bureau. Though purportedly operating in the administrative realm, the Bureau is essentially a policing agency that, by virtue of its multi-agency composition, is able to draw upon an extensive array of powers to pursue criminal law objectives. Not only does the Bureau have significant powers, so too is it lacking in transparency and accountability, which further reinforces concern surrounding the Irish approach to targeting 'criminal' assets outside the confines of the criminal justice system. In the rush to enact legislation to "hit back" at organised crime groups, inevitably it is the rights of the individual that suffer most.

The Irish legislation has been on the statute book for almost seventeen years and, during that time, there has emerged a wealth of information on the legalities of the legislation and how it withstands constitutional scrutiny. The Irish experience has proved influential on the international stage, with many other jurisdictions influenced by the Irish model (in respect of both the civil forfeiture legislation and the multi-agency approach personified by the Criminal Assets Bureau), as well as members of the judiciary elsewhere being influenced by Irish judicial dicta (Simser, 2009; Kennedy, 2006). The Irish model is now undergoing a review under the auspices of the Department of Justice and Equality "*to consider the effectiveness of the legislation utilised by the Bureau and whether or not a Bill with suggested amendments should be submitted to the Dáil.*" (CAB, 2011: para.5.12) This presents an ideal opportunity to consider the impact of both civil forfeiture and the Criminal Assets Bureau in disrupting the activities of crime groups – something which is long overdue. This chapter has pointed to the significant impact that civil forfeiture and the Criminal Assets Bureau have had upon the rights of the individual. Much less is known as to the extent and/or nature of organised criminal activity in Ireland. Reliable data concerning economic cost, market size, criminal income and wealth is notably absent (cf. Naylor, 1999; Vander Beken, 2004). This is an area that merits immediate scrutiny, before the State can make any meaningful pronouncements as to the effectiveness of civil forfeiture.

References

Ashe, M. and P. Reid, Ireland: The Celtic tiger bites – The attack on the proceeds of crime. *Journal of Money Laundering Control*, 2001, 4 (3), 253 - 263

Ashe, M. and P. Reid, *Money laundering: Risks, liabilities and compliance* (First Law, Dublin, 2007, 2nd (ed)

Ashworth, A., Four threats to the presumption of innocence. *International Journal of Evidence and Proof*, 2006, 10 (4), 241-279

Barrett, R., Proceedings taken by the Criminal Assets Bureau. *Judicial Studies Institute Journal*, 2007, 229 - 238

Bowling, B. and C. Murphy, Serious organised crime under New Labour. *Criminal Justice Matters*, 2007, 32 - 33

Blumenson, E. and E. Nilsen, Policing for profit: The drug war's hidden economic agenda. *University of Chicago Law Review*, 1998, 65 (1), 35 - 114

Boer, M. den, Towards an accountability regime for an emerging European policing governance. *Policing and Society*, 2002, 12 (4), 275 - 289

Campbell, L., Criminal justice and penal populism in Ireland. *Legal Studies* 2008, 28 (4), 559 - 573

Campbell, L., Re-configuring the pre-trial and trial processes in Ireland in the fight against organised crime. *International Journal of Evidence and Proof*, 2008b, 12 (3), 208 - 233

Criminal Assets Bureau *Annual Report 2005* (Stationery Office, Dublin, 2006)

Criminal Assets Bureau *Annual Report 2007* (Stationery Office, Dublin, 2008)

Criminal Assets Bureau *Annual Report* 2009 (Stationery Office, Dublin, 2010)

Criminal Assets Bureau *Annual Report* 2010 (Stationery Office, Dublin, 2011)

European Commission, Proceeds of Organised Crime: Ensuring that 'crime does not pay' Com. (2008) 766

Farley, T.P., Asset forfeiture reform: A law enforcement response. *New York Law School Law Review*, 1994, 149 - 162

Fellmeth, A.X., Civil and criminal sanctions in the constitution and courts. *Georgetown Law Journal*, 2005, 94 (1), 1 - 66

Fellmeth, A.X., Challenges and implications of a systemic social effect theory. *University of Illinois Law Review*, 2006, 691 - 750

Harfield, C., SOCA: A paradigm shift in British policing. *British Journal of Criminology*, 2006, 46 (4), 743 -761

Hart, H.M. Jr., The aims of the criminal law. *Law and Contemporary Problems*, 1958, 401 - 441

Hederman Committee, *Report of the Committee to Review the Offences Against the State Acts, 1939-1998 and Related Matters* (Stationery Office, Dublin, 2002)

Jensen, E.L. and J. Gerber, The civil forfeiture of assets and the war on drugs: Expanding criminal sanctions while reducing due process protections. *Crime and Delinquency*, 1996, 42 (3), 421 - 434

Joint Committee on Human Rights, *Scrutiny: First Progress Report. Fourth Report of Session 2004-05.* Stationery Office, London, 2005

Joint Committee on Human Rights, *Scrutiny: Fourth Progress Report. Eighth Report of Session 2004-05.* Stationery Office, London, 2005b

Kennedy, A., Designing a civil forfeiture system: an issues list for policymakers and legislators. *Journal of Financial Crime*, 2006, 13 (2), 132 - 163

Kilcommins, S. and B. Vaughan, Reconfiguring state-accused relations in Ireland. *Irish Jurist*, 2006, (n.s.), 90 - 124

Law Reform Commission, *Report on the confiscation of the proceeds of crime (LRC 35-1991)* (Law Reform Commission, Dublin, 1991)

Lea, J., Hitting criminals where it hurts: Organised crime and the erosion of due process. *Cambrian Law Review*, 2004, 81 - 96

Lemieux, F., Tackling transnational drug trafficking effectively: assessing the outcomes of the Drug Enforcement Administration's international cooperation initiatives. In: F. Lemieux (ed.) *International police cooperation: Emerging issues, theory and practice*. Willan Publishing, Devon, 2010

Lusty, D., Civil forfeiture of proceeds of crime in Australia. *Journal of Money Laundering Control*, 2002, 5(4), 345 - 359

Mahmutaj, K., Cash forfeiture following acquittal: an 'affront to public perception' or a breach of a fundamental human right? *Criminal Law Review*, 2009, 783 - 793

Meade, J., Organised crime, moral panic and law reform: The Irish adoption of civil forfeiture. *Irish Criminal Law Journal*, 2000, 11

Murphy, F. and B. Galvin, Targeting the financial wealth of criminals in Ireland: The law and practice. In: McCutcheon and Walsh (eds.), *The confiscation of criminal assets: Law and procedure*. Round Hall Sweet and Maxwell, Dublin, 1999

Naylor, R.T., Wash-out: A critique of follow-the-money methods in crime control policy. *Crime, Law and Social Change*, 1999, 32 (1), 1 - 58

O'Donnell, I and E. O'Sullivan, The Politics of intolerance – Irish Style. *British Journal of Criminology*, 2003, 43 (1), 41 - 62

O'Higgins, Michael, The Proceeds of Crime Act 1996. *Bar Review*, 1996, 12

Performance and Innovation Unit, *Recovering the Proceeds of Crime*. Cabinet Office, London, 2000

Piety, T.R., Scorched earth: How the expansion of civil forfeiture doctrine has laid waste to due process. *University of Miami Law Review*, 1991, 45(4), 911 - 978

Simser, J., Perspectives on civil forfeiture. In: S. Young, (ed.), *Civil forfeiture of criminal property: Legal measures for targeting the proceeds of crime*. Edward Elgar, Cheltenham, 2009

Stahl, M., Asset forfeiture, burdens of proof and the war on drugs. *Journal of Criminal Law and Criminology*, 1992-93, 83(2), 274 - 337

Vander Beken, T., Risky business: A risk-based methodology to measure organized crime. *Crime, Law and Social Change*, 2004, 471- 516

Peculiarities of unjustified wealth confiscation policy in Romania

Radu Nicolae[1]

Introduction: the issue of unjustified wealth

In the last decade, corruption has become one of the most researched and debated crime all over the world due to its proven negative impact on economic development and rule of law (Nicolae, 2010). Corruption is essentially a profit-driven crime. Corrupt profits are estimated €120 billion per year only in the European Union (European Commission, 2011). Thus, fighting corruption seems to require an approach that is different to the classic criminal policy model(Brun and Gray, 2011). This new approach's primary goal is confiscation of corrupt money because recovery of proceeds and full compensation to victims are presumed to have a strong deterrence effect. Merely sentencing someone to prison may be ineffective once the corrupt individuals are left to secure or hide their corruption profits arising from corruption.

At the international level, several confiscation instruments have been developed: extended confiscation, third party confiscation, asset recovery policy, illicit enrichment policy, non-conviction based confiscation. These instruments entail extensive human rights restrictions but are widely promoted by international organisations and recommended as appropriate reform measures in countries facing rampant corruption (Young, 2009). It is, however, vital to assess how these instruments perform in such countries as their implementation might produce collateral damages, such as reinforcing state abuses, strengthening old power structures or weakening the support for democracy.

This chapter analyses how the non-conviction based confiscation instrument has been applied in Romania, an E.U. member state that continues to register high

1 Radu Nicolae is the anticorruption program manager at the Centre for Legal Resource, a Romanian independent foundation. He holds a PhD in political science and used to teach an anticorruption academic course at SNSPA University in Bucharest.

level of corruption.[2] Romanians perceive corruption to be widespread[3] and the primary source of wealth acquisition.

Beginning with the 1989 revolution, there developed a growing demand for justice in Romania as the country experienced a harsh economic transition from communism/socialism to capitalism. The economic transition came with dubious privatisations, job losses, inequality and polarisation of wealth. People thought that those who benefited from transition made their fortune by corrupt means and their wealth should therefore be taken back by the state: 69% of the Romanians consider that rich people have acquired their wealth by breaking the law and 17% consider wealth is acquired by those with inside connections (Pro-Democracy Association, 2010). At the same time, international organisations, especially the European Union, pressured the Romanian government to take strong measures against corruption. Facing this double pressure from both inside and outside the country, local politicians engaged in an extensive anti-corruption policy agenda.

One of the tools used against corruption in Romania is *non-conviction based (NCB) confiscation*. This NCB confiscation instrument has been labelled in Romania as "*confiscation of unjustified wealth*" and by its nature it has generated an intensive debate that drained the energy of Romanian policy makers over the last 15 years. Complicated polices, obscure laws and procedures have been developed and a sizeable governmental apparatus has been put to work. Although the unjustified wealth policy generated much noise in the public arena, it was never subjected to an impact assessment, an evaluation or even a brief policy analysis. The available public data on the policy results are scarce and dispersed, and the agencies implementing the policy are reluctant to display any transparency.

Our chapter sheds light on the actual results generated by the unjustified wealth policy in Romania. The main issue under discussion is how to manage cases in which the acquisation of assets cannot be reasonably justified from official income but, at the same time, it cannot be proven that the assets are derived from specific illegal activities for which the owners have been convicted. Naturally, such cases hurt feelings, in particular when the persons involved have a public function in the administration, government or parliament. Should it be possible to strip such persons of their unaccountable assets without a criminal conviction?

---

2 Romania scores 3,6 in TI Corruption Perception Index 2011 and 0.6 at Absence of Corruption Factor in WJP Rule of Law Index 2011. World Bank's Trends in Corruption and Regulatory Burden in Eastern Europe and Central Asia reports corruption in Romania to be a third major problem in doing business.

3 2012 Special Eurobarometer on corruption report that 96% of the Romanians consider corruption to be a major problem in their country (European Commission, 2012a: p. 14). Romania is the first country in Europe from the personal experience of corruption point of view: 31% of Romanians report they have been asked or expected to pay bribe over the last 12 months (European Commission, 2012a: p.61).

Non-conviction based (NCB) confiscation is gaining increased attention internationally (see Wilsher, 2006; Jorge, 2007; Greenberg, Samuel, Grant and Gray, 2009; Hamilton, 2011); European Commission, 2012b; Muzila, Morales, Mathias and Berger, 2012 and the chapter of Colin King in this volume).[4] In the international academic literature, the Romania NCB confiscation system is rarely mentioned, though the NCB confiscation policy has been in force since 1996. How did it function in a country perceived as being highly corrupt, assuming that corruption is one of the contributors to unaccountable increase of wealth?

Some principles of unaccountable wealth and confiscation

The basic thesis of non-conviction based (NCB) asset forfeiture is that unjustified wealth is presumed to derive from (unproven) crime. This problem is solved differently from country to country, but several common characteristics may be drawn. Lacking criminal conviction of the person, the action is a civil procedure directed against a 'thing' which has to be dispossessed (Greenberg *et al.*, 2009), but also against the owner to whom the burden of proof is shifted (Hamilton, 2011): (s)he must prove the legal resources with which the 'thing' was acquired. In the case where he is unable to provide such prove, the state can conclude there is unexplained wealth, which is assumed to be illegal, without specifically identifying the criminal activity that produced such wealth.

This system implied an increase in state power and was therefore subject to serious human rights concerns. NCB confiscation "*enable interferences with the right to property, in the meaning of Article 17 of the Charter* [of Fundamental Rights], *without the said property being linked to a specific criminal conviction. Since NCB does not relate assets to a criminal conviction it raises the question of the presumption of innocence guaranteed by Article 48(1) of the Charter and Article 6(2) ECHR*" (European Commission, 2012c). NCB confiscation implies a restraint of basic human rights and, for this reason, it requires proper justification (broader grounds), proportionality (reasonable means considering the objective sought) and adequate safeguards (public hearing, possibility to rebut the presumption, effective legal remedies). The compatibility between NCB confiscation and European Convention on Human Rights (ECHR) has not been settled in principle by the European Court of Human Rights (ECtHR). Thus, NCB confiscation has to be allowed only in very

4 NCB confiscation is one of the accepted articles in the United Nations Convention against Corruption (UNCAC) (UNODC, 2004). Article 54(1)(c). Romania ratified UNCAC in 2004 by Law no. 365/2004.

limited circumstances where a criminal conviction cannot be obtained. What system did Romania choose and when?

The Romanian legal and institutional framework

Romania has no good memories of the state meddling with one's property. The Wealth Verification Law of 1968 was one of the tools that allowed the communist regime to control its citizens, endorse fear and induce conformity with the decisions of the Regime. Following the revolution of 1989, the law was not repealed, however, it ceased to be effective. After the 1989 revolution, the fear of abuses induced the Constituent Assembly to pass a constitutional article stating that the assets of a person are presumed to be lawfully acquired (Jorge, 1997). Such a presumption was deemed necessary to prevent the state from abusing the shift of the burden of proof as under the old Law of 1968.

Changing the constitutional safeguards did little to address the widespread corruption, which potentially contributes to 'unaccountable wealth'. As the rampant corruption led to broad dissatisfaction, pressure was exerted on the government to respond to it. The result was the 1996 Wealth Verification Law. While the 1968 law had applied to all citizens, the 1996 law was only applicable to politicians and employees of the public sector, including magistrates. Each public sector employee had to make a wealth statement covering all property (land, houses, apartments, commercial or production venues, live stock, shares in companies, art collections – paintings, stamps, coins, antiquities, furniture–gold, silver, platinum, jewellery, deposits of over $ 3.000[5], vehicles, electronic equipment of over $ 1.500), all paid activities (other than their daily job) and debts (debts over $3.000). The statement was confidential – it was to be handed over in closed envelope. Submitting a wealth statement was mandatory at the beginning and at the end of the term of office (a 15 days submission deadline was established). If the mandate was longer than 4 years, the statement had to be updated after a period of four years.

Despite the confidentiality, these wealth statements have become public documents from the beginning of 2003 and are published on the official websites. The wealth statement form was improved in 2005 by adding a chapter on income and making the rest of the declaration more precise. Further improvements to the wealth statements submission rules were made in 2010, the statements being submitted annually until June 15 and also at the beginning and at he end of the term of office but with a 30 days deadline instead of 15 days.

5 November 1996: 1 US$ = 3.268 lei.

Anyone failing to observe the deadline for submitting the statement was to be subjected to a *wealth verification procedure*, either requested by the chief prosecutor of the Court of Appeal Prosecution or by the head of the public authority for the employees of that authority. As under the previous communist law, an investigation could also be initiated at the request of any official or public sector employee against whom public allegations of unjustified wealth were made. If someone else, a citizen, NGO activist or journalist, had reasons to suspect unjustified wealth, he/she had to send the complaint to the prosecutor's office or to the head of the public authority for review. The wealth verification was carried out by 16 Wealth Investigation Commissions organised within the Courts of Appeal and High Court (15 Courts of Appeal in Romania). The High Court Commission was competent to investigate high level officials. Each Wealth Investigation Commission was composed of two Court of Appeal judges, appointed by the Court president and a prosecutor, appointed by the chief prosecutor of the Prosecutor's Office related to the Court of Appeal. One of the judges acted as president of the commission.

For the high ranking state officials[6], a special Wealth Investigation Commission for wealth verification was established under High Court of Justice.[7] It was similarly composed of two High Court judges and a prosecutor, all appointed by this institution. This special Wealth Investigation Commission could receive complaints only from the Ministry of Justice and General Prosecutor. Anyone else had to submit the complaint to the Ministry of Justice or/and General Prosecutor, who forwarded justified cases to the special Wealth Investigation Commission.

The procedure followed by the Wealth Investigation Commissions, referred to as *Commissions* hereafter, consisted in summoning witnesses (the person who filed the complaint, the person investigated, as well as others who could give information about the assets under investigation), analysing the documents and requesting an economic report from an independent expert; together with on the spot investigations of each asset by the Commission. Article 10 of the law automatically extended the investigation to the common property if the person investigated was married. The works and documents of the Commissions were not public.

---

6 The Romanian President, members of Parliament, members of Government, heads of public institutions appointed by the President, Parliament or Prime-Minister, Constitutional Court judges, Court of Account members, High Court judges, and prosecutors form the General Prosecutor's Office, Court of Appeal Judges and prosecutors form the Prosecutor's Offices related to the Courts of Appeal.

7 After the 2003 amendments to the Constitution, the official name of the High Court of Justice has become High Court of Cassation and Justice (HCCJ).

Following the wealth verification, a motivated decision supported by a majority of votes, within a maximum of three months, the Commissions could:

- close the file, when all assets were found to be justified by the lawful income;
- send the file to the Court of Appeal (High Court for high rank officials) in the jurisdiction of the person' residence if they found evidence of illicitly or unjustifiably obtained wealth;
- suspend the case and refer it to the competent unit of prosecution, if there was a crime in connection with the assets investigated.

The Commissions had the right to freeze the property of persons investigated and could, when closing a case, reverse the measure of freezing property (article 13).

The Ministry of Finance and the Chief Prosecutor of the Court of Appeal / General Prosecutor to the High Court of Justice could challenge the Commission's decision to close a case. The decision to send the file to court could be contested only during the first Court proceedings.

The Court of Appeal could determine that (1) the assets were legally acquired and close the file, (2) the assets were illegally obtained and decide on their confiscation, (3) refer the case to the competent unit of prosecution, in case of a suspected asset-crime connection or other crime. Appeals against the Court of Appeal ruling could be referred to the High Court of Justice. The confiscation was conducted under a civil procedure.

On paper, all seemed reasonable and enforceable so, in 1996, the Parliament passed the Law on Wealth Verification with an overwhelming majority, there being only two votes against. Nonetheless, concerns about the constitutionality of the law had been raised during parliamentary debates. Basically, the law sanctioned unaccountable discrepancies between wealth and lawful income in cases where no connecting criminal offence could be proven.

Law in (*in*-)action

From 1996 until 2003 the law functioned without public scrutiny or noticeable effect as no final confiscation order had been issued by Courts during this period. The Centre for Legal Resources (CRJ) published in 2004 a report on the activity of the Commissions.[8] Several findings are worthy to remark.

Firstly, during that period, the wealth was found to be justified by lawful income in 85% of the cases. All 16 Commissions had processed 254 cases in seve

8 Centre for Legal Resources, *Wealth Investigation Commissions – monitoring the implementation no. 115/1996*, Bucharest, Didactical and Pedagogical Publishing House, 2004

years: on average two cases per year/commission. Only in 15 cases (6%) did the Court of Appeal reach a first instance decision. 3% of the cases were still under investigation at the time of CRJ report (2004). Nevertheless, in those 9% of the cases that were not finalized in 2004, in appeal only *three binding decision* of confiscation were made of approximately $ 8.000, $ 130.000 and €14.500 in respectively 2006, 2011 and 2012, after five, nine and eight years of procedings. Detailed statistics are provided in Table 1. Most of the complaints (over 90%) were submitted by the heads of public organisations. Only 4% of the complaints (11 cases) came from the Prosecutor's Office/General Prosecutor. 5% of the cases (12 cases) were initiated at the request of a person against whom public allegations of unjustified wealth were made.

Table 1

Wealth verification cases in 2004

Commissions under the Court of Appeal	Total no. of cases submitted to Commissions	Cases closed	Sent to Court of Appeal	Cases under investigation by the Commissions	Cases sent back for additional information	Cases rejected
Commissions (15)	249	217	15	6	7	4
Commission under High Court	5	0	0	2	1	2
Commission under the Court of Appeal	Total N handled by Commissions	Cases closed	To Court Appeal	Under investigation Commission	Sent back for information	Cases rejected
Total: N Percent	**254** **100%**	**217** **85,4%**	**15** **5,9%**	**8** **3,2%**	**8** **3,2%**	**6** **2,4**

Secondly, the persons investigated by the Commissions were not high level officials and most procedures were initiated because public servants did not submit their wealth statements. Thus, at the beginning of 1997, after the 1996 autumn elections, the new Government requested the Commissions to investigate all 45 former county prefects and vice-prefects because they failed to submit their wealth statements. All 45 cases were closed by the Commissions and the Government did not appeal, raising doubts about the willingness of the Government to really pursue the cases. The other broad category investigated was that of police officers (over 150 cases but 99% of the files were closed).

Thirdly, the Commissions did not follow a unified organisational and verification procedure. To begin with, the Commissions were not all established in the same year: 12 were established in November 1996, the other four were established in 1997, 2000 and 2001. Each Commission had a three years mandate but in four cases the Court President 'forgot' to nominate another Commission after the mandate had expired. In addition, the Commissions developed divergent interpretations of the same law regarding the following subjects: how an *ex-officio* investigation could be initiated, the period of wealth verification (from 1989 or 1996 until the date of the investigation, the term of office period or the period specified in the complaint), types of investigation (closing the file without any investigation, on subjective grounds[9], shallow investigation, rigorous investigation). The Commissions accepted all sorts of justifications for the assets acquired, more or less unreasonable or even frivolous. Many of the persons investigated argued that they acquired assets from money borrowed from friends or relatives (between 15.000 and 30.000 DM[10]); from money saved during communist times (*e.g.*. $ 10.000 in one case); from working in agriculture and animal farms, after office hours, and selling informally the products (*e.g.* selling the pigs, sheep and chicken raised in households; selling their wheat, sugar beet, corn, onion, sunflower and potato harvest; selling wine, wood or grassland); money from buying and informally selling second-hand cars; in-kind help from neighbours; money received from friends as gifts at weddings and baptisms (*e.g.* DM 9.000 in one case).

The complex legal framework determined the Court's processing time (almost ten years in one case[11]). Under the system of procedural law a case could be sent to and fro from the First Court, back to the Commission, the Ministry of Finance and Prosecutor's Office, Appellate Court and back again to the First Court for re-trial. For instance, there were several cases where the file had been sent back on two occations to the Wealth Commission or Court of Appeal (first instance Court) for restarting the investigation or re-trial. These procedures proved to be time consuming.

These findings called for a reform of the unjustified wealth confiscation policy and opened up a debate around two major issues: the policy alternatives able to ensure confiscation of unjustified assets and the constitutionality of the policy. Most of the policy makers admitted that the Commissions did not take their role seriously but they were reluctant to make any change except for a legislative one

9 For instance, in one case of failure to declare property at the end of mandate, the Commission concluded that: "given the complex evidences, it is clear that the delay in submitting the asset declaration was not the result of reasons attributable to the person investigated. Between December 1996-March 1997 the person investigated was overload with physical and mental activity due to the election campaign, the release from office and the subsequent challenge of finding and adapting to a new job, which combined with worsening personal problems – worsening health of the mother-in-law, whose chronic illness advanced, he had to deal directly and repeatedly with hospital admissions and the follow-up of the treatment" (File no. 3 / 1997).

10 DM = Deutsch Mark, currency of West Germany till the adoption of the euro in 2002.

11 The case against Simionovici has been initiated in 2003 and it is not finalized.

because it is preferable to build something new than to fix something broken.[12] In fact, unwilling to change anything partly because of ill-will, partly because of indifference, the decision-makers were happy to hide the power structures and current state of affairs behind a veil of draft legislation and good intentions, nicely embellished to cool down the European Union's concerns.[13] Such a pattern of behaviour, namely promising new legislation instead of making genuine reforms, is not as uncommon as one might expect. Indulging in ritual legislation and building anti-corruption institutions as Potemkin villages was the general coping strategy of Romania in dealing with European Union's concerns about corruption. It seems that this coping strategy is not so unique; Serbia is facing similar corruption problems and employing similar coping strategies (Van Duyne *et al.*, 2010; 2012). Bulgaria has also established anticorruption organisations with little success in delivering results (European Commission, 2012b).[14] In any case, in order to better understand how it was possible for the Romanian decision-makers to deceive the EU with the idea of the integrity agency and how the EU embraced the idea, we have to examine in more detail against the background of the Romania and Romania-EU relationship in 2004. The next section explains the genesis of the integrity agency idea.

Foot dragging in European context

The 2004 context was very favourable for a broad reform of anticorruption policies as Romania had been struggling to close the negotiations with the EU, especially the "justice and home affairs" chapter. At the conclusion of the accession negotiations on 14 December 2004 Romania accepted several specific requirements.[15] Among these requirements, the following anti-corruption provisions were included:

12 NIA draft law rationale: PL-x nr. 616/2006.

13 The idea of NIA emerged in 2004 as a solution of the Romanian Government to close the accession negotiations. The EU took that solution for granted. See also: Realitatea TV, Rehn cere intervenţia lui Tăriceanu în adoptarea legii ANI/Rehn asked Tariceanu to intervene for the adoption of the NIA law, 22.12.2006.http://www.realitatea.net/rehn-cere-interventia-lui-tariceanu-in-adoptarea-legii-ni_32019.html#ixzz2BCYaWX8O

14 "The track record of decisions and penalties in cases related to high-level corruption, fraud and organised crime under investigation and in court does not yet provide the convincing results needed to provide effective dissuasion" (European Commission, 2012b: p. 2).

15 Act concerning the conditions of accession of the Republic of Bulgaria and Romania and the adjustments to the treaties on which the European Union is founded, Annex IX Specific commitments.

"(5) To conduct an independent audit of the results and the impact the current National Anti-Corruption Strategy has generated; to reflect the conclusions and recommendations of this audit in the new multi-annual anticorruption strategy which must be one comprehensive document, in place no later than March 2005".

In the same year, Romania ratified the UN Convention against Corruption that has special provisions related to unjustified wealth

In 2004, Romania also adopted an Anticorruption Strategy 2005-2007. However, that was never put into practice due to the conclusions of the accession negotiations on 14 December 2004. The plans was full of good intentions, such as an independent audit of the results and the impact of the National Corruption Prevention Program 2001-2004 and international harmonisation concerning the criminalisation of illicit enrichment,[16] never implemented, however.

During 2004, Transparency International (T.I.) Romania and the Ministry of Justice negotiated a set of anticorruption policies. One of the policies aimed at increasing the relevance of the wealth verification policy by "*establishing a body with jurisdictional powers, composed of judges, designed to ensure continuity, impartiality and effectiveness*" (Transparency International Romania, 2004).

In July 2004, the Ministry of Justice announced that six anti-corruption draft laws negotiated with T.I. Romania were going to be adopted (Iordache, 2004). Among them, a new body would cover issues of wealth verification, conflicts of interests and incompatibilities of all civil servants, officials and magistrates. That proposal was cancelled by the Ministry of Finance because of its costs (Freedom House, Inc., 2005: 11). Nonetheless, the idea to establish an agency competent to deal with wealth verification, conflicts of interests and incompatibilities continued to preoccupy the policy makers.

In 2005, the Ministry of Justice commissioned to Freedom House Washington the independent audit of the National Corruption Prevention Program 2001-2004 which was requested in the conclusions of the accession negotiations. The audit recommended the creation of an "Integrity Agency" under the control of an "Integrity Council" (Freedom House, Inc., 2005: 10).

Based on the independent audit, in March 2005, the Ministry of Justice drafted the new anticorruption strategy requested by the European Union. In the end of March 2005, the Government passed the "National Anticorruption Strategy 2005-2007" which stated the establishment of a "*single and independent entity to verify the wealth, conflicts of interest declarations and the incompatibilities and the annual assessment of its activity*" (Objective 8 - Combating corruption through administrative means).

16 Government Decision no. 1944/2004, Measure 2.2.5, Objective II.5

Collective paralysis, activism and coping strategis

While policy makers had been struggling to build a legislative agenda to improve this policy, several NGOs, among which the Centre for Legal Resources, started to monitor the implementation policy. The assumption was that the failure of the unjustified wealth confiscation policy could be better explained by lack of transparency, monitoring and public pressure, on the one hand, and lack of good practices, involvement and responsibility of the Wealth Investigation Commissions and prosecutors, on the other hand. In fact, in most of the Romanian public service sector organisations, initiatives and activism is penalised while indifference and laziness is regarded as wisdom and consequently rewarded or at least not punished. In our particular case, a display of intensive activities by the Wealth Investigation Commissions and prosecutors would have been disrupting high level interests of officials. The investigators in the front line of the anti-corruption war would be exposed without having any additional benefit. No surprise that prosecutors are more inclined to play a waiting game than pursue an anti-corruption agenda on their own. The stakeholders from civil society are poorly structured and unable to raise a strong demand for integrity and monitor the results of the anti-corruption if there are any. The political-entrepreneurs have maintained in power in the last 20 years because of the current state of affairs and are averse to changes, while a new generation of political-entrepreneurs have not emerged yet.

The NGO mentioned before thought the policy needed an increased pressure. Beginning from 2004, the Centre for Legal Resources acted in partnership with local NGOs and journalists to uncover cases of unjustified wealth, published numerous reports, and submitted numerous complaints. It managed to secure *two final confiscation decisions* regarding a mayor and a vice-mayor as well as a ruling form the High Court's Commission stating that an ex-minister failed to justify € 1 million: the case had bounced to and fro since 2007. In three years, due to transparency and public pressure, the policy generated more results than in all the previous eight years. It was a *démasqué* of the indifference and ineffectiveness of the authorities' anti-corruption policy. Although these results caught the headlines of all major mass-media in Romania, they did not trigger any public debate on the concrete measures available at the implementation level. Instead, policy-makers were very keen to be busy with changing legislation, irrespective of alternative simpler solutions. As always, the European Commission had condoned the government plans despite knowing the double standards of the Romanian authorities: developing a pretentious legislative agenda against corruption but in fact maintaining the status-quo and covering the indifference and lack of implementation.

The two final confiscation decisions mentioned above are the only confiscation orders enforced by the Ministry of Public Finance. The 2006 confiscation decision also mentioned before was not enforced by the Ministry of Public Finance. After the Centre for Legal Resources (CRJ) struggled four months to find data using the Freedom of Information Act, the Ministry of Public Finance officially confirmed that it 'forgot' to enforce the relevant civil confiscation decision of the Bucharest Court of Appeal, which remained irrevocable by a civil decision of the High Court of Cassation and Justice. In March 2012, the Ministry of Finance began the enforcement of this confiscation decision after pressure from the CRJ. The 2011 and 2012 confiscation orders are also awaiting execution. This neglect demonstrates even more convincingly the basis lack of will to make the mere appearance of interest.

At the same time, the debate on unjustified wealth confiscation policy continued to intensify at legislative level. During the period June 2005 - June 2006, the Ministry of Justice published several drafts of the law on the National Integrity Agency (NIA), the body intended to replace the Wealth Investigation Commissions. Its painful development reflected incompetence but was cleverly advertised as an impetus to reform the corrupt establishment.

A first draft published by the Ministry of Justice on 5 July 2005 was challenged because it did not observe the legislative techniques regarding constitutional aspects.

A second draft was published on 2 March 2006: envisaged the establishment of a National Integrity Directorate under the Fiscal Authority. The second draft was challenged too because it replaced the confiscation sanction for unjustified wealth with a 32% tax on these assets.

The third draft was published on July 3rd 2006 and it prescribed the establishment of National Integrity Agency (NIA) managed by a President, appointed by the Romanian President, after a contest organised by the planned National Integrity Council. This Council was intended as an autonomous representative body with non-permanent activity. The Parliament finally adopted the law establishing the National Integrity Agency alongside the National Integrity Council on 9 May 2007.

This was just in time: at the end of 2006, the European Commission issued Decision no. C(2006) 6569 of 13 December 2006 establishing a mechanism for cooperation and verification of progress in Romania to address specific benchmarks in the areas of judicial reform and the fight against corruption. One of the benchmarks was the establishment of National Integrity Agency.

The debate around NIA became highly politicised: critics argued that the Agency will become a convenient political tool used by the Government against opposition figures (Jorge, 2007, p. 58). Supporters state that promoting this policy is in agreement with the European Commission. Soon after this, the debate became irrational with smearing accusations from both sides.

To sum up the facts so far, we have explained how the Romanian political elite managed legislating NCB confiscation, thus, making the appearance of a tough anticorruption reform when, in fact, nothing changed in the practice of not giving account for the unaccountable wealth. During the period 1996-2007 period, the Wealth Investigation Commissions had not worked properly and lacked basic transparency and public scrutiny. Only, after 2004, due to civil society pressures, the unjustified wealth policy rendered final confiscation orders. Unfortunately, these actual results came out too late to be able to influence the reform agenda. In 2004, the Romanian Government had acknowledged the failure of the policy in front of EU and it was in the process of introducing draft after draft to modify the law so that the Wealth Investigation Commissions to be replaced by an integrity agency. This feverish drafting process managed to generate controversies between the politicians. In the next section, we will see the main arguments in dispute.

Knights, Conservatives and the NIA law

The conflict over the NIA law is rooted in a more general disagreement in the Romanian society regarding the compatibility between the anti-corruption work and human rights.

In themselves, the anticorruption objectives are legitimate in a "*rechtsstaat*". Disagreement emerges concerning the means to ensure the anti-corruption objectives. Is non-conviction based confiscation an appropriate instrument to counter unjustified wealth or does it imply excessive state power and illegitimate human rights restrictions? The fight against corruption must respect the generally valid human rights framework and not turn into a witch hunt. As long as the anti-corruption legal instruments provide all procedural, legal and constitutional safeguards, as long as prosecutors employ legitimate means to collect evidence, as long as the right to defence is respected, as long as judges are independent and there is transparency of the process, fighting corruption is fully compatible with human rights. What happens when there are indications that the fight against corruption is about to turn into a witch hunt or that anti-corruption agencies are used for political or personal settling of accounts; that the means they use are illegal, abusive and lack basic transparency? What happens when there is evidence that innocent individuals are accused resulting in an irreparably damaged public reputation?

'Anti-corruption knights' and 'human rights conservatives'

These questions are at the core of the anti-corruption debate in Romania, which has become the field for a confrontation between the '*anti-corruption knights*' and '*human rights conservatives*'.

'*Anti-corruption knights*' say that those who raise human rights concerns are those while being actually corrupt, are afraid of law and impartial justice. Consequently they encourage justice to continue delaying *sine die* the corruption files, want to keep judges unaccountable for the judgments they issue, strive to disband anti-corruption agencies, and want to make less drastic laws.[17] '*Knights*' say the Romanian state is weak, lacks repressive means. In their view, the state is powerless in front of the offenders, so the state power against citizens must grow. The '*knights*' base their argument the adage: "If you have nothing to hide, you have nothing to fear." In other words, for the innocents there is no need for safeguards or procedures. For the '*anti-corruption knights*' the means employed to prove the guilt are less important as long as guilt is obvious – on audio-video recordings, for instance. It does not matter whether the means are excessive, abusive, and illegal as long as the defendant/respondent is clearly guilty.

'*Human rights conservatives*', on the other hand, focus on means and procedural justice. Guilt must be proved by legal means. They accuse the anti-corruption agencies and secret services of parallel criminal prosecution, illegal phone tapping, arrangement of evidence, intimidation and blackmail, monitoring and prosecution on political grounds (all who are against the establishment), lacking transparency (restricting access to evidences in defence), manipulating mass-media to demonize political opponents, and filling in public authorities with undercover agents.[18] '*Conservatives*' say that the balance is broken and that '*knights*' are trying to establish a repressive system veiled by a 'velvet glove'. '*Knights*' are then just corrupt political entrepreneurs that have high-jacked the fight against corruption to protect their own cliques and to crucify all others.

In this tense political environment, two basic myths have developed:

1. The Agency has powerful enemies in the Parliament that seek to shut down NIA because the work of the Agency undermines their corruption deals.
2. The Agency is the creation of European Commission and any other policy alternative is a blasphemy and could jeopardise the Romania statute in the European Union.

---

17 Monica Macovei (European deputy), Ziare.com, public declarations on 21st of July 2010, 27th of October 2011 and 09th of December 2011.

18 György Frunda (president of the Senate standing commission on human rights), Mediafax, public declaration on 12th of October 2011.

These myths have been wisely disseminated even before the establishment of the Integrity Agency [19] and consolidated soon after. What started as legitimate democratic debate over a draft law, transformed after 2007 into an institutional fight between the Integrity Agency and its creator, the Romanian Parliament. During the first two years of its functioning the Agency leadership is taken over by "*anticorruption knights*" that are eager to increase their legal competences, being under constant pressure by the EU to deliver results. They consider that the Parliament allowed only 'soft powers' to the Agency. They are reluctant to provide any Member of Parliament with control and are adverse to any criticisms. Any such criticism is regarded as interference in the investigative independence of the Agency (Centre for Legal Resources, 2009). The event that inflamed the already tense environment was the attempt of Alice Draghici, a member in the National Integrity Council - NIC (the committee that oversees the Agency), to influence a case pending to the Agency. Alice Draghici was nominated in the NIC by a political party and it was the perfect occasion to point a finger at the enemies of NIA as coming from Parliament. Soon after this unfortunate event, NIA begins to compile files against Alice Draghici and her colleagues from the Conservative Party.[20] NIA's aggressive behaviour increases after several Agency employees blew the whistle and revealed to Transparency International Romania evidence of abuses of the Agency's leadership. TI Romania and the whistleblowers went public with the accusations (illegal budget spending, procurement irregularities), which were soon confirmed by a final Court of Account audit. [21] Nevertheless, the whistleblowers were immediately fired and even though the Courts established by final decisions that the dismissals of the whistleblowers were abusive and illegal, the NIA re-hired and fired them back in the same day[22] in order to lose again in the

[19] Cronica Romana newspaper, Monica Macovei vrea sa retraga legea ANI, 30th of October 2006 (http://www.9am.ro/stiri-revista-presei/Actualitate/46758/Monica-Macovei-vrea-sa-retraga-legea-ANI.html); Academia Catavencu magazine, Peter Eckstein: 'Sefii UDMR impotriva ANI. Din misoginism. Legile in Senat, la cheremul Opozitiei', Eugen ISTODOR, 1st November 2006 (http://www.9am.ro/stiri-revista-presei/Politica/46915/Peter-Eckstein-Sefii-UDMR-impotriva-ANI-Din-misoginism-Legile-in-Senat-la-cheremul-Opozitiei.html); Newsin, Monica Macovei: Legea ANI nu e mai severă, 2nd of June 2007 (http://www.realitatea.net/monica-macovei-legea-ani-nu-e-mai-severa_65963.html#ixzz2Bf3ZNY00); Hotnews, L. Pirvu, Legea ANI controleaza averile demnitarilor, dar este subordonata Senatului, 9th of May 2007 (http://www.hotnews.ro/stiri-arhiva-1080795-legea-ani-controleaza-averile-demnitarilor-dar-este-subordonata-senatului.htm).

[20] Ziare.com, Alice Draghici a demisionat din Consiliul National de Integritate, 27th of January of 2009

[21] Fundatia pentru dezvoltarea societății civile, Carta alba a sectorului ONG, 2012, p. 44

[22] National Integrity Agency letter no. 608/07.03.2011, National Integrity Agency President Order no. 176/14.03.2011 and Civil decision no. 2150/14th of March 2012, file no.25108/3/2011

Court. They were ordered to pay to the whistleblowers their full salary from the moment of first abusive dismissal. In the following months the NIA compiled cases against the executive director of TI Romania and against the civil society representative in NIC, also member of TI Romania Board. These later files proved unjustified, being definitively closed by the Prosecutor's office or Courts.[23] Later on, almost all the critics of the Agency 'benefited' by the same treatment, especially those from Parliament. The Agency became more and more aggressive toward Parliament, threatening its members.[24] In all this period, the EU did not react to the abuses but encouraged the Agency to continue with this approach. On the other hand, apart from several incidents[25], the Parliament did not take a strong stance against NIA abuses but institutionally it reacted rather submissively. The Parliament (specifically the Senate) did not exert its powers to control provided by the law over the Agency (it never requested an audit, for instance, or tried to revoke the Agency leadership). More than that, in 2012, the Parliament appointed the former general secretary of the Agency as the NIA president, a person well-known for his declarations against Parliament[26] and a person publicly accused of unaccountable wealth.[27] The representatives of political parties in NIC are also very constructive in supporting the agency initiatives instead of verifying the numerous

---

23 Criminal files no. 145/D/P/2009, 577/P/2010, 1633/II-2/2010, 810/P/2010, 764/P/2011 against Codru Vrabie, the civil society representative in NIC and member of TI Romania Board have been closed. Transparency International Romania, pres-release, Victor Alistar: Am câştigat irevocabil procesul cu Agenţia Naţională de Integritate / Victor Alistar: I have won definitively the trail with National Integrity Agency, 18th of May 2012.

24 Newsin, *ANI reclama interferente ale Senatului in activitatea sa*, 7th of December 2011 (http://www.ziare.com/articole/macovei+lege+agentia+nationala+integritate); Hotnews, *Horia Georgescu: Peste 20-30 de parlamentari au probleme cu Legea ANI*, 2nd of November, 2012 (http://revistapresei.hotnews.ro/stiri-radio_tv-13537599-horia-georgescu-peste-20-30-parlamentari-probleme-legea-ani-cazul-diaconu-creat-precedent-periculos.htm).

25 Unsuccessful attempts to reduce NIA budget: Hotnews.ro, Ministerul Justitiei: *Reducerea bugetului ANI s-ar reflecta negativ in raportul pe Justitie al Comisiei Europene*, 6 December 2011 (http://www.hotnews.ro/stiri-esential-10869864-ministerul-justitiei-reducerea-bugetului-ani-reflecta-negativ-raportul-justitie-comisiei-europene.htm)

26 Realitatea.net, *Horia Georgescu, despre respingerea bugetului ANI: Interesele personale ale unor certaţi cu legea*, 5 December 2011 (http://www.realitatea.net/horia-georgescu-despre-respingerea-bugetului-ani-interesele-personale-ale-unor-certati-cu-legea_892714.html#ixzz2BfZDhWrC);
Newsin, Horia Georgescu (ANI): MCV pentru Romania ar trebui inasprit, 27 September 2011 (http://www.ziare.com/stiri/justitie/horia-georgescu-ani-mcv-pentru-romania-ar-trebui-inasprit-1123284)

27 Antena3, Exces de putere: Averea "Integrului" de la Integritate, Horia Georgescu, 3 November 2012 (http://www.antena3.ro/romania/exces-de-putere-averea-integrului-de-la-integritate-horia-georgescu-a-cumparat-de-la-parinti-cu-bani-de-la-nasi-pe-care-ii-da-inapoi-de-la-parinti-190662.html).

complaints about NIA. Portraying the Parliament as the corrupt body that holds back NIA activity is heavily overstated.

The second myth derives logically from the first. If the Parliament is full of corrupt individuals that are afraid of NIA, how can you let them mess with the NIA law? Any proposed change in the legislation is seen from the very beginning as an illegitimate attempt to take over the NIA legal status[28] thus affecting irremediably the Cooperation and Verification Mechanism (CVM), jeopardising Romania joining Schengen or the Romania's very status of EU member state.

This intensively politicised quarrel between "*who is good and fights corruption*" and "*who is bad and corrupted*" has almost nothing to do with the reality and actual results of NIA, of which the basic provisions of the 2007 NIA law are examined below.

The law itself

NIA was established as an autonomous administrative authority with legal personality, under the overview of the Senate, and received the mandate to investigate wealth, incompatibilities and conflict of interests' cases. Wealth Investigation Commissions had been disbanded. Wealth was defined as all property and rights and obligations of economic value owned by a person (article 2). The investigations were carried out by integrity inspectors (article 2). Any natural or legal person could submit a complaint to NIA regarding unjustified wealth, incompatibilities or conflict of interests. NIA could also initiate ex-officio investigations (Article 4).
The NIA wealth verification procedure had three stages:

1. the designated integrity inspector had to compare the information provided in the complaint or written report of notification, and for *ex-officio* investigations, with the data from the wealth statement and interest declaration. If there were inconsistencies between data, the integrity inspector had to request from the person under investigation new information or evidence;
2. the integrity inspector compared the initial data with the supplementary information provided by the person under investigation. If the inspector had found differences of at least € 10.000 between the wealth acquired during the term of

28 Romania Curata, *Avertismentele secretarului general al ANI, Horia Georgescu, devenite realitate: Deputatul UDMR Marton Arpad vrea sa reteze puterile Agentiei Nationale de Integritate*, 4th of October 2011 (http://www.romaniacurata.ro/ltfont-colorblackgtavertismentele-secretarului-general-al-ani-horia-ge-1839.htm); Ziare.com, Presedintele ANI: Nu suntem de acord cu Codexul. Ministrul Pivniceru va da explicatii, 24th of October 2012 (http://www.ziare.com/ stiri/ ani/presedintele-ani-nu-suntem-de-acord-cu-codexul-ministrul-pivniceru-va-da-explicatii-1197705).

office and the legal income, he/she had to further investigate the wealth. During this stage, the Agency could require all documents and information;

3. if the inspector found unaccountable differences then the Agency could notify the competent court (Court of Appeal or, for high level officials, the High Court of Cassation and Justice) in order to establish whether and what the part of the wealth was acquired unjustifiably and to request the confiscation thereof. The confiscation was done under the administrative procedure. The decision of the Court of Appeal could be challenged at the High Court of Cassation and Justice.

The integrity inspector could suspend the verification procedure and could notify the prosecutor's office when there was evidence or solid grounds for suspecting criminal offences. Also, the integrity inspector had to notify the fiscal authorities if she/he found indications of fiscal fraud. If the inspector found no evidence of an unjustified difference between the assets obtained during the term of office and legal income in the same period, he could dismiss the action.
The law prescribed several due legal process guarantees:

- the scope of the verification shall not exceed the limits of the notification;
- the documents and works made by the inspectors of the Agency are not public, except for the ascertaining act;
- the person verified has the right to be informed at the beginning of the verification procedure, of the documents and works included in the file, and to be assisted or represented by an attorney;
- the reports drawn up by the inspectors after the start of the verification procedure shall be void, *de iure*, unless the verified person is informed about the opening of the verification procedure. This provision ensures the right to defence as the verified person has the right to submit documents in defence.
- the person under verification has to consent to an order for an expert report to be commissioned by the NIA but has the right to choose an assistant expert at his/her own expenses.
- cases shall be assigned to inspectors at random.
- wealth investigations may be opened no later than 5 years from the end of office/employment or dismissal.

Regarding the organisational structure, the NIA is led by a president, assisted by a vice-president, both appointed by the Senate for a 4-year non-renewable term of office, at the proposal of the National Integrity Council, following a competition or an examination. The National Integrity Council (NIC) is a representative body under Parliamentary authority exercised by the Senate, with non-permanent activity, acting as a supervising board of the NIA. A special commission composed of five NIC members is designated to verify the illicit enrichment, incompatibilities and conflicts of interests of Agency's personnel, including the president and vice-president. The NIC has 16 members appointed by the Senate for a three years term, renewable once.

Exercises in impotence

NIA became operational in 2008. During the period 2008-2010, NIA found six cases of unjustified wealth and send the files to the courts: four police officers, one university rector and one former senator. In 2010 the NIA law has been declared unconstitutional so it has been replaced by a new Wealth Verification Law the same year. A short description of these cases sheds light on the inefficiency of applying the NIA Law.

One case concerned a former senator whose file had been initially investigated by the former Wealth Verification Commissions and was send to the NIA in 2008 by the Court which considered that the file has to be reinvestigated under the 2007 NIA law. The former senator was accused of having an unjustified difference of over € 3,5 million between his wealth and lawful income. The NIA had sent the file to the Bucharest Court of Appeal at the end of 2008[29] but the former senator raised a constitutionality exception of the NIA law. The case had been suspended until 2010 when the Constitutional Court decided the matter and found the NIA law unconstitutional, reviving the debate around the constitutionality of unjustified wealth confiscation policy. Taking into account the constitutional court judgment, the Bucharest Court of Appeal sent the second time the file to NIA to be investigated under the 2010 new Wealth Verification Law. Due to this entire procedural ordeal, the file finally reached the statute of limitations and was closed by the Wealth Commission, confirming the adage: "*Justice delayed, justice denied.*"

The files regarding the four police officers were initiated by the NIA after the National Anticorruption Directorate (NAD), a special anticorruption department within the General Prosecutor's office, uncovered a corruption network in the Arges police office handling driving licences and vehicle registers. Special confiscation in criminal cases allows only the confiscation of assets related to a specific crime for which the person is convicted. The criminal forfeiture system is object-based. Thus, the NAD managed to freeze only the proceeds and instrumentalities of the crimes investigated representing only a small part of the unaccountable wealth of the police officers involved in the corruption network.

---

29 Court file no. 5544/2/2008

The NAD suspected that the entire wealth of the police officers involved was acquired illicitly, a result of their long term criminal behaviour, but they were unable to prove this fact "*beyond reasonable doubt*".[30] Therefore the NAD referred the cases to the NIA. In two out of four cases the NIA secured final confiscation decisions, all amounting approximately € 1 million. In one confiscation order, the former chief of Arges police office was found by the Court to have € 994.735 as unjustified wealth, while, in the second confiscation order, other police officer was found to have an unjustified wealth of € 63.932. Another file involving a policeman from that corruption network has been sent twice to re-trail by the High Court of Cassation and Justice (HCCJ). The fourth case has been sent once to re-trial. In the re-trial, the Court closed the case but the NIA appealed. At the time of writing, the appeal is considered by the High Court of Cassation and Justice.

In the last case the head of a public university from Iasi, Iasi Court of Appeal declined jurisdiction in favour of HCCJ. HCCJ declined the case in favour of Bucharest Court of Appeal. Bucharest Court of Appeal declined jurisdiction in favour of Iasi Court of Appeal. Iasi Court of Appeal decided again that it does not have legal competence to solve the case and asked the HCCJ to solve the negative conflict of competence. The procedural conflict emerged because the defendant was member of Romanian Parliament and, at the time of the NIA's ex-officio investigation member of the European Parliament. According to the article 46 of the NIA, in case of a deputy or a senator, the file is decided in first instance by the High Court of Cassation and Justice in a panel of three judges, the appeal being concluded also by the HCCJ in a panel of nine judges. This case shows how legislation is unable to solve anything where there is incompetence and lack of interest. NIA's investigative activity had been suspended in May 2010 as a consequence of the Constitutional Court's Judgment publication in the Official Journal of Romania. In the next section, we will discuss the constitutionality problem of NCB confiscation.

The constitutional dilemma

As mentioned earlier the "shifting of the burden of proof" issue is central to the discussion of unjustified wealth confiscation in Romania. How can the state disregard the presumption of wealth legality written in the Constitution? Is the wealth legality presumption compatible with NCB confiscation? How, during the

30 Romania has only recently adopted an extended confiscation law (March 2012).

proceedings, we can respect the Constitution and, in the same time, request the respondent to justify his/her wealth? In practice he has to, otherwise his disputed wealth is 'unjustified'. These continue to be unanswered questions mostly because the practice of the Constitutional Court shifted progressively over the 2008 – 2010 period. We will give a brief account of these changes.

In 2006, the 1996 law on wealth verification was subject to the first constitutional test. This test was requested by the Ombudsman who challenged the law on lack of clarity and uniformity. Specifically, the Ombudsman argued that the law uses interchangeably the following concepts: origin of assets – acquisition of assets, legal/illegal wealth/assets – justified/unjustified wealth/assets. These concepts are not, whatsoever, synonymous as "the wealth origin is justified" is not equal to "the wealth is legally acquired". People cannot be forced to justify their assets because this contradicts art. 44, paragraph 8 from the Constitution that prescribes the assumption of the legality of wealth acquired. The Court rejected the challenge claiming that the provisions of law on wealth verification are written with enough precision and clarity for invoking effectively the constitutional protection. Nevertheless, the Court admitted that the law uses "inadequate formula, which, indeed, could lead to problems and difficulties in their application" but it is up to judges to decide on the interpretation and application of legal rules.

From 2008 onward, after the National Integrity Agency became functional, the Court changed progressively the jurisprudence regarding the confiscation. Firstly, the Court ruled that a draft law amending the Law on Wealth Verification is unconstitutional.[31] The draft law changed the term "illicit wealth" with the term "unjustifiable differences between income and wealth". This change was challenged in front of the Constitutional Court by 71 deputies. They argued that "*using expressions such as* 'unjustifiable differences' *contradicts the constitutional norm established by paragraph (8) of article 44*". In their opinion, simply identifying "unjustifiable differences" does not mean the wealth is illicit, but it may mean that the source of income cannot be proven because of negligence. As a result, the "unjustifiable differences" cannot be confiscated. The Constitutional Court shared this opinion. Therefore, the Court ruled that the criticised law has an excessively coverage, is poorly developed, sometimes impossible to implement, with obviously unconstitutional effects. The provisions of criticised law aim to shift the burden of proof on the legality of the assets, providing the confiscation of the assets whose acquirement from lawful income cannot be justified. As a consequence, it follows that one's wealth is presumed to be gained illegal until proven otherwise by the

---

31 Judgment no. 453/2008 on the complaint of unconstitutionality of provisions of the Law amending the Law no. 115/1996 for declaration and control of the assets acquired by officials, magistrates, of people with management and control duties and public servants.

holder himself. The Constitutional Court also extends the argument and changes the jurisprudence when it emphasises that confiscation is possible under the Constitution "only if there is an offence or misdemeanour". Thus, the procedure of NCB confiscation is left outside the Constitution.

In 2010, the Constitutional Court, calling upon the 2008 judgment, declared unconstitutional the unjustified wealth confiscation policy, namely the functioning of the National Integrity Agency law. In the motivation of the judgment, the Court referred to the Constitution that says "*assets intended, used or resulted from offences and misdemeanour may be confiscated only according to the law*". The Court stressed that no confiscation is possible without a final Court decision attesting an offence or misdemeanour, and "*the law [National Integrity Agency Law] extends the cases of confiscation [. . .] also to the unjustified assets*". The Court also argued that the criticised law shift the burden of proof which "*contradicts the presumption of licit acquirement of wealth, prescribed by article 44, paragraph 8 from the Constitution*".

The Constitutional Court made other interesting points. It considered that NIA had quasi-judicial powers and the wealth investigations activities carried out by NIA's integrity inspectors were of a jurisdictional nature. Under paragraph 4, article 21 of the Constitution, the special administrative jurisdictions are not mandatory but the NIA jurisdiction is mandatory. Thus, the NIA law breached the Constitutional separation of powers.

This late clear-cut judgment put a tremendous pressure on the Government and Parliament to find a solution to ensure the continuity of the unjustified wealth confiscation policy. European Commission hinted at the commitments made at the time of accession and Romania's responsibility to solve this problem. The judgment appears to outlaw confiscation on merely "*grounds of discrepancies between wealth and lawful income*". The Court allows only confiscation assets acquisition is related an offence or misdemeanours. How did the Parliament handle this constitutional dilemma.

The 2010 bill: a fresh start or a short term compromise

After the Constitutional Court's judgment the Government submitted a concept law amending the National Integrity Agency law[32] to Parliament, which was debated and adopted in May 2010. This revised version of the law was criticised because it deprived the NIA of the power to send files of unjustified wealth

32 Draft law no. 207/2010 on enhancing the integrity in performance of public office.

increase to the courts for confiscation.[33] The NIA could refer such files only to prosecutors' office, tax authorities or to Wealth Investigation Commissions that were re-established. Although the Romanian President had decided not to promulgate the revised version of the law and had returned it to Parliament for re-examination, the Parliament adopted the revised version of the law once again with several unimportant changes. Then, the Romanian President challenged the revised version of the law to the Constitutional Court on procedural grounds, namely because the Parliamentarian procedures were not respected. In July 2010 the Constitutional Court ruled that the revised version of the law is unconstitutional[34] but not on the grounds put forward by the Romanian President but on the fact that the revised version of the law maintained several regulations that were also previously declared unconstitutional. The Parliament re-examined the draft law for the second time and adopted a new law on wealth verification (the third law), namely Law no. 176/2010.[35]

After all this bickering and sending 'to and fro', it is surprising to notice that the wealth investigations procedures under the new law resemble the previous ones declared unconstitutional. The NIA has the same organisation and competences described before (section 'the law itself'') with the several changes. First, the NIA does not investigate anymore, it just assesses. Second, the integrity inspectors have to submit the wealth evaluation reports to Wealth Investigation Commissions (15 Commissions) that are again re-established after being disbanded just three years ago.

The new the NIA wealth assessment procedure has three stages. First, the designated integrity inspector has the right to make assessments of wealth only based on public available information (*e.g.* wealth statement). If the inspector finds differences of at least € 10.000 between the wealth acquired and legal income gained during the term of office, he has to notify the person under wealth assessment in order to be able to continue the assessment and request documents and information from all public authorities involved and from other public or private legal entities.

Second, only after the person under assessment is notified the integrity inspector invites him/her to submit information he/she finds appropriate.

33 Supporting document accompanying the report from the Commission to the European Parliament and the Council on progress in Romania under the Co-operation and Verification Mechanism, ROMANIA: Technical Update, SEC(2010) 949, p. 9.

34 Judgment no. 1018 of 19 July 2010 over the objection of unconstitutionality of the law on the integrity in performance of public office, amending and supplementing the National Integrity Agency LAW on the establishment, organisation and functioning of the National Integrity Agency and to amend and supplement other normative acts.

35 Law no. 176/2010 on the integrity in performance of public office, amending and supplementing the National Integrity Agency Law.

Third, if the inspector still finds differences between wealth and income, he submits an assessment report to the assessed person and to the competent Wealth Investigation Commission of the respondent's region. The inspector may send the wealth assessment report also to the tax authorities and to the prosecutor's office. Under the new law, the authorities have the obligation to assess the recommendations of the wealth assessment reports and decide on the appropriate measures. The new law maintains all former procedural guarantees presented above.

The procedure outlined in Figure 1 allows for the confiscation of unjustified assets without connecting them to an offence or misdemeanour, thus, now bypassing the Constitutional Court judgement. The *sole difference* between the former and the new law is that the power to request the Court to confiscate a particular unjustified asset or a specified portion of property is transferred from NIA to the Wealth Investigation Commissions. Otherwise, apart from wording nothing has changes in practical terms. Three years were lost, providing a good example of the Romanian coping strategy with anti-corruption concerns.

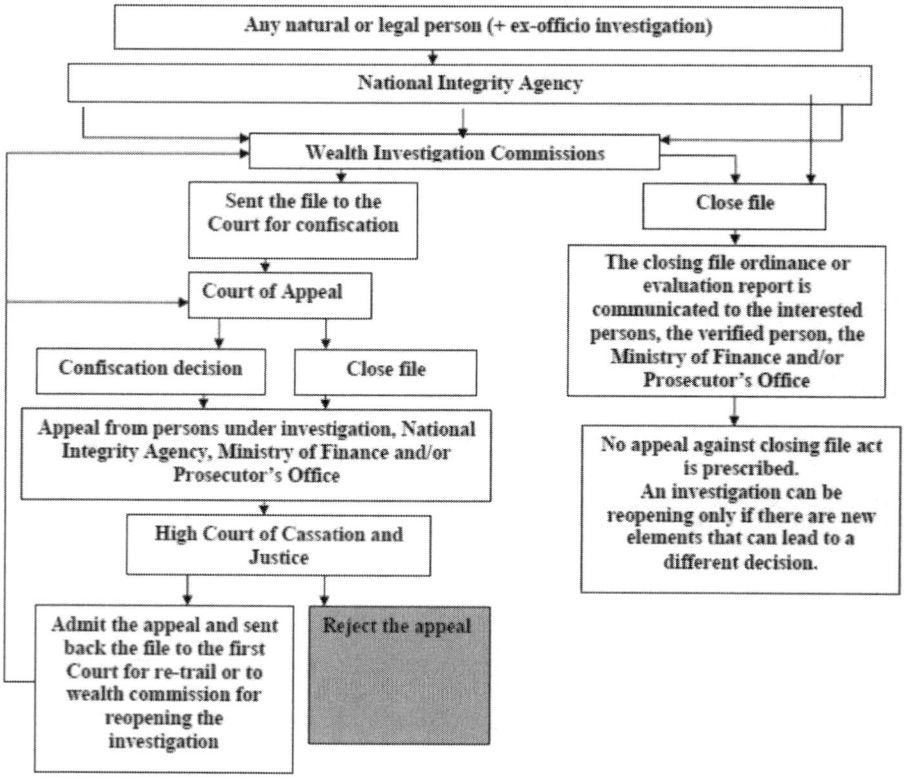

Figure 1 – The route of an unjustified wealth file: from the complain to final Court decision – 2010 law

Legally, it remains unclear whether the assessed person is compelled to give an account before the Wealth Investigation Commission/courts of the origin of his/her wealth against the evidence of a difference between wealth and income. It also remains unclear whether the respondent has a legal or evidential burden or if he/she has a burden of proof at all. The 2010 law as well as previous laws does not employ any presumptions of law. The difference between wealth and income is not legally presumed to be acquired from corruption or other forbidden acts. At the same time, the law omits any reference to "*mens rea*".

The jurisprudence on confiscation shows that the Courts analyse the dynamics of income and spending during certain periods of time and if expenditure is much higher than income in that period and the assessed person is unable to explain the difference or the Court finds the explaining evidence unsatisfactory, then that difference is confiscated. The courts dismissed the evidences provided by the assessed persons on the following grounds:

- income derived from close relatives labour and commercial activities that were not properly recorded to the tax authorities or otherwise not properly recorded;
- implausible references to other relatives' financial support or money transfers;
- unrecorded savings;
- unreported loans, which should have been mentioned in the Wealth Statement;
- unreported money transfers from one's own enterprise to the private person.

The above-mentioned jurisprudence certify that once the NIA or the Wealth Investigation Commissions establish a difference between wealth and income then the legal burden of proof is totally reversed to the assessed person. In practice, the assessed person faces strict liability for excess wealth per se: an official is liable it he/she fails to keep proper records of his/her financial dealings.

This state of affairs, namely failure to give a full income declaration, is regularly dealt with by the tax authority. The tax authority also keeps records of income from all sources as well as of the most valuables individual possessions (houses, vehicles, land, other property, etc.). If there are discrepancies between the assets acquired during a fiscal year and the income declared, the tax authority may search, under the Fiscal Code, the fiscal status of an individual.[36] If the tax authority identifies unjustified differences exceeding € 10.000, it asks the tax payer for explanations. If the tax payer is unable to clarify or he/she does not give clarifications within 60 days, the tax authority has the right to estimate the real income, tax it according to the law and impose an additional fine. This procedure

36 Fiscal status is defined by art. 1091 of the Fiscal Procedural Code as "*all financial rights and obligations, cash flow and other factors likely to determine the state of the taxpayer's actual tax for the period checked*".

does not require the intervention of the Court, it is swifter than the NIA procedure and it has strong constitutional back-up. The fiscal procedure resembles the NIA procedure, both of them covering the same thing – the unjustified wealth. Unfortunately, the fiscal authority is scarce in giving data on the results obtained, if any.

The Wealth Investigation Commissions are not judicial authorities but administrative bodies with the peculiarity of being composed of two judges and one prosecutor. By law, they are not hierarchically subordinated to the Court of Appeal or part of the judicial authority. Also, their members exercise only administrative duties during the Commission's proceedings. Wealth Investigation Commissions do not have a statute different from the former statute of the NIA just because the members of the Commissions are during most of their professional time judges and prosecutors. From our point of view, the investigation activities conducted by the Wealth Investigation Commissions have a jurisdictional nature and may have the same constitutionality vulnerability discussed before.

The unconstitutional dilemma is still at hand but left aside for political reasons. It may be a matter of time before the 2010 new Wealth Verification Law will again be challenged to the Constitutional Court on the grounds just mentioned. Then, the Constitutional Court will have two options, depending on the political context and on the stakes involved: to maintain their new jurisprudence and declare the Wealth Investigation Commissions unconstitutional or to return to their former jurisprudence and rule that unjustified assets can be confiscated by civil or administrative procedure.

The NIA case-law 2011 - 2012

NIA resumed its activities in late 2010 and it has deployed a feverish level of activity. NIA issued 17 assessment reports about unjustified wealth regarding five customs officers, five local councillors, two members of Parliament, one police officer, one mayor, one director of a state owned company, one union leader and one Parliament councillor. On average NIA needs 245 days in order to complete a wealth assessment. The quickest assessment took 98 days and the slowest 372 days. Several years are needed for the Wealth Investigation Commissions to build a relevant track-record.

All reports were sent to the Wealth Investigation Commissions. In several cases NIA assessment reports have been challenged in courts. The file against a local councillor was dismissed by the Bucharest Wealth Investigation Commission. NIA challenged the Commission's decision in Court. The rest of the files are currently under investigation by the Wealth Investigation Commissions.

The policy is lacking basic transparency as the statistics on cases dismissed by NIA are not publicised. NIA does not inform the public about the number of cases closed or the reasons for closing the unjustified wealth files. The names and positions of the officials whose files had been closed is not public information. Centre for Legal Resources demanded form 2009 onward the "opening of the books" but NIA constantly rejected the demand.

Defining the Romanian system of unjustified wealth confiscation

The Romanian "unjustified wealth" confiscation system is definitely a non-conviction based confiscation/forfeiture system. It resembles both the classic NCB-confiscation system as described by Greenberg *et al.* (2009) and the unexplained wealth system. Nevertheless it cannot be placed in one category. It shares common characteristics with classic NCB-confiscation: the judicial action is not related to a criminal charge against a person, the unlawful conduct is established on an intimately 'convinced' standard of proof.[37] It has also common traits with "unexplained wealth" system: "*in personam*" forfeiture proceeding (judicial action is filed against a person), the action is filed at a civil or administrative court, the burden of proof is shifted, specific assets or their money equivalent are confiscated. It has specific traits as a financial disclosure system (each public servant or official has to regularly fill in wealth statements and interest declarations that are publicly available on the Internet) or a scope limited only to public officials.

The compatibility between the Romanian policy and the ECHR is still a subject of debate as thus far no confiscation case from Romania has been taken into consideration by ECtHR.

Conclusion

Beginning from 1996, Romania developed for public officials only an unjustified wealth confiscation policy resembling other civil confiscation policies developed internationally. The Romanian policy has twice been seriously amended, in 2007

37 "*Assessment of evidence is the mental operation done by the Court in order to determine the strength and value of each proof in hand, and of all the evidence together. In other words, during the stage of deliberation, the judge must assess the evidences given by all parties. [. . .] The removal of evidences does not mean infringement of defence [. . .] as long as the judge shall state the factual and legal reasons that led the court to be intimately convinced of that*" (Decision no. 4519/2006).

and 2010, without altering its core characteristics: a financial disclosure system, the procedure conducted in a civil/administrative setting, establishing differences between spending and income, lack of presumptions of law of innocence, lack of interest for intent for or underlying excessive wealth ("*mens rea*").

Although seriously amended, the policy continues to be poorly drafted because it lacks clarity on several key issues: the burden of proof (conditions for shifting the burden and the compatibility with Constitution), the requirements necessary for overriding the constitutional presumption of wealth legality, and the conditions for liability (what type of behaviour triggers liability because failing to keep proper records of financial dealings is not a legitimate reason for confiscation). The policy is lacking basic transparency provisions as the statistics on cases dismissed by the NIA are not publicised.

The jurisprudence on confiscation shows that the courts analyse the dynamics of legal income and spending in certain periods of time and if expenditure is much higher than income and the defendant provides no or insufficient explanation, the courts confiscate that difference. This procedure is commonly used by tax authorities, which check if a tax payer maintains a standard of living above that which is commensurate with his/her present or past official income.

Following the letter of the law, the 'unjustified wealth' should not be considered illicit by default. Despite these facts, the analysis of the courts' decisions proved that in most cases judges chose to equate unjustified and illicit. This practice is bound to change however, especially after the recent rulings of the Constitutional Court.

The first two laws on wealth verification have generated seven final confiscation decisions: five confiscation orders were issued in cases initially raised under the 1996 law and two confiscation orders issued in cases raised under the 2007 law. The total amount ordered to be confiscated reached approximately € 1.224.000 but the Ministry of Finance has thus far recovered only € 40.000. Many cases from the period 1996 – 2010 are still pending in court. Probably, the 2010 law will have similar results as many confiscation files are pending at the offices of the Wealth Commissions. The analysis suggests that all the legislative and constitutional struggles have proved futile as the underlying problem of the unjustified wealth policy has rested in the first place on the flaw in the implementation. As Jorge (2007, 58) puts it "*The main obstacle of Romanian legal framework in controlling illicit enrichment is not the lack of an offence but rather the lack of an efficient procedure for detecting illicit enrichment*".

The policy has remained controversial form the Constitutional point of view because the Romanian Constitution presumes wealth to be legally acquired. Thus, the Constitutional Court admits only confiscation of assets intended to be used,

used or resulted from offences and misdemeanour. Nevertheless, the Constitutional court jurisprudence changed in 2010, and the lack of predictability hinders the development of the unjustified wealth confiscation policy in the long run.

In the last 15 years, the political elite managed to maintain the *status quo* of unaccountable wealth impunity and at the same time engage on paper and in public declarations in ambitious reforms intensively debated and monitored by Romanian society and European Union. It is a sad lesson about how to do nothing by doing lot of nonsense and 'ritual political dancing'. The Romanian experience with using new criminal policy instruments highly recommended for countries with rampant corruption remains a bungling – abusive affair.

References

Brun, Jean-Pierre and Gray, Larissa, *Asset recovery handbook: a guide for practitioners*, The International Bank for Reconstruction and Development / The World Bank, 2011

Centre for Legal Resources, *Wealth Investigation Commissions - monitoring the implementation no. 115/1996*. Bucharest, Didactical and Pedagogical Publishing House, 2004

Centre for Legal Resources, *The performance of the anticorruption bodies in Romania*. Bucharest, Cornelius Publishing House, 2006

Centre for Legal Resources, *Local Public Administration Integrity I*, Bucharest , Didactical and Pedagogical Publishing House, 2007

Centre for Legal Resources, *Integritatea, încotro? Perspective asupra funcționării Agenției Naționale de Integritate și a Consiliului Național de Integritate*, 2009

Centre for Legal Resources, *Local Public Administration Integrity II*, Bucharest, Didactical and Pedagogical Publishing House, 2010

Duyne, P.C. van and E. Stocco, *Corruption in Serbia. From black box to transparent policy making*. Nijmegen, Wolf Legal Publishers, 2012

Duyne, P.C. van, E. Stocco, M. Milenović and M. Todorova, Searching for the contours of the anti-corruption policy in Serbia. *Journal of Financial Crime*, 2010, vol. 17, issue 1, pp. 22-46

European Commission, Fighting Corruption in the EU, Communication from the Commission to the European Parliament, the Council and the European economic and social Committee. COM (2011) 308 final, Brussels, 2011

European Commission, Special Eurobarometer on corruption, 2012a

<http://ec.europa.eu/public_opinion/archives/ebs/ebs_374_en.pdf> (last accessed March 30, 2012)

European Commission, *Report from the Commission to the European Parliament and the Council interim report on progress in Bulgaria under the Co-operation and Verification Mechanism*. COM (2012) 57 final, Brussels, European Commission, 2012b

European Commission, Commission staff working paper accompanying document to the Proposal for a directive of the European parliament and the Council on the freezing and confiscation of proceeds of crime in the European Union. Impact assessment, COM(2012) 85 final, 2012c.

Freedom House, Inc., *The anticorruption policy of the Romanian Government*. Assessment report, Washington, D.C., Freedom House, Inc. 2005

Greenberg, Th.S., L.M. Samuel, W. Grant and L. Gray, *Stolen asset recovery: A good practices guide for non-conviction based asset forfeiture*. Washigton, D.C. the International Bank for Reconstruction and Development / The World Bank, 2009

Hamilton, B.A., *Comparative evaluation of unexplained wealth orders*. Report commissioned by US Department of Justice, Washington, D.C., National Institute of Justice, 2011

Iordache, N., *Ministry of Justice proposes new laws and institutions against corruption, because those that exist today are not effective - anticorruption exercises*. Cotidianul newspaper, July 28, 2004.

Jorge, G., *The Romanian legal framework on illicit enrichment*, American Bar Association Central European and Eurasian Law Initiative, 2007 < http://apps.americanbar.org/rol/publications/romania-illegal_enrichment_framework-2007-eng.pdf> (last accessed May 1, 2012)

Muzila, L., M. Morales, M. Mathias and T. Berger, *Illicit enrichment*, Washington, D.C., StAR Initiative, the World Bank, 2012

Nicolae, R., *Coruptia si politicile anticoruptie*, Polirom, Iasi, 2010

Pro-Democracy Association, *After 20 years: survey on democracy, citizenship and civic participation in Romania after 20 years since the fall of communism*, Bucharest, Pro-Democracy Association, 2010

The World Justice Project, *Rule of Law Index*, Washington, D.C., The World Justice Project, 2011

The World Bank, *Trends in Corruption and Regulatory Burden in Eastern Europe and Central Asia*, 2011, <http://siteresources.worldbank.org/ECAEXT/Resources/2011_report_fullreport.pdf>(last accessed May1, 2012)

Transparency International, *Corruption Perceptions Index 2011*, Berlin, Transparency International, 2011

Transparency International Romania, *For Transparency International and the European Commission counts only the facts*, press release, June 6, 2004.

United Nations Office on Drugs and Crime (UNODC), *United Nations Convention against Corruption,* 2004<http://www.unodc.org/documents/treaties/ UNCAC /Publications/Convention/08-50026_E.pdf> (last accessed November 25, 2011)

Wilsher, D., Inexplicable wealth and illicit enrichment of public officials: A model draft that respects human rights in corruption cases. *Crime, Law and Social Change*, 2006, vol. 45, 27-53

Young, S.N.M., *Civil forfeiture of criminal property: Legal measures for targeting the proceeds of crime*. Edward Elgar Pub, 2009

Serbian anti-corruption policy: Welcome to Potemkin village?

Petrus C. van Duyne[1]

Corruption: a matter of general concern?

Surveying the numerous reports, memos and papers on corruption in Europe, one cannot escape the impression that it is a matter of real concern to all, whether institutions, the business community or the citizens. At present this is reflected in the National Integrity System assessments that are carried out in the EU, supported by the EU and coordinated by Transparency International in Berlin. Given this generally shared attitude one would expect a Europe-broad approach to this phenomenon. However, this appears to be a too optimistic view. As a matter of fact, given that corruption is to a large extent (also) a political concern, political opportunism always slips in. While the European Union first allowed two highly corrupt countries, Romania and Bulgaria, to enter the Union, and only after this event took severe measures against corruption in these countries, it turned a blind eye on corruption in Greece and Italy. The case of Italy hardly needs further illustration: for almost two decades the EU heads of governments and states resigned to the presence of a(n allegedly) corrupt Prime Minister amidst their ranks. No token of concern being expressed though the Italian corruption is very well documented while 'innocent until proven guilty' meant in Italy that the prime-minister could orchestrate his own innocence through an equally corrupt Parliament. Given the blatant openness of corruption in Italy, this resignation is the more blameworthy. Does this also apply to Greece? Politically high-level corruption cases have come to light in the country, but systematic literature or research is very scarce. No general concern was expressed, until Greece proved to have defrauded its national financial statistics, though right 'under the nose' of

1 The author is emeritus professor of Criminal Law at Tilburg University and visiting professor at Manchester University. This paper is based on two research projects, supported respectively by the OSCE and the Dutch Embassy. See Van Duyne *et al.* (2010) and Van Duyne and Stocco (2012).

Eurostat. Only then was Greece's rampant corruption and nepotism brought to the open.

What sparked the concern for corruption in these countries were the enormous financial risks which emerged and not the immorality of corruption itself. The same applies to Bulgaria and to a lesser extent Romania: (fear of) embezzlement evoked action from 'Brussels'. These observations shed doubt on the pretention that corruption is a concern of us all: it is mostly subjected to opportunistic political considerations instead of a genuine worry.

In the EU an important consideration is the state of affairs of the situation of corruption in the countries that want to join the EU. At the moment these are the countries of the western Balkan, the largest of them being Serbia. There are many worries about this country, one of them about the relationship with the new state of Kosovo, the other being corruption, which is considered as a matter of great concern. However, where the previous section cast doubt on the degree to which this is a genuine international worry, the same question has to be raised at national and local level: the daily level of policy makers and citizens. The relevance of this question is the plausible assumption that any genuine policy of change must find its roots in the daily life and feelings of the common people. If they feel corruption is not really their concern, why should the political elite, policy makers and politicians, care to make efforts? True, there is external pressure from 'Brussels' which matters, but this forms only an external motivation. The internal motivation must come from the people: they can either resign themselves to corruption, be part of it or make their dissatisfaction known, for example during elections, assuming that there are non-corrupt political alternatives. Few Serbians think so: opinion surveys show that 77% of the respondents consider the political parties corrupt (UNODC, 2011). This lack of trust is a stable given over the past decade (Vuković, 2002): in the perception of the people little has changed. Against this background Van Duyne and Stocco (2012) raised the question: "*who cares about corruption*?" in Serbia.

So, this chapter will first address this question: "Who cares". Then the subject itself must be described: corruption as far as brought to light and the way it has been handled by the institutions of law enforcement. Subsequently I will return to the initial question to compare intentions, pretentions and reality.

After Milošević: a decade of hope, deception and indifference

The era of Milošević was one of decay and cynicism. The economy of Serbia was ruined, not only by the sanctions, which lasted only until the Dayton Agreements in 2005, but by a government under whose leader the national economy became criminalised (Juda, 1997, ch. 14; LeBor, 2002, ch 17). Interactions with criminal organisations were hardly veiled (Logonder, 2008). Corruption, nepotism and misappropriation of state funds were rampant while the population became impoverished (Pesić, 2007; Begović and Mijatović, 2007).

After the fall of Milošević, in 2000, there was new hope of a return to the 'rule of law': justice without corruption. People began to turn against the 'ugly face of corruption' and launched complaints against all kinds of corruption, covering all kinds of *abuse of office* as well as nepotism: for example against the judiciary, privatisation agencies, utility companies or the health service. Did this herald a reform movement against a general corrupt governance?

The picture is very ambivalent and weighing progress and stagnation, the scales tip towards the latter. At the beginning this did not look like that. There was improvement of some indices, however imprecise these are. These concern the World Bank rating of control of corruption in Serbia as well as the Corruption Perception Index since respectively 2000 and 2003 (Sadiku, 2010). Indeed, there was optimism in the air, if not a '*post-October euphoria*' as Begović *et al.* (2007) called it. Anti-corruption legislation was extended and various organs, such as the Anti Corruption Council (Oct. 2001) and mobile anti-corruption teams were established and the role of the state in the market was reduced, which also lowered its corruption potential. The perception of the prevalence of corruption became slightly more favourable. However, this did not last. Later Begović *et al.* (2007) observed a waning of the anti-corruption spirit.

This is understandable as behind the stage decors of the reform much remained the same. The reformist premier Đinđić is said to have moved too fast to the taste of many and was killed by members of Beograd organised crime, in 2003. Still, also under Đinđić, rich criminals were well served: in 2001, the Extra Profit Tax legalised with one stroke of the pen, much crime-money by simply taxing (and effectively pardoning) those who had taken advantage of the corruptive previous regime. This did not eliminate the need for money-laundering, which continued unabated, irrespective of the Serbian Financial Intelligence Unit which proved to be little effective (Van Duyne and Stefano, 2008). Public institutions continued to fare badly, whether for entrepreneurs or the 'sick and needy', creating a demand to buy those services. According to research (Vuković, 2002), 89% of the entrepreneurs bought services from corrupt civil servants, acting as if they were the 'rightful owners' of their position, sometimes 'by heritage' from parents or other relatives.

On the other hand, foreign (EU) pressure contributed to a modest and steady progress, in particular as far as legislation and the establishment of institutions are concerned. As paper won't blush, much remained on paper: throughout the past decade and up until now, the laws are fine but the implementation remains defective. Whether it concerned the National Anti-corruption Strategy, the Government Audit Institution or the Anti-corruption Agency, every development looks like a hurdle race, but then in slow motion. Or was it mainly a *Potemkin Village*-like acting? Or perhaps a bit of improvement and a bit of acting and pretending at the same time? I think that this is the most plausible interpretation, given the lower corruption perception data in the middle of the previous decade (Begović, 2007, Figure 7). At the political level, there was still stagnation, which is understandable if Pesić's (2007) description of Serbia as a 'feudalistic state' is correct. In such a state political bosses act like medieval Lords, bestowing favours (positions) to their political retainers. Likewise, in Serbia the political leadership grabbed the state as a property, divided it in 'fiefs' which were bestowed on followers as vassals. Small wonder that with so many broadly shared interests at stake, progress was smothered behind the settings of laws and institutions. The latter proved to be ineffective, not only against political corruption, but also the lower level 'executive' corruption: bribery in the form of the selling medical services, school or university diplomas, or buying off traffic fines.

This state of affairs, a mixture of some progress and much stagnation, does not reflect much enthusiasm for fighting corruption, as observed by Trivunović *et al.* (2007, 73). The authors remark with clear disappointment that "*there is little interest, both within the government, but also civil society in participating* [in the fight against corruption] . . . *let someone else do it.*"

With disappointment came indifference. Research on corruption disappeared from the Serbian academic radar: there were (and are) no funds nor interest. As one respondent conveyed to me: "*Corruption is no longer a sexy subject for my students. They do not care.*" Correctly, who cares for things which are not sexy?

We are not short of solemn official proclamations of how serious the authorities takes the corruption issue. This chapter will investigate this claim later by comparing it with the latest research findings. For the moment it is informative to juxtapose this claim with the outcomes from opinion surveys discussed below. Of these the most important findings concern the *seriousness* ratings and the *own experience.*

- *Seriousness*

  Do the people think of corruption as the most important problem of the country? No. In all the opinion surveys corruption as 'most important problem of the country' ended up at the *third* place. That was the case in 2001, 2006 (Begović *et al.*, 2007) and with the recent surveys carried out in the *TNS-Medium Gallup* and *UNDP* project (2010), by Transparency International or UNODC. While poverty and unemployment, respectively, were rated by 20-30% of the respondents as the 'most serious' problem in the country, corruption achieved a rating of 9-18% with only in the UNODC survey exceeding the 10%-mark. In the 2001 and 2006 surveys the seriousness rating remained at 10%, while in 2006 only 5% thought it a problem experienced personally.
- *Own experience*

  The surveys also asked for personal experience, broadly formulated as "*did you or someone of your household pay a bribe in the past . . .*" Depending on the project the period was set at three or 12 months. Alternatively, the score was related as a percentage of the *real contacts* with civil servants. This method is realistic: more contacts, more exposure. While in the former method the direct and indirect experience approached 20%, relating the experience to the frequency of real contacts resulted in a lower figure of 8%. This does not mean that the other figures are wrong, but that other denominators were used.

Summarised: a sizeable part of the population has a personal experience with corruption, which may be annoying, but not as the most prominent problem for themselves or the country. But how bad is that experience? When bribes are not extorted, it is a voluntary barter transaction: indeed, 85% admitted to have taken the initiative, for example to get the desired medical treatment or to avoid problems with the police (TNS-Medium Gallup and UNDCP, 2011).

Hence, many 'do it' – and as initiator! This must be weighed against statements of disapproval or resentment. To what extent do these statements reflect political correctness? This is important, because it is difficult to pursue an anti-corruption policy which is mainly based on political correctness. We meet here an ambivalent situation. On one side of the balance we have the political correctness: 'corruption is bad' and police, prosecution and courts should do something about it. On the other side it appears that citizens think these branches of law enforcement too corrupt to handle corruption cases: the perception of the morality of the legal professions is very low (only politicians and doctors are less trusted). This is an enduring phenomenon reflecting a deeply rooted reputation problem (Begović *et al.*, 2004; chapter IV; Trivunovic *et al.*, 2007; 21). This perception itself reinforces the attitude of the citizens concerning reported cases to the police: of the bribe payers 35% thought reporting to the police pointless: "*Nobody would care*" (UNODC report,

Figure 22; p. 32). Perception creates reality which again reinforces perception. "*Many do it and few care.*" This reflects the major obstacle of the past decade: indifference, displayed either openly or behind the stage settings of law and institutions.

The black box conception of the law enforcement

The previous section outlined a decade of expectations sliding down to indifference as far as the citizens are concerned. During the same decade a corruption policy has been formulated, related laws have been enacted and institutions established (*e.g.* Anti Corruption Council; Ombudsman; Board for Freedom of information of public interest), with the Anti-Corruption Agency as the last 'acquisition'. If all these measures and institutions are effective these constitute important developments, though they fail to impress the population. Of importance are also the institutions of law enforcement, functioning as the '*ultimum remedium'* in the whole anti-corruption strategy. As a matter of fact, little is known about the functioning of the 'rule of law', except that in all opinion surveys the related institutions end invariably in 'the top five of distrust'. But these are subjective ratings and do not inform us about the functioning of the law enforcement agencies, as far as it concerns tackling corruption.

This chapter will focus on the criminal law enforcement by the prosecution and the courts. Though we intended to involve the police too, the Ministry of Interior pursued such a 'byzantine' procedure that this intention was effectively blocked. As the Ant-Corruption Agency has a monitoring function in the implementation of the Anti-Corruption Strategy, also concerning criminal law enforcement, the chapter will also relate the Agency's findings in this field.

With so little knowledge it is difficult to formulate hypotheses about the functioning of law enforcement. Even with the beginning of insight from our first OSCE supported research project (Van Duyne *et al.*, 2010), the institutions of prosecution and the judiciary are still a kind of *black box*. That may not look positive, though in experimental psychology it is a neutral concept used to denote the 'mind' which is closed to direct observations and therefore a 'black box'. All we can do is to observe what kind of stimuli are exerted upon someone (input) and what kind of conduct follows as a result (output). In between we must speculate about inner mechanisms. The same approach can be used to address the prosecution and courts embedded in a surrounding anti-corruption strategy. It is plausible to expect that this strategy exerts stimuli on the law enforcement and that as a consequence, there is a related output, consisting of prosecutions, verdicts and sentences. Of course, this output will be related to a description of the input of cases, which in its turn should be a function of the surrounding strategy.

Method of research

As remarked in the previous section, there is not much research tradition in this field in Serbia. Apart from the OSCE-project, there have been no research projects of any significance since 2006/7. In a country, in general characterised by opaqueness, when it comes to corruption one has to throw a wide net in a muddy pool and fish up bits and pieces of empirical evidence. In a way, the methodology is itself a kind of anthropological finding, which tells us about the corruption attitude of the people we addressed.

Given the state of the knowledge and the data management in the country, we had to knock on the doors of many institutions. Could their reactions be considered as a kind of attitude measurement? I think this is permissible with institutions and functionaries having a direct responsibility for the corruption policy. Can one scale this attitude? That would be too intuitive and a bit of 'wisdom by hindsight'. Lining up the addressed institutions we get the following:

- *Ministry of Interior*, essential for getting cooperation with the police: failed. To obtain a few obsolete and useless data the research team was sucked into a bizarre correspondence that even involved the Dutch embassy;
- *Ministry of Justice*, important for obtaining access to the Republic Public Prosecution Offices (RPPO). The addressed persons, whether high-up or humble-down, did not respond to or requests. The Minister is the national anti-corruption coordinator.
- The Republic Prosecution Office, *Anti-Corruption Department*: should have about 2.200 cases archived for inspection and coordination, but denied the possession of any data, except annual frequencies which do not match with any other data. Letters with requests, delivered in person, were not responded to.
- The *Anti-Corruption Agency*: the staff showed no interest in data or research, even if it has a *monitoring and coordinating task* (art. 66 Act on the Anti Corruption Agency). How to carry out such a task without data is a mystery.

These are central organs, tasked with coordination and having as their mission to "*inform the general public*", as a glossy booklet of the Republic Public Prosecution states (The Republic Prosecutor's Office, 2011). However, no trace of task fulfilment could be identified. Searching the websites of the ministries and RPPO with 'corruption' and all the synonym search words only produced blanks: no public informed and no evidence of coordination.

The following organisations displayed more responsiveness and cooperation:

- The *Anti-Corruption Council*, which is a governmental advice body, but acting independently. The ACC collects and investigates cases with a team of experts. If its findings are relevant for further criminal investigation, it passes the case to the RPPO, which rarely responds. It also advises the government, which never replies (ACC, 2011). We obtained full insight into the cases processed by the ACC.
- The *Special Prosecutor for Organised crime*, also competent for serious corruption cases provided us with the indictments of all 26 corruption cases.
- The *Courts*: the First Basic Court and the Belgrade Higher Court allowed us to study 65 verdicts, from which we selected 31. The Second Basic Court denied having any corruption cases, though from the database of the Statistical Office we could extract 109 processed by this court.
- The *Statistical Office of the Republic of Serbia* cooperated fully by providing us with the raw excel databases of the years 2007-2009. From these databases we omitted the records of *un*known perpetrators. The remainder was converted into an SPSS database. The databases of the Prosecution Offices and the Courts could not be integrated as their input format is different, excluding a fusion. The relevant offences were the articles 359-369 from the chapter "Criminal offences against official duty" which is a broader concept than corruption itself. These offences can be considered as an equivalent of 'violations of integrity in office'. Because of the low frequencies, the data from the Basic Courts had to be put together according to the District Court to which they belong. They will be called 'Court Regions'.

Results: from black box to random box

From the perspective outlined above this chapter will first give a general overview of the past decade concerning the reported cases of 'crimes against official duty' and the decisions of the Prosecution and the Courts as presented in Table 1 and Figure 1.

Table 1

Crimes against official duty: reported offenders, charged and convicted 1998-2009

	Offenders			%		
ear	eported	charged	convicted	Charged/ reported	Convicted/ charged	Convicted/ reported
1998	4.303	1.860	1.242	43	67	29
1999	3.169	1.566	1.133	49	72	36
2000	3.312	1.583	1.101	48	70	33
2001	4.640	1.473	983	32	67	21
2002	5.312	1.553	1.031	29	66	21
2003	5.535	1.566	1.038	28	66	19
2004	5.356	1.796	1.170	33	65	22
2005	5.253	1.839	1.126	35	61	21
2006	4.343	1.896	1.147	44	60	26
2007	4.244	1.564	994	37	64	23
2008	4.114	1.661	1.079	38	58	22
2009	3.980	1.833	878	46	48	22
Average	4.463	1.683	1.076	37	64	24

Source: Statistical Yearbook 2010

Do these figures tell us something about what happened in society and within law enforcement? Let us follow the timeline. With the regime change in 2000 we also see a change in reporting conduct: the frequency of reported offences rose steeply, till 2003. After the murder of Đinđić in that year the curve reduces steadily. In 2005/6 even markedly, corresponding with the growing disappointment. And what happened with the Prosecution and the Courts? Almost nothing: a virtual flat line suggesting a non-responding black box. Of course, these numbers must be related to the total number of reported crimes, for which we only have the years 2006 - 2009. For these years the percentage of crimes against official duty went gradually down from 6,8% in 2006 to 6,1% in 2009.

Figure 1
Trends in reports, charges and convictions of crime against official duty

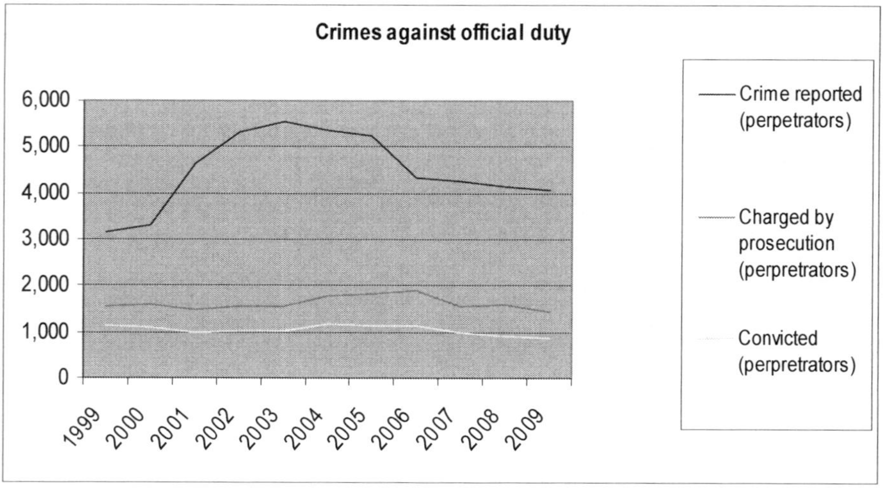

These are aggregate figures which may veil local differences between the Prosecution and the Courts. These will now be discussed in two sections.

a. The prosecution offices

Table 2 (below) show the input of corruption reports, broken down by district. Differences between the districts are clearly present, though very unsystematically: at the low end of the range we find Pančevo (2,8%), Subotica (2,9%), Zrenjanin (3%) and Belgrade (3,5%). At the high end we have Vranje (11,4%), Leskovac (10,6%) and Požarevac (10,5%). But viewed over the years there are no regular high- and low-frequency districts. Jagodina being on top in 2007, with 15% crimes against official duty, Požarevac heading the year after with 10,2%, and in 2009, Leskovac with 14%.

When we look at the 2007-2009 database for a comparison of increases and decreases per Prosecution Office in the districts, we see a similar unsystematic variability. Between 2007 and 2009 Leskovac showed an *increase* of cases from 159 to 249, while in the same time span Negotin experienced a *decrease* from 155 to 81. In percentages: an increase of 57% versus a decrease of 48%. Table 2 provides the full picture.

Large increases (≥ 40%) can also be observed in the districts of Čačak, Kraljevo, Pito, Užece and Valjevo. Decreases of more than 30% are observed in Kragujevac and Niš. On average there is more decrease than increase resulting in a slightly lower figure in 2009 compared to 2007.

Table 2
Reported offenders against official duty at Prosecution and bribery cases: per court region 2007-2009

	Reported offenders against official duty			Difference 2007-2009 in %	**2007-2009**	
Districts (regions)	2007	2008	2009		Taking bribes	Giving bribes
Belgrade	426	473	436	2	35	24
Čačak	83	150	120	45	2	1
Kragujevac	123	94	85	-31	1	1
Kraljevo	73	55	112	53	19	15
Kruševac	144	134	165	15	6	1
Leskovac	159	180	249	57	17	9
Negotin	155	103	81	-48	18	9
Niš	115	112	77	-33	6	5
Novi Pazar	71	46	60	-15	10	10
Pirot	50	35	70	40	0	1
Požarevac	195	218	198	2	26	23
Prokuplje	110	120	87	-21	6	2
Smederevo	179	182	131	-27	41	51
Jagodina	239	154	207	-13	25	10
Šabac	254	303	259	2	28	10
Užice	106	154	150	43	7	4
Valjevo	152	187	219	44	5	8
Vranje	388	315	361	-7	18	45
Zaječar	166	193	163	-2	9	2
Novi Sad	217	222	173	-20	12	5
Pančevo	66	59	54	-18	5	4
Sombor	95	75	102	7	8	14
Sr. Mitrovica	232	229	184	-21	16	10
Subotica	85	67	77	-9	5	2
Zrenjanin	98	91	77	-21	1	2
Total	**3981**	**3951**	**3897**	**-2**	**326**	**268**

There are no explanations for these sudden increases or decreases which look rather like an unpredictable weather forecast in the autumn than a trend of an underlying stable phenomenon let alone the outcome of an anti-corruption strategy. Statistically the input of black box appears to be quite at random.

Given their relevance the frequencies of the reported bribery (taking and giving) are added in the last two columns, albeit measures by their numbers their relevance looks less convincing. That must be reduced with about 20% non-indictment. In about half the Court regions there are less than ten cases for both taking and giving bribes together. Some of the Court regions handle only one or two cases in three years.

Table 3
Type of prosecution decision per Court district: 2007-2009

Court region	Dismissal report %	Disrupt investigation %	Terminating investigation %	Indictment %	Total = 100%
Belgrade	31,8	1,4	9,0	57,8	1316
Čačak	41,5	0,6	8,3	49,6	337
Kragujevac	26,2	0	10,3	63,5	301
Kraljevo	32,1	0	2,5	65,4	240
Kruševac	38,5	0,2	7,9	53,3	418
Leskovac	60,5	0	6,0	33,4	583
Negotin	66,2	0,3	3,3	30,3	337
Niš	65,3	0	4,3	30,3	300
Novi Pazar	44,5	0,6	2,3	52,6	173
Pirot	58,7	0	11,0	30,3	155
Požarevac	70,9	0	2,9	26,2	595
Prokuplje	46,6	0,3	14,2	38,8	309
Smederevo	34,2	1,3	6,7	57,8	479
Jagodina	64,6	1,0	3,4	31,0	594
Šabac	64,0	2,3	5,3	28,4	791
Užice	43,8	0	13,9	42,3	404
Valjevo	69,3	0	3,1	27,5	541
Vranje	50,2	0	12,8	37,0	1033
Zaječar	63,2	0,2	9,3	27,2	503
Novi Sad	31,2	0,5	6,2	62,1	593
Pančevo	33,5	0	9,1	57,4	176
Sombor	29,6	0	13,7	56,7	270
Sr. Mitrovica	47,9	3,1	11,3	37,7	639
Subotica	46,2	0	1,8	52,0	223
Zrenjanin	37,5	0	6,4	56,2	251
Total	5652 48,9%	78 0,7%	886 7,7%	4945 42,8%	11561 100,0%

Given this seemingly random input, what will the output look like? The output consists of the decision whether to pursue the prosecution by filing an indictment; dismissing the report; or by suspending or terminating the investigation. Looking for a 'system', the next question concerns the pattern of indictment rates differentiated per Court district. This is presented in Table 3 (above).

Almost 60% of the reports do not result in an indictment. However, the picture is again very diverse with large differences between the districts. The indictment rate ranges between the extremes with on the low end Požarevac with 26,2% and at the other extreme Kraljevo with a 65,4% prosecution chance. Of course, we do not know potential underlying causes. Kraljevo has less cases reported than Požarevac. Is there an underlying policy? Such as: Kraljevo filters out weak cases resulting in a high indictment percentage. Požarevac on the contrary the report frequency is high and therefore the likelihood of weak cases which must be dismissed for lack of evidence is higher. But this assumes that the inflow of cases is subjected to a management strategy. This assumption is not corroborated: neither in the previous research, nor in this one did we ever found a trace of any strategy.

The correlation between the percentage of indictments and the total case input is slightly negative (Spearman's Rho = -0,27), but not significant.

The large differences in indictment percentages may be related to differences in deciding on certain categories of cases: do the same offence categories have more or less the same chance of indictment or are the decision outcomes different per court. For this reason the extremes of Požarevac (highest) and Kraljevo (lowest) are compared, though their case frequencies differ widely: 595 against 240 cases. Table 3 presents the comparison.

Table 4
Type of decision of Požarevac and Kraljevo: 2007-2009

	Požarevac				**Kraljevo**			
Type of offence	Dismissal report %	Stop investigati on %	Indict ment %	Total	Dismis s report %	terminating investingati on %	Indict- ment %	Total
Abuse of office	67,2	4,4	28,4	*229*	26,6	2,3	71,1	*128*
Law breaking court	91,7	0	8,3	*241*	92,3	2,6	5,1	*39*
Dereliction duty	84,2	0	15,8	*19*	71,4		28,6	7
Ill.collection payment	100	0	0	*1*				*0*
Fraudulent serv.				*0*	33,3		66.7	*3*
Embezzl.	17,0	13,2	69,8	*53*	4,0	4,0	92	*25*
Offence by civ. servant	0	0	100	*2*			100	*4*
Influence trading			100	*1*				*0*
Taking bribe	57,7	0,0	42,3	*26*			100	*19*
Giving bribe	26,1	0,0	73,9	*23*		6,7	93,3	*15*
Total	422	17	156	*595*	77	6	157	*240*
	70,9%	2,9%	26,2%		32,1%	2,5%	65,4%	

As can be observed in the findings of Table 4, the main difference appears to be the decisions on *abuse of office* cases, with a low indictment rate in Požarevac and a high one in Kraljevo: 28,4% against 71,1%. With the exception of complaints against judges and prosecutors, embezzlement and bribery, the other crime categories have too low absolute frequencies in either of the two regions (or in both) for presenting relative frequencies.

Bribery cases show also marked differences: in Kraljevo almost all cases are indicted, while in Požarevac taking and giving bribes are prosecuted in 42,3 and 73,9%. *Embezzlement* is also prosecuted more often in Kraljevo: 92% against 69,8% in Požarevac.

To explore a frequency effect (240 against 595 cases), the team also looked at the district with a similar high prosecution percentage but with a comparable case frequency: *Novi Sad*, with 593 cases, does not differ much from Požarevac, but has an indictment percentage of 62,1%. Now the main difference is determined by *abuse of office* with also a high indictment rate in Novi Sad: 64,3%. Other categories do not differ essentially or the absolute numbers are so small as to make a comparison futile. For example, in Novi Sad there are only 15 cases of taking bribes and 5 cases of giving bribes over a three year period.

Inspection of the whole of the decision outcomes of the Court districts broken down per offence categories shows that the absolute frequencies are very low (making percentages meaningless) except for *abuse of office* and *embezzlement*. Their indictment percentages also display different but large ranges between the Court districts: *abuse of office* ranges from 27,2% to 71,2%; embezzlement starts with a much higher threshold of 50% with the maximum of 90% of the reported cases leading to indictments. The variance between the courts is similar, but the threshold differs.

Before we move on it is good to pause for a moment and look back: what do we see? Mainly a bundle of case processing institutions with a low frequency input for a high priority policy, with – unknown – differences in decision outcomes. The statistical view is somewhat troubled by the dominance of the 'umbrella article' of abuse of office, though this does not veil the very low figure of the key offences such as taking and offering bribes which then must be reduced with 20% non-indictment.

b. The courts

The above section looked at the prosecution output, which concerned the indictments that should be the input of the Courts: indictments out of the Prosecution and into the Courts should therefore match. However, that is not the case: in this database there is a difference of 402 cases between Prosecution output and Court input. This difference is also unsystematic: some courts 'missing' more than others. This makes clear that the Prosecutor and Court databases must be treated as different – statistical – populations, even if dealing with the same suspects.

As is the case with the prosecutions, the 'turnover' of the courts went gradually down: from 2007-2009 a reduction from 1.558 to 1.420, a difference of 9%. And also with the Courts, the difference was not spread evenly over the local units: Niš saw a reduction of 63 cases while Zaječar had an increase of 42. The increases and decreases of the courts did not correlate with that of the related Prosecution offices in the same district (Spearman's Rho = ,05): within the same locality, the Prosecution could have an increase and the Courts a decrease.

The most important criterion variable is the decision outcomes of the courts: verdict and sentencing. The decision categories in the verdicts are very refined: 13 categories, which can then be broken down per year and municipality and district. Given the low frequencies in most of them these were reduced to three categories (see Table 5 below). Noticing not much difference between the years (57,9% in 2008 to 63,6% in 2007), these categories were again fused. Concerning the District and the Municipal Courts, the percentage of guilty verdicts were 60,6 and 60,7 respectively for which reason we grouped the Courts again into regions (District plus Municipal Courts).

Table 5
Category of verdict: guilty or not guilty

	Category of verdict			
Regions (district + municipal courts)	Guilty %	Charge lifted/denied %	Other end not guilty %	**Total** = 100%
Belgrade	53,8	16,7	29,5	593
Cačak	56,8	34,8	8,3	132
Kragujevac	41,6	38,3	20,2	243
Kraljevo	63,9	23,6	12,5	144
Kruševac	62,8	23,0	14,2	113
Leskovac	52,9	39,2	7,8	204
Negotin	54,9	33,3	11,8	102
Niš	69,4	17,6	12,9	255
Novi Pazar	63,4	26,8	9,8	41
Pirot	45,6	30,4	24,1	79
Požarevac	73,0	16,4	10,7	122
Prokuplje	66,7	29,4	3,9	51
Smederevo	82,9	17,1	0	105
Jagodina	62,9	31,7	5,4	224
Šabac	63,1	23,6	13,3	195
Užice	65,4	26,2	8,4	107
Valjevo	56,3	30,4	13,4	112
Vranje	72,1	24,5	3,4	265
Zaječar	63,0	20,3	16,7	227
Novi Sad	53,5	29,8	16,7	467
Pančevo	70,4	18,4	11,2	152
Sombor	69,2	26,6	4,2	143
Sremska Mitrovica	65,8	16,9	17,3	266
Subotica	56,8	24,2	18,9	95
Zrenjanin	62,6	28,7	8,7	115
Total	2.759	1.141	652	4.552

First we have to look at the comparison of the guilty verdict rank order of the Court regions with the rank order of the indictments of the Prosecution Offices: is a high (or low) indictment score indicative for a high guilty score? Not necessarily: prosecutors may charge too many weak cases resulting in a higher percentage of non-guilty verdicts. That would result in a negative correlation. The comparison between the rank order of indictments and guilty verdicts (Spearman's Rho) shows a slightly negative correlation of -0,091, however it is non-significant. There is no support for the hypothesis of coherence between the decisions of the Prosecution Offices and the Courts, lending support to the hypothesis of a *random* functioning of the institutions of criminal justice.

Subsequently there are the differences between the Court regions. As can be observed in Table 5, around the average of 60,6% guilty verdict, the interregional differences are again large, ranging from 82,9% (Smederevo) to 41,6% (Kragujevac). These differences are compounded by differences between the offences. The guilty verdict rate of abuse of office, being the most prevalent offence category, scores with 55% below the average of 60,6%. This can be observed in all Court regions, though the largest percent differences can be observed in Belgrade, Zrenjanin and Pirot (-15% to -16%).

Comparing guilty verdicts against the Court regions is hampered by low frequencies of most offences per cell (< 10). Only *abuse of office* and *embezzlement* have sufficient frequencies for further comparison. Concerning abuse of office with an overall 55% guilty verdict, Pirot has the lowest guilty percentage, 30,2% against 77% for Smederevo. For embezzlement the overall guilty percentage is 75, with a range from 56% (Prokuplje) to 97 and 100% (Požarevac, respectively Smederevo, though only 15 cases). It demonstrates again the large differences between the court regions.

Are such differences also to be expected when it comes to sentencing? Given the previous findings, such disparity would not come as a surprise. There are many sentence modalities, which can be simplified to: prison, fine and a (suspended) punishment on parole or under conditions. The fines can be discarded, as only three fines have been imposed. Hence, with prison as the main category, we can differentiate between an unconditional and a conditional prison sentence: 78,6% (2167) of the prison sentences were conditional (probation). In this modality we find again the usual differences. Four Courts are the most *lenient* by meting out mostly conditional prison sentences:

- Prokuplje 94%
- Valjevo 94%
- Vranje 92%
- Subotica 91%

The three most *severe/strictest* courts in terms of lower *conditional* sentences are:

- Čačak 45%
- Sombor 51%
- Kraljevo 64%

Further breaking down per offence category is again hampered by low frequencies, with the exception of abuse of office and embezzlement.

In *abuse of office cases* Sombor and Čačak, with 50% and 52% unconditional sentences, respectively, are the most strict, against 100% conditional sentences in Prokuplje, and Novi Pazar.

With *embezzlement* Čačak was even more implacable and had with only 21% conditional punishments the most severe score. It was in this regard followed by Niš: 45%. In contrast, Subotica with only conditional sentences handed down, was very lenient, followed by the other lenient courts: Vranje and Valjevo (95%). And Prokuplje? It had only five embezzlement cases, three of them conditionally punished. Small frequency constraints prevent us from further breaking down the data.

These findings seem to point at some within-court consistency. Is that also the case if the length of prison sentence is taken into account? To make comparisons on this dimension all the crime types are put together, which produces the following picture for *unconditiona*l prison sentences (Table 6).

Though sentencing intervals used by the Statistical Office are unequal, while for a number of Court regions the absolute numbers are very small, it seems that Belgrade, Kragujevac and Požarevac tend to impose more unconditional prison terms in the 6–12 months category, while Novi Sad imposed prison sentences of more than one year in 44,3% of the cases, mainly pertaining to *abuse of office*: of the 56 unconditional prison sentences for this offence, 43% were longer than one year. This Court region can be considered as one of the severest in Serbia; in terms of the length of prison sentence, but not regarding the conditional/unconditional division.

Table 6

Unconditional prison sentences per court region, all years

	Length prison term									
Court regions	Till 30 d %	1 - 2 months %	2 - 3 months %	3 - 6 months %	6 - 12 months %	1 - 2 years %	2 - 3 years %	3 – 5 years %	5 - 10 years %	Total Courts 100%
Belgrade		2,6	5,1	30,8	43,6	15,4	2,6			39
Čačak		2,4	19,5	34,1	19,5	12,2	12,2			41
Kragujevac		9,1	9,1	36,4	45,5					11
Kraljevo		3,1	12,5	37,5	21,9	18,8		6,3		32
Kruševac			11,1	66,7		11,1	11,1			9
Leskovac	6,5	12,9	16,1	45,2	12,9	6.5				31
Negotin		7,7	15,4	46,2	23,1			7,7		13
Niš		1,3	11,7	46,8	31,2	6,5	1,3	1,3		77
Novi Pazar				66,7	33,3					3
Pirot			44,4	22,2	33,3					9
Požarevac			9,1	40,9	45,5	4,5				22
Prokuplje			50,0			50,0				2
Smederevo			18,2	36,4	36,4			9,1		11
Jagodina		6,7	13,3	20,0	33,3	16,7	10,0			30
Šabac		4,8	23,8	52,4	9,5		4,8	4,8		21
Užice			13,0	43,5	26,1	17,4				23
Valjevo			25,0	50,0		25,0				4
Vranje			23,1	46,2	23,1	7,7				13
Zajecar			26,1	43,5	30,4					23
Novi Sad			4,9	21,3	29,5	23,0	14,8	4,9	1,6	61
Pančevo			6,3	56,3	12,5	25,0				16
Sombor	2,0	2,0	10,2	26,5	24,5	25,5	4,1	4,1		49
Sr. Mitrovica			5,6	44,4	33,3	5,6	5,6	5,6		18
Subotica				50,0	50,0					4
Zrenjanin			25,0	41,7	8,3	16,7	8,3			12
Total	3	14	76	216	155	72	25	12	1	574
	0,5%	2,4%	13,2%	37,6%	27,0%	12,5%	4,4%	2,1%	,2%	

c. The time variable: justice delayed is justice denied

Time is a very important variable in all legal matters: being tried within a reasonable time is a basic right. But what is reasonable? There are complaints about the slow functioning of the Serbian justice system. These are moral issues, which must come after the facts. Our question is: what is the processing time of our judicial black box of cases concerning crimes against official duty. Of course, answers to this question must be related to the total processing times in all criminal cases as a base line. The Statistical Office reported as follows.

- for *all* criminal cases finished in 2007-2009 by the Courts around 45% lasted more than one year. Half of these lasted more than two years (23% of the total number of cases);
- acquittals last systematically longer: For the non-guilty verdicts only 39% were processed within one year. Of that 60% lasting more than one year, 40% of the defendants had to wait for more than 2 years for an acquittal. The guilty ones were served quicker in relative terms: 59% of the *guilty* verdicts were pronounced within one year. Still 20% had to wait for more than 2 years.
- the average duration of criminal proceedings in the Basic Courts is 1,47 years; in the Higher Court in the first instance it is 1,6 years and in the second instance it is 1 year.[2] There is no information about the accumulation of processing times in cases of more instances.

Not all the time data could be converted into SPSS variables. But we could retrieve the *date of receiving the charge* and the *date of decision* as a full day-month-year time variable. This was not possible for the *offence* and the *finalisation* date: these were only available as a full *year* variable. This entails some rough rounding off.

There are some additional *caveats* to mention: (a) the year of finalisation may sometimes be the next year; (b) the year of offending is not necessarily the year in which the case has been registered. In addition, we do not know the investigatory or procedural part of the time span before the day of receiving the charge: the pre-charge phase. Naturally, this pre-charge phase has also its division of 'time slices': the 'police time' and the 'prosecutor time'. This precludes attributing the length of the procedure to either the police or prosecution. This makes it impossible to answer the "who delays" question.

Nevertheless, we have three interesting time spans: (a) the *total time span* from the year of offending to the year of finalisation and within that (b) the time span *before* receiving the charge (pre-charge) and (c) the time span from the day of receiving the charge till the day of the finalisation (post charge). How do these relate? Table 7 provides an interesting insight.

2 Answers given to the European Commission questionnaire: question 23. (EU *Commission Staff Working Paper. Analytical Report.*)

Table 7

Processing times in years: from year offence till finalisation; from year offence till receiving of charge and year receiving charge till finalisation.

Court District	N	Mean: total time	Mean pre-charge	Mean post-charge	Maximum total time
Beograd	592	5,20	2,60	2,95	18,00
Čačak	132	5,62	3,16	2,84	14,00
Kragujevac	242	5,59	2,65	3,31	13,00
Kraljevo	164	5,99	2,88	3,32	14,00
Kruševac	113	4,53	2,24	2,69	11,00
Leskovac	204	4,72	2,55	2,51	13,00
Negotin	102	4,59	2,23	2,79	12,00
Niš	255	4,72	2,39	2,68	17,00
Novi Pazar	41	3,83	1,68	2,68	9,00
Pirot	79	5,23	2,30	3,49	14,00
Požarevac	122	4,13	2,23	2,18	13,00
Prokuplje	51	3,82	2,68	1,61	10,00
Smederevo	105	5,58	2,72	3,18	12,00
Jagodina	223	4,49	2,66	2,06	15,00
Šabac	195	4,78	2,73	2,26	18,00
Užice	107	4,63	2,81	2,22	13,00
Valjevo	112	5,39	2,64	3,07	12,00
Vranje	265	4,89	2,22	3,01	17,00
Zaječar	227	4,17	2,67	1,84	12,00
Novi Sad	467	5,64	3,09	2,93	14,00
Pančevo	152	5,01	2,78	2,53	14,00
Sombor	143	6,57	3,20	3,57	14,00
Sremska Mitrovica	266	6,76	2,87	4,24	16,00
Subotica	95	5,36	2,79	2,75	15,00
Zrenjanin	115	4,48	2,59	2,31	11,00
Total	4569	5,16	2,67	2,83	18,00
Median		5.00	2,14	2,00	

Despite the fact of high maximum total processing times for single cases, the median is close enough to the mean to use that index.

A few observations can be made. In the first place, the difference between the averages of these cases and *all* criminal proceedings is very wide: 5,16 versus 1,47 years for the Basic Courts and 1,6 for the Higher Courts. A methodological warning must be made: our Court regions (District Courts + Municipal Courts) are not the same as the Higher and Basic Courts after the judicial reform of 2010, while many corruption cases are not handled by the lower courts. Nevertheless, assuming that the answers of the Ministry of Justice given to the EU Commission are correct, we must face the hypothesis that in corruption related cases the procedures last much longer than in 'normal' cases. This is an important finding which needs to be investigated in-depth by applying the analysis of this research on all other criminal cases. As we do not have the total criminal database, we have to continue with this subset which is likely to consist of another statistical offender population.

In the second place, the difference between the means of the two processing time spans should be noted: the difference between the pre-charge phase and the charge-end phase was significant (T-test, 2 tailed, $p < 0{,}000$). This means that the processing time of the Courts deviates not just 'by change' from the prosecution-and-police time. If justice is delayed, it is significantly delayed by judges.
Further observations concern:

- the *total* processing time: the between-court differences range from 3,8 (Prokuplje) to 6,8 years (Sremska Mitrovica), a two years difference;
- the time span of the *pre-charge* ranges from 1,68 (Novi Pazar) to 3,2 year (Sombor), just more than one year and half;
- the processing time *from charge to finalisation* ranges from 1,61 year (Prokuplje) to 4,24 years (Sremska Mitrovica), a difference of 2,63 years.

Apart from Prokuplje, every time another district appears to be at the low or high end of the division. Where is the system? In statistical terms there is none. The correlation between the two processing time spans (pre-charge and post-charge) was r_{xy} .021 and not significant (Pearson, 2 tailed, $p = 0{,}16$) for the whole database of single cases. When we do the same for the 25 Court districts and compare the pre-charge and post-charge means, there is some trend (Spearman's rho as well as Pearson: .17 respectively .15) but statistically also not significant: police, prosecution and judges, they all can be delaying factors in all *at random* combinations. Finally we checked whether there is a correlation between the *number* of processed cases per Court region and the processing times: the turnover volume which tested against the total time, the pre-charge and the post-charge means. Here we found stronger, but statistically still not-significant trends:

- total time and N cases: Pearson .29 and Spearman's Rho .27
- pre-charge time and N cases: Pearson .22 and Spearman's rho .24
- post-charge time and N cases: Pearson .38 and Spearman's rho .31

Taken together, these findings do not appear to represent a coherent ordering of the lengths of the processing times, either in the pre-charge phase or the charge-to-end phase (the 'Court time') or between them. In fact, nothing correlates with anything. In the correlation between total turnover and processing times some trend seems to dawn, though: if cases can drag on for years, the more so in 'busy' districts even if statistically not-significant.

Once the charge has been received, it is of interest to learn (a) how long it takes for a (not)-guilty verdict, (b) for what crimes and (c) with what punishments. This implies that we shrink our database to the post-charge phase while using the full day-month-year measures. Changes in missing variables may cause some variation in totals.

First, we dichotomise the type of sentence into guilty and not-guilty. This results in the following average case processing time:

- Guilty: 2,48 years
- Not-guilty: 3,36 years

Apparently, reaching a guilty verdict takes less time than a non-guilty verdict (t-test $p < .000$). This is in line with the observation of the Statistical Office for all criminal cases. Also on this criterion variable no such correlation between the turnover of the Court regions and guilty/not-guilty verdicts was observed. (Spearman's rho, -0,034 for the 'guilty'; 0,317 for the not-guilty. sign. = 0,123; two tailed).

Differentiating according to type of offence reveals a considerable variation. In cases of fraud-within-service or taking bribes it takes respectively 5,5 and 3 years before being acquitted. For staff of Courts or Prosecution Offices this takes only 11 months. Table 8 (see next page) also shows that awaiting a prison sentence the 'waiting time' for the sentence increases with the length of the prison term imposed.

Justice delayed, justice denied? This question can only be raised, as there are no standards for a fair term within which a case must be processed. Also the European Convention of Human Rights or the European Court does not provide general standards. Notwithstanding that, the high average and extreme maximum processing times as well as the lack of consistency between most variables should raise concern. From the perspective of rule of law and equality of justice, these findings more than justify deeper and more detailed research.[3]

---

3 A more extensive analysis can be found in *Criminal corruption policy in Serbia* (Van Duyne and Stocco, 2012).

Table 8
Mean processing time and sentence modality

Prison term category	N total	Mean all	Mean parole	Mean not parole
up to 30 days	36	1,81	1,85	1,43
1- 2 months	63	2,15	2,26	1,77
2 – 3 months	415	2,43	2,45	2,35
3 – 6 months	1411	2,40	2,35	2,65
6 – 12 months	631	2,60	2,54	2,78
1 – 2 years	147	3,10	2,79	3,60
2 – 3 years	25	2,64	2,41	2,64
> 3 years	12	3,07	1,85	3,07
Total average		**2,48**	**2,26**	**2,75**
Total N	**2.740**		**2.167**	**573**

Summarising the outcomes of this statistical analysis of the input and output of the judicial black box, we find an overwhelming inconsistency: hardly anything correlates with anything. Whatever may go on inside the black box, in its outward functioning it behaves like a slow *random (black) box*. This applies to the general patterns as well as to the Prosecution and the Courts: the two random boxes interacting as two different entities without coherence and together producing this total randomness. One may indentify one consistency: above average and often extreme processing times, but also randomly distributed. This refutes the priority claim of the anti-corruption policy: 'high priority', yes, but: 'haste slowly'.

One of the aspects of this black box characteristic is the rate of responsiveness, as we have already sketched. The next section will address whether this pertained to this particular research or should be considered as a basic characteristic.

The non-responding random black box

We are not alone in our attempt to make the black box 'speak'. The agency which supported us throughout, the Anti-Corruption Council, has been knocking on the doors of its own government as well as the Republic Public Prosecution Office since its beginning. It reported more than two hundred cases of highly dubious financial dealings to the Government. The reports were summarily neglected, as was also observed by Transparency International (2011). Do the authorities share the "who cares?" attitude of the people? Sometimes the reverse occurs and the authorities do care, albeit in a foul way: it turns itself actively against those who blow the whistle, as illustrated by the following ACC report.

> Zoran K. submitted four times (2004, 2005 and 2006) criminal complaints to the II Municipal Prosecution office in Belgrade against officials for dereliction of duty and corruption related to building permits in his building, which is in private ownership. These criminal complaints were not processed. However as soon as Zoran K. had gone public in the news paper DANAS, the President of the Executive Board submitted a criminal charge for slander. Now the police reacted without delay and called Zoran immediately for an interview.
> Likewise, in the case of JUGOREMEDIJA, the prosecution did not process the criminal charge that the Association of Small Shareholders of that company has filed in 2004 against the director of the company for abuse of office and falsifying official documents. The conflict escalated and became violent and in the end the prosecution proceeded at short notice against the strike committee. The complaint of the Association of Small Shareholders were investigated only after two years.
> The President of the ACC added: "*This example is not the only one; the same situation can be found in many cases the Council is familiar with, from the complaints of citizens.*" The President can draw on her own experience: she saw her efforts against the machinations around the Port of Belgrade responded to by a criminal investigation against herself. (Letter to the Government 26 October 2009).

Compared with the long processing times discussed in the previous section, the authorities do show a capacity to act fast and firmly – against those who act against foul play.

How does the ACC work and what happens next? The ACC regularly receives complaints from concerned and/or aggrieved citizens and carries out an investigation by its own experts to determine the seriousness. From 2001 till 2009, 212 complaints were considered to be serious enough to be presented as criminal charges to the Republican Public Prosecution Office (RPPO). The complaints were classified as represented in Table 9.

Table 9

Complaints from the public to the ACC about law breaking

submitter	Field/subject of complaint	N
Unions/small shareholders	Privatisation and bankruptcy	46
Tenants ass. and individuals	Urbanisation and construction	55
n.a.	Courts: intentional stalling procedures	51
n.a.	Economy	23
n.a.	Other economic and public interests	37
Total		212

Source: ACC report 2009. n.a. = not available

Apart from informing the government (which does not respond), the ACC sends its reports to the RPPO. It is interesting to look at the persons and institutions who were accused of wrong-doing.

Table 10

Persons and institutions being accused.

2001-2007

Municipal management	16
Directors	28
Representatives	31
Judges and prosecutors	35
City planning management	10
other	25
Total	145

Sourse: Anti Corruption Council

Indeed, this represents the very elite.

How did the RPO respond? The special Anti-Corruption Department was most reluctant to inform the research team, but eventually it was told that of the 147 cases sent to the Prosecution Offices, only in 22 cases a response was received: 11 of which mentioned a *rejection* of the charge; the other reports were forwarded to the Prosecution District Office, to another agency for information gathering or fused with an existing file. There were no reports about the finalisation of these cases, unless rejected.

The underlying material is poor in terms of content and does not allow far reaching conclusions, though it certainly justifies a further investigation if only to exclude the not all too implausible hypothesis of an apparent *elite class bias*.

About the flow of communication between the ACC and the RPPO there is no jumping to conclusions: on the side of the RPPO it reflects anything but responsiveness or a sense of urgency, unless it can move against complainants.

The Anti Corruption Agency: monitoring and coordination in Potemkin Village

The situation described in the previous section may be puzzling against the background of a multitude of coordinating actors: the Minister of Justice, the specialised Anti-Corruption Department within the Republic Public Prosecution Office and above all that the Anti-Corruption Agency. Together they should be able to turn the *random box* into a more coherently operating apparatus. Is that the case?

Looking at the latest implementation of the Anti-corruption Strategy, the Anti-Corruption Agency (not to be confused with the Anti Corruption Council), we have to rely on their own task description and own account of its functioning as described in their annual report. In its annual report 2010 ACA, Annex I mentioned 21 tasks entrusted to it. From our perspective the most important ACA task concerns the "*monitoring and coordination of the work of state authorities*" in the fight against corruption. That is a potentially powerful role, because it implies also the monitoring and coordination of the organs of criminal law enforcement: the police, the Republican Prosecution and the Courts. As the ACA became operational in January 2010, it cannot be held accountable for the 'random black box' performance uncovered in our research. But how would it fulfil this function at present, assuming that the criminal justice institutions still operate at random? During the conduct of the research project no sign of monitoring or coordination could be observed, so we have to turn to ACA's annual report to find information we may have missed.

In its report (Annex I) the ACA accounts for an important monitoring fulfilment: a survey, the methodology of which was described in 28 lines. It sent out a questionnaire, which is not presented in an addendum, to an undisclosed number of 'implementing entities' (implementing the National Strategy), of which there might be 11.000. In total 78 entities replied (0,7%) and only after some prodding of ACA; not on their own initiative. This 'observation instrument' did not appear to be working very well: ACA complained about "*uneven usefulness and meagreness . . . . diversity and lack of relevant databases . . . most entities gave descriptive answers i.e. without providing valid data and sources to support their assessments. The reporting was thus reduced to self-evaluation.*" To make up for these deficiencies (which should have halted the whole undertaking), the ACA interviewed 'experts' without mentioning who and how many.

It should be remarked that ACA's task of assessing the implementation of the recommendations of the Strategy and the Action Plan was certainly not to be envied. Nevertheless, ACA's staff made a valiant attempt while being frank about obstacles. However, given these adverse circumstances, a responsible Board of ACA should never have pursued this undertaking.

Given the methodological qualities of this survey, what relevant observations were communicated about the fulfilment of the National Strategy and the related Action Plan activities against corruption? The police, prosecution and the judiciary are taken together which obfuscates the account as they operate independently.

As far as the *National Strategy* recommendations for the police, prosecution and justice sectors are concerned, 29% was listed as completely fulfilled, 13% was not fulfilled, 46% only partly, at which one can think of 'a glass half full or half empty'. Below we will give reasons for holding the glass half empty, or even less than that. The remaining 13% was qualified as "permanent tasks", though unspecified.

Of the *Action Plan Activities* 30% was fulfilled, 19% not fulfilled, 12% partly and of 21% there were no data. The remaining 18% were unspecified 'permanent tasks' (p. 37).

Implemented activities were only clarified with some examples, and these were far from reassuring. One example: the judicial reform counts as a fulfilled activity, which is only formally correct. Actually, this reform was criticised from virtually all sides: the Serbia 2010 Progress Report of the EU (p. 10) as well as GRECO expressed great concern, which makes one think of a fulfilled failure.

Another fulfilled strategy recommendation is the special Anti-corruption Department within the RPPO. We have encountered this non-responding body several times in the previous sections and could not but get the impression of a lasting non-functionality (see also Van Duyne *et al.*, 2010)

The same impression is conveyed by the ACA report when it describes the fulfilment of the recommendation of the *ex post fact checks*: the extra control in case of dismissal or other discontinuation of prosecution. Not only we, but also ACA could find no trace of this fulfilled recommendation except for the mentioning of its existence: "*The Agency, however, was unable to obtain data whether a system to review reports of such* [political] *pressures* [not to prosecute] *has been introduced.*" (p. 40) According to our estimate the Anti Corruption Department of the RPO would have handled or at least archived more than 2.200 cases between 2007 and 2009.[4]

[4] *Work of Public Prosecutions in combating crime and the protection of constitutionality and legality in 2009.* (29 page of electronic version of report. Section: *The Work of the Anti Corruption*

In view of this important information gathering role this department could not fail to have the relevant information. But it failed: the RPPO denied having any cases in their premises.[5]

Unless proven differently, we must apply here the principle of *esse est percipi*, or to be is to be perceived, implying that we are dealing here with a spook-fulfilment we cannot see. Or we are looking at the stage decor of a Potemkin village.

All together, I share the reservations of the EU in its 2010 report. The ACA methodology casts great doubt on the reliability of its mentioned achievements, in particular if they are described as "partly fulfilled". It would be more realistic to consider in these cases the glass less than 'half empty'. Nobody knows: the glass is stained and few care.

Europe: welcome to Potemkin Village?

The title of the concluding section is not a rhetorical question: it is intended as factual and needs to be investigated and answered from a fact based perspective, even if it is a historical metaphor. Because it is so sensitive, it is best to give the floor to the institution which is supposed to be the most knowledgeable: the ACA. If the ACA does not know, who else knows?

Though this study criticised ACA's survey and consequently the execution of its monitoring and coordination task, this does not imply that the agency fails to shed any light on the broader landscape which I also highlighted in the first sections. Connecting beginning and end we come full-circle.

Reading the account of the ACA of its ill-fated attempt at fact finding, one must allow for ACA's sensitive position. The ACA is independent, but to what extent can it play a hard game? Anyhow, from ACA's report a feeling of disappointment is clearly conveyed.

In the first place, the ACA reports "*direct and indirect challenges*", which is a euphemism for serious societal and political shortcomings, "*the most important being the low anti-corruption activism in the society as a whole.*" [. . .] "*lack of incentives to fight corruption at the state administration level.*" [. . .] "*the bureaucracy lacks the will to change.*" (p. 6) This is important for a realistic valuation of the many *partly* implemented

---

Department). A high representative of the RPO requested us not to disclose the actual figures, for which reason we rounded them.

5 In the previous research project (Van Duyne *et al.*, 2010), we basically asked for the same information. After first stating there were no files, we unexpectedly got a handful of them. Then we got a whole collection of unsorted, partly irrelevant reports "from the field" about 2007 and 2008, after which the flow of information dried up again.

recommendations: how many of these are carried out half-heartedly or mentioned only for social-desirability reasons?

In the second place, the ACA encountered the same indifference as we did on many occasions during this research project: "*Not one of them* [of the obliged 'entities'] *fulfilled the obligation to report* [. . .] *at their own initiative.*" Information is provided reluctantly, bit by bit which 'eats away one's time'.

In the third place, whether this is due to understaffing or a general disinterest, this finding has the methodological consequences mentioned before: the quality of the given information is of questionable quality: "*Most answers were descriptive and assessments were not corroborated by valid data and sources.*" What was the proportion of such low-grade responses to the whole and what has finally been used for ACA's assessment? This may compromise parts of the report, though one cannot know to what extent.

In the fourth place, the ACA observed that the Strategy failed to focus on two very important fields, namely the education and health systems, while additionally characterising its Action Plan in all regards as "*too broad and too vague*", whether it concerns recommended activities or the formulation of indicators. In our metaphor: in the absence of clear indicators the ACA had to assess the random box of the criminal law enforcement administration while being surrounded by fog.

Notwithstanding, above that fog we find a recorded achievement of 30% recommendations fulfilled. Is this real or is it just a house front in the main street of the village? But what does 'fulfilment' really mean against the background of a steady decline of registered and processed related corruption cases and above average processing times of which nobody appeared to be aware? What is behind the façade if there is nobody to give answers?

Judging the corruption policy in Serbia requires an unprejudiced realism: maybe the village has real houses too. But that must be investigated one by one. That would be an appropriate task for the Anti-Corruption Agency.

References

Anti Corruption Agency. *Annual report of the Anti Corruption Agency for 2010.* Belgrade, 2011

Anti Corruption Agency: Annex Report on the Implementation of the National Anticorruption Strategy and the Action Plan for the Implementation of the National Anticorruption Strategy, Belgrade, 2011

Anti Corruption Council, *Report on pressures on and control of the media.* Belgrade, 2011

Begović, B. and B. Mijatović, (eds.), *Corruption in Serbia; five years later.* Beograd, Center for Liberal Democratic Studies, 2007

Begović, B., B. Mijatović and D. Hiber, *Corruption in Judiciary.* Center for Liberal-democratic Studies, Belgrade, 2004

Begović, B., Corruption: concepts, types, causes and consequences. *Cadal*, 2005, 1 March, 2-7

della Porta, D., and A. Vannucci, The resources of corruption: some reflections from the Italian Case. *Crime, Law and Social Change*, 1997, 27, 231-254

Corruption in health sector in Serbia. Report by the Center of Antiwar Action. Belgrade, 2005

Commission staff working paper. Analytical report. *Commission Opinion on Serbia's application for membership of the European Union.* COM (2011) 668 Brussels, 2011

Datzer, D., A, Maljević, M. Budimlić and E. Muratbegivić, Police corruption through the eyes of the bribers: the ambivalence of the sinners. In: P.C. van Duyne, J. Harvey, A. Maljevic, K. von Lampe and M. Scheinost (eds.), *European crime-markets at cross-roads. Extended and extending criminal Europe.* Nijmegen, Wolf Legal Publishers, 2008

Duyne, P.C. van, Will 'Caligula go transparent?' Corruption in acts and attitude. *Forum on Crime and Society*, 2001, vol. 1, *no. 2*, 73-98

Duyne, P.C. van, E. Stocco, M. Milenović, M. Todorova, Searching for contours of anti-corruption policy in Serbia. In: P.C. van Duyne *et al.* (eds.), *Cross-border crime inroads on integrity in Europe.* Nijmegen, Wolf Legal Publishers, 2010

Duyne, P.C. van, E. Stocco and M. Milenović, Corruption in Serbia: unique or a shared Balkan disease? *Temida*, 2009, *no. 2*, 29-56

Duyne, P.C. van and S. Donati, In search of crime-money management in Serbia. In: P.C. van Duyne, J. Harvey, A. Maljevic, K. von Lampe and M. Scheinost (eds.), *European crime-markets at cross-roads. Extended and extending criminal Europe.* Nijmegen, Wolf Legal Publishers, 2008

Gelemerova, L., Fighting foreign bribery. The stick or the carrot. In: P.C. van Duyne *et al.* (eds.), *Cross-border crime inroads on integrity in Europe.* Nijmegen, Wolf Legal Publishers, 2010

Hulten, M. van, *Corruptie. Handel in macht en invloed.* Den Haag, SDU-uitgevers, 2011

Juda, T., *The Serbs: History, myth and the destruction of Yugoslavia.* New Haven, Yale University Press, 1997

LeBor, A., *Slobodan Milošević – A biography.* London, Bloomsbury

Logonder, A., Who is "Yugo" in "Yugo-mafia"? A comparative analysis of Serbian and Slovene offenders. In: P.C. van Duyne, J. Harvey, A. Maljevic, K. von Lampe and M. Scheinost (eds.), *European crime-markets at cross-roads. Extended and extending criminal Europe.* Nijmegen, Wolf Legal Publishers, 2008

Pesić, V., *State capture and widespread corruption in Serbia.* Centre for European Political Studies, 2007

Sadiku, L., *Serbia*, Civil society against corruption. School of Governance, 2010

Serbia corruption bench marking, TNS Gallup and UNDP. Belgrade, October 2010

The Republic Prosecutor's Office. Belgrade, 2010

Transparency Serbia, *The National Integrity System of the Republic Serbia.* Belgrade, 13 September 2011

Trivunović, M., V. Devine, H. Mathisen, *Corruption in Serbia 2007. Overview of problems and status of reforms.* Bergen, Chr. Michelsen Institute, 2007

UNODC, *Corruption in the Western Balkans. Bribery as experienced by the population.* Vienna, 2011

UNODC, *Technical Assessment Report*, Vienna, June 2010

Vuković, S., Corruption in Serbia, *South-East Review*, 2002, *no. 1*, 135-146

Joining the EU: is corruption a problem from the Turkish perspective?

Ugur Omurgonulsen[1]

Introduction

In many countries, like Turkey, with the encouragement and support of various regional and international organisations, recently serious attempts have been made by governments to equip their national bureaucracies against corruption with some legal instruments (*i.e.* a legal ethical infrastructure, including laws, international conventions, codes of ethics) and institutional mechanisms (*i.e.* an institutional ethical infrastructure, including anti-corruption agencies and ethics councils); and then to make them work in practice through various awareness, cultural change and training programmes (*i.e.* cultural ethical infrastructure). The implementation of formal anti-corruption arrangements, including strategies, laws, conventions, institutions and procedures are in fact heavily influenced by both the culture and traditions among public officials and citizens. Therefore, exploration of the effects of cultural traditions and public attitudes on facilitating or inhibiting corrupt or unethical conduct is a significant task (see Omurgonulsen and Doig, 2012a).

Accession of Turkey to the EU has brought a new focus on the issues of corruption which is both a long-standing and continuing issue. Given that such an issue has been concerning the EU both before and after the accession of other countries, the current Turkish context is usually assessed in terms of laws, institutions and strategies. The legal adoption (and possible perceptions of the imposition) of Western liberal democratic standards in this area is important to understand. However, those standards are applied to public officials and citizens while the raising of awareness and acceptance among them is another serious issue.

This chapter argues that Turkey is well-served in terms of laws, institutions and strategies but that there are issues relating to the continuing *strong state* tradition and socio-political and administrative culture in terms of implementation of laws and the effectiveness of institutions. Therefore, the question of changing current

1 Associate Professor, Hacettepe University, Department of Political Science and Public Administration omur@hacettepe.edu.tr

tradition and culture of both politicians and public officials and citizens are central to Turkey's progress in meeting European concerns and expectations (see Omurgonulsen and Doig, 2012b and Doig and Omurgonulsen, 2012). In this paper, the issue of tradition and culture in respect to corruption will be examined from the following perspective: "Is corruption regarded as a significant problem from the Turkish perspective?" (*i.e.* opinion and attitudes of politicians, public officials and citizens in relation to corruption). In this context, socio-political and administrative traditions and prevailing attitudes among both politicians, public officials and citizens about corruption will be reviewed and their effects on reforms in this area as a driver or inhibitor will be clarified. In other words, the issues about the implementation of legal instruments and the operation of institutional mechanisms will be explored in relation to the role of culture and traditions among both politicians, public officials and citizens in the development and sustainability of public ethics and anti-corruption understanding in Turkey. Finally, the perceived effect of corruption from the Turkish side, particularly in the accession process of Turkey to the EU (*i.e.* a real and primary or secondary problem), will be discussed.

The perspective from the external actors:

Legal and institutional infrastructure and its implementation[2]

The Turkish public administration has experienced serious and gradually expanded corruption scandals and ethical crises as an indicator of corruption in the political-bureaucratic system since the second half of the 1970s (see Aktan, 1992: Chp.2 and 1999; İTO, 1997; TÜGİAD, 1997). These scandals and crises are not only a part of global ethical crises in public administration, but also a result of a broad structural and operational degeneration of the Turkish political-bureaucratic system (Emre, Hazama and Mutlu, 2003: 438). The rapid social and economic transformation of society since the early 1980s has contributed to the erosion of social values in Turkey. Such eroded social values have also influenced all activities of the Turkish bureaucracy. Therefore widespread bureaucratic corruption and unethical conduct has become a feature of the political-administrative culture of Turkey (see Omurgonulsen and Oktem, 2005 and 2006). Different types of corruption and unethical conduct in various subsectors of the Turkish public sector (*e.g.* public

2 For an elaborated review of legal and institutional anti-corruption and ethical infrastructure of Turkey (i.e. the formal anti-corruption arrangements, including strategies, laws, institutions, procedures and adherence to international standards), see Omurgonulsen (2008, 2009, 2011) and Omurgonulsen and Doig (2012b).

bidding, planning at local level, law enforcement, health services, title/land registry, customs services) have come to be regarded as ordinary by the public.

However, a new wave of anti-corruption measures and related ethics has emerged in Turkey during the last decade. On the one hand, both recent struggles for accession to the EU and structural adjustment programmes demanded by international financial institutions (*i.e.* the IMF and the World Bank) in the face of the serious economic crisis of 2001 have been real turning points in Turkey's efforts to combat corruption and unethical conduct (*i.e.* external factors furthering recent anti-corruption initiatives). Turkish governments are required to adjust Turkish national anti-corruption legislation to that of the EU in the process of accession to the EU. Developing a European-style legal-institutional infrastructure in this field is seen as one of the significant criteria for enhancing the administrative capacity of the Turkish public administration. Also, Turkish governments are encouraged to take some institutional and legal-administrative measures for an anti-corruption policy in order to receive financial aid from international financial institutions such as the International Monetary Fund (IMF) and the World Bank in the process of economic recovery. On the other hand, the widespread political and bureaucratic corruption and unethical conduct are regarded by the Turkish public as the main cause of the economic and financial crisis of 2001 and this opinion (*i.e.* internal factor furthering recent anti-corruption initiatives) has facilitated the recent anti-corruption and ethics initiatives of various governments (see Omurgonulsen and Oktem, 2005 and 2007: 112-113). In this context, the legal and institutional aspects of the anti-corruption and ethical infrastructure of Turkey have been updated and fortified.

Consecutive Turkish Governments have made an effort to fill up the holes in the anti-corruption and ethical infrastructure of Turkey with mostly hard and also some soft ethics management measures during the 2000s. As for the fight against corruption, this is a significant development (see ABGS, 2008). As a matter of fact, Turkey's scores and rank in the Corruption Perception Index (CPI) by Transparency International have gradually improved in the second half of the 2000s (www.transparency.org). The relative improvement in public perception concerning corruption and unethical conduct in the late 2000s has also been detected by several empirical studies in various areas of public services (see CEPS, 2009 and TEPAV, 2009). There are also some early signs that the number of corruption cases have decreased (see KOM, 2010) as a consequence of the measures taken. However, this does not necessarily mean that corruption and unethical conduct has in fact been diminished in the Turkish public sector. Whether or not the attempts of the Turkish governments produce the intended results in practice, largely depends on the strength of political will of governments in this issue (Omurgonulsen, 2003: 40; Omurgonulsen, 2009: 39).

Although progress in combating corruption and unethical conduct are generally appreciated in various reports written recently by independent foreign reviewers who work on behalf of the European Commission (EC) and the OECD, corruption and unethical conduct still remains a problem also in the external observers' view as cited below. Major efforts are still required in both legislative and institutional aspects and their implementation, as is also emphasised by the EC's Progress Reports for Turkey since 2002 (European Commission, 2002, 2003, 2004, 2005, 2006, 2007, 2008, 2009, 2010 and 2011), UNDESA Report (2004), recent OECD-FATF (2010) and OECD-GRECO (2010a and 2010b) and Reports and by international associations (see www.business-anti-corruption.com). According to the EC as a major external actor for pushing anti-corruption initiatives[3], the independence, competence and effectiveness of various political, administrative and judicial bodies established to combat corruption remain a matter of concern. The consistency of policies and strategies and integration and co-ordination of various rules and institutions are weak. Turkey is invited to set up an 'independent anti-corruption body' and to adopt a 'general anti-corruption law'. An 'Ombudsman' is considered an important institution for combating corruption. Furthermore, the dialogue between the parliament, government, public administration and civil society should be strengthened and a general 'code of ethics' for all public officials both elected and appointed should be developed. In addition, more action should be taken to raise public awareness of corruption as a serious criminal offence. For the EC, continuous support at the highest political level for the fight against corruption would be welcome since this is explicitly or implicitly regarded as one the most important deficiencies in anti-corruption initiatives (*e.g.* European Commission, 2004: 146; and 2005: 13, 125, 128-129). This comment is repeated in various sections of the following Progress Reports of the European Commission for Turkey (see European Commission, 2006, 2007, 2008 and 2009). The expectation of EC from the Turkish authorities in respect to the accession process is not only the adjustment of political, economic and administrative regulations, but also the proper and effective implementation of those regulations in practice (see *Hürriyet*, a Turkish daily, 18 October 2003). This expectation is also valid for combating corruption and unethical conduct.

As examples of recent progress in a few areas should be mentioned: the application of the right to information, the preparation of a general strategy for combating corruption and the assignment of the *Prime Ministry Inspection Board*

---

3 (EC issues detailed progress report every year for Turkey because of its candidacy for full-membership of EU.

(PMIB) as a co-ordination unit in combating corruption, and ethical inquires conducted by the Council of Ethics for the Public Service (CEPS) in accordance with the principles of ethical behaviour. Despite these achievements in some areas problems continue according to the EU and GRECO. These concern among others financing political parties and their election campaigns, the political immunity of parliamentarians and the scope of authority and the administrative, technical and financial capacities of the CEPS (see European Commission, 2006, 2007, 2008 and 2009; and GRECO, 2010c). Allegations of corruption and unethical conduct against national and local politicians of different political affiliations and bureaucrats have not been significantly reduced. Whether or not the attempts of the current government do actually produce their intended results in the near future will depend on the strength of the government's commitment (Omurgonulsen, 2009: 39-40). Thus, not only legal-institutional measures but also mentality changes as a fundamental element of integrity-based management are essential in combating corruption and unethical conduct (Omurgonulsen and Alemdar, 2011: 14). Effective implementation of anti-corruption laws and strategies also contribute to the changing mentality and then to the behaviour of public officials, so that it promotes and protects public ethics and reduces opportunities for corrupt practices in the long-run.

The perspective from the internal actors:
The effects of culture and tradition

In spite of deficiencies in the anti-corruption infrastructure and its operation, which were pointed out above by both regional and international organisations and Turkish authors, Turkey has a made some progress in terms of rectifying ethical, audit, inspection and anti-corruption framework (Omurgonulsen and Doig, 2012b: 16, 17) in the process of accession to the EU (Omurgonulsen and Oktem, 2005 and 2007: Chp.5). If so, the question can be raised why the Turkish public administration has still infected with corruption?. As Omurgonulsen and Doig asked, "*[W]hy this environment does not, certainly to the EU, GRECO and other external agencies, appear to be addressing corruption to their satisfaction – why does there appear to be a gap between the formal position and the reality?*" (2012b: 16).

These questions can partly be answered through an external reason (*i.e.* the high expectations of many EU's and GRECO's reviews and expectations from Turkey) (see Omurgonulsen and Doig, 2012b: 16). They can also be answered through several internal reasons (*i.e.* the limited enforcement of legislation and a continuing weakness of existing institutions to take responsibility for legislative implementation;

and the continuing lack of connectedness between institutions) (see Omurgonulsen and Doig, 2012b: 16-21). One of the internal reasons for this gap is particularly related to our topic in this paper: "*culture and tradition*" (see Omurgonulsen and Oktem, 2006; and Omurgonulsen and Doig, 2012b: 16-21). "*Part of the reason that [legal and institutional means] do not appear to have significantly impacted on corruption may be countervailing influences of enduring cultural traditions within the public sector and among citizens.*"(Doig and Omurgonulsen, 2012: 1)

The Turkish bureaucratic culture relevant to corruption[4]

Although Turkish governments have launched numerous reform initiatives (*i.e.* new legal-administrative regulations and institutional reorganisations) in order to cope with structural and operational dysfunctions in the public sector since the World War II, these attempts could not produce a successful result because of their neglect of the cultural dimension of the problems. Combating corruption and other manifestations of unethical conduct is one of those areas of cultural neglect. Since within the public service ethics in general and corruption in particular concern the values and attitudes of public servants, they should be analysed not only in a legal-administrative context but also within a cultural context (see Emre, Hazama and Mutlu, 2003). Most of the authors on the issue of public service ethics and corruption advise considering cultural relativity when searching for applicable prescriptions for combating corruption and unethical conducts, particularly in non-Western settings (for example, see Kernaghan and Dwivedi, 1983; Khassawneh, 1989; Cooper, 1990; and Emre, Hazama and Mutlu, 2003). Therefore, in an examination of value change in the Turkish public administration, analysing some features of the Turkish bureaucratic culture is helpful to understand the feasibility of proposed solutions to those problems (Emre, 1993; Emre, Hazama and Mutlu, 2003: 438).

Public bureaucrats, depending on the bureaucratic tradition of the country concerned, may adopt various personal missions, which are not always in accordance with the general interest of the public, given the lack of well-defined ethical codes for the public service. Either they become an elite group isolated from the public and identify their personal interests with the public interest in accordance with their worldview (*i.e.* modernising mission) or they become an entrepreneurial group and clearly put their personal or group interests before the public interest (*i.e.* enterprising mission) (see Stever, 1988: 88).

---

4 For an elaborated review of Turkish bureaucratic culture relevant to public service ethics, see Omurgonulsen and Oktem (2009: 142-146).

With the transition to multi-party politics in Turkey after World War II, the 'bureaucratic ruling tradition' which was inherited from the Ottoman Empire and shared with the founders of the Republic, began to crumble. However, the new political elite, which was the representative of periphery rather than a central elite, could not substitute it with democratic public values (see Heper, 1985). As Emre and his colleagues point out, political turmoil and rapid socio-economic transsformation in the Turkish society after 1950 led to the corrosion of public service values, particularly ethical values, in the bureaucracy on the one hand, and the opening of the door for elements of traditional social values to enter into the bureaucracy on the other. This meant the stabilisation of an 'allaturca' administration (*i.e.* a type of administration with heterogeneous cultural values) (2003: 440). Although Turkey has been suffering from big, interventionist, and cumbersome government (see Aktan, 1995), launching some neo-liberal economic and managerial strategies since the early 1980s, without questioning enough the essence of the policy of withdrawal of government, resulted in further corruption through damaging public service ethics rather than implanting new professional public service values such as efficiency and effectiveness to the public service.

Corruption in the *economic* sphere has increased rapidly since the early 1980s in paralel with widespread corruption in other spheres of the Turkish society. In the triangle of corrupt politicians, corrupt bureaucrats and corrupt businessmen many legal and ethical rules and standards were ignored in the name of sorting out the economic and domestic security problems of the country (Emre, Hazama and Mutlu, 2003: 440-442). In brief, political and economic instabilities have accelerated social disintegration and caused erosion in the value system of the Turkish society. Political and administrative corruption has increased with the degeneration of the judicial system and bureaucratic control mechanisms. This is obviously not an optimistic picture of Turkey particularly in relation to corruption.

Many questions might come to mind about the socio-political and cultural factors hindering the enforcement of legal-administrative regulations and mechanisms for combating corruption. A few research projects on the cultural base of the values in the Turkish bureaucracy (see Emre, 1993; and Ozen, 1996) have provided us an opportunity to make an assessment on this issue. The results of these researches show that the significant element of Turkish bureaucratic culture is 'collectivism, solidarity and harmony' in 'community' or 'groups'. The literature on the Turkish culture also supports this finding (see Ergun, 1991; and Guvenc, 1993). In contrast to 'individualistic' culture, the special characteristics of 'collectivist' culture are: loyalty to his/her own community, solidarity and harmony with the other members of the community, and less individual accountability. In a collectivist culture, a community (*i.e.* family in the broader sense, friendship groups, membership of a profession or a government department) is responsible for taking care of individuals and community leaders have an extraordinary prestige in the communities concerned (see Emre, 1993: 136-137). Like ordinary Turkish people, the Turkish bureaucrats themselves feel secure only in a community. They try to develop good interpersonal relations in the community (*i.e.* the public bureaucracy) in order to survive in the political and bureaucratic arena. The guardianship for group interests is also the easiest way to get beneficial posts in the bureaucracy. This also means the development of negative attitudes against other communities or groups. The forming of a community or a group as a way of getting extra benefits makes impartiality impossible in practice in the Turkish bureaucracy. That is why, independent or impartial ethics committees might not properly function in Turkey. The extraordinary prestige of political and bureaucratic elite and their poor personal accountability also facilitate the expansion of corruptive activities in the public sector (Emre, Hazama and Mutlu, 2003: 450-451).

The '*unquestionable state*' is another strong cultural value, which is a negative aspect of the bureaucratic ruling tradition in Turkey by itself. This is the main obstacle to transparency and accountability of the government (see Emre, Hazama and Mutlu, 2003: 451-452; and Gormez et al., 2009: 283). "Protecting the interests of the State" is one of the official duties of civil servants. Every kind of activities which are done in the name of protecting the interests of the State, even if it is a crime or offence, might be seen, not legally but morally right. Also, some other cultural values encourage the concealment of transgressions committed in the name of the State. A Turkish proverb clearly defines the collectivist mentality of the Turkish people on this manner: "a broken arm should remain inside the sleeve". It means "you should not wash your dirty linen in public" (Emre, Hazama and Mutlu, 2003: 451-452). As Omurgonulsen and Doig note (2012: 22), this dimension also emerges in a number of academic papers on the influence of the state over perceptions of the value and intentions of external influences (Johnson, 2008), the tensions over the EU accession process (Patterson, 2008; and Acar and Emek, 2008), and the levels (or absence of) pluralist and democratic development (Onen, 2008).

In spite of the existence of a value such as 'the unquestionable state', it should be emphasised that ordinary people who long occupied a place at the periphery of the society and were isolated from the government of the country by the state elite do not show any respect, in practice, to the protection of public money and property against any kind of corruption. A general expression, "the property of the State belongs to everybody but nobody" might explain this attitude. Furthermore, ordinary people do not refrain from capturing some parts of it in illegal ways since they regard that public resources were controlled by the Sultans or the State elite for a long time in the history and now it is their time to use them. As a matter of fact, another Turkish proverb perfectly explains this manner: "the property of the State is plentiful and the one who does not possess it is obstinate". It is obvious that nothing is easier than spending uncontrolled public funds. This distorted understanding is expected to contribute to the serious deterioration of democratic and ethical public service values such as rule of law and protection of public funds and property.

In brief, a number of interconnected trends within the public sector, including political penetration of the administrative and judicial arenas, economic liberalisation favouring economic elites close to government and a collectivist and networked culture in the public sector, all serve to reinforce rather than evolve the enduring concept of 'the unquestionable state' (Omurgonulsen and Oktem, 2006 and 2009; Omurgonulsen and Doig, 2012b). The 'centralist nature of public administration', which has been inherited from the Ottoman period and developed and enhanced by Republican administrations in both single and multi-party regimes during the consolidation of the nation state, has contributed to the concept of 'the unquestionable state' (UNDESA, 2004: 17). Evidence suggests the pervasive potential for the political penetration and dominance, and which led to the possibility that "*Turkey, through an act of democracy ended up with an ineffective, politicised, and de-institutionalised bureaucracy, which started to experience erosion of its professional norms and values*" (Kalaycıoğlu, 2003: 15).

Turkey's accession process to the EU has also accelerated the administrative reform efforts in Turkey. International actors like IMF, World Bank and OECD have also had great effects in the reformation process. Due to this development, the words like globalisation, liberalisation, democratisation, good governance, and market-type and managerial solutions have entered more into the language of the Turkish public administration when compared to the past. In this context, new public service values have emerged to decrease the influence of traditional public service values (Oktem, Omurgonulsen and Yıldız, 2007).

Cultural strategies as a means of combating corruption

Ethical perception does not develop free from the social culture. For this reason in public administration ethical principles should be taken as cultural values. Every individual in the society, especially politicians and public officials should be aware of which purpose they serve in fulfilling their task. Every individual in his or her decisions on behalf of the public and should pose the question whether performing a specific task in the own interest or for the public interest. In order to prevent corruption and unethical conduct in public administration, the cultural infrastructure should be institutionalised and based on the principles of justice, equality, transparency and accountability (Gormez et al., 2009: 318).

The most important aspect of the fight against corruption is not only enacting anti-corruption legislation, but also the enforcement of legal provisions and the continuous monitoring of activities of all public officials in the light of this legislation. In spite of improvements which were recently made in the legal and institutional infrastructure, most of the legal-administrative institutions and mechanisms are not operated properly in practice. In addition to the fragmented ethical structure (*i.e.* lack of connectedness between legal rules and control institutions), defective enforcement is one of the most serious obstacles to establishing an ethical administration in Turkey, which mainly stems from 'cultural factors' (see Omurgonulsen and Oktem, 2005, 2006, 2009). Therefore, it can be argued that cultural factors are other important elements for an ethical administration. Combating corruption and unethical conduct has to be supported with "cultural strategies" (*i.e.* soft-measures) as well as legal-administrative strategies (*i.e.* hard-measures) (see, Omurgonulsen and Oktem, 2005 and 2006; Omurgonulsen, 2008: 28-29). So, the consolidation of ethical culture is a significant task in the public sector (see Eryılmaz, 2008). Public service ethics is not only concerned with the conscience of individual public servants or with legal-institutional measures. The prevention of unethical conduct among public servants must be maintained not only through punishing those who have committed corrupt actions, but through understanding the 'cultural dimension of ethical administration'. The most important thing is to establish an administrative climate based on ethical values in public administration; and even to create an understanding based on ethics in society as a consequence of legal-institutional measures and cultural-behavioural efforts.

Recent empirical evidence:
Is corruption a problem for Turkish citizens and public officials?

Fact based evidence of corruption and prevailing attitudes among both citizens and public officials is scarce in Turkey. There is no central database in the public administration. There is a limited amount of media and public opinion survey material on corruption and unethical conduct: much of the latter is nearly a decade old. There are a number of surveys conducted by international organisations but their reliability and validity are questionable (see Omurgonulsen and Doig, 2012a: 5).

With the TYEC Project[5], which aimed to contribute to the prevention of corruption in Turkey in accordance with European and other international standards, a number of research studies[6] were commissioned to develop a greater understanding of various issues concerning the development of public ethics in Turkey, the drivers/inhibitors of reform, the institutions involved and the role of the media and civil society in combating corruption and unethical conduct. With those research studies undertaken in 2008 and 2009, the available empirical data have increased to some extent. They essentially explored what is or is not seen as corruption, what are attitudes to corruption, relations between the public and public officials to understand how far prevailing cultures and attitudes would be suitable to the continuing reform process.

So, all the research studies themselves drew attention to the question of culture, reflecting a continuing general acceptance in society that the standards and conduct expected of citizens or among public officials that reflects the Western democratic model are not yet in place. The practice of paying bribes for public services (usually to expedite the process or ensure the right result) continued to be seen as acceptable in a culture where the relationship is primarily directly between the citizen and the public official dealing with his or her business. More specific standards in the the Code of Ethics prepared and executed by the CEPS (*e.g.* standards about gift-taking) were still non-contextualised or internalised in the minds of public officials (Omurgonulsen and Doig, 2012b: 23). As Genckaya points out, some concepts in the Code, particularly 'avoiding conflict of interest' and 'accountability' are new to the Turkish administrative culture as well as to the Turkish society and they are in the process of taking their forms. Public officials do not refer them as a priority for the fulfillment of their duties (2009. 375).

Although public officials and citizens generally condemn corruption as being morally wrong, some traditional forms of corruption such as accepting gifts are still tolerated. At the same time, citizens also have a weak sense of public interest, evincing a dual morality toward what is generally acceptable or not acceptable, and what is acceptable or not acceptable in terms of their own direct interests. So, pragmatic morality rather than public ethics is the basis of the relationship between citizens and public officials. As a result, sometimes corrupt or, at least, unethical behaviour simply reflects custom and practice in certain public organisations such as

5 TYEC (Ethics for the Prevention of Corruption in Turkey) Project, which was mainly funded by the European Commission and implemented by the Council of Europe in co-operation with the Turkish Council of Ethics for the Public Service in 2008 and 2009. See Doig (2009).

6 A recent special issue of Turkish Studies (*Corruption, Public Ethics and Changing Cultures*, 13/1, March 2012), which was edited by U. Omurgonulsen and A. Doig, was mainly developed from these research studies.

title offices, urban and physical planning offices of municiplaities and customs (see Doig and Omurgonulsen, 2012: 105).

While there is some evidence that both public officials and the public understand the distinction between gift-giving and bribery, the continuing and accepted use of payments and middlemen, as well as the belief that social status, political influence and connections could continue to influence public decisions or actions all this generally contributes to poor or negative images of the public sector among the citizens. In particular, the perceived power of the public officials, and slowness, opacity and complexity of decision-making and other procedures, as allowing public officials to control and misuse their authority, will dilute or even negate the reform process. The articles in the recent special issue of an international journal, Turkish Studies (13/1, March 2012), based on these studies, explore why this is so, and what are the missing components from the current anti-corruption reform process of which both the government, and external review mechanisms, need to take cognisance of in order to work toward a more effective and sustainable implementation (and, with it, toward accession of the EU) (Omurgonulsen and Doig, 2012b: 23).

As Doig and Omurgonulsen emphasised, such a cultural perspective is missing from the various EU and GRECO reviews.(This is not out of context; on the contrary, it shows the major difference between the perspectives of external and internal actors.) There is no doubt that corruption in Turkey has a continuing and pervasive presence, with less evidence that it is diminishing and more evidence that corruption continues to be embedded in the political and administrative structures which have heavily been affected by cultural norms (2012: 101, 107).

It is also clear that Turkey has substantial legal and institutional means to address corruption. Part of the reason that they do not appear to have significantly impacted on corruption may be, as noted above, the countervailing influences of enduring cultural traditions within the public sector and among citizens. These will in turn impact on the nature of the developmental trajectory and the question of the nature of the reform process. In other words, the effectiveness of the reform process and the consolidation of substantive democracy, rather than a veneer over continuing practices, may now require significantly more attention to ethics and culture as two dimensions necessary to address corruption in the Turkish context and establish a more ethical environment. Failure to spread and embed ethical awareness could lead to a longer-term loss of trust in the state and will encourage not only the continuation of existing bad practices but creates a context where new types of misuse can easily become established (Doig and Omurgonulsen, 2012: 107).

Conclusion

In this chapter, we have raised the question how far the cultural dimension (*i.e.* socio-political culture and traditions) shapes the reform process. Of the core components to the reform process, the continuing traditions within the political and administrative spheres shape the implementation and effectiveness of reform initiatives (Omurgonulsen and Doig, 2012b: 22). Thus, mentality changes through awareness and training programmes in public ethics for both citizens and public officials (*i.e.* soft measures of integrity-based ethics management as a complementary to hard mesures of compliance-based ethics management) is necessary to combat corruption and unethical conduct (Doig and Omurgonulsen, 2012: 107) though this evolves only very slowly.

Turkish public opinion has recently become more aware of the need of combating corruption and unethical conduct, partly with the positive effects of the contributions of mass media, civil society institutions and the academic circle as well as that of public organisations such as the CEPS and PECs. In particular, academic interest in and support for the creation of ethical awareness and the consolidation of ethical culture in both society and the public sector has increased gradually in Turkey, thanks to the activities of the CEPS (see Sakarya Üniversitesi İİBF, 2005; CEPS, 2009; and TODAİE, 2009). However, this does not mean that there is substantive evidence that corruption and unethical conduct is substantially diminishing. On the contrary, they continue to be embedded in the political and administrative structures (Doig and Omurgonulsen, 2012: 107).

One of the consequence of economic development and democratisation in Turkey in the past decades is to create potential breaks between payments as part of continuing particularistic relationships as well as to create groups who not only resist such traditions but also expect 'the unquestionable state' to change. This process has also exacerbated the conflicts or contrasts between the continuing and emerging perceptions and expectations. However, it should be noted that also developed liberal democracies continue to provide evidence of traditional types of corruption and also face new types of corruption (*e.g.* from party funding to professional lobbying as related to the interface between the State and the private sector) as well as new controversies that emerged as a result of the applications of new public management practices in recent decades. In other words, economic development and democratisation do not automatically produce a clean environment (see Doig and Omurgonulsen, 2012: 102, 103). "*Within such as context, therefore, understanding the nature and potentially enduring strength of cultural dimension of change, and how citizens and public officials view conduct and expectations, may have a significant impact on the future of Turkish public administration*" (see Doig and Omurgonulsen, 2012: 103).

Corruption was on the agenda, even with repugnance, of politicians from governing parties in the first half of the 2000s due to the accession process of Turkey to the EU. With the slow down of accession process since the mid of 2000s due to recent serious economic-financial crisis of EU countries as well as the EU's hidden or open negative attitudes against the Turkey's full-membership and the current Turkish government's hesitated approach to the EU membership, corruption is no longer considered as significant problem and subsequently a priority for the government. Corruption is, nowadays, only expressed in the discourse of the main opposition party leader. In fact, corruption is regarded as a serious disease by real tax payers (urbanised and educated upper middle classes). For lower classes which form the majority of voters and traditionally represent the periphery of the social and political system, corruption has never been regarded as serious problem for the society and even anti-corruption and/or public ethics policies are seen as an obstacle for populist policies of governments. Therefore, traditions, interwoven with economic and political interests of masses as well politicians, have very deep cultural effects on corruption and unethical conduct.

References

ABGS, *2008 National Programme of Turkey for the Adoption of the EU Acquis*. Ankara, The Prime Ministry, Secretariat General for EU Affairs, (http://www.abgs.gov.tr), 2008.

Acar, M. and U. Emek, Building a clean government in Turkey: Pillars, perils, and prospects. *Crime, Law and Social Change*, 2008, 49(3).

Aktan, C.C., *Politik yozlaşma ve kleptokrasi: 1980-1990 Türkiye Deneyimi*. Ankara, Yeni Türkiye, 1992.

Aktan, C.C., *21.Yüzyıl İçin Yeni Bir Devlet Modeline Doğru: Optimal Devlet*. İstanbul, TÜSİAD, 1995.

Aktan, C.C., *Kirli Devletten Temiz Devlete*. Ankara, Yeni Türkiye, 1999.

CEPS, *Academic researches on public ethics*. Two Volumes, Ankara, CEPS, and Council of Europe and European Union, 2009

Cooper, T. L. (ed.), *The responsible administrator*. San Fransisco: Jossey-Bass, 1990.

Doig, A., *Review of sanctions for the Council of Ethics for Public Service*, Long-Term Advisor's study report for Ethics for the Prevention of Corruption in Turkey (TYEC) Coe Project No. Ec/1062, September 2008, Ankara, 2008

Doig, A., *Corruption report: Findings, analysis and recommendations.* Ethics for the Prevention of Corruption in Turkey (TYEC), Ankara, Council of Europe and European Union and Council of Ethics for the Public Service, 2009.

Doig, A., and U. Omurgonulsen, Conclusion: Development, ethics and culture, *Turkish Studies*, 2012, 13(1), 101-108.

Emre, C., *Toplumsal Kültürel Etmenler Açısından Türk Kamu Yönetimi Üzerine Bir İnceleme.* (unpublished PhD Thesis). Ankara: Ankara Üniversitesi, Sosyal Bilimler Enstitüsü, 1993).

Emre, C., Y. Hazama, and S. Mutlu, Cultural values, morality and public administration in Turkey. In: C. Emre, *Yönetim bilimi yazıları*, İmaj, Ankara, 2003. (The original edition of this article was published in: Y. Hazama, Emerging changes in Turkish politics and society, IDE, Tokyo).

Ergun, D., *Türk Bireyi Kuramına Giriş*, İstanbul, Gerçek, 1991.

Eryılmaz, B., Etik kültürü yerleştirmek", *Türk İdare Dergisi*, 2008, nr. 459, 1-12

European Commission, *2002 Regular report on Turkey's progress towards accession.* Brussels, Commission of the European Communities, 2002, (http://www.abgs.gov.tr).

European Commission, *2003 Regular Report on Turkey's Progress Towards Accession.* Brussels, Commission of the European Communities, 2003, (http://www.abgs.gov.tr).

European Commission, *2004 Regular Report on Turkey's Progress Towards Accession.* Brussels, Commission of the European Communities, 2004, (http://www.abgs.gov.tr).

European Commission, *Turkey 2005 progress report.* Brussels, Commission of the European Communities, 2005 (http://www.abgs.gov.tr).

European Commission, *Commission staff working document, Turkey 2006, progress report.* Brussels, Commission of the European Communities, 2006 (http://www.abgs.gov.tr).

European Commission, *Commission staff working document, Turkey 2007 progress report, accompanying the Communication from the Commission to the European Parliament and the Council enlargement strategy and main challenges 2007-2008.* Brussels, Commission of the European Communities, 2007, (http://www.abgs.gov.tr)

European Commission, *Commission staff working document. Turkey 2008 progress report, accompanying the Communication from the Commission to the European*

Parliament and the Council enlargement strategy and main challenges 2008-2009. Brussels, Commission of the European Communities, 2008, (http://www.abgs.gov.tr).

European Commission, *Commission staff working document, Turkey 2009 progress report, accompanying the Communication from the Commission to the European Parliament and the Council enlargement strategy and main challenges 2009-2010.* Brussels, Commission of the European Communities, 2009, (http://www.abgs.gov.tr).

European Commission, *Commission staff working document, Turkey 2010 progress report, accompanying the Communication from the Commission to the European Parliament and the Council enlargement strategy and main challenges 2010-2011.* Brussels, Commission of the European Communities, 2010, (http://www.abgs.gov.tr).

European Commission, *Commission staff working document, Turkey 2011 progress report, accompanying the Communication from the Commission to the European Parliament and the Council Enlargement strategy and main challenges 2011-2012.* Brussels, Commission of the European Communities, 2011, (http://www.abgs.gov.tr).

Genckaya, O. F., Conflict of interest, In: *Academic researches on public ethics.* Vol. I, Council of Ethics for the Public Service; Council of Europe; European Union, Ankara, 2009.

Gormez, K. *et al.*, Ethics, culture and society, In: *Academic researches on public ethics,* Vol. II, Council of Ethics for the Public Service; Council of Europ; European Union, Ankara, 2009

Güvenç, B., *Türk Kimliği.* Ankara, Kültür Bakanlığı, 1993.

Heper, M., *The state tradition in Turkey.* Walkington, Eothen Press, 1985.

İTO, *Araştırma.* İstanbul, İTO, 1997

Johnson, R., "Driving towards the EU using its rear-view mirror: Turkey's 'foreigner' policy". *Turkish Policy Quarterly*, 2008, 7(1), 33-43

Kalaycıoğlu, E., The political criteria: Fair or strict conditionality? In: *Conference on Turkey, the EU and the 2004 milestone: Is this time for real?*", St. Antony's College, University of Oxford, Oxford, 2003

Kernaghan, K. and O.P. Dwivedi, Public service ethics: Issues and ideas, In K. Kernaghan and O.P. Dwivedi, *Ethics in the public service: Comparative perspective,* IIAS, Brussels, 1983

Khassawneh, A. S., A sociocultural approach to the study of bureaucratic corruption in the developing countries, *METU Studies in Development*, 1989, 16(3-4), 127-146

KOM, *2010 Yılı Raporu*. Ankara, Emniyet Genel Müdürlüğü Kaçakçılık ve Organize Suçlarla Mücadele (KOM) Daire Başkanlığı, 2010

OECD-FATF, *Improving global AML/CFT compliance: On-going process*. Paris, OECD-FATF, 2010.

OECD-GRECO, *Third evaluation round: Evaluation report on Turkey: Theme I*. Strasbourg, Council of Europe, 2010a

OECD-GRECO, *Third evaluation round: Evaluation report on Turkey: Theme II*. Strasbourg, Council of Europe, 2010b.

OECD-GRECO, *Report of 47th plenary meeting of Greco (7-11 June 2010)*. Strasbourg, OECD-GRECO, 2010c.

Oktem, M. K., U. Omurgonulsen, and H.H. Yıldız, Public service values in Turkey. 27th *International Congress of Administrative Science*, Panel on Virtues and Values, 9-14 July 2007, Abu Dhabi-UAE

Omurgonulsen, U., Public service ethics: The feasibility of an ethical administration in Turkey. *1st International Business and Professional Ethics Congress of Turkey*, September 17-19, 2003, Ankara-Turkey, Hacettepe University, Research Centre for Business and Professional Ethics

Omurgonulsen, U., Legal and institutional infrastructure of ethical administration in Turkey: Adequate or not? *International Conference on Social Sciences,* 21-22 August 2008, İzmir-Turkey, Social Sciences Research Society (SOSRES)

Omurgonulsen, U., *System studies report: An evaluation of the effectiveness of anti-Corruption measures implemented in recent years, including the Code of Ethics, the Public Information Act, Criminal Law Measures and Disciplinary Provisions*. Ethics for the Prevention of Corruption in Turkey (TYEC). Ankara, Council of Europe; European Union; Council of Ethics for the Public Service, 2009

Omurgonulsen, U., and S. Alemdar, *Technical assistance for the needs assessment for the Public Ethics Commissions*. Ankara, CFCU;Particip; Council of Ethics for the Public Service, 2011

Omurgonulsen, U., and A. Doig, Editors' note. *Turkish studies*, 2012a, 13(1), 5-6.

Omurgonulsen, U., and A. Doig, Why the gap? Turkey, EU accession, corruption and culture., *Turkish Studies*, 2012b, 13(1), 7-25

Omurgonulsen, U., and M. Kemal Oktem, The Feasibility of an ethical administration in Turkey: Legal-institutional and cultural pillars of public service ethics. *The Conference on Ethics and Integrity of Governance: The First Transatlantic Dialog*, 2-5 June 2005, Leuven-Belgium, Catholic University of Leuven-Public Management Institute, ASPA, IIAS-EGPA

Omurgonulsen, U., and M. Kemal Oktem, Towards an understanding of the cultural pillars of ethical administration in Turkey: A qualitative research endeavour. *EGPA Annual Conference: Public Managers under Pressure between Politics, Professionalism and Civil Society*, 6-9 September 2006, Milan-Italy, Bocconi University

Omurgonulsen, U., and M. Kemal Oktem. *Avrupa Birliği'ne Üyelik Sürecinde Türk Kamu Yönetimi*. Ankara, İmaj, 2007

Omurgonulsen, U., and M. Kemal Oktem, Is there any change in the public service values of different generations of public Administrators? The case of Turkish governors and district governors. *Special Issue: Professional Ethics in Business and Socil Life-The EBEN 21st Annual Conference in Antalya, Journal of Business Ethics*, 2009, 88(1), 137-156.

Omurgonulsen, M., and U. Omurgonulsen, Critical thinking about creative accounting in the face of a recent scandal in the Turkish banking sector. *Critical Perspectives on Accounting, Special Issue, Accounting for the Global and the Local: The Case of Turkey*, 2009, 20(5), 651-673

Onen, H., The long path ahead in Turkey's integration with the world", *Turkish Policy Quarterly*, 2008, 7(1), 65-75.

Ozen, S., *Bürokratik Kültür 1: Yönetsel Değerlerin Toplumsal Temelleri*.Ankara, TODAİE, 1996

Patterson, R., Rising nationalism and the EU accession process", *Turkish Policy Quarterly*, 2008, 7(1), 131-138

Sakarya Üniversitesi-İİBF, *2. Siyasette ve Yönetimde Etik Sempozyumu Bildiriler Kitabı*. Sakarya, Sakarya Üniversitesi İİBF, 2005

Stever, J., *The end of public Administration: Problems of the profession in the post progressive era*. New York, Transnational Pub. Inc., 1988

TEPAV, *Hanehalkı Gözünden Kamu Hizmetleri ve Yolsuzluk*. (Eds. F. Adaman, A. Çarkoğlu, B. Şenatalar, Ankara, TEPAV, 2009

TODAİE , *Kamu Etiği Sempozyumu Bildirileri*. 2 Cilt. Ankara, TODAİE, 2009

TÜGİAD, *2000'li Yıllara Doğru Türkiye'nin Önde Gelen Sorunlarına Yaklaşımlar: Kamu Yönetiminde Yozlaşma ve Rüşvet*. Ankara, TÜGİAD, 1997

UNDESA, *Assessment of public administration in Turkey*. New York, UNDESA/UNPAN (Division for Public Administration and Development Management, UN Department of Economic and Social Affairs), 2004

It depends where you stand: Corruption, Turkey and EU accession

Alan Doig and Brendan Quirke[1]

> *Turkey has always given priority to the fight against corruption. Turkey is strongly committed to the fight against corruption and has taken all legislative and operational measures in order to stamp out domestic corruption and to contribute to the international efforts to tackle the problem, as it has increasingly assumed a transnational character.*
> *[Source: Turkish Ministry of Foreign Affairs, 2008]*

> *AKP swept to power by promising to root out corruption. However, in increasing numbers AKPers from ministers on down, and people close to the party, are telling us of conflicts of interest or serious corruption in the party at the national, provincial and local level and among close family members of ministers.*
> *[Source: Wikileaks 2010 from 2004-05 cables from US Ambassador]*

Introduction

This chapter is linked to that presented by Ugur Omurgonulsen, and reviews perceptions of corruption and Turkey. Corruption, as with other accession countries, has been an integral part of issues to be addressed. The EU discusses corruption in its annual accession progress reports and it is a constant feature in a number of reviews, reports and research outputs from the Council of Europe, OECD and from authors such as Doig (2010) and Michael (2004).

---

1 Alan Doig is Hon. Research Fellow, International Development Department, University of Birmingham. Brendan Quirke is Senior Lecturer, Liverpool Business School, Liverpool John Moores University.

As a starting point, this chapter takes the 2008 report from the European Commission which essentially summarised the internal and external perceptions on corruption in Turkey in stating that "*overall, there has been limited progress in the area of anti-corruption. Corruption remains a widespread issue*" (Commission Staff Working Document, 2008: 11).

The question posed is how corruption is perceived internally and externally, whether or not the responses address the concerns, and whether the responses are likely to be sufficient in terms of other countries satisfying EU accession expectations.

External reviews and sources

There is a limited range of relevant non-Turkish academic material (see Doig, 2010a and 2010b) although what there is ranges from why corruption is not being addressed to drivers for reform. One approach makes the point that, "*in Turkey, a number of executive bodies deal with anti-corruption. However, none of these has been given a definitive leadership role and the relationship between these entities is ambiguous*" (Michael, 2004, 8). Another argues that there is a 'disproportionate emphasis on culture', used by the EU to impose 'extraneous guidance' on how to reform the Turkish economic and administrative frameworks, and allow the increased involvement of European capital (Jacoby, 2010).

There is more material produced by international NGOs or international institutions like Transparency International and the OECD that relates to anti-corruption quantitative assessments. These present a more detailed picture which suggest that Turkey shares with a number of other countries both low scores in the direct corruption rankings, as well as a poor performance in corruption-context indicators – those areas whose level, up or down, such as the degree of freedom of the media or informal economy activity, are considered to suggest a propensity for corruption. Such assessments are also reflected in terms of the number of countries which appear ranked with Turkey in more than one survey in both corruption-associated and corruption surveys. Individually, most surveys have little intrinsic value, offering generalised snapshots that offer neither explanation of country-specific causes, nor country-specific bases for reform proposals, although collectively they indicate corruption as a pervasive issue.

More narrative based reviews range from the IMF reporting on fiscal transparency to the US Chamber of Commerce reporting on export issues relating to Turkey. Most are conducted on a regular basis by organisations of which Turkey is a member, or as part of the European Union accession process. These include the

EC Council Decision of 23 January 2006 on the principles, priorities and conditions contained in the Accession Partnership with Turkey (Council Decision, 2006), the 2006 SIGMA report (SIGMA, 2006) on the Elements of a Public Integrity System, the Group of States against Corruption (GRECO) reports for Turkey and various EC Progress Reports on Turkey.

Most reports have noted a continuing and pervasive concern over administrative opacity and delay, the presence of corruption and successive governments' limited efforts to address these issues. Many would endorse the findings of the 2008 SIGMA follow-up assessment to its 2006 review when it reported that "*no significant achievement was recorded during the assessment period*" in relation to anti-corruption projects and initiatives between 2006 and 2008, that anti-corruption policies seriously lacked ownership and that corruption "*continued to be a matter of concern*". On the other hand, the earlier SIGMA report (SIGMA, 2006) noted that, except in some areas, such as asset declaration and the financing of political parties, there was overall a sufficient legal basis for fighting corruption. What was missing, it suggested, was a long-term anti-corruption policy that had clear political support, and included a range of initiatives to address corruption such as a comprehensive strategy that addressed civil society, judicial independence, public sector reforms, simplification of administrative procedures and legally-binding codes of conduct.

Probably the most important reviews are the GRECO review in 2006 and subsequent compliance reports (GRECO, 2006, 2008, 2010a) and 2010 reviews (GRECO, 2010b, 2010c, 2012), and those initiated by the EU as part of the accession process. The 2006 review was the most comprehensive[2], noting a number of areas for reform, including: a national strategy and implementing body; coordination and monitoring of anti-corruption work with a specialised investigative agency; the establishment of the Ombudsman; training of investigators; enhanced independence of judges from the Ministry of Justice and training of judges; revising MPs' immunities; reviewing the criteria for investigating public officials; improving confiscation; lowering fees for accessing official information and strengthening the independence and capacity of the relevant agency; strengthening the independence and capacity of the Council of Ethics and promoting codes of conduct and ethics training; enhancing the role of Inspection Boards; introducing whistle-blowing; improving company registration; complying with the Criminal Law Convention on Corruption; training tax officials and engaging with accountants and auditors to report money laundering offences.

In the subsequent compliance reviews, GRECO noted that 'out of the 21 recommendations issued to Turkey, in total 15 recommendations have now been

2 The 2010 reviews were more restricted, focussing on Incriminations and Political Funding.

implemented satisfactorily or dealt with in a satisfactory manner.[3] GRECO notes that Turkey has made further efforts to ensure the practical implementation of a number of recommendations since the adoption of the Compliance Report. The measures required are substantial and include constitutional reform (GRECO, 2010a, 12).

Further to its 2008 concerns, the 2009 EC report noted a number of areas where progress had not been made, such as those relating to ethics rules, fraud cases, improving state audit, and stated: "*Overall, the legislative framework designed to prevent corruption has been improved. However, corruption remains prevalent in many areas. Turkey needs to finalise an anticorruption strategy and to develop a track record of investigations, indictments, prosecutions and convictions*" (Commission Staff Working Document,2009, 13).

The latest, October 2011, report summarized the current assessment of external agencies in what had - and had not - been achieved:

- In line with the 2010-2014 Strategy and Action Plan, an Executive Committee for Increasing Transparency and Fighting Corruption has coordinated working groups preparing proposals on 28 corruption-related issues. The Committee of Ministers on anti-corruption policy approved all the proposals. However, there was no increase in the strength or independence of institutions involved in the fight against corruption, which are not sufficiently staffed. Participation by civil society, particularly in the Executive Committee and in implementing the strategy, needs to be strengthened.
- Turkey has implemented 19 of the 21 recommendations made in the 2005 first and second evaluation reports by the Group of States against Corruption (GRECO). There has been no progress in limiting the immunities of Members of Parliament or of senior public officials in corruption-related cases and establishing objective criteria setting the conditions under which their immunity could be lifted. Two major sets of GRECO recommendations on 'Incrimination' and 'Transparency of Party Funding' remain to be implemented after the third evaluation round adopted in March 2010.
- Legislation on political parties imposes some restrictions on the amount and nature of donations parties may receive. However, there has been no progress concerning the transparency of financing political parties. Auditing of political parties remains weak and there is no legal framework for auditing election campaigns or the financing of individual candidates. There is no limit on general

3 The review noted that the recommendations relating to a single lead anti-corruption agency, the independence of the judiciary, the independence of the Ethics Council, and reforming the Inspection Board system had only partly been implemented. Those relating to a specialised investigation unit and the immunities of MPs had not been implemented.

party and campaign-related spending. In particular, the legislation contains no specific provisions on campaign financing. Parties declare their campaign-related income and expenditure in their general financial statements as part of their annual report to the Constitutional Court. The Constitutional Court itself focuses primarily on compliance with reporting requirements and with parties' internal regulations. It does not verify the data and source documents submitted or review them for undisclosed income and expenditure.

- Civil servants working for central and local government received training on ethics between October 2010 and July 2011. However, no progress has been made on extending codes of ethics to academics, military personnel or the judiciary.
- The Law on the Turkish Court of Accounts (TCA) adopted in December 2010 should significantly strengthen the transparency and accountability of public administration.
- However, the exclusion of the Foundation for Strengthening the Armed Forces from the audit mandate of the TCA is a major shortcoming of the revised Law on the TCA [. . .] There is no administrative act to freeze suspicious assets.
- No steps have been taken to build up a track record of investigations, indictments or convictions related to corruption cases (Commission Staff Working Document, 2011)[4].

The tenor of the report was a re-iteration of 'limited progress' in terms of both implementing the strategy and the action plan to combat corruption, with particular reference to the lack of transparency relating to political party financing and the scope of MPs' immunities. The report called for greater political support for strengthening the legislative framework to fight corruption and the implementation of the framework in practice.

4 It is also worth noting that the FATF continued to be concerned about Turkey's capacity to address money laundering and illicit money flows: "Despite Turkey's high-level political commitment to work with the FATF to address its strategic CFT deficiencies, Turkey has not made sufficient progress in implementing its action plan, and certain strategic CFT deficiencies remain. Turkey should work on addressing these deficiencies, including by: (1) adequately criminalising terrorist financing; and (2) implementing an adequate legal framework for identifying and freezing terrorist assets. Given Turkey's continued lack of progress in these two areas, if Turkey does not take significant actions by October 2012, the FATF will call upon its members to apply countermeasures proportionate to the risks associated with Turkey" (FATF, 2012).

How has Turkey responded to the concerns?

The 2010 GRECO and 2011 EC reviews note that Turkey has made progress although primarily against the agendas set by the two organisations. Nevertheless addressing corruption has been an agenda issue for successive governments and the Turkish Parliament (TGNA) which have undertaken a number of initiatives in the past decade.

The 57th Government Programme included an intention to address corruption. A Guidance Committee was set up and a Prime Ministry Circular (2001/38) was issued in July 2001, seeking opinions of the state institutions in respect to effective public management and anti-corruption within their areas of jurisdiction. A Working Group was established and an international conference was organised in September 2001 whose outcomes were also used in drafting an anti-corruption plan. As a consequence the Council of Ministers issued an Action Plan in January 2002 – "*Increasing Transparency in Turkey and Enhancing Good Governance in Public Sector* (2002/3)". It covered the following areas: public service delivery; regulation of public agencies and foundations; personnel; access to information and transparency; healthcare; inspection and audit; judiciary; money laundering; party and campaign finance; financial disclosure statements; local government. The various activities to be undertaken within the designated areas were all required to be completed by December 2004 (of which a number were either completed or begun). In the same month another circular set up the Ministerial Commission for Enhancing Transparency and Improving Good Governance (2002/56), supported by a Technical Commission (public officials from various ministries headed by the PMIB) to provide the secretariat to the Ministerial Commission.

In 2003 there was also TGNA Inquiry Commission on Corruption which submitted a report containing number of reform proposals to the Presidency of Parliament (TGNA – the Turkish Grand National Assembly) in mid-2003 but on which there was no progress. The proposals included: amendments in various laws and requests for the parliamentary investigations into former politicians, a permanent parliamentary commission (and consideration of an independent inspection agency to undertake inspections for parliament), along with the establishment of the Ombudsman, a Code of Conduct, the role of NGOs, an enhanced role for Inspection Boards (with the possibility of an independent status, common approach, and performance and risk-based inspections), media campaigns to raise public awareness, specialist prosecutors, legislative reform (*e.g.*, to banking secrecy, parliamentary immunity, procurement, approval before the investigation of public officials, post-retirement activities, gift-giving, and asset disclosure), quicker judicial processes and use of asset confiscation. While a limited number of the proposals were later addressed by government, most were not and Parliament did not engage in any further substantive work on anti-corruption proposals.

The 58th Government Programme campaigned in part on an anti-corruption platform and its Emergency Action Plan was announced after winning the election. This was intended to provide a "*roadmap whose milestones will be followed by politicians, bureaucrats and the concerned sections of the society*" and stated that the following actions would be undertaken: ratification of two European Conventions (the Council of Europe's Criminal Law Convention on corruption and Civil Law Convention on corruption); penalties concerning corruption and irregularity; the fields where public officials are not allowed to work would be expanded and applied very effectively; financing of the politics would be given a transparent nature; the concept of confidential information would be re-defined in legislation; a dialogue would be developed among government – public administration – judiciary – media and civil society in terms of non-corruption efforts; the justification of the law would include the benefits and costs to be brought by the law. The reforms were to be implemented within 12 months.

In April 2006 the 9th Reform package was announced by the government. The proposals included changes to the law and procedures for public procurement, asset declaration, and the financing of election campaigns and political parties as well as draft laws on the Ombudsman and the Court of Accounts. On August 2007 another circular (2007/23) appointed the Minster of the Interior as head of the Ministerial Commission for Enhancing Transparency and Improving Good Governance. By 2008 the main reforms introduced included: the law (and associated agency) on access to information; establishing the Council of Ethics in Public Service (and associated Regulation); establishing the laws, units and procedures on financial management and internal audit control; banking; money laundering; and renewal of the Criminal Code and the Procedure Code (including harmonisation with the OECD Convention of Foreign Overseas Officials). The Council of Europe's Criminal and Civil Law Conventions, and the EU Convention on money laundering and proceeds of crime, and the UNCAC were ratified. Generally, as indicated in Table 1, the response collectively to identified concerns was up to 2009 was piecemeal and primarily focused on legislative reform.

Table 1
Strategy Recommendations

Area	Recommendations (✓)					Status up to 2009
	Parliamt.	2002	2004	2006	2008	
Procurement	✓	–	–	✓		Law
Asset Disclosure	✓	✓	–	✓	✓	N.a.
Party finance		✓	✓	✓	✓	N.a.
Ombudsman	✓	–	–	✓	–	N.a. constit.
Court of Accounts	✓	–	–	✓	–	N.a.
Code of Conduct (Council of Ethics)	✓	✓	–	–	✓	Partial: Law, Regulation & Agency
Role Inspect. Boards	✓	–	–	–	✓	N.a.
Access Information/reviewing access confidential information	✓	✓	✓	–	✓	Law, Procedures & Agency established
Money Laundering	✓	✓	–	–	–	Partial: Law, Proc. & Agency established
Council of Europe Conventions	–	–	✓	–	–	Partial: Ratified not fully converted
Permission to invest. public officials	✓	–	–	–	✓	N.a.
Post-retirement	✓	✓	–	–	✓	N.a.
Civil Soc; education, awareness, surveys	✓	–	✓	–	✓	N.a.
Debarment	–	–	–	–	✓	N.a.
Reform Crim. Law	✓	–	✓	–	–	Partial
Agency Capacity	–	–	–	–	✓	N.a.
Disciplinary database	–	–	–	–	✓	N.a.
Cooperation/information-sharing	✓	–	–	–	✓	N.a.
Booklet	✓	–	–	–	✓	N.a.
Law on Investigating Public Officials	✓	–	–	–	✓	N.a.
Whistle blowing	–	–	–	–	✓	N.a.
Specialism in LEA & Prosecutors	✓	–	–	–	✓	N.a.
Parliament immunity	✓	–	–	–	–	N.a.

N.a. = no action

In mid-2009, however, a more comprehensive approach was undertaken when with the Prime Minister's circular 2009/19, the Prime Ministry Inspection Board (PMIB) was appointed as the secretariat to the Commission for Enhancing Transparency and Reinforcing the Fight against Corruption, a committee of Ministers, chaired by the Deputy Prime Minister, and take responsibility for drafting a national anti-corruption strategy (NACS), as well chairing working groups, developing the NACS action plans and coordinating all relevant institutions.

The PMIB prepared a draft NACS which appeared to seek to address areas where no reform had been delivered from the previous initiatives, and also in those areas where it had identified a need for further reform. These included: improving openness and transparency in the financing of political parties and election campaigns, completing work on official secrecy, political ethics, conflict of interest and post-public office appointments, setting up the Ombudsman, revising the public procurement system, increasing transparency, accountability and ethics at local level, changing regulations governing the investigation of public officials, introducing whistle-blower protection, encouraging inter-agency coordination and cooperation, promoting citizen awareness and education.

In terms, therefore, both of the work of the PMIB and in terms of the areas covered when compared to the earlier initiatives (see Table 2 next page), the Turkish approach would appear not only to be identifying what reforms are still needed but also to be addressing most if not all those areas that GRECO and other bodies have raised as requiring attention.

Formally, therefore, it could be argued that Turkey has taken or is taking those steps necessary to address corruption that have long been identified as of concern, particularly in terms of the EU accession process, and has developed a broad-ranging strategy to implementing the reforms in practice. The question that the EU reports raise, however, are not only are the proposed reforms enough but also why corruption remains a significant aspect of Turkish politics and public administration.

Table 2
Mapping Turkish Anti-corruption Initiatives

Area	TGNA Commission	2002	2004	2006	2009/11
Procurement	✓	–	–	✓	✓
Asset Disclosure	✓	✓	–	✓	✓
Party finance		✓	✓	✓	✓
Ombudsman	✓	–	–	✓	✓
Court of Accounts	✓	–	–	✓	–
Code of Conduct (Council of Ethics)	✓	✓	–	–	✓
Role of Inspection Boards	✓	–	–	–	✓
Access to Information/ reviewing access to confidential information	✓	✓	✓	–	✓
Money Laundering	✓	✓	–	–	–
Council of Europe Conventions	–	–	✓	–	–
Permission to investigate public officials	✓	–	–	–	✓
Post-retirement	✓	✓	–	–	✓
Civ. Soc.; education, awareness, surveys	✓	–	✓	–	✓
Role of Media	✓	–	–	–	✓
Debarment for contracts	–	–	–	–	✓
Reform Criminal Law	✓	–	✓	–	✓
Agency Capacity	–	–	–	–	✓
Disciplinary database	–	–	–	–	✓
Cooperation/information-sharing	✓	–	–	–	✓
Booklet	✓	–	–	–	✓
Law on Investigating Public Officials	✓	–	–	–	✓
Whistle blowing	–	–	–	–	✓
Specialism in LEA and Prosecutors	✓	–	–	–	✓
Immunity of MPs	✓	–	–	–	–
Use of risk assessment	✓	–	–	–	✓
Local government	✓	–	–	–	✓
Role of audit	✓	–	–	–	✓

Has Turkey done enough to address corruption?

The first, and obvious, question is who is to judge if (and when Turkey) has done enough to address corruption. It is worth noting that many of the surveys, reviews, and evaluations of current projects, usually involving external agencies, only have a basic understanding of the laws, institutions and reform processes in Turkey. There is some concern about the role of the reviews and reviewers/evaluators who should be, but often are not, acting as 'intelligent customers' – *i.e.*, not possessing sufficient knowledge and expertise to make critical assessments. The question of detailed local knowledge, acceptance at face value of statements made to the evaluators, the absence of evidence-based findings and a lack of understanding of the workings of Turkish political and administrative institutions, laws and procedures and how they work in practice raise issues about the credibility and relevance of authority of some of their conclusions and recommendations.

The second issue is whether or not the external reviews are demanding standards that are not in fact, for example, EU norms but aspirational expectations that most European countries cannot satisfy. Currently, GRECO is demanding that all members address in legislation a number of areas relating to party financing, including the transparency of some sources of income of parties, such as donations in kind, party membership fees, loans or sponsorship, anonymous donations, local party bodies and other entities involved in election campaigns, accessible financial information and an independent supervisory body (GRECO, 2011). Turkey was criticised by GRECO in 2012: "*in the present absence of final achievements, further significant material progress is necessary to demonstrate that an acceptable level of compliance with the recommendations within the next 18 months can be achieved*" (2012, 12).

Yet the Transparency International (TI) assessment in the same year noted that Turkey was not only in failing to match expectations and reported that the relationship between 'political parties and businesses exhibit the highest risks of corruption across Europe; with few exceptions they are rated among the weakest sectors when it comes to anti-corruption safeguards. One of the intersections at which parties and businesses meet – political party financing – is a particularly high-risk area, which even countries often described as "*low corruption contexts*" have not managed to insulate themselves against' (TI, 2012, 22). It may be pertinent to ask if external agencies are expecting or demanding levels of reform by Turkey that not even established EU member states have achieved and whether or not a more incremental approach to the evaluation and compliance process should be taken.

Certainly, Turkey has undertaken a wide range of anti-corruption initiatives, including the current strategy/action plan. A number of the laws, procedures and institutions proposed in previous initiatives have been established. Various ministries as part of their modernisation and public service delivery focus are addressing procedures, one of whose consequences will be to reduce the opportunities, incentives and opacity that facilitate corruption. The Council of Ethics in Public Service has provided ethics training through a Council of Europe project. A further project is intended to start in 2012 and all ministries have set up both internal audit units and ethics commissions to progress work on internal control procedures and on ethics training. Both the UNDP and Council of Europe are, or will be, running projects with the *Prime Ministry Inspection Board* (PMIB) in 2012-2013 to improve its capacity as the owner and coordinator of the anti-corruption strategy, and to facilitate its anti-corruption work.

On the other hand, and despite the now substantial legal and institutional means to address corruption, there are still concerns from the external reviews. The 2012 GRECO review on criminalisation of corruption and party funding noted that Turkey had 'implemented satisfactorily none of the seventeen recommendations' required of it while the Business Anti-corruption Portal, funded by a number of European countries' aid agencies, notes that "*corruption in Turkey remains rampant and enforcement of anti-corruption policies remains weak.*"

What may inhibit the reform process?

Why this is the case may be the consequence of a number of immediate reasons. First, much of the responsibility falls on a small agency within the Turkish public administration, the PMIB. The PMIB is the lead Inspection Board; it can instigate, lead and coordinate complex inquiries and cross-ministry inquiries under the formal authority of the Prime Minister who must also authorise any investigation (and who also provides the authority for implementing findings from a report). It sets the principles of the IB system and reviews the legal procedural frameworks under which they operate. It covers all public bodies, NGOs and private companies. It has, however, has less than 100 staff and now has two additional functions: that relating to the *National Anti Corruption Strategy* (NACS) and as the counter-part institution of OLAF (the European Union's anti-fraud office), responsible for inquiring into cases relating to EU-funded projects. This has meant that the NACS, which is very much concerned with the introduction of laws, codes or procedures, is not effectively monitored to in terms of the implementation of the NACS in practice, and nor on how it is to be measured in terms of performance and effectiveness.

Second, many ministries see the NACS as something to be completed, rather than an on-going responsibility, largely because the NACS was not discussed with individual public sector organisations, either in terms of its preparation or implementation, but issued as a formal requirement. In such circumstances, the issue was more one of compliance than an iterative process in developing and reviewing the NACS in practice. In terms of assessing the strength or effectiveness of the NACS, therefore, the following two dimensions have not been addressed: (a) vertically by measuring each institution's 'fitness for purpose' and the quality of their vertical accountability; (b) horizontally, by assessing how the institutions inter-relate and support one-another, especially through horizontal accountability mechanisms.

This means that the identification of specific institutions in terms of their centrality to the working of the NACS, the added-value of institutional interaction both in terms of addressing corruption and the wider NACS goals, promoting co-ordinated support to institutions to deliver the NACS, developing institutional action plans to implement NACS anti-corruption measures, measuring individual institutional and the NACS performance, and revising the NACS as a consequence, has also not yet taken place. One consequence has been that there is no common understanding of anti-corruption strategy and no common reporting of data to the Prime Ministry Inspection Board (PMIB), so that cross-sectoral analyses of corruption by the effective implementation of the Strategy could be developed.

This in turn may well reflect the compartmentalism and departmentalism that are core Turkish public sector traditions. These form only part of the continuing dynamics of the nature of the Turkish state, the enduring cultural traditions within the public sector, the development of a public ethics environment, where corruption as a policy issue appears on the list of competing demands on and priorities of government, the question of ownership of the reform process, the lack of coordination, communication and *connectedness* between existing institutions involved in whole or in part in addressing corruption, and whether a holistic or comprehensive anti-corruption approach may also be necessary. Yet, such fragmentation is also typical of many established EU member states (Quirke and Doig, 2011; Quirke, 2009). Here three wider and enduring influences may have relevance.

First, the development of the Turkish state is one of strong centralised control with a collectivist culture based on solidarity and traditional spoils culture, 'administrative traditions' (*e.g.* patronage in entering the public service, gift giving and taking, and keeping business relations with the government department after retirement), and 'legal uncertainties' (*e.g.* lack of definitions of confidential information or lack of formal guidance on undue infleunce by senior political or administrative figures). This is compounded by the application of new management practices and procedures onto existing administrative cultures without assessment, adaptation and a realignment of the control environment. A number of interconnected trends are also noted within the public sector, including political penetration of the administrative and judicial arenas, economic liberalisation favouring economic elites close to government and a collectivist and networked culture in the public sector which serve to reinforce rather than evolve the enduring concept of the 'unquestionable state' (see Omurgonsulen and Oktem, 2007).

The question of administrative culture is equally relevant. Research on public and public official perceptions of culture report an acceptance that the standards and conduct expected of society or among public officials that reflects the western democratic model are not in place (see *Turkish Studies*, 2012). More specific standards, including those introduced through the Council of Ethics for Public Service are even more, as a 2009 Conflict-of-Interest Research Study noted, non-contextualised or internalised in the minds of public officials: "*it is striking that 'avoiding conflict of interest', 'accountability' and 'unlawful benefit/gift receiving', which are the most important principles of the Regulation and the Ethics Contract, none referred to them in priority. The first two concepts are new to Turkish administrative culture as well as to the society and they are in the process of taking their forms*" (Genckaya, 2009, 375).

Thirdly and finally, is the question of how far governments are under pressure from society to reform. External reviews from bodies such as the World Bank Institute Working Group (2010) have stressed the importance of the role of civil society in the fight against corruption. Civil Society should take on a watchdog role and monitor the efforts of government, the public and private sector in the fight against corruption. The World Bank takes the view that civil society organisations should make the general public aware of the benefits of fighting corruption and help bring different actors such as government and business together. To be successful in the long run, all actors have to build an alliance and act collectively in the fight against corruption.

Karaman and Aras (2000) observe that Turkey has problems with respect to a fully functioning civil society. In their judgement, there is an unstable democratic process, rigid bureaucratic centralisation and perpetuation of a state ideology. Turkey has not yet achieved, however, the full fledged existence of civil society that exists in the West. Their assessment is that civil society remains underdeveloped and still constrained to some extent by the state. The state allows the organisational appearance of civil society, it even encourages it, yet the dominance that the state exercises over individuals and groups in society results in it very often turning a deaf ear to – and even take legal action against – those groups that it does not favour or which challenge its authority (which, in the recent Turkish context, have ranged from the armed services, to journalists and businessmen).

This view is supported by Levant Korkut, the Chairman of the Civil Society Development Centre (STGM) in an interview in *Today's Zaman* newspaper on April 6th, 2010 who believes that civil society organisations in Turkey face many shortcomings, not only in finding sources of funding and new members, but also in the area of legal obstacles. Korkut emphasises the impact of the modernisation process of Turkish society throughout the twentieth century which has led to the dominance of state bureaucracy and the emergence of the state elite. The state is not opposed to the emergence of civil society, but it has to be under the control of the state.

Is too much being asked from Turkey, too quickly?

This view reflects a much more significant developmental issue. The external assessments of, and pressures for reform of corruption in Turkey are, in developmental terms, relatively immediate but may not take full cognisance of a country's developmental trajectory. At the core is the question of the state – whether its propensity to address and prioritise the development agenda as well as the wider likelihood of accepting the need to move toward a 'limited, legitimate, honest, strengthened and transparent state' as the vehicle to deliver the development agenda – continues to raise issues about the pace, linear direction, focus, effectiveness and sustainability of the reform process and the relevance of the prevailing governance approach. In a number of the country studies the veneer of democracy is being cemented over the old political systems and power plays which continue to operate beneath the surface or parallel to the democratic transition.

To address such trajectories with reform proposals based on a pre-determined template or on assumptions about why and how other countries' practice may work effectively in the Turkish context, reflects a lack of understanding of the institutional landscape, the organisational cultures, as well as issues of prioritisation, sequencing, timing, resourcing and achievability. This may mean that the effectiveness of a NACS or work on anti-corruption projects, or reviewing progress, is filtered through enduring cultural and other issues. This will require other reforms or will only become fully effective within wider social, political and other developments. This is a phenomenon that the EU has come to discover when dealing with other EU accession countries too.

Michael (2004) likens Turkey to its near neighbours, Romania and Bulgaria, in terms of steps taken to combat corruption, perceptions of corruption and so on. Bulgaria and Romania, both had high levels of public support for EU membership and accession to the EU became a number one foreign policy objective. This gave the EU an opportunity to pressurise both the Romanian and Bulgarian governments to try to tackle the problem of corruption and to take effective measures against it in both the legal and administrative spheres (Quirke and Doig, 2011).

Like Turkey, both Romania and Bulgaria ratified international conventions and implemented and amended national anti-corruption strategies and also implemented new laws and amended the criminal code and so on in order to satisfy the demands of the EU and its external inspectors. However, just because something exists on paper, does not mean that it is implemented in reality. When the goal of EU accession had been achieved, despite the measures both countries had signed up to, corruption remained as a big a problem as it had before and together with the added attraction of billions of EU funds that could be used for purposes other than those intended, then major problems ensued which led to EU funds to Bulgaria being suspended in 2008, until there were discernible improvements in the situation (Quirke and Doig, 2011).

Turkey has experienced similar corruption problems to the Bulgaria and Romania experience, such as high profile cases involving politicians like the former Prime Minister Nastase in Romania (Quirke, 2009) and former Turkish Prime Minister Yilmaz (Sarlak and Bali, 2008), immunity from investigation and prosecution for parliamentarians in both Romania and Turkey, a huge 'black' economy, a web of patronage based networks (Sarlak and Bali, 2008), lack of transparency in the funding of political parties etc. As well as similarities, there are also differences. The influence of organised criminal gangs is nothing like as pervasive in Turkey as it is in Bulgaria for example, where Orenstein and Buniewicz (2009) comment that there appears to be high level penetration of government and society by such groups.

This recent experience of near neighbours, where once accession was achieved, commitments entered into on paper, in terms of tackling corruption in a serious and systematic way, were quickly pushed to one side, does not inspire confidence that the situation in Turkey will improve, just because laws and strategies exist on paper, or accession to the EU is a distinct possibility.

Also, in Turkey, the role of civil society organisations is more fragmented and not as influential as it is in countries like Bulgaria and Romania. In Romania for example, there have been coalitions of civil society organisations such as the Romanian Coalition for a Clean Parliament to try and prevent politicians (blacklisted for corrupt behaviour and activity) from being elected to Parliament (Mungiu-Pippidi, 2010). Also, in Bulgaria, the Center for the Study of Democracy in Sofia has published a number of damning reports on the efforts of the Bulgarian authorities in terms of fighting corruption. There does not appear to be the same influence in Turkey from civil society which is tolerated as long as it does not challenge the authority of the state. Civil society in Turkey has not had the impact of civil society in Eastern European countries, where such organisations banded together and helped bring down the communist authorities at the end of the 1980s (Mungiu-Pippidi, 2010).

The EU accession process was keen to integrate Romania and Bulgaria long before their developmental trajectories were even aligned with, let alone substantively reflecting, EU requirements and expectations. Part of this was an assumption that enthusiasm for membership would provide a leadership committed to EU expectations and another part of the thinking was that the weak states could be shaped and directed by EU requirements. Both expectations do not apply to Turkey as in fact and practice, Turkey is a much larger country with a much stronger economy and state, which evinces a very different set of issues (and reactions from more established EU states), while its public cultures and traditions may be less amenable to reform, certainly in the shorter-term, than either Romania or Bulgaria. In all three cases, however, although for different reasons, the pressure to accelerate the developmental trajectory of any country may have hidden or adverse consequences for which the timetable for reform, and the reforms demanded, have yet to demonstrate flexibility and time.

Conclusions

Corruption has been seen as a major issue which Turkey needs to address effectively, before it can accede to membership of the EU. In the reports produced by various international NGOs and institutions, corruption has been identified as a pervasive issue as has the limited efforts of successive governments in addressing the issue. In seeking to respond to these concerns, Turkey has devised an anti-corruption strategy and action plan, she has implemented the majority of the recommendations from the first and second GRECO evaluation reports. However, there has not been a great deal of progress on the transparency of the financing of political parties. Ethics training although it has been extended for civil servants, has not been introduced for academics, military personnel or the judiciary. On balance there has been limited progress.

So, does the fact that Turkey has signed up to various international conventions and protocols and amended its criminal code amount to a serious effort on her part to tackle corruption, or is it just window-dressing in an attempt to appease international actors such as the EU, or has insufficient time been provided to allow the embedding of the reforms so that organisational cultures can be amended, following the changes to laws and procedures? The recent experience of Bulgaria and Romania in this respect, does not inspire confidence. The relative weakness of civil society which does not appear to have the impact and influence of that of its Balkan neighbours and is fragmented and not capable of building coalitions, is problematic in terms of holding the state to account in the anti-corruption policy and activity arena. From the Western European perspective, it appears that Turkey still has much to do in order to fight corruption and to attempt to control it effectively. The questions the EU now needs to ask are: can Turkey demonstrate how its developmental trajectory has changed sufficiently to reflect EU requirements and expectations; have the reforms sought by the EU been the right reforms to effect the changes; and what more needs to be done, over what timeframe, for the reforms to be seen to be working in practice.

References

Commission Staff Working Document, *Turkey 2008 Progress Report Accompanying the Communication from the Commission to the European Parliament and the Council: Enlargement Strategy and Main Challenges 2008-2009 {COM (2008) 674}*, Commission of the European Communities, 2008

Commission Staff Working Document, *Turkey 2009 Progress Report Accompanying the Communication from the Commission to the European Parliament and the Council; Enlargement Strategy and Main Challenges 2009-2010,* Commission of the European Communities, Brussels, 14 October 2009, pp12-13, 2009

Commission Staff Working Document, *Turkey 2011 Progress Report Accompanying the Communication from the Commission to the European Parliament and the Council; Enlargement Strategy and Main Challenges 2011-2012,* Commission of the European Communities, Brussels, 12 October 2011, pp19-20, 2011

Council Decision of 23 January 2006 on the principles, priorities and conditions contained in the Accession Partnership with Turkey (2006/35/EC), Brussels, Commission of the European Communities.

Doig, A., *Corruption Report: Findings, Analysis and Recommendations.* Strasbourg, Council of Europe, 2010a (http://www.coe.int/t/dghl/cooperation/economiccrime/corruption/projects/TYEC/TYEC_en.asp).

Doig, A., *Background review to corruption Report.* Strasbourg, Council of Europe, 2010b (http://www.coe.int/t/dghl/cooperation/economiccrime/corruption/projects/TYEC/TYEC_en.asp).

FATF, *FATF Public Statement,* FATF, 2012 (http://www.fatf-gafi.org/documents/repository/fatfpublicstatement-2june2012.html#Turkey).

Genckaya, O. F., Conflict of interest. In: A. Doig (ed.), *Academic researches on public ethics, Vol. I.* Ankara: Council of Ethics for the Public Service, Council of Europe and European Union, 2009

GRECO, *Joint First and Second Round Evaluation Report on Turkey (GRECO Eval I-II Rep (2005) 3E).* Council of Europe adopted 6-10 March 2006, 2006

GRECO, *Joint First and Second Round Evaluation Report on Turkey: Compliance report on Turkey.* Council of Europe adopted 31 March – 4 April 2008

GRECO, *Joint First and Second Round Evaluation Round: Addendum to the Compliance Report on Turkey,* Council of Europe adopted 7-11 June 2010, 2010a

GRECO, *Third Evaluation Round: Evaluation Report on Turkey on Transparency of Party Funding (theme II),* Council of Europe adopted 22-26 March 2010, 2010b

GRECO, *Third Evaluation Round: Evaluation Report on Turkey (GRECO ETS 173 and 191, GPC 2) (theme I),* Council of Europe adopted 22-26 March 2010, 2010c

GRECO, *Twelfth General Activity Report, Strasbourg,* Council of Europe, 2011

GRECO, *Third Evaluation Round: Evaluation Report on Turkey: compliance report on Turkey,* Council of Europe adopted 20-23 March 2012, 2012

Jacoby, T., Turkey and Europe: Culture, Capital and Corruption, *Review of International Studies.* 2010, vol 36, *no* 3, pp 663-684

Karaman, M.L. and B. Aras, The crisis of civil society in Turkey, *Journal of Economic and Social Research,* 2010, vol. 2, no 2, pp 39-58

Michael, B., Anti-corruption in Turkey's EU Accession, *Turkish Policy Quarterly,* 2004, vol 3, no 4, 2004 (www.turkishpolicy.com/images/stories/2004-04-EUodyssey2/TPQ2004-4-michael.pdf; no page numbers).

Mungiu-Pippidi, A. *The experience of civil society as an anti-corruption actor in East Central Europe.* Working paper, Romanian Academic Society and Hertie School of Governance, 2010.

Omurgonsulen, U. and M.K. Oktem, Is there any change in the public service values of different generations of public administrators? The case of Turkish governors and district-governors. Conference paper for Fifth workshop of the EGPA Study Group on Ethics and Integrity of Governance. *Subtheme: "Research methods in corruption and integrity",* Madrid, Spain, 2007

Orenstein, M.A. and N. Buniewicz, *Case study: Funding the fight against corruption in Romania and Bulgaria.* School of Advanced International Studies Working Paper, Johns Hopkins University, 2009

Quirke, B. J. *Romania and the fight against EU Fraud: A Balkan success story.* In P.C. van Duyne, J. Harvey, M. Maljevic and K. von Lampe (eds.) *Crime, money and criminal mobility in Europe.* Nijmegen: Wolf Legal Publishers, 116-134, 2009.

Quirke, B.J. and A. Doig, *Bulgaria and EU fraud: A case of better late than never.* In G. Antonopoulos, M.S. Groenhuijsen, J. Harvey, T. Kooijmans, A. Maljević, and K. von Lampe (eds.) *Usual and unusual organising criminals in Europe and beyond.* Maklu Publishers, 187-206, 2011

Sarlak, Z. and B.B. Bali, *Corruption in Turkey: Is the donor content when the recipient is content.* Crime and Culture Discussion Paper, Discussion Paper Series No. 9, University of Konstanz, 2008

SIGMA, *Elements of the Public Integrity System: Assessment,* SIGMA/OECD, 2006

Transparency International, *Money, Politics, Power: Corruption Risks in Europe*, Berlin: Transparency International Secretariat. 2012

Turkish Studies, Special Issue. *Corruption, public ethics and changing cultures,* vol. 13, no 1, 2012

World Bank Institute Working Group, *Collective Action in the fight against Corruption,* Washington DC, World Bank, 2010

Go with the e-waste flow. The governance reality of illegal transports of e-waste in a European trade hub

Lieselot Bisschop[1]

Introduction

A number of behaviours have been identified as comprising major forms of environmental crime (White, 2011),[2] many of which are inherently transnational and linked to global trade (Beirne and South, 2007). Capital, goods, people and information flow swiftly having potentially – and often unpredictable – worldwide consequences (Keohane and Nye, 2000). The impact of the illegal transports of e-waste resides on ecological, social as well as on economic levels (Bisschop, 2012). Moreover, the e-waste supply chain illustrates the interconnectedness of environmental crime flows consisting of: of producers; distributors; consumers; collectors; refurbishers; waste brokers; shipping companies; recyclers; downstream vendors and finally actors responsible for final – often far distant – disposal (Schluep *et al.*, 2008). Different legal-illegal interfaces present themselves in the illegal transports of e-waste (Bisschop, 2012). The complexity becomes clear once one realises why actors become involved in illegal transports of e-waste. Although profit or its lure play a very important role, elements on all levels combine to shape the flows (Bisschop, 2012; Gibbs, McGarrell, and Axelrod, 2010). Given these complexities, this chapter sets out to analyse the 'governance[3] reality' of illegal e-waste transportation.

---

1 Lieselot Bisschop is a researcher at University College Ghent, Department of Public Administration, research group Governing and Policing Security and a PhD candidate in Criminology at Ghent University. lieselot.bisschop@ugent.be.

2 Directive of the European Parliament and Council on the protection of the environment through criminal law (COM(2007) 51/Final).

3 Governance equals the intentional activities designed to shape the flow of events (Wood and Shearing, 2007, p. 6). Governance differs from government, because it includes different social and political units (governments, corporations, international organisations, NGOs, etc.) as governing social interactions (Holley, Gunningham, and Shearing, 2012; Parker and Braithwaite, 2003).

Criminal policy has long been dominated by public institutions, but in face of the worldwide complexities a shift was required from single governments to governance arrangements involving multiple actors (Loader and Sparks, 2002; Sheptycki, 2007). Environmental issues are one global dynamic with new actors (corporations, NGOs) taking up responsibilities formerly reserved for the nation state (Bartley, 2007; Gunningham *et al.*, 2003; Holley *et al.*, 2012). This has resulted in various regulatory hybrids where responses to (transnational) environmental crime may come from the administration (*e.g.* criminal justice system), but also from regulators and private actors.

To provide an empirical underpinning, this chapter examines how the governance of security framework – in the sense of preventing the illegal transports of e-waste from occurring[4] – is organised. To this end, this chapter reports on a study that carried out a nodal-networked governance analysis (Shearing and Johnston, 2010). This implies an analysis of the separate nodes[5] (nodal governance analysis) and their characteristics before moving to an analysis of their interactions (networked governance analysis). Throughout this analysis attention is paid to the local and global context that shapes the governance across the environmental flows (Aas, 2007; Spaargaren, Mol, and Bruyninckx, 2006; White, 2011). First, the nodal governance analysis examines how the nodes problematise the topic (mentalities), what they set as objectives (finalities) and what strategies they use to reach that goal (Johnston and Shearing, 2003). Governance actors involved in transnational environmental crime could well be driven by different objectives, interpreting behaviour differently and responding in various ways. The nodal governance analysis will make clear which government, corporate and third party actors take up governance responsibilities and within this, who takes a leading role (Braithwaite, 2002; Gunningham *et al.*, 1998; Wright and Head, 2009). Second, this chapter examines the interaction between these governance actors (networked governance analysis). This examines whether their interaction is cooperative, competitive or non-existent (Braithwaite, 2008; Crawford, 2006; Mazerolle and Ransley, 2006; Shearing and Johnston, 2010). Moreover, the networked governance analysis allows for an assessment whether there are individuals or groups (missing nodes) currently not mobilised in governance despite their relevant knowledge, capacity and resources.

---

4 It is not a reference to the general governance of economic flows or trade.

5 Instead of the term actor, 'node' will be used as well. Nodes are actors involved in governance.

Theoretical framework for regulation and governance

In many security matters, states are no longer single governing actors but there is a diversity of actors each involved in different interactions (Crawford, 2006; Wood and Dupont, 2006). Although hybrid arrangements seem logical in terms of the present and future arrangements, many authors still attribute a central role to state actors (Braithwaite, 2008; Gille, 2006; Jänicke, 2006). The governance of e-waste flows is thus at a crossroad between the management of trade flows and the prevention and control of illegality. A diverse range of actors can play a role within this governance framework. Traditionally, governmental institutions have a central responsibility for crime and security (Shearing and Johnston, 2010). Because illegal transports of e-waste have been subject to international conventions [6], the administration remains responsible, but this is in conjunction with other actors. In fact, a lot of the environmental issues have been dealt with centrally, assuming uniform compliance backed up by consistent punishment (Grabosky and Gant, 2000). This, however, provides only part of the solution to the complexity of environmental problems (Gunningham, 2004). The globalised e-waste flow challenges the states in drafting global governance frameworks (Sassen, 1996). This then allows other actors to play a role. Through self-regulation, corporate actors involved in the e-waste supply chain can contribute to the prevention and control of illegal transports. Corporations often prefer clarity in regulations in order to have a level playing field (Delmas and Young, 2009). Some are concerned about their reputation and see self-regulation as a way to distinguish themselves from the 'bad apples'. In these cases, they sometimes choose to pre-empt state initiative for regulation (Gunningham *et al.*, 2003). Moreover, self-regulation is a way for corporations to present themselves as responsible giving them a competitive advantage over non-compliant firms. In the face of a lack of government initiatives, non-state actors have sought alternative solutions for environmental issues (*e.g.* multi-stakeholder initiatives) (Bernstein and Cashore, 2007). Third actors such as consumers and non-governmental organisations (NGOs) also play a role in governance through labelling, certification initiatives, awareness raising and consumer boycotts.

The social reactions to transnational or corporate environmental crime can thus develop into a mixture of criminal law, civil law, administrative law and self-regulation, varying from controlling strategies (*e.g.* whistle-blowing or sanctioning) to stimulating strategies (Grabosky and Gant, 2000; Ponsaers and Hoogenboom,

6 See for instance the Basel Convention, Montreal Convention and the European Waste Shipment Regulation (WSR) and Waste Electric and Electronic Equipment (WEEE) Directive.

2004; Van de Bunt and Huisman, 2004). The governance reality can equally have developed into a regulatory hybrid where private actors play a role. The following briefly discusses two theoretical models about governance hybrids: responsive regulation and networked governance. These models were used in this e-waste case study.

A very influential theoretical model for dealing with corporate crime, and by extension with environmental crime, is the *responsive regulatory pyramid.* In responsive regulation, the approach is attuned to the motivations and characteristics of particular sectors and/or situations (Ayres and Braithwaite, 1992) thus avoiding the inflexibility and inefficiency of command and control (Wright and Head, 2009). The basic assumption is that the choice of regulatory strategy should be responsive to what is more appropriate for any given situation (Braithwaite, 2002). At the basis of the pyramid, there is ample room to act responsibly and for an appropriate restorative justice. By allowing corporate actors to self-regulate and having other actors meta-regulate[7], regulatory burdens are intended to be avoided. This is assumed to be the most successful by 'going beyond compliance' (Gunningham, Grabosky, and Sinclair, 1998).

In order to grasp the new reality of contemporary governance, Braithwaite (2008) suggested using a network rather than a pyramid metaphor, where the focus is less on the vertical dimension and more on the horizontal (Van Erp, 2008). The state is then just one actor within this hybrid governance arrangement, since corporate and civil society actors also have a role to play a role. A pre-requisite remains the competence of the state for punitive reactions when actors fail to regulate themselves and/or do not owne up to their responsibility (Braithwaite, 2008).

This networked governance[8] is the second model that embraces the idea of governance arrangements that go beyond the nation state paradigm and looks at the role played by non-state actors such as corporations and NGOs (Mazerolle and Ransley, 2006; Wood, 2006; Wood and Shearing, 2007). The basic assumption in networked governance is that different stakeholders act together towards achieving commonly defined and agreed goals. There could also in addition be coalitions of non-state actors, which set regulatory standards and their enforcement, independent of governments but not limited to self-regulation (Bartley, 2007). Others have referred to this as plural and fragmented policing (Loader, 2002), nodal and networked governance (Shearing and Johnston, 2010) or polycentric or de-

7 Meta-regulation is regulated self-regulation which means that controls happen on a higher level either by 3rd actors, by government or through public scrutiny, and are based on the own management system of the corporation (Gunningham, et al., 2003).

8 Networked governance owes many of its basic assumptions to the theory about the network society developed by Castells (2000).

centred governance referring to the multiple sites of regulation (Black, 2008). This networked governance model uses the concept of governance nodes in reference to non-governmental organisations, corporations, government agencies and citizen associations. The core focus is on the capacity of these nodes within the regulatory networks. This framework is particularly interesting for studying transnational environmental crime because complexity and (global) interdependency are core themes of the model (Holley *et al.*, 2012).[9]

Methodology

This research is based on a multi-method approach combining a document analysis, with interviews and field visits. By corroborating different perspectives and opinions about the cases, the arguments were exposed to validation or indeed falsification at different times (King, Keohane, and Verba, 1994; Yin, 2003). The respondents represent different segments of society – government, corporations and civil society.

The document-analysis gathers in-depth knowledge about the governance of the cases and is based on governmental sources (reports of inspectorates, police and customs, data-bases of waste crimes, policy plans), research reports (World Customs Organisation (WCO), Secretariat of the Basel Convention (SBC), United Nations Environmental Programme (UNEP), INECE[10], IMPEL(-TFS)[11], Interpol, the World Bank, independent consultants and academics), corporate documents (press releases, websites, year reports, policy plans, ethical codes) and documents by civil society actors (environmental organisations, nongovernmental organisations (NGO), media).

A total of 56 semi-structured interviews[12] were conducted: 27 interviews with 34 government actors, 16 interviews with 23 corporate actors, 13 interviews with and 14 civil society actors.[13] The governmental actors are national and international government agencies such as customs, environmental inspectorates, police

9 They detected five basic characteristics: collaboration of different stakeholders; participation of different groups on different levels of governance; deliberation about the goals and practice of governance; learning from practice; and accountability.

10 International Network for Environmental Compliance and Enforcement.

11 IMPEL is the European Network for the Implementation and Enforcement of Environmental Law; IMPEL-TFS is the subgroup of IMPEL that focuses on the inspection and enforcement of Transfrontier Shipments of Waste.

12 Interviews ranged from 45 minutes to 2 hours.

13 The number of interviews and number of respondents differ because some actors chose to address the researcher in pairs and 6 actors were interviewed twice. In addition, there was one group interview with 13 government respondents, 4 of which had already been interviewed separately.

organisations, prosecutor service and environmental administrations. The civil society respondents comprised scientists, representatives of national and international environmental NGOs, labour unions and investigative journalists. The corporate representatives are producers of (inter)national computer hardware, e-waste collectors, refurbishers and recyclers, and transport corporations.[14] These respondents were located within the Belgian research setting as well as in other EU countries, as locations of origin, together with Ghana as one of the countries of destination.

This research included 'field visits', limited to crucial sites and actors throughout the transnational e-waste flows. The researcher was present at the customs and the federal environmental inspectorate in the port of Antwerp. This part of the research focused on the export and transit of e-waste, relevant to the research setting of the port of Antwerp.[15] In addition, field visits in the port of Antwerp were carried out. Also the country of destination (Ghana) was visited because of its importance for the export from or transit in Belgium.[16] The port of Tema, the informal recycling and refurbishing firms and e-goods markets of Tema and Accra and the Agbogbloshie dumpsite were observed. Observations were triangulated with the data obtained from interviews and document analysis, integrating data about Belgium, Ghana and elsewhere in the analysis[17] (Mortelmans, Decorte, and Zaitch, 2009).

Nodal governance analysis of the e-waste flows

A range of authorities govern the illegal transportation of e-waste from countries of export and transit, in this case Belgium, to countries of import, in this case Ghana. This section provides the results of the nodal governance analysis, the examination of the reality of the separate governance nodes: governmental, corporate and civil

---

14 At the outset of this study, the respondents were guaranteed anonymity. For quotations they are referred to by the general stakeholder category (government (G), corporate (C) and civil society respondents (S)) and a number. This case study is part of a broader PhD research on transnational environmental crime, which also included another case (tropical timber). There is one list of respondents for both cases and respondents were number consecutively.

15 Import flows are predominantly destined for the major recycling facilities in the EU and therefore do not refer to the transnational environmental crime flows subject of this research.

16 See for example Bisschop (2012) and Gibbs et al. (2010).

17 More information about the data gathering and analysis can be found in the author's PhD thesis: *Governance of transnational environmental crime: Case study research on the illegal trade in e-waste and tropical timber* (Ghent University: Faculty of Law).

society actors. Their roles and responsibilities, strengths and weaknesses in dealing with e-waste are highlighted.[18]

a. Government actors (together) in the director's chair

The control and prevention of illegal e-waste transports involves a diverse range of government actors. Environmental administrations and inspectorates, customs, the harbourmaster's office, police and judiciary each play a role in Antwerp and Belgium. The following discusses the governance reality of these nodes. The role of the Ghanaian government actors is discussed separately.

a1. Environmental administrations

The Flemish public waste authority (*Openbare Vlaamse Afvalstoffenmaatschappij - OVAM*) is responsible for Flanders' waste policy and coordinates all Belgian statistics (*e.g.* for European Commission). OVAM is responsible for notification procedures of Flemish waste exports and imports. The notifications for transit are with the administration of the federal environmental inspection. Licenses are also one of the responsibilities of OVAM and is executed in close cooperation with the regional inspectorates. The most important function of OVAM for e-waste is in policy preparation, implementation and advice. They have an advisory function for authorities across Flanders. OVAM's policy preparation has influence across the regional borders.

a2. Environmental inspectorates

The Belgian responsibility for environmental inspection of waste transports is divided between the federal and the regional level. The control for transit is with the Federal Environmental Inspectorate (FEI/FLI/IFE) and the control for import and export is with the Flemish Environmental Inspectorate (EID/MI), Brussels Environmental Inspectorate (IBGE/BIM) and Walloon Environmental Inspectorate (DPE/URP).[19] For e-waste transports, 20% of containers and 10% second hand vehicles originate in Belgium, the rest is in transit. The responsibilities of these inspectorates were recently updated in order to stimulate a coherent policy and determine effective, proportionate and deterrent sanctions for breaches of the EU waste legislation.

---

18 In the scope of this chapter, it is impossible to discuss all governance characteristics of these nodes. Therefore, this is focused on those elements relevant to the e-waste case.

19 In view of the research setting of the port of Antwerp, the Flemish (FLI) and Federal inspectorate (MI) are most relevant. The other inspectorates are not discussed separately, but were contacted for interviews. FLI and MI, the Dutch abbreviations, are used.

The Federal Environmental Inspection (FLI) is responsible for transit of waste. Four FLI inspectors focus on the Belgian harbours, two of which work in the harbour of Antwerp and focus on all waste issues, e-waste being one of these. Their powers include stopping vehicles for cargo controls, requesting all documents for inspection, entering premises where waste in transit is temporarily stocked and interviewing staff. With the new law on the transit of waste, they became officers of judicial police, which allows them to give warnings, levy administrative fines, determine a deadline for compliance with the law, and block, secure, send back, take into custody or destroy goods and vehicles without compensation. The selection of shipments for inspection is made either by walking the quays and selecting units or by studying the documents. Selected containers and vehicles are scanned by customs using either their fixed or mobile scanners. The inspectorate interprets the images and unblocks the unit when the equipment is legal. In case of further suspicions, the units[20] are physically inspected.[21] When controlled transit shipments turn out to be illegal, they require details on the states of origin in order that the waste can be returned and a decision is made on whether to prosecute. This is, however, often to no avail. Therefore, if it is environmentally irresponsible to send the shipment back or if no responsible owner is found within reasonable time, the FLI makes sure the waste is treated within nearby licensed facilities. More recently, FLI has also been able to impose fines on shippers.[22] Given the limited staff that are available, the inspectors have to be selective: *e.g.* limiting scans to a maximum of 10 units or not unloading scanned units having few electronic devices. The administrative follow-up of the units is cniducted by the same inspectors. FLI selects the offences they think may secure a fine or prosecution.

The Flemish environmental inspectorate (MI) is crucial to address governance earlier in the supply chain, because this node deals with (import and) export of e-waste. They have the same powers as the federal inspectorate, mainly focusing on checks early in the chain through certification and licensing. Physical checks in the port are mainly carried out upon the request of other actors such as customs, maritime police or FLI.[23] In case other actors observe illegal imports or exports of waste the administrative control follow-up is the task of MI (LNE, 2010). When the facility is outside the Flemish territory, other Belgian or European authorities need to follow up. Road controls, controls in the harbour and site inspections of

20 Units can either be containers or vehicles.

21 Another factor they consider for physical checks is whether the suspicious unit was notified to them by other authorities (within Belgium or in countries of export).

22 This measure was new at the time of field visits and interviews. The impact could not be assessed.

23 Several times a year there are 'action days' in the ports. FLI, MI, customs, HMO and police then particularly focus on illegal waste shipments.

waste facilities is the task of two full time inspectors (LNE, 2011).[24] Approximately 5 to 6% of MI inspections results in police reports, but the core of their activities is administrative. Prosecution of waste cases is very difficult and therefore MI often prefers to address the license.

Both inspectorates are the go-to agency for advice, expertise and administrative follow-up up if other government actors detect suspicious units. Several respondents deemed this to be a bottleneck in the control of illegal transports of e-waste.

a3. Customs

The customs authorities are responsible for the clearance of the goods. Their core function is taxation and, therefore, they need to check whether the goods correspond with the bill of lading. They have also other tasks such as the protection of society's health, the environment and safety.[25] The respondents (G18) explained how the renewed focus seems to have repositioned customs within the security framework, which also has implications for their role in the governance of illegal e-waste transports. Faced with an enormous trade volume and limited staff, most customs controls concern documents and are led by a risk analysis system. Currently less than 1% of shipments are controlled and even a marginal increase would require a significant increase in staff. Automation and informatisation recently reoriented the customs' system from a transaction based to a system based control, which was intended to address both increased workload and the need to safeguard security. The system based control uses the management system of the corporations to determine control density. This changed focus on the quantity of controls had implications for their quality as well (Sluis, Marks, Gilleir, and Easton, 2012). The new system based control considers the most of transactions OK and uses 'green lanes' with limited checks. Automatic Economic Operators (AEO) form the core of the system based control. Producers, exporters, shipping agents, storage facilities, transporters and importers can all be granted the AEO certificate. It aims to stimulate self-regulation by rewarding integer behaviour with quicker processing and random checks.[26] Government respondents told me this AEO certification is not a watertight system because waste handlers who had been fined

24 In comparison, the Dutch inspectorates has 23 FTE responsible for waste matters.

25 Missie, http://fiscus.fgov.be/interfdanl/nl/publications/missie.htm (last consulted on December 29th 2011) and European Customs Information Portal http:// ec.europa.eu /ecip/ (last consulted on January 21st 2012).

26 Holders of the AEO certificates get certain advantages such as quicker customs simplified procedures, less physical verification and other controls. In case of controls, AEO certified companies get priority and can ask for a physical check of the goods at a particular location. AEO – Wat. Douane and Accijnzen. http://fiscus.fgov.be/interfdanl/nl/aeo/wat.htm (last consulted on 8 February 2012).

in Belgium received an AEO certificate in other EU countries, which grants them trade priorities across the EU.

In this system, customs use a risk analysis on the customs declarations, which contain information about the origin and destination of goods, goods codes, value, etc.[27] For (e-)waste, the system checks for particular countries of destination, descriptions of the goods, VAT-numbers, text selection (*e.g.* suspicious streets) and the value[28] of the goods. These criteria are informed by the legislation, by Risk Information Forms (RIF) and are further refined based on the past experience of customs in negotiation with environmental inspectorates and administrations. Note that this system applies only to import and export and not to transit data because the documents in countries of transit do not contain enough information for an effective risk analysis. The risk analysis is the responsibility of the EU country of export. For goods in transit, customs (need to) trust the export checks of other EU states, as foreseen in the European waste legislation. This is problematic because 80% of e-waste shipments are in transit in Antwerp.

Another critique of the system is that the customs' scanners are not used to their full potential.[29] "*If you ask me, it's merely a matter of good logistic planning. The only costs you have are the customs' staff and that's where the shoe pinches. As long as this does not cause delays in shipment, we applaud the use of scanners*" (C4). Some respondents called these "*mere teething problems*" and found other critiques more fundamental. For instance, they said the system does not allow enough discretion to determine the checks from the bottom up. "*Personnel on the ground know the flows very well and are able to assess whether or not to expect trouble. Practical knowledge and experience seems to be referred to playing the second fiddle*" (G17). The risk analysis system, however, still allows input based on practical experience and leaves room for individual choices whether via documents, scan or physical control.

Customs have an autonomous stop-function for illegal waste transports, but are not a first line service that acts autonomously for environmental issues. The administrative follow-up is for the inspectorates. The reality is, of course, that customs have more staff than other law enforcement nodes in this field. Customs have already demonstrated that waste transports can be intercepted when they focus on this intensely. "*The involvement of customs in environmental matters to a major extent depends on the motivation and passion of individual officers. Hierarchical leaders tell them not to focus on non-fiscal matters too much, because it is not their core priority*" (S10).

A final critique of the role of Antwerp customs as a governance node for e-waste is the possibility of having a 'late bill of lading' – which in practice means

---

27 For waste transports, attachment 7 and notification documents are required.

28 In case a container of electronic equipment is reported with a value of 500 euro this will give a warning, because it is likely to be of low quality.

29 In 2010, 30.529 containers were scanned whereas the total capacity is 70.000 containers.

you can deliver the cargo in the port and provide the necessary documentation afterwards. The respondents were not clear about this: some said it was everyday practice while others thought it not possible, reflecting a lack in coherence in policy.[30]

a4. Harbourmaster's Office

The Harbourmaster's Office (HMO), part of the Antwerp Port Authority (APA), has the responsibility for safeguarding the safety, peace, public order, integrity and environment of the port area. The Harbourmaster and his deputies are officers of judicial police and have the authority to investigate criminal offences and submit police reports (Verstraeten, 2007). The policing authority of HMO is limited to the nautical context and to the territory of the harbour. HMO handles about 550 offences each year of which 75% result in police reports. Most of these concern violations of environmental legislation, the vessel traffic system or the dangerous goods regulation. As part of the APA, HMO has the difficult task of uniting both economic and safety rationalities.[31] Economically this actor advertises the flexibility of the port in Antwerp which does not always coincide with the governance reality of preventing and controlling illegal e-waste transports. Other respondents feared the fragmented policy at the terminals[32] in Antwerp furthers criminal activity. "*There are currently vehicles that are driven from Greece or Italy to be shipped in Antwerp, so there has to be a reason for making this trip worthwhile*" (G15). Of particular importance for the case of e-waste, is the new police regulation that was issued by HMO to address worries about the port of Antwerp's reputation as a waste hub in second hand vehicles and their cargos. The extra cargo in the vehicles now requires a bill of lading that needs to be accessible and controllable. It stipulates that CFC-holding equipment is not allowed and all used electric and electronic equipment (UEEE) has to be functional. A particular advantage of this new regulation is that it allows for immediate fines in case of transgressions up to a maximum of 1.500 euro per offence. It remains to be seen how the new regulation of this governance node will work in practice, since the newly hired staff were not employed at the time of the empirical research. Transport corporations (C4) fear the effect of increased controls on trade and the potential diversion to lower control ports.

30 Antwerp is known as a flexible part where "*you can put a container on the ship of yesterday*" (S10). Particularly, units that arrive on Friday afternoon have a chance of being on the ship without checks.

31 http://www.portofantwerp.com/portal/page/portal/POA_EN/Havenhandboek/ Haven lexicon (last consulted on December 28th 2011).

32 The terminals have different policies, whereas other European ports (e.g. Rotterdam) have a more integrated policy for the entire port area.

a5. Federal environmental and maritime police

Within the harbour, the maritime police are responsible for (e)waste cases as one amongst many environmental on which they focus.[33] When the shipper or location of loading is located near the Antwerp harbour, local police can also be involved. The police focus mainly on major criminal cases in which the federal judicial police are responsible for gathering information. Waste fraud has been listed as a police priority in the national security plan, implying that the police focus on it proactively and reactively. In practice, the police focus is on serious environmental crimes, which means they are organised, linked to a corporate setting, involve high profits, are international, repetitive, related to other criminal behaviour and have an impact on the environment as well as citizens' health. The police as a governance node is confronted with different challenges in preventing and controlling e-waste transports. There is limited staff and resources available, located in different municipal and judicial districts. Many of the respondents, also in other government agencies, were worried about the potential implications of future priority changes and are concerned about a lack of hierarchical support (G18). Given the limited resources, it should come as no surprise that proactive controls are limited. In these investigations the police try to target the offender and attempt to calculate the illegal profits. It is often very difficult to retrospectively prove that earlier waste transports were illegal as well or to follow the trace to the source. Moreover, the environmental police officers are experts on police investigations, but not on environmental issues for which they need environmental administrators and inspectors, whose reports are added to the police files. When checks by the maritime police point towards illegal shipments the container can be blocked, but the follow-up is the responsibility of the appropriate authorities.

a6. Judicial authorities

The port of Antwerp is located both on the left and right banks of the Scheldt estuary, which translates into separate judicial and municipal districts, with its own law enforcement priorities. Depending on the *locus operandi*, the prosecution has judicial authority in either the districts of Antwerp or Dendermonde. The judicial authorities of Antwerp took the initiative to set up a project approach for waste fraud in the port of Antwerp. This plan stipulates that prosecution priority is with those offences that are so serious that available administrative sanctions or procedures are considered insufficient. Moreover, these need to involve either criminal intent by the perpetrator, imply a real risk for the environment or public

33 De Scheepvaartpolitie http://www.polfed-fedpol.be/org/org_dga_spn_nl.php (last consulted January 21st 2012)

health, cause abnormal hindrance for the surrounding area or result in significant financial benefits. This plan stresses the importance of partnerships and follow-up of cases through the (criminal) justice chain. It lists both quantitative and qualitative micro-indicators to follow up the actions taken by the different governance nodes, although they cannot hold each other to account. The follow-up is the responsibility of the working group on waste fraud. Preventive aspects do not form part of this plan. The success of the judicial approach depends on the information provided by other actors, gathered from different perspectives and therefore of limited value.[34] Information from different relevant sources is gathered by the prosecutor at which level information can be integrated.

In principle, all possible means will be used to prosecute import and export cases and also transit issues will be met with sanctions. In practice prosecution of transit cases is problematic and the focus is mainly on export. Out-of-court settlements are given whenever possible, in which also economic motivations play a role.

> "The objective is to investigate the potential criminal networks involved in it and find those 'big fish', but there are many intermediaries in different (international) locations. There is cooperation needed with different actors and it is a very media sensitive topic. Moreover, in everything we do, we feel the threat of the economic lobby. An enforcement actor who wants a new regulation to be imposed in the harbour gets a lot of critique. Economic actors are often protected by powerful people up in the government hierarchy" (G19).

In practice the cases thus hardly ever result in successful court cases, while fines[35] are too low and prosecution is too slow to be effective, similar to that found in other environmental cases (Faure, 2012). This is a problem not only for Belgium, but applies throughout Europe: "*If you get fined for a WSR-breach, a fine of 1.000 euro is very unlikely and hardly ever imposed. If you are in the illegal waste business, you can make that part of your business plan*" (S20).

---

34 This relates to the 'administrative dependence of the environmental criminal law' (Faure, 1991).

35 Sanctions can be as high as 8 days to 3 years imprisonment and/or a fine of 52 to 4.000.000 euro for breaches of article 7 and 9 of the Belgian law on transit of waste and breaches of WSR articles and other EU regulations. Breaches of articles 10, 16, 17 and 18 of the WSR and other EU laws are met with imprisonment of 8 days to 1 year and a fine of 40 to 120.000 euro.

a7. Government actors in Ghana as a country of destination

Despite signing the international conventions, there is currently no Ghanaian legislation that regulates e-waste or second hand transports. As long as that is not in place, checking transports is to no avail since no fines can be imposed.

The Ghanaian Environmental Protection Agency (EPA) aims to play a similar role as the inspectorates in countries of origin or transit, but has very limited staff. Two full time employees work on waste issues. In absence of a legal basis to act, their main concern is with raising awareness among government actors about the dangers of e-waste since many consider them as profitable second hand products. The EPA's current enforcement focus is on licensing recycling facilities and analysing where WEEE/UEEE is sold and refurbished. However, these actors are numerous, very flexible and spread out across Ghana. Other respondents think this licensing by means of environmental impact assessments is too high a barrier for many recycling facilities pushing them into informality. This was observed in Belgium as well, where small scale collectors could not answer to the high standards imposed. The EPA therefore reaches out to these informal actors and shows them how to improve the working conditions with simple tools similar to what local NGOs do. "*The core idea is to support them instead of criminalize them*" (G29).

Ghanaian customs are less concerned with e-waste, despite their governance potential. The researchers observed how containers of WEEE/UEEE are inspected and unloaded by customs. E-waste is not their first concern, especially because they can impose high taxes on imports of electronics and also given the low level of training. The scanning facilities are present, but only homogenous shipments are inspected. In face of this governance reality, customs will need more incentives (*e.g.* rewards for seizing low quality goods): "*Customs are paid very low wages so they want a piece of the cake for themselves.*"(G28). In the event that a law is passed, awareness raising and training of these enforcers will be crucial. Even then, the problem remains that seized goods will have to be recycled locally, often ending up in the same system.

As for other governance nodes, the Ghana Ports and Harbours Authority (GPHA) focuses on environmental safety in the port. Their main concern is the dumping of waste and release of waste water. A few of their employees are concerned about e-waste, but this depends on their own interest in the topic. Ghanaian police do not work on environmental issues and there are no cases going to court.

b. Corporations as (passive) governance nodes

This section examines the governance reality of corporate actors in e-waste flows. The roles of shipping agents, shipping lines and e-goods producers and recyclers are analysed. This will make clear that the governance of the flows is not really a priority for these nodes, since their role is often limited to responding to requests of government actors. Others take more initiative, mostly when it coincides with their core business (Gunningham *et al.*, 2003).

b1. Shipping agents

A shipping agent is paid by the buyer or seller to organise the transport. Their tasks can involve drafting the bill of lading, taking care of the transport documentation and arranging the payments and deposits. A number of observations can be made. Commodity handlers in Antwerp recognise they have a responsibility in the transport of second hand vehicles containing e-waste. "*In the past, some of these vehicles were definitely filled with goods, amongst others e-waste. But meanwhile, a code of conduct was drafted which was later used as a basis for the new regulation*" (C2). As witnessed in the field visits, not all shipping agents however agreed the shipments were a bad thing: "*Inspectors themselves should go to Africa to see how difficult life is*" (C23). The fact that many shipping agents are unaware of the issue or even facilitate regular illegal transports was made obvious by a terminal operator in Ghana (C19).

The shipping agents' business is based on trusting the shippers and shifting the responsibility to actors earlier in the chain: the shipper. Shipping agents, and especially those that do the handling and storage as well, however, have the opportunity to know both the content and the customers. Some shipping agents take the initiative to know their clients, refusing the problematic ones or undertake to inform them about what is allowed, warning them about possible fines.[36] Some even anticipate potential trouble and ask their customers for a guarantee (*e.g.* € 3.000), because the terminal will charge the shipping agent for the costs of unloading.[37] Others, however, work with whatever clients they can get. Both government and corporate respondents suggested installing a system of minimum prerequisites for shipping agents "*You would quickly see who is willing to go the extra*

36 They do this by providing the port regulations of Antwerp to their clients (translated in English, French or German) and by distributing ads and warning notices in their office and on their website which explain what is allowed and what is not (e.g. CFC, missing cables).

37 In addition, port authorities can block their financial guarantee and revoke their license. The Belgian judicial system also tries to deal with them as accomplices.

mile, and then you know enough to target controls. This would have to be EU-wide to avoid economic consequences of stricter controls in Antwerp" (C2).

b2. Shipping lines

The sector of international maritime transports and trade through ports is known for its somewhat in-transparent way of communication (Denoiseux, 2010). "*Although environmental issues could be part of this broader denominator of security, it is still not a major concern*" (C5). It is indeed true that contacting shipping lines for this research was challenging. One major shipping line was however, willing to talk. Together with the interviews of the other governance actors, this allowed us to analyse their role in the illegal e-waste flows. Some shipping lines take the initiative to self-regulate and several incentives stimulate this. This however does not necessarily mean the entire shipping industry is influenced by these incentives. Economic, ethical and political considerations guide them to refuse certain shipments (Bartley, 2007). A first motivation is their concern to be a sustainable and responsible actor. The reputational risk also plays an important role. Shipping lines do not strictly have a legal responsibility in illegal e-waste flows, but they feel subject to criticism from their stakeholders. Being recognised as a responsible actor is seen as being economically beneficial. They also face the financial risk of fines and of costs of transports not being refunded. For a shipping line, the container itself (not the content) is an asset and it is important to get this back. Moreover, shipping lines are sometimes targeted in countries of destination because judges choose to target them for a case of illegal waste transport, as the closest actor in proximity, chaining their vessels until the costs are paid for. The shipping lines' involvement (or some of them) is also guided by both the society's tendency to increasingly challenge shipping lines on legal and ethical issues and the fact that the 21st Century provides a hyper-transparent community. Shipping lines however, worry how much they can engage without taking up a responsibility that is not theirs. To a certain extent, they choose to remain pragmatic while staying within the existing legal framework. Similar to the shipping agents, shipping lines do not have the authority to open containers and they are even at a greater distance to the initial shipper. They rely on the trustworthiness of shippers and shipping agents. "*Many shipping lines are not intrinsically motivated to know what is inside containers*" (S20). Other respondents believed these actors use tricks to hide behind their commercial practicalities and know they transport illegal waste, but until recently were not challenged on this by their stakeholders.

b3. European producers and recyclers

European recyclers' corporations are also increasingly involved as governance nodes in e-waste, although their motivations are linked to the raw materials discussion rather than the environment. Their incentive is the availability of metal scrap. Therefore, they try to influence EU policy and aim for the continued criminalisation of transports of e-waste in protection of the 'urban mine'.[38] This economic factor is a major part of the current policy discussion and is critical for success, together with addressing corporations on their (loss of) reputation. Many corporations may even be stricter because customers increasingly ask for end-use information or take other measures to boost their corporate image. Recyclers are setting up take-back initiatives in (West) Africa, partly for the environment, but also to save labour costs for dismantling the equipment. Monitoring is, therefore, important. This could be connected to formal collection and dismantling initiatives that have emerged in Ghana as well as to the informal sector, which collects 90% of e-waste (Rufener, 2012, 9).

A central concern for recyclers is with the establishment of a level playing field. Currently, EU countries are perceived to protect their own market and hamper the enforcement of the EU waste legislation. Similarly, recycling corporations across the EU have difficulty in focussing their efforts because they suspect competitors of feeding into illegal transportation. Others believe self-regulatory initiatives to be a promising alternative. The European recycling industry therefore proposed a scheme for controls on e-waste transport, in which the percentage of controls is tailored to both the destination (low-medium-high risk) and the exporter (low-medium-high risk) (Euromettaux, 2012).[39] It proposes that controls should take place at the EU port of departure at the exporter's costs and that second hand equipment should be identifiable in the customs documents for more thorough inspection.

Producers of EEE could also choose to self-regulate. They are required to take steps because of their extended producer responsibility as determined by the Waste Electronic and Electric Equipment (WEEE) Directive, which makes producers

38 The urban mine are the (raw) materials from products, buildings and waste in a society. Urban mining is the idea of using those compounds and elements as resources for new production, thereby avoiding these materials from going to waste. E-waste exports can thus be seen as a loss in raw material.

39 Low risk exporters, which are those with AEO certificates, should have 0,0001% chance of control when they ship to low risk countries (OECD), 0,001% chance when they ship to medium risk (other non-OECD) countries and 0,01% when shipping to high risk (West-African countries). Medium risk exporters are manufacturers, producers and important traders and they should respectively have a 0,01%; 0,1% and 1% chance of control when shipping to low, medium and high risk countries. High risk exporters (all other) should respectively have a 1%, 10% and 100% chance of control.

responsible for take-back and recycling of their products, and the Regulation on Hazardous Substances (RoHS) that requires manufacturers to phase out the use of the most hazardous components, though it is difficult to trace these products. Two government and three NGO respondents mentioned that they would prefer producers to set-up a take back system for their products which would make all other take back uninteresting. Some producers are currently moving into that niche, similar to refurbishers on the other end of the supply chain. In countries of destination, some producers take their extended producer responsibility seriously. Other producers however claim they are not responsible and blame the shippers. A Ghanaian waste collector (C25) puts it as follows: "*currently producers are cherry picking what they will and won't take back. [. . .] Producers should be encouraged to take back their equipment, take the metal, circuit boards and plastic casings. The main problem is that they don't care about their image*" " (C25).

c. Civil society actors as crucial (but waning) support

Besides the role for government and corporate nodes in the governance of illegal transports of e-waste, the question remains over role played by civil society actors. It seems rather clear to most of the respondents that NGOs continue to have a crucial role to play in distributing information and continuing to raise awareness. In the 1970s and 1980s, NGOs scandalised illegal waste shipments and played an essential role in negotiations for the Basel Convention. Their current importance is in keeping up pressure. NGOs like Greenpeace have already used GPS trackers to follow e-waste around the world and to bring the topic to the public attention. Similarly, they publish the tags that were found on dumped e-waste or confront previous owners with their old data. This technique could be used to track containers as well (Auld, Cashore, Balboa, Bozzi, and Renckens, 2010). The focus on (e-)waste however sometimes seems to be limited as opposed to concerns for animals. One of the Ghanaian respondents (G28) explained that they saw fluctuations in transports depending on the amount of attention for e-waste in countries of origin.

For NGOs based in Western countries, their role seems to be one of contributing to the achievements of other governance nodes (Young, 2009) and in the meanwhile continuing their environmental advocacy (Holley *et al.*, 2012). These NGOs, however, do continue to be involved as stakeholders in policymaking on both EU and UN level. By their presence at these levels, they can help to broaden policy maker's traditional attention to narcotics or terrorism. Similarly, they could play a role in converting the international legislation to national laws in countries of destination, while furthering the often neglected implementation (S22).

Several of the respondents raised the concern that NGOs are western centred, disregarding the local context. "*Involving the informal collection and dismantling sector can help towards lowering the environmental harm. Stopping the inflow of e-waste is then only secondary to teaching them how to recycling more environmentally and health friendly*" (S21) NGOs based in the local settings have a good chance of involving those communities affected by illegal e-waste flows – but not recognised as such and getting them involved in the governance process as a complement to the conventional strategies (Braithwaite, 2000; Holley *et al.*, 2012). Local Ghanaian NGOs working on e-waste try to involve informal actors as well as reach out to recyclers for support. Their intention is to reduce the illegal imports, but even then the problem of recycling the domestic consumption of new products will remain a problem. Therefore, they set-up capacity building projects (for example, by providing informal actors with the tools to dismantle or burn e-waste). NGOs should be self critical as well. Several NGOs or smaller scale charity projects have been associated with illegal transports of e-waste.

> "There are so many do-good initiatives in Europe that are actually doing wrong. Out-of-use and all those so-called charities that ask you to send your phone, it is for a so-called good cause but so much disappears into the pockets of those that organise it. The question is why people, and mind you, major corporations and NGOs, continue to be fooled by this. Even investment funds finance recyclers who don't necessarily practice what they preach" (G22).

The role of civil society actors thus seems to be in shaming and blaming illegal e-waste transports as well as in attempting to find the best governance approach attuned to the local context (cf. capacity building). Braithwaite (2008) referred to this as balancing the responsive regulatory pyramid with a strength-based pyramid.

Networked governance analysis

In the departure, transit and destination locations of e-waste, different nodes have a governance responsibility. The roles governments, corporations and civil society actors play were discussed above. The following networked governance analysis examines the interactions within the governance reality of illegal e-waste flows.

a. Same intentions and different realities in inter-agency cooperation

The analysis of the governance reality shows cooperation between the nodes. Each of the government actors analysed in this study made clear that their work on illegal transports of e-waste is only one part of the entire control mechanism. In the first place there are the environmental inspectorates and administration. Flemish inspectorates (export) will usually address corporations on their license by following the e-waste flow back to its source. The inspectorates negotiate licenses of facilities. Of course, this inevitably relates back to the management systems – and self-regulation of corporations. Similarly, the AEO system of customs gives corporations the opportunity to make sure a management system is in place which influences the degree of control. Neither of these, however, applies easily to the multitude of small scale (often individual) shippers of UEEE/WEEE because they are difficult to trace. The federal inspectorate (transit) – which deals with 80% of the e-waste shipments in Antwerp – moreover relies on other EU states to trace the transports back to their origin. Depending on the features of the case one or another actor takes up a leading role. This can merely be a result of a practical reality, of the available expertise or can genuinely be out of concern for an integrated approach. The judiciary clearly takes a leading role in the approach to waste fraud in the port of Antwerp. Customs takes a leading role in the risk analysis system. Inspectorates and administrations have the expertise on environmental issues. Hence, the primary role in the governance of illegal e-waste flows seems to be that of law enforcement rather than of the administrative level. Belgium has the advantage of having an environmental administration (OVAM) that takes up a role that other countries reserve for local administrations. The administrative/ preventative aspects are developed into policy by the Flemish and Federal Administrations and are of course highly influenced by the European framework. The risk is that local authorities in Belgium are not fully engaged in the process (Braithwaite, 2008).

Transparency and clear delineation of tasks and objectives is crucial to avoid government actors from fighting each other instead of crime (Sluis *et al.*, 2012). The question is then whether these actors work with the same intentions and the same realities at hand. Environmental inspectorates both clearly focus on illegal transports of e-waste for environmental reasons, but work in different surroundings. Whereas the regional inspectorates are in the position to address the topic earlier in the chain, the federal inspectorate only has the location of the port within which to work. OVAM is similarly oriented towards environmental issues but focuses on initiatives earlier in the chain (licences) as well as policy making. The customs' focus on illegal transports of e-waste is rather recent and struggles with balancing concerns for security and the economy. Customs specialises in customs-related responsibilities, is at the front line in import and export of waste, has the technical means to control (scanning of containers and risk analysis) and has many 'eyes and ears'. Note however, that a system based on trust does not match the approaches of other government actors. A question remains whether this system of trust in economic operators by customs and even the system of trust in compliance by the environmental administrations can be united with the strategies of judicial actors that work on a basis of distrust.

The HMO's priority is with safety and compliance. E-waste is a rather recent concern and they have to maintain a balance with economic interests. HMO can now control for e-waste in second hand vehicles and their increased resources are important. Customs as well as HMO, however, rely on the environmental inspectorates for the follow up of the cases they find suspicious. Unless these agencies equally receive additional resources, the extra focus of customs and HMO risks becomes futile. Finally, the police and the judiciary are both clearly concerned with the illegal transport of e-waste because they are environmental crimes and have a potential or alleged link to 'organised crime'. This only concerns the serious and extensive cases. The police expertise on strategic analysis could prove useful for all data on illegal e-waste trade.

One of the criticisms of corporations is that the implementation of the law seems to be valued higher than the environmental interest. Corporations experience an extra burden in terms of administration because of the fragmentation of agencies and perceive the staff resources invested in controls as inefficient. This efficiency of the network will get increasingly important, given the planned expansion of the Antwerp harbour and its associated commodity flows. The governance involves different layers of authority and faces different objectives and means. Although these nodes are all part of the governmental response to these issues, their methods and everyday work floor reality are different. Their cooperation determines whether there is coherence in governance.

b. Starting cooperation between shipping lines and governments

As witnessed during the field visits and interviews, many port actors do not know what e-waste is and are unaware of the potential harms. Some company brochures and websites are already mentioning sustainability and the like, but the translation into practice lags behind in both Belgium and Ghana. "*[P]ractical advice [should be] directed not only at the managers of these companies but also at the actual cargo handlers.*

This might not stop crafty criminals from shipping e-waste illegally, but might address 'low hanging fruit'" (S20). As a testimony to the governance potential of shipping lines, the UK shipping lines are partners of the waste enforcement agencies. They provide them with information about their clients and in this way help to keep their business clean and help to trace waste back to its origin. It is, however, not possible to replicate this in Antwerp. Stimulated by Dutch inspectorates a seminar was organised (IMPEL-TFS) to look at options for future cooperation with shipping lines. A similar approach is taken in countries of destination where shipping lines are increasingly providing the authorities with information to facilitate controls or even warn their clients in case of suspicions.

c. The challenge of (better) information exchange

Information exchange between governance nodes is crucial for success (Holley *et al.*, 2012). Government agencies are faced with the challenge of better exchange, because the agencies gather information from different perspectives and on the basis of different objectives. Information exchange between private actors and government agencies is even more complex. Information led investigations are a core issue for policing illegal transports of e-waste. The current systems are capable of detecting and sanctioning individual perpetrators of waste legislation, though insufficient to tackle the repeat offenders. The information led policing strategy is also applied by environmental inspectorates, particularly the regional ones, because they follow the goods in the supply chain and go in search of the source. Currently, different databases and systems for information exchange are in use, but the respondents complained that these systems do not always work both ways. Administrative information does flow towards police or judicial actors, but the former do not always get feedback. Different agencies currently gather data, often with limited resources, but databases are not always interconnected. The coordination and communication platform in the port of Antwerp is an important trigger for this, but by extension this requires the analysis of data across national borders in case of internationally operating perpetrators (G29). Not all EU countries however, allow for the exchange of administrative information. Each authority has to go through the respective national channels to get access to police files, customs files, etc. (Ponsaers *et al.*, 2008). Recently, a platform for information exchange and cooperation on environmental crime was set up at Europol, called *Envicrimenet*. This is intended to gather and analyse information and coordinate actions and strategies. At the moment however, not all individual member states provide information about environmental crime to Europol, so no strategic analysis is yet possible. When fully functional, this could take the governance system to a nodal level, taking responsibility for the meta-perspective. Using this intelligence could be difficult, since it was gathered for different objectives and exchange is often not allowed.

Increased information exchange illustrates which observations should raise suspicion with shipping lines and agents.[40] Examples of suspicious cargos abound: *e.g.* clients offer to pay cash for 10 containers or provide a hotmail-address as contact details; the destination of the recycling is the 9th floor of an office building; shippers refuse to provide information on the destination. Respondents mentioned that some shipping lines already have informal 'black lists' that are fed with generic information from both corporate and government contacts such as descriptions of cargo and destinations. They make sure that they do not share personal information. "*Although corporations and governments might be walking a thin privacy line in this matter, the risk of negative publicity gives them enough incentive. This information is, however, not shared lightly*" (S20). Once again concerns were raised about the one-sidedness of the communication. A concern for shipping lines was that, despite the increasing information exchange, they did not get the impression a lot was done with it. A concern for recyclers and waste traders is the protection of data against competitors.[41]

d. The exceptions to the rule

Despite e-waste fraud being an issue of national and international importance, resources are limited as is political will (Griffiths and Jenks, 2012). Compared to other international crimes such as drugs, the law enforcement resources invested in environmental crime are limited (Faure, 2012; White, 2011). Both in countries of origin and destination, there are a limited number of people involved. Despite their field knowledge and experience being crucial for the governance framework, they are bound by their limited resources affecting particularly the follow-up of initial detections. "*The problem is not that we don't know where the illicit traffic is, know where to find it or know how to check it. The problem is that we don't have the means to guarantee the follow-up, that's the bottleneck*" (G14).

All agents are crucial sources of information, but this intelligence is limited, fragmented and not always put to good use. These exceptions to the rule are passionate about their job, but frustration looms. Taken to the extreme, this implies

40 Privacy issues pose a problem here. Discussing the judicial possibilities of and limits to information exchange was not the intent of this study.

41 Business to business information exchange exists also, but only applies to a limited number of metals. "*Certain compositions are as accurate as a fingerprint. For other e-waste flows however, the situation is totally different because many actors are involved and in mixing waste, relabeling it, etc. modus operandi are multiple*" (C16).

that the success of this entire networked governance depends on these 'exceptions' (sources of information). This goes against the requirements of effective environmental governance as identified by Holley, Gunningham and Shearing (2012).

e. The harmonisation of policy rather than implementation

The flows of goods – e-waste amongst them – are difficult to govern by national authorities (Brown, 2010). Implementation of governance in more complex arrangements is often problematic (Holley *et al.*, 2012). Katja Franko Aas (2011, 333) moreover warned that supranational governance systems should not be met with limitless optimism, because they are often "*negotiated, rendered less efficient and even sabotaged by sovereignty games played by individual nation states*". The e-waste case illustrates that the conversion from paper to practice entails many challenges. Electronics are a very dynamic topic, where new inventions become e-waste a few years later. The policy that defines what type of equipment is e-waste therefore needs to adapt to this dynamic governance reality. Currently, that is not the case given that "*by the time CRTs will be considered e-waste by European law, the major share of CRTs – and thus the lead it contains - will already have been exported as second hand goods and dismantled in unacceptable circumstances*" (G24). Every European country is supposed to do thorough checks of exports of e-waste, implying that transit countries can trust their judgement. Government, corporate and civil society respondents, however, notice a North-South and West-East schism in Europe with respect to how seriously inspections and transport controls are taken and the existing problems with e-waste transit in Antwerp testify to this. Both environmental inspectors and shipping agents responsible for sending back the units even come across authorities that doubt that the shipment originated in their country. This led different respondents to refer to the need for further harmonisation of EU policy implementation to avoid displacements. The continued harmonisation on the level of implementation is politically very sensitive. Even if definitions and interpretations would be the same, Europe – let alone the global policy – is a long way from harmonization of implementation. Not all member states use complementary interventions besides the traditional environmental inspection and when controls become more severe in one country, illegal flows shift to another.

Another field with lacking EU harmonization is sanctioning. Although the European waste legislation requires sanctions to be set, there are major differences. Fines differ by up to a factor of 100 across the EU. Even within countries there are considerable differences in decision-making (Sander and Schilling, 2010). It would be beneficial to organise the controls on EU level for more unity, but this is a politically a very sensitive topic. As a consequence, "*[t]hey risk becoming a mere paper tiger, a mere increase of administration that makes unpractical suggestions*" (S20). Besides the various initiatives for international networking, the responsible authorities cooperate bilaterally with their neighbouring countries as well as with countries of destination such as Ghana, but given the limited staff and resources this is difficult.

Different international guidelines and soft measures exist and are stimulated by networks such INECE[42], IMPEL-TFS[43], Secretariat of the Basel Convention[44], the WCO[45] and the StEP-initiative[46]. These initiatives organise training sessions in countries of destination and fund capacity-building projects. Despite their realisations, a challenge to these international networking initiatives is their voluntary character. Unambiguous measures (*e.g.* inspections and controls) are more difficult to agree on.

Discussion

This chapter examined the governance reality of the illegal trade in e-waste in a European trade hub. Throughout the flows different nodes have a governance responsibility. The analysis of the governance reality illustrated how the control and prevention of illegal e-waste flows is primarily taken up by government actors, which is not surprising given its criminalisation. Similar to what Holley *et al.* (2012) found, the state is crucial for definitional guidance, for inducing corporate actors to participate through both positive and negative incentives and for using their enforcement capacity. An important challenge is the underfunding of the government actors with consequences for training, resources and effective follow-up throughout the flows (Brack and Hayman, 2002). Despite the good intentions of many, the actual governance of illegal transports of e-waste remains limited. Governments are perceived to be too slow to respond. An important characteristic

42 INECE stimulates trainings and exchange of expertise to increase the interception of vessels.

43 IMPEL-TFS plays a role in standardizing control practices in ports concerning the export of UEEE/WEEE to non-EU countries and is involved in trainings in countries of destination.

44 Its Partnership for Action on Computing Equipment (PACE) focuses on criteria for reuse of personal computers and aims to draft further regulation of export (Basel Convention Secretariat, 2011). It invests in capacity building projects in countries of destination (e.g. e-waste for Africa).

45 The World Customs Organisation supports the fight against transnational organised crime (e.g. hazardous waste) (Otterson and Meiser, 2009; WCO, 2009).

46 Governments, corporations, NGOs and researchers jointly operate in the StEP initiative of the United Nations University, a discussion platform to advice for policy making.

of responsive regulation is its punitive reaction in case of (continued) non-compliance (Braithwaite, 2008; Nielsen and Parker, 2009). As it has been argued, that is not at all certain for illegal trade in e-waste, at least not in countries of origin and even less likely in countries of destination.

This analysis of the governance reality in the port of Antwerp inevitably opened up the scope to a larger scale approach. It cannot be analysed without relating it to the global trade flows. The sheer scale of global trade makes it very challenging to base the governance framework only on governmental basis (Sassen, 1996), let alone narrow it down to a penal law perspective. Governance actions by one country are necessarily limited in their effectiveness. Due to the global interdependencies of the flows of e-waste, governance activities on one end are vulnerable to governance activities at the other end (Urry, 2003; Yar, 2011). Illegal e-waste flows and their governance are inherently transnational, but much of the implementation remains local and fragmented. As a consequence, corporate actors perceive an absence of a level playing field.

To engage corporate actors in the governance of these flows, carefully designed incentives are needed, both positive and negative, because economic and environmental interests do not necessarily coincide (Gunningham *et al.*, 1998; Holley *et al.*, 2012). A part of the governance reality is the supply chain of electronics where producers, recyclers and consumers play a role (van Erp and Huisman, 2010). Corporate actors already contribute to the governance of illegal e-waste flows, although not all producers, recyclers as well as transporters play an equally proactive role. For producers and recyclers, the governance involvement largely depends on their estimated profitability, as well as their corporate image. The economic importance of the subject for these corporate actors can be used to the benefit of the environment. The raw material discussion can also contribute to make recycling facilities more efficient and encourage eco-design. Transport actors could be encouraged to be diligent and transparent.

Reducing demand is very complicated, because dismantling e-waste and second hand electronics in search of precious metals is a sole source of secure livelihood for many (Bisschop, 2012). In face of this complex governance reality, it is useful to consider governance nodes that are not primary stakeholders (*cf.* so-called missing nodes, Wood, 2006). Capacity building in developing countries – addressing the structural causes – is already partially part of the current governance reality, but a lot of these initiatives are still small scale and *ad hoc*. The strength of these capacity building projects is their potential to engage local actors, for instance the informal workers in countries of destination. NGOs seem to be the most suitable actors to engage them in this process. NGOs already play a role in raising consumer awareness and in keeping both corporations and governments attentive.

Corporations are increasingly involving informal actors as well, since they see the economic advantages. Involving the informal sector risks becoming unbalanced (*e.g.* exploitation) and requires installing monitoring initiatives (Holley *et al.*, 2012; Wood and Shearing, 2007).

Given the enormous amount of goods and the complexity of this transnational flow in case of law breaking, a mere re-active approach will always be lagging behind, one step short of the newest route or technique used by the transporters of e-waste. This is evident from this case study of the port of Antwerp and its illegal e-waste flows towards Ghana. The governance reality of illegal transports of e-waste is about much more than this reactive approach. The analysis showed how actors earlier in the flow and throughout the supply chain – producers, consumers, collectors, informal dismantlers – can be involved. The leading role is taken up by government actors – and law enforcement more in particular – but in looking to address the contextual characteristics that shape this environmental flow, a broader diversity of governance nodes becomes relevant.

References

Aas, K.F., Analysing a world in motion - Global flows meet 'criminology of the other'. *Theoretical Criminology, 11*(2), 283-303, 2007

Aas, K.F., 'Crimmigrant' bodies and bona fide travelers: Surveillance, citizenship and global governance. *Theoretical Criminology, 15*(3), 331-346, 2011

Auld, G., B. Cashore, C. Balboa, L. Bozzi and S. Renckens, Can technological innovations improve private regulation in the global economy? *Business and Politics, 12*(3), Article 9, 2010

Ayres, I. and J. Braithwaite, *Responsive regulation: transcending the deregulation debate.* New York: Oxford University Press, 1992

Bartley, T., Institutional emergence in an era of globalization: The rise of transnational private regulation of labor and environmental conditions. *American Journal of Sociology, 113*(2), 297-351, 2007

Basel Convention Secretariat. Partnership on Computing Equipment (PACE). (2011).Retrieved 13 February, 2012, from http://archive.basel.int/industry/compartnership/

Beirne, P. and N. South, (Eds.).*Issues in green criminology. Confronting harms against environments, humanity and other animals.* . Portland: Willan Publishing., 2007.

Bernstein, S. and B. Cashore, Can non-state global governance be legitimate? An analytical framework. *Regulation and Governance, 1*(4), 347-371, 2007

Bisschop, L., Is it all going to waste? Illegal transports of e-waste in a European trade hub. *Crime, Law and Social Change, 58*(3), 221-249.

Black, J., Constructing and contesting legitimacy and accountability in polycentric regulatory regimes. *Regulation and Governance, 2*(2), 137-164, 2008.

Brack, D. and G. Hayman, *International environmental crime: The nature and control of environmental black markets.* Paper presented at the Sustainable Development Programme, RIIA workshop, 27-28, May 2002. 2002

Braithwaite, J., The New regulatory state and the transformation of criminology. *British Journal of Criminology, 40*, 222-238, 2000

Braithwaite, J., *Restorative justice and responsive regulation.* New York: Oxford University Press, 2002

Braithwaite, J., *Regulatory capitalism: how it works, ideas for making it work better.* Cheltenham: Edwar Elgar, 2008

Castells, M., *The Rise of the network society, The information age: Economy, society and culture. vol. I* (2 ed.). Cambridge (MA)/Oxford (UK): Blackwell Publishers, 2000

Crawford, A.. Networked governance and the post-regulatory state?: Steering, rowing and anchoring the provision of policing and security. *Theoretical Criminology, 10*(4), 449-479, 2006

Delmas, M. and O. Young (eds.). *Governance for the environment: New perspectives* Cambridge: Cambridge University Press, 2009

Denoiseux, D., L'exportation de déchets dangereux vers l'Afrique: de las du Probo Koala. *Courrier hebdomadaire, 2071*, 47, 2010

Euromettaux. Recycling for a resource efficient EU economy. European recycling industries' position on the challenges of secondary raw materials markets and policies needed to enable resource efficiency. In E. EuPC, CEPI, CIRFS, Euromettaux, EuPR (Ed.), *http://www.eurometaux.org/DesktopModules/Bring2mind/DMX/Download.aspx?TabID=57andCommand=Core_DownloadandEntryId=2126andPortalId=0andTabId=57* (pp. 9). Brussels: Position Paper, 2012.

European Commission - Taxation and Customs Union. Implementing risk management in the EU. (2012, 13 February 2012). Retrieved 13 February, 2012, from http://ec.europa.eu/taxation_customs/customs/customs_controls/risk_management/implementing/index_en.htm#rif

Faure, M., De gevolgen van de 'administratieve afhankelijkheid' van het milieustrafrecht: een inventarisatie van knelpunten. In: M. Faure, J. Oudijk and D. Schaffmeister (eds.), *Zorgen van heden. Opstellen over het milieustrafrecht in theorie en praktijk* (pp. 91-150). Arnhem: Gouda Quint, 1991

Faure, M., Instruments for environmental governance: What works? In P. Martin, Z. Li, T. Qin, A. Du Plessis and Y. Le Bouthillier (eds.), *Environmental governance and sustainability* (pp. 3-23). Cheltenham, UK and Northampton, USA: Edward Elgar Publishing, 2012

Gibbs, C., E.F. McGarrell and M. Axelrod, Transnational white-collar crime and risk. Lessons from the global trade in electronic waste. *Criminology and Public Policy, 9*(3), 543-560, 2010

Gille, Z. Detached flows or grounded place-making projects? In G. Spaargaren, A. Mol and F. Buttel (Eds.), *Governing environmental flows. Global challenges to social theory* (pp. 137-156). London/Cambridge (MA): MIT Press, 2006

Grabosky, P. and F. Gant, *Improving environmental performance, preventing environmental crime.* Canberra: Australian Institute of Criminology Research and Public Policy Series., 2000

Griffiths, H. and M. Jenks, *Maritime Transport and Destabilizing Commodity Flows* Solna: Stockholm International Peace Research Institute, 2012

Gunningham, N., Beyond compliance: next generation environmental regulation. In R. Johnstone and R. Sarre (Eds.), *Regulation: Enforcement and Compliance* (pp. 49-60). Canberra: Australian Institute of Criminolog, 2004

Gunningham, N., P. Grabosky and D. Sinclair, *Smart regulation: designing environmental policy.* Oxford: Clarendon press, 1998

Gunningham, N., R. Kagan and D. Thornton, *Shades of green: Business, regulation and environment.* Standford: Stanford University Press, 2003

Holley, C., N. Gunningham and C. Shearing, *The new environmental governance.* Abingdon - New York: Routledge, 2012

Jänicke, M., The environmental state and environmental flows: the need to reinvent the nation-state. In G. Spaargaren, A. Mol and F. Buttel (Eds.), *Governing environmental flows. Global challenges to social theory* (pp. 83-105). London /Cambridge (MA): MIT Press, 2006

Johnston, L. and C. Shearing, *Governing security: explorations in policing and justice.* London/New York: Routledge, 2003

Keohane, R. and J. Nye, Introduction. In: J. Nye and J. Donahue (Eds.), *Governance in a globalizing world* (pp. 1-27). Washington, D.C.: Brookings Institution, 2000

King, G., R. Keohane and S. Verba, *Designing social inquiry: scientific inference in qualitative research.* Princeton (NJ): Princeton University Press, 1994

LNE. (2010). *Milieuhandhavingsrapport 2009.* Brussel: Vlaamse Overheid - Departement Leefmilieu, Natuur en Energie - Afdeling Milieu-inspectie

LNE. *Milieu-inspectieplan 2011*: Departement Leefmilieu, Natuur en Energie. Afdeling Milieu-inspectie, 2011

Loader, I., Policing, securitization and democratization in Europe. *Criminology and Criminal Justice, 2*(2), 125-153, 2002

Loader, I. and R. Sparks, Contemporary landscapes of crime, order and control: Governance, risk and globalization. In M. Maguire, M. Morgan and R. Reiner (eds.), *The Oxford handbook of criminology*. Oxford: Oxford University Press, 2002

Mazerolle, L. and J. Ransley, *Third party policing*. Cambridge: Cambridge University Press, 2006

Mortelmans, D., T. Decorte and D. Zaitch, D. Observaties. In: T. Decorte and D. Zaitch (Eds.), *Kwalitatieve methoden en technieken in de criminologie* (pp. 261-286). Leuven: Acco, 2009

Nielsen, V.L. and C. Parker, Testing responsive regulation in regulatory enforcement. *Regulation and Governance, 3*(4), 376-399, 2009

Otterson, K. and U. Meiser, *UNODC - WCO. Container Control Programme.* Vienna: UNODC - WCO, 2009

Parker, C. and J. Braithwaite, Regulation. In P. Cane and M. Tushnet (Eds.), *The Oxford Handbook of Legal Studies* (pp. 119-145). Oxford: Oxford University Press, 2003

Ponsaers, P., M. Easton, M. Cools and F. Gilleir, *Onuitgegeven onderzoeksrapport: Nodale politie in de Antwerpse haven*: uitgevoerd in onderaanneming voor Universiteit Nyenrode en in opdracht van Programma Politie en Wetenschap (Nl.), 2008

Ponsaers, P. and B. Hoogenboom, Het moeilijke spel van wortel en stok—Organisatiecriminaliteit en handhaving-strategieën van bijzondere inspectie- en opsporingsdiensten. *Tijdschrift voor Criminologie, 46*(2), 165-181, 2004

Rufener, S., *Overview of existing and planned activities in the field of formal e-waste recycling in Accra, Ghana*. Zurich: NADEL – Centre for Development and Cooperation, 2012

Sander, K. and S. Schilling, *Transboundary shipment of waste electrical and electronic equipment / electronic scrap – Optimization of material flows and control*: The Federal Environment Agency (Germany) - Ökopol GmbH, 2010

Sassen, S., *Losing control? Sovereignty in an age of globalization.* New York: Colombia University Press, 1996

Schluep, M., D. Rochat, A.M. Wanjira, S.E. Laissaoui, S. Wone and C. Kane, *Assessing the e-waste situation in Africa*. Paper presented at the Electronics Goes Green 2008+. 2008

Shearing, C. and L. Johnston, Nodal wars and network fallacies. A genealogical analysis of global insecurities. *Theoretical Criminology, 14*(4), 495-514, 2010

Sheptycki, J., Criminology and the transnational condition: A contribution to international political sociology. *International Political Sociology, 1*(391-406), 2007

Sluis, A. van, P. Marks, F. Gilleir and M. Easton, Nodal security in the ports of Rotterdam and Antwerp. In V. Bekkers and H. Fenger (eds.), *Beyond fragmentation and interconnectivity: public governance and the search for connective capacity* (pp. 73-94). Amsterdam: IOC Press, 2012

Spaargaren, G., A. Mol and H. Bruyninckx, Introduction: Governing environmental flows in global modernity. In G. Spaargarten, A. Mol and F. Buttel (eds.), *Governing environmental flows. Global challenges to social theory* (pp. 1-36). London/Cambridge (MA): MIT Press, 2006

Urry, J., Global complexity. (pp. 172). Cambridge: Polity Press, 2003

Van de Bunt, H. and W. Huisman, Organisatiecriminaliteit. *Tijdschrift voor Criminologie, 46*(2), 106-120, 2004

van Erp, J. Lessen voor toezicht in de 21e eeuw. Actuele inzichten van Braithwaite en Sparrow. *Justitiële Verkenningen, 34*(6), 9-21, 2008

van Erp, J. and W. Huisman, Smart regulation and enforcement of illegal disposal of electronic waste. *Criminology and Public Policy, 9*(3), 579-590, 2010

Verstraeten, R., *Handboek strafvordering.* Antwerpen-Apeldoorn: Maklu, 2007

WCO., *Operation Demeter yields tons of illegal shipments of hazardous waste.* Brussels: WCO, 2009.

White, R. *Transnational environmental crime. Towards an eco-global criminology.* London and New York: Routledge, 2011

Wood, J., Research and innovation in the field of security. In J. Wood and B. Dupont (eds.), *Democracy, Society and the Governance of Security* (pp. 217-240). Cambridge/New York: Cambridge University Press, 2006

Wood, J. and B. Dupont, (eds.).*Democracy, society and the governance of security.* Cambridge/New York: Cambridge University Press, 2006

Wood, J., and Shearing, C. *Imagining security.* Cullompton: Willan Publishing, 2007.

Wright, J. and B. Head, Reconsidering regulation and governance theory: a learning approach. *Law and Policy*, 2009, *31*(2), 192-216

Yar, M., From the governance of security to governance failure: refining the criminological agenda. *Internet Journal of Criminology*, 19, 2011

Yin, R., *Applications of case-study research.* (2nd ed.). Thousand Oaks (CA): Sage Publications, 2003

Yin, R. *Case study research: design and methods.* (4th ed.). Thousand Oaks (CA): Sage, 2009

Young, O. Governance for sustainable development in a world or rising interdependencies. In M. Delmas and O. Young (Eds.), *Governance for the environment: new perspectives.* Cambridge: Cambridge University Press, 2009

A dysfunctional system of data collection as an obstacle to tackle crime

Exploring the dilemma of a good Ukrainian policeman

Anna Markovska and Alexey Serdyuk[1]

Introduction

During the last twenty years researchers have explored different dimensions of crimes in transition societies. A lot of attention has been paid to the peculiar nature of crimes in post soviet countries (Los, 2003; Aslund, 2005; Pridemore and Kim, 2006; Oleinik, 2006; Rawlinson, 2010). State formation and corruption have been analysed in great details, providing a number of labels to the post-Soviet countries, from the captured state concept (World Bank, 2000) to the criminal or bandit state (Los, 2003).

Los (2003) writes how for most people leaving in communist countries the dream was not to get fabulously rich, but to live their lives freely. Los also describes how the notion of freedom has been transformed or rather distorted, to include the development of a criminal state or 'captured' state, where certain powerful groups obtained unprecedented political and economic freedoms that they have abused. Analysing the transition journey for most of the post soviet countries Los (*ibid.*, 161-162) writes that "*the state and law are simultaneously undermined and fortified, dwarfed and augmented, supplanted and made indispensable by the quasi-marketisation of corruption, crime and security.*" To what extent does this also apply to Ukraine?

The legal system established in Ukraine has been described by Foglesong and Solomon (2001, 39-40) as the one where "*most legislation consisted of 'frame laws', which failed to supply the details needed for application and left crucial specifications to bureaucratic regulations*". Legal ambiguity and "*a new scope for bureaucratic discretion*" have armed public officials with more power and less accountably frame of conduct

---

1 Dr. Anna Markovska is a Senior lecturer in Criminology, Department of Humanities and Social Sciences, Anglia Ruskin University; Dr Alexey Serduyk is a Senior Lecturer, Head of the Department of Sociology and Social Work, Faculty of Psychology, Management and Socio-informational Technologies Kharkiv National University of Internal Affairs.

(*Ibid.*). Many Western democracies consider powerful public officials who are not accountable for their actions as the remnants of the distant past. Fukuyama (2012) describes the way the late seventeenth Century England dealt with corruption and reversed the patrimonialism. The crucial reforms named are "*an external environment that puts fiscal pressure on the government to improve its performance, . . . reform champions within the government who have sufficient political support to carry out their programme, and finally strong political pressure from below on the part of those who are paying taxes to the government and don't want to see their money wasted*" (*Ibid.*, 416). Fukuyama comments that many of the current anti-corruption initiatives fail because they lack one of the elements mentioned. Strong state and democratic elections are not enough to achieve democratic principles, the leaders of the state should themselves be bound by a rule of law (Ibid.). This is a missing link for Russia as well as Ukraine. On the one hand, Ukraine had moved away from an authoritarian regime, but om the othe hand, it has not quite reached a democratic regime either. It is interesting to observe the way certain social institutions still function in the 'grey zone' of transition (Carothers (2002), as quoted in Fukuyama, 2012, 4).

Organised crime and corruption use to be addressed from a one-dimensional threat perspective. That may be politically correct, however does have limited explanatory power. The explanatory powers to understand organised crime and corruption have increased with the arrival of an institutional choice approach and the development of interdisciplinary theory of the causes of corruption (Collier, 2002). Collier (2002, 25) combines "*theories of political, economic and cultural behaviours into an interdisciplinary social theory*". This approach provides different angles to view corruption and to understand the ways how to tackle it.

Policing as an institution of social control in Ukraine presents a very peculiar example where the old Soviet legacy is still alive and sustained by the state as it forms the protective mechanisms for those in power. In Soviet times police were "*corrupt, unprofessional, centralised, bureaucratic, politicized and militarized*", serving to protect the party-state from its subjects (Harasymiw, 2003, 319). In Soviet times, as well as in post Soviet Ukraine police were accountable to the state, and to no one else (Harasymiw, 2003). The main claim was that crime in Soviet times was relatively low (Los, 2003). In the late 1980s, "*revelations of fraud in recording crime showed that police claims were much inflated and that the system's performance was not exemplary*" (Foglesong and Solomon, 2001, 65). It is not surprising that in this situation there is a deficit of trust in the police (Goldsmith, 2005). Where democratic governments rest on the accountability and informed consent, captured states depend on the corruption and dysfunctional systems of data collection to sustain the power.

This chapter aims to analyse the work of the law enforcement agencies in Ukraine, discussing the system of data collection in operation within the Ukrainian police force and the way to measure the success of the Ukrainian police officers. We start with a brief overview of the way the success of the Ukrainian law enforcement agencies has been measured during Soviet and post-soviet times. The institutional analysis and development framework is then applied to understand the nature of the law enforcement work in Ukraine. The authors suggest that one of the ways to challenge political culture and revive the issues of accountability and trust is by analysing the existent methods of measuring the success of the law enforcement agencies in Ukraine, specifically looking at the ways to measure the performance of the Ministry of Internal Affairs.

Law enforcement agencies in Ukraine: how to show success in fighting crime?

In Soviet times (up until the end of the 1980s) in Ukraine, as in many other countries of the former Soviet Union, criminal statistics were difficult to obtain. In 1994, the National Academy of Internal Affairs in Ukraine published criminal statistics for the use of the general public for the first time, using data from 1972 to 1993. Since then, certain statistical data have been published in various periodicals, as well as the annual reports of the Ministry of Internal Affairs.

Foglesong and Solomon (2001, pp. 64-65) write how if one had to measure the effectiveness of the Ukrainian criminal justice in fighting crime, one would be surprised how 'spectacularly successful' the police were.

> "In most years, the clearance rate hovered above 90 percent; for certain offences, it was close to 100 percent . . . Until 1988 the police could 'solve' crimes without sending cases or criminals to court. Between 1970 and 1980, the Ministry of Internal Affairs considered a crime 'solved' from the moment a decision was made to open a criminal investigation. Between 1980 and 1988, a crime was deemed solved once charges were formally presented to the accused. The police were not required to obtain a conviction in order to be favourably evaluated".

This has changed, and at present a case is considered to be solved when it ends with a guilty verdict.

The problem of measuring the performance of the Ministry of Internal Affairs in Ukraine occupied researchers during the Soviet times (for example, Berekashvili, 1981; Barnov, *et al.*, 1977), and in the independent Ukraine (Zakalyuk, 1999;

Boiko, 2003; Kukushka, 2004). Researchers share the opinion that, both during the Soviet times and in modern day Ukraine, there has been no real progress in measuring the performance of the Ministry of Internal Affairs. Currently, the work of law enforcement agencies is often measured on the basis of known statistical data ('specific indicators') stressing the importance of certain area of the work of the law enforcement. This approach is also limited in its ability to access performance metrics of the agency (Boiko, 2003), and may not prevent the manipulation of statistical data.

On the whole, the system of collection and recording crimes is centred around the Ministry of Internal Affairs. The Ministry is obliged to count the recorded crimes by the citizens as well as crimes recorded by other law enforcement agencies. Generally speaking, the police in Ukraine will not only record crimes, but will also regulate the targets imposed by the Ministry of Internal Affairs and crime recording issues. The performance of the police is measured on the basis of the cases solved, and the number of cases that have to be solved is directly imposed by the relevant ministry. Foglesong and Solomon (2001) analyse the crime statistics in Ukraine in 1990-98, note that "*the rise in levels of reported crime was not matched by a comparable rise in registered crime*". It either means that the public is reporting "*false or frivolous incidents at a growing rate*" (*Ibid.* 75), or police is following their own rules on the number of crimes to report (possibly the rules and quotas imposed from above).

Such a system is only useful for the ministries if it confirms the effectiveness of their work, but it has nothing to do with the reality of the crime situation in the country (KhISR, 2010). For example, the designated units to fight economic crime should identify more contraband goods for each reported period. The necessity to 'provide' the indicators is 'hanging' above each law enforcement officer (Ibid.). As a result, the work of the police officer is a race for the 'positive dynamics' in crime records.

Selective registration of crimes is a serious concern. It can either be a "*de facto decriminalisation or something more corrupt and worrisome*" (Foglesong and Solomon, 2001, 75). Assessing the system's performance in fighting crime has been proved to be difficult in other countries, such as the United States and many European countries (Fogleson and Solomon, 2001, Goldsmith, 2005, von Lampe, 2005). Discussing the methodological difficulties in assessing organised crime in Germany, von Lampe (2005) comments on a susceptibility of official police recorded statistics "*to differential priority setting and bias in tactical and strategic police work*". In Soviet Ukraine the difficulties had a very strong ideological background, and at present it is the endemic nature of corruption coupled with the old centrally imposed and controlled targets that make the situation in Ukraine rather challenging.

The use of qualitative indicators, together with the percentage of the solved cases, leads to 'percentage-mania' (Shostko, 2004), or the 'run' towards the indicators. One would expect that this would lead to an unbridled number inflation. However, that is not the case. There are important counterweights that keep the spread narrow. It works as follows. The current work should always be slightly better than during the previous period (otherwise there would be a disciplinary procedure), but it shouldn't be much better than before, because such a progress will be difficult to sustain. This problem is especially acute in the area of the organised crime, as it is latent in nature, and official statistics only uncover a small part of it. In order to achieve the targets suggested by the authorities, the officers are interested in the less serious crimes, as they can provide the necessary numbers. In cases of serious crime, the investigation can last from one month to one year or more, and unfortunately this may not be acknowledged in the reports for the certain period. The following case study illustrates this problem.

In 2007, a study of the system of free legal advice available to Ukrainian citizens, was conducted in the Kharkiv region (Kobzin *et al.*, 2007), including an analysis of criminal files (605 cases covering the period from 2002 to 2007 were selected using random sample), expert interviews (120 investigators), 5 focus group interviews and 15 detailed interviews with the investigators (Ibid.). Analysis identified a number of features of the law enforcement activity provoked and sustained by the deficiencies in the way the criminal statistics is compiled (*Ibid.*).

Kobzin, *et al.* (2007) noted that the peculiarity of registration of the final verdicts suggests that the Ukrainian judicial system has become focussed on guilty verdicts. Currently, the acquittal rate in Ukraine is from 0,2 to 0,3 %. During Stalin's repression, the acquittal rate was 10%, and during the 19th Century and the beginning of the 20th Century in the Russian Empire it was around 40% (Aleinikov, 2007). The formal way to measure the success of the work of police investigators is to base it on the number of cases sent to court. The researchers have found that in reality the success is measured by the number of guilty verdicts. Police officers risk disciplinary procedures against them in cases where a not-guilty verdict is given, because the solved case is the case that ends up with a guilty verdict (Kobzin *et al.* 2007). 57% of the cases found guilty had conditions attached, such as a suspended sentence or a delay in the execution of the verdict (*Ibid.*). Judges suggest that the reason for this is the fact that the courts receive cases with minor crimes. The judges seemed to be aware that for a long period of time the majority of the cases based on Article 309 of the Criminal Code: Illegal production, transportation, and supply of narcotic substances, or the analogues *without the aim to supply* would reach the court in order for the militia and the office of public prosecutor to achieve the targets suggested by the Ministry (*Ibid.*). By implications these are the minor cases.

This practice of production of criminal cases for minor crimes keeps the whole system of the law enforcement in a workable mode, or to be more precise: in the condition of self-reproduction (Ibid.). These are the cases militia officers, investigators, public prosecutors and judged are working on. The problem is that the state expenditure on these crimes cannot be compared to the seriousness of these crimes to society. To illustrate this point Kobzin, *et al.* (2007) use the following example of a criminal case open under the Article 358 of the Criminal Code *Forgery of the documents, stamps, its sale and the usage of forged documents.*

> The defendant was a disabled person, who in order to use the free pass on the public transport available to the second category of disability, corrected the category of his disability from the third to the second.[2] When using his disability ID to enter the underground metro, he was stopped by the militia who transported him to their local office. During this period two experts studies were conducted, and four witnesses interviewed. The public prosecutor had signed the charge, and this individual was found guilty in court. The case was about 152 pages long and took around 52 days. The example illustrates that the system is completely out of balance.

The question is: what was more costly to the state? The answer to this question will be: the cost of investigation. However, the justification for the police to carry on with the case is that the case is good in terms of reaching the targets.

During the study, researchers noticed that a large proportion of serious cases with a substantial damage resulted in a suspended sentence, suggesting corruption in the court (Kobzin, *et al.*, 2007). In a simplified way, the more you steal, the more likely you have enough money to pay the bribes on different stages of the criminal justice process, so that at each stage you find that the risk of punishment and actual imprisonment is minimised. The suggested bribe to the police is around \$1.000 per year of possible imprisonment (*Ibid.*).

Without studying the context of a criminal case, it will be difficult to consider the success of the criminal justice system. What is known is that the criminal was caught, and a crime was recorded and solved. The case transferred to the office of public prosecutor and then to the court, with the latter finding a verdict of guilty. In each stage, the targets are met and the indicators are officially recorded. Only the context of these cases might suggest that bribes were paid to delay and reduce the severity of the sentence. In the current situation, the main worry for the police will

2 The third category of disability does not entitle a person for a free travel on public transport, but the second category does.

be delivering the targets because it may directly impact the managerial decision. Good results mean positive career progression bad results can mean dismissal (*Ibid.*).

The Institutional Analysis and Development (IAD) Framework: rational choice and the Ukrainian reality.

Collier (2003, 3) argues that the Institutional Analysis Development (IAD) framework not only demonstrates how varied institutional structures affect agent decision making, but also how agent decisions affect (change) the institutional structures themselves. Explaining how structure and agents work, Collier writes:

> "a principal constructivist tenet is that people (agents) and society (structure) co-constitute (construct) each other in a continuous process" (Ibid.). Rules the agents use are very important in this case. "Rules make people active participants, or agents, in society, and they form agent's relations into the stable arrangements, or institutions, that give society a recognizable pattern or structure" (*Ibid.*, 4).

This is the neutral or formal formulation, which may get a distorted content, as is the case in the Ukrainian police force.

In the case of a Ukrainian police officer and the rules on how to measure their performance, by complying with the rules that 'do not make sense' or 'are unrealistic' and by supplying the system with the data collected on the basis of these rules, the agents (the police officer) inadvertently support the dysfunctional system (the system of the data collection by the Ministry of Internal Affairs). The system is dysfunctional because police as an institution of social control should be aiming among the other things to "*defend citizen's rights and freedoms, preserve public order, prevent and investigate crimes*" (Harasymiw, 2003, 319). Instead their activities are centred around the production of the crime quotas imposed from above.

Amongst the three types of rules discussed by Collier (2003), there are directive rules that provide specificity to the instruction-rules principles, beliefs and norms. This is what the agents must do; otherwise there are sanctions to follow. This is what sustains the dysfunctional system in Ukraine. By following the rules in the situation where lack of resources coupled with systemic corruption, provides fertile grounds for power abuse and preferential treatment as well as mistreatment. The KhISR (2010, 10) study quotes one of the expert participant:

> "I think to work in order to reach the performance target can lead to paradox situation, where instead of providing law and order, the police is constantly involved in the number game. Here is a good example: a couple of days ago in

one of the central locations in the city centre was a traffic jam. The problem was that one driver parked the car in a wrong spot. So, in the absence of any police/road officers, some drivers turned to the street with the one way traffic. When the road police arrived they stopped at the end of that one way street to catch the drivers, and inevitably to seek bribes, instead of moving a few metres away and solving the situation. In a way that particular road officer was dealing with the offences, but not with the cause. So, the whole system in Ukraine is built on the same principle: to provide the data on the number of crimes and the illusion of the work".

The short-term consequence of this situation is the individual satisfaction (the exercise of power and bribe seeking), but the long term organisational consequences are stagnation in development and spread of dysfunctional characteristics to other social institutions. Directive rules are not for questioning, they are to be observed. Going back to the example discussed earlier, the dilemma of a good police officer, would either be to go and solve the traffic jam problem, or step aside, catch those who in a critical situation move to the wrong side of the road and offer some sort of corrupt exchange or following the rules register and solve the offences.

Figure 1:
Corruption institutional choice analytical frame: police and performance targets (adopted from Collier, 2002, p.4)

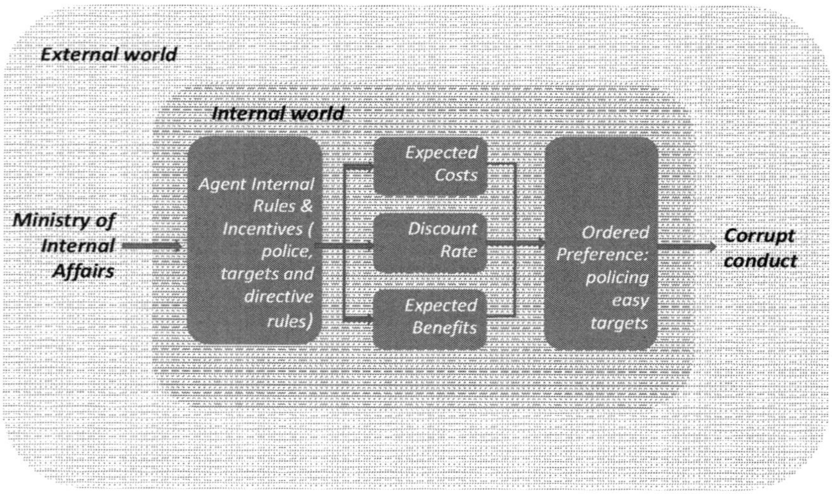

By continuing to measure the activities of the police according to the directive rules, the Ministry of Internal Affairs engages in the grey area of social control. The only target of this type of control is to control the police (even more precisely, to control the production of statistics on crimes), and not the social order or the criminality. The police officers interpret the rules of measuring the costs and benefits of certain investigations on the basis of two premises: (a) they know that mechanisms of social control do not work and (b) they know they are only accountable to the Ministry (see Figure 1) that determines their career path. Expected costs and benefits of engaging in serious and lengthy criminal investigations are measured against expected performance targets imposed by the Ministry. As a result, the ordered preference of conduct is to police minor crimes, police easy targets with the possibility to engage in corrupt conduct.

The issue is complicated even further if one considers the relationship between the targets for the preventative measures and targets for the number of crimes solved. The preventative measures aim to reduce the level of crimes. However, the Ukrainian police experience a rather different way of measuring the preventative success. The expert study conducted by the KhISR (2010) showed that preventative measures have been identified as a big part of the police work, however, the measures undertaken should not change the number of registered crimes. The reason for this is that the decrease in the number of crimes registered will be criticised by the relevant bosses and considered as an attempt to cover the real level of (expected) crimes (*Ibid.*). Even though, what is measured is not necessarily 'a real level of crime'. The system makes sense but only in a rather distorted way.

Following is a quote from the expert interviews (KhISR, 2010), suggesting how preventative measures could go wrong.

> "In the 1990s we had a very high level of street crimes, it was really dangerous to get out of the house. It should be said, that the police worked well and if not successfully solved the problem, they have managed to 'suffocated' it. They have exchanged the roles. The illegal business, illegal drug trade, prostitution, and other illegal activities that can be profitable have changed hands and the so called 'roof' is now provided by police and public prosecution office".

In other words, a displacement of the organisation of the criminal enterprise took place, and what previously was known to be a part of service provided by the local organised crime groups, currently the service is supplied by the organised police groups. Foglesons and Solomon (2001, 69-71) argue that in some cases "*officers and even entire police units have either betrayed law enforcement or been captured by criminal groups*". The old Tramadol[3] case is a good illustration of the absence of political will coupled with the dysfunctional system of law enforcement system.

3 The drug Tramadol has a ten year history of abuse in the country. Tramadol is a synthetic opioid, similar to heroin and morphine, and due to assumed pressure from manufacturers,

On the 4th June 2008 the Cabinet of Ministers of Ukraine declared Tramadol to be a narcotic substance. According to investigators, in 2006, the eight largest Ukrainian pharmaceutical companies produced 151 million capsules and 4,4 million ampoules of Tramadol. In 2008 the producers officially declared and made 150 million capsules, and 14 million ampoules of tramadol. The established legal medical need of this drug in Ukraine is 10 million capsules and four million ampoules a year (Panashyk, 2008). These sources suggested that in the second half of the 2008, Ukraine had enough raw materials to produce 690 million doses. The volume of Tramadol production as suggested in the Decree of the Ministry of Health No. 236 from 5 May 2008 was 19,5 million capsules and 6,5 million ampoules (26 million dosages), this being 6,5 times higher than the genuine medical need (four million dosages) (Linskij, 2008).

Despite the obvious side effects of abusing Tramadol, any attempts to change the classification of this drug were ineffective. The causes of this situation were the 'narcomafia' lobby (reported to consists of the MPs with connections to the pharmaceutical companies), as well as the sizable profits from the legal (prescription sales) and illegal sale (on the black market supervised by certain legally registered pharmacies) of this drug (Panashuk, 2008). Even the former Chief Narcologist of Ukraine, Anatolii Vievskii, suggested that Tramadol use does not lead to dependency (Protyag, 2007). However, Kravchenko (2008) named the case of Tramadol as the crime of the Ukrainian government against their own people (cited in Panashuk, 2008). This exemplifies the potential problems of measuring police performance with regards to the proscribed use of illegal drugs within country. Kuchniruk (2008) argues that there was (and still is) a well-known structure in place promoting the sale of illegal drugs through the legally registered pharmacies, where the pharmacy would be 'protected' by the local police force (as quoted in Panashuk, 2008).

The Tramadol case illustrates the macro and micro levels of the problem of corruption. At the macro level, the interested parties among the high level officials failed to change the classification of the drug, and at the micro level, the support of police was crucial to protect the interests of the officials from one side and to establish the corrupt surveillance mechanisms to provide security for the pharmacies known to sell the drugs to addicts from another side. In this case, the whole pyramid of criminal activities escapes from the official data on crime.

---

it was listed as a 'potent medical substance' rather than as a narcotic. For a decade, the production and sale of this drug was not controlled (Panashuk, 2008).

The Pirates of the Ukraine

The Tramadol case leads us to consider the political culture or the lack of one in Ukraine. Collier (2002) describes three types of political culture: collectivist, individualistic and egalitarian. Ukraine can fit the collectivist model, as

> "*social and economic transactions in collectivist cultures are organised around small groups defined by familial, kinship, tribal, ethnic, religious, or other social relationships. Each group tends to have its own narrow base of interest*" (Collier, 7). "*In collectivist cultures, there is virtually no sustained elite or mass opinion to condemn corrupt behaviour . . . the ruling elites are likely to act as pirates – those that operate mainly on the illegal side of the law and pillage their society's resources through their access to public office*" (*Ibid.* 12).

The clan based political system in Ukraine ensures that 'the frame laws'[4] protect the interest of their own group. There are laws that will work for the elite only, and the rest is for the members of general public. An ordinary market seller or small entrepreneur understands this, but mass condemnation of the corrupt conduct is rather rare and does not lead to proactive or challenging actions.

Obviously, official statistics on corruption do not reflect the real life situation. One of the reasons for that is public opinion about the work of police and other law enforcement agencies is rarely a subject of interest, let alone of debate. In 2005 there was an attempt to introduce a public opinion survey as one measure of the success of the traffic police (The Decree of the Ministry of Internal Affairs of Ukraine no. 214 from 28-02-2006). The idea was that the work of the traffic police will be measured on the basis of the public satisfaction in the local area (where public satisfaction will is a form of the public opinion). Between 2007 and 2008, researchers from Kharkiv University's Department of Internal Affairs studied corruption in the work of the State Automobile Inspection (Road traffic police) in the Kharkiv region (Serdyuk *et al.*, 2007; Serdyuk *et al.*, 2008). The results of the study suggest that between 56% to 73% of all official contacts with the road traffic police is accompanied with the bribing of officials. However, according to official statistics, during the same period, there was not a single case of bribery of the road traffic police officer known to the authorities. This particular initiative was short lived. Nevertheless, it shows that the Ministry of Internal Affairs began thinking about alternative ways of measuring the success of the work of certain departments. This may be a long journey. So that road traffic police may continue to operate as pirates of the roads, knowing, that as long as the 'pirates above' would keep the old

---

4 Discussed by Foglesons and Solomon (2001) as the once that 'failed to supply the details for application and left crucial specifications to bureaucratic regulation' (pp. 39-40). ?? Explain.

system alive, everyone will be fine. As in Tramadol case discussed earlier this is the problem of corruption within, as well as the problem of capturing the level of certain crimes.

Currently, one of the new performance indicators introduced is about "*the formation of positive image of the departments of Internal Affairs*", and it has also been suggested that "*the results of the public opinion surveys should be introduced as a measure of police performance*" (Decree of the Ministry of Internal Affairs N 279 26.09.2010). However, police leaders do not see how they can use the public opinion, because they believe that the public, 'the civilians', are not capable to adequately measure the success of their work.

Concluding remarks

Recording practices in cases of serious crimes, as well as measuring police performance and identifying successful practices may have implications on different levels. For example, within a country it might concern the integrity of the law-enforcement agencies and the accountability to the public and government, as well as fighting crime and providing justice. Lack of integrity at one level, *e.g.* recording, may pervade all other levels. Discussing successful policing of organised and transnational crimes Harfield (2008, 487) noted the "*strategic prerequisite of legitimacy: the expectation on the part of citizens that State agents and organisations, having been invested with significant coercive powers, will use those powers with integrity, free from corrupt influence, only when it is lawful, necessary and proportionate to do so*". Collaboration between the jurisdictions can also be very different, as in some countries the prerequisites identified above are not common, as is the case in Ukraine. So, how do we begin to challenge the conduct of the pirates in the uniforms? We argue that it is important to start with something and the way to start will be from challenging the performance targets, and thus the way the rules are imposed.

Figure 2:
Corruption institutional choice analytical frame: police and performance targets challenged
(on the basis of Collier, 2002, p.4)

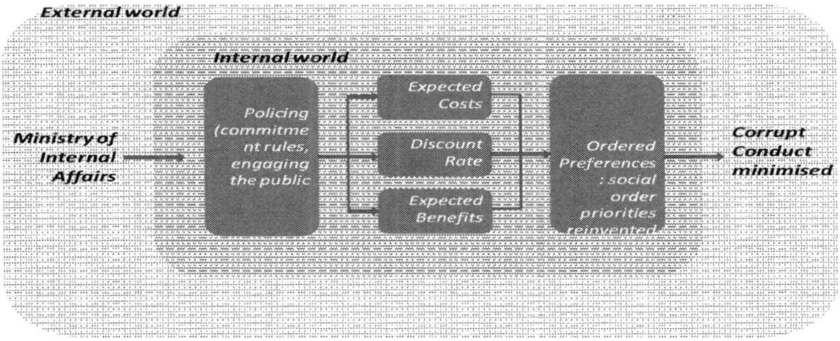

We propose moving away from directly imposed targets by the Ministry of Internal Affairs as the only way to measure the success of police work to the system that acknowledges public opinion and people's experience of crime (See Figure 2). It has a potential to minimise the old preferences of policing and maximise the importance of a new way collecting the data. In this case, the directive rules are changing to the commitment rules that "*tell the agents what they have a right or duty to do. Commitment rules give some agents well defined powers, while assuring other agents that those powers will not be abused*" (Collier, 2003, 5).

Ukrainian examples show a distorted work ethic that is often perceived as a lack of interest to policing serious crimes, or an absence of adequate prosecution strategy in case of serious crimes. It seems that authorities are competent in delivering the targets and bringing the case to prosecution, however the details of some trials suggest that competent investigations can be undermined by corruption within the trial process. Van Dijk (2007, 39) notes the "*strenuous efforts . . . made by international organisations such as Europol and the United Nations Office on Drugs and Crime to harmonise official data of police and courts on transnational organised crime and corruption. It seems doubtful that such administrative data will ever produce useful indicators of the level of these types of crime across countries.*" For example, as discussed earlier, suspended sentences for serious crimes in Ukraine can be a questionable success from the point of view of the members of the general public, but for the relevant authorities it means that the trial took place and targets were met. When analysing the response to serious crimes and developing new strategies, one has to acknowledge the availability of the rule of law and the indicators of good governance.

It can be argued that following a brief spell of a transition mode for many social institutions in Ukraine the reality is a rather dysfunctional nature of their work. The dysfunctionality of the institutions is also sustained by the rational decision making of the individual actors involved. Destructive social needs (for example, production of illegal drugs) provide one of the bases for the dysfunctional social institutions. For example, corruption is functional in short term, as it provides those involved with a personal enrichment, but from the long-term perspective of a state it cultivates bad governance and discourages transparency. The tendency to police vulnerable groups, coupled with a number of peculiar features inherited from the Soviet times, turn the system of the law enforcement into the system of the target enforcement for the self-fulfilling obligations of the Ministry in charge. The existent system supports the "*directive-ruled authoritarian structures of the states – the source of a ruling elite's political power*" (Collier, 2003, 25). We submit that it is possible to shake this culture by changing the way the police performance is measured, and the way public opinion is recognised in the new performance indicators. As argued by Van Dijk (2007, 40) "*the case of measuring levels of crime independently of the police is even stronger regarding organised crime and corruption than regarding common crimes*". Perhaps the all-Ukrainian Crime Survey is the next step forward. Similar to the British Crime Survey this alternative way of measuring the level of crime in the country should be an essential tool in assessing the threat and the scale of common and organised crimes.

References

Aleinikov, G.E., Vupravdyvlnuj vurok u kruminalnomy processi Ukrainu. [Not guilty verdicts in the criminal process in Ukraine]. Herson: Fond miloserdya ta zdorovya, 2007

Aslund, A., The Economic policy of Ukraine after the Orange Revolution. *Eurasian Geography and Economics*, 2005, vol. 46, *no. 5*, 327-353

Baranov, N.N., Kondratyuk, L.V., Methods to measure the effectivenss of the investigation unit. Moscow: Vestnik MVD, USSR, 1977, 44-46

Berekashvilli, L.S., Problems with the effectiveness of the departments of the internal affairs. Moscow: Academy MVD USSR, 1981, 33-37

Boiko, I.V., The main criteria of measuring the activities of the units within the Ministry of Internal Affairs in Ukraine. *Pravova Informatika*, 2003, vol. 1, 9-22

Collier, M.W. Explaining corruption: an institutional choice approach. *Crime, Law and Social Change*, 2002, vol. 38, pp.1-32

Dijk, J.J.M. van, Mafia markers: assessing organised crime and its impact upon societies. *Trends in Organised Crime*, 2007, vol. 10, 39-56

Foglesong, T.H. and J. Solomon, Crime, criminal justice, and criminology in post-Soviet Ukraine. Washington, DC: US Department of Justice, 2001

Fukuyama, F., The origins of political order. London: Profile Books, 2012

Harasymiw, B., Policing, democratisation and political leadership in Post-communist Ukraine. *Canadian Journal of Political Science*, 2003, vol. 36, 2, 319-340

Harfield (2008) The organisation of 'organised crime policing' and its international context. *Criminology and Criminal Justice*, 2008, vol. 8 (4), pp. 483-507

KhISR (2010) Public opinion survey about the activities of the police officers in the city of Kharkiv. Kharkiv: KhISR

Kobzin, D. Y. Belousov, A. Chernousov and A. Serdyuk, A., Monitoring sistemu bezoplanoj pravovoi dopomogu v Kharkivskij oblasti: resultatu sociologichnogo doslidzhennya. [in Ukrainian] Monitoring of the system of free legal advise in Kharkiv region: results of sociological survey. Kharkiv: Kharkiv National University of Internal Affairs, 2007

Kukushka, E., Problemu ocenki deyatelnosti poreformennoj sistemu MVD Ukrainu. [Post-reform problems in measuring the performance of the Ministry of Internal Affairs of Ukraine].Yuridicheskaya Ukraina, 2004, *no. 12*

Linskij, I., Tramadol kak zerkalo nacionalnoj politicki v otnoshenii narkotikov. [Tramadol as a mirror of the national drug policy]. Zerkalo nedeli No. 22. [ON-line]. 2008, Available at: (http://www.zn.kiev.ua/3000/3450/63245/)

Los, M., Crime in transition: the Post-Communist state, markets and crime. Crime, Law and Social Change, 2003, vol. 40, 145-169.

Von Lampe, K., Making the second step before the first. Assessing organised crime: case of Germany. Crime Law and Social Change, 2003, vol. 42, 227-259

Von Lampe, K., Criminals are not alone. Some observations on the social microcosm of illegal entrepreneurs. In P.C. van Duyne, *et al.* (eds.), *Crime business and crime money in Europe: the dirty linen of illicit enterprise.* Nijmegen: Wolf Legal Publishers, 2007

Oleinik, A., A plurality of total institutions: towards a comparative penology. *Crime, Law and Social Change*, 2006, vol. 46, 161-180

Panashyk, Tramadoil- eto desyatki tusyash iskalechennuh sudeb. [Tramadol - thousands of ruined lives]. 2008 [On-line]. Avaliable at: http:/ /iz vestia.com.ua/?/articles/2008/07/10/184320-15

Pridemore, W. and S. Kim, Democratization and political change as threats to collective sentiments: testing Durkheim in Russia. *The ANNALS of the American Academy of Political and Social Science*, 2006, vol. 605, *no. 1*, 82-103

Protyag, Mediki ne hotyat priznavat tramadol narkotikom. [Doctors do not want to accept that tramadol is an addictive susbstance]. Gazeta №313 [On-line]. 2007, Available at:
http://gazeta.ua/index.php?id=150981&eid=313&lang=ru

Rawlinson, P., *From fear to fraternity: a Russian tale of crime, economy and modernity.* London: Pluto Press, 2010

Shostko, A.Y., Organizovannyay prestypnost v Ukraine:nekotorue voprosu otnositelno effektivnosti borbu s nej. [Organised crime in Ukraine; some questions regarding the effectiveness of the fight against it. Problemu zakonnosti, 2004, vup. 68

Serdyuk, O., Y. Svezhenceva and D., Kobzin, Korupciya v dijalnosti Derzhavnoi avtomobilnoi inspekcii: resultatu sociologichnogo monitoringy.[Corruption in the work of the State Automobile Inspection: the results of sociological research].Harkiv:HICD, 2007

Serdyuk, O., Y. Svezhenceva and A. Chernousov, Antikorupciinui monitoring diyalnosti Derzhavnoi avtomobilnoi inspekcii.[Anti-corruption monitoring in the work of State Automobile Inspection. Harkiv:HICD, 2008

Serdyuk, O. and A. Markovska, Migrant workers and police relationship. *Visnuk Kharkiv National University*, 2012, no.999, Issue 30, 131-136

The European Neighbourhood and Partnership Instrument, Ukraine: National Indicative Programme 2007-2010. [On-line] 2007 Available at:
http://ec.europa.eu/world/enp/pdf/country/enpi_nip_ukraine_en.pdf

The World Bank, *Anticorruption in transition. A contribution to the policy debate.* Washnigton, D.C. :The World Bank, 2000

Zakalyuk, A. P., Pro zavprovadhzennya v Ukraini kriminologichnoi ekspertizu. [About introducing criminological expertise in Ukraine]. *Pravo Ukraine* 1999, *no.* 7

Volume Overview Cross-Border Crime Colloqium

Usual and unusual organising criminals in Europe and beyond. Profitable crimes, from underworld to upper world. Liber amicorum Petrus C. van Duyne. Georgios Antonopoulos, Marc Groenhuijsen, Jackie Harvey, Tijs Kooijmans, Almir Maljevic & Klaus von Lampe (eds.), Maklu Uitgevers, Antwerpen 2011, ISBN: 978-90-4660-429-8

Flesh and Money. Trafficking in Human Beings. Petrus C. van Duyne and on Spencer (eds.), Wolf Legal Publishers, Nijmegen 2011, ISBN: 978-90-5850-655-9

Cross-border crime inroads on integrity in Europe. Petrus C. van Duyne, Georgios A. Antonopoulos, Almir Maljevic, Jackie Harvey, Tom Vander Beken, Klaus von Lamp, (Eds.) Wolf Legal Publishers, Nijmegen 2010, ISBN: 978-90-5850-577-4

Crime, Money and Criminal Mobility in Europe, Petrus C. van Duyne, Stefano Donati, Jackie Harvey, Almir Maljević and Klaus von Lampe (Eds.), Wolf Legal Publishers, Nijmegen 2009, ISBN: 978-90-5850-477-7

The criminal smoke of tobacco policy making. Cigarette smuggling in Europe. Petrus C. van Duyne and Georgios A. Antonopoulos (eds.), Wolf Legal Publishers, Nijmegen 2011, ISBN: 978-90-5850-476-0

European crime markets at cross-roads: extended and extending criminal Europe. Petrus C. van Duyne, Jackie Harvey, Almir Maljevic, Klaus von Lampe, Miroslav Scheinost (Eds.) Wolf Legal Publishers, Nijmegen 2008, ISBN: 978-909-5850-392-3

Crime business and cime money in Europe. The dirty linen of illicit enterprise. Petrus C. van Duyne, Almir Maljevic, Maarten van Dijck, Klaus von Lampe, Jackie Harvey (Eds.) Wolf Legal Publishers, Nijmegen, 2007, ISBN: 978-90-5850-305-3

The organisation of crime for profit. Conduct law and measurement. Petrus C. van Duyne, Almir Maljevic, Maarten van Dijck, Klaus von Lampe, James L. Newell (Eds.) Wolf Legal Publishers, Nijmegen 2005, ISBN: 978-90-5850-220-9

The organised crime economy. Managing crime markets in Europe. Petrus C. van Duyne, Klaus von Lampe, Maarten van Dijck, James L. Newell (Eds.) Wolf Legal Publishers, Nijmegen 2005, ISBN: 978-90-5850-144-8

Threats and Phantoms of Organised Crime, Corruption and Terrorism; Rhetoric and critical perspectives. Petrus C. van Duyne, Matjaz Jager, Klaus von Lampe, James L. Newell (Eds.) Wolf Legal Publishers, Nijmegen 2004, ISBN: 978-90-5850-077-9

Criminal Finances and Organising Crime in Europe. Petrus C. van Duyne, Klaus von Lampe, James L. Newell (Eds.)Wolf Legal Publishers, Nijmegen 2003, ISBN: 978-90-5850-045-8

Upperworld and underworld in cross-border crime. Petrus C. van Duyne, Klaus von Lampe, Nikos Passas (Eds.) Wolf Legal Publishers, Nijmegen 2002, ISBN: 978-90-5850-030-4

Cross-border Crime in a Changing Europe. Petrus C. van Duyne, Vincenzo Ruggiero, Miroslav Scheinost, Wim Valkenburg (Eds.), Nova Science Publishers, Huntingdon, New York 2001, ISBN: 978-1-56072-966-2

The Manchester Cross-border Crime Colloquium, 2012

9 789058 509833
13W21704/ T2/ 9789058509833